WESTERN CANADA
Saskatchewan and Manitoba

0   100   200km

N

Worth a visit ★★
Interesting ★

ULYSSES

Suns
Vanc
a pro
moder
- *Walte*4)
Bibikov

Nature and the
ocean are never
far away in
Vancouver, even
in the heart of
the city.
- *Michel Gascon*

Then the locomotive whistle sounded again and a voice was heard to cry: "All aboard for the Pacific."
It was the first time that phrase had been used by a conductor from the East... The official party obedi-
ently boarded the cars and a few moments later the little train was in motion again, clattering over the
newly laid rail and over the last spike and down the long incline of the mountains, off towards the
dark canyon of the Fraser, off to broad meadows beyond, off to the blue Pacific and into history.

Pierre Berton
The Last Spike

Research and Writing
Julie Brodeur
Alexis de Gheldere
Paul-Eric Dumontier
Jacqueline Grekin
Mark Heard
Stephanie Heindenreich
Paul Karr
Pierre Longnus
Jennifer McMorran
Lorette Pierson
Corinne Pohlmann
François Rémillard
Collaboration
Amber Martin

Publisher
André Duchesne

Translation
Cindy Garayt

Corrector
Jennifer McMorran

Page layout
Isabelle Lalonde

Cartographer
Isabelle Lalonde

Computer Graphics
André Duchesne

Illustrations
Lorette Pierson
Myriam Gagné
Jenny Jasper
Marie-Annick Viatour

Photographs
Cover Page
Robert Glusic
(PhotoDisc)
Inside Pages
M. Michaelnuk
(Megapress Images)
Walter Bibikow
Michel Gascon
Derek Caron
Sean O'Neill
Tibor Bognár
Troy and Mary Parlee

Artistic Director
Patrick Farei (Atoll)

Acknowledgements: Ulysses Travel Guides gratefully acknowledges the many wonderful Westerners who assisted with the production of this guidebook. In particular, we take our hats off to: Lana Cheong (Tourism Vancouver Island); Heather McGillivray (Tourism Victoria); Kate Colley Lo (Tourism Vancouver); Danielle Oberle (Tourism Calgary) Kathy Cooper & Shannon Harrison (BC Rockies); Kelly Reid (Tourism Development Services Penticton & Wine Country). Thanks also to Marla Daniels, Elinor Fish, Tammy Campbell, Nancy Cameron, Lynda Trudeau & Sharon Williams, Karen Cook, Jennifer Groundwater, Colette Fontaine, David Freeman, Chris Brown, Blain Sepos, Jennifer Senycz, Virginia Haar, Casie Murdoch, Mary Ann Bell and Sue & Drew too.

We acknowledge the financial support of the Government of Canada through the Book Publishing Industry Development Program (BPIDP) for our publishing activities. We would also like to thank the government of Québec for its SODEC income tax program for book publication.

Symbols

≡	Air conditioning
bkfst incl.	Breakfast included
⇄	Fax number
🔥	Fireplace
⊘	Fitness centre
fb	Full board (lodging + 3 meals)
½b	Half board (lodging + 2 meals)
K	Kitchenette
🐾	Pets allowed
≈	Pool
pb/sb	Both private and shared bathrooms*
sb	Shared bathroom
ℝ	Refrigerator
ℜ	Restaurant
⌂	Sauna
☼	Spa
☎	Telephone number
🚢	Ulysses's favourite
⊛	Whirlpool

*Note that all establishments have private bathrooms unless otherwise indicated.

Attraction Classification

★	Interesting
★★	Worth a visit
★★★	Not to be missed

Hotel Classification

$	$50 or less
$$	$51 to $100
$$$	$101 to $150
$$$$	$151 to $200
$$$$$	more than $200

Unless otherwise indicated, the prices in the guide are
for one standard room, double occupancy in high season.

Restaurant Classification

$	$10 or less
$$	$11 to $20
$$$	$21 to $30
$$$$	more than $30

Unless otherwise indicated, the prices in the guide are for a
three-course meal for one person, not including drinks and tip.

All prices in this guide are in Canadian dollars.

Table of Contents

Table of Contents *(continued)*

List of Maps

List of Maps *(continued)*

Map Symbols

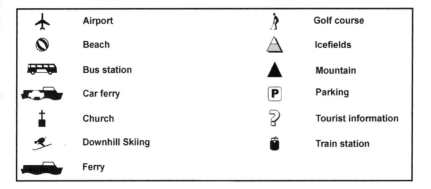

✈ Airport

◉ Beach

🚌 Bus station

🚗 Car ferry

✝ Church

⛷ Downhill Skiing

🚤 Ferry

🏌 Golf course

△ Icefields

▲ Mountain

P Parking

? Tourist information

🚂 Train station

Write to Us

The information contained in this guide was correct at press time. However, mistakes can slip in, omissions are always possible, places can disappear, etc. The authors and publisher hereby disclaim any liability for loss or damage resulting from omissions or errors.

We value your comments, corrections and suggestions, as they allow us to keep each guide up to date. The best contributions will be rewarded with a free book from Ulysses Travel Guides. All you have to do is write us at the following address and indicate which title you would be interested in receiving.

Ulysses Travel Guides
4176 St. Denis Street
Montréal, Québec
Canada H2W 2M5
www.ulyssesguides.com
E-mail: text@ulysses.ca

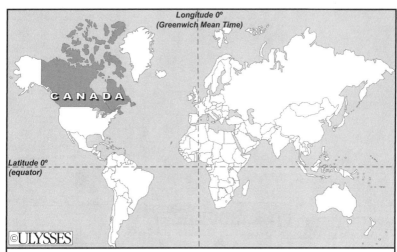

 # Where is Western Canada?

British Columbia
Capital: Victoria
Population: 3,900,000 inhab.
Area: 950,000 km²

Saskatchewan
Capital: Regina
Population: 990,000 inhab.
Area: 651,900 km²

Alberta
Capital: Edmonton
Population: 2,600,000 inhab.
Area: 661,000 km²

Manitoba
Capital: Winnipeg
Population: 1,114,000 inhab.
Area: 649,950 km²

Travel better, enjoy more

ULYSSES
Travel Guides

Western Canada is

a difficult region to pin down. Some define it as British Columbia and Alberta, some as everything west of Ontario (the generally accepted centre of Canada), while still others would further divide that version of Western Canada into the Prairies, the mountains and the coast.

The version of Western Canada described in this guidebook adopts the wider definition, including the provinces of British Columbia, Alberta, Saskatchewan and Manitoba, so that we may introduce you to the range of landscapes found across this part of Canada.

The fabulous chain of mountains, the Rockies, is an easy focus for any trip to this part of the world. But what trip to Canada's West would be complete without also experiencing Calgary and the world-famous Stampede, the rolling plains, magnificent lakes and rivers of southern Alberta, Saskatchewan and Manitoba, the metropolis of the Pacific, Vancouver, the stunning coastline, Gulf Islands or the fruit-bearing valleys of southern British Columbia?

This region has only been known to Europeans for the last 200 years. In fact, the sons of the French explorer La Vérendrye did not set eyes on the Rocky Mountains until the end of the 18th century, and England's George Vancouver only explored the Pacific coast and Columbia River in the last decade of the same century. White settlement of the region is even more recent, going back just over 100 years in Alberta, which, like Saskatchewan, has only existed as a province since 1905. Aboriginal peoples have inhabited this territory for at least 11,000 years, but never in large numbers; there were only 220,000 of them in all of Canada when explorer Jacques Cartier arrived in 1534.

Geography

This guide covers the four most westerly provinces of Canada: British Columbia, located on the Pacific coast and covered by vast mountain chains; Alberta, which begins on the eastern slopes of the Rocky Mountains and extends into the vast Canadian prairies, Saskatchewan, and finally Manitoba, which borders the central province of Ontario. These provinces are bordered to the south by the U.S. states of Washington on the coast, and heading eastward Idaho, Montana, North Dakota and Minnesota. British Columbia borders Alaska to the northwest and the Yukon to the north. The northeastern corner of British Columbia and the entire northern border of Alberta and Saskatchewan are shared with the Northwest Territories, while Manitoba's northern border is shared by the newly created Inuit territory of Nunavut.

British Columbia is the largest of these provinces with an area of 950,000km². And Alberta, Saskatchewan, and Manitoba cover some 650,000km².

Carved out by countless fjords and dotted with hundreds of islands, British Columbia's jagged coastline is 7,000km long, not counting the shores of the islands. The largest of these is Vancouver Island, about the size of the Netherlands and home to the provincial capital, Victoria. Despite its name, the city of Vancouver is not on the island but rather lies across the Strait of Juan de Fuca, on the mainland. The Queen Charlotte Islands lie to the north. The maritime nature of the province is foremost in many minds, but in actuality three quarters of the province lie an average of more than 930m above sea level, and a 3,000m-high barrier of mountains is visible from the coast. A succession of mountain ranges stretches from west to east, all the way to the famous Rocky Mountains, whose summits reach up to 4,000m. This chain was named for its bare, rocky eastern slopes.

During the Precambrian era, the Pacific Ocean covered most of Western Canada. Over a period of about 500 million years, the ocean advanced and receded, depositing sediment on the Precambrian rock of the Canadian Shield, one of the oldest rock formations on earth. Microscopic organisms in the sea died, creating enormous amounts of decaying organic matter, at the source of Alberta's huge oil deposits. By

the Cretaceous period, some 75 million years ago, the Arctic Ocean had flooded most of Alberta, creating a vast inland sea known as the Bearpaw.

Dinosaurs thrived along the shores of this subtropical sea and along the rivers that emptied into it. They lived there for millions of years, until about 70 million years ago when the Pacific Plate collided with the North American Plate and was forced upwards, forming the mountain ranges of present-day British Columbia and western Alberta. This gradually altered the climate, cooling things down and eventually killing off the dinosaurs around 63 million years ago. Then, about a million years ago, four polar ice caps advanced across the region, eroding the mountain ranges and carving out the rivers and lakes that make up the present landscape as they receded.

These rivers divide the province of Alberta into regions. The Mackenzie, Peace and Athabasca Rivers make the land arable as far as the Boreal forests of the north and eventually empty into the Arctic Ocean. The North Saskatchewan and Red Deer Rivers provide most of the irrigation for Alberta farms, and empty into Hudson Bay, along with the South Saskatchewan, Oldman and Bow Rivers.

Flora and Fauna

There is a section devoted specifically to the flora and fauna of the Rockies at the beginning of the chapter describing that region (see p 266).

Despite the limited extent of the plains in British Columbia, 56% of the province's territory is covered by forest. The forest growing along the coast, Haida Gwaii (Queen Charlotte Islands) and on the west coast of Vancouver Island is so

lush that it is called the northern rain forest, the counterpart of the tropical rain forest. Douglas firs and western red cedars abound, as does the Sitka spruce. The Douglas fir can grow to up to 90m in height and 4.5m in diameter. This forest receives up to 4,000mm of rain per year and many of its trees are more than 1,000 years old, though most of the ancient Douglas firs were cut down in the last century. Much higher and drier, the province's interior is home to vast pine, spruce and hemlock forests.

Larches grow in the subalpine forests found at higher altitudes. The larch is the only coniferous tree in Canada that loses its needles in the fall, after they turn yellow. They grow back in the spring.

Sheltered by Vancouver Island, the southern Gulf Islands have a relatively dry, mild climate. You'll even find certain varieties of cacti here, including the prickly pear. Flowers bloom in this area all year round, especially in the months of April and May.

The prairies stretch from southeast Alberta to Ontario. Grasses cover the land, except along the rivers, where cottonwood and willows trees grow. Cacti are also common here. The prairies rise and become hilly as you head west into the foothills, where aspen, white spruce, lodgepole pine and Douglas fir trees grow.

A belt of aspen parkland acts as a transition zone between the grasslands of the south and the Boreal forest of the north. Aspen and grasslands cover most of this area.

Beyond this, more than half the territory is covered with Boreal forest dotted with lakes, bogs, and marshland. In the northern mixed forest, it is not uncommon for an invasion of parasites, a heavily logged

Bighorn sheeps

area, or a forest fire to spawn a pioneer forest which will initiate the regeneration of the original forest. White spruce, lodgepole pine and balsam fir are the most common trees. Finally, parts of this region are strewn with bushes bearing raspberries and Saskatoon berries.

Wildlife abounds throughout Alberta and travellers with cars should look out for muledeer and white-tailed deer. Even just outside the city of Calgary these animals can often be found close to highways. Pronghorns scampering across grasslands are a common sight, and coyotes and occasionally wolves can also be spotted near highways, especially farther north. Black bears are found in forested areas throughout the province, while grizzly bears inhabit Waterton Lakes National Park along with cougars and bighorn sheep.

Warmed by the Japanese current, the waters of the Pacific maintain a higher temperature than those of the Atlantic which are cooled by the Labrador current. As a result, this region features very distinctive marine life. For example, this is the only place in Canada where sea otters are found, even though they were almost completely exterminated by hunting. Sea lions are also indigenous to the Pacific coast.

The Northern sea lion is often the subject of fishers' griping, since it is the main predator of salmon. It is true that some sea lions can weigh up to a tonne and never seem to stop eating, but many other animals feast on the abundant salmon on the coast and in the rivers where they spawn. Grizzly bears, for example, gather for a feast when the rivers are teeming with salmon, and gourmets that they are, eat only the roe and the head! Wolves, black bears, raccoons, gulls and bald eagles eat the leftovers.

Speaking of bald eagles, the Pacific coast is home to Canada's largest population of these majestic birds, which have all but disappeared from the Atlantic coast.

Countless orcas inhabit the waters around Vancouver Island and are commonly spotted from the ferries that link this island with the mainland. They are the only marine mammals that eat warm-blooded animals like seals, belugas and other smaller whales, which probably explains their more common appellation, killer whales.

With the arrival of fall, certain marine mammals, like the grey whale, migrate from Alaska to Baja California in Mexico. They make their way back up to Alaska in the winter.

Orca

Large numbers of cougars (see p 267) inhabit British Columbia's forests, particularly on Vancouver Island, where they feed on Columbia blacktail deer.

An impressive variety of birds and mammals inhabits Alberta. Some of the more noteworthy winged species are bald eagles found around the northern lakes, prairie and peregrine falcons, which can often be seen in and around the plains either diving for prey or waiting patiently on a fence post by the highway. Finally, the migratory path of the trumpeter swan passes through Alberta.

To the delight of anglers, the lakes and rivers of this region are teeming with countless freshwater fish, including eight different varieties of trout.

History

The First Inhabitants

The region's first human inhabitants are believed to have arrived at least 11,000 years ago when the Wisconsin glacier receded, though they may have arrived on the American continent earlier. These people found large numbers of buffalo and other game animals here, as well as berries and roots. They did not waste any of these resources, using hides for clothing, storage and shelter, bones as tools, horns for spoons, antlers for handles, plants for medicines, sinew for thread and clay for pottery.

There is some doubt, however, as to whether native civilization on the West Coast came with these same vast waves of immigration. According to one theory, the ancestors of the West Coast tribes came here more recently (around 3000 BC) from islands in the Pacific. Proponents of this hypothesis base their argument on Aboriginal art, traditions and spoken languages, which are not unlike those of the indigenous peoples of the Pacific islands.

In the 18th century, five First Nation's families occupied the area between Hudson Bay and the Rocky Mountains. The part of the Canadian shield covered by vast forests is Ojibway land. The Assiniboins occupied the plains and prairies and the Western Crees lived in the forests and plains south of present-day Manitoba and Saskatchewan. Southwest of these two groups lived the Blackfoot and in the far north, the Athapaskans.

The arrival of the European colonists drastically disrupted these nations. They were either brought into direct conflict with the colonists or other displaced Aboriginal groups, or were affected by the ensuing profound changes in the environment, such as the near extinction of the Prairie buffalo herds.

The arrival of traders around Hudson Bay introduced items like metal tools and weapons to some of Alberta's First Nations before they had even laid eyes on a single European. The horse was unknown to Alberta's First Nations, and its arrival in the early 1700s following the Spanish conquest of Mexico changed their hunting methods forever. The traditional buffalo jump, during which buffalo were herded over a cliff to their death, thus became obsolete.

Canadian history is marked by a series of treaties between First Nations and Europeans. In the West, the first treaties were drawn up in the 19th century, when the Aboriginal peoples, seeing themselves on

the brink of assimilation, had to give up much of their land to the Crown. This is when the first reserves were created, which, to this day, are still home to many First Nation's peoples.

When the first Europeans arrived on the coast in the 18th century, the territory that was to become British Columbia was occupied by Nootka, Coast Salish, Kwakiutl, Bella Coola, Tsimshian, Haida and Tlinkit. Tagish, Tahltan, Testsaut, Carrier, Chilcotin, Interior Salish, Nicola and Kootenays occupied the interior. Slavery seems to have been practised among the Interior Salish, who had three social classes.

The region that would become Vancouver was inhabited by the Salish. Like their compatriots, they favoured this region for its remarkably mild climate and abundance of belugas, salmon, seals, fruit and other resources. This beneficial environment, combined with the barrier formed by the nearby mountains, enabled the coastal nations to thrive. Not only was their population quite large, but it was also significantly denser than that of other First Nations in central and eastern Canada.

In 1820, there were some 25,000 Salish living on the shores of the Fraser River, from its mouth south of Vancouver all the way up into the Rockies. Like other native tribes, the Salish were sedentary and lived in villages of red cedar longhouses. They traded with other natives along the coast during potlatches, festive ceremonies lasting weeks on end and marked by the exchange of gifts.

Fur and Exploration

In 1670, the territory now known as the prairies, made

up of the provinces of Manitoba, Saskatchewan and Alberta, was ceded by the British Crown to the Hudson's Bay Company (HBC), which took over the economic and political administration of the region.

The HBC controlled trade in Rupert's Land, which encompassed all land that drained into Hudson Bay, therefore covering much of present-day Canada. In 1691, Henry Kelsey, an employee of the company was the first to set sight on the eastern boundary of Alberta. HBC traders, however, had competition from French fur trappers, known as *voyageurs*, who headed inland to the source of the fur instead of waiting for the natives to bring the pelts to the trading posts. Encouraged by favourable reports, independent fur traders in Montreal formed the North West Company in 1787, and then founded the first trading post in Alberta, Fort Chipewyan, on Lake Athabasca.

These trading posts eventually came to serve as bases for exploration and in 1792 Alexander Mackenzie crossed Alberta by the Peace River, becoming the first man to reach the Pacific overland. The trading companies' sole interest in the West lay in the fur trade, which continued unabated, even receiving a boost when the North West and Hudson's Bay Companies merged in 1821. By the late 1860s, however, beaver stocks had begun to dwindle, and merchants turned their attention to buffalo.

After only 10 years of buffalo hunting and trading, there were almost no more of these majestic animals which had once roamed wild. This had dire consequences for the Aboriginal peoples, who depended on the buffalo for their survival and were ultimately left with no choice but to negotiate treaties with Canada, give up their land and move onto reserves.

Furthermore, the fur-trading companies were only interested in fur and offered nothing in the way of law enforcement. Whisky traders from the United States were thus drawn north to this lawless land. With dwindling buffalo herds, Aboriginal peoples were exploited and generally taken advantage of by the Americans, not to mention the deleterious effect the whisky trade had on them. Uprisings, including the Cypress Hills Massacre (see p 360), prompted the formation of the Northwest Mounted Police and the March West began. Starting from Fort Garry in Winnipeg, the police crossed the plains lead by James Macleod. Their presence got rid of the whisky traders at Fort Whoop-Up in 1874, and they then set about establishing four forts in southern Alberta, including Fort Macleod and Fort Calgary.

The fur trade being the principle activity of the HBC, the Company did all it could to discourage colonization in the region, so that they could pursue their activities unimpeded. At the time, the United States had just ended its civil war and was clearly interested in conquering the British part of North America, present-day Canada. They had purchased Alaska from Russia in 1867, and in 1868, Minnesota drew up a resolution favouring the annexation of the Canadian prairies.

These vague American impulses were enough to worry the leaders of the fledgling Canadian Confederation (1867) who negotiated with Great Britain and the Hudson's Bay Company to acquire the Northwest Territories (which at the time included present-day Alberta, Saskatchewan, Manitoba and the

Northwest Territories) in 1868 without so much as consulting the people who had settled there, for the most part French-speaking Metis. These people resisted and prevented the governor appointed by Canada from taking power.

Their leader, Louis Riel, tried to obtain a land title for his people, but the Canadian government paid no attention. With his troops, Riel then declared himself leader of Manitoba and forced Ottawa to negotiate. Finally, on July 15, 1870, the bilingual province of Manitoba was created. Its territory, not much larger than present-day Belgium, was small, and, except for some control over land development and natural resources, it had little of the power the other provinces had. These circumstances have continued to influence relations between the federal and provincial governments of what would one day be the Prairie provinces of Manitoba, Saskatchewan and Alberta.

Some 15 years later, the Metis called back their exiled leader to confront a similar situation, this time in Saskatchewan. Ottawa was faring better this time and sent troops to quash the rebellion. Under of an old British law, Riel was found guilty of treason and hung.

The Isolation of the Pacific Coast

The 18th century saw an increase in exploration and colonization all over the world by European sea powers, but there was an immense area that still seemed inaccessible: the far-off and mysterious Pacific Ocean. Some of the many peoples inhabiting its shores were completely unknown to French, Spanish and English navigators. The Panama Canal had not yet been dug, and sailing ships had to cover incredible distances,

Alberta Treatys

Under Treaty No. 6, the Crees, Assiniboines and Ojibwas surrendered all lands in central Alberta. The next year, in 1877, the Blackfoot, Blood, Peigan, Sarcee and Stoney signed Treaty No. 7, surrendering all lands south of Treaty No. 6. The northern lands of the Beaver, Cree, Slavey and Chipewyan were surrendered in Treaty No. 8, signed in 1899. For the most part, the size of reserves was based on a five-people-per-square-mile rule. Today, more than 35,000 Aboriginal people live on reserves, representing about 60% of the province's total Aboriginal population.

their crews braving starvation, just to reach the largest of the Earth's oceans.

In 1792, English explorer James Cook's compatriot George Vancouver (1757-1798) took possession of the territory surrounding the city that now bears his name for the King of England, thereby putting an end to any claims the Russians and Spaniards planned to make. The former would have liked to extend their empire southward from Alaska, while the latter, firmly entrenched in California, were looking northward. Spanish explorers had even made a brief trip into Burrard Inlet in the 16th century. This far-flung region was not coveted enough to cause any bloody wars, however, and was left undeveloped for years to come.

The Vancouver region was hard to reach not only by sea, but also by land, with the virtually insurmountable obstacle of the Rocky Mountains blocking the way. Imagine setting out across the immense North American continent from Montreal, following the lakes and rivers of the Canadian Shield, and exhausting yourself crossing the endless Prairies, only to end up barred from the Pacific by a wall of rock several thousand metres high. In 1808, the fabulously wealthy fur merchant and adventurer Simon Fraser became the first person to reach the site of Vancouver from inland. This belated breakthrough had little impact on the region, though, since Fraser was unable to reach any trade agreements with the coastal nations and quickly withdrew to his trading posts in the Rockies.

The Salish thus continued to lead a peaceful existence here for many more years before being disrupted by white settlers. In 1808, except for sporadic visits by Russians, Spaniards and Englishmen looking to trade pelts for fabrics and objects from the Orient, the Aboriginal people were still living according to the traditions handed down to them by their ancestors. In fact, European influence on their lifestyle remained negligible until the mid-19th century, at which point colonization of the territory began slowly.

In 1818, Great Britain and the United States created the condominium of Oregon, a vast fur-trading zone along the Pacific bounded by California to the south and Alaska to the north. In so doing, these two countries excluded the Russians and the Spanish from this region once and for all. The employees of the North West Company combed the valley of the Fraser River in search of furs. Not only did they encounter the coastal Aboriginals, whose precious resources they were depleting, but they also had to adapt to the tumultuous waterways of the Rockies, which made travelling by canoe nearly impossible. In 1827, after the Hudson's Bay Company took over the North West Company, a large fur-trading post was founded in Fort Langley, on the shores of the Fraser, some 90km east of the present site of Vancouver, which would remain untouched for several more decades.

Unlike the Prairies, which were simply annexed to the Canadian Confederation in 1868, British Columbia was already a British colony and was thus able to negotiate its entrance into confederation. Isolated on the Pacific coast, British Columbia's principal trading partner was California. As its population grew with the gold rush of the 1850s, certain residents even dreamed of creating an independent country. But these hopes were dashed at the end of this prosperous period, when in 1871, British Columbia's population was only 36,000. Great Britain had already joined its colony on Vancouver Island with British Columbia in anticipation of their eventual integration into the new Canadian Confederation.

Due to American protectionism, local industrialists and merchants could not distribute their products in California, while Montréal was too far away and too hard to reach to be a lucrative market. The only favourable outlets, therefore, were the other British colonies on the Pacific, which paved the way for Vancouver's present prosperity.

With a promise from Canada that a Pan-Canadian railway would reach the coast by 1881, British Columbia joined confederation in 1871. However, all sorts of problems delayed the construction of the railroad, and in 1873, as a severe recession gripped Canada, causing major delays in the railway, British Columbia threatened to separate. It wasn't until November 7, 1885 that the railway from Montréal to Vancouver was finally completed, four years late.

Expanding Confederation

As the railway expanded, more and more farmers settled in the region known as the Northwest Territories, which had no responsible government on the provincial level. You will recall that Canada had annexed the territories (Prairies) without giving them provincial status, except for a small parcel of land, which became the province of Manitoba. Inevitably, Canada had to create the provinces of Alberta and Saskatchewan and enlarge the province of Manitoba in 1905.

Most settlers arrived in Alberta when the Canadian Pacific Railway reached Fort Calgary in 1883 and eight years later in 1891 when the Grand Trunk Railway's northern route reached Edmonton. Ranchers from the United States and Canada initially grabbed up huge tracts of land with grazing leases that, in the

case of the Cochrane Ranch, west of Calgary, occupied 40,000ha. Much of this open range land was eventually granted to homesteaders.

To easterners, the West was ranches, rodeos and cheap land, but the reality was more often a sod hut and loneliness. Though a homestead could be registered for $10, a homesteader first had to cultivate the land, and own so many head of cattle. But the endless potential for a better future kept people coming from far and wide. Alberta's population rose from 73,000 in 1901 to 375,000 in 1911.

Hard Times

Life in Western Canada was hard around the turn of the century. The coal mines of Alberta and British Columbia were the most dangerous in the Americas: by the end of the century there were 23 fatal accidents for every million tonnes of coal extracted, while in the United States there were only six. In British Columbia, a strike by 7,000 miners looking to improve their working conditions lasted two years, from 1912 to 1914, and finally had to be broken by the Canadian army.

For the farmers who came here to grow wheat, the high cost of rail transport, lack of rail service, low wheat prices and bad harvests, along with duties too high to protect the fledgling industry in central Canada, all came together to make for miserable and desperate times. Certain arrangements improved the situation, like the establishment in 1897 of the Crow's Nest Pass rate for grain transport.

The First World War created a temporary boom, which lasted until 1920, causing a rise in the price of raw materials and wheat. The workers remained dissatisfied, though,

and in 1919, the workers' unions of the West created their own central union, the One Big Union. As supporters of Russian Bolsheviks, the union's goal was to abolish capitalism. However, a general strike in Winnipeg, Manitoba quickly created a rift between the workers with respect to their objectives, and demonstrated Canada's determination not to let the country adopt Marxist ideology.

The 1920s again proved prosperous for the West, and Alberta and the prairie provinces, whose economies were essentially agricultural at the time, were able to finish clearing their territory.

The great crash of 1929 had a profound effect on Western Canada, in particular the Prairie provinces, which saw their agricultural revenues drop by 94% between 1929 and 1931! And the fact that their farms specialized almost exclusively in wheat made the situation even worse.

This period was marked by the evolution of two Western Canadian political movements, both of which remained almost exclusively local, the Social Credit and the Cooperative Commonwealth Federation (CCF).

The doctrine of the Social Credit, which supported the small farmers' and workers' stand against the capitalist ascendancy by providing interest-free credit, reached its height under William Aberhart, who was elected premier of Alberta in 1935. His government dared to defy the capitalist system like no Canadian government ever had before (or has since). In 1936, Alberta refused to redeem any bonds, unilaterally cut the interest it was paying on its loans in half, started printing its own money, prohibited the seizure of assets for non-payment and even went

so far as to force provincial newspapers to print the government's point of view. One by one, these Albertan laws were voided by the federal government or the Supreme Court of Canada, but Aberhart was so successful in making the population believe it was the victim of a conspiracy involving the federal government and capitalists that he was re-elected in 1940. He died in 1943 and was replaced by Ernest Manning, elected in 1944.

Manning got the party in order and eliminated all the anti-capitalist rhetoric from the party line. He dealt with all the controversy surrounding Alberta's debt, enabling the province to benefit once again from investment capital.

In 1947, large oil deposits were discovered, and from then on the province enjoyed unprecedented prosperity, thanks to royalties and foreign investment in the gas and petroleum industries.

The CCF, for its part reached its pinnacle in 1933 when it became the official opposition in British Columbia. An outgrowth of the Socialist Party, workers' unions and farmers' associations, the party was never elected to power, but nevertheless influenced the political agenda and gave rise to the New Democratic Party (NDP).

At the beginning of the 20th century, Vancouver's economic focus shifted from Gastown to the Canadian Pacific Railway yards. Nevertheless, most local residents still earned their livelihood from the lumber and fishing industries and lived in makeshift camps on the outskirts of town. Economic ups and downs caused by the opening of the Panama Canal (1914), the end of World War I and the crash of 1929 plagued British Columbia, as the country began to focus its energies on its status as the railway terminal of Canada.

The Modern Era

Neither the Social Credit nor the CCF, two western parties, ever came to play an important role in federal politics. The arrival of John Diefenbaker, the first Canadian prime minister from the West, only further marginalized the two parties. Under Diefenbaker, a true representative of the West (Saskatchewan), as well as under the leadership of his successor, Lester B. Pearson, who truly understood the need to give the provinces more powers, the demands of the West almost seemed a thing of the past. They came to the fore once again, however, during the 1970s, when the oil crisis caused world markets to reel. Residents of oil-rich Alberta took particular offense at Prime Minister Trudeau's various attempts to weaken the provinces by imposing unpopular policies such as the transfer of control over natural resources to the federal government.

At the end of the 1970s, the oil boom, combined with an economic slowdown in Ontario and Québec, gave Alberta almost total employment and made it the province with the highest revenue per capita. This record performance cost Alberta some credibility when it came to its demands for larger control of its oil and gas. The split between the province and the federal government widened, and in the 1980 federal elections, the Liberal Party, the party ultimately brought to power, failed to elect any members of parliament from British Columbia or Alberta. The Liberals thus led the country until 1984 without any representation from these two provinces.

The National Energy Program tabled by the Trudeau government was the straw that broke the camel's back as far as Albertans were concerned. Under this program, the federal government was to claim a greater and greater share of the price of Canadian oil and natural gas, leaving only a very marginal amount of the profits generated by the explosion of the world markets for the provinces and producers. This appropriation by the federal government of natural resources that had been regulated and private since Confederation was strongly repudiated by Alberta and was one of the reasons, along with the repatriation of the Constitution without the consent of Québec in 1982, for the federal Liberals' defeat in the 1984 election. In the early '80s, separatist movements in Alberta succeeded in gaining the support of 20% of the population and in electing a member to the Alberta legislature in 1981.

Pierre Trudeau's Liberal government, which had led Canada almost continuously for 17 years, was succeeded by the Progressive Conservative government of Brian Mulroney, which did away with the much hated National Energy Program. Mulroney was unable, however, to maintain the support of westerners beyond his second mandate. The reasons for this are the same ones that cost him the federal elections of 1993: an inability to reduce the deficit left by the Trudeau government, large-scale corruption and discontent with many of his major decisions, including free trade with the United States and the Meech Lake constitutional accord.

Drawing on Western Canada's sense of alienation and the extreme-right's disappointment with the weakness of the Mulroney government, Preston Manning, an Albertan,

founded the Reform Party in Vancouver in 1987. This party advocated, among other things, a smaller, less costly federal government and the reduction of federal expenditures. Westerners massively supported the Reform Party during the 1993 and 1997 elections.

By 2000, Reform had morphed into the Canadian Alliance, a new party with a new leader, Stockwell Day. In 2002, after a brief period as the party's golden boy and an extended period of embarrassing in-fighting, party members replaced Day with Stephen Harper, now the Leader of the Opposition. While still largely a Western force, two members of the Alliance were elected in Ontario in the 2000 federal elections.

At the same time, Quebecers massively supported the Bloc Québécois party, which favours an independent Québec. In the 1993 election the Bloc formed the official opposition in the federal parliament, while in 1997, the position was taken over by Reform, which maintained its popularity in the West and also gained ground in other regions of Canada. This last election, and the parliamentary distribution that resulted, illustrate the regionalism that exists in Canada and the potential risk of disintegration.

Talk of British Columbia separating first surfaced in the late 1980s and has resurfaced many times since. As a province whose economic wellbeing is more dependent on Asia than on the rest of Canada, it is naturally less interested in what goes on in Ottawa. This is further emphasized by the fact that its industries are heavily based on the exploitation of natural resources, and that these are for the most part provincially regulated, except fisheries.

And the feeling goes both ways; Ottawa is not implicated in and therefore rarely spends much time on B.C. issues; its endless constitutional wrangling is that much more resented by British Columbians.

The New Democratic Party (NDP), a social-democratic party, is the governing party of both Saskatchewan and Manitoba. While British Columbia had an NDP government throughout the 1990s (part of a 30-year pattern of alternation between left- and right-wing governments in that province), in 2001, a Liberal government was sworn in. In its first year in power, and facing a $2 billion deficit, the Liberals cut personal income tax, announced drastic cuts to the provincial government workforce, slashed spending on health and social services and made no friends in the labour movement by illegalizing teacher strikes.

Alberta is presently led by one of the most right-wing governments in Canada, Ralph Klein's Conservatives.

The Canadian Political System

The constitutional document that forms the basis of the Canadian Confederation of 1867, the British North America Act, established a division of power between the two levels of government. This means that in addition to the Canadian government, located in Ottawa, each of the 10 provinces has its own government capable of legislating in certain areas. The Confederative Pact originally allowed for a decentralized division of powers, however, over the last 50 years, the Canadian government has tended away from this decentralization in areas traditionally within the jurisdiction of the provinces, thereby creating tensions

between the two levels of government.

Based on the British model, Canada's political system, like those of the provinces, gives legislative power to a parliament elected by universal suffrage according to a single ballot vote with a simple majority. This method of voting usually leads to an alternation of power between two political parties. Besides the House of Commons, the federal government also consists of an Upper Chamber and the Senate, whose real powers are presently being curtailed and whose future remains uncertain.

The Economy

In the early 1980s, Alberta was the richest province in Canada, followed by British Columbia. While Alberta continues to lead the pack, it is now followed by Ontario. By 1998, British Columbia's GDP per person had tumbled below the Canadian average. Analysts point to factors such as the decline in prices and demand for commodities, like lumber, fish and minerals, on which the province's wealth was based; the prolonged recession in Japan, an important export market; and provincial policies in the 1990s that alienated business leaders. Most recently (2002), the United States Commerce Department slapped a 29% duty on softwood lumber imports from Canada, to make up for what it ruled were Canadian subsidization of lumber production and unfair pricing. British Columbia's lumber mills, and those who depend on them for their livelihood, were hit hard.

In British Columbia, only 2% of the territory is used for agriculture, but it is carried out very efficiently. Dairy and poultry farms make up the majority of the province's

agricultural production, while the cultivation of small fruits, vegetables and flowers represents an important share as well. Orchards and vineyards fill the Okanagan Valley, while vast sheep and cattle ranches stretch across the centre of the province.

Forestry remains British Columbia's most important economic activity, representing more than 30% of the province's GDP. Tourism now occupies second place, and mining third.

Alberta, Saskatchewan and Manitoba are important grain producers; the Prairies produce almost all of Canada's wheat.

Manitoba's economy is not only agriculture-based but has a strong service sector and mining industry; 75% of its mining concentrates on metals such as copper and zinc, and the province is the world's leading producer of nickel.

In addition to wheat, Saskatchewan grows canola, rye, oats, barley and flax. Its land feeds pigs and large herds of cattle and the dense northern forests keep the timber industry strong. Saskatchewan's subsoil is rich in minerals, such as petroleum, uranium, coal, natural gas and it is one of the largest exporters of potash.

Alberta is also the province with the most cattle ranches. Some 4 million head of cattle represent the largest portion of Alberta's agricultural output. These ranches are concentrated in the southern half of the province and in the foothills of the Rockies, where dry conditions and steep slopes make for poor farming conditions.

Although the oil boom is over, the petroleum industry is still vital to Alberta's economy, representing more than 10% of the GDP. Tourism, natural gas, coal, minerals, forestry and agriculture complete Alberta's economic pie.

The Population

In the huge land mass that makes up Western Canada, the total population wavers around 9.2 million. While most are British, French or First Nations origins, many come from Asian or European families who immigrated here in the early 20th century or since.

Saskatchewan has a total population of 1,024,000; along with Newfoundland and Labrador, it is experiencing negative population growth. This province stands out from other Canadian provinces in that most of its population has origins other than British, French or First Nations. A substantial part of the population has German, Ukranian, Scandinavian, Dutch, Polish or Russian origins.

Sixty per cent of Manitoba's 1,150,000 inhabitants live in or around the capital, Winnipeg. Interestingly, it is home to the largest Ukrainian cultural centre outside of the Ukraine. There is also an important Mennonite community, not to mention the 128,000 Metis and First Nations people.

The majority of Alberta's nearly 3 million inhabitants lives in the southern part of the province, while 20% of the population lives in rural areas. Greater Edmonton has more than 938,000 residents, Calgary has 952,000 residents. Alberta's population is among the youngest in the western world; nearly two-thirds of the population is under 40 years of age

Alberta's largest ethnic group is represented by descendants of homesteaders from the British Isles lured to the province at the turn of the 20th

century. The second largest group consists of Germans who migrated over a longer period. German Hutterites today live in closed communities throughout central and southern Alberta. They are recognizable by their particular, traditional dress. Ukrainians are the third largest group. They left their homeland, attracted by the promise of free land. The fourth largest ethnic group is French. Early French fur traders and missionaries were actually the first permanent settlers in the province. Other large ethnic groups include Chinese, Scandinavian and Dutch.

British Columbia has more than 4 million inhabitants, or 13% of Canada's total population, more than half of whom live in Vancouver and Victoria. Vancouver has a population of nearly two million; the city itself numbers 543,000. Victoria has 312,000 people. Over 90% of the province's territory belongs to the provincial government.

Even early on, British Columbia had a multi-ethnic population, but in the wake of the colonial era, residents of British descent still formed a large majority. A number of Americans came here during the gold rush, and soon after, the first wave of Chinese immigrants established Vancouver's Chinatown, which grew considerably after the completion of the Canadian Pacific railway (1886), a good part of which was built by Asian labourers. Before long, a Japanese community was born, further diversifying the city's "Pacific" profile. Today, Vancouver has over 300,000 residents of Asian descent.

British Columbia's cultural mosaic became that much richer in the 20th century, when immigrants from Europe (especially Germany, Poland, Italy and Greece) began arriving. Today, Vancouverites of

British descent make up less than one third of the total population. The French Canadian population, which has always been small in British Columbia, stands at about 60,000.

Only a small minority of westerners are able to express themselves in both of Canada's official languages, English and French. The English language dominates in this part of Canada. There is, however, a significant French presence in the province of Manitoba.

The West was settled in a few short years by people from a variety of ethnic backgrounds, and with no forerunners to either absorb or alienate them, these newcomers found that geography and history had created a Western Canadian subculture. They have always been inspired by their common future, rather than by their disparate pasts.

First Nations

After coming within a hair's breadth of vanishing completely, due to the illnesses to which they were exposed through their contact with European settlers in the late 19th century, the First Nations of the West are now seeing a substantial growth in their population. In 1870, there were fewer than 80,000 Aboriginals in British Columbia. In 1934, illnesses like scarlet fever, tuberculosis and smallpox, against which their immune system had not developed any antibodies, drove their population below 24,000. It has since climbed back up to nearly 140,000 (1996), accounting for about 3.5% of the province's total population.

Though the Aboriginal population is growing considerably, it would be incorrect to speak of a real "renaissance", since a number of nations, like the Coast Salish, who once inhabited the Vancouver region, have vanished forever, taking their rites and traditions along with them. Other communities have become highly visible, but their future is still uncertain.

Two thirds of western Aboriginals live on reservations. Some of these pieces of land are the size of Switzerland, while others aren't even as big Manhattan. A notable case in point is the Capilano reservation in North Vancouver, which barely covers three blocks and is completely surrounded by the city. The reservations were created by the Indian Act, adopted in 1867 by the federal government of Canada, and do not always correspond to the traditional territory of the various nations. Some have been laid out on the sites of former Catholic and Protestant missions, while others were stuck in remote and sometimes inhospitable locations. All the reservations

Totem

are administered by a band council answerable to the Canadian Ministry of Indian and Northern Affairs.

Aboriginals living on reservations are entitled to certain privileges. They pay no income tax, nor any goods and services taxes. They also have the right to free education from primary school through university. Finally, health-related expenses such as eye exams, glasses and dental care are paid by the State. Until the 1950s, the Indian Act also attempted to strip Aboriginal people of their traditional culture, by forbidding their languages, ceremonies and rituals. Children were separated from their families and sent to boarding schools, where they were forced to learn and speak only English and to wear western clothing, to the extent that when the families were reunited, the parents and the children could no longer understand each other.

Since 1960, the Aboriginals of British Columbia have been struggling to revive their culture and traditions. The Haida artists of the Queen Charlotte Islands have become known around the world for their carving, especially totem poles and jewellery. In addition, a number of First Nations have become involved in protecting the province's magnificent forests, viewed by some as a place of peace and harmony and by others as raw material waiting to be turned into shingles, furniture and paper. The demonstrations organized to preserve the old-growth forests of Vancouver Island have been marked by numerous clashes, pitting natives and ecologists on one side against loggers and big business on the other.

The only treaty signed in British Columbia in modern times came into effect in 2000, and not without controversy. The

Nisga'a Nation was awarded 2,000km^2 of land in the lower Nass Valley, in northern British Columbia, subsurface rights and powers of self-government. In 2002, the Haida Nation initiated a lawsuit in which they claim title to Haida Gwaii, also known as the Queen Charlotte Islands, an archipelago they inhabit, along with non-natives, off Prince Rupert, also in northern British Columbia. Some 50 other First Nations land claims are outstanding in the province.

The Aboriginals of the Prairies face a gloomier situation than their British Columbian compatriots. Relegated to bleak lands in the late 19th century, after giving up their vast ancestral hunting grounds, these former nomads, who were forced to settle in one place, never really adapted to their new way of life. Serious drug and alcohol problems are undermining these individuals and communities, as can be seen, for example, on the streets of downtown Winnipeg.

The gradual disappearance of traditional grounds has given rise to aggressive territorial claims in most of Canada's provinces. With the help of the Assembly of First Nations, made up of several band chiefs, the First Nations are trying to advance their cause with government authorities, both federal and provincial.

Arts and Culture

Many Canadians have ambiguous feelings when it comes to their U.S. neighbours. American popular culture is omnipresent in their everyday lives. It is fascinating, but also troubling, and much time and energy is invested in defining just what distinguishes Canadian culture from that found south of the border. Nevertheless, countless extremely talented artists of all kinds have

Hockey

Canada's national sport, without a doubt, is ice hockey. The National Hockey League (NHL) originally had only six teams, two of which were in Canada: the Montréal Canadiens and the Toronto Maple Leafs.

During the 1960s and 1970s, expansions doubled the number of franchises, eventually bringing the number of teams up to 21. Today the league includes 28 teams divided between two associations. The Edmonton Oilers were a part of the second wave of expansion when the World Hockey Association (WHA) joined up with the NHL.

The Oilers and three other WHL teams joined the NHL in time for the 1979-80 hockey season. The Oilers were a well-managed, young team that knew how to scout recruits from the minor leagues. The team's owner even declared that his team would win the Stanley Cup (the trophy awarded to the winner of the finals) within five years or less. This was a bold prediction in a league where the championship title passed back and forth between the dynasties of the

Montréal Canadiens and the New York Islanders.

But while those teams were ageing, the Oilers were building their future. Their captain, Wayne Gretzky, soon earned the nickname "The Great One" due to his incredible natural talent. He accumulated record after record, and even scored five goals in one game on December 30, 1981. That day, he became the first player in hockey history to score 50 goals in such a short period of time: 39 games. He ended the season with 92 goals and 120 assists, an unprecedented record.

However, Oilers fans had to wait until their players matured, and it was not until 1984 that the Oilers finally broke the domination of the New York Islanders, who had just won four consecutive championships. The rest is history: the Oilers won five Stanley Cups in seven years, broke numerous records and had the satisfaction of winning the coveted trophy again in 1990, while Gretzky had been playing for the Los Angeles Kings for two years.

Since these glory years, Canadian teams have remained competitive, but have not frequently won top honours in competition. Money prevailed over passion, and the teams with the largest budgets now attract the best players – nearly all of them millionaires – who all hope to run off with the Stanley Cup.

Canadian hockey in particular suffers from this new business environment since its markets are much smaller than those of the American megalopolises, not to mention the weakness of the Canadian dollar against the American currency. For these reasons, the Québec Nordiques and Winnipeg Jets had to move to the United States at the beginning of the 1990s.

Having broken every imaginable record, Wayne Gretzky retired from competition in 1999. After toying with the idea of renaming their town "Gretzkyville," Edmonton instead decided to name a highway after him. And why not?! The highways can turn to ice on cold winter days in northern Alberta!

gained international renown and have established cultural trends that are uniquely Canadian.

In the following pages we have identified some of the distinc-

tive elements of the culture of this young region, in the hopes that travellers will be tempted to learn more during their visit.

Aboriginal Culture

Totemic culture is surely one of the greatest legacies of Canada's First Nations. This culture reached its height at the middle of the 19th century, and it is easy to imagine the wonder that the sight of 30 to 40 totem poles along the rivers leading to each Aboriginal village must have engendered in the first Europeans to settle in British Columbia. The totems were not revered like idols but featured elements relating to Aboriginal beliefs. The celebrated British Columbian painter Emily Carr (see below) visited many native villages, and some of her most beautiful paintings were inspired by totemic culture.

Unfortunately, totem poles do not stand up well against the ravages of weather, and those that have survived to this day have been preserved in parks and museums; there are also some standing in Gwaii Haanas National Park Reserve, under the watchful protection of the Haida Watchmen. Aboriginal art has always been linked to the beliefs of its producers, which were consistently viewed with suspicion by European missionaries, who did all they could to convert Aboriginal people. This ultimately led to a loss of interest in their art among Aboriginals themselves. Efforts were made in the 1960s and 1970s to revive First Nations' cultures in northwestern British Columbia with the KSAN project, centred in the village of Hazelton (see p 247).

Visual Arts

Emily Carr

At the beginning of the 20th century, Emily Carr, who had travelled extensively throughout British Columbia, produced magnificently beautiful paintings reflecting the splendid landscapes of the Pacific coast and revealing certain aspects of Aboriginal spirituality. Her blues and greens portray the captivating atmosphere of British Columbia.

Several rooms at the Vancouver Art Gallery (see p 70) are devoted exclusively to her work. A pioneer of the West Coast art scene, she was followed by such great artists as Jack Shadbolt and Gordon Smith, whose work illustrates the unique vision that all inhabitants of this region have of the landscapes that surround them.

Chinese-Canadian Art

Canadians of Chinese extraction are the largest ethnic group in British Columbia. They are divided into two distinct groups. On the one side, there are the Cantonese, who settled in Canada after the construction of Canadian Pacific's transcontinental railroad at the end of the 19th century. These individuals suffered from poverty and pervasive racism until the 1960s, and were long restricted to thankless jobs. On the other side, there are the wealthy immigrants from Hong Kong, who display an almost arrogant confidence in re-establishing themselves and all their money in Canada.

This duality is reflected in the many and varied works of art produced by the Chinese-Canadian community. In addition, certain artists of Chinese origins want to develop their individual style and no longer wish to be associated with a particular ethnic group. One example is Diana Li's work *Communication* (from the exhibition Self not Whole, presented at the Chinese Cultural Centre in Vancouver in 1991). Other artists are more concerned with exorcising past injustices suffered by the Chinese community, like Sharyn Yuen, whose installation entitled *John Chinaman* (1990) looked back on the dismal lot of Chinese-Canadians living in the 1920s.

Literature

One of the earliest pieces of literature from the Canadian West is *David Thompson's Narrative of his Explorations in Western North American 1784-1812*. Earle Birney was born in Alberta in 1904, and was brought up there and in British Columbia. His belief that geography links people to their history is evident in his poetry and its attempts to define the significance of place and time.

Born in 1920 in the Yukon, which was overrun by gold-diggers in the 19th century, to a father who participated in the Klondike gold rush, Pierre Berton lived in Vancouver for many years. He has written many accounts of the high points of Canadian history including *The Last Spike* which recounts the construction of the pan-Canadian railway across the Rockies all the way to Vancouver.

Renowned for her powerful paintings of Canada's Pacific coast, Emily Carr wrote her first book at the age of 70, just a few years before her death. The few books she wrote are autobiographical works, which vividly portray the atmosphere of British Columbia and exhibit her extensive knowledge of the customs and beliefs of the First Nations.

Robert Kroetch and Rudy Wiebe are two of Alberta's most well-respected writers. Kroetch is a storyteller above all, and his *Out West* trilogy offers an in-depth look at Alberta over four decades. *Alberta* is part travel guide, part wonderful collection of stories and essays, and captures the essence of the land and people of Alberta. *Seed Catalogue* is another of his excellent works.

Rudy Wiebe was born in Saskatchewan in 1934, but has spent most of his life in

Alberta. He was raised as a Mennonite, and the moral vision instilled in him by his religious background is the most important feature of his writing. *The Temptations of Big Bear*, for which he won the Governor General's Award, describes the disintegration of native culture caused by the growth of the Canadian nation.

Nancy Huston was born in Calgary, where she lived for 15 years. More than 20 years ago, after a five-year stay in New York City, she decided to relocate to Paris, where she finished her doctoral studies in semiology under the tutelage of Roland Barthes. After winning the Governor General's Award in 1993 for her novel *Cantique des Plaines* (*Plainsong* in English) she became a major contributor to French-language literature. Though an anglophone, she writes fist in French and then translates her own work into English.

The writings of Jane Rule, an American who has lived in British Columbia since 1956, reflect a mentality that is typical of both the American and Canadian west. However, she is better known for her efforts to bridge the gap between the homosexual and heterosexual communities. Other notable western writers include poets Patrick Lane from British Columbia and Sid Marty from Alberta. Douglas Coupland is perhaps the province's best-know contemporary writer. (see inset)

Vancouver playwright George Ryga's play *Ecstasy of Rita Joe* marked a renewal for Canadian theatre in 1967. This work deals with the culture shock experienced by Aboriginal communities, who are inherently turned towards nature yet existing in a dehumanized western society. Albertan Brad Fraser's powerful play *Unidentified Human Remains or the True Nature of*

Douglas Coupland

Vancouver can be proud of its native son, Douglas Coupland, who, in 1991, at the age of 30, published his first novel, *Generation X*. His work coined a new catch-phrase that is now used by everyone from sociologists to ad agencies to describe this young, educated and underemployed generation.

Coupland's novel *Microserfs* (1995), is just as sociologically relevant, but this time he turns his attention to the world of young computer whizzes, which he describes, with sweeping, ironic generalizations about American popular culture mixed with a dash of admiration. Coupland's observations struck a chord with many Canadians, who have mixed feelings about their giant neighbour to the south.

Life After God (1995) explores spirituality in a

modern world and the impact of a generation raised without religion. *Girlfriend in a Coma* (1997) criticizes society's "progress" through a woman who wakes up from an 18-year coma to find out nothing has changed for the better. Coupland's other works include *Polaroids From the Dead* (1996) and *Shampoo Planet* (1993). His most recent novel is *Miss Wyoming* (2000).

Coupland has recently shifted focus somewhat, having taken to photography and writing about his city and his country. In *City of Glass*, published in 2000, Coupland writes with typical humour and irony about his home town and accompanies his texts with his own photographs. Coupland's most recent work, *Souvenir of Canada* (2002), marries textual observations and memories with images of Canadian icons.

Love analyzes contemporary love in an urban setting. The play was adapted for the cinema by Denys Arcand under the title *Love and Human Remains*.

Music

The Canadian Radio-television and Telecommunications Commission (CRTC) supervises all types of broadcasting in Canada, ensuring, among other things, Canadian content. For example, non-Canadian songs are limited to 18 airplays per week. Though this may seem restrictive, it has gone a long way to promoting Canadian music and television in all its forms and languages, and to ensuring that Canadian artists get a fair chance in an area that is all too often dominated by the giant to the south.

Western Canada is a cultured place with orchestras, operas and theatre. British Columbia, and more particularly cosmo-politan Vancouver has pro-duced a variety of significant mainstream stars. Bryan Adams was actually born in Kingston, Ontario, but eventu-ally settled in Vancouver. This Grammy-nominated rock 'n' roll performer is known the world over. Grammy-winner Sarah McLachlan, herself born in Halifax, Nova Scotia, now calls Vancouver home and has set up her own record label, Nettwerk, in the city.

Born in 1964 in Nanaimo, north of Victoria, pianist and singer Diana Krall has become a jazz superstar. Her captivat-ing vocals give new life to jazz standards and have won her many fans who were not familiar with the genre. She won three Juno Awards (the Canadian version of the American Grammy Awards) in 2002 for *The Look of Love*, and a Grammy Award for best jazz

vocal performance in 1999 for *When I Look in Your Eyes*.

In the case of Alberta, how-ever, country music is perhaps more representative of the culture. This music has re-cently experienced a revival, entering the mainstream and moving up all sorts of country charts as well as pop charts. Calgarian Wilf Carter became famous in the United States as a yodelling cowboy. k.d. lang, of Consort, Alberta, became a Grammy-winning superstar in the 1990s. In her early days with the Reclines she was known for her outrageous outfits and honky-tonk style, but of late, her exceptional voice and blend of country and pop are her trademarks. A rarity in show business, she has always had the courage to be open about her homosex-uality. Alberta also has its share of more mainstream stars, among them Jann Arden.

Loreena McKennitt, whose recordings featuring haunting Celtic melodies, have sold by the million in over 40 coun-tries, was born and raised in Morden, Manitoba. She cur-rently lives in Stratford, On-tario. Chantal Kreviazuk, a Juno-award- (Canadian equiv-alent of the Grammy) winning songstress and pianist, hails from Winnipeg, as do the Crash Test Dummies, whose first hit was the catchy *Super-man's Song* in 1991.

As for Saskatchewan, its most famous daughter by far is popular folk singer Joni Mitch-ell. Born Joan Anderson in Fort McLeod, Alberta, Mitchell grew up in Saskatoon, Sas-katchewan before heading south of the border, where she found fame and fortune.

Movies and Television

The low Canadian dollar compared to the U.S. dollar has earned Vancouver the nickname "Hollywood North." Indeed, Hollywood produc-ers, also established on the West Coast of the North American continent, rush to Vancouver, where they can shoot movies and television shows for half of what it would cost them in Los Angeles or San Francisco. Thanks to its diverse landscape, the city has played several roles; in the past years, it has become Washington, D.C., Chicago, Milwaukee and even Santa Fe.

Architecture

The sharp geographical con-trast – it could even be called a clash – between British Columbia and the Prairies has led to the development of two very different styles of archi-tecture – as is true of the other arts as well. The blanket of forests and mountains that covers two thirds of the Cana-dian West, combined with the coastal climate, which is much

"Hollywood North"

The fact that the US dollar is stronger than the Canadian dollar has enabled Vancou-ver to become "Hollywood North". Hollywood produc-ers have been flocking north to Vancouver, where they can shoot movies and television shows for a fraction of the cost of filming in Los Angeles or San Francisco.

The diversity of its cityscape has won Vancouver all sorts of honours. Over the years, it has masqueraded as Washington D.C., Chicago, Milwaukee and even Florida in various television series

and films. According to the British Columbia Film Commission, B.C. is the third-largest film and TV production centre in North America, after New York and Los Angeles. In 2001, there were nearly 200 productions in the province, accounting for revenues totaling $1.1 billion, of which foreign productions accoun-ted for $857 million.

This industry may be lucra-tive, but it has lead some Vancouver residents to wonder when their city will star as itself in a movie.

milder than in the rest of Canada, is juxtaposed with the bare Prairies, where the climatic conditions are among the harshest in Canada, and the deep snow is blown by violent winds during the long winter months.

The Aboriginal people were the first to adapt to these two extremes. Some developed a sedentary architecture with openings looking out onto the sea and the natural surroundings; others, a nomadic architecture designed primarily to keep out the cold and the wind. Thanks to the mild climate along the coast and the presence of various kinds of wood that were easy to carve, the Salish and the Haida were able to erect complex and sophisticated structures. Their totem poles, set up in front of long-houses made with the carefully squared trunks of red cedars, still stood along the beaches of the Queen Charlotte Islands near the end of the 19th century. These linear villages provided everyone with direct access to the ocean's resources. The ornamentation of the houses, sometimes reminiscent of Polynesia, indicates possible links between the Aboriginal peoples of British Columbia and the inhabitants of those faraway islands.

On the other side of the Rocky Mountains, the Prairie peoples turned the hides of bison to good account, using them to make clothing, build homes and even to make shields with which to defend themselves. Their homes, commonly known as tipis, could be easily taken down and packed up for transportation. They consisted of a thin cone-shaped structure made with the woody stems of shrubs and covered with hides sewn together with animal tendons.

The first Europeans to exploit the natural resources of the Canadian West took refuge in palisaded forts that doubled as fur trading posts during peacetime. They erected these rectangular structures between the mountains and the plains during the first half of the 19th century to protect themselves from warlike Aboriginals. Some interesting reconstructions can be found in a number of places.

On the West Coast, peace and easy living provided a fertile environment for the introduction of Loyalist architecture from Upper Canada, as evidenced by Victoria's St. Ann Schoolhouse (1848) and Wentworth Villa (1862). These structures are shingled and painted white, and have sash windows with small panes of glass. During the second half of the 19th century, this type of building quickly gave way to elaborate Victorian architecture, which made maximum use of the region's abundance of soft wood, which was easy to cut and turn mechanically.

Numerous sawmills in British Columbia started producing Gothic Revival balconies, Renaissance Revival cornices, Second Empire dormer windows and Queen Anne gables. California, located a few hundred kilometres to the south, left its mark starting in 1880, with the appearance of multiple oriels on British Columbia's facades. These big, multi-level windows project out over the sidewalks, thus letting in lots of natural light.

With Canadian Pacific's construction of a transcontinental railroad and the opening of coal mines in Alberta and British Columbia, all sorts of new towns sprang up, each with its own destiny in store. During their first years of existence, all of them had boomtown architecture, character-

ized by rows of buildings with prefabricated wooden structures, often imported from eastern Canada, and a false front that concealed a smaller interior. Some of these façades were adorned with a prominent cornice or a whimsically shaped parapet.

The inauguration of the transcontinental railroad was also marked by the dismissal of the thousands of Chinese-born workers who had helped build it. These people settled in the towns of the West Coast, where they developed a hybrid architecture, adding deep Cantonese loggias and tiled roofs with turned-up edges to North American buildings (Chinese School of Victoria, 1909). This curious mixture marked the beginning of an oriental influence that continues to be felt to this day throughout the region.

In 1890, anxious to rid themselves of their backward, uncouth Far West image, the fledgling towns of the West destined for a bright future started using local and imported stone (red sandstone from Scotland, beige sandstone from Calgary, grey granite from Québec, limestone from Indiana) and adopting the Richardsonian Romanesque Revival style, in fashion in the rest of North America at the time. Calgary's Stephen Avenue Mall is still lined with these massive, rustic stone buildings, which are adorned with multiple arches framed by small columns with medieval-looking capitals. In the same spirit, but more Beaux-Arts in style, Vancouver, which only had 120,000 inhabitants in 1912, became the home of the tallest skyscraper in the British Empire (Sun Tower).

Upon completing its transcontinental railway in 1886, Canadian Pacific began building a nationwide network of luxury hotels and took particular interest in the Canadian West from the outset. It erected hotels and train stations in the Château style, which over the years became the company's trademark and the country's "national" style.

The Banff Springs Hotel, erected in 1903, and the Empress Hotel in Victoria (1908), both graced with tall, sloping roofs and adorned with Renaissance details, at once reminiscent of the manors of Scotland and the châteaux of the Loire, are the finest examples.

These palaces contrast sharply with the modest Prairie farmhouses hastily erected by immigrants from Central Europe, large numbers of whom settled all over the Prairies in the early 20th century. The lines of some of these houses, now either abandoned or converted into museums, were vaguely inspired by the traditional architecture of old German, Hungarian, Polish

and Ukrainian villages. In those days, the rural landscape was punctuated with thatched and orange-tiled, hipped roofs. In villages, it was not unusual to see wooden churches topped with onion domes.

Since then, Alberta's cattle ranches and farms have become gigantic businesses. The owner's house, often covered with standard white aluminum siding, is surrounded by several modern farm buildings, also covered with metal. The centres of these villages are no longer dominated by the bell tower of the local church, but rather by the huge grain elevators next to the railroad tracks.

At the beginning of the 20th century, British Columbia residents of English and Scottish extraction began developing a taste for the temperate natural environment in which they were living, and also seem to have become infatuated with the first part of their province's name. Lovely landscaped gardens full of flowers

that couldn't survive anywhere else in Canada became all the rage, particularly in Vancouver and Victoria. In the midst of these magnificent green spaces, huge Tudor Revival and Arts and Crafts houses were built. These two styles originated in the so-called "back to basics" movement led by British immigrants.

The Tudor Revival style was inspired by the manors built in the English countryside under the reign of Henry VIII, and was characterized by the use of red-brick facing, bay windows with stone mullions and surbased gothic arches.

The Arts and Crafts movement, which could be described as both a craze for rural British crafts and a rejection of the industrialization of big cities, produced an organic architecture featuring extensions covered with different materials, ranging from half-timbering to walls made of stones from the beach. Everything was skillfully designed to

Prairie Cathedrals

There used to be a grain elevator and a town every 16km along the railway line that follows Highway 61, and throughout the prairies for that matter.

The old elevator system was established in the 1880s and based on the premise that a farmer and his horsedrawn carriage could only haul grain about 16km, in one day. Longhaul trucks put an end to the need for so many elevators and the phasing out of a government transporta-

tion subsidy has forced the construction of a new generation of elevators.

The more sophisticated "high throughputs" can hold more grain, handle the drying and cleaning and load the grain more quickly into the railcars. As a result, grain elevators are being torn down so quickly that they will be extinct within 25 years, maybe sooner. The prairie towns that once depended on the elevators for the better part of their tax base

are also losing a significant part of their histories.

The Provincial Museum of Alberta is searching for old photographs to preserve these cathedrals before the 1,153 elevators that still stood in the Prairies in the summer of 1997 are gone.

In Inglis, Manitoba, a dedicated volunteer group has gone a step further, by restoring a row of grain elevators, which has become a National Historic Site.

produce an overall effect of great charm. The Vancouver architects Maclure and Fox excelled in this domain (Walter Nichol House, 1402 The Crescent, Shaughnessy Heights, Vancouver).

The public buildings erected during the same period, shaped more by their function, are more urban in style. Here, too, however, the emphasis was on British styles and architects. Sir Francis Rattenbury, who designed Victoria's Legislature and Vancouver's former courthouse (now the Vancouver Art Gallery), was the leading light of this prosperous era.

Due to the severe economic crisis that hit British Columbia and the Prairies in the 1920s and 1930s, Art Deco, popular at the time in the rest of the western world, did not make much of an appearance here. There are, however, a few noteworthy examples of this style, including St. James Anglican Church (Adrian Gilbert Scott, 1935) and especially the Marine Building (McCarter and Nairne, 1929), both in Vancouver.

The end of World War II marked the beginning of a new era of unprecedented prosperity throughout the region. The birth of the oil industry in Alberta and the migration of thousands of Canadians to the West Coast, lured by the wonderfully mild climate and remarkable quality of life here, stimulated architectural research. Vancouver soon became one of the country's principal testing grounds for modern architecture. Influenced once again by nearby California, as well as by the Japan of the shoguns and by Haida art, West Coast architects started moving in a new direction.

Using wood, and then concrete, individuals like Robert Berwick, C.E. Pratt, Ron Thom and more recently

Arthur Erickson designed buildings according to the elementary post and beam method, and erected them on the Coast Mountains. The pure lines of these structures blend into the luxuriant greenery that envelops the communal rooms, while the wall-to-wall picture windows that fill in the voids highlight the panoramas of the Pacific Ocean (Robert Berwick, Berwick House, 1560 Ottawa Avenue, Vancouver, 1939; Erickson and Massey, Gordon Smith house, The Byway, Vancouver, 1965). Until that time, only houses in the fishing ports of Vancouver Island had had any openings looking out onto the sea.

In Alberta, the prosperity of the 1970s and 1980s led to massive development in the cities of Edmonton and Calgary. Skyscrapers sprang up like mushrooms, changing both skylines considerably in just a decade. In Calgary, a network of skywalks known as the "+15" was put in place, so that office workers and shoppers could make their way from one building to another despite the winter cold. In addition, the sprawling suburbs of the two rival cities gobbled up several kilometres of the surrounding countryside. Both places are steeped in mainstream North American culture, as evidenced so clearly by the enormous West Edmonton Mall, where the "teachings" of Disneyworld and Las Vegas blend together in a whirl of gaudy commercialism.

However, since 1985, individuals like Douglas Cardinal, an Aboriginal architect from Red Deer, have been trying to develop a style more in harmony with the particularities of

the Alberta plains. The undulating shapes of Cardinal's buildings, which look as if they have been sculpted by the violent winds that sweep the Prairies, have gained international recognition (Canadian Museum of Civilization, Hull, Quebec 1989). In the same spirit, Robert Leblond's design for the interpretive centre of Head-Smashed-In Buffalo Jump (see p 352) blends seamlessly into the land on which it is built.

Two events also drew the world's attention to the region in the 1980s. Expo '86 left Vancouver with a magnificent convention centre (see p 68) shaped like a sailing ship, while Calgary equipped itself with a saddle-shaped stadium, appropriately called the Saddledome (opened in 1983; see p 330) for the 1988 Winter Olympics. Both buildings clearly illustrate that the interaction between architecture and geography endures to this day in the Canadian West.

Concord Pacific Place, located on the former Expo 86 site, was named "Best Master-Planned Community in British Columbia" by the Urban Development Institute in 2000. Its master plan is truly a great success. To get more information on this project, stop by the Concord Pacific Place Presentation Centre.

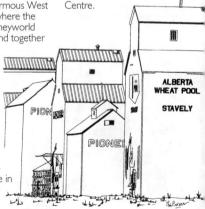

ALBERTA
WHEAT POOL

STAVELY

Practical Information

Information in this

section will help visitors better plan their trip to Western Canada.

Entrance Formalities

Passport and Visa

A valid passport is usually sufficient for most visitors planning to stay less than three months in Canada. U.S. citizens do not need a passport, but it is, however, a good form of identification. US citizens and citizens of Western Europe do not need a visa. For a complete list of countries whose citizens require a visa, see the **Canadian Citizenship and Immigration** Web site *(www.cic.gc.ca)* or contact the Canadian embassy or consulate nearest you.

Extended Visits

Visitors must submit a request to extend their visit **in writing before** the expiration of the first three months of their visit or of their visa (the date is usually written in your passport) to an Immigration Canada office. To make a request you must have a valid passport, a return ticket, proof of sufficient funds to cover the stay, as well as the $65 non-refundable filing fee. In some cases (work, study), however, the request must be made **before** arriving in Canada.

Customs

If you are bringing gifts into Canada, remember that certain restrictions apply:

Smokers (minimum age is 18, 19 in British Columbia) can bring in a maximum of 200 cigarettes, 50 cigars, 200g of tobacco, and 200 tobacco sticks.

For **wine,** the limit is 1.5 litres; for **liquor,** 1.14 litres. The limit for beer is 24 355ml cans or 341ml bottles. The minimum drinking age in Canada is 19 years, except in Manitoba and Alberta, where it is 18 years.

For more information on Canadian customs regulations, contact the **Canada Customs and Revenue Agency** *(☎800-461-9999 within Canada, ☎204-983-3500 or 506-636-5067 outside Canada, www.ccra-adrc.gc. ca).*

There are very strict rules regarding the importation of **plants, flowers**, and other **vegetation**; it is therefore not advisable to bring any of these types of products into the country.

If you are travelling with your **pet**, you will need a rabies-vaccination certificate. For more information on travelling with animals, plants or food, contact the **Canadian Food Inspection Agency** *(www.cfia-acia.agr. ca)* or the Canadian embassy or consulate nearest you before your departure for Canada.

Finally, visitors from out of the country may be reimbursed for certain taxes paid on purchases in Canada (see p 43).

Embassies and Consulates

Canadian Embassies and Consulates Abroad

For a complete list of consular services abroad, visit the Canadian Goverment web-site: *www.dfait-maeci.gc.ca/world/embassies*

Australia
Canadian Consulate General
Level 5, Quay West, 111 Harrington Road, Sydney, N.S.W. Australia 2000
☎*(612)9364-3000*
⇌*(612)9364-3098*

Great Britain
Canada High Commission
1 Grosvenor Square, London W1X 4AB, England
☎*(207)258-6600*
⇌*(207)258-6333*

United States
Canadian Embassy
501 Pennsylvania Ave. NW, Washington, DC, 20001
☎*(202)682-1740*
⇌*(202)682-7701*

Canadian Consulate General
1175 Peachtree St., Suite 1700, 100 Colony Square, Atlanta, Georgia, 30361
☎*(404)532-2000*
⇌*(404)532-2050*

Canadian Consulate General
Three Copley Place, Suite 400, Boston, Massachusetts, 02116
☎*(617)262-3760*
⇌*(617)262-3415*

Canadian Consulate General
Two Prudential Plaza, 180 N., Stetson Ave., Suite 2400, Chicago, Illinois, 60601
☎*(312)616-1860*
⇌*(312)616-1877*

Canadian Consulate General
750 N. St. Paul St., Suite 1700, Dallas, Texas 75201
☎*(214)922-9806*
⇌*(214)922-9815*

Canadian Consulate General
600 Renaissance Center, Suite 1100, Detroit, Michigan, 48243
☎*(313)567-2340*
⇌*(313)567-2164*

Canadian Consulate General
300 South Hope St., 9th Floor, California Plaza, Los Angeles, California, 90071
☎*(213)346-2700*
⇌*(213)346-2767*

Canadian Consulate General
Suite 901, 701 Fourth Ave. S, Minneapolis, Minnesota, 55415-1899
☎*(612)332-7486*
⇌*(612)332-4061*

Canadian Consulate General
1251 Avenue of the Americas, New York, New York, 10020
☎*(212)596-1600*
⇌*(212)596-1793*

Canadian Consulate General
HSBC Center, Suite 3000, Buffalo, New York, 14203-2884
☎*(716)858-9500*
⇌*(716)858-9562*

Canadian Consulate General
412 Plaza 600, Sixth Ave. and Stewart Sts., Seattle, Washington, 98101
☎*(206)443-1777*
⇌*(206)443-9735*

Foreign Consulates in Western Canada

Australia
Australian Consulate
Suite 1225, 888 Dunsmuir St., Vancouver, BC, V6C 3K4
☎*(604)684-1177*
⇌*(604)684-1856*

Great Britain
British Consulate General
1111 Melville St., Suite 800, Vancouver, BC, V6E 3V6
☎*(604)683-4421*
⇌*(604)681-0693*

United States
U.S. Consulate General
1075 West Pender, Vancouver, BC, V6E 2M6
☎*(604)685-4311*
☎*800-283-4356*
⇌*(604)685-7175*

U.S. Consulate General
615 Macleod Trail SE, Suite 1000, Calgary, AB, T26 4T8
☎*(403)266-8962*
⇌*(403)264-6630*

Tourist Information

Each of the four provinces covered in this guide has a Ministry of Tourism in charge of promoting tourism development in its respective province. Tourist information is distributed to the public by regional offices. You can get details on the sights, restaurants and hotels in the region. Besides these numerous information centres, most large cities also have their own tourism associations. These offices are open year-round whereas the regional offices are generally only open in the high season. The addresses of the various regional tourist information offices are located in the "Practical Information" section of each chapter.

Before Leaving

The following provincial and federal tourism offices will gladly send you general information on Canada or the provinces.

Canada

www.canadatourism.com

British Columbia

Hello BC
Suite 601, 6th Floor, 1166 Alberni St.
Vancouver, BC
☎*(250)387-1642*
☎*(604)435-5622 in Vancouver*
☎*800-435-5622*
www.hellobc.com

Super, Natural British Columbia
Box 9830, Station Province-Government, Victoria, BC, V8W 9W5
☎*(604)435-5622*
☎*800-663-6000*
www.travel.bc.ca

Alberta

Travel Alberta
PO Box 2500, Edmonton, Alberta, T5J 2Z1
☎*(403) 297-2700*
⇌*(403) 297-5068*
www.travelalberta.com

Manitoba

Travel Manitoba
155 Carleton Street, 7th Floor, Winnipeg, MB, R3C 3H8
☎*(204)943-1970*
☎*800-665-0040*
www.travelmanitoba.com

Winnipeg Tourism
279 Portage Ave.,Winnipeg, MB R3B 2B4
☎*(204)943-1970*
☎*800-665-0204*
⇌*(204)942-4043*

Saskatchewan

Tourism Saskatchewan
1900 Albert Street, Suite 500, Regina, S4P 4L9
☎*(306)787-2300*
☎*877-2ESCAPE*
⇌*(306)787-5744*
www.sasktourism.com

Getting to Western Canada

By Plane

From Europe

There are two possibilities: direct flights or flights with a stop over in Montreal, Toronto or Calgary. Direct flights are of course much more attractive since they are considerably faster than flights with a stopover (for example expect about nine hours from Amsterdam for a direct flight compared to 13 hours). In some cases, however, particularly if you have a lot of time, it can be advantageous to combine a charter flight from Europe with one of the many charter flights within Canada from either Montréal or Toronto. Prices for this option can vary considerably depending on whether you are travelling during high or low season.

The major airlines flying to western Canada are **Air Canada**, **KLM**, **Air France** and **British Airways.**

For more information:

Canada
Air Canada
☎*800-361-8620*
www.aircanada.ca

From the United States

American Airlines, Delta Airlines, Northwest Airlines, United Airlines, Air Canada
and their affiliates offer daily direct or connecting flights between major US. and western Canadian cities.

From Oceania

Air Canada, in cooperation with United Airlines, offers three daily flights from Sydney to Vancouver via Los Angeles or San Francisco; one continues on to Calgary.

Qantas *(www.qantas.com)* flies twice daily between Sydney and Los Angeles, from where there are connector flights to Vancouver and other western Canadian cities.

Air Canada Offices

Australia
Level 12 - 92 Pitt St., Sydney
☎*(61-2) 9232 5222*
Inwats: 1-300 656 232
⇌*(61-2) 9223 7606*

New Zealand
Dingwall Building 3/F, 87 Queen Street, Auckland
☎*(64-9) 379 3371*
⇌*(64-9) 302 2912*

From Asia

Air Canada offers direct flights between Vancouver and Hong Kong.

Within Canada

Daily flights to Vancouver as well as many other cities are offered from all the major cities in the country. Flights from Eastern Canada often have stopovers in Montreal or Toronto. The following airlines offer regular flights to Vancouver from within Canada:

Air Canada
☎*888-247-2262*
☎*800-361-8620*
www.aircanada.ca

Tango (Air Canada's no-frills carrier)
☎*800-315-1390*
www.flytango.ca

WestJet
☎*888-937-8538*
☎*800-538-5696*
www.westjet.ca

Jetsgo
☎*866-440-0441*
www.jetsgo.net

During the high season, the aforementioned flights are complemented by many others offered by the charter

The Airlines

Air Canada	☎888-247-2262
Delta Airlines	☎800-221-1212
Northwest Airlines	☎800-225-2525
American Airlines	☎800-433-7300
US Airways	☎800-428-4322
Lufthansa	☎800-563-5954
British Airways	☎888-334-3448
Air France	☎800-667-2747
Qantas	☎800-227-4500
Air New Zealand	☎800-663-5494

company **Air Transat** (☎866-847-1919, www.airtransat.ca). These flights are subject to change with respect to availability and fares.

Air Canada Jazz (☎888-247-2262, www.flyjazz.ca), Air Canada's regional partner, offers flights within British Columbia on Air BC.

Airports

Vancouver International Airport

Vancouver International Airport (☎604-207-7077, www.yvr.ca) is served by flights from across Canada, the United States, Europe and Asia. Nineteen airline companies presently use the airport. The airport is located 15km from downtown. It takes about 30 minutes to get downtown by car or bus. A taxi or limousine will cost you about $25-$30, or you can take the **Airporter** (*$12 one way or $18 return; departures: every 20min from 9am to 8pm and every 30min from 9pm to 11:30pm;* ☎604-946-8866 or 800-688-3141, www.yvrair porter.com), which offers shuttle service to the major downtown hotels, the bus depot and the ferries. To

reach downtown by public transit take Bus #100 for downtown and points east and Bus #404 for Richmond, Delta and points south. It costs between $2 and $4 depending on the destination and time of the day.

Take note: even if you have already paid various taxes included in the purchase price of your ticket, Vancouver International Airport charges every passenger an **Airport Improvement Fee (AIF)**. The fee is $5 for flights within B.C. and to the Yukon, $10 for flights elsewhere in North America, and $15 for overseas flights; credit cards are accepted, and most in-transit passengers are exempted.

Besides the regular airport services (*duty-free shops, cafeterias, restaurants, etc.*) you will also find an exchange office. Several car rental companies also have offices in the airport, including Avis, Thrifty, National, Hertz, Alamo Rent-a-Car and Budget (see p 55).

Victoria International Airport

Victoria International Airport (☎250-953-7500, www.cyyj.ca) is 27km from downtown Victoria and the second largest

airport in British Columbia. There is an exchange office open from 6am to 9pm. Several car rental companies, including Avis, Budget, Hertz and National Tilden have offices at the airport. Taxis and limousines can bring you downtown for about $38. The **AKAL Airport Shuttle** (☎250-386-2525) provides transportation to the major downtown hotels. The cost is $13 one-way or $23 return for adults.

Calgary International Airport

Calgary International Airport (☎403-735-1200, www.calgaryairport.com) is the largest airport in the province of Alberta and the fourth busiest in Canada. There is a currency exchange office open from 6am to 9pm. Taxis and limousines can take you downtown for about $25, while the **Airport Shuttle Express** (*$14 downtown; every day 4am to 2am;* ☎403-509-4799 or 888-642-5252) shuttle bus takes passengers downtown. Several car rental companies have offices at the airport, these include Avis, Thrifty, Hertz, Budget, National and Alamo (see p 324). Two shuttles run between Calgary International Airport and Banff, Lake Louise and Jasper:

Brewster (☎403-762-6700 or 800-661-1152, www. brewster.ca) charges $40 to Banff, $47 to Lake Louise and $75 to Jasper, all one-way, and the **Banff Airporter** (☎888-449-2901 or 403-762-3330) charges $40 one-way to Banff.

Calgary International Airport charges an **Airport Improvement Fee (AIF)** of $12 which is included in the price of your ticket.

Edmonton International Airport

Edmonton International Airport (☎ 780-890-8382 or 800-268-7134, www. edmontonairports.com) is the second largest airport in the province. A taxi or limousine from the airport to downtown is about $30, while the **Sky Shuttle** (☎ 780-465-8515 or 800-268-7134) costs $13 one-way or $20 return. It passes every 20 min on weekdays and every 30min during the weekends. Several car rental companies have offices at the airport. These include Avis, Thrifty, Budget, National and Hertz (see p 388).

Edmonton International Airport collects a $15 **Airport Improvement Fee (AIF)** which is included in the price of your ticket.

Saskatoon John G. Diefenbaker International Airport

To get to Saskatoon John G. Diefenbaker International Airport (☎ 306-975-8900, www.yxe.ca), head directly north of the city approximately 7km. A chain of motels marks the approach. It is about a $12 taxi ride from downtown. There is no shuttle bus.

Regina International Airport

Regina Airport (☎ 306-761-7561, www.yqr.ca) lies just southwest of the city, about five kilometres away (15min); a cab costs $10.

Winnipeg International Airport

Winnipeg Airport (☎ 204-987-9402, www.waa.ca) is situated surprisingly close to the downtown area, only about 5km away. Air Canada has an office inside the airport.

By Train

Travellers with a lot of time may want to consider the train, one of the most pleasant and impressive ways to discover Western Canada. Via Rail Canada is the only company that offers train travel between the Canadian provinces. This mode of transportation can be combined with air travel (various packages are offered by Air Canada) or on its own from big cities in Eastern Canada like Toronto or Montreal. This last option does require a lot of time however, it takes a minimum of five days to get from Montreal to Vancouver. The transcontinental railway passenger service runs three times a week. Note that it does not travel through Calgary, it follows a more northern route through Edmonton and Jasper and then on to Vancouver.

The **CanRailpass** is another particularly interesting option. Besides the advantageous price, you only need to purchase one ticket for travel throughout Canada. The ticket allows 12 days of unlimited travel in a 30-day period. At press-time the CanRailpass was $719 in the high season and $448 in the low season. CanRailpass holders are also entitled to special rates for car rentals.

For further information on VIA trains:

In Canada

☎ 888-842-7245
www.viarail.ca

In the United Kingdom

Leisurail
☎ 0870 7500222
≈ 0870 7500333
www.leisurail.co.uk

Airsavers
☎ 0141-303-0308
≈ 041-303-0306

In the United States

Amtrak
☎ 800-872-7245
www.amtrak.com

Trains from the United States and eastern Canada arrive at the intermodal **Pacific Central Station** (Via Rail Canada, 1150 Station St., ☎ 800-561-8630) in Vancouver where you can also connect to buses or the surface public transportation system known as the **SkyTrain**. The cross-country Via train, **The Canadian**, arrives in Vancouver three times a week from Toronto. The trip from Edmonton to Vancouver is a spectacular trip through the mountains along the rivers and valleys. Those in a rush should keep in mind that the trip takes 24hrs, and is more of a tourist excursion than a means of transportation. It costs less than $200 one-way; check with VIA, however, about seasonal rates.

BC Rail
1311 West First St., North Vancouver
☎ 984-5246 or 800-663-8238
BC Rail trains travel the northwest west coast. Schedules vary depending on the season.

During the summer, the **Great Canadian Railtour Company Ltd.** offers **Rocky Mountaineer Railtours** ($729 per person double occupancy; ☎ 604-606-7245 or 800-665-7245, www.rockymountaineer.com) between Calgary and Vancouver. Passing through the Rockies, it's an extraordinary experience.

Amtrak US Rail
☎ 800-USA-RAIL
☎ 800-872-7245 (toll-free in North America)
There is daily service aboard **Amtrak's Mount Baker International** from Seattle, Washington; the trip takes 3hrs and follows a scenic route.

Practical Information

By Car

By car is the best way to see Western Canada at your own pace, especially when you consider the excellent road conditions and the price of gas, which is three times cheaper than in Europe. An extensive network of roads links the United States and Canada as well as the eastern provinces with the rest of the country. The most famous of these is by far the impressive TransCanada Highway which links Saint John's in New-foundland with Victoria in British Columbia.

Driver's licenses from western European countries are valid in Canada and the United States. While North American travellers won't have any trouble adapting to the rules of the road in Western Canada, European travellers may need a bit more time to get used to things.

Here are a few hints:

Pedestrians: Drivers in West-ern Canada are particularly courteous when it comes to pedestrians, and willingly stop to give them the right of way even in the big cities, so be careful when and where you step off the curb. Pedestrian crosswalks are usually indi-cated by a yellow sign. When driving pay special attention that there is no one about to cross near these signs. Turning right on a red light when the way is clear is per-mitted in Western Canada.

When a school bus (usually yellow in colour) has stopped and has its signals flashing, you must come to a complete stop, no matter what direction you are travelling in. Failing to stop at the flashing signals is considered a serious offense, and carries a heavy penalty.

Wearing of seatbelts in the front and back seats is manda-tory at all times.

Almost all highways in West-ern Canada are toll-free, and just a few bridges have tolls. The speed limit on highways is 100km/h. The speed limit on secondary highways is 90km/h, and 50km/h in urban areas.

Gas Stations: Because Canada produces its own crude oil, gasoline prices in Western Canada are much less expen-sive than in Europe, and only slightly more than in the United States. Some gas sta-tions (especially in the down-town areas) might ask for payment in advance as a security measure, especially after 11pm.

Winter driving: Though roads are generally well plowed, particular caution is recom-mended. Watch for violent winds and snow drifts and banks. In some regions gravel is used to increase traction, so drive carefully.

Always remember that wildlife abounds near roads and high-ways in Western Canada. It is not unheard of to come face to face with a deer only min-utes from Calgary. Pay atten-tion and drive slowly especially at nightfall and in the early morning. If you do hit any large animal, try to contact the **Royal Canadian Mounted Police (RCMP)**. Dial *0* or *911* to reach the police.

Certain roads in northern British Columbia and Alberta are not paved. Make sure you rent the appropriate vehicle (4-wheel drive, high clear-ance) if you plan on covering any rough terrain.

Car Rentals

Packages including air travel, hotel and car rental or just hotel and car rental are often less expensive than car rental

alone. It is best to shop around. Remember also that some companies offer corpo-rate rates and discounts to auto-club members. Some travel agencies work with major car rental companies (Avis, Budget, Hertz, etc.) and offer good values; contracts often include added bonuses (reduced ticket prices for shows, etc.).

When renting a car, find out if the contract includes unlimited kilometres, and if the insur-ance provides full coverage (accident, property damage, hospital costs for you and passengers, theft).

Certain credit cards, gold cards for example, cover the collision and theft insurance. Check with your credit card company before renting.

Warning

To rent a car you must be at least 21 years of age and have had a driver's license **for at least one year**. If you are between 21 and 25, certain companies (for example Avis, Thrifty, Budget) will ask for a $500 deposit, and in some cases they will also charge an extra sum for each day you rent the car. These conditions do not apply for those over 25 years of age.

A credit card is extremely useful, and in many cases required, for the deposit to avoid tying up large sums of money.

Most rental cars come with an automatic transmission, how-ever you can request a car with a manual shift.

Child safety seats cost extra.

See the "Finding Your Way Around" sections throughout this guide for local car rental outlets.

Table of distances (km/mi)
Via the shortest route

	Banff (AB)	Calgary (AB)	Dawson Creek (AB)	Edmonton (AB)	Flin Flon (MB)	Jasper (AB)	Kamloops (BC)	Lethbridge (AB)	Medicine Hat (AB)	Prince Albert (SK)	Prince George (BC)	Regina (SK)	Saskatoon (SK)	Vancouver (BC)	Victoria (BC)
Calgary (AB)	129														
Dawson Creek (AB)	1022	893													
Edmonton (AB)	407	278	597												
Flin Flon (MB)	1260	1130	1547	950											
Jasper (AB)	267	396	964	365	1317										
Kamloops (BC)	480	609	1399	802	1739	435									
Lethbridge (AB)	345	216	1109	512	1165	612	825								
Medicine Hat (AB)	414	285	893	581	1001	681	894	164							
Prince Albert (SK)	884	755	1172	575	375	942	1364	790	626						
Prince George (BC)	644	773	1341	744	1694	377	525	989	1058	1319					
Regina (SK)	872	743	1371	774	748	1139	1352	622	458	373	1518				
Saskatoon (SK)	742	613	1110	513	517	880	1222	648	484	142	1257	261			
Vancouver (BC)	819	948	1738	1141	2078	774	339	1063	1227	1703	777	1685	1561		
Victoria (BC)	886	1014	1804	1207	2144	840	405	1129	1293	1769	843	1751	1627	66	
Winnipeg (MB)	1465	1336	1885	1288	756	1732	1945	1215	1051	834	2032	593	775	2278	2344

Exemple: The distance between Edmonton (AB) and Saskatoon (SK) is 513 km.

Accidents and Emergencies

In case of serious accident, fire or other emergency dial ☎*911* or *0*. If you run into trouble on the highway, pull onto the shoulder of the road and turn the hazard lights on.

If it is a rental car, contact the rental company as soon as possible. Always file an accident report. If a disagreement arises over who was at fault in an accident, ask for police help.

By Ferry

BC Ferries serves 47 ports of call on 25 routes throughout coastal British Columbia. The crossings between Vancouver Island and B.C.'s Lower Mainland take between 90 minutes and two hours. Shorter hops include service to the Gulf Islands, and to communities along the Sunshine Coast, northwest of Vancouver. For more of a cruise experience, you can travel British Columbia's majestic Inside Passage, from Port Hardy at the northern end of Vancouver Island to Prince Rupert. Reservations are a must for this trip and for the eight-hour crossing from Prince Rupert to the Queen Charlotte Islands. BC Ferries has introduced a new summer route between Port Hardy and Bella Coola, this area is called the Discovery Coast Passage, because it reveals a part of the province that until now was difficult to reach.

For information on all these routes contact:

BC Ferries
☎*250-386-3431*
☎*888-BCFERRY*
≈*250-381-5452*
www.bcferries.bc.ca

Also see the appropriate "Finding Your Way Around" sections in this guide.

By Bus

Extensive and inexpensive, buses cover most of Canada. Except for public transportation, there is no government run service; several companies service the country.

The company **Greyhound** (☎*800-661-8747, www.greyhound.ca*) services all the lines in Western Canada in cooperation with local companies.

It is important to book at least one day in advance to take advantage of cheaper fares. Here are some sample adult fares:

Vancouver - Calgary
one way $126.51
return $233

Calgary - Regina
one way $93.14
return $186.29

Regina - Winnipeg
one way $67.41
return $134.82

See the "Finding Your Way Around" sections throughout this guide for local bus stations.

Smoking is forbidden on all lines and pets are not allowed. Generally children five years old or younger travel for free and people aged 60 or over are eligible for discounts. An economic way of travelling long distances by bus in Canada is with the International Coach Pass, a package offering discounts on selected trips between seven days and two months. Tickets can be purchased in Canada and many other countries.

Insurance

Cancellation Insurance

Your travel agent will usually offer you cancellation insurance when you buy your airline ticket or vacation package. This insurance allows you to be reimbursed for the ticket or package deal if your trip must be cancelled due to serious illness or death.

Theft Insurance

Most residential insurance policies protect some of your goods from theft, even if the theft occurs in a foreign country. To make a claim, you must fill out a police report. It may not be necessary to take out further insurance, depending on the amount covered by your current home policy. As policies vary considerably, you are advised to check with your insurance company. European visitors should take out baggage insurance.

Health Insurance

This is the most useful kind of insurance for travellers, and should be purchased before your departure. Your insurance plan should be as complete as possible because health care costs add up quickly. When buying insurance, make sure it covers all types of medical costs, such as hospitalization, nursing services and doctor's fees. Make sure your limit is high enough, as these expenses can be costly. A repatriation clause is also vital in case the required care is not available on site. Furthermore, since you may have to pay immediately, check your policy to see what provisions it includes for such situations. To avoid any problems during your vacation, always keep proof of your insurance policy on your person.

Climate and Packing

Climate

The climate of Western Canada varies widely from one region to another. The Vancouver area benefits from a sort of micro-climate thanks to its geographic location between the Pacific and the mountains. Temperatures in Vancouver vary between 0°C and 15°C in the winter and much warmer in the summer.

The high altitudes of the Rocky Mountains and the winds of the Prairies make for a varied climate throughout the rest of the region. Winters are cold and dry and temperatures can drop to -40°C, though the average is about -15°C. Winters in southern Alberta are often marked by the phenomenal Chinook wind which can melt several feet of snow is a matter of hours. Summers are dry, with temperatures staying steady around 25°C on the plains and lower in the mountains.

Winter

December to March is the ideal season for winter-sports enthusiasts (skiing, skating, etc.). Warm clothing is essential during this season (coat, scarf, hat, gloves, wool sweaters and boots). Winnipeg and Saskatoon are the coldest cities in Canada in winter. Vancouver on the other hand, has a particularly wet winter so don't forget your raincoat. In southwestern British Columbia the mercury rarely falls below 0.

Spring and Fall

Spring is short (end of March to end of May) and is characterized by a general thaw leading to wet and muddy conditions. Fall is often cool. A sweater, scarf, gloves, windbreaker and umbrella will therefore come in handy.

Summer

Summer lasts from the end of May to the end of August. Bring along t-shirts, lightweight shirts and pants, shorts and sunglasses; a sweater or light jacket is a good idea for evenings. If you plan on doing any hiking, remember that temperatures are cooler at higher altitudes.

Health

General Information

Vaccinations are not necessary for people coming from Europe, the United States, Australia and New Zealand. On the other hand, it is strongly suggested, particularly for medium or long-term stays, that visitors take out health and accident insurance. There are different types so it is best to shop around. Bring along all medication, especially prescription medicine. Unless otherwise stated, the water is drinkable throughout British Columbia, Alberta, Saskatchewan and Manitoba.

During the summer, always protect yourself against sunburn. It is often hard to feel your skin getting burned by the sun on windy days. Do not forget to bring sun screen!

Canadians from outside British Columbia, Alberta, Saskatchewan and Manitoba should take note that in general your

province's health care system will only reimburse you for the cost of any hospital fees or procedures at the going rate in your province. For this reason, it is a good idea to get additional private insurance. In case of accident or illness make sure to keep your receipts in order to be reimbursed by your province's health care system.

Emergencies

In case of emergency (police, fire department, ambulance), dial ☎911.

Accommodations

A wide choice of accommodations to fit every budget is available in most regions of Canada. Most places are very comfortable and offer a number of extra services. Prices vary according to the type of accommodation and the quality/price ratio is generally good, but remember to add the 7% GST (federal Goods and Services Tax) and the provincial sales tax, which varies from province to province. The Goods and Services Tax is refundable for non-residents in certain cases (see p 43).

A credit card will make reserving a room much easier (strongly recommended in summer!), since in many cases payment for the first night is required.

Most tourist information centres provide a free hotel-room reservation service.

Prices and Symbols

All the prices mentioned in this guide apply to a **standard room for two people in peak season**. Prices are indicated with the following symbols:

Practical Information

$	$50 or less
$$	$50 to $100
$$$	$100 to $150
$$$$	$150 to $200
$$$$$	$200 and over

The actual cost to guests is often lower than the prices quoted here, particularly for travel during the off-peak season. Also, many hotels and inns offer considerable discounts to employees of corporations or members of automobile clubs (CAA, AAA). Be sure to ask about corporate and other discounts, as they are often very easy to obtain.

The various services offered by each establishment are indicated with a small symbol, which is explained in the legend in the opening pages of this guidebook. By no means is this an exhaustive list of what the establishment offers, but rather the services we consider to be the most important.

Please note that the presence of a symbol does not mean that all the rooms have this service; you sometimes have to pay extra to get, for example, a whirlpool tub. And likewise, if the symbol is not attached to an establishment, it means that the establishment cannot offer you this service. Please note that unless otherwise indicated, all lodgings in this guide offer private bathrooms.

The Ulysses Boat

The Ulysses boat pictogram is awarded to our favourite accommodations. While every establishment recommended in this guide was included because of its high quality and/or uniqueness, as well as its good value, every once in a while we come across an establishment that absolutely wows us.

These, our favourite establishments, are awarded a Ulysses boat. You'll find boats in all price categories: next to exclusive, high-price establishments, as well as budget ones. Regardless of the price, each of these establishments offers the most for your money. Look for them first!

Hotels

There are countless hotels across Canada, and they range from modest to luxurious. Most hotel rooms come equipped with a private bathroom. The prices we have listed are rack rates in the high season. In the majority of establishments, however, a whole slew of discounts, up to 50% in some cases, is possible. Weekend rates are often lower when a hotel's clientele is mostly business people. There are also corporate rates, rates for auto-club members, and seniors discounts to take advantage of. Be sure to ask about package deals, promotions and discounts when reserving.

Bed and Breakfasts

Bed and breakfasts are well distributed throughout Canada, in the country as well as the city. Besides the price advantage, is the unique welcoming atmosphere. They can be a wonderful option for those who want to get to know local people and get personalized service. Credit cards are not always accepted in bed and breakfasts. Unlike hotels or inns, rooms in private homes do not always have a private bathroom.

Youth Hostels

Youth hostel addresses are listed in the "Accommodations" section for the cities in which they are located.

Motels

There are many motels throughout the country, and though they tend to be cheaper, they often lack atmosphere. These are particularly useful when pressed for time.

University Residences

Due to certain restrictions, this can be a complicated alternative. Residences are only available during the summer (mid-May to mid-August) and reservations must be made several months in advance, usually by paying the first night with a credit card.

This type of accommodation, however, is less costly than the "traditional" alternatives, and making the effort to reserve early can be worthwhile. Visitors with valid student cards can expect to pay approximately $20 plus tax, while non students can expect to pay around $30. Bedding is included in the price, and there is usually a cafeteria in the building (meals are not included in the price).

Staying in Aboriginal Communities

The opportunities for staying in Aboriginal communities are limited but are becoming more popular. As reserves are managed by band councils, in some cases it is necessary to obtain authorization from them prior to your visit.

Camping

Next to being put up by friends, camping is the least expensive form of accommodation. Unfortunately, unless you have winter-camping gear, camping is limited to a short period of the year, from

June to early September. Services provided by campgrounds can vary considerably. Campsites can be either privately or publicly owned, fully serviced (showers, electricity hookups) or not at all. The prices listed in this guide apply to campsites without hookups for RVs, and vary depending on additional services.

Restaurants

Many restaurants offer set menus, complete meals for one price, which is usually less expensive than ordering individual items from the menu. The price usually includes a choice of appetizers and main dishes, plus coffee and sometimes dessert.

There are several excellent restaurants throughout western Canada. The local specialties are without a doubt Pacific salmon and Alberta beef. Every city has a wide range of choices for all budgets, from fast food to fine dining.

Prices in this guide are for a typical three-course meal for one person, excluding drinks and tip.

$	$10 or less
$$	$11 to $20
$$$	$21 to $30
$$$$	$30 and over

These prices are generally based on the cost of evening set menus, but remember that lunchtime meals are often considerably less expensive.

The Ulysses Boat

The Ulysses boat pictogram is awarded to our favourite restaurants. To find out more about it, see p 40.

Entertainment

In most cases there is no cover charge, aside from the occasional mandatory coat-check. However, expect to pay a few dollars to get into discos on weekends. The legal drinking age is 19 in British Columbia and Saskatchewan and 18 in Alberta and Manitoba; if you're close to that age, expect to be asked for proof.

Most provinces stop the sale of alcohol at 2am. Some bars remain open past these hours but serve only soft drinks. Drinking establishments that only have a liquor license must close at midnight. In small towns, restaurants also frequently serve as bars. For entertainment come nightfall consult the "Restaurant" and "Entertainment" sections in every chapter.

Wine, Beer and Alcohol

Beer, wine and alcohol can only be purchased in liquor stores run by the provincial governments.

Shopping

What to Buy

Salmon: you'll find this fish on sale, fresh from the sea, throughout the coastal areas of British Columbia.

Western wear: Alberta is the place for cowboy boots and hats and other western leather gear.

Local crafts: paintings, sculptures, wood-working items, ceramics, copper-based enamels, weaving, etc.

Native Arts & Crafts: beautiful native sculptures made from different types of stone, wood and even animal bone are available, though they are generally quite expensive. Make sure the sculpture is authentic by asking for a certificate of authenticity issued by the Canadian government.

Wine: British Columbia has a well established wine industry. Vineyard tours are possible and the wines can be purchased throughout the province.

Mail and Telecommunications

Canada Post provides efficient mail service across the country. At press time, it cost $0.48 to send a letter elsewhere in Canada, $0.55 to the United States and $1.25 overseas. Stamps can be purchased at post offices and in many pharmacies and convenience stores.

Telecommunications

There are two area codes in Alberta: **403** for Calgary, southern Alberta and parts of central Alberta **780** for Edmonton, parts of central and northern Alberta.

There are two area codes in the province of British Columbia. The area code for the lower mainland and Vancouver is **604**; the area code for Vancouver Island, eastern, central and northern British Columbia is **250**.

The area code for Manitoba is **204** and **306** for Saskatchewan.

Long distance charges are cheaper than in Europe, but more expensive than in the U.S. Pay phones can be found

Practical Information

everywhere, often in the entrances of larger department stores, and in restaurants. They are easy to use and most accept credit cards. Local calls to the surrounding areas cost $0.25 for unlimited time. 800 and 888 numbers are toll free.

Telus (in British Columbia and Alberta), SaskTel (in Saskatchewan) and MTS (in Manitoba) sell local- and long-distance phone cards in various denominations for use in pay phones, or you can use coins. Bell Canada also sells cards for local- and long-distance calls, available in most variety stores, newspaper stands, etc. Many pay phones also take credit cards.

Calling Abroad

When calling abroad you can use a local operator and pay local phone rates. First dial 011 then the international country code and then the phone number, except for the United States for which you simply dial 1 the area code and the phone number.

Country Codes	
United Kingdom	44
Ireland	353
Australia	61
New Zealand	64
Belgium	32
Switzerland	41
Italy	39
Spain	34
Netherlands	31
Germany	49

Another way to call abroad is by using the direct access numbers below to contact an operator in your home country.

United States

AT&T
☎ *1-800-CALLATT*

Sprint
☎ *1-800-859-8888*

MCI
☎ *1-800-888-8000*

Britain

British Telecom Direct:
☎ *1-800-408-6420 or 1-800-363-4144*

Australia

Australia Telstra Direct:
☎ *1-800-663-0683*

Money and Banking

Currency

The monetary unit is the dollar ($), which is divided into cents ($\cent$). One dollar = 100cents.

Bills come in 5-, 10-, 20-, 50-, 100-, 500- and 1000-dollar denominations, and coins come in 1- (pennies), 5- (nickels), 10- (dimes), 25-cent pieces (quarters), and in 1-dollar (loonies) and 2-dollar coins.

Exchange

Most banks readily exchange American and European currencies but almost everyone of these will charge a commission. There are, however, exchange offices that do not charge commissions and keep longer hours. Just remember to ask about fees and to compare rates.

Traveller's Cheques

Traveller's cheques are accepted in most large stores and hotels, however it is easier and to your advantage to change your cheques at an exchange office. For a better exchange rate buy your traveller's cheques in Canadian dollars before leaving.

Credit Cards

Most major credit cards are accepted at stores, restaurants and hotels. While the main advantage of credit cards is that they allow visitors to avoid carrying large sums of money, using a credit card also makes leaving a deposit for a car rental much easier and some cards, gold cards for example, automatically insure you when you rent a car (check with your credit card company to see what coverage it provides). In addition, the exchange rate with a credit card is generally better. The most commonly accepted credit cards are Visa, MasterCard, and American Express.

Banks

Banks can be found almost everywhere and most offer the standard services to tourists. Visitors who choose to stay in Canada for a long period of time should note that non-residents cannot open bank accounts. If this is the case, the best way to have money readily available is to use traveller's cheques. Withdrawing money from foreign accounts is expensive. However, several automatic teller machines accept foreign bank cards, so that you can withdraw directly from your account. Money orders are another means of having money sent from abroad. No commission is charged but it

Exchange Rates*

$1 CAN = $0.75 US		$1 US	= $1.33 CAN
$1 CAN = £0.41		£1	= $2.46 CAN
$1 CAN = 0.61 € (euro)		1 € (euro)	= $1.64 CAN
$1 CAN = 4.53 DKK		1 DKK	= $0.22 CAN

*Samples only—rates fluctuate

takes time. People who have resident status, permanent or not (such as landed immigrants, students), can open a bank account. A passport and proof of resident status are required.

Taxes

The ticket price on items usually does not include tax. There are two taxes, the G.S.T. or federal Goods and Services Tax, of 7%, which is payable in both provinces, and the P.S.T. or Provincial Sales Tax of 7% in British Columbia and Manitoba, and 6% in Saskatchewan; Alberta has no provincial sales tax. They are cumulative and must be added to the price of most items and to restaurant and hotel bills. Some hotels charge an additional 8% provincial room tax.

There are some exceptions to this taxation system, such as books, which are only taxed with the G.S.T. and food (except for ready made meals), which is not taxed at all.

Tax Refunds for Non-Residents

Non-residents can be refunded for taxes paid on their purchases made while in Canada. To obtain a refund, it

is important to keep your receipts. A separate form for each tax (federal and provincial) must be filled out to obtain a refund.

Conditions for refunds are different for the GST and the PST. It is important to note that to be eligible, your purchases must total at least **$200**. For further information, call ☎*800-668-4748* or visit *www.ccraadrc.gc.ca/visitors.*

Tipping

In general, tipping applies to all table service: restaurants, bars and night-clubs (therefore no tipping in fast-food restaurants). Tips are also given in taxis and in hair salons.

The tip is usually about 15% of the bill before taxes, but varies of course depending on the quality of service.

Business Hours

Stores

Generally stores remain open the following hours:

Mon to Wed	*10am to 6pm*
Thu and Fri	*10am to 9pm*
Sat	*9am or 10am to 5pm*
Sun	*noon to 5pm*

Well-stocked convenience stores that sell food are found throughout Western Canada and are open later, sometimes 24 hours a day.

Banks

Banks are open Monday to Friday from 10am to 3pm. Most are open on Thursdays and Fridays, until 6pm or even 8pm. Automatic teller machines are widely available and are open night and day.

Post Offices

Large post offices are open Monday to Friday from 9am to 5pm. There are also several smaller post offices located in shopping malls, convenience stores, and even pharmacies; these post offices are open much later than the larger ones.

Holidays

The following is a list of public holidays in the four western provinces. Most administrative offices and banks are closed on these days.

New Year
January 1 and 2

Easter Monday

Good Friday

Victoria Day
the 3rd Monday in May

Canada Day
July 1st

Practical Information

Civic holiday
1st Monday in August

Labour Day
1st Monday in September

Thanksgiving
2nd Monday in October

Remembrance Day
November 1

Christmas Day
December 25

Boxing Day
December 26

Advice for Smokers

As in the United States, cigarette smoking is considered taboo, and it is being prohibited in more and more public places:

- in most shopping centres;
- in buses;
- in government offices

Most public places (restaurants, cafés) have smoking and non-smoking sections. However, the city of Vancouver has recently passed a by-law prohibiting smoking in all restaurants. Cigarettes are sold in bars, grocery stores, newspaper and magazine shops.

Safety

By taking the normal precautions, there is no need to worry about your personal security. If trouble should arise, remember to dial the emergency telephone number ☎*911*.

Disabled Travellers

There isn't actually an association in Western Canada that lists the establishments that are accessible for disabled travel-

lers. For information on wheelchair access at miscellaneous attractions, banks, churches, parks, restaurants, shops and theatres, pick up an *Accessibility Awareness Vancouver Guide*. This guide can be found at **BC Coalition of People with Disabilities** *(204-456 W. Broadway, Vancouver, BC, V5Y 1R3,* ☎*604-875-0188, www.bccpd.bc.ca).*

For more information, contact the following organizations:

Access to Travel
www.accesstotravel.gc.ca

Canadian Foundation For Physically Disabled Persons
731 Runnymede, Toronto, Ontario, M6N 3V7
☎*(416) 760-7351*
⇰*(416) 760-9405*
www3.sympatico.ca/whynot

Disabled Peoples International
3516 42a Ave NW, Edmonton, Alberta, T6L 4N7
☎*(780) 462-4853*
www.dpi.org

Children

As in the rest of Canada, facilities exist in Western Canada that make travelling with children quite easy, whether it be for getting around or when enjoying the sights. Generally children under five travel for free, and those under 12 are eligible for fare reductions. The same applies for various leisure activities and shows. Find out before you purchase tickets. High chairs and children's menus are available in most restaurants, while a few of the larger stores provide a babysitting service while parents shop.

Calgary is the only city in North America to have a "Child Friendly Business Accreditation Program" called the **Child & Youth Friendly Calgary** *(Kahanoff Centre, 8th floor, 1202 Centre St., Calgary,*

AB, T2P 1A7, ☎*403-266-5448, www.childfriendly.ab.ca)* Essentially every restaurant, museum and attraction is rated by children.

Seniors

Seniors get various discounts on transportation and entertainment. Ask around or contact the **Canadian Association of Retired Persons** *(27 Queen E, Toronto, ON, M5C 2M6,* ☎*416-363-8748,* ⇰*416-363-8747, www.fifty-plus.com)*

Gay and Lesbian Life

In 1977, Québec became the second place in the world, after Holland, to include in its charter the principle of not discriminating on the basis of sexual orientation. Other Canadian provinces later followed suit (most recently Alberta).

Canadians are generally open and tolerant towards homosexuality. Over the years, legislation, particularly at the federal level, has been reformed, to an extent, in favour of gays and lesbians, thus reflecting changing attitudes in society, especially in Québec, Ontario and British Columbia. However, the government sometimes seems to be living in the dark ages when Canada Customs does everything in its power to ban the importation of Marcel Proust's novels in English Canada! Little Sisters bookstore in Vancouver has been putting up a brave legal battle against these inspectors who believe they are the authority on censorship.

Generally speaking, rural areas tend to be more homophobic and Western Canada is not as tolerant of gays and lesbians. Yet, the Prairies have their share of queer celebrities, including country-singer, k.d.

lang. Vancouver has the largest established gay community in Western Canada. It is mainly in the West End.

British Columbia

Little Sister Book and Art Emporium:
1235 Davie St., Vancouver, BC, V6T 1Z2
☎*(604) 669-1753*
☎*800-567-1662*
⁼*(604) 685-0252*

Gay Lesbian Transgendered Bisexual Community Centre
1170 Bute St., Vancouver, BC, V6Z 2L9
☎*(604) 684-4901*

Alberta

Gay & Lesbian Community Centre of Edmonton Society
9912 106th St. NW, Suite 45, Edmonton, AB, T5K 1C5
☎*(780) 488-3234*
⁼*(780) 482-2855*
www.freenet.edmonton. ab.ca/glcce

Gay & Lesbian Community Services
223 12 Ave. SW, Suite 205A, Calgary, AB, T2R 0G9
☎*(403) 234-8973*
www.glc.sa.org

Saskatchewan

Gay & Lesbian Community of Regina
2070 Broad St, Regina, SK, S4P 1Y3
☎*(306) 569-1995*
www3.sksympatico.ca/ glcr1

Manitoba

Rainbow Resource Centre
#1-222 Osborne St. S.
☎*(204) 284-5208*
☎*888-339-0005*
⁼*(204) 478-1160*
www.mts.net/~wglrc

Pets

The restrictions on animal companions vary from one province to another. Pets are not allowed in restaurants.

Note that in this guide, the following pictograph 🐾 appears with the description of accommodations in which pets are permitted. In some cases, there is a small extra charge or restrictions apply on the size of the animal. For the safety of your pet and that of those to follow you, make sure that your pet is treated for fleas with a reliable product (available from your veterinarian) before bringing it to any commercial lodging.

Time Zone

Western Canada covers two different time zones: **Mountain Time** and **Pacific Time**. Alberta is therefore two hours behind Eastern Standard Time, while British Columbia is three hours behind. Continental Europe is nine hours ahead of British Columbia and eight hours ahead of Alberta. The United Kingdom, on the other hand is eight and seven hours ahead respectively. **Daylight Savings Time** (+ 1 hour) begins the first Sunday in April.

Illegal Drugs

Recreational Drugs are against the law and not tolerated (even "soft" drugs). Anyone caught with drugs in their possession risk severe consequences.

Electricity

Voltage is 110 volts throughout Canada, the same as in the United States. Electricity plugs have two parallel, flat pins, and adaptors are available here.

Laundromats

Laundromats are found almost everywhere in urban areas. In most cases, detergent is sold on site. Although change machines are sometimes provided, it is best to bring plenty of quarters (25¢) with you.

Movie Theatres

There are no ushers and therefore no tips.

Museums

Most museums charge admission. Reduced prices are available for people over 60, for children, and for students. Call the museum for further details.

Newspapers

Each big city has its own major newspaper:

Vancouver
Vancouver Sun
Vancouver Province

Calgary
Calgary Sun
Calgary Herald

Edmonton
Edmonton Journal

Regina
The Leader Post

Winnipeg
Winnipeg Free Press

The larger newspapers, for example *The Globe and Mail*, are widely available, as are many international newspapers.

Practical Information

Pharmacies

In addition to the smaller drug stores, there are large pharmacy chains which sell everything from chocolate to laundry detergent, as well as the more traditional items such as cough drops and headache medications.

Restrooms

Public washrooms can be found in most shopping centres. If you cannot find one, it usually is not a problem to use one in a bar or restaurant.

Weights and Measures

Although the metric system has been in use in Canada for several years, some people continue to use the Imperial system in casual conversation.

Weights and Measures

Although the metric system has been in use in Canada for more than 20 years, some people continue to use the Imperial system in casual conversation. Here are some equivalents:

Weights
1 pound (lb) = 454 grams (g)
1 kilogram (kg) = 2.2 pounds (lbs)

Linear Measure
1 inch (in) = 2.54 centimetres (cm)
1 foot (ft) = 30 centimetres (cm)
1 mile (mi) = 1.6 kilometres (km)
1 kilometre (km) = 0.63 miles (mi)
1 metre (m) = 39.37 inches (in)

Land Measure
1 acre = 0.4 hectare (ha)
1 hectare (ha) = 2.471 acres

Volume Measure
1 U.S. gallon (gal) = 3.79 litres
1 U.S. gallon (gal) = 0.8 imperial gallons

Temperature

To convert °F into °C: subtract 32, divide by 9, multiply by 5.
To convert °C into °F: multiply by 9, divide by 5, add 32.

The four provinces

of Western Canada boast vast, untouched stretches of wilderness protected by national and provincial parks, which visitors can explore on foot, by bicycle or by car.

You'll discover coasts washed by the waters of the Pacific Ocean (Pacific Rim and Gwaii Haanas National Parks), vast rain forests harbouring centuries-old trees (Vancouver Island), majestic mountains that form the spine of the American continent (Banff, Jasper, Kootenay and Yoho National Parks), some of the world's richest dinosaur-fossil beds in the Badlands of the Red Deer River Valley (Dinosaur Provincial Park), huge stretches of forest, prairies and lakes (Prince Albert National Park; Lac La Rouge Provincial Park; Grasslands National Park) beaches (Grand Beach Provincial Park) and immense northern expanses of rivers, lakes and lush forests (Grass River Provincial Park).

The following pages contain a description of the various outdoor activities that can be enjoyed in these unspoiled areas.

Parks

In Western Canada, there are 15 national parks, run by the federal government, and more than 400 provincial parks, each administered by the government of the province in question. Most national parks offer facilities and services such as information centres, park maps, nature interpretation programmes, guides, accommodation (B&Bs, inns, equipped and primitive camping sites) and restaurants. Not all of these services are available in every park (and some vary depending on the season), so it is best to contact

park authorities before setting off on a trip. Provincial parks are usually smaller, with fewer services, but are still attractively located.

A number of parks are crisscrossed by marked trails stretching several kilometres, perfect for hiking, cycling, cross-country skiing and snowmobiling. Primitive camping sites or shelters can be found along some of these paths. Some of the campsites are very rudimentary, and a few don't even have water; it is therefore essential to be well equipped. Take note, however, that in the national parks in the Rocky Mountains, wilderness camping is strictly forbidden due to the presence of bears and other large animals. Since some of the trails lead deep into the forest, far from all human habitation, visitors are strongly advised to heed all signs. This will also help protect the fragile plant-life. Useful maps showing trails, camping sites and shelters are available for most parks.

National Parks

There are 15 national parks in Western Canada: Glacier National Park (British Columbia), Yoho National Park and Kootenay National Park (in the Rockies, in British Columbia), Mount Revelstoke National Park (in the Columbia River Valley in British Columbia), Pacific Rim National Park (on Vancouver Island), Gwaii Haanas (in the Queen Charlotte Islands), Waterton Lakes National Park (on the U.S. border in Alberta), Banff National Park and Jasper National Park (in the Rockies), in Alberta, Elk Island National Park (east of Edmonton), Wood Buffalo National Park (in Northern Alberta, on the border with the Northwest Territories), Prince Albert National Park (in northern Saskatchewan), Grasslands National Park (in southwestern Saskatchewan), Riding Mountain National Park (in southwestern Manitoba) and finally Wapusk National Park (in northern Manitoba). In addition to these parks, the Canadian Park Service also oversees a number of national historic sites, which are described in the "Exploring" section of the appropriate chapters.

For more information on national parks, you can call ☎800-651-7959 or visit the Parks Canada Internet site at *www.parkscanada.ca*

Provincial Parks

Each of the four provinces manages a wide variety of parks. Some of these are small, day-use areas, while the larger ones offer a broader scope of activities. These parks provide visitors with access to beaches, campsites, golf courses, hiking trails and archaeological preserves. Throughout this guide, the most important parks are described in the "Parks and Beaches" section of each relevant chapter. For more information on provincial parks, contact:

British Columbia

Ministry of Water and Air Protection
P.O. Box 9339
Stn. Provincial Government
Victoria, V8W 9M1
☎*250-387-1161*
www.gov.bc.ca/wlap

Alberta

Environmental Protection and Natural Resources administer the provincial parks, but travellers are better off contacting **Travel Alberta** at ☎*800-661-8888* for information.

Saskatchewan

Travel Saskatchewan
☎*800-667-7191*

Manitoba

Travel Manitoba
☎*800-665-0204*
www.travelmanitoba.com

For information regarding parks, fauna, hunting and fishing in Manitoba, call ☎204-945-6784

Summer Activities

When the weather is mild, visitors can enjoy the activities listed below. Anyone intending to spend more than a day in the park should remember that the nights are cool (even in July and August) and that long-sleeved shirts or sweaters will be very practical in some regions. In June, and throughout the summer in northern regions, an effective insect repellent is almost indispensable for an outing in the forest.

Hiking

Hiking is an activity open to everyone, and it can be enjoyed in all national and most provincial parks. Before setting out, plan your excursion well by checking the length and level of difficulty of each trail. Some parks have long trails that require more than a day of hiking and lead deep into the wild. When taking one of these trails, which can stretch dozens of kilometres, it is crucial to respect all signs.

To make the most of an excursion, it is important to bring along the right equipment. You'll need a good pair of walking shoes, appropriate maps, sufficient food and water and a small first-aid kit containing a pocket knife and bandages.

Bicycling

Visitors can go bicycling and mountain biking all over Western Canada, along the usually quiet secondary roads or the trails crisscrossing the parks. The roads offer prudent cyclists one of the most enjoyable means possible to tour these picturesque regions. Keep in mind, however, that distances in these vast provinces can be very long.

If you are travelling with your own bicycle, you are allowed to bring it on any bus; just be sure it is properly protected in an appropriate box. Another option is to rent one on site. For bike rental locations, look under the heading **"Bicycling"** in the "Outdoor Activities" section of the chapters on each region, contact a tourist information centre or check under the "Bicycles-Rentals" heading in the *Yellow Pages*. Adequate insurance is a good idea when renting a bicycle. Some places include insurance against theft in the cost of the rental. Inquire before renting.

Canoeing

Many parks are strewn with lakes and rivers which canoe-trippers can spend a day or more exploring. Primitive camping sites have been laid out to accommodate canoers during long excursions. Canoe rentals and maps of possible routes are usually available at the parks' information centres. It is always best to have a map that indicates the length of the portages in order to determine how physically demanding the trip will be. Carrying a canoe, baggage and food on your back is not always a pleasant experience. A 1 km portage is generally considered long, and will be more or less difficult depending on the terrain.

Beaches

Whether you decide to stretch out on the white sand of Long Beach on Vancouver Island, or prefer the more family-oriented atmosphere of Qualicum Beach, with its calm waters, or Wreck Beach, the driftwood-carvers' rendez-vous, you'll discover one of Western Canada's most precious natural attractions, British Columbia's Pacific Coast. Swimming is not always possible, however, because of the heavy surf and cold water temperatures.

Fishing

In the West, anglers can cast their line in the ocean or in one of the many rivers and lakes. Don't forget, however, that fishing is a regulated activity. Fishing laws are complicated, so it is wise to request information from the four provinces ahead of time and obtain the brochure stating key fishing regulations. Furthermore, keep in mind that there are different permits for fresh water and salt water fishing. Most permits or licenses can be purchased at major sporting-goods stores.

For more information on salt water fishing, contact:

Fisheries and Oceans Canada
Suite 200 - 401 Burrard Street Vancouver, BC, V6C 3S4
☎*(604) 666-0384*

or

501 University Cr.
Winnipeg, Manitoba, R3T 2N6
☎*(204)983-5000*
www.dfo-mpo.gc.ca

For more information on fresh water fishing, contact:

Ministry of Water, Land and Air Protection
P.O. Box 9339
Stn. Provincial Governement
Victoria BC, V8W 9M1
www.gov.bc.ca/wlap

Alberta Fish and Wildlife Services
South Tower, Petroleum Plaza, 9915 108th St., Edmonton, AB T5K 2G8

Saskatchewan Environment
☎*800-205-7070 or*
(306) 787-2700
www.se.gov.sk.ca

Manitoba Conservation Fisheries Branch
☎*(204) 945-6640*
www.gov.mb.ca/ conservation

As a general rule, however, keep in mind that:

• it is necessary to obtain a permit from the provincial government before going fishing;

• a special permit is usually required for salmon fishing;

• fishing seasons are established by the ministry and must be respected at all times;

• the seasons vary depending on the species.

Fishing is permitted in national parks, but you must obtain a permit from park officials beforehand (see regional office addresses in this chapter, or in the parks section of the chapter on the provinces); for more information, look under the "Fishing" heading in the "Outdoor Activities" section of the relevant chapter.

Outdoors

Birdwatching

The wilds of Western Canada attract all sorts of birds, which can easily be observed with the help of binoculars. Some of the more noteworthy species that you might spot are hummingbirds, golden eagles, bald eagles, peregrine falcons, double-crested cormorants, pelicans, grouse, ptarmigans, countless varieties of waterfowl, including the mallards, barnacle geese, wild geese, trumpeter swans (which migrate from the Arctic to Mexico) and finally the grey jay, a little bird who will gladly help himself to your picnic lunch if you aren't careful. For help identifying them, purchase a copy of *Peterson's Field Guide: A Field Guide to Western Birds*, published by Houghton Mifflin. Although parks are often the best places to observe certain species, bird-watching is an activity that can be enjoyed throughout.

Whale-Watching

Whales are common along the coasts of British Columbia. Visitors wishing to catch a closer view of these impressive but harmless sea mammals can take part in a whale-watching cruise or go sea-kayaking. The most commonly sighted species are orcas (also known as killer whales), humpbacks and grey whales. These excursions usually start from the northeastern end of Vancouver Island, in the Johnstone Strait, or from Long Beach. Ensure that the company you organize your tour with is a reliable one that respects the space and safety of the whales.

Seal-Watching

Seals are also found along British Columbia's coasts, and anyone wishing to observe them from close up can take part in an excursion designed for that purpose. Occasionally, attracted by the boat, these curious mammals will pop their heads out of the water right nearby, and gaze, with their big, black eyes, at the passengers.

Golf

Magnificent golf courses, renowned for their remarkable natural settings, can be found throughout British Columbia and Alberta. Stretching along the ocean, or through narrow mountain valleys, these courses boast exceptional views and challenging holes. A few courses have been laid out in provincial parks (in Kananaskis Country) and near the parks of the Rockies (in the valley of the Columbia River), where peace and quiet reign supreme and luxurious hotels are just a short distance away.

Horseback Riding

Trail riding through the Canadian Rockies is a unique experience. You can sleep under the stars and get a taste of the cowboy and pioneer ways of life. A ranch vacation is another exciting introduction to life in the west.

The relevant chapters contain some suggestions for pack-trip outfitters and ranches. For more information call the relevant provincial travel office.

Winter Activities

In winter, most of Western Canada is covered with a blanket of snow creating ideal conditions for a slew of outdoor activities. Most parks with summer hiking trails adapt to the climate, welcoming cross-country skiers. The mountainous regions boast world-class resorts that will satisfy even the most demanding downhill skiers.

Cross-Country Skiing

Some parks, like those in Kananaskis Country and in the Rocky Mountains, are renowned for their long cross-country ski trails. The cross-country skiing events of the 1988 Winter Olympics were held in the small town of Canmore, Alberta. Daily ski rentals are available at most ski centres.

Downhill Skiing and Snowboarding

Known the world over for its downhill skiing, the mountains of Western Canada attract millions of downhill skiers and snow-boarders every year. The most popular ski hills are around Banff and Jasper and outside of Vancouver at Whistler and Blackcomb.

Fans of powder skiing are whisked to the highest summits by helicopter, and deposited there to enjoy the ski or snowboard of their lives.

Snowmobiling

This winter activity has many fans in the West. Each province is crisscrossed by thousands of kilometres of trails.

Don't forget that a permit is required. It is also advisable to take out liability insurance. The following rules should be respected at all times: stay on the snowmobile trails; always drive on the right side of the trail; wear a helmet; all snowmobiles must have headlights.

The following association can provide further information on the provincial trail system, clubs and events.

British Columbia

BC Snowmobile Federation
☎*(250) 860-8020*

Alberta

Alberta Snowmobile Association
☎*(780) 427-2696*

Saskatchewan

Saskatchewan Snowmobile Association
☎*800-499-7533*

Manitoba

Snowmobilers of Manitoba Inc.
☎*(204) 940-7533*

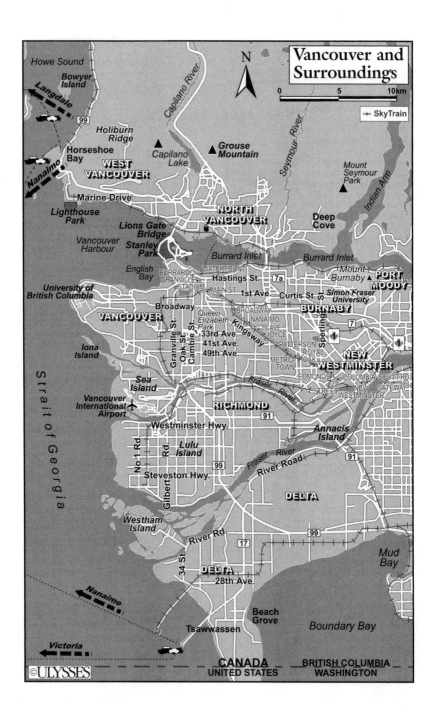

Vancouver and Surroundings

0   5   10km

SkyTrain

Howe Sound
Bowyer Island
Langdale
99
Holiburn Ridge
Horseshoe Bay
WEST VANCOUVER
Nanaimo
Capilano Lake
Grouse Mountain
Capilano River
Seymour River
Mount Seymour Park
Indian Arm
Marine Drive
Lighthouse Park
NORTH VANCOUVER
Deep Cove
Lions Gate Bridge
Vancouver Harbour
Stanley Park
Burrard Inlet
Burrard Inlet
English Bay
BURRARD STADIUM
WATERFRONT
GRANVILLE
Hastings St.
Mount Burnaby
PORT MOODY
University of British Columbia
MAIN ST.
1st Ave.
Curtis St.
Simon Fraser University
7a
Broadway
BROADWAY
NANAIMO
29 AVE
JOYCE
BURNABY
VANCOUVER
Queen Elizabeth Park
Kingsway
Sperling St.
7
Iona Island
Granville St.
Oak St.
Cambie St.
33rd Ave.
41st Ave.
49th Ave.
PATTERSON
ROYAL OAK
METRO TOWN
NEW WESTMINSTER
Sea Island
EDMONDS
COLUMBIA
SCOTT RD.
NEW GATEWAY
Vancouver International Airport
STREET
NEW WESTMINSTER
Fraser River
RICHMOND
91
Westminster Hwy.
Annacis Island
No.1 Rd.
Gilbert Rd.
Lulu Island
99
Fraser River
River Road
91
Steveston Hwy.
DELTA
Westham Island
River Rd.
99
34 St.
17
Mud Bay
DELTA
28th Ave.
Beach Grove
Boundary Bay
Nanaimo
Tsawwassen
Victoria
CANADA
UNITED STATES
BRITISH COLUMBIA
WASHINGTON
©ULYSSES

Strait of Georgia

Vancouver

Vancouver ★★★
is truly a new city, one framed by the mighty elements of sea and mountains.

As part of one of the most isolated reaches on the planet for many years, the city has, over the last 100 years, developed close ties with the nations of the largest ocean on Earth, and is one of the most multicultural metropolises of the Pacific Rim. Its history is tied to the development of British Columbia's natural resources. Most residents were lured here by the magnificent setting and the climate, which is remarkably mild in a country known for its bitter winters and stifling summers. Vancouver, where Asia meets America, is a city well worth discovering.

Geography

Pacific-minded though it is, Vancouver does not actually face right onto the ocean, but is separated from the sea by Vancouver Island, where Victoria, the capital of British Columbia, is located. Vancouver, the province's economic hub, lies on the Strait of Georgia, an arm of the sea separating Vancouver Island from the mainland. Its population is scattered across two peninsulas formed by Burrard Inlet to the north and False Creek to the south.

Point Grey, the larger, more southerly peninsula, is home to the University of British Columbia and sprawling residential neighbourhoods. On the smaller peninsula to the north, visitors will discover a striking contrast between the east end, with its cluster of downtown skyscrapers, and the west end, occupied by the lovely, unspoiled woodlands of Stanley Park. The city's location, surrounded by water and connected to the rest of the country by bridges and ferries, has led to a steady increase in the price of land in the centre and to major traffic problems for commuters from the city's suburbs and satellite towns. Finally, it is worth noting that Vancouver is only about 30km from the U.S. border (and less than 200km north of Seattle).

Vancouver boasts an exceptionally mild climate, with average temperatures of 3°C in January and 17°C in July. There is very little snow, though there is a lot of rain (annual average: 163 days of precipitation) and the summers are temperate and sunny. Clouds that form over the ocean are blown inland by westerly winds, when they hit the Coast Mountains they precipitate causing generally grey weather.

History and Economy

When the first Europeans arrived here in the late 18th century, the region that would become Vancouver was inhabited by the Salish First Nation (the other linguistic groups on the Pacific coast are Haida, Tsimshian, Tlingit, Nootka-Kwakiutl and Bellacoola). In 1820, there were some 25,000 Salish living on the shores of the Fraser River, from its mouth south of Vancouver all the way up into the Rockies.

The voyages of French navigator Louis Antoine de Bougainville and English explorer James Cook, removed some of the mystery surrounding these distant lands. After Australia (1770) and New Zealand (1771), Cook explored the coast of British Columbia (1778). He did not, however, venture as far as the Strait of Georgia, where Vancouver now lies.

In 1792, Cook's compatriot George Vancouver (1757-1798) became the first European to trod upon the soil that would give rise to the future city. He was on a mission to take possession of the territory for the King of England.

The Vancouver region was hard to reach not only by sea, but also by land. A belated breakthrough by Simon Fraser in 1808 had little impact on the region. European influence on native lifestyle remained negligible until the mid-19th century, at which point colonization of the territory began slowly.

In 1827, after the Hudson's Bay Company took over the North West Company, a large fur-trading post was founded in Fort Langley, on the shores of the Fraser, some 90km east of the present site of Vancouver, which would remain untouched for several more decades.

The 49th parallel was designated the border between the United States and British North America in 1846, cutting the hunting territories in half and thereby putting a damper on the Hudson's Bay Company's activities in the region.

It wasn't until the gold rush of 1858 in the hinterland that the region experienced another era of prosperity. When nug-

gets of the precious metal were discovered in the bed of the Fraser, upriver from Fort Langley, a frenzy broke out. In the space of two years, the valley of the golden river attracted thousands of prospectors, and makeshift wooden villages went up overnight. Some came from Eastern Canada, but most, including a large number of Chinese Americans, were from California.

In the end, however, it was contemporary industrialists' growing interest in the region's cedar and fir trees that led to the actual founding of Vancouver. In 1862, Sewell Prescott Moody, originally from Maine (U.S.A), opened the region's first sawmill at the far end of Burrard Inlet, and ensured its success by creating an entire town, known as Moodyville, around it. A second sawmill, called Hastings Mills, opened east of present-day Chinatown in 1865. Two years later, innkeeper Gassy Jack Deighton arrived in the area and set up a saloon near Hastings Mills, providing a place for sawmill workers to slake their thirst. Before long, various service establishments sprang up around the saloon, thus marking the birth of Gastown, later Vancouver's first neighbourhood.

In 1870, the colonial government of British Columbia renamed the nascent town Granville, after the Duke of Granville. The area continued to develop, and the city of Vancouver was officially founded in April 1886. It was renamed in honour of Captain George Vancouver, who made the first hydrographic surveys of the shores of the Strait of Georgia. Unfortunately, a few weeks later, a forest fire swept through the new town, wiping out everything in its way. In barely 20 minutes, Vancouver was reduced to ashes. In those difficult years, local residents were

still cut off from the rest of the world, so the town was reconstructed with an eye on the long term. From that point on, Vancouver's buildings, whether of wood or brick, were made to last.

The end of the gold rush in 1865 led to a number of economic problems for the colony of British Columbia. In 1871, British Columbia agreed to join the Canadian Confederation on the condition that a railway line linking it to the eastern part of the country be built.

Recognizing the potential of this gateway to the Pacific, a group of businessmen from Montréal set out to build a transcontinental railway in 1879. Canadian Pacific chose Port Moody (formerly Moodyville) as the western terminus of the railway. On July 4, 1886, the first train from Montréal reached Port Moody after a tortuous journey of about 5,000km.

A few years later, the tracks were extended 20km to Vancouver in order to link the transcontinental railway to the new port and thereby allow greater access to the Asian market. This change proved momentous for the city, whose population exploded from 2,500 inhabitants in 1886 to over 120,000 in 1911! Many of the Chinese who had come to North America to help build the railroad settled in Vancouver when the project was finished; they were soon joined by Asians from Canton, Japan and Tonkin. The city's Chinatown, which grew up between Gastown and Hastings Mills, eventually became the second largest in North America after San Francisco's.

At the beginning of the 20th century, the city's economic activity gradually shifted from Gastown to the Canadian Pacific Railway yards, located around Granville Street. Within a few years, lovely stone buildings housing banks and department stores sprang up in this area. In 1913, the city was much like a gangling adolescent in the midst of a growth spurt. It was then that a major economic crisis occurred, putting an end to local optimism for a while. The opening of the Panama Canal (1914) and the end of World War I enabled Vancouver to emerge from this morass, only to sink right back into it during the crash of 1929. During World War II, residents of Japanese descent were interned and their possessions confiscated. Paranoia prevailed over reason, and these second- and sometimes even third-generation Vancouverites were viewed as potential spies.

Nevertheless, the city's dual role as a gateway to the Pacific for North Americans and a gateway to America for Asians was already well established, as evidenced by the massive influx of Chinese immigrants from the 19th century onwards and the numerous import-export businesses dealing in silk, tea and porcelain. The name Vancouver has thus been familiar throughout the Pacific zone for over a century.

With the explosive economic growth of places like Japan, Hong Kong, Taiwan, Singapore, the Philippines, Malaysia and Thailand, especially in regards to exportation, Vancouver's port expanded at lightning speed. Since 1980, it has been the busiest one in the country; 70.7 million tonnes of merchandise were handled here in 1991.

Vancouver (especially the downtown core) has enjoyed continued growth since the late 1960s. Even more than San Francisco or Los Angeles, Vancouver has a strong, positive image throughout the

Pacific. It is viewed as a neutral territory offering a good yield on investments and a comfortable standard of living.

Finding Your Way Around

By Car

Vancouver is accessible by the **TransCanada Highway 1**, which runs east-west. This national highway links all of the major Canadian cities. It has no tolls and passes through some spectacular scenery. Coming from Alberta you will pass through the Rocky Mountains, desert regions and a breathtaking canyon.

The city is generally reached from the east by taking the "Downtown" exit from the TransCanada. If you are coming from the United States or from Victoria by ferry, you will enter the city on Hwy. 99 North; in this case expect it to take about 30min to reach downtown.

Getting around Vancouver by car is easy. Although take note that the government has decided not to build any expressways through downtown which is exceptional for a city of two million people; as a result, rush-hour traffic can be quite heavy. If you have the time, by all means explore the city on foot.

Car Rental Companies

National Car Rental
1130 W. Georgia St.
☎(604) 685-6111
☎800-227-7368
at the airport
☎(604) 273-3121

Budget
450 W. Georgia St.
☎668-7000
at the airport
☎800-527-0700 or
(604) 668-7000

No Frills Auto Rentals
5730 Marine Dr., Burnaby
☎877-663-7457 or
(604) 873-6622

Thrifty
1400 Robson St.
☎(604) 681-4869
at the airport
☎(604) 606-1655

Avis
757 Hornby St.
☎(604) 606-2847
at the airport
☎(604) 606-2847

By Taxi

Taxis are usually easy to find, either near large downtown hotels or on the main streets such as Robson and Georgia. The following are the main companies:

Yellow Cab
☎(604) 681-1111

McLure's
☎(604) 731-9211

Black Top
☎(604) 731-1111

Public Transit

BC Transit *(www.bctransit. com)* bus route maps are available from the **Vancouver Travel InfoCentre** or from the BC Transit offices in Surrey *(13401 108th Ave., 5th floor, Surrey, ☎604-953-3333 or 953-3000)*. BC Transit also includes a rail transit system and a marine bus. The **Skytrain** runs east from the downtown area to Burnaby, New Westminster and Surrey. These automatic trains run from 5am to 1am all week, except Sundays when they start at 9am. The **Seabus** shuttles run

Vancouver

frequently between Burrard Inlet and North Vancouver.

Tickets and passes are available for **BC Transit**, including Skytrain and Seabus tickets from the coin-operated machines at some stops, in some convenience stores or by calling ☎*(604) 521-0400*.

The fares are the same whether you are travelling on a BC Transit bus, the Skytrain or the Seabus. A single ticket generally costs $2, except at peak hours (Mon to Fri before 9:30am and 3pm to 6:30pm) when the system is divided into three zones and it costs $2 for travel within one zone, $3 within two zones and $4 within three zones.

BC Transit
lost and found
☎*(604) 682-7887*

Blue Bus
☎*(604) 985-7777*
serving West Vancouver

Car and Van Pooling
☎*(604) 879-RIDE*

Transportation for Disabled Travellers

Handydart *(300-3200 E. 54th St., ☎604-430-2742 or 430-2692)* provides public transportation for wheelchair-bound individuals. You must reserve your seat in advance.

Vancouver Taxis *(2205 Main St., ☎604-255-5111 or 874-5111)* also offers transportation for disabled individuals.

By Plane

Vancouver International Airport

Vancouver International Airport *(☎604-276-6101)* is served by flights from across Canada, the United States,

Europe and Asia. The airport is located 15km south of downtown. It takes about 30min to get downtown by car or bus. To reach downtown by public transit take bus #100 for downtown and points east and bus #404 or #406 for Richmond, Delta and points south. The fare varies between $1.75 and $3.50 depending on the time of departure and the chosen destination.

Take note: even if you have already paid various taxes included in the purchase price of your ticket, Vancouver International Airport charges every passenger an Airport Improvement Fee (AIF). The fee is $5 for flights within B.C. and to the Yukon, $10 for flights elsewhere in North America, and $15 for overseas flights; credit cards are accepted, and most in-transit passengers are exempted.

By Train

Trains from the United States and Eastern Canada arrive at new intermodal **Pacific Central Station** *(Via Rail Canada, 1150 Station St., ☎800-561-8630)* where you can also connect to buses or the Skytrain. The cross-country Via train, **The Canadian** arrives in Vancouver three times a week from Eastern Canada. The trip from Edmonton to Vancouver is a spectacular trip through the mountains along the rivers and valleys. Those in a rush should keep in mind that the trip takes 24hrs, and is more of a tourist excursion than a means of transportation. It costs less than $200 one-way; check with VIA, however, about seasonal rates.

BC Rail *(1311 West First St., North Vancouver, ☎604-984-5246 or 800-663-8238, www. bcrail.com)* trains travel the northern west coast. Sched-

ules vary depending on the seasons.

During the summer, the **Great Canadian Railtour Company Ltd**. offers **Rocky Mountain Railtours** *($784 per person, $729 per person double occupancy; ☎604-606-7245 or 800-665-7245, www.rocky mountaineer.com)* between Calgary and Vancouver.

The steam locomotive **Royal Hudson** *(1311 West First St., North Vancouver, ☎604-631-3500)* is very well-known in Vancouver tourist circles. Dating from the beginning of the 20th century, but restored, it takes passengers from its station in North Vancouver to Squamish, 65km away. The journey allows passengers to discover the splendid **Howe Sound** fjord, as the railway skirts the shore.

By Ferry

Two ferry ports serve the greater Vancouver area for travellers coming from other regions in the province. Horseshoe Bay, to the northwest, is the terminal for ferries to Nanaimo (crossing time 90min), Bowen Island and the Mainland Sunshine Coast. Tsawwassen, to the south, is the terminal for ferries to Victoria (Swartz Bay crossing time 95min), Nanaimo (crossing time 2hrs) and the Southern Gulf Islands. Both terminals are about 30min from downtown. For information on these routes contact **BC Ferries** *(☎250-386-3431 or 888-BCFERRY)*.

By Bus

Greyhound Lines of Canada
Pacific Central Station
1150 Station St.
☎*(604) 482-8747 or*
800-661-8747
www.greyhound.ca

Practical Information

Area Code: **604**

Take note: you must always dial the area code when calling in Vancouver

Tourist Information

Super, Natural British Columbia
P.O. Box 9830, Station Province-Government, Victoria, V8W 9W5
☎*800-663-6000*
www.hellobc.com

Vancouver Tourist InfoCentre
May to Sep, every day 8am to 6pm; Sep to May, Mon to Fri 8:30am to 5pm, Sat 9am to 5pm
Plaza Level, Waterfront Centre, 200 Burrard St.
☎*683-2000*
⁼*682-6839*
www.tourism-vancouver.org

Vancouver Parks & Recreation
☎*257-8400*
www.city.vancouver.bc.ca/parks
Vancouver Parks & Recreation can provide information about sports and recreation activities.

Emergencies

Police, ambulances and firefighters
☎*911*

Crime Stoppers
☎*669-8477*

Emergency Dental Service
☎*736-3621*

Poison Control Centre
☎*682-5050 or 682-2344*

Emergency Veterinary Clinic
24 hour service
☎*734-5104*

Children's Emergency Helpline
dial **0** and ask **Zenith 1234**

Women's help
☎*872-8212*

Legal Help
24 hour service
☎*687-4680*
Information about British Columbia's laws.

Road Assistance
☎*295-2222*

Exploring

The following seven tours, each covering a different part of Vancouver, will help you fully enjoy the local sights:

Tour A: Gastown ★

Tour B: Chinatown, Downtown Eastside and East Vancouver ★★

Tour C: Downtown ★★

Tour D: The West End and Stanley Park ★★

Tour E: Burrard Inlet ★★

Tour F: False Creek ★★

Tour G: West Side ★★★

These are primarily walking or cycling tours, although you will need a car or other transport to tour Burrard Inlet (Tour E) and parts of The West Side (Tour G). Also, to get from Chinatown to East Vancouver (Tour B) you will need to take the SkyTrain or other means of transportation.

Tour A: Gastown

This walking tour can easily be combined with Tour B, Chinatown, Downtown Eastside and East Vancouver.

Long before there were the glass towers, housing million-dollar condos on the shores of Burrard Inlet, there was Gastown, the birthplace of the city of Vancouver. The area dates back to 1867 when John Deighton, known as "Gassy" Jack for his talkative nature, opened a saloon for the employees of a neighbouring sawmill, the **Hastings Mill**. Gastown was destroyed by fire in 1886, but this catastrophe did not deter the city's pioneers. They rebuilt from the ashes and started anew the development of their city, this time in brick and stone, rather than wood; the city was incorporated several months later.

By 1887, when the Canadian Pacific Railway reached its new western terminus, Gastown was booming. Like any true Wild West town, its streets surged with hotels, saloons and shops that catered to the sawmill workers, lumberjacks, railway workers, land speculators and other hopefuls.

In the late 19th century, Gastown's economic development was driven by rail transport and the gold rush. The neighbourhood then became an important commercial distribution centre, whose warehouses eventually became so crowded that a second warehouse district was established in **Yaletown** (see p 78), which eventually supplanted Gastown. Long since abandoned and neglected, the restoration of Gastown began in the mid-1960s and continues to this day.

Vancouver

Located a short walk from downtown and the Cruise Ship Terminal, Gastown is high on the agenda of many sightseers and cruise-ship passengers on a day pass. Today, Gastown is a historic district with many handsome late-19th and early 20th-century Victorian and Edwardian commercial vernacular buildings, which narrowly escaped the wrecker's ball in the late 1960s. Although many of these buildings now house some good restaurants and popular nightspots, the district has somehow managed to retain a whiff of that "Wild West" atmosphere, as a decidedly seedy feel permeates its rundown hotels and tacky souvenir stores. Gastown is also home to a number of First Nations art galleries, though before making any serious purchases, you'd be well advised to check out Gallery Row, south of the Granville Street Bridge.

Some of Gastown's commercial heritage buildings have been converted to residential use, particularly along Alexander and Water streets, contributing to the viability of local businesses but also creating tensions with long-term, low-income residents.

Despite the caveats, many of our readers will still enjoy a little stroll along its cobblestone streets lined with gas-lit lanterns.

Start off your tour at the corner of Water and West Cordova streets, at the west edge of Gastown (the eastern limit of downtown), which is accessible from the Waterfront station of the SkyTrain. It can also be reached from downtown by walking north on Richards Street until Water Street.

Note that if you prefer a guided tour, the Gastown Business Improvement Society (131 Water St., ☎683-5650) offers free walking tours of Gastown once a day during the months of

June, July and August. Tours last about 2hrs.

The **Landing** (375 Water St.), with its brick and stone facade, was a commercial warehouse at the time of its construction in 1905; today it is a fine example of restoration. Since the late 1980s, it has housed offices, shops and restaurants.

Walk east along Water Street.

Like many other 19th-century North American buildings, **Hudson House** (321 Water St.) has its back to the water and the natural setting. Erected in 1897 as a warehouse for the Hudson's Bay Company, it was renovated in 1977 in order to accentuate the pure lines of its red brick arches. Today it houses a souvenir shop, an antique shop and a restaurant.

Gastown Steam Clock

The **Gastown Steam Clock**, at the corner of Cambie Street, uses steam conducted through an underground network of pipes to whistle the hours. The clock is far from historic, however, having been built in 1977. In clear weather, this spot affords a stunning view of the mountains north of the city. It's also a favourite stop for photographs.

The intersection of Water and Carrall streets is one of the liveliest parts of Gastown. Long **Byrnes Block** (2 Water St.), on the southwest corner, was one of the first buildings to be erected after the terrible fire of 1886; it was also one of Vancouver's first brick buildings. It was built on the site of Gassy Jack's second saloon, torn down in 1870; a rather crudely rendered **statue** of the celebrated barkeep graces tiny **Maple Tree Square**, the city's first public gathering place. The thick cornice on the brick building is typical of commercial buildings of the Victorian era. Rising in front is the former **Europe Hotel** (4 Powell St.), a triangular building erected in 1908 by a Canadian hotel-keeper of Italian descent. Its leaded-glass windows bejewel what remains a strikingly elegant building; it now provides affordable housing.

Head south on Carrall Street.

Nip into **Gaoler's Mews**, a peaceful brick courtyard surrounded by heritage buildings. As its name indicates, Gaoler's Mews was the site of Vancouver's first jail and customs house. The city's first telegraph office and fire station were also located here. The **Irish Heather pub** (see p 101) backs onto it, as do some offices and a café or two.

Turn right onto West Cordova.

Lonsdale Block (8-28 West Cordova St.), built in 1889, is one of the most remarkable buildings on this street. Its early tenants included the city's first synagogue. Despite the 1974 restoration of its classical-style facade, today it looks pretty run down and is occupied by a military surplus store.

Turn left on Abbott Street.

At the corner of Hastings Street stands the former

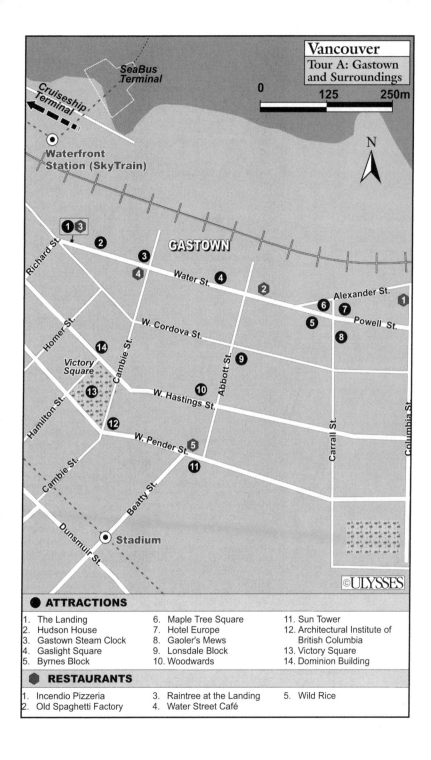

Vancouver
Tour A: Gastown and Surroundings

0   125   250m

N

SeaBus Terminal

Cruiseship Terminal

Waterfront Station (SkyTrain)

GASTOWN

Richard St.
Homer St.
Hamilton St.
Cambie St.
Cambie St.
Beatty St.
Dunsmuir St.

Water St.
W. Cordova St.
W. Hastings St.
W. Pender St.
Abbott St.
Carrall St.
Columbia St.
Alexander St.
Powell St.

Victory Square

Stadium

©ULYSSES

● **ATTRACTIONS**

1. The Landing
2. Hudson House
3. Gastown Steam Clock
4. Gaslight Square
5. Byrnes Block
6. Maple Tree Square
7. Hotel Europe
8. Gaoler's Mews
9. Lonsdale Block
10. Woodwards
11. Sun Tower
12. Architectural Institute of British Columbia
13. Victory Square
14. Dominion Building

◆ **RESTAURANTS**

1. Incendio Pizzeria
2. Old Spaghetti Factory
3. Raintree at the Landing
4. Water Street Café
5. Wild Rice

Woodwards department store *(101 West Hasting St.),* founded in 1892 by Charles Woodward. It closed exactly 100 years later, following the death of the Woodward family patriarch, and now belongs to the provincial government. In the 1990s, the provincial NDP government had plans to redevelop the building and turn it into 350 affordable housing units. Since 2002, however, the Liberal government has planned to sell it to a private developer. Frustration with the situation led to some 50 homeless people squatting in the building in the autumn of that year.

The south end of Abbott Street is dominated by the **Sun Tower ★** *(100 West Pender St.),* erected in 1911 for the *Vancouver World* newspaper. It later housed the offices of the local daily, *The Vancouver Sun,* after which it was named. At the time of its construction, the 17-storey Sun Tower was the tallest building in all of the British Empire.

Continue south on Abbott until West Pender Street.

Turn right on West Pender Street and continue to Cambie Street, where you turn right, passing the **Architectural Institute of British Columbia** *(440 Cambie St.,* ☎683-8588*),* which has a small gallery and offers guided tours of Vancouver during the summer. Opposite is **Victory Square**, in the centre of which stands **The Cenotaph**, a memorial to those who lost their lives in the two World Wars. It was sculpted by Thornton Sharp in 1924. The square separates the streets of Gastown from those of the modern business district. Facing onto the north side is the elegant **Dominion Building ★** *(207 West Hastings St.)* whose mansard roof is reminiscent of those found on Second Empire buildings along the boulevards of Paris.

Continue north on Cambie Street to return to the Gastown Clock.

On your way, you can turn left on West Cordova, where you'll find several triangular buildings. They're shaped in accordance with the streets, which intersect at different angles. Other buildings, with their series of oriel windows, are reminiscent of San Francisco.

Tour B: Chinatown, Downtown Eastside and East Vancouver

This tour takes in three distinct neighbourhoods, Chinatown and the adjacent Downtown Eastside, as well as East Vancouver which is further to the east. Each tour can be enjoyed on foot, but you'll need to drive or take the SkyTrain to get from Chinatown and the Downtown Eastside to East Vancouver.

Also note that Chinatown extends from Gore Street, in the east, to just beyond Carrall Street in the west, and south from East Pender to East Georgia Street. Vancouver's notorious Downtown Eastside is centred just a block beyond, on the corner of East Hastings and Main streets. When wandering around Chinatown, it's quite easy to stumble upon this area, which, though not dangerous to the passer-by, may not be a choice destination for visitors with delicate sensibilities. If this describes you, keep your eyes open and avoid the area altogether.

A good way to get to know Chinatown is by taking part in a **guided walking tour**. Tours last 90min *($6; Jun to Sep every day 10:30am and 2:30pm;*

Chinese Cultural Centre, 50 E. Pender St, ☎658-8883*).*

This tour starts on West Pender Street, between Abott and Carrall streets; at Carrall, West Pender becomes East Pender.

On East Pender Street, the scene changes radically. The colour and atmosphere of public markets, plus a strong Chinese presence, bring this street to life. The 1858 Gold Rush in the hinterland drew Chinese from San Francisco and Hong Kong; in 1878, railway construction brought thousands more Chinese to British Columbia. This community resisted many hard blows that might have ended its presence in the province. At the beginning of the 20th century, the Canadian government imposed a heavy tax on new Chinese immigrants, and then banned Chinese immigration altogether from 1923 to 1947. Today, the local Chinese community is growing rapidly due to the massive influx of immigrants from Hong Kong.

But while Vancouver's Chinatown is one of the largest in all of North America, much of Vancouver's Chinese population now lives in Richmond, south of Vancouver.

For an unusual way to experience Chinatown, visit the **Chinatown Night Market** *(Jun to Sep Fri-Sun 6:30pm to 11pm),* where you can shop for exotic products you won't find at the grocery store. A festive atmosphere reigns.

The western entrance to Chinatown, at West Pender and Taylor streets, has recently been marked by the addition of the **Chinatown Millenium Gate**. Designed by architect Joe Wai, who is also responsible for the Dr. Sun Yat-Sen Classical Chinese

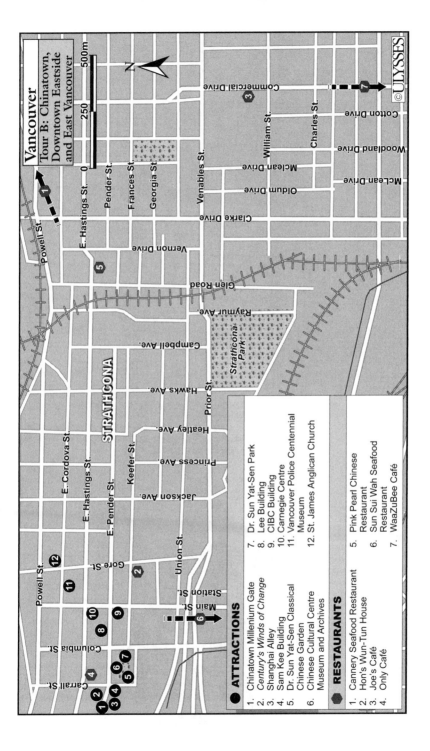

Vancouver
Tour B: Chinatown, Downtown Eastside and East Vancouver

0   250   500m

N

STRATHCONA

Strathcona Park

E. Cordova St.
E. Hastings St.
E. Pender St.
Keefer St.
Jackson Ave.
Princess Ave.
Heatley Ave.
Hawks Ave.
Campbell Ave.
Raymur Ave.
Glen Road
Vernon Drive
Clarke Drive
Prior St.
Union St.
Main St.
Station St.
Gore St.
Columbia St.
Carrall St.
Powell St.
Powell St.

E. Hastings St.
Pender St.
Frances St.
Georgia St.
Venables St.
Oldum Drive
McLean Drive
McLean Drive
William St.
Charles St.
Commercial Drive
Woodland Drive
Cotton Drive

© ULYSSES

● ATTRACTIONS

1. Chinatown Millenium Gate
2. Century's *Winds of Change*
3. Shanghai Alley
4. Sam Kee Building
5. Dr. Sun Yat-Sen Classical Chinese Garden
6. Chinese Cultural Centre Museum and Archives
7. Dr. Sun Yat-Sen Park
8. Lee Building
9. CIBC Building
10. Carnegie Centre
11. Vancouver Police Centennial Museum
12. St. James Anglican Church

⬡ RESTAURANTS

1. Cannery Seafood Restaurant
2. Hon's Wun-Tun House
3. Joe's Café
4. Only Café
5. Pink Pearl Chinese Restaurant
6. Sun Sui Wah Seafood Restaurant
7. WaaZuBee Café

Garden and the Chinese Cultural Centre Museum and Archives, the gate is being funded by three levels of government and the local community in an effort to revitalize the area. The design is based on 19th- and 20th-century tomb and burial ground gates in Beijing, and, following local concern about this being a bad omen, was approved, with minor changes, by a Feng Shui master.

On your left, just past the gate, is the **Century's Winds of Change Mural**, depicting the history of Chinese integration into Canada. Duck into **Shanghai Alley**, just past the gate to your right. In the early 1900s, Chinese merchants moved into this alley, as well as Canton Alley, which ran parallel one block west, as a result of pressure from White merchants on Hastings Street. Most of the buildings, including restaurants, stores, a theatre and several tenements, had double fronts, opening onto both the alley and Carrall Street. They were demolished in the 1940s.

The alley's walkway is made of coloured asphalt imprinted with a template to give it the look of paving stones; its original surface consisted of wood blocks sealed with sap and covered with tar. The walkway leads to **Allan Yap Circle**, site of a replica of the 2,200-year-old Western Han Dynasty bell. This was a gift from the City of Guangzhou, Vancouver's twin city and the place where the original bell was unearthed in 1983. Also in the circle are panels recounting Chinatown's social and architectural history from 1870 to 1940.

On your way into Chinatown, you'll see the strange little **Sam Kee Building** (8 West

Pender St.), which occupies a leftover piece of land 1.8m deep. The Sam Kee Company, one of the wealthiest firms in late-18th-century Chinatown, bought a standard-sized lot here in 1903. When the City expropriated 7m from the front of the lot to widen the street, the determined owner vowed to build regardless. This 1.8m-wide building was erected about 10 years later. According to *Ripley's Believe It or Not* and the *Guinness Book of Records*, it is the narrowest commercial building in the world. Its interior space is augmented by oriel windows overhanging the sidewalk and a basement that extends under the street, which once harboured public baths; sunlight was provided by glass blocks that are still embedded in the sidewalk. Today, the building houses an insurance company and is not open to the public. This area was once home to several famous brothels as well as to a number of opium dens.

Take East Pender Street into the heart of Chinatown.

It is well worth stopping in at the **Dr. Sun Yat-Sen Classical**

Dr. Sun Yat-Sen Classical Chinese Garden

Chinese Garden ★ *($7.50; every day early May to mid-Jun 10am to 6pm, mid-Jun to end Aug 9:30am to 7pm, early Sep to end Sep10am to 6pm, early Oct to end Apr 10am to 4:30pm; several tours scheduled daily, call for times; 578 Carrall St., ☎689-7133)* behind the traditional portal of the **Chinese Cultural Centre** *(50 East Pender St.)*. Built in 1986 by Chinese artists from Suzhou, this garden is the only example outside Asia of landscape architecture from the Ming Dynasty (1368-1644). This green space is surrounded by high walls that create a virtual oasis of peace in the middle of bustling Chinatown. It is worth noting that Dr. Sun Yat-Sen (1866-1925), considered the father of modern China, visited Vancouver in 1911 in order to raise money for his newly founded Kuomintang ("People's Party").

Those who are unfamiliar with Chinese gardens will appreciate the guided tours; docents provide a wealth of information to help neophytes appreciate and understand the significance of every element. Reflecting the Daoist philosophy of yin and yang, classical Chinese gardens represent a balance of opposing forces: human beings versus nature, heaven versus earth, light versus dark, hard versus soft. Its water and plants represent yin, its covered walkways, yang. Built as private gardens by scholars, such gardens were meant to inspire reflection; the unusually shaped, eroded limestone rocks throughout the garden were referred to as "moon rocks" and displayed as sculptures meant to influence artistic creativity. Note that there is not a nail in the place: all of the structures were built using mortise-and-tenon construction. The water in the pond was intentionally made jade-coloured and opaque by lining the bottom of the pond with clay, in order to increase the water's reflectivity and enhance the mystery of the underwater world, enriching the garden experience. In the summer, water lillies cover the water—symbols of purity, growing from its murky depths. The intricately patterned paving stones beneath your feet were collected from stream beds in China; the white flower designs in the pattern were created with pottery shards. It's a charming spot to contemplate your own place in the world. Call for a schedule of events.

Leaving the garden, turn left onto Keefer Street, and left again onto Columbia Street, where you'll find the **Chinese Cultural Centre Museum and Archives** ★ (*$4; Tue-Sun 11am to 5pm; tours by prior arrangement; 555 Columbia St., ☎658-8880*). On the first floor of this facility, designed in a style that was popular during the Ming Dynasty (1368-1644 CE), there are changing exhibits on such subjects as painting, calligraphy and music, all beautifully presented. The permanent exhibit on the second floor (while you're there, take a peek at the gardens from the observation deck) traces the history of Vancouver's Chinese population from 1788 to modern times. You'll find photographs, including one of a brand-new Sam Kee Building, mounted press clippings and a variety of 19th-century artifacts, such as a wooden abacus handmade by a miner and tiny models of a Chinese funeral procession. Here you'll learn that British Columbia's first Chinese immigrants mined for gold in the Cariboo area of northern British Columbia; the town of Barkerville, where they lived, is today a historic site. Chinese immigrants were long subjected to discrimination on many fronts; the concentration of Chinese in Chinatowns across North America is itself

testament to the hostility they faced. Only in 1947 did the B.C. government allow the Chinese to vote in federal elections. There is also a small military history museum on site, which documents the role played by Chinese Canadians in World War II.

Next to the museum is **Dr. Sun Yat-Sen Park** (*free admission; corner Columbia and Keefer Sts.*), which adjoins the garden of the same name. Attractively landscaped, it's a pleasant place for a stroll, but no substitute for the genuine article next door. Chances are good, however, that you might also encounter neighbourhood vagrants, who similarly enjoy the park.

Leaving the park, turn left on Columbia and left again on East Pender.

The architecture of the buildings along East Pender Street reflects the background of Vancouver's first Chinese immigrants, most of whom were Cantonese. Take, for example, the deep, multi-storey loggias on a number of the facades, such as that of the **Lee Building** (*129 East Pender St.*), built in 1907. Gutted by fire in 1972, its original facade conceals the completely new structure behind it. This is a fine example of successful private preservation of a heritage building.

To the left of this building is a passageway leading to an inner court surrounded by shops. Many of these buildings feature historical plaques; right across the street from the garden is the oldest building in Chinatown, built in 1889.

During Chinese festivals, the loggias along East Pender Street are packed with onlookers, heightening the lively atmosphere.

Continue along East Pender Street until Main Street.

At the corner of Main Street, to your right, stands a branch of the **CIBC (Canadian Imperial Bank of Commerce)** (*501 Main St.*), whose architecture was inspired by the English baroque style. Faced with terra cotta, this colossal edifice was designed by architect Victor Horsburgh and erected in 1915.

If you turn left onto Main Street, you will approach East Hastings Street. One of the country's most notorious corners, Main and Hastings is also referred to as "Pain and Wastings" by residents of the area. The nerve centre of Vancouver's Downtown Eastside, the poorest community in Canada, it is alight with panhandlers, drug dealers and prostitutes. The police claim that it is not a dangerous place for tourists (although the same cannot necessarily be said for residents) and that the worst that might happen is being harassed to buy drugs or for spare change. Nevertheless, some may prefer to avoid the area altogether. The drug dealing is concentrated around the Carnegie Library (see below) on the west side of Main Street, in plain view of Vancouver Police headquarters, so if you'd rather not be confronted with it at close hand, cross Main Street at East Pender, and stay on the east side of the street.

Another example of the English baroque revival style is the former **Carnegie Library** (*at the corner of Main and East Hastings*), now used as a community centre (the Carnegie Centre). This building owes its existence to American philanthropist Andrew Carnegie, who financed the construction of hundreds of neighbourhood libraries in the United States and Canada. If you're not put off by the goings-on outside, enter the building and take a look at the stained-glass portraits of Shakespeare, Robert Burns

Vancouver

Pain and Wastings

The Downtown Eastside is Vancouver's skid row. Considered the poorest neighbourhood in Canada, it is home to a disproportionate number of drug addicts and HIV/AIDS sufferers, and is rife with poverty, prostitution and crime. Over 80% of its households are considered "low income" by Statistics Canada, compared with 31% in Vancouver as a whole (1996 census).

The neighbourhood is defined by Burrard Inlet to the north, East Hastings Street to the south, Clark Drive to the east and Main Street to the west. Its nerve centre is the corner of Main and Hastings, known to residents as "Pain and Wastings." There, in front of the Carnegie Centre (Vancouver's former public library) and in full view of Vancouver Police headquarters on Main Street, is where drug dealers and clients congregate.

Walking through the area, any visitor will be alarmed by its many detox centres, rundown rooming houses and staggering poverty. Its handsome Victorian buildings, however, testify to a once-vibrant neighbourhood. Vancouver's first downtown developed here in the early 20th century, near the nucleus of the growing city. It was home to the municipal courthouse, city hall, the Carnegie Public Library, several theatres and Woodward's department store. It was also the transportation hub of the city, with the streetcar station at Hastings and Carrall streets, and the ferry and pier just north on Burrard Inlet.

The westward shift of downtown and the consequent decline of the Eastside began with the opening of the new courthouse on Georgia Street in 1907 (today the Vancouver Art Gallery), and accelerated in the late 1950s, when the library moved to Burrard and Robson streets, the streetcar service was terminated and the ferry service discontinued (today the SeaBus leaves from the foot of Seymour Street, further west). As a result, some 10,000 fewer people passed through the neighbourhood each day. By the time Woodward's department store closed in 1992, taking with it many other stores and restaurants, the Downtown Eastside had seen better days. As the area declined, housing became increasingly affordable here, attracting those on fixed incomes who could not afford the soaring rents in other parts of the city.

The community's problems were brought to national attention in 1999 with the release of the award-winning documentary *Through a Blue Lens*. A National Film Board production, it was filmed by a number of Vancouver constables who captured the lives of addicts on their Eastside beat for use as an anti-drug educational tool. The film compellingly portrays the squalor, desperation and fear in which these people live. The neighbourhood has made national headlines more than ever lately, as a result of the case of the more than 50 missing women, mostly drug addicts and prostitutes, who have disappeared from the Downtown Eastside since 1983.

A number of community organizations work tirelessly to improve the lot of residents. The Vancouver Agreement, a five-year plan signed by three levels of government in 2000, will address the community's needs by providing a new health program and treatment centre, street clean-ups, improved housing, and stepping up police efforts against drug dealers.

The election in 2002 of a new mayor, for whom the clean-up of the Downtown Eastside is a priority, is another sign that change is on the horizon.

and Sir Walter Scott, which illuminate the main stairwell inside.

If you'd rather skip this corner, continue along East Pender Street to Gore Street, one block east of Main Street, and turn left on Gore Street until East Cordova Street. Otherwise, turn right on East Cordova Street, past the Salvation Army, several detox centres and rundown rooming houses.

If the poverty, suffering and addiction you see around here aren't bleak enough for you, head into the **Vancouver Police Centennial Museum ★** *($6; year-round Mon-Fri 9am to 3pm, early May to end Aug also Sat 10am to 3pm)*, (although it bills itself as a place of "mystery, history and intrigue" it's more like "sordid, morbid and graphic"). Located in the former coroner's courtroom and autopsy laboratory, the exhibit begins harmlessly enough with memorabilia tracing the history of the Vancouver Police Department (VPD), punctuated by rather spooky models dressed in historical police uniforms. This exhibit is likely to be of local interest only, and one hopes that this, rather than what comes later, is the focus of the popular tours given to local schoolchildren. Interestingly enough, however, one learns that in 1912, the first woman constable in the entire British Empire was hired right here in Vancouver.

The exhibit then takes a turn for the gory, with its collection of weapons, many hideously crude, that were seized on the streets of Vancouver. Other "delights" include a re-created murder scene in a Downtown Eastside rooming house, black-and-white photographs of past murder scenes, and a forensic display in the autopsy lab, with mounted organs and autopsies being performed by dummies—definitely not for the squeamish. If you're wondering why there's a portrait

of late Hollywood actor and notorious ladies' man Errol Flynn, it's because the actor died in Vancouver in 1959 and his autopsy took place in this very lab. Rumour has it that some of Flynn's genital warts were harvested as souvenirs by lab staff after his death, but promptly stitched back on before his body was sent back home for burial. These days, Hollywood stars such as Brad Pitt, Jack Nicholson and Gwyneth Paltrow make "live" appearances at the former morgue, shooting scenes for films. You can buy your very own VPD paraphernalia at the Cop Shoppe.

Across East Cordova, at the corner of Gore Street, stands **St. James Anglican Church ★** *(303 East Cordova)*, one of the most unusual buildings erected in Canada between the two World Wars. A tall, massive structure made of exposed reinforced concrete, it was designed by British architect Adrian Gilbert Scott in 1935.

Head south on Gore Street to admire all the exotic products displayed along East Pender Street or enjoy a meal in one of the many Chinese restaurants there.

If you wish to leave no stone unturned in your exploration of Vancouver's ethnic neighbourhoods, take Gore all the way to Keefer, turn right, then take a left on Main Street to reach Pacific Central Station (about a 5min walk). Take the SkyTrain toward Surrey, and get off at the next station (Broadway). If you're driving, head east on Georgia Street, turn onto Prior Street at the viaduct, then take a right on Commercial Drive. When you get off the SkyTrain, head north up Commercial Drive.

The next part of town you'll pass through is known as **Little Italy**, but is also home to Vancouverites of Portuguese, Spanish, Jamaican and South American descent. In

the early 20th century, the **Commercial Drive** area became the city's first suburb, with middle-class residents building small, single-family homes with wooden siding here. The first Chinese and Slavic immigrants moved into the neighbourhood during World War I, and another wave of immigrants, chiefly Italian, arrived at the end of World War II. North Americans will feel pleasantly out of their element in the congenial atmosphere of Little Italy's Italian cafés and restaurants.

Today, "The Drive," between Venables and 12th Avenue, is awash with the flavours of Italy, Portugal, Greece, Mexico, India, the Caribbean and Vietnam, to name but a few, with Italian coffee houses and markets, little bars where East Vancouver hipsters converge on patios in dry weather, vegetarian cafés and restaurants galore, and groovy shops of every variety—but not a sushi bar in sight! There aren't any attractions to be visited here per se—it's the street life that warrants a slow-paced afternoon here, ensconced among the locals. The view of Vancouver's skyline, to the west, and the mountains to the north, is indeed grand from **Grandview Park** *(William and Charles sts.)*, especially when the sun is setting.

Tour C: Downtown

On May 23, 1887, Canadian Pacific's first transcontinental train, which set out from Montréal, arrived at the Vancouver terminus. The railway company, which had been granted an area roughly corresponding to present-day downtown Vancouver, began to develop its property. To say that it played a major role in the development of the city's business district would be an understatement.

Vancouver

Canadian Pacific truly built this part of town, laying the streets and erecting many very important buildings. Downtown Vancouver has been developing continually since the 1960s. It's a sign of the city's great economic vitality, which can be attributed to Asian capital and the Canadian population's shift westward to the mild climes of the Pacific coast.

This tour starts at the corner of West Hastings and Seymour streets. This tour can easily be combined with Tour A, which covers Gastown and ends nearby.

Begin your tour at Harbour Centre. Vancouver's tallest building, topped by what looks like a flying saucer hovering above, is hard to miss. The building is home to Simon Fraser University's downtown campus. **The Lookout! at Harbour Centre** *($10; 555 West Hastings St.,* ☎*689-0421),*

Vancouver's version of Toronto's CN Tower, offers a "360-degree view" of Vancouver and surroundings. A glassed-in elevator whisks you to a height of 174m, almost too quickly to enjoy the ride. Those who enjoy observation towers may well not balk at the $9 admission fee, but others might find this a little steep (no pun intended), particularly when, after reluctantly coughing it up and becoming a captive audience, you are bombarded by advertisements for shopping centres, tour companies and various other costly Vancouver attractions. Furthermore, those unfamiliar with the city could use more user-friendly plans indicating the precise location of many of the landmarks or sectors referred to in the panels. Nevertheless, the view of English Bay and the fjords of the North Shore is really quite lovely from the top. To get the most out of your ticket,

save it and return later in the evening to see the city lights.

Located opposite Harbour Centre, the former regional headquarters of the **Toronto Dominion Bank** *(580 West Hastings St.)* exemplify the classical elegance of early 20th-century financial banking halls. The bank abandoned this registered heritage building in 1984 for one of the modern skyscrapers along Georgia Street. It is now held by Simon Fraser University. One block west, the former regional headquarters of the **Canadian Bank of Commerce** *(698 West Hastings St.),* a veritable temple of finance, met the same fate and now houses the elegant Henry Birks and Sons shop. Also a heritage building, it was renamed the Birks Building in 1994. With its massive Ionic columns, this building was erected in 1906 according to a design by Darling and Pearson, whose

● ATTRACTIONS		
1. The Lookout! at Harbour Centre	12. Christ Church Cathedral	22. Granville Mall
	13. Cathedral Place	23. Pacific Centre
2. Toronto Dominion Bank	14. Canadian Craft and	24. The Bay
3. CIBC Building	Design Museum	25. Vancouver Centre
4. Royal Bank	15. Robson Street	26. Sears Downtown
5. Sinclair Centre	16. BC Hydro Building	27. Commodore Theatre
6. Crédit Foncier Franco-Canadien	17. St. Andrew's Wesley United Church	28. Orpheum Theatre
		29. Vogue Theatre
7. Vancouver Club	18. First Baptist Church	30. Library Square
8. Marine Building (R)	19. Provincial Law Courts	
9. Canada Place	20. Robson Square	(R) establishment with
10. Bentall Centre	21. Vancouver	restaurant
11. Royal Centre	Art Gallery (R)	(see description)

○ ACCOMMODATIONS		
1. Faimont Hotel Vancouver (R)	5. Sheraton Vancouver Wall Centre	(R) establishment with restaurant
2. Kingston Hotel Bed & Breakfast	6. Terminal City Club	(see description)
	7. Victorian Hotel	
3. Le Soleil Hotel	8. Wedgewood Hotel (R)	
4. Pan Pacific Hotel Vancouver	9. Westin Grand	
	10. YWCA	

● RESTAURANTS		
1. Aqua Riva	6. Joe Fortes Seafood & Chop House	9. Olympia Seafood
2. Bin 941 Tapas Parlour		10. Raku
3. Diva at the Met	7. Kitto Japanese House on Granville	11. Subeez Café
4. Elbow Room		
5. India Gate Restaurant	8. Lucy Mae Brown	

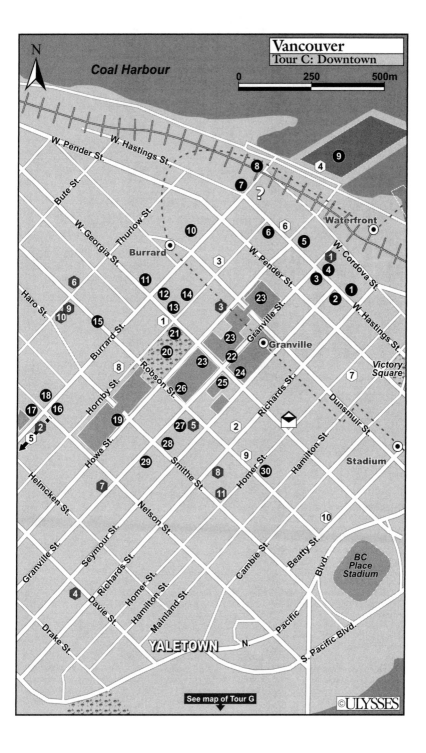

N

Coal Harbour

Vancouver
Tour C: Downtown

0   250   500m

W. Pender St.
W. Hastings St.

Bute St.

W. Georgia St.

Thurlow St.

Burrard

Haro St.

Burrard St.

Hornby St.

Robson St.

Howe St.

Helmcken St.

Granville St.

Seymour St.

Richards St.

Homer St.

Hamilton St.

Mainland St.

Davie St.

Drake St.

Nelson St.

Smithe St.

YALETOWN   N.

Pacific

S. Pacific Blvd.

W. Pender St.

Granville St.

Richards St.

Dunsmuir St.

Hamilton St.

Cambie St.

Beatty St.

Blvd.

W. Cordova St.

Waterfront

W. Hastings St.

Granville

Victory
Square

Stadium

BC
Place
Stadium

See map of Tour G

©ULYSSES

Sinclair Centre

credits include the Sun Life Building in Montréal. Opposite stands the massive **Royal Bank ★** (*675 West Hastings St.*) building, designed by S. G. Davenport. The Italian Renaissance–style banking hall is stunning and well worth a look.

The **Sinclair Centre ★** (*701 West Hastings St.*) is a group of government offices. It occupies a former post office, and its annexes are connected to one another by covered passageways lined with shops. The main building, dating from 1909, is considered to be one of the finest examples of the neo-baroque style in Canada.

A little further, at the corner of Hornby Street, is an austere edifice built in 1913 by the **Crédit Foncier Franco-Canadien** (*850 West Hastings St.*), a financial institution jointly founded by French and Québecois bankers. On the other side of the street, the

Vancouver Club (*915 West Hasting St.*) is dwarfed by the skyscrapers on either side of it. Founded in 1914, it is a private club for businessmen modelled after similar clubs in London.

Facing you as you head west on West Hastings Street, is the **Marine Building ★★** (*355 Burrard St.*), a fine example of the Art Deco style. It's characterized by vertical lines, staggered recesses, geometric ornamentation and the absence of a cornice at the top of the structure. Erected in 1929, the building lives up to its name in part because it is lavishly decorated with nautical motifs, and also because its occupants are ship-owners and shipping companies. Its facade features terra cotta panels depicting the history of shipping and the discovery of the Pacific coast. The interior decor is even more inventive, however. The lights in the lobby are shaped like the prows of ships, and there is a stained-glass window showing the sun setting over the ocean. The elevators will take you up to the mezzanine, which offers an interesting general view of the building.

Turn right on Burrard Street, heading toward the water, and duck into the **Vancouver Tourist Info Centre** (*200 Burrard St.*, ☎683-2000) to stock up on any additional information you might need.

Take Burrard Street toward the water to reach **Canada Place ★★** (*999 Canada Place*), which occupies one of the piers along the harbour and looks like a giant sailboat ready to set out across the

waves. This multi-purpose complex, which served as the Canadian pavilion at Expo 86, is home to the city's Convention Centre, the cruiseship terminal, the luxurious **Pan Pacific Hotel Vancouver** (see p 92) and an IMAX theatre. Even if you're not setting sail, take a walk on the "deck" and drink in the magnificent panoramic view of Burrard Inlet, the port and the snow-capped mountains.

Take Burrard Street back into the centre of town and continue southward to West Georgia Street.

On your way, you'll see the giant **Benttal Centre** (*at the corner of Pender St.*), made up of three towers designed by architect Frank Masson and erected between 1965 and 1975.

On your right, you'll also see the **Royal Centre** (*1055 W. Georgia St.*), which includes the 38-storey Royal Bank tower. These skyscrapers have to be "low" and squat in order to withstand the seismic activity in the Pacific Ring of Fire.

On your left, just before West Georgia Street, stands tiny **Christ Church Cathedral** (*690 Burrard St.*). This Gothic Revival Anglican cathedral was built in 1889, back when Vancouver was no more than a large village. Its skeleton, made of Douglas fir, is visible from inside. What is most interesting about the cathedral, however, is neither its size nor its ornamentation, but simply the fact that it has survived in this part of town, which is continually being rebuilt. It now also functions as a community centre.

Across West Georgia Street and dwarfing the cathedral, stands the imposing, 23-storey **Fairmont Hotel Vancouver ★** (*900 W. Georgia St.*) (see p 92), a veritable monument to the Canadian railway companies that built it between 1928 and 1939. For many years, its high copper roof served as the principal symbol of Vancouver abroad. Like all major Canadian cities, Vancouver had to have a Château-style hotel. Make sure to take a look at the gargoyles near the top and the bas-reliefs at the entrance, which depict an ocean liner and a moving locomotive. Note that this is actually the third Hotel Vancouver built by the Canadian Pacific Railroad, the first one having been built at the corner of Georgia and Granville streets in 1887 and the second near the current hotel, on the site of the Pacific Centre (1916-1949).

Flanking the cathedral to the east are the shops and offices of **Cathedral Place** *(925 West Georgia St.)*, built in 1991. Its pseudo-medieval gargoyles have not managed to make people forget about the Art Deco-style Georgia Medical Building, which once occupied this site, and whose demolition in 1989 prompted a nation-wide outcry. Even with rock singer Bryan Adams's help, a major campaign to save the building proved futile. Cathedral Place is thus a building that is trying to gain acceptance. Its pointed roof was modelled after that of the neighbouring hotel, and is adorned with the stone nurses that once graced the Georgia Medical Building. The **Canadian Craft and Design Museum** *($5; Mon-Sat 10am to 5pm, Sun and holidays noon to 5pm, Thu to 9pm, Sep to May closed Tue; 639 Hornby St., ☎687-8266)* lies behind in a

pretty little garden integrated into the project. (You can also get there by turning left on Hornby Street.) This small museum houses a sampling of Canadian handicrafts and a few decorative elements that were part of the Georgia Medical Building. It stages rotating exhibits with eclectic themes, ranging from cookie-cutter design to architectural furniture. On-site craft shop.

Head west on West Georgia Street.

Turn left on Thurlow Street and left again on **Robson Street ★**, which is lined with fashionable boutiques, elaborately decorated restaurants and West Coast-style cafés. People sit at tables outside, enjoying the fine weather and watching the motley crowds stroll by. This activity has become a veritable mania among coffee lovers. American celebrity Bette Midler, passing through Vancouver once marvelled at the number of cafés on Robson Street, going so far as to declare that Vancouverites are addicted to coffee. If this is true, it hasn't changed the tempo of life here, which is known to be quite laid back. In the mid-20th century, a small German community settled around Robson Street, dubbing it

Canada Place

Robsonstrasse, a nickname it bears to this day.

Return to Burrard Street, turn right and continue to Nelson Street. Or, turn left on Robson and window shop until you reach Burrard Street.

At the intersection of Thurlow and Robson streets, notice the triumvirate of coffee shops on three of the four corners, two of which are Starbucks! How long can the boutique on the fourth corner withstand the onslaught?

The former **B.C. Hydro Building ★** *(970 Burrard St.)*, at the corner of Nelson and Burrard streets, was once the head office of the province's hydroelectric company. In 1993, it was converted into a 242-unit co-op and renamed The Electra. Designed in 1955 by local architects Thompson, Berwick and Pratt, it is considered one of the most sophisticated skyscrapers of that era in all of North America. The ground floor is adorned with a mural and a mosaic in shades of grey, blue and green, executed by artist B.C. Binning. Kitty-corner stands **St. Andrew's Wesley United Church**, which was built in 1931 and houses a window created by master glassworker Gabriel Loire of Chartres, France in 1969. The **First Baptist Church** *(969 Burrard St.)*, located opposite, was erected in 1911.

Walk east on Nelson Street.

Turn left on Howe Street to Smithe Street, to view the **Provincial Law Courts ★** *(800 Smithe St.)*, designed by talented Vancouver architect Arthur Erickson and completed in 1978. The vast interior space, accented in glass and steal, is worth a visit. The courthouse and **Robson Square** *(on the 800 block of Robson St.)*, by the same architect, form a lovely ensemble. Vancouver's luxuriant vegeta-

Vancouver

tion (sustained by abundant rainfall and a temperate climate) which is unlike anything else in Canada, is put to maximum use here. Plants are draped along rough concrete walls and in between multiple little stepped ponds over which little waterfalls flow. Shops, restaurants and a skating rink welcome passers-by.

Continue along Howe Street to Robson Street.

The **Vancouver Art Gallery** ★ *($12.50; end Apr to mid-Oct every day 10am to 5:30pm, mid-Oct to end Apr closed Mon, year-round Thu until 9pm; 750 Hornby St.,* ☎*662-4700, www.vanartgellery. bc.ca)*, located north of Robson Square, occupies the former Provincial Law Courts. This big, sumptuous, neoclassical-style building was erected in 1908 according to a design by British architect Francis Mawson Rattenbury. His other credits include the British Columbia Legislative Assembly and the Empress Hotel, both located in Victoria on Vancouver Island. Later, Rattenbury returned to his native country and was assassinated by his wife's lover.

The building was renovated by Arthur Erickson in the 1980s. Make sure to peer up into the rotunda as you climb the stairs. Painted gray and white and ornately decorated with bas-relief, it is quite simply magnificent. The same can be said of the Emily Carr gallery on the fourth floor, decorated in the same style and fondly referred to by the staff as the "wedding cake room." The gallery is home to an important Emily Carr collection of more than 200 works, most of which are paintings. Selections are displayed on a rotating basis. Emily Carr (1871-1945) was a major Canadian painter whose primary subjects were the Aboriginal peoples and landscapes of the West Coast. One look at her

magnificent red cedars, vividly rendered with expressive swooshes of blue and green, and you'll immediately understand why her work is so cherished by Westerners. The gallery also hosts very contemporary travelling exhibits, which you'll either like...or you won't. In short, fans of Emily Carr and of contemporary art will not be disappointed. There is a lovely café, with a reasonably priced menu, on site (see p 96).

Continue along Howe Street.

Turn right on West Georgia Street, then right again on the **Granville Mall** ★, the street of cinemas, theatres, nightclubs and retail stores. Its busy sidewalks are hopping 24hrs a day. The black skyscrapers at the corner of West Georgia belong to the **Pacific Centre** *(on either side of Georgia St.)*, designed by architects Cesar Pelli and Victor Gruen (1969). Beneath the towers lie the beginnings of an underground city modelled after Montréal's, with 130 shops and restaurants. Opposite stands the Hudson's Bay Company department store (1913), better known as **The Bay**. The company was founded in London in 1670 in order to carry out fur-trading operations in North America. In 1827, it became one of the first enterprises to set up shop in British Columbia. Across the street stands the **Vancouver Centre** *(650 West Georgia St.)*, which contains Scotia Bank's regional headquarters, and the **Vancouver Block** *(736 Granville St.)*, topped by an elegant clock. Finally, south of the Pacific Centre, you can't miss the massive **Sears Downtown** department store, occupied until 2002 by **Eaton's**, one of a chain of Canadian department stores that started in Toronto in 1869 and went bankrupt in 1999. This branch was one of a handful across the country that held out until 2002.

Stroll along the Granville Mall heading south past Robson Street.

The portion of Granville Street from Georgia to Nelson streets (700 to 900 block) is known as the Theatre Row Entertainment District, as indicated on the banners strung up along the street. The City has so zoned the area in an attempt to concentrate the bars, dance clubs and theatres away from residential districts. Looking for some nightlife? Just stroll along Granville, check out the crowd that invariably gathers in front of these venues and take your pick. The scene is largely made up of college kids—he in baggy pants, she in merciless hiphuggers—but you'll also find a thirtysomething-friendly venue or two. Also attracted here are homeless people asking for change, self-described dope heads politely requesting money for pot, forlorn guitarists stubbornly trying to bring the music of the 1960s to the hip-hopping masses, the occasional flamenco duo and, always, flower vendors. It's a moveable feast of sights and sounds that some may find more interesting than the scene inside the clubs! Inevitably, it's a mob scene at 2am, when the bars close. (For a review of selected venues, see **Entertainment**, p 101.)

You'll pass the **Commodore Theatre** *(870 Granville St.)* and the **Orpheum Theatre** ★ *(601 Smithe St., free group tour upon reservation* ☎*665-3050)*. Behind the latter's narrow facade, barely 8m wide, a long corridor opens onto a 2,800-seat Spanish-style Renaissance Revival theatre. Designed by Marcus Priteca, it was the largest and most luxurious movie theatre in Canada when it opened in 1927. After being meticulously restored in 1977, the Orpheum became the concert hall of the Vancouver Symphony Orchestra and stages musical performances of all genres. The theatre turned 75 on November 7, 2002. Further south, you'll see the vertical sign belonging to the **Vogue Theatre** *(918 Granville St.)*, erected in 1941. Today, popular musicals are presented in its streamlined Art Deco hall.

Retrace your steps along Granville Street, turning right on Robson Street.

At the corner of Robson and Homer streets is a curious building that is more than a little reminiscent of Rome's Coliseum—the **Vancouver Public Library ★ ★** *(free admission; year-round, Mon-Thu 10am to 8pm, Fri and Sat 10am to 5pm, Sun 1pm to 5pm; free tours can be arranged, ☎331-4041; 350 West Georgia St., ☎331-3603, www.vpl.vancouver.bc.ca)*, known as **Library Square**. This impressive building, completed in 1995, is the work of Montréal architect Moshe Safdie, known for his Habitat '67 in Montréal and the National Art Gallery in Ottawa. The project stirred lively reactions both from local people and from architecture critics. The design was chosen after finally being put

Library Square

to a referendum. The six-storey atrium is positively grandiose.

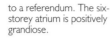

Tour D: The West End and Stanley Park

This tour starts at the corner of Thurlow and Davie. Head west on the latter.

The population of the West End is a mixture of students and professionals, many of whom made a fortune on new technologies and the various new therapies now in fashion. The gay community is also well represented here.

This tour starts at **Barclay Heritage Square**, bounded by Barclay, Nicola, Haro and Broughton streets.

There are eight heritage houses on this square, which is actually an Edwardian garden with its very own gazebo, all of which date from the 1890s. One of them has been reborn as a museum showcasing furnishings from the Victorian period. Built in 1893, the **Roedde House Museum ★ ★** *($4; admission by tour only, Wed-Fri 2pm to 4pm; 1415 Barclay St., ☎684-7040)* was the family home of Gustav and Matilda Roedde and their family until 1925. Gustav was the first book binder and printer in Vancouver, a vocation profitable enough to permit the construction of a comfortable upper-middle-class home. The house was designed by notable architect and family friend Francis

Rattenbury, known for his design of the rather more grand Empress Hotel and the Parliament Buildings in Victoria and the Vancouver Art Gallery (see p 70). Ten of the home's 12 rooms are furnished with period pieces, most of which were donated to the museum by individuals; others are on loan from the Vancouver Museum and some are original to the house. The attention to detail is astounding and anyone with an interest with Victoriana and Art Nouveau will be delighted by this charming little museum.

Leave the square, heading south on Broughton Street until Davie Street.

Vancouver's gay village, known as **Davie Village**, extends along Davie Street just east of Broughton Street and as far east as Thurlow Street. You can't miss it: just look for the rainbow banners strung up along the street lamps *(turn left from Broughton Street)*. The village is a pleasantly shabby-looking mix of cafés, diners and discount stores punctuated by high-rise apartment buildings.

Retrace your steps and head west along Davie.

Head west on Davie Street, then left on Bidwell Street and follow the dogs, human companions in tow, to **Alexandra Park ★** which forms a point south of Burnaby Street. It boasts a pretty wooden bandstand (1914) for outdoor concerts, as well as a marble fountain adorned with a brass plaque honouring Joe Fortes, who taught several generations of the city's children to swim.

The east end of **English Bay Beach ★ ★** *(along the shore between Chilco and Bidwell sts.)*, whose fine sands are crowded during the summer, is just opposite the park. Here you'll find an enormous

Vancouver

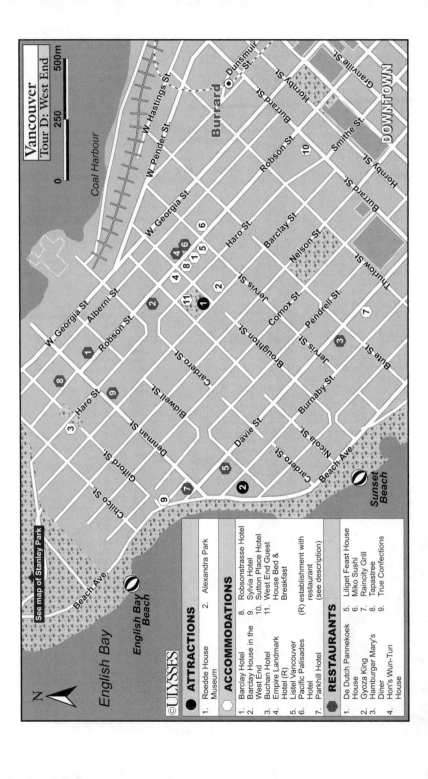

Vancouver
Tour D: West End

0   250   500m

Coal Harbour

English Bay

English Bay Beach

Sunset Beach

See map of Stanley Park

DOWNTOWN

Burrard

© ULYSSES

● **ATTRACTIONS**

1. Roedde House Museum
2. Alexandra Park

○ **ACCOMMODATIONS**

1. Barclay Hotel
2. Barclay House in the West End
3. Buchan Hotel
4. Empire Landmark Hotel (R)
5. Listel Vancouver
6. Pacific Palisades Hotel
7. Parkhill Hotel
8. Robsonstrasse Hotel
9. Sylvia Hotel
10. Sutton Place Hotel
11. West End Guest House Bed & Breakfast

(R) establishment with restaurant (see description)

● **RESTAURANTS**

1. De Dutch Pannekoek House
2. Gyoza King
3. Hamburger Mary's Diner
4. Hon's Wun-Tun House
5. Liliget Feast House
6. Miko Sushi
7. Raincity Grill
8. Tapastree
9. True Confections

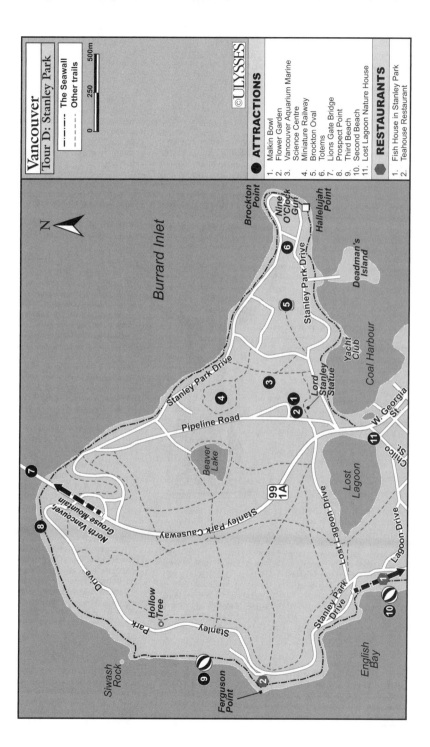

Vancouver
Tour D: Stanley Park

- ·─·─· The Seawall
- ·─·─· Other trails

0   250   500m

©ULYSSES

⬡ ATTRACTIONS
1. Malkin Bowl
2. Flower Garden
3. Vancouver Aquarium Marine Science Centre
4. Miniature Railway
5. Brockton Oval
6. Totems
7. Lions Gate Bridge
8. Prospect Point
9. Third Beach
10. Second Beach
11. Lost Lagoon Nature House

⬡ RESTAURANTS
1. Fish House in Stanley Park
2. Teahouse Restaurant

N

Burrard Inlet

Brockton Point

Nine O'Clock Gun

Hallelujah Point

Deadman's Island

Stanley Park Drive

Yacht Club

Coal Harbour

Lord Stanley Statue

Stanley Park Drive

Pipeline Road

W. Georgia St.

Chilco St.

Lost Lagoon

Lost Lagoon Drive

Beaver Lake

99 1A

North Vancouver, Grouse Mountain

Stanley Park Causeway

Hollow Tree

Stanley Park Drive

Park Drive

Stanley

Lagoon Drive

Siwash Rock

Ferguson Point

English Bay

inukshuk created by Alvin Kanak for the Northwest Territories pavilion at Expo 86; it was moved to this site the following year. The apartment high-rises behind the beach give beach-goers the illusion that they are lounging about at a seaside resort like Acapulco, when they are actually just a short distance from the heart of Vancouver. Few cities can boast beaches so close to their downtown core. Fleets of sailboats skim across the magnificent bay, which has recently been cleaned of pollutants. To the west, it is bordered by the verdant expanse of Stanley Park.

Lord Stanley, for whom the National Hockey League's Stanley Cup was named, founded **Stanley Park ★★★** on a romantic impulse back in the 19th century when he was Canada's Governor General (1888-1893) and dedicated it "to the use and enjoyment of people of all colours, creeds and customs for all time." Like New York's Central Park and Montréal's Mount Royal, Stanley Park was largely designed by Frederick Law Olmsted.

Stanley Park lies on an elevated peninsula stretching into the Georgia Strait, and encompasses 405ha of flowering gardens, dense woodlands and lookouts offering views of the sea and the mountains. Obviously Vancouver's many skyscrapers have not prevented the city from maintaining close ties with the nearby wilderness.

A 9km waterfront promenade known as the **Seawall ★★** runs around the park, enabling pedestrians to drink in every bit of the stunning scenery here. The **Stanley Park Scenic Drive** is the equivalent of the Seawall for motorists. This road runs one-way in a counter-clockwise direction. There are numerous parking

lots along the road *($1/2hrs, $3/day)* and although parking is inexpensive, traffic is heavy in the park on summer weekends. A good alternative is to take the bus from downtown (nos. 23, 123, 35 or 135) and once in the park, to take advantage of the free **Stanley Park Shuttle Bus**, which provides transportation between 14 of the park's most popular attractions *(every 15min, mid-Jun to mid-Sep, 10am to 6:30pm)*. You can also take the **express bus to Stanley park**, which operates from about a dozen downtown

Lord Stanley monument

hotels and is free of charge for those heading to the Vancouver Aquarium or the Horse-Drawn Tour. Speaking of which, if a splurge is in order, hop aboard a **Stanley Park Horse-Drawn Tour** *($20.55; mid-Mar to late Oct; ☎681-5115)*, which will take you around in style. Tours last 1hr.

The best way to explore Stanley Park, however, is by bicycle. You can rent one from **Spokes Bicycle Rental** *(corner of West Georgia and Denman sts., ☎688-5141)*. Remember that the path is also one-way

for cyclists, counter-clockwise from Coal Harbour to English Bay.

Another way to discover some of the park's hidden treasures is to walk along one of the many footpaths criss-crossing the territory. There are numerous rest areas along the way.

From West Georgia Street, walk along Coal Harbour toward Brockton Point.

You'll be greeted by the sight of scores of gleaming yachts in the Vancouver marina with the downtown skyline in the background. This is the most developed portion of the park, where you'll find the **Malkin Bowl** (inland from the rowing club), where **Theatre Under the Stars** performs *(about $30; Jul and Aug; ☎687-0174)*.

Near the Malkin Bowl, Stanley Park harbours some lovely **flower gardens ★** that are meticulously tended by a team of gardeners.

Continue along the Seawall.

Follow the footpath to the renowned **Vancouver Aquarium Marine Science Centre ★★★** *($14.95; Jul and Aug, every day 9:30am to 7pm; early Sep to end Jun, every day 10am to 5:30pm; ☎659-3474, www.vanaqua. org)*, appropriately located by the ocean. (Sign indicating the way via the footpaths can be hard to find—ask someone to direct you. Directions by car are well indicated from West Georgia Street.) It displays representatives of the marine animal life of the West Coast and the Pacific as a whole, including magnificent killer whales, belugas, dolphins, seals and exotic fish.

You'll want to leave a couple of hours for the visit. There are shows or feeding sessions scheduled every 30min (subject to change), so if you have your heart set on seeing a dolphin-training session or a beluga show, call first. Make sure to visit the outside exhibit, home to harbour seals, Spinnaker the dolphin, sea otters and belugas, all of which face particular challenges that prevent them from being released into the wild. Inside, there are underwater viewing areas for the belugas and dolphins. The Treasures of the B.C. Coast displays representative ecosystems, one tank for each area, complete with interpretive panels. There is a section on the shores of Stanley Park, supplied by seawater piped in from Burrard Inlet. Finally, don't miss the Amazon gallery, where rainforest residents of all kinds make their home, including free-flying Costa Rican butterflies. Take the time to look for the sloths in the trees.

While you're at the aquarium, don't miss the new **BC Hydro Salmon Stream Project**, a salmon run created as a public education project. From the B.C. Forest Headwaters

Totem Pole

Exhibit, visitors can follow a man-made stream through the park to Coal Harbour, near the Vancouver Rowing Club, where 10,000 hatchery-bred chinook and coho salmon fry were released in 1998. A pheromone was released into the water to help the mature salmon find their way to their home stream, which they began to do in November 2001. This marked the first time in over a century that salmon returned to downtown Vancouver! The salmon hatchery is located in the former bear pit, part of the now defunct **Stanley Park Zoo**, which closed in the early 1990s.

There are several food concessions that actually offer more imaginative fare than hot dogs (although hot dogs are available too) at reasonable prices.

North of the aquarium are the **Miniature Railway**, **farmyard** and **playground**, all a real hit with kids.

From here, you can head south and return to the Seawall or take one of the interior footpaths toward the east, leading to the **Brockton Oval**, where rugby and cricket are played. Further east are the famous **Totem Poles** ★ which are reminders of a sizeable Aboriginal population on the peninsula barely 150 years ago. Most of these totem poles, however, are fairly modern, having been carved since 1987. Note that one was carved by famed Haida artist Bill Reid and his assistants in 1964.

The **Nine O'Clock Gun** goes off every day at 9pm on Hallelujah Point (it is best not to be too close when it does). This shot used to alert fishermen that it was time to come in.

Continue along the Seawall, passing Brockton Point and some lovely landscapes to

photograph. About 2.5km further, you will pass beneath **Lions Gate Bridge ★ ★**, an elegant suspension bridge built in 1938. Measuring 1,527m long and 111m high, it spans the First Narrows, linking the affluent suburb of West Vancouver to the centre of town. At the entrance to the bridge, artist Charles Marega sculpted two immense lion heads. The bridge was rehabilitated between 1999 and 2002, following extensive study by the government, which examined and finally rejected proposals that the bridge be widened or replaced. It remains an enduring symbol of the city. **Prospect Point ★ ★ ★**, to the west, offers a general view of the bridge, whose steel pillars stand 135m high.

The **Seawall Promenade** runs along the edge of the park, and after rounding a 45-degree bend offers a panoramic view of the Georgia Strait, with Cypress Park and Bowen Island visible in the distance on clear days. Next, it passes **Third Beach ★**, one of the most pleasant beaches in the region. The numerous cargo ships and ocean liners waiting to enter the port complement the setting. From here, stairs lead up to the **Third Beach Café**, where snacks can be purchased.

We recommend stopping at the **Teahouse Restaurant ★** (see p 98), located between Third Beach and **Second Beach ★**. In the 1850s, the British government, fearing an American invasion (the U.S. border is less than 30km from Vancouver), considered building artillery batteries on this site. The risk of such a conflict had diminished by the early 20th century, so a charming tearoom was erected here instead. The Swiss-chalet-style building, surrounded by greenery, dates from 1911.

Vancouver

From Second Beach, complete the loop by following the signs to Georgia Street/Seawall, which will take you past **Lost Lagoon ★**, which was once part of Coal Harbour but was partially filled in during the construction of Lions Gate Bridge. It is now a bird sanctuary where large numbers of Canada geese, mallards and swans can be seen frolicking about.

On your way out of the park you'll see signs indicating the **Lost Lagoon Nature House**, home to the Stanley Park Ecology Society *(Jul to Sep Mon-Fri noon to 7pm, Sat and Sun 11am to 7 pm, fall and spring Fri-Sun 11am to 5 pm, Dec to Feb Sat and Sun 9 am to 4 pm, ☎257-8544)*, which has a small nature display and organizes thematic walks through the park *($5; call for schedule).*

Tour E: Burrard Inlet

Burrard Inlet is the long and very wide arm of the sea on which the Vancouver harbour—Canada's most important port for over 20 years now—is located. The Atlantic was once a favourite trading route, but the dramatic economic growth of the American West Coast (California, Oregon, Washington) and even more importantly, the Far East (Japan, Hong Kong, Taiwan, China, Singapore, Thailand, etc.), has crowned the Pacific lord and master of shipping.

Beyond the port lie the mountainside suburbs of North and West Vancouver, which offer some spectacular views of the city below. Along their steep, winding roads, visitors can admire some of the finest examples of modern residential architecture in North America. These luxurious houses, often constructed of posts and beams made of local

wood, are usually surrounded by lofty British Columbian firs and a luxuriant blend of plants imported from Europe and Asia.

There are two ways to take this tour. The first is by foot: hop aboard the SeaBus, the ferry that shuttles back and forth between downtown Vancouver and the north shore of Burrard Inlet, enjoy the open air and take in some exceptional views of both the city and the mountains. The other option is to drive across Lions Gate Bridge, take Marine Drive east to Third Street and head south on Lonsdale Avenue. The following descriptions refer to the walking tour, unless otherwise indicated.

Start off your tour in front of the neoclassical facade of the former **Canadian Pacific Station ★** *(601 West Cordova St.),* which dates from 1912 and was designed by Montréal architects Barrott, Blackader and Webster.

This station, Canadian Pacific's third in Vancouver, occupies a special place in the city's history. Before ships arriving from the west took over, trains arriving from the east fuelled the area's prosperous economy. In keeping with the times, the station no longer welcomes trains, but provides access to the Granville terminal of the SeaBus. It also provides indirect access to the Waterfront terminal of the SkyTrain (at the far end of Howe Street), but that's somewhat of a meagre consolation prize. Above the latter terminal is tiny **Portal Park** and its azaleas. **Granville Square**, the skyscraper immediately to the west, is the only completed portion of a major real-estate development project (1971) which was to include the demolition of the train station.

Follow the signs for the **SeaBus**. The crossing *($1.75)* to **North Vancouver ★★** takes barely 15min, though you'll wish it were longer. The ferry lands at its northern terminal near the pleasant **Lonsdale Quay Market ★**, built on a quay stretching out into Burrard Inlet. The cafés surrounding the market offer an unimpeded view of Vancouver and the mountains as well as all the activity at the nearby port, with the colourful tugboat dock flanking the market to the east. Built in 1986, Lonsdale Quay Market was the brainchild of architects Hotson and Bakker, who wanted to satisfy every basic human need here: food (ground floor), clothing (second floor) and lodging. From here, Vancouver really looks like a Manhattan in the making.

If you are travelling by car, return to Marine Drive heading west and go up Capilano Road until you reach the **Capilano Suspension Bridge and Park** *($13.95; mid-May to early Sep 8:30am to 8pm, reduced hours the rest of the year, call first; 3735 Capilano Rd., ☎985-7474).* If you are on foot at Lonsdale Quay Market, take bus number 236, which stops across the street from the entrance. Buses depart every half hour, on the quarter hour. Paths lead to this metal-cabled bridge, suspended 70m above the Capilano River, which replaced the original bridge of rope and wood built in 1899.

This heavily advertised, privately owned attraction draws some 800,000 visitors a year, each of whom pays a small fortune for the not-so-thrilling opportunity to walk across a shaky suspension bridge for all of two minutes. The admission fee is outrageous and the place is clearly a tourist trap. Its only redeeming feature, although just barely, are its planked walkways through the forest—negligible for hikers, but for seniors, or those with

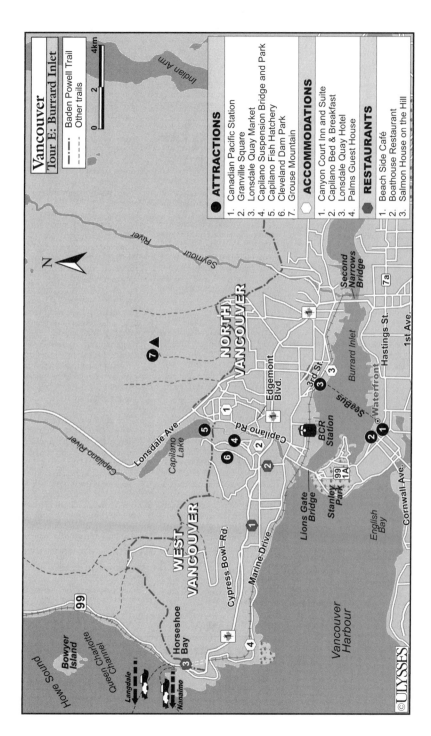

Vancouver
Tour E: Burrard Inlet

—·—·— Baden Powell Trail
————— Other trails

0 2 4km

● ATTRACTIONS
1. Canadian Pacific Station
2. Granville Square
3. Lonsdale Quay Market
4. Capilano Suspension Bridge and Park
5. Capilano Fish Hatchery
6. Cleveland Dam Park
7. Grouse Mountain

⬡ ACCOMMODATIONS
1. Canyon Court Inn and Suite
2. Capilano Bed & Breakfast
3. Lonsdale Quay Hotel
4. Palms Guest House

⬢ RESTAURANTS
1. Beach Side Café
2. Boathouse Restaurant
3. Salmon House on the Hill

Indian Arm

Seymour River

N

Capilano River

Howe Sound

Bowyer Island

Queen Charlotte Channel

Langdale

Nanaimo

99

Horseshoe Bay

3

WEST VANCOUVER

Cypress Bowl Rd.

Marine Drive

Lions Gate Bridge

Stanley Park

99
1A

English Bay

Cornwall Ave.

Vancouver Harbour

Capilano Lake

Lonsdale Ave.

Capilano Rd.

Edgemont Blvd.

NORTH VANCOUVER

3rd St.

BCR Station

SeaBus

Waterfront

Burrard Inlet

Hastings St.

1st Ave.

Second Narrows Bridge

7a

© ULYSSES

physical limitations, they do provide readily accessible exposure to the forest. That said, however, the shaky bridge itself is probably not suitable for anyone who is unsteady on their feet. Save your money and take a lovely walk (free!) through Stanley Park instead. But if you insist on visiting, make sure to walk down to the lookout to the right of the bridge, for a good view of it from below. And if you actually found the experience thrilling, visit the gift shop, where you can purchase your very own "I survived" T-shirt.

A good alternative, though substantially more physically challenging because it actually involves a hike, is the suspension bridge at **Lynn Canyon Park** (see p 87).

Three kilometres to the north is the **Capilano Fish Hatchery** ★ *(free; 4500 Capilano Park Rd., ☎666-1790)*, the first salmon hatchery in British Columbia. This well laid-out spot provides visitors with an introduction to the life cycle of the salmon. In the summer, Pacific salmon wear themselves out as they make their way up the Capilano River to reach their spawning grounds, making for an exceptional spectacle for visitors.

The upper part of Upper Capilano Road was renamed Nancy Greene Way after the Canadian skier who won the gold medal for the giant slalom at the 1968 Olympics in Grenoble, France. On the left, a road leads to **Cleveland Dam Park** ★★ on the shores of Lake Capilano. The construction in 1954 of the impressive 100m-high dam at the centre of the park led to the creation of the lake, Vancouver's main source of drinking water. Spectacular views of the neighbouring mountains surround the park.

At the north end of Nancy Greene Way, there is a **cable car** *($21.95; $5 down only; if you arrive here by city bus, no. 236, present your transfer for a 20% discount; every day 9am to 10pm; ☎980-9311)* that carries passengers to the top of **Grouse Mountain** ★★★, for a small fortune. At an altitude of 1,250m, skiers and hikers can contemplate the entire Vancouver area as well as Washington State (in clear weather) to the south. At this price, make sure you head up on a clear day! The view is particularly beautiful at the end of the day. Wilderness trails lead out from the various viewing areas. During summer, Grouse Mountain is also a popular spot for hang-gliding.

Climbing the mountain is a popular option (and a popular way to avoid the rather steep cable-car charge) (see p 87) instead. Remember that this is primarily a ski mountain, so during the winter, be prepared for crowds with ski equipment to jostle you about in the cable car. While you're up there, head into the Theatre in the Sky (in the chalet) to view the rather decent film *Born to Fly* (which provides a bird's-eye view of B.C.), shown hourly (free admission). But don't bother with the very-brief tractor-driven sleigh ride (departure from chalet in the winter), which, though free, isn't worth your five minutes (plus waiting time).

To return to Vancouver, get on the bus again, then take the SeaBus back the other way.

Tour F: False Creek

False Creek is located south of downtown Vancouver and, like Burrard Inlet, stretches far inland.

The presence of both water and a railroad induced a large number of sawmills to set up shop in this area in the early 20th century. These mills gradually filled a portion of False Creek, leaving only a narrow channel to provide them with the water that is needed for sawing. Over the years, two thirds of False Creek, as explorer George Vancouver had known it in 1790, have disappeared under asphalt.

By the early 1980s, the sawmills and other industries had disappeared and a century's worth of industrial pollution had left the area a mess. The City purchased the site, quickly cleaned it up, and during the summer of 1986 hosted Expo 86, a world's fair that attracted several-million visitors in the space of a few months. The vast stretch of unused land along the north shore of False Creek was occupied by dozens of showy pavilions with visitors crowding around them.

The City then rezoned the land for residential and commercial use and sold it to a Hong Kong tycoon for $145 million.

Our tour of the False Creek area begins in Yaletown, southeast of downtown and bordering on False Creek. From downtown, take Robson street east until Homer and turn right.

Yaletown ★ stretches between Homer to the west, Pacific Boulevard to the east, Nelson to the north and Drake to the south, but the two blocks of Mainland and Hamilton streets between Davie and Nelson are probably the most interesting for visitors.

Originally, Yaletown was located just south of its current location, on Drake Street between Granville Street and

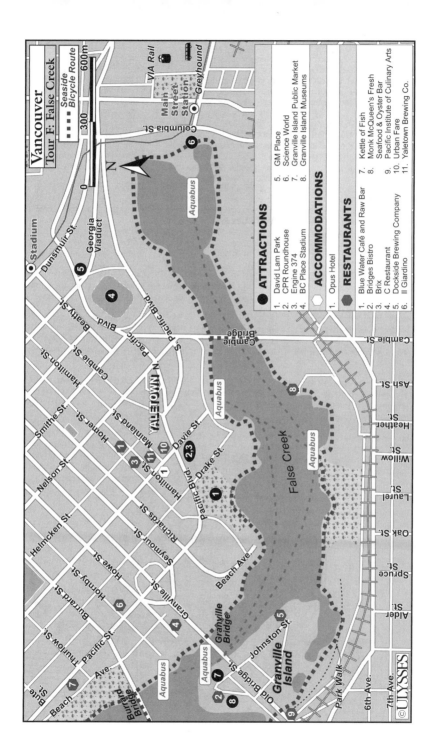

Vancouver

Tour F: False Creek

Seaside
Bicycle Route

0   300   600m

● ATTRACTIONS

1. David Lam Park
2. CPR Roundhouse
3. Engine 374
4. BC Place Stadium
5. GM Place
6. Science World
7. Granville Island Public Market
8. Granville Island Museums

◇ ACCOMMODATIONS

1. Opus Hotel

⬡ RESTAURANTS

1. Blue Water Café and Raw Bar
2. Bridges Bistro
3. Brix
4. C Restaurant
5. Dockside Brewing Company
6. Il Giardino
7. Kettle of Fish
8. Monk McQueen's Fresh Seafood & Oyster Bar
9. Pacific Institute of Culinary Arts
10. Urban Fare
11. Yaletown Brewing Co.

© ULYSSES

False Creek

YALETOWN

Granville Island

Park Walk

Pacific Boulevard; in fact, even before that, "Yaletown" was actually the town of Yale, in the Fraser River Canyon. It was there that the western terminus of the Canadian Pacific Railway (CPR) was located until 1886, when Vancouver took over that role. The CPR then moved its facilities from Yale to Yaletown, where a community of railway workers grew. The **Yale Hotel** *(1300 Granville St., near Drake St.)*, today a popular blues venue, was originally the Colonial Hotel, a rooming house for these workers. Built in 1890, it is one of the oldest buildings in Vancouver. In the early 1900s, the City erected a warehouse district next to the original community, in the area commonly considered Yaletown today. Its warehouses were built with loading docks at the rear, sheltered by permanent canopies, where goods from the boxcars could be directly loaded and unloaded.

The growth of the trucking industry shifted business away from Yaletown's big warehouses and the area declined. The train tracks were removed in the 1980s, around the time "loft livers" discovered the area. The loading docks of Hamilton and Mainland streets have since been transformed into

outdoor cafés and restaurants and a new group of tenants now occupies the old brick warehouses; designers, architects, film production companies and business people in general have brought this area back to life. Trendy cafés and restaurants have followed suit.

After exploring Yaletown's historic buildings, boutiques and restaurants, take Homer Street down to False Creek and you'll find yourself in **David Lam Park**, a pleasant spot for dog walkers, cyclists, soccer players and stone skippers, equipped with plenty of spots to sit and witness it all.

The new **Marinaside Crescent seawalk** is the latest extension to the seaside waterfront path, linking David Lam Park 220m east to Coopers' Park, near the Cambie Bridge. The new seawalk is lined with a number of innovative public art installations and numerous benches.

Continue to Davie Street and turn left.

On your left, at the corner of Pacific Street, you'll see an

interesting semi-circular structure. The beautifully restored **CPR Roundhouse** ★ *(at the corner of Davie St. and Pacific Blvd.)*, located opposite, is all that remains of the Canadian Pacific Railway (CPR) marshalling yard once located on this site. Erected in 1888, it was used for the servicing and repair of locomotives.

The roundhouse was built in this shape to allow grouping the inside tracks in a semicircle. In front of the roundhouse, locomotives were driven onto a turntable that directed them into a number of service bays.

Before you reach the entrance to the Roundhouse, you'll see the glassed-in **Engine 374 Pavilion** ★ *(donations accepted; summer every day 11am to 3pm, rest of the year Thu-Sat 11am to 3pm; hours subject to change; Davie St. and Pacific Blvd., ☎684-6662)*, home to the locomotive that pulled the very first train to reach Vancouver, in 1887. Engine 374, built by the Canadian Pacific Railway in 1886, was restored by volunteers in time for Expo 86 after a period of neglect and deterioration in Kitsilano Park. Kids enjoy climbing aboard and tooting the whistle.

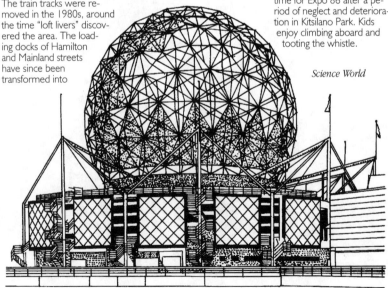

Science World

At the bottom of Davie Street is a marina served by the **Aquabus** *($2–$5; ☎689-5858)*, tiny little put-put ferries that look more like bath toys than seaworthy vessels. The Aquabus serves **Science World** *($3 one way; Sat and Sun only, departures 10:10am to 6:15pm every 30min, similar return schedule)* as well as **Granville Island** *($3 one way; every day departures every 30min on the hour and half hour 7am to 8:30pm, every 15min from 8:45am to 6:15pm, similar return schedule; ferry stops at Stamps Landing en route).* If you choose to visit both sites, you can also take the Aquabus from one to the other on Saturdays and Sundays *($5 one way; departs Granville Island 10am to 6pm every 30 min, departs Science World 10:30am to 6:30pm).* **False Creek Ferries**, *($5 one way; ☎684-7781)*, however, also runs the latter route and departs every day *(from Science World every 30min, at 15 and 45 past the hour; from Granville Island at 25 and 55 past the hour).*

If the ferry schedule doesn't suit you, you can conceivably walk all the way to Science World. Continue your promenade to Cooper's Park, in the shadow of the Cambie Bridge, also a favourite for dogs and their walkers. The paving stones and lights of the walkway continue until the Plaza of Nations, but beyond that you'll have to duck your way in and out of fenced-off areas until Science World, about a 12min walk from the Plaza.

On your way to Science World, you can spot the gray dome of GM Place and the white dome of BC Place Stadium, next to it. The 60,000 seats in **BC Place Stadium** *(777 Pacific Blvd. N., ☎669-2300, 661-7373 or 661-2122)* are highly coveted by fans of Canadian football, who come here to cheer on the B.C. Lions. Large trade fairs and rock concerts are also held in the stadium. Beside it is **GM Place** *(Pacific Blvd. at the corner of Abbott St., ☎899-7400)*, a 20,000-seat amphitheatre that was completed in 1995 and now hosts the home games of the local hockey and basketball teams, the Vancouver Canucks and Grizzlies respectively.

Science World ★ *($12.75 or $15.75 with movie; 1455 Québec St., ☎443-7440)* is the big silver ball at the end of False Creek. Architect Bruno Freschi designed this 14-storey building as a welcome centre for visitors to Expo 86. It was the only pavilion built to remain in place after the big event. The sphere representing the Earth has supplanted the tower as the quintessential symbol of these fairs since Expo 67 in Montréal. Vancouver's sphere contains an **OMNIMAX** theatre that presents films on a giant, dome-shaped screen. The rest of the building is now occupied by a museum that explores the secrets of science from all different angles.

Included are both high- and low-tech puzzles and displays for kids, many of which have a strong environmental message, including a display demonstrating the enormous waste of water involved in the simple act of flushing a toilet, a film called *Burgerworks*, which explains the energy and resources that go into the making of a hamburger, and an explanation of how electricity runs household appliances. The majority of Science World's visitors are school-aged children under 14, for whom most of the exhibits are geared. Don't leave without spending a few moments watching the delightful Tower of Bauble, a giant kinetic sculpture located outside the main entrance.

If you're heading to the market at **Granville Island** ★ ★ *(every day 9am to 6pm,* *www.granville-island.net)* by ferry, take the ramp down to the False Creek Ferries dock. If you're driving (a bad idea, as traffic is heavy and parking is limited) or cycling (possible via the Seaside Bicycle Route), just take the Granville or Burrard Bridge and follow the signs from there. To reach the island without following the False Creek tour, take bus number 50 heading south from Howe Street downtown. You'll notice the vaguely Art Deco pillars of the Burrard Street Bridge (1930).

In 1977, this artificial island, created in 1914 and once used for industrial purposes, saw its warehouses and factories transformed into a major recreational and commercial centre. The area has since come to life thanks to a revitalization project. A public market, museums, many shops and all sorts of restaurants, plus theatres and artists' studios are all part of Granville Island.

The **Granville Island Market** ★ ★ is a must-see. Grab yourself a herbal chai at the Granville Island Tea Co. or an organic fair-trade coffee at Origins Coffee Company, and feast every sense: there are stalls of oriental orchids, fishmongers with salmon in every shade of red (the Indian candy is a must), focaccia and fig-anise loaf at the wonderful Terra Breads, bowls of smoked-salmon chowder at Stock Market, and atmosphere to spare. Sit yourself down on a bench by False Creek and partake of the festive atmosphere. The view of the development's high- and low-rises on the north shore is not particularly inspiring, but with such creature comforts in hand, chances are you won't really mind.

Take Anderson Street south beneath the Granville Bridge, then turn left on Park Walk.

The museum is at the junction, to your right.

Granville Island Museums ★ *(1502 Duranleau St., Granville Island,* ☎*683-1939)* is actually three separate museums in one location, a stone's throw from the market: the Sport Fishing Museum, the Model Trains Museum and the Model Ships Museum. While they are quite clearly special-interest museums, those of us uninitiated in the joys of fishing, model trains and model ships will still find some pleasure here.

Tour G: West Side

The culture of the Pacific as well as the history and traditions of the Aboriginal peoples are omnipresent throughout this tour, which follows the shore of the vast peninsula that is home to the majority of Vancouver's residents. Posh residential neighbourhoods, numerous museums, a university campus and several sand and quartz beaches from which Vancouver Island is visible on a clear day all make up this tour. This is a driving tour, as it extends over 15km. The first four attractions are accessible aboard bus no. 22 from downtown or by taking bus no. 4 directly to the University of British Columbia campus. You can also get to the starting point in Vanier Park via False Creek Ferries *(departure at Aquatic Centre, foot of Thurlow St.; ☎684-7781 for schedule).*

Exit the downtown area by the Burrard Street Bridge.

Keep right, and immediately after going down the roadway leading off the bridge, take a right on Chestnut Street to get to **Vanier Park** (directions well indicated), which is home to three museums.

The **Vancouver Museum ★ ★** *($10; Tue-Sun 10am to 5pm, Thu until 9pm; 1100 Chestnut St., in Vanier Park,* ☎*736-4431)* forms its centrepiece. This delightful museum, whose dome resembles the head-dress worn by the Coast Salish First Nation, presents exhibitions on the history of the different peoples who have inhabited the region.

In the Orientation Gallery, you'll find an eclectic collection, including items from all over the world that were once collected by Vancouverites. You'll also see a photograph of **Engine 374**, which pulled the first transcontinental train into Vancouver (see p 65), on May 23, 1887. Children will be delighted by this gallery, which features a collection of toys, thoughtfully displayed in child-height glass exhibit cases. You'll also be treated to some wonderful views of the West End and Stanley Park.

Much of the rest of the museum is divided into Vancouver Story Exhibits, each focused on a period in Vancouver's history and imaginatively arranged with enough realism to enthral both children and adults. You'll see replicas of the steerage quarters of an immigrant ship, circa 1860, complete with seasickness-inducing sound effects; an early-19th-century fur-trading post, complete with howling wolves; an actual "colonist car" locomotive; the facade of a Victorian home (1890), recreated from demolished downtown and Eastside homes; and the interior of an Edwardian home. And if you enjoy it, you'll be pleased to know that the museum is planning to tell six new Vancouver stories in the coming years.

Also in the park is the **H.R. MacMillan Space Centre** *($12.75; Tue-Sun 10am to 5pm;* ☎*738-7827, www.pacific-space-centre.bc.ca)*, which

houses the H.R. MacMillan Planetarium and relates the creation of the universe. It has a telescope through which you can admire the stars. The **Maritime Museum** *($8; mid May to early Sep, every day 10am to 5pm; Nov to mid May Tue-Sat 10am to 5pm, Sun noon to 5pm; 1905 Ogden Ave.,* ☎*257-8300, www.vmm.bc.ca)* completes the trio of institutions in Vanier Park. Being a major seaport, it is only natural that Vancouver should have its own maritime museum. The key attraction is the **Saint-Roch**, the first boat to circle North America by navigating the Panamá Canal and the Northwest Passage.

Get back on Chestnut Street and turn right on Cornwall Avenue, which becomes a scenic road named Point Grey Road.

You will now pass through **Kitsilano** *(between Burrard and Alma sts.)*, bordered to the north by a public beach on English Bay and to the south by 16th Avenue. This area, whose wooden Queen Anne and Western Bungalow Style houses are typical of the West Coast, was a middle-class neighbourhood in the early 20th century. By the 1960s, it was the centre of Vancouver's flower-power scene. Today, polar fleece has largely replaced paisley, but the area still has a strong counter-culture feeling to it. Around the corner of First Avenue and Yew Street, there are a number of restaurants, cafés and bars, conveniently located close to the beach.

The area west of Alma Street as far as the University of British Columbia gates is known as **Point Grey ★ ★ ★**.

Fourth Avenue runs alongside lovely **Jericho Beach Park ★ ★**, a green space and beach rolled into one at the edge of English Bay. Turn right on Northwest Marine Drive,

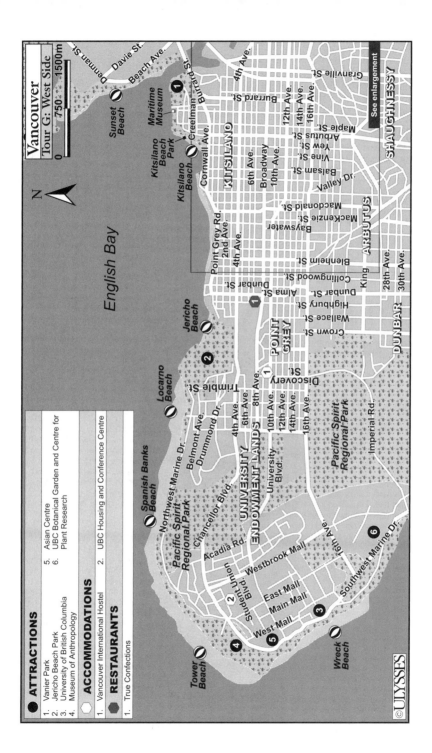

Vancouver
Tour G: West Side

0   750   1500m

See enlargement

English Bay

ATTRACTIONS
1. Vanier Park
2. Jericho Beach Park
3. University of British Columbia
4. Museum of Anthropology
5. Asian Centre
6. UBC Botanical Garden and Centre for Plant Research

ACCOMMODATIONS
1. Vancouver International Hostel
2. UBC Housing and Conference Centre

RESTAURANTS
1. True Confections

© ULYSSES

N

Sunset Beach

Maritime Museum

Kitsilano Beach Park

Kitsilano Beach

Cornwall Ave.

KITSILANO

Point Grey Rd.
2nd Ave.
4th Ave.

Bayswater St.
MacKenzie St.
Macdonald St.

ARBUTUS

Blenheim St.
Collingwood St.
Dunbar St.
Alma St.

DUNBAR

Highbury St.
Wallace St.
Crown St.

POINT GREY

Discovery St.

4th Ave.
6th Ave.
8th Ave.
10th Ave.
12th Ave.
14th Ave.
16th Ave.

University Blvd.

Trimble St.

Jericho Beach

Locarno Beach

Spanish Banks Beach

Pacific Spirit Regional Park

Northwest Marine Dr.
Belmont Ave.
Drummond Dr.

Chancellor Blvd.
Acadia Rd.

UNIVERSITY ENDOWMENT LANDS

Student Union Blvd.
Westbrook Mall
East Mall
Main Mall
West Mall

16th Ave.

Pacific Spirit Regional Park

Imperial Rd.

Southwest Marine Dr.

Tower Beach

Wreck Beach

Davie St.
Denman St.
Beach Ave.

Greer Ave.
Creelman Ave.
Burrard St.

4th Ave.

Granville St.

Burrard St.

12th Ave.
14th Ave.
16th Ave.
Maple St.
Arbutus St.
Yew St.
Vine St.
Balsam St.

6th Ave.
Broadway
10th Ave.

Valley Dr.

King

28th Ave.
30th Ave.

SHAUGHNESSY

then left on Belmont Avenue, driving up the hill, to see some of the loveliest houses on the West Side.

Return to Northwest Marine Drive and head west to **Spanish Banks Beach ★★**, where you'll get an unimpeded view of Vancouver and the north shore. It's a favourite place to watch the sunset. Just beyond Spanish Banks is **Pacific Spirit Regional Park ★★** (☎224-5739), also known as the University Endowment Lands. This 763ha parcel of land encompasses the rocky beaches on the perimeter of UBC as well as an inland section that contains more than 40km of gentle hiking and biking trails. The beaches are unsupervised and clothing is optional. From here, you get a full panoramic view of the Strait of Georgia.

The tour continues onto the grounds of the **University of British Columbia ★**, or UBC. The university was created by the provincial government in 1908, but it was not until 1925 that the campus opened its doors on this lovely site on Point Grey. An architectural contest had been organized for the site layout, but the First World War halted construction work. It took a student demonstration denouncing government inaction on this matter to get the buildings completed. Only the library and the science building were executed according to the original plans. To this day, the UBC campus is constantly expanding, so don't be surprised by its somewhat heterogeneous appearance. Quite frankly, the only redeeming feature of the campus is its view. If you're interested in a campus tour, nontheless, **Set Foot for UBC** (May to Aug, ☎822-TOUR) offers free tours organized by students.

There are, however, a few gems on the campus, including the **Museum of Anthropology ★★★** (*$7, free admission Tue 5pm to 9pm; mid-May to early Sep every day 10am to 5pm, Tue until 9pm, beg Sep to mid-May Tue 11am to 9pm, Wed-Sun 11am to 5pm; 6393 NW Marine Dr.; from downtown, take bus no. 4 UBC or bus no. 10 UBC; it's a 10 to 15min walk from the UBC bus terminal;* ☎822-3825). It's not to be missed both for the quality of Aboriginal artwork displayed here, including totem poles, and for the architecture of Arthur Erickson. Erickson designed the Great Hall

Raven and the First Men

with big concrete posts and beams to imitate the shape of traditional Aboriginal houses. Inside are immense totem poles gathered from former Aboriginal villages along the coast and on the islands. Here you will learn that there are three types of totem poles, classified according to function: supporting house poles, frontal beams, and memorial totem poles. Visitors are cautioned that "only those who know and have the right to the stories can tell the meaning of a totem pole." Some are

contemporary, others over a century old.

A highlight of the museum is the *Raven and the First Men*, by renowned Haida artist Bill Reid and several assistants. This impressive yellow cedar piece depicts the Raven, an infamous trickster in Haida history, coaxing fearful human beings out of a clam shell after a great flood. This huge piece was lowered into the museum through the skylight above it. In addition to wooden sculpture, you'll also find some fabulous carved silver and gold jewellery; the contemporary pieces you see in jewellery stores around the city have their roots in silver and gold coins, which the Haida hammered into bracelets and other objects and engraved as early as the 1860s.

In addition to objects related to the First Nations of B.C., including many pieces of intricate basketry, you'll also be astounded by the museum's rich collection of artifacts from other Canadian First Nations, as well as international items, such as Japanese dolls and masks, Chinese porcelain and representational art, and Polynesian, Australian, Southeast Asian and Indian art.

The museum's collection has exceedingly outgrown its display space; much of the collection, particularly the above-noted items, is crammed together in "visible storage," either in glass-topped drawers or squeezed into display cases. Each piece has a code, which can be looked up in a large book, something of a labourious process not usually found in contemporary museums. The process is soon to be computerized, and much more of the collection will be displayed in the coming years, thanks to upcoming renovations. It's a

Vancouver

Tour G: West Side enlargement

N

0   250   500m

Burrard Bridge

Cornwall St.

York Ave.
1st Ave. W.
2nd Ave. W.
3rd Ave. W.
4th Ave. W.
5th Ave. W.
6th Ave. W.
7th Ave. W.
8th Ave. W.
10th Ave. W.
11th Ave. W.

Balaclava St.
Bayswater St.
Trafalgar St.
Larch St.
Stephens St.
Macdonald St.
MacKenzie St.
Carnarvon St.

Yew St.
Vine St.
Balsam St.
Larch St.
Arbutus St.
Maple St.
Cypress St.
Burrard St.
Pine St.
Fir St.
Granville St.
Hemlock St.
Birch St.
Alder St.
Spruce St.
Oak St.
Laurel St.
Willow St.
Heather St.
Ash St.
Cambie St.
Yukon St.

16th Ave. W.
17th Ave. W.
18th Ave. W.
19th Ave. W.
20th Ave. W.
21st Ave. W.
22nd Ave. W.
23rd Ave. W.

17th Ave. W.

King Edward Ave. W.

Puget Dr.
Quesnel Dr.
King Edward Ave. W.

Matthews Ave.
Balfour Ave.
Laurier Ave.
Granville St.
Oak St.

12th Ave. W.
13th Ave. W.
14th Ave. W.
15th Ave. W.

Laurel St.
Willow St.
Heather St.
Broadway W.
7th Ave. W.
8th Ave. W.
Alberta St.
Columbia St.
Manitoba St.
Tupper St.

Trafalgar St.
Macdonald St.
MacKenzie St.

ACCOMMODATIONS

1. Accommodation by Pillow Suites
2. Johnson Heritage House B&B
3. Penny Farthing Inn
4. Plaza 500 Hotel

RESTAURANTS

1. Banana Leaf Malaysian Restaurant
2. De Dutch Pannekoek House
3. Habibi's
4. Incendio West
5. Lumière
6. Naam
7. Salade de Fruits
8. Seasons in the Park
9. Smoking Dog
10. Sophie's Cosmic Café
11. Tomato Fresh Food Café
12. Vij's

© ULYSSES

good idea to participate in a guided museum tour because the museum's interpretive signage is rather limited. There are political reasons for this: all cultural groups in British Columbia (there are seven major First Nations and a great number of language-based culture groups) must agree to any cultural interpretation—a long, contentious process.

On your way out (leave by the main entrance and turn right, turning again on the path), don't miss the outdoor exhibit, a 19th-century Haida house complex.

On the edge of the West Mall is the **Asian Centre** (*1871 West Mall*), capped with a big pyramidal metal roof. It houses the department of Asian studies and an exhibition centre. Behind the building is the magnificent **Nitobe Memorial Garden ★ ★** (*$2.75 summer, free winter; $6 with Botanical Garden admission, see below; mid-Mar to mid-Oct, every day 10am to 6pm; winter, Mon to Fri 10am to 2:30pm; ☎822-9666*) which symbolically faces Japan on the other side of the Pacific.

The southwestern edge of the campus harbours a spot unlike any other—**Wreck Beach ★** (*NW Marine Dr. at University St.*)—where students come to enjoy some of life's pleasures. Nudists have made this their refuge, as have sculptors, who exhibit their talents on large pieces of driftwood. Vendors hawk all sorts of items next to improvised fast-food stands. A long stairway, quite steep in places, leads down to the beach.

Just beyond Wreck Beach is the **UBC Botanical Garden and Centre for Plant Research** (*$4.75, $6 with Nitobe Memorial Garden admission; every day mid-Mar to mid-Oct 10am to 6pm; free admission mid-Oct to mid-Mar, open daylight hours; guided tours Apr to mid-Oct, Wed and Sun at 2pm*

from the main gatehouse; 6804 SW Marine Dr., ☎822-3928), an attractive place for a stroll and a popular place to find many species that are extremely rare in Canada, many of which are for sale in its Shop in the Garden. Its annual Mother's Day perennial plant sale is a popular event.

Outdoor Activities

For general information on all outdoor activities in the Greater Vancouver area, contact **Sport B.C.** (*409-1367 W. Broadway, Vancouver, V6H 4A9, ☎737-3000, www.sportbc.ca*) or the **Outdoor Recreation Council of B.C.** (*334-1367 W. Broadway, Vancouver, V6H 4A9, ☎737-3058, www.orcbc.ca*). Both organizations offer many suggestions and information.

Vancouver Parks & Recreation
☎257-8400
www.city.vancouver.bc.ca/parks
Vancouver Parks & Recreation provides information on sports and recreation activities.

Beaches

The Vancouver shoreline is made up in large part of easily accessible sandy beaches. All these beaches lie along English Bay, where it is possible to walk, cycle, play volleyball and, of course, take a dip in the sea to fully enjoy the setting. Stanley Park is fringed by **Third Beach** and **Second Beach**, and then, further east, along Beach Avenue, by **First Beach**, where hundreds of bathers brave the icy water to celebrate the New Year on January 1. A little farther east,

Sunset Beach celebrates the day's end with gorgeous sunsets. At the southern edge of English Bay are **Kitsilano Beach**, **Jericho Beach**, **Locarno Beach**, **Spanish Banks Beach**, **Tower Beach** and, finally, **Wreck Beach** at the western edge of the University of British Columbia campus.

Kitsilano Beach is enlivened by beach volleyball tournaments and by an assortment of sports facilities, including a basketball court. Locarno, Jericho and Spanish Banks beaches are quieter spots for family relaxation, where walking and reading are key activities.

Hiking

Stanley Park is definitely the best place go hiking in Vancouver with over 50km of trails through forest and greenery along the seashore, lakeshores, including the **Seawall**, an outstanding 9km trail flanked by giant trees.

There are lots of places to go walking in the Point Grey area. Myriad trails crisscross the **University of British Columbia (UBC) Endowment Lands**, now known as **Pacific Spirit Regional Park** (*access via Northwest Marine Dr. and Southwest Marine Dr., east of the UBC campus, as well as 16th Ave., where there is parking, and the Park Centre; ☎224-5739*). Pick up a trail map from the centre or download one from *www.gvrd.bc.ca*. There is a 40km network of trails through the forest, and since UBC is located on a peninsula, all trails ultimately lead to the beach.

On the other side of Lions Gate Bridge, in North Vancouver, Capilano Road leads to **Capilano River Regional**

Park *(☎224-5739)*, where you'll find a trail offering sweeping views of the Capilano River. During summer, you can see the salmon swimming upriver. Maps are available on the following Web site: *www.gvrd.bc.ca*.

Mountain hiking is also accessible near the city centre. **Cypress Provincial Park** *(☎924-2200)*, north of the municipality of West Vancouver, has several hiking trails, among them the Howe Sound Crest Trail, which leads to different mountains, including The Lions and Mount Brunswick. The views over the west shore of Howe Sound are really quite spectacular. You must wear good shoes and bring food and water for these hikes. To get to Cypress Park by the Lions Gate Bridge, follow the signs west along the Trans-Canada Highway and take the Cypress Bowl Road exit. Take the time to stop at the lookout to contemplate Vancouver, the Strait of Georgia and, on a clear day, Mount Baker in the United States.

The hike up **Grouse Mountain** ★ ★ ★ *(☎984-0661)*, known as the Grouse Grind, is not particularly difficult, but the incline is as steep as 25° in places, so you have to be in good shape. It takes about 2hrs to cover the 3km trail, which starts at the parking lot for the cable car. The view of the city from the top of the mountain is fantastic. If you are too tired to hike back down, take the cable car for the modest sum of $5. Note that the trail is subject to closures due to inclement weather or other dangerous conditions.

Mount Seymour Provincial Park ★ ★ *(☎986-2261)* is another good hiking locale, offering two different views of the region. To the east is Indian Arm, a large arm of the sea extending into the valley.

A little further east in this marvellous mountain range on the north shore, magnificent **Lynn Canyon Park** ★ ★ ★ *(☎981-3103)* is scored with forest trails. It is best known for its footbridge, which stretches across an 80m deep gorge. Definitely not for the faint of heart! There is also an ecology centre on-site. To get there, take Highway 1 from North Vancouver to the Lynn Valley Road exit and follow the signs, then turn right on Peters Road.

Lighthouse Park, in West Vancouver, is well suited to hiking on flatter terrain. From this site, you will be facing the University of British Columbia, the entrance to English Bay, and the Strait of Georgia. Take the Lions Gate Bridge and follow Marine Drive West, crossing the city of West Vancouver and hugging the seashore until you reach the western edge of English Bay. Turn left at Beacon Lane toward Lighthouse Park.

If you get off Highway 99 just after West Vancouver and head west to Horseshoe Bay, you'll come to lovely little **Whytecliff Park**, located on the seashore. Most people come here to go picnicking or scuba diving. For an interesting little excursion, follow the rocky trail out to **Whyte Island** at low tide. Before heading out to this big rock, make sure to check what time the tides are due to come in, or you'll end up with wet feet.

A 15min **ferry** *(BC Ferries, ☎888-223-3779)* ride from Horseshoe Bay transports you to **Bowen Island** ★ ★ ★ *(☎947-2216)*, where hiking trails lead through a lush forest. Although you'll feel as if you're at the other end of the world, downtown Vancouver is only 5km away as the crow flies.

Cycling

The region has a multitude of mountain-biking trails. Just head to one of the mountains north of the city.

A pleasant 9km ride runs along the Seawall in Stanley Park, part of Vancouver's oldest, and no doubt best, bike path, the **Seaside Bicycle Route**. It extends from Coal Harbour, just west of the Pan Pacific Hotel, west to the Stanley Park Seawall, and from there along English Bay and False Creek to Spanish Bank West. If you include the Stanley Park Seawall, the entire route measures about 30km and is an excellent way for visitors to explore the beauty of the city. Shortcuts can be taken along the Cambie and Burrard bridges, the latter being a good choice if you want to head directly to Granville Island. A handy map of bike paths in Vancouver can be obtained by contacting the **Bicycle Hotline** at ☎871-6070.

Bicycle rentals are available at **Spokes Bicycle Rental** *(1798 West Georgia St., corner of Denman, ☎688-5141)*.

Bird-watching

Birders should make a trip to the **George C. Reifel Bird Sanctuary** ★ ★ *(5191 Robertson Road, Delta, ☎946-6980)* on Westham and Reifel islands. Dozens of species of migratory and non-migratory birds draw orthinology enthusiasts year-round to see aquatic birds, birds of prey, and many other varieties. Further south, several species can also be observed at Boundary Bay and Mud Bay as well as on Iona Island closer to

Vancouver

Vancouver, next to the airport.

Paddling

Like the mountains, the water is a key part of life in Vancouver, and there is an almost unlimited number of ways to get out and enjoy the sea. One option is to tour the city by sea kayak. **False Creek** stretches all the way to Main Street and Science World, and you'll pass Granville Island along the way; by paddling around **Stanley Park**, you can reach Canada Place and the skyscrapers downtown. More courageous visitors can set out along **Indian Arm ★★★** from Deep Cove, an expedition likely to include a few encounters with seals and eagles.

A completely no-hassle way to get there is to take part in an organized expedition, such as the ones available from:

Lotus Land Tours Inc.
2005-1251 Cardero St.
Vancouver V6G 2H9
☎*684-4922*
Knowledgeable guide Peter Loppe and his staff will pick you up from your hotel and take you kayaking in scenic Indian Arm. A barbecued-salmon lunch is provided ($145). No experience required.

Ecomarine Ocean Kayak Centre
1668 Duranleau St.
Granville Island
☎*689-7520*
This Granville Island outfit offers kayak rentals as well as 2.5hr and 4hr tours (*$49 and $89 respectively*) of False Creek and English Bay. This company also offers instruction.

Sailing

Sailing is the best way to visit some of the lovely spots in **Vancouver Harbour**. Jericho Beach, in the Kitsilano area, is an excellent starting point. You can rent your own sailing dinghy or Hobie Cat at the **Jericho Sailing Centre Association** (*1300 Discovery St.*, ☎*224-4177*), or climb aboard a larger sailboat for a cruise of several hours or several days. The **Cooper Boating Centre** (*1620 Duranleau St., Granville Island*, ☎*687-4110*) is a good place to keep in mind.

Pleasure Boating

Renting an outboard **motor boat** is as easy as renting a car. No special permit is required for you to putter around at your leisure or speed across the water, as long as you stay near the shore. You'll find everything you need at **Granville Island Boat Rentals** (*16296 Duranleau Street, Granville Island*, ☎*682-6287*).

Fishing

Salt-water Fishing

Vancouver is the starting point for unforgettable fishing. When it comes to sea fishing, salmon reigns supreme. Before casting your line, you must obtain a permit from a specialized outfitter from whom you can also rent out the necessary equipment. They have boats, know the best locations, and supply equipment and often meals, too. Make sure you are dressed appropriately. Even

when the sun is out, it can get very cold on the open sea. It is also essential that you not forget your fishing license. You will find a mine of information from:

Sport Fishing Institute of British Columbia
Sport Fishing Museum
200-1676 Duranleau St.,
Granville Island, V6H 3S4
☎*689-6438*
www.sportfishing.bc.ca

The following charter companies can make all the arrangements for you:

Bites-On Salmon Charters
1128 Hornby St.
Granville Island
☎*877-688-2483*
A 5hr trip will run you about $425.

Westin Bayshore Yacht Charters
1601 West Georgia St.
☎*691-6936*
Westin Bayshore Yacht Charters has an impressive fleet of fishing yachts.

Fresh-water Fishing

With an infinite number of lakes and rivers, trout fishing in British Columbia is always excellent. Licenses are sold in all camping equipment stores as well as at **Ruddik's Fly Shop** (*1077 Marine Dr., N. Vancouver*, ☎*985-5650*), a good shop for this sport. Thousands of flies for catching every kind of fish in the area can be purchased here. The owner will gladly offer advice. Vancouver is the starting point to equip yourself and make inquiries, though you will have to leave the city to fish on a river or lake. The interior region and Cariboo Country are prime destinations for anglers from Vancouver. You can also purchase an issue of *BC Outdoors Sports Fishing* magazine at almost any newsagent's or call on fishing clubs or outfitters.

For more information on fresh-water fishing, contact the **Sport Fishing Institute of British Columbia** (see above).

Mountaineering

A trip to Vancouver without tackling the snow-covered peaks that surround the city would be a real shame. The **Federation of Mountain Clubs of B.C.** *(47 W. Broadway, Vancouver, V5Y 1P1, ☎737-3053, www.mountainclubs. bc.ca)* is a very reliable club with experienced instructors. Excursions are organized on a regular basis.

Helicopter Sightseeing

If Vancouver's scenery has already won you over, here is something that will truly take your breath away!: a glacier-skimming helicopter ride over snow-covered peaks and turquoise lakes! Some agencies even offer landings on the glaciers. Though somewhat pricey, you will have unforgettable memories and extraordinary photographs too.

Vancouver Helicopters
5455D Airport Rd. S., Richmond
☎270-1484 or 800-987-4354
Vancouver Helicopters is located right near Vancouver International Airport. This enterprise has a fine reputation and will take you anywhere you want to go.

Kite Flying

With its 26km of beaches, Vancouver is the perfect place to go fly a kite. The most

renowned spot for this activity is **Vanier Park**, which borders the beaches on English Bay, behind the Vancouver Museum. To get there, take the Burrard Bridge out of the downtown area and follow Chestnut Street through the pretty neighbourhood of Kitsilano.

In-line Skating

In-line skating is a popular activity in Vancouver. Although you'll see skaters all over, the most popular place to go is around Stanley Park on the **Seawall**, a scenic, 9km trail flanked by a century-old forest. Skaters must travel counter clockwise (from Coal Harbour to English Bay), keep to the bicycle lane and not travel faster than 15km/hr. Skate rentals are available at many places along the beach, as well as near the entrance to the park at **Bayshore Bike Rentals** (*$13.50/4hrs; 745 Denman St., ☎688-2453*).

Golf

Vancouver is unquestionably the golf capital of Western Canada, with golf for all tastes and budgets. Golf courses in Vancouver and its surrounding areas are virtually all hilly and offer spectacular views of the ocean and especially the mountains that loom over all parts of the region. It should be noted that all golf clubs require appropriate attire. There are very few courses in Vancouver itself, but the suburbs boast one at practically every turn.

University Golf Club
5185 University Blvd.
☎224-1818
The University Golf Club is one of the best-known in town and among the priciest. It is situated a stone's throw from the University of British Columbia (UBC). Sean Connery has played here.

Peace Portal Golf Course
16900 Fourth Avenue, Surrey
☎538-4818 or 800-354-7544
The oldest public golf course, the Peace Portal Golf Course was founded in 1928 and is open year-round. It lies along Highway 99, near the U.S. border, in the suburb of Surrey.

Mayfair Lakes Golf and Country Club
5460 No. 7 Road, Richmond
☎276-0585
In Richmond, another of the city's southern suburbs, the Mayfair Lakes Golf and Country Club has a top-notch green surrounded by water.

Furry Creek
Britannia Beach
☎922-9576 or 922-9461
No golf course boasts a more spectacular setting than Furry Creek, located just past the village of Lions Bay, on **Howe Sound**, (Highway 99 N). Nestled away in a splendid landscape, this course is more than just pleasant; imagine the sea stretched out beside towering, snow-capped peaks. Amazing.

Fraserview Golf Course
7800 Vivian Dr.
☎280-1616
The Fraserview Golf Course is an affordable golf course, managed by the City and located at the southern tip of Vancouver.

Langara Golf Course
6706 Alberta St.
☎280-1818
The Langara Golf Course is also a municipal golf course, situated southeast of town.

Vancouver

Gleneagles
6190 Marine Dr., West Vancouver
☎*921-7353*
Right near the lovely village of Horseshoe Bay and 15min from Vancouver, this very inexpensive golf course is sometimes jam-packed on weekends, but the scenery makes playing here worth the wait.

Cross-country Skiing

Less than a 30min drive from Vancouver, three ski resorts welcome snow-lovers from morning to evening. In **Cypress Provincial Park**, on Cypress Mountain (*$15;* ☎*926-5612*) there are nearly 25km of mechanically maintained trails suitable for all categories of skiers. These trails are frequented day and evening by cross-country skiers. There are also trails at *Grouse Mountain (*☎*984-0661)* and *Mount Seymour Provincial Park (*☎*986-2261)*.

Downhill Skiing

What makes Vancouver a truly magical place is the combination of sea and mountains. The cold season is no exception, as residents desert the beaches and seaside paths to crowd the ski hills, which are literally suspended over the city. There are four ski resorts close to the city: **Mount Seymour** (*$29; 1700 Mount Seymour Rd., North Vancouver; Upper Level Hwy. heading east, Deep Cove Exit,* ☎*986-2261)*, a family resort with beginner trails, situated east of North Vancouver, above Deep Cove; **Grouse Mountain** (*$35; 6400 Nancy Greene Way, North Vancouver;* ☎*984-0661)*, a small resort accessible by cable car, which offers an

unobstructed view of Vancouver that is as magnificent by day as it is by night; **Cypress Mountain** (*$42; from North Vancouver, take Trans-Canada Highway 1, heading west for 16km, then follow road signs;* ☎*926-5612)*, a resort for the most avid skiers, also offers magnificent views of Howe Sound and of the city. For more affordable skiing, try the village-style **Hemlock Valley Resort** (*$34.50; Hwy. 1 heading east, Agassizou Harrisson Hot Springs Exit;* ☎*515-6300 or 866-515-6300)*. Situated at the eastern tip of Vancouver's urban area, in the heart of the Cascade Mountains, this resort boasts an abundance of snow and a spectacular view of Mount Baker in the United States. As soon as enough snow blankets the slopes, in late November or early December, these four ski resorts are open every day until late at night, thanks to powerful neon lighting. It should be noted, however, that the first three resorts do not provide accommodation (consult the section for Burrard Inlet in p 94 for the nearest hotels).

Accommodations

There are more than 10,000 hotel rooms in the downtown core and another 8,000 in the surrounding area. They include hotels, motels, bed and breakfasts, inns and hostels. According to Tourism Vancouver, the average rate is just over $100, with the lowest at around $60. In our experience, however, during peak summer season, you'll pay well over $150 for a decent room and over $200 for really top-notch digs. We've included reviews in all price ranges for those looking for the best value for their money,

as well as for those looking for the best the city has to offer.

Accommodations can be booked for you by **Super, Natural British Columbia Reservation and Information Service**:

☎*800-HELLO-BC (North America)*
☎*(250) 387-1642 (overseas)*
☎*(604) 663-6000 (Greater Vancouver)*

Downtown

YWCA
$$-$$$
pb/sb, ℝ, ≡
733 Beatty St.
☎*895-5830 or 800-663-1424*
≈*681-2550*
www.ywcahotel.com
Forget whatever images you had of lodgings beginning with a *Y*. Far from dreary, this purpose-built (1995) high-rise offers 155 private rooms on 11 floors, each simply but brightly decorated and equipped with all the essentials. Open to men, women and families, it's safe and centrally located across from BC Place Stadium. In addition, it's a non-profit establishment, with proceeds invested in YWCA community programs. Guests have access to three common kitchens and can choose from a variety of room types. Discounts for seniors and students. The only competition in the vicinity is the Kingston and the Victorian (see below), and a number of dreary motels and motor inns. Inexpensive private parking.

Kingston Hotel Bed and Breakfast
$$-$$$ bkfst incl.
sb/pb, △
757 Richards St.
☎*684-9024 or 888-713-3304*
≈*684-9917*
www.kingstonhotelvancouver.com
This family-owned hotel, built in 1910, is a favourite with budget-conscious travel-

lers—and with good reason. It offers 55 clean rooms, which range in size from a very small room with a sink and a shared bathroom (down the hall) to a large double-bedded room with desk, TV, armchairs, hair dryer and bathtub. All rooms have telephones and windows that open, and guests have access to a coin-operated laundry, storage and sauna. Strictly no frills, however, this four-storey hotel has no elevator. A courtyard patio with a pub is in the works. Excellent downtown location. Continental breakfast.

Victorian Hotel
$$-$$$ bkfst incl.
pb/sb, K
514 Homer St.
☎*681-6369 or 877-681-6369*
⇰*681-8776*
www.victorian-hotel.com
More charming than the Kingston and the YWCA but still in the budget category, the Victorian Hotel is without a doubt the best deal in downtown Vancouver. Spotless and attractive, all rooms feature feather duvets, hardwood floors, high ceilings and sinks; some have antique furniture, bay windows and bathtubs. All rooms have telephones and TVs and there are laundry facilities on-site and reasonably priced, secure parking ($10). Bike rentals are also offered. A continental breakfast is included. Your hosts Miriam and Andrew speak German, French, Dutch, Czech and Slovak, to the delight of their many European guests. A real find.

Westin Grand
$$$$-$$$$$
K, ≡, =, ⊙, ℜ, △
433 Robson St.
☎*602-1999 or 888-680-9393*
⇰*647-2502*
www.westingrandvancouver.com
A new kid on the block (1999), the all-suite Westin Grand has become a highlight among downtown hotels in no time at all. Its suites offer

floor-to-ceiling windows for some incredible city views. Decorated in warm sand tones with beech and walnut furnishings and original artwork, they are tasteful and understated, and the beds, linens, showers and soaker tubs are designed with the utmost comfort in mind. Furthermore, the service is friendly and professional throughout. An excellent spot for business travellers, 23 of its 207 suites are fully equipped "guest offices." Conveniently located within easy walking distance of Yaletown, the heart of the downtown core, Gastown and Chinatown. Highly recommended.

Terminal City Club
$$$$$
ℜ, ⊙, ≈, ≡, △, K, ⊛
837 West Hastings St.
☎*681-4121*
⇰*681-9634*
www.tcclub.com
The favourite place for business travellers, this luxurious establishment has an elegant style. It has 60 cozy rooms with a cheerful decor. Its poolroom, golf simulator, ocean view and attentive service will make your stay memorable.

Sheraton Wall Centre Hotel
$$$$$$
ℜ, ⊙, ✖, △, ≡, ℝ, K, ✪, ≈
1088 Burrard St.
☎*331-1000 or 800-663-9255*
⇰*331-1001*
www.sheratonwallcentre.com
With the recent addition of a second tower (2001), this mega-hotel now offers over 700 guest rooms and takes up an entire city block. The best feature of the guest rooms is their floor-to-ceiling windows, offering an unequalled city view and as much natural light as you can get in this frequently overcast city. The contemporary decor is understated, warm and tasteful, with beige tones, gorgeous linens and duvets, and original photographs taken on site. The

decor in the original south tower, which dates from 1996, is still fresh and attractive. All rooms have safes, bathrobes, irons, hair dryers and coffee makers, as well as high-speed, ethernet Internet access via a TV screen and wireless keyboard. A plethora of meeting rooms and upgraded "club" rooms make this a choice lodging for business travellers with a hefty expense account.

Le Soleil Hotel
$$$$$$
ℜ, ≡, ✖
567 Hornby St.
☎*632-3000 or 877-632-3030*
www.lesoleilhotel.com
The Sun King would have been so proud. This swish and stylish boutique hotel, housing 119 suites, was purpose built in Vancouver's financial district in 1999, on the vanguard of Vancouver's burgeoning boutique hotel scene. From its opulent, gilded lobby to the 18ft vaulted ceilings and black whirlpool bath in its magnificent penthouse suite, each suite is magnificently done up in shades of gold or crimson, with blond-wood furniture and brocade duvets on beds with padded headboards. Each has an in-room safe, two TVs so you never have to miss your favourite programs, bedside cordless phone, deep soaker tub, high-speed Internet hookups, as well as the usual accoutrements (coffee makers, ironing boards, etc.). True to European style, the rooms are a tad on the cozy (i.e. small) side, but their style and comfort is undeniable. The daily newspaper is delivered to your door, along with fruit and bottled water. While the price tag is clearly beyond the reach of many, inquire about the off-peak rates, which may actually be a relatively good deal.

Vancouver

Wedgewood Hotel
$$$$$$
☺, △, ≡, ℜ, ℝ
845 Hornby St.
☎689-7777 or 800-663-0666
≈668-3074
www.wedgewoodhotel.com
The Wedgewood Hotel is small enough to have retained some character and style. In particular, It features a lovely lobby complete with shiny brass accents, cozy fireplace and distinguished art, and is large enough to offer a certain measure of privacy and professionalism. This is a popular option for business trips, with an on-site business centre, and romantic weekend getaways.

Fairmont Hotel Vancouver
$$$$$$
≈, ☺, △, ℜ, ✖, ☺, ≡
900 West Georgia St.
☎684-3131 or 800-441-1414
≈662-1929
www.fairmont.com
The storied Hotel Vancouver, formerly a Canadian Pacific Hotel, is actually the third incarnation of the hotel by this name. Completed in 1939 in the château-style characteristic of Canadian railway hotels, it replaced two earlier Hotel Vancouvers, the first located at Georgia and Granville (1887), the second nearby on the site of Pacific Centre Mall (1916). Soon after opening, it hosted George VI and Queen Elizabeth, the first British monarchs to visit Canada. You will find tranquillity and luxury in the heart of downtown near Robson Street and Burrard Street. The hotel has some 550 rooms and a popular on-site bar.

Pan Pacific Hotel Vancouver
$$$$$$
≡, ☻, ☺, ≈, △, ℜ, ✖, ℝ
300-999 Canada Place
☎662-8111
☎800-663-1515 in Canada
☎800-937-1515 in the US
≈685-8690
www.panpacific.com
The luxurious Pan Pacific Hotel Vancouver is located in Canada Place, on the shore of Burrard Inlet facing North Vancouver. Everyone from Elizabeth Taylor to Sly Stallone has called the landmark Pan Pacific home. Connected to Canada Place and the Vancouver Convention and Exhibition Centre, its fabulous atrium lobby with fountain and armchairs looks out over the harbour, where sea planes land and cruise ships dock, and the Coastal Mountains to the north—apparently, Liz couldn't tear herself away from the window of her deluxe suite. All of the 504 rooms were recently redecorated and feature tasteful neutral tones, with bird's-eye maple furnishings and feather duvets. High-speed Internet access in all rooms.

West End

Buchan Hotel
$$
sb/pb, ℜ
1906 Haro St.
☎685-5354 or 800-668-6654
≈685-5367
Buchan Hotel is located in the West End residential area, near Stanley Park, beneath the trees. At the end of Haro Street, on Lagoon Drive, three municipal tennis courts are accessible to guests. Other tennis courts, a golf course and hiking trails can be found near this 61-room, three-storey hotel. Smoking on the premises is prohibited. Children under 12 free.

Barclay Hotel
$$$
≡, ℜ, ℝ
1348 Robson St.
☎688-8850
≈688-2534
www.barclayhotel.com
Of the handful of budget accommodations concentrated at the intersection of Robson and Broughton streets, the Barclay, along with the Robsonstrasse (see below) are probably the least objectionable choices. That being said, its 90 rooms are rather shabby—the tiny windows and the flickering fluorescent lights make for a dark, uninviting ambiance, adequate only for those who plan on spending more time in nearby Stanley Park than in their room.

Sylvia Hotel
$$$
K, ℜ, ✖
1154 Gilford St.
☎681-9321
≈682-3551
www.sylviahotel.com
Located just a few steps from English Bay, this charming old hotel, built in the early 1900s, offers unspoiled views and has 118 simple rooms. People come for the atmosphere, but also for food and drink at the end of the day. For those on lower budgets, rooms without views are offered at lower rates. The manager of this ivy-covered hotel is a Frenchman who is fully and justifiably dedicated to his establishment. Request a southwest-facing room (one facing English Bay) in order to benefit from magical sunsets over the bay.

Robsonstrasse Hotel
$$$
K, ≡, ☺
1394 Robson St.
☎687-1674 or 888-667-8877
≈685-7808
www.robsonstrassehotel.com
The Robsonstrasse Hotel is another relatively affordable Robson Street option.

Oceanside Hotel
$$$
K, ≡, ✖
1847 Pendrell St.
☎682-5641
The Oceanside Hotel is a small hotel offering complete apartments, with separate bedrooms. Well located in the West End a walk away from the major attractions.

West End Guest House Bed & Breakfast
$$$$ bkfst incl.
⊛

1362 Haro St.
☎681-2889 or 888-546-3327
⇄688-8812
www.westendguesthouse.com
This Victorian-style B&B houses eight cozy guest rooms, all decorated with the requisite flowered wallpaper and antiques, as well as ceiling fans and luxurious linens. Some of the rooms are a bit small, however, and most have showers rather than baths. Attentive host Evan Penner likes his guests to socialize, so he offers an informal afternoon sherry service by the cozy gas fire in the living room. An elaborate full breakfast is served and cookies await at bedtime. A popular, gay-friendly spot. Children over 12 are welcome.

Parkhill Hotel
$$$$
⊘, ℜ, ⌂, ≈, ≡, ℝ

1160 Davie St.
☎685-1311 or 800-663-1525
⇄681-0208
www.parkhillhotel.com
The Parkhill Hotel is right in the middle of Vancouver's gay village. Despite their purely utilitarian furnishings, the rooms are comfortable and offer a truly phenomenal view of English Bay from the 18th floor upwards ($20 surcharge). Originally built as apartments, each guest room is actually a very spacious studio suite with a king-size or two queen-size beds, ordinary furnishings and a balcony for you to really appreciate the view. Inexpensive parking available. A very good, mid-range option. Don't bother with the overpriced buffet breakfast, though—there are plenty of much better options right nearby.

Barclay House in the West End
$$$$ bkfst incl.
ℨ

1351 Barclay St.
☎605-1351 or 800-971-1351
⇄605-1382
www.barclayhouse.com
This five-room Victorian bed and breakfast provides personalized service and a conservative, neutral-toned decor. From the West room, a small room with king-size sleigh bed and its own balcony, to the garden suite, a cozy hideaway with its own entrance and gas fire place, all rooms are furnished with antiques, and equipped with luscious down duvets, bathrobes, telephones, VCRs and CD players. A three-course breakfast is served, and sherry and cookies await in the sitting room, by the grand piano. Off-season rates are a super value.

Listel Vancouver
$$$$$$
≡, ℜ, ⊘

1300 Robson St.
☎684-8461 or 800-663-5491
⇄684-7092
www.listel-vancouver.com
This six-storey, 129-room hotel has recently decked out most of its rooms with works of art from local galleries (fourth and fifth floors) and the Museum of Anthropology (sixth floor). The latter, our favourite, achieve a contemporary, minimalist look by means of pale, neutral colours, cedar and hemlock furnishings (most B.C.-made), natural fabrics and Northwest Coast artwork (for sale). Gallery rooms have a more traditional hotel decor, albeit spruced up by mahogany furnishings, comfortable armchairs, window seats and original artwork. Strangely enough, however, the museum floors are the less expensive of the two. There are also two floors of standard rooms awaiting renovations. On site, O'Doul's Restaurant and Bar stages jazz acts Thursdays to Saturdays.

Empire Landmark Hotel
$$$$$
⊛, ⊘, ℜ, ⌂, ≈, ≡, ℝ

1400 Robson St.
☎687-0511 or 800-830-6144
⇄687-2801
www.asiastandard.com/hotel/vancouver
The recently renovated Empire Landmark Hotel truly is a landmark, with 40 floors and a revolving restaurant and bar at the top. The view is wonderful and quite an experience!

Pacific Palisades Hotel
$$$$$$
≈, ℜ, ℝ, K, ⊘, ≡, ⊛, 🐾

1277 Robson St.
☎688-0461 or 800-663-1815
⇄688-4374
www.pacificpalisadeshotel.com
The Pacific Palisades Hotel is part of the Kimpton Group Hotels chain. Its two towers, totalling 233 rooms, offer peekaboo views of the sea and the mountains. Recently completely revamped, the new decor is clearly meant to endear the establishment with a young (or young at heart), well-heeled clientele. Described as "South Beach meets Stanley Park," its look is fun, modern and retro, with a little whimsy thrown in for good measure. The guest rooms, all suites, are decked out in lime-green and yellow, with furnishings straight out of the Ikea catalogue. It is entirely too big to be a boutique hotel, as the PR would have you believe, but this truly is a fun place, unique in the city. A big pool and a well-equipped gymnasium are available to guests. The staff is friendly and professional.

Sutton Place Hotel
$$$$$$
⊛, ⊘, ≈, ⌂, ℝ, ℜ, ≡, 🐾

845 Burrard St.
☎682-5511 or 800-961-7555
⇄682-5513
www.suttonplace.com
The Sutton Place Hotel has 397 rooms and the full range of five-star services normally provided by the top hotel

Vancouver

chains. The decor, all peachy pinks, coffered ceilings, elaborate mouldings, golden chandeliers and marble, drips with traditional European elegance. Next to the main hotel is La Grande Résidence, a travel apartment for stays of a week or more. It's a favourite with film crews. If you are a chocolate lover, don't miss the chocolate buffet *(Thu-Sat 6pm and 8:30pm)*. And not only can you bring Whiskers, you can even regale her with Alberta T-bone or fresh tuna steak and caviar!

Burrard Inlet

Canyon Court Inn and Suites
$$$
≡, ≈, *K*
1748 Capilano Rd., North Vancouver
☎988-3181 or 888-988-3181
⇄904-2755
www.canyoncourt.com
Canyon Court Inn and Suites is located right next to the Capilano Suspension Bridge, the Lions Gate Bridge and the Trans-Canada Highway. It is very comfortable and reasonably priced.

Lonsdale Quay Hotel
$$$
≡, ☉, ℜ, ℝ
123 Carrie Cates Court
North Vancouver
☎986-6111 or 800-836-6111
⇄986-8782
www.lonsdalequayhotel.com
The Lonsdale Quay Hotel is a lovely hotel set magnificently near the shores of Burrard Inlet, above the huge covered Quay Market. The rooms enjoy extraordinary views of downtown Vancouver.

Capilano Bed & Breakfast
$$$ bkfst incl.
K, ℝ
1374 Plateau Dr.
☎990-8889 or 877-990-8889
⇄990-5177
www.capilanobb.com
The Capilano Bed & Breakfast is located close to Lions Gate Bridge. Skiers can easily get to Cypress Mountain (15min)

and Grouse Mountain (8min). Except during rush hour, the hotel is 5min from Stanley Park, 10min from downtown and Chinatown, and about 25min from the airport. The rooms are attractive, and some have nice views. The complete breakfasts are delicious. Prices for weekly stays can be negotiated.

Palms Guest House
$$$$ bkfst incl.
≡, ℝ, ℜ, ⊛
3042 Marine Dr.,
West Vancouver
☎926-1159 or 800-691-4455
⇄926-1451
www.palmsguesthouse.com
Palms Guest House offers luxurious, if somewhat overdecorated, rooms with private balconies and a view of the ocean. Inquire about off-season prices. Conveniently located for attractions in North and West Vancouver.

False Creek

Opus Hotel
$$$$$$
ℜ, ≡, ℨ, ☉, 🐾
322 Davie St.
☎642-6787 or 866-642-6787
⇄642-6780
www.opushotel.com
Vancouver's newest boutique hotel opened during the summer of 2002. Purpose-built to blend in with the neighbouring industrial brick buildings of Yaletown, its 97 innovatively designed rooms and suites sport one of five different decor schemes to appeal to different lifestyle types, all of them packing thick wallets. Each provides contemporary furnishings, European bedding, robes and slippers, 24-hour room service, cordless telephones with private voice mail, high-speed Internet connections, 27" televisions and CD players. On-site bar and brasserie-style restaurant to see and be seen in. For the spoilt starlet in you.

West Side

Vancouver International Hostel Jericho Beach
$
pb/sb
1515 Discovery St.
☎224-3208 or 888-203-4303
⇄224-4852
www.hihostels.ca
Located in Jericho Park, this youth hostel is open day and night; take bus no. 4 from downtown to reach it. With Locarno and Jericho beaches nearby, this is a great spot for budget travellers. There are co-ed, men-only and women-only dormitories as well as private rooms. The cafeteria is open from April to October. Members $18, non-members $22.

UBC Housing and Conference Centre
$-$$$
sb/pb, *K*, ℝ
5961 Student Union Blvd.
☎822-1001
⇄822-1010
www.conferences.ubc.ca
In addition to a year-round 48-suite hotel, the UBC campus offers rental apartments from May to August. Inexpensive and well located near museums, beaches and hiking trails, this spot also provides tranquility.

Penny Farthing Inn Bed & Breakfast
$$$ bkfst incl.
sb/pb, ℝ, ℨ
2855 W. Sixth Ave., V6K 1X2
☎739-9002 or 866-739-9002
⇄739-9004
www.pennyfarthinginn.com
A warm welcome awaits at Penny Farthing Inn, situated in lovely Kitsilano, a short distance from downtown. Easy-going host Lyn Hainstock has four guest rooms in her 1912 home, all brightly and cheerfully decorated. An experienced cook, Lyn prepares full breakfasts, which can be enjoyed in the dining room or the English garden. Three cats

in residence. British-style country ambiance guaranteed.

Johnson Heritage House
Bed & Breakfast
$$$ bkfst incl.
𝕊, ⊛
May to Nov
2278 West 34th Ave., Kerrisdale
☎/≈*266-4175*
www.johnsons-inn-vancouver.com
The Johnson Heritage House Bed & Breakfast occupies a magnificent, fully renovated house from the 1920s with an extra floor added. The owners, Sandy and Ron Johnson, carried out the work and furnished the place with antiques.

Accommodations by Pillow Suites
$$$
ℝ, K, 𝕊,
2859 Manitoba St.
☎*879-8977*
≈*897-8966*
www.pillow.net
Accommodations by Pillow Suites is three adjacent heritage houses dating back to the early 1900s, and the decor and ambiance attest to it. Individually decorated with taste and originality, they are complete apartments with kitchens and living rooms. Not only lovely, they are also good value, especially for families or a small group of friends. Monthly rates available.

Plaza 500 Hotel
$$$$
ℜ, ℝ, ≡
500 W. 12th Ave.
☎*873-1811 or 800-473-1811*
≈*873-5103*
www.plaza500.com
Located 15min by car from downtown just after the Cambie bridge, this recently renovated hotel has attractive rooms, many with balconies, and a view of the city. Broadway Street, only 2min away, has a variety of shops, restaurants and bars. The perfect place for large groups or conferences.

Restaurants

Gastown and Surroundings

The Old Spaghetti Factory
$-$$
53 Water St.
☎*684-1288*
With posters and photography on the walls and a cozy atmosphere, this restaurant serves up pasta at reasonable prices. Main courses come with hot sourdough bread, soup or salad, coffee or tea and ice cream.

Incendio Pizzeria
$$-$$$
103 Columbia St.
☎*688-8694*
(see review in "West Side p 100)

Water Street Cafe
$$$
300 Water St.
☎*689-2832*
The freshly baked bread that comes from the ovens of the Water Street Cafe accompanies the pasta and fish dishes. This contemporary-style restaurant has a laid-back, friendly ambiance.

Wild Rice
$$$
117 W. Pender St.
☎*642-2882*
Located on the edge of Chinatown (in more ways than one), Wild Rice is one of Vancouver's hippest, most exciting restaurants. Abandon all preconceived notions of what Chinese cuisine looks and tastes like. Wild Rice has subdued lighting, groovy music, high ceilings and an ice-blue glow-in-the-dark resin bar—yes, it's a Chinese restaurant-cum-martini bar! The food isn't like anything you'll find in Chinatown either: you can order a selection of

tapas-sized dishes (*$9 and less*) or larger, main dishes (*$10-$18*). While the staples of Chinese cuisine are here, they are given a twist; even more exciting are the many highly original menu items, such as the high-elevation-tea-smoked-duck salad on a tasty assortment of greens, or a B.C. sablefish roasted with ginger and served on a golden fried-rice paddy and sautéed moo qua—both delicious.

Chinatown and East Vancouver

Chinatown

Hon's Wun-Tun House
$
268 Keefer St.
☎*688-0871*
This restaurant has been a Vancouver institution for more than 20 years. Its reasonably priced dishes, including traditional Chinese specialities, are all excellent. Sample some of the dishes in the noisy, jam-packed, canteen-style atmosphere. Efficient service.

The Only Café
$
20 E. Hastings St.
☎*681-6546*
A little hole in the wall in a not particularly appetizing part of the city, The Only Café is a local institution that offers some of Vancouver's best fish and chips. Takeout recommended.

Pink Pearl Chinese Restaurant
$$
1132 E. Hastings St.
☎*253-4316*
This enormous seafood restaurant is a Vancouver institution. Dim sum is served daily and Cantonese and Szechuan cuisine are specialties.

Vancouver

East Vancouver

Joe's Café
$
1150 Commercial Dr.
☎255-1046
This spot is frequented by a regular clientele of intellectuals and Sunday philosophers, among others. What brings them together, most of all, is Joe's coffee.

WaaZuBee Café
$
every day 11:30am to 1am
1622 Commercial Dr.
☎253-5299
The WaaZubee Café is an inexpensive treat. The innovative cuisine combined with the "natural-techno-italo-bizarre" decor are full of surprises. The pasta dishes are always interesting.

Sun Sui Wah Seafood Restaurant
$$
3888 Main St., at 23rd Ave.
☎872-8822
Authentic Chinese food, lobster, crayfish, crab, oysters and, of course, Peking duck, are served in a bright dining room. One of Vancouver's most highly rated Chinese restaurants.

The Cannery Seafood Restaurant
$$$
2205 Commissioner St.
☎254-9606
The Cannery is one of the best places in town for seafood. It is located in a renovated, century-old warehouse. The view of the sea is fantastic.

Downtown

India Gate Restaurant
$$
616 Robson St.
☎684-4617
At India Gate, you can get a curry dish for as little as $5.95 at lunchtime. In the evening, this restaurant is rather de-

serted. The decor is not at all exotic.

Kitto Japanese House on Granville
$
833 Granville St.
☎687-6622
All kinds of Japanese delicacies such as *sushi*, *robata* and *yakisoba* are available at Kitto. Reasonable prices and fast service.

Elbow Room
$
560 Davie St.
☎685-3628
The motto of this unique Vancouver institution is "service is our name, abuse is our game." Patrons who are brave enough to venture into the Elbow Room for all-day breakfast (try the B.C. Benny) will be mercilessly abused (read gently teased), particularly if they don't follow house rules (outlined in the menu). Single diners risk being auctioned off and those who don't finish their meals must make a donation to charity. Among its many honours and awards, most notable is its award for "best surly and indifferent service." And if that doesn't make you feel at home, nothing will!

Gallery Café
$
8:30am to 5:30pm, Thu until 9pm
Vancouver Art Gallery, 750 Hornby St.
☎688-2233
Weary shoppers, downtown office workers and harried travel writers alike steal away from the crowds on Robson Street and into this lovely café, an oasis of calm in the Vancouver Art Gallery. In addition to cakes and squares at church-bake-sale prices, they also prepare sandwiches, quiches, salads and light entrées. Lovely patio.

Olympia Seafood
$
820 Thurlow St.
☎685-0716
Fishing for fast food like they make in the old country? Stop by this conveniently located downtown chippy for some very respectable cod, halibut or sole with chips.

Subeez Cafe
$-$$
891 Homer St.
☎687-6107
This enigmatic spot, a favourite casual hangout among locals, is open late for drinks (great selection of B.C. beers, including choice from the wonderful Storm Brewery) and early enough for a late breakfast (11am) or brunch on weekends. The post-industrial decor features sky-high ceilings with suspended fans and eclectic art. All-day breakfast, interesting sandwich and salad selection, and ample vegetarian options.

Raku
$$
838 Thurlow St.
☎685-8817
A young Japanese clientele meets in this noisy bar with an open kitchen, where they prepare creative, delicious Japanese dishes, beyond what you'd get at a typical sushi bar. The grilled meats are recommended, as is the *yakisoba* (fried udon noodles).

Bin 941 Tapas Parlour
$$
closed Sun
941 Davie St.
☎683-1246
Tapas and tasty Pacific Northwest dishes are served in this popular spot, which is great for a late-night bite. Although long and narrow and short on leg room, the dining room is big on energy and atmosphere.

Victoria's Market Square, a charming little street full of colourful banners and...Victorian homes!
- *Walter Bibikow*

Whistler has an authentic mountain atmosphere, lively and geared towards the outdoors.
- *Derek Caron*

Dawn gently breaks the mist over Pacific Rim National Park
where the ocean meets endless beaches and dense forests. - *Sean O'Neill*

Lucy Mae Brown
$$$-$$$$ (restaurant)
$$ (lounge)
closed Mon
862 Richards St.
☎899-9199
Lucy Mae Brown may have been the keeper of a simple boarding house; she may also have been a madame with this address as her brothel. In fact, Lucy Mae has a double identity today, too: in the basement you'll find a lounge that attracts a young crowd (see p 101) while upstairs, a slightly older, more conservatively dressed crowd enjoys intimate tête-à-têtes to the strains of soft jazz from the cozy confines of circular blue-velvet booths. The much-lauded menu features simply prepared pasta and very reasonably priced, heartily prepared fillet of halibut Basquaise, free-range chicken and organic beef tenderloin. Reservations recommended.

Imperial Chinese Seafood
$$-$$$$
355 Burrard St.
☎688-8191
Located in the Marine Building, an Art Deco architectural masterpiece (see p 68), this Chinese restaurant also has several Art Deco elements. It is the big windows over looking Burrard Inlet, however, that are especially fascinating. In this very elegant spot, young men in livery and discreet young women perform the *dim sum* ritual. Unlike elsewhere, there are no carts here: the various steamed dishes are brought on trays. You can also ask for a list, allowing you to choose your favourites among the 30 or so offered. The quality of the food matches the excellent reputation this restaurant has acquired.

Aqua Riva
$$$-$$$$
200 Granville St., next to Canada Place
☎683-5599
Enjoy roasted and grilled meats, fish and seafood in a colourful ambiance with a magnificent view of Burrard Inlet.

Joe Fortes Seafood and Chop House
$$$$
777 Thurlow St., at Robson
☎669-1940
Joe Fortes is renowned for its oysters and other seafood. With its turn-of-the-century decor and heated upstairs terrace, this bistro has an appetizing menu. This is a popular meeting place for young professionals.

Diva at the Met
$$$$
Metropolitan Hotel, 645 Howe St.
☎602-7788
Good contemporary Pacific Northwest cuisine and fine wine served up in a pleasant ambiance with elegant decor. A perennial favourite of Vancouver's jet set.

West End and Stanley Park

De Dutch Pannekoek House
$
1725 Robson St.
8am to 3pm
☎687-7065
De Dutch Pannekoek House is a specialist in pancake breakfasts. Big beautiful pancakes are made to order, plain or with your favourite fillings. There are several of these restaurants, in Vancouver (see p 99). The $5 Tuesday special is a great deal.

 True Confections
$
until 1am
866 Denman St.
☎682-1292
True Confections is a dessert place par excellence that serves huge slices of mile-high cakes that look like cartoon versions of themselves. They put those at competitor Death by Chocolate *(1001 Denman St. and other locations)* to shame. Be sure to try the divine chocolate Belgian mousse.

Bread Garden
$
24hrs/day
1040 Denman St.
☎685-2996
812 Bute St.
☎688-3213
These cafés sell bread, pastries and tasty prepared dishes, such as quiches, lasagnas, sandwiches, and fruit plates, to enjoy in-house or to go. Good vegetarian selections. Good service and low prices.

Hamburger Mary's Diner
$-$$
1202 Davie St.
☎687-1293
Mary's is a popular neighbourhood joint with a 1950s-diner decor and a huge menu that includes breakfast items, burgers (organic, if you so desire), sandwiches and milkshakes. Daily specials and a few surprises to boot.

Gyoza King
$$
1508 Robson St.
☎669-8278
Interested in Japanese food but sick of sushi? Take your place in line amongst the Asian students and get ready for Japanese comfort food like ubon and ramen, served in handmade stoneware bowls, and other non-raw-fish-based staples. Oh, and don't forget the gyoza, a Japanese version of the pot stickers you'll find at **Hon's Wun-Tun House** (see p 95). Doughy pockets filled with meat, seafood or veggies, they're served either pan-fried or baked. And if the menu leaves you bewildered, just point at someone else's bowl and enjoy!

Vancouver

Miko Sushi
$$
Mon to Sat
1335 Robson St.
☎*681-0339*
Meticulously prepared Japanese food, extremely fresh sushi and sashimi, and impeccable service are all in store at this small restaurant. Reservations recommended.

Tapastree Restaurant
$$-$$$
1829 Robson St.
☎*606-4680*
As the name suggests, this cozy West End establishment specializes in tapas—appetizer-size dishes, creatively concocted in the Pacific Northwest style. Tapastree is frequented by a local crowd that includes chefs on their night off—always a good sign.

Liliget Feast House
$$$-$$$$
1724 Davie St.
☎*681-7044*
Liliget is a First Nations restaurant that offers authentic Aboriginal-style food: salmon grilled on a wood fire, smoked oysters, grilled seaweed, poached black Alaskan cod and wild Arctic caribou. Makes for a unique dining experience and quiet evening out.

Raincity Grill
$$$$
1193 Denman St.
☎*685-7337*
The Raincity Grill specializes in grilled fish and meats in true West Coast tradition. Renowned for its selection of British Columbia wines and by-the-glass offerings.

Stanley Park

Teahouse Restaurant
$$$-$$$$
Ferguson Point, Stanley Park
☎*669-3281*
During World War II, the Teahouse was a garrison and officers' mess. Today, the Teahouse Restaurant serves delicious food and offers

stunning views of English Bay within a charming dining room with pale yellow walls and huge windows. Rather complicated menu hours are worth noting: brunch *($$)* is served every day until 2:30pm; high tea *($20)* as well as a simpler tea break *($12; Mon-Sat 2:30pm to 4:30pm)* are served at the same time as a light lunch menu *($-$$; Mon-Fri)*. Full-dinner menu features seafood, lamb, steak and vegetarian dishes. Call ahead for reservations and for precise directions as it can be tricky to find. And if you're cycling, note that there is regrettably nowhere to lock your bike nearby.

The Fish House in Stanley Park
$$$$
8901 Stanley Park Dr.
☎*681-7275*
The Fish House in Stanley Park is located in a Victorian house right in the heart of the park and just a few steps from the Seawall. Fine seafood and fish dishes are served in a lovely, opulent decor.

Burrard Inlet

West Vancouver

Beach Side Café
$$-$$$$
1362 Marine Dr.
☎*925-1945*
The Beach Side Café in West Vancouver is a lovely restaurant with original recipes prepared from local produce, as well as meat and fish dishes. Pub menu, bistro menu or fine dining.

The Salmon House
$$$$
2229 Folkestone Way
☎*926-3212*
The Salmon House offers unique, creative cuisine that focuses on salmon in a superb, Canadian-cedar decor. A view of the ocean, the city and Stanley Park adds to the pleasure of the palate.

Horseshoe Bay

Boathouse Restaurant
$$
6695 Nelson Ave.
☎*921-8188*
The Boathouse is a large glassed-in restaurant at the heart of the quaint community of Horseshoe Bay. Seafood is its specialty: oysters, halibut, salmon...

False Creek

Il Giardino
$$$
1382 Hornby St.
☎*669-2422*
This popular restaurant has a reputation for its attractive Italian-style decor, charming patio, inspired dishes with local and European accents and its vast selection of pasta. Always crowded. Warm, friendly ambiance.

Monk McQueens
$$$-$$$$
601 Stamps Landing
☎*877-1351*
This restaurant overlooks the inlet and has the decor of a small sailing club. Very pleasant inside and on the patio. Impeccable service and delicious food—specialties are fish and oysters. A jazz pianist accompanies your meal *(Thu-Sat)*.

Kettle of Fish
$$$-$$$$
900 Pacific Blvd.
☎*682-6661*
Kettle of Fish has a cozy winter-garden-style ambiance with plenty of flowers. The menu includes tasty fish and fresh seafood and the wine list is excellent. Good service.

C Restaurant
$$$$
1600 Howe St.
☎*681-1164*
This "contemporary fish" restaurant, whose name evokes the sea, is the talk of the town, and for good reason. The chef has created innovative and unique recipes

with a Southeast Asian influence. If you come for lunch, served at the stroke of noon, the C-style Dim Sum is a real delight. Tidbits of fish marinated in tea and a touch of caviar, vol-au-vents with chanterelles, curry shrimp with coconut milk, and the list goes on... All quite simply exquisite. Desserts are equally extraordinary. For those who dare, the crème brûlée with blue cheese is an unforgettable experience. This restaurant is an absolute must.

Yaletown

Urban Fare
$
177 Davie St.
☎**975-7550**
This yuppie food emporium is a good place to stop for lunch or a snack during your tour of Yaletown. The self-serve counter features panini, wraps and other trendy items. Brunch served weekends and holidays *(7am to 2pm)*.

Yaletown Brewing Co.
$$
1111 Mainland St.
☎**681-2739**
The Yaletown Brewing Co. is a veritable yuppie temple in the post-industrial neighbourhood of Yaletown and a fun place to spend an evening. There's a cozy bar on one side (with a huge fireplace) and a restaurant on the other. Try the pizza from the wood-burning oven.

 Brix
$$$-$$$$
1138 Homer St.
☎**915-9463**
This lovely restaurant features a cool and soothing decor of exposed brick, wood and tile, cream-coloured walls adorned with vivid, modern portraits, and a cozy courtyard patio. In addition to inspired lunches (including the chef's excellent daily duos: try anything with ahi tuna and/or Indian candy!) and dinners (mango-curry seared ahi tuna, porcini-dusted

wild B.C. caribou), tapas are available all day. Extensive wine list, including many B.C. vintages, a good many of which are available by the glass. Reservations recommended for dinner *(Fri-Sun)*. A truly delicious choice.

Blue Water Café and Raw Bar
$$$$
1095 Hamilton St.
☎**688-8078**
A well-heeled Yaletown crowd keeps the Pellegrino flowing like water in this new favourite for fresh, local seafood. In addition to an oyster and a sushi bar, you'll find entrées such as smoked B.C. sablefish, Dover sole, striped marlin and albacore tuna, all fresh rather than farmed, as well as Alberta steaks. The dining room is attractively done up with terra cotta tiles, brick, exposed pipes, wood tables and leather booths, and the service is thoughtful and professional. Reservations recommended on weekends. While you're there, check out the impressive wine cellar.

Granville Island

 Bridges
$$-$$$$
1696 Duranleau St.
☎**687-4400**
Bridges Bistro boasts one of the loveliest patios in Vancouver, right by the water in the middle of Granville Island's pleasure-boat harbour. The food and setting are decidedly Pacific Northwestern.

Dockside Brewing Company
$$$
1253 Johnston St.
Granville Island Hotel
☎**685-7070**
You'd think that any restaurant that brews its own beer might neglect the food side of the equation—wrong! The new Dockside Brewing Company serves up surprisingly good soups and salads (the smoked-salmon chowder is a lovely surprise, as is the dockside salad) that make for good

lunches, as well as rotisserie chicken and fish dishes, among other selections. Excellent patio on False Creek with heat lamps.

Pacific Institute of Culinary Arts
$$$-$$$$
1505 West Second Ave.
☎**734-4488**
The Pacific Institute of Culinary Arts offers a different gourmet menu every day prepared by its students. The dishes are exquisite and the service is excellent. The three-course fixed-price menu is available for lunch *($20)* Monday to Friday and dinner seven days a week *($30, Mon-Fri; $34, Sat and Sun)*. And there's a patio, too!

West Side

De Dutch Pannekoek House
$
2622 Granville St.
☎**731-0775**
3192 Oak St.
☎**732-1915**
See review under "West End," p 97.

True Confections
3701 W. Broadway
☎**222-8489**
See review under "West End," p 97.

Sophie's Cosmic Café
$
2095 W. Fourth Ave.
☎**732-6810**
This is a weekend meeting-spot for the Kitsilano crowd, who come to stuff themselves with bacon and eggs. 1950s decor, relaxed atmosphere.

The Naam
$-$$
24hrs/day
2724 W. Fourth Ave.
☎**738-7151**
The Naam blends live music with vegetarian meals. This little restaurant, decorated with ceiling fans and wooden tables, has a warm peaceful atmosphere, friendly service,

Vancouver

and is frequented by a young clientele. Service can be slow.

Salade de Fruits
$$
closed Sun evening and Mon
1551 W. Seventh Ave.
☎714-5987
Located within the Maison de la Francophonie de Vancouver, Salade de Fruits is not the easiest place to find (there's no sign) but you'll be very glad when you do! One of Vancouver's best-kept secrets is run by affable Frenchmen Antoine and Pascal, who clearly take great pride in offering down-to-earth bistro food at more than reasonable prices. At lunch, the place is packed to the rafters with locals chowing down on the excellent house specialty, *moules frites*, or other dishes such as quiches and poutine. For dinner, a weekly table d'hôte is offered, which may feature anything from confit of duck to *raclette savoyarde*. All desserts (homemade by Pascal) are only $3.99 and a glass of wine is an astonishing $3.75. Dinner reservations recommended.

Habibi's
$$
closed Sun
1128 W. Broadway Ave.
☎732-7487
If you think Lebanese food is limited to meat shaved off a spit, think again. This cheerful, cozy restaurant lovingly offers delectable vegetarian Lebanese specialties that will put your neighbourhood kebab house to shame. Order the dinner special ($13), which allows you to choose any three dishes. Among the tasty items are the delicious smoky-flavoured *baba ganoush* (eggplant purée), *loubieh* (green beans sautéed in garlic and tomatoes) and *fatbe* (chick peas with garlic-infused yogurt and pine nuts). Finish your meal with a cup of Arabic tea served in a brass *rakwy*, brought by Richard, the chef/owner, from Lebanon. A delight.

Tomato Fresh Food Café
$$-$$$
3305 Cambie St.
☎874-6020
Tomato's is a cheerful diner-style café boldly decorated in yellow and red. Open for three meals a day, you can start your day with an *omelette du Pacifique* (with wild B.C. salmon and cream cheese), return for a sandwich or homemade soup at lunch, and end your day with a *bouillabaisse du Pacifique*, a much-raved-about dinner offering. Reasonable wine list.

Incendio West
$$-$$$
2118 Burrard St.
☎736-2220
The second branch of this popular pizzeria (the other is in Gastown, see p 95) offers 25 different kinds of pizza, from an Athenian to a volcana, fresh from a wood-burning brick oven. There are also a variety of pastas, as well as some good salads and appetizers (the pan-seared calamari is delicious). Ceiling fans, tile floors and subdued lighting make for an intimate but casual atmosphere that tends to get a bit loud with the sound of friends catching up.

Banana Leaf Malaysian Restaurant
$$-$$$
820 W. Broadway Ave.
☎731-6333
If there's no Malay restaurant back home, make sure to head out to the Banana Leaf for a taste of something new. Malay cuisine, which has Chinese and Indian influences, can be rather spicy, but you'll find a mostly toned-down version here. An excellent choice is the delicious sambal tiger prawns fried in chili, garlic and dry shrimp sauce and served with green beans and Chinese eggplant. The Singapore fried chili crab also has an extremely devoted following. Cheerful service, reasonable prices, and pleasant, casual ambiance.

The Smoking Dog
$$$
1889 W. First Ave.
☎732-8811
The Smoking Dog has a warm, lively atmosphere, lovely decor and reasonable prices for its carefully prepared *table d'hôte*. Exquisite steak, copious salads and creative daily specials. The *pommes frites* that accompany every dish are golden brown on the outside and tender on the inside. Jean-Claude, the owner, is a friendly Marseillais.

Seasons in the Park
$$$$
Queen Elizabeth Park, Cambie and 33rd sts.
☎874-8008
Seasons in the Park is a pleasant restaurant with classic, elegant decor and an unhindered view of the city. Succulent Pacific Northwest cuisine. Reservations required. Also open for lunch and weekend brunch.

Lumière
$$$$ (restaurant)
$$$ (tasting bar)
Tue-Sun
2551 W. Broadway Ave.
☎739-8185
Lumière is probably the brightest light on Vancouver's burgeoning restaurant scene. Praise has been lavished on chef Rob Feenie and his lovely restaurant from far and wide, most recently by *Vancouver Magazine*, which named it Restaurant of the Year (2001). Furthermore, Lumière has recently been awarded a Relais Gourmands designation by the prestigious Relais et Chateau association. The Asian-inspired, minimalist interior allows the food to shine, and shine it does! The fresh, local ingredients used in each dish make for creative and honest, yet very refined cuisine. There are four different tasting menus—vegetarian, seafood, chef's and signature—which consist of small portions of eight to 13 courses ($80-$120). But don't

let those prices scare you off: Feenie recently opened a much more accessible tasting bar adjoining his dining room, complete with a glowing Jetsons-style lime-green bar. Here, foodies with small appetites (or budgets) can sample as many as 12 appetizer-size items (such as confit of lamb shoulder, or seared marinated sablefish) each for $12. Servers will gladly tell you which are the most substantial dishes. The wine list is extensive and the service is remarkably warm and professional.

 Vij's
$$$$
1480 W. 11th Ave.
☎736-6664
One look at Vij's minimalist blue neon sign and you'll be hip to the fact that this is no ordinary Indian restaurant. Inside the spare dining room you'll find a decor unlike other East Indian restaurants in this country: instead, a 700lb Himalayan teak door from an Indian temple takes centre stage in a dark room punctuated by hanging lanterns splashing colour onto the walls. Vij doesn't take reservations so everyone—local celebrities included—is led to the bar area to comfortably await a table while drinking complimentary sweet chai and tasty hors d'oeuvres. The menu is a meeting of East and West: wine-marinated lamb popsicles in fenugreek cream curry with turmeric spinach and potatoes; tea-braised sablefish in ginger and black chick-pea curry. A glass of locally brewed IPA from the Storm Brewery is a wonderful accompaniment. Ultra-professional service.

Entertainment

Bars and Nightclubs

Note that the majority of bars and nightclubs in Vancouver are non-smoking.

Irish Heather
217 Carrall St.
☎688-9779
This casual pub has a cozy, brick-lined upstairs seating area and plenty of little nooks and crannies to hide away in, including a glassed-in terrace backing onto Gaoler's Mews, site of the city's first jail. They pour a good pint of Guinness but their lack of B.C. brews is regrettable. Rather sophisticated Irish-style pub menu.

Steamworks Brewing Co
$$$
375 Water St.
☎689-2739
Conveniently located right by Waterfront Station, Steamworks is the best excuse yet for a pre- (or post-) trip sup. On hand is a wide selection of beers brewed right on site. On the main floor there's a view across Burrard Inlet, while downstairs is a super cozy dining area, ensconced in stone and brick, next to shiny copper beer vats and spinning pizza dough. There's a full dinner menu as well as a pub menu.

The Purple Onion Cabaret
$8 weekends, $5 weekdays
15 Water St., third floor
☎602-9442
The Purple Onion is a popular two-room venue featuring live music and DJs. Wednesdays are dedicated to live music and DJ-spun funk; on Fridays and Saturdays, DJs spin R&B and hip hop in the club and electronica, house and hip hop in the lounge. A perennial favourite.

Sonar
66 Water St.
☎683-6695
This very big Gastown venue offers an alternative and underground DJ format as well as some live shows. Gay-friendly.

Bacchus Lounge
845 Hornby St., Wedgewood Hotel
☎608-5319
This plush lounge and piano bar, lined with cherrywood panelling and decorated with rich burgundy fabrics, attracts the glitterati as well as the rest of us mere mortals seeking a romantic spot. Excellent cocktails and bar food are served while a pianist entertains.

Gerrard Lounge
845 Burrard St., Sutton Place Hotel
☎682-5511
This cozy bar oozes with the atmosphere of a gentleman's club, with leather armchairs to sink into, dark wood panelling and professional service. A good place to spot celebrities and wannabees.

Lucy Mae Brown
862 Richards St.
☎899-9199
This much-celebrated new restaurant just off Robson Street houses a basement lounge, with retro furnishings of the type that were stashed away in basements across the nation with the fading of the 1970s. Here, a young dressed-for-success crowd grooves to the latest sounds while sipping martinis, appealing appetizers and reasonably priced mains.

Ginger Sixty Two
1219 Granville St.
☎688-5494
This groovy lounge for thirty-somethings is named for Ginger, the boopsy starlet played by Tina Louise, who was shipwrecked on *Gilligan's Island*; her floor-to-ceiling portraits grace a wall in this lusciously funky, stylish lounge with plenty of cozy seating. Good Asian-style lounge

Vancouver

menu. Wednesdays feature house music, Thursdays are for 1960s favourites, particularly R&B, while Fridays and Saturdays feature electronica. Dress is relaxed, smart casual.

Cardero's
1583 Coal Harbour Quay
☎669-7666
At the end of the day, when nothing but a pint and a harbour view will do, make your way down to Coal Harbour on Burrard Inlet (at the foot of Nicola Street, by the Westin Bayshore). Baseball caps and hardhats mix with suited gentlemen and women on the wood and tan leather of this nautically themed harbourfront bar and restaurant. And if your cocktail whets your appetite, there's a casual restaurant with an open kitchen and patio adjoining.

O'Doul's Restaurant and Bar
1300 Robson St.
☎661-1400
Located in the Listel Vancouver hotel, O'Doul's is a popular spot for live jazz, presented most summer evenings and weekends the rest of the year.

DV8
515 Davie St.
☎682-4388
This cool, sparsely lit spot is popular with a mainly young, alternative crowd. DV8 hosts record launches and features an art space, which changes every few weeks. Good food, too, served (a little slowly) until late, making it a good after-hours spot.

Georgia Street Bar & Grill
801 West Georgia St.
☎602-0994
This bar is really popular with its downtown regulars, who gather here to decompress at the end of the work day. Its well-dressed clientele flocks here in the evening to guzzle down beer, nibble on grilled dishes and listen to live R&B.

Luv-a-Fair
1275 Seymour St.
☎685-3288
For a heady night of techno and alternative music and dancing, check out Luv-a-Fair. Young, gay-friendly crowd.

Railway Club
$3 to $8
579 Dunsmuir St.
☎681-1625
An eclectic musical menu, ranging from folk and blues to pop, punk and rockabilly, is presented in an oblong spot that brings to mind a railway car. A miniature electric train runs in a loop above customers' heads as they enjoy the live music. A popular spot for an after-work beverage.

Richard's on Richards
$10
1036 Richards St.
☎687-6794
Richard's on Richards is an institution in Vancouver. Theme nights, such as wet T-shirt contests, hip-hop and Top 40 keep the twentysomething crowd entertained. Dress is mainly casual.

The Roxy
$4 to $8
932 Granville St.
☎331-7999
The Roxy is a boisterous rock club where the beer flows abundantly. Regulars don't seem to mind cooling their heels on the sidewalk a spell. Cruising appears to be one of the favourite pastimes here.

The Yale Hotel
1300 Granville St.
☎681-9253
The big names in rhythm and blues regularly play at this locale—the undisputed R&B mecca of Vancouver. Great ambiance on the weekends. The cover charge varies depending on the performers.

Yaletown Brewing Co.
1111 Mainland St.
☎681-2739
The Yaletown Brewing Co. is a popular yuppie hangout in Yaletown and the ideal spot for an evening of brews with some friends.

Gay and Lesbian Bars

Numbers Cabaret
$3 cover on Fri and Sat
1042 Davie St.
☎685-4077
This large cabaret is frequented by gay men of all ages.

Odyssey
$3-$5
1251 Howe St.
☎689-5256
The Odyssey is a gay dance club where young people go to meet in a fun-loving atmosphere. Theme nights and performances include retro-disco on Mondays, Hot House on Tuesdays, drag show at midnight on Wednesdays, Homo Homer with Go Go Boys on Fridays, Fallen Angel night on Saturdays and female impersonators on Sundays. Straight-friendly.

Royal Hotel
1025 Granville St.
☎685-5335
A gay crowd packs the Royal Hotel, which boasts a "modern" decor. Monday nights feature the Diva Inc. drag show, while Tuesdays play host to a fundraising Bingo night, with all proceeds going to the Friends for Life charity. Friday nights are also very popular, when people wait in line as early as 8pm; Sunday evenings are a better bet.

Oasis Pub
1240 Thurlow St.
☎685-1724
This friendly, comfortable bar is discreetly located above street level, just off Davie Street. While they have a pub-style menu, the main attraction here is the extensive list of

evocatively named martinis. You and a friend can treat yourselves to an "Oasis" martini, served in a glass the size of a goldfish bowl. Live piano player Wednesday to Saturday. Rooftop patio.

Pumpjack Pub
1167 Davie St.
☎685-3417
Tough on the outside, Pumpjack is warm and fuzzy on the inside (at least, the bartenders are!). The decor is spare (the underwear hanging from the ceiling is a nice touch), leather is the fabric of choice, and the pool table is front and centre. Ask about the racy in-house calendar.

Fountainhead Pub
1025 Davie St.
☎687-2222
The Fountainhead's lesbian and straight clientele gather in casual surroundings dominated by neon beer signs and a window-framed view of Davie Street. Inexpensive pub menu.

Cultural Activities

Theatres

Arts Club Theatre
1585 Johnston St., Granville Island
☎687-1644
Arts Club Theatre is a steadfast institution on the Vancouver theatre scene. Located on the waterfront on Granville Island, this theatre presents contemporary works with social themes, as well as lighter fare like musicals. Audience members often get together in the theatre's bar after the plays.

Stanley Theatre
2750 Granville St.
The younger sibling of The Arts Club Theatre Company's Granville Island stage (see above), the Stanley Theatre stages classic, mainstream plays. A movie theatre when it opened in 1930, it features a

rococo design typical of the period.

Malkin Bowl
Stanley Park
☎687-0174
Theatre Under the Stars has been performing amateur Broadway musicals (around $29) in this open-air venue right in Stanley Park (Jul and Aug), for more than 50 years.

Bard on the Beach
301-601 Cambie St.
☎737-0625 or 739-0559
Bard on the Beach is an annual event in honour of Shakespeare. Plays are presented, all in period costume, under two huge tents on a peninsula with a view of English Bay (mid-Jun to end Sep).

Vancouver East Cultural Centre
1895 Venables St.
☎251-1363
"The Cultch" is an arts centre that has built a solid reputation over the years for the quality of the shows presented. Theatre, dance, singing and music all take place in this cozy, dimly lit performance space. A great experience.

Centre culturel francophone de Vancouver
1551 W. Seventh Ave.
☎736-9806
www.ccfv.bc.ca
The French cultural centre of Vancouver stages a full schedule of visual and performing arts events and exhibitions representing French culture from around the world. They also organize an annual festival of music and dance (mid-Jun), house a library and a good bistro (see p 100) and offer French courses.

Centre in Vancouver for the Performing Arts
777 Homer St.
☎602-0616
www.centreinvancouver.com
After a prolonged blackout period, the Ford Centre for the Performing Arts has recently reopened under new

ownership and with a new name. This performing arts venue hosts major international productions, like Show Boat, Les Misérables and Phantom of the Opera.

Calendar of Events

From spring to fall, Vancouver hosts a wide range of festivals. Below you will find just a sample of what's scheduled. For more details, contact Tourism Vancouver or check out the following Web site: www.tourismvancouver.com

January

Polar Bear Swim
every year on the morning of January 1
Hundreds of people actually choose to take a dip in the frigid winter waters of English Bay. If you don't feel brave enough to challenge this icy water yourself, you can always go there and watch or see it on television.

Chinese New Year
☎658-885
Gung Hai Fat Choy! means "Happy New Year!" in Cantonese. The date is determined by the lunar calendar, and therefore varies every year, but celebrations are usually held around the end of January or the beginning of February. Traditional Dragon parades are organized in Chinatown and in Richmond.

February

The **Spring Home Show** is the biggest home show in Western Canada, which takes place under the BC Place Stadium dome.

April

The **Vancouver Playhouse International Wine Festival** (☎873-3311) is an important festival where bottles of wine are auctioned and hundreds of wine growers gather to dis-

Vancouver

cuss their art and offer samples.

The Vancouver Sun Run

(☎689-9441) takes place during the third week of April, when over 10,000 people celebrate sport and spring.

May

Cloverdale Rodeo and Exhibition

☎576-9461
www.cloverdalerodeo.com
If you're in Vancouver and have never been to a rodeo, this is definitely the occasion. It's considered one of the most important in North America.

Vancouver International Marathon

☎872-2928
The Vancouver International Marathon starts at the Plaza of Nations, then goes through Stanley Park to North Vancouver, and back to Vancouver. Thousands of runners take part in this major sporting event on the first Sunday in May.

Vancouver International Children's Festival

Vanier Park
☎708-5655
www.youngarts.ca/vicf
The Vancouver International Children's Festival takes place the last week of May under red-and-white tents in beautiful Vanier Park. Drawing over 70,000 people each year, this big festival is a hit with children from all over British Columbia.

May

Spike & Mike's Animation Festival

Ridge Theatre
3131 Arbutus St.
☎738-6311
Held every year throughout the month of May, Spike & Mike's Animation Festival presents the best "sick and twisted" short animation films from all over the world.

June

International Dragon Boat Festival

False Creek, Concord Pacific Place and Plaza of Nations
☎688-2382
Long dug-out boats in the Chinese tradition, from all over the world, compete in these friendly races on the calm waters of False Creek.

Vancouver International Jazz Festival

☎888-GET-JAZZ
Fans can come and satisfy their hunger for jazz at this distinguished festival. Artists perform throughout the city and the surrounding area.

Bard on the Beach

Vanier Park
☎737-0625 or 739-0559
www.bardonthebeach.org
Bard on the Beach is an annual event in honour of Shakespeare. Plays are presented under two large tents against the spectacular backdrop of English Bay.

July

Benson & Hedges Symphony of Fire

English Bay
☎738-4304
The Benson & Hedges Symphony of Fire is an international fireworks festival. Two barges on English Bay serve as the staging ground from which the fireworks are launched to music. Dazzling show, guaranteed thrills.

Vancouver Chamber Music Festival

☎736-6034
www.vanrecital.com/chamber
In the last week of July and the first week of August, six concerts are presented featuring talented young musicians.

Vancouver Early Music Festival

☎732-1610
The music department of the University of British Columbia (UBC) hosts a series of baroque and medieval concerts performed with period instruments.

Vancouver Folk Music Festival

Jericho Beach Park
☎602-9798
www.thefestival.bc.ca
The Vancouver Folk Music Festival has become a tradition in Vancouver. It takes place during the third week of July and features musicians from all over the world who play from sunrise to sunset on Jericho Beach.

Molson Indy Vancouver

Concord Pacific Place
☎684-4639
www.molsonindy.com
tickets:
☎280-INDY
In the heart of downtown, a course is set up where Indy racing cars (the North American equivalent of Formula 1) compete in front of hundreds of thousands of enthusiastic spectators.

Vancouver International Comedy Festival

☎683-0883
www.comedyfest.com
Every year on Granville Island in late July, comics from around the world provide several days of laughs on outdoor stages.

August

Vancouver Pride Parade

☎687-0955
www.vanpride.bc.ca
This colourful, popular annual event attracts more than 120,000 participants and spectators. Begins at Denman and Nelson streets in the West End.

Abbotsford International Airshow

Abbotsford
☎852-8511
www.abbotsfordairshow.com
In Abbotsford, approximately 100km east of Vancouver, both young and old will be dazzled by F-16s, F-117

Stealths, and MiGs. There are also old airplanes and clothing accessories. Don't forget your aviator glasses and sunscreen.

Greater Vancouver Open
Northview Golf and Country Club, Surrey
☎*575-0324*
At the Greater Vancouver Open, the biggest names in golf compete on a splendid course.

September

Terry Fox Run
from Ceperley Park to Stanley Park
☎*888-836-9786*
The Terry Fox Run, a fund-raising event for cancer research, takes place on foot, bicycle or in-line skates and is from one to 10km in length. The run is in memory of the young athlete, Terry Fox, who initiated it.

Vancouver Fringe Festival
☎*257-0350*
www.vancouverfringe.com
The Vancouver Fringe Festival presents 10 days of theatre, including original pieces by contemporary playwrights and performers.

Vancouver International Film Festival
☎*685-0260*
www.viff.org
"Hollywood North" plays host to this increasingly significant festival which offers film buffs up to 250 films from all over the world.

October

Vancouver International Writers (and Readers) Festival
☎*681-6330*
For five days during the third week of October, more than 90 authors from Canada and abroad meet with the public for conferences and readings.

October

Vancouver Waterfront Antique Show
Vancouver Trade & Convention Centre
☎*800-667-0619*
This annual antique show features furniture and *objects d'art* from the 18th and 19th centuries, as well as from the beginning of the 20th.

November

Vancouver Storytelling Festival
☎*776-2272*
www.vancouverstorytelling. org
Storytellers gather in the West End andpractise their art in front of a captivated audience during this three-day event.

December

VanDusen Botanical Garden's Festival of Lights
☎*878-9274*
www.vandusengarden.org
The VanDusen Botanical Garden's Festival of Lights is another festival for the whole family. Throughout the Christmas season, the garden is decorated with seasonal displays and illuminated with millions of twinkling lights.

Shopping

You'll surely come upon all manner of interesting shops as you explore the city. To help you discover some of the best bets in Vancouver, however, read on...

Malls, Department Stores and Markets

Downtown

Pacific Centre
corner of Howe St. and W. Georgia St.
☎*688-7236*
The Pacific Centre is the largest shopping centre in the city. Approximately 300 quality boutiques offer a complete range of everything from jewellery and clothes including top-of-the-line clothing and accessories at the Hermès and Louis Vuitton boutiques in Holt Renfrew. A fitness equipment store, a Ticketmaster, The Bay and Sears, as well as Le Château, which mainly caters to a young clientele, are all here. Parking fee.

The Bay
at Granville and W. Georgia Sts.
☎*681-6211*
Right downtown, this large department store offers over six floors of designer and brand-name clothing and accessories and a huge perfume department with Chanel, Lancôme, Saint-Laurent, Clinique and more. There are restaurants on various floors, and a catering service with coffee tables in the basement. They offer many promotions on Saturdays and Sundays.

Waterfront Centre
at the base of the Waterfront Hotel
900 Canada Pl. Way
☎*646-8020*
Waterfront Centre is home to souvenir shops, flowers, cigars, a tourist information counter, a hair salon, shoe repairs, a Starbucks coffeeshop, and a handful of small fast-food counters featuring various national cuisines.

East Vancouver

If you're looking for your very own sari, or simply some colourful silks from India, head to the **Punjabi Market** *(Main St., between 48th and 51st* *aves.),* Vancouver's "Little India." You'll also find plenty of Indian jewellery and food stores.

Burrard Inlet

Lonsdale Quay Market
123 Carrie Cates Court
North Vancouver
at the SeaBus terminal
☎985-2191
A charming market, beautiful shops, a multitude of fast-food counters—all of it made a little more lively by artists performing on the seaside terrace.

False Creek

Granville Island Market
every day 9am to 6pm
Granville Island
☎666-5784
Granville Island Market is Vancouver's best-known and most popular market. It is an immense commercial area surrounded by water with a fairground atmosphere. Everything is available here—prepared food, organic vegetables, fresh fish and meat, wholesome breads, as well as fast-food counters and pleasant shops selling jewellery, clothing and equipment for water sports and outdoor activities. Take a day to look, sample and wander. Street parking is hard to find but there are two indoor parking *(fee)* lots nearby. Better yet, take the ferry downtown (see p 81).

West Side (Oakridge)

Oakridge Centre
Cambie St. and 41st Ave.
☎261-2511
Here, you'll find clothing boutiques, some of which feature French or British designers, such as Rodier Paris; an optical wear boutique; restaurants; The Bay; and Zellers. In all, 150 shops and services. Free parking.

Art Galleries

Gallery Row

The stretch of Granville Street leading south from the Granville Bridge until around 16th Avenue is known as **Gallery Row**. Some 20 galleries are located right on Granville or in the vicinity. Many of them specialize in the works of First Nations artists from the Northwest Coast. They offer a wonderful selection of high-quality items and probably your best chance of finding that perfect piece to take home.

Douglas Reynolds
2335 Granville St.
☎731-9292
This gallery has magnificent Aboriginal works of art, including a good collection of masks. If the totems are too heavy to take home with you, the gallery carries an excellent selection of prints by Aboriginal artists, many of which are quite affordable.

Granville Island

A good many art galleries are concentrated on Granville Island. At the **Crafts Association of British Columbia** *(1386 Cartwright St.,* ☎687-7270) you'll find some gorgeous merchandise, including silver jewellery and works of glass and wood. Nearby is the **Federation of Canadian Artists** *(1241 Cartwright St.,* ☎681-8534) where a selection of paintings is displayed; the **Gallery of BC Ceramics** *(1359 Cartwright St.,* ☎669-5645), which sells original works in clay; and next to it, **Joel Berman Glassworks Ltd.** *(1244 Cartwright St.,* ☎684-8332), home to colourful, pricey glassworks.

The Raven and The Bear
1528 Duranleau St., Granville Island
☎669-3990
Excellent-quality Aboriginal works at reasonable prices. Lithographs, sculptures and natural stonework.

The Walrus & the Carpenter
1518 Duranleau St.
Granville Island Shopping Centre
☎687-0920
Beautiful reproductions of animals indigenous to Canada (bears, beavers, ducks).

Leona Lattimer
1590 West Second Ave.
west of Granville Island
☎732-4556
Leona Lattimer is a lovely gallery where you can admire some fine, expensive Aboriginal art, quality jewellery and prints.

Other Areas

Coastal Peoples Fine Arts Gallery
1024 Mainland St.
☎685-9298
This lovely Yaletown shop offers an excellent selection of gold and silver jewellery, masks and totems made by the First Nations of the Pacific Northwest. Personalized service.

Marion Scott Gallery
481 Howe St.
☎*685-1934*
Marion Scott Gallery has a beautiful Aboriginal art collection, including superb sculptures.

Khot-La-Cha
270 Whonoak St., North Vancouver
☎*987-3339*
Beautiful sculptures by First Nation's artists, including the Coast Salish. One block from Marine Drive and McGuire Street.

Spirit Wrestler Gallery
8 Water St.
☎*669-8813*
Attractive sculptures and paintings by Inuit and Northwest Coast artists.

For First Nations works in silver and gold, see "Jewellery" bellow.

Bookstores

Duthie Books
2239 W. Fourth Ave.
☎*732-5344*
This independent bookstore is a favourite among Vancouverites.

Granville Book Co.
850 Granville St.
☎*687-2213*
Right downtown on Theatre Row, Granville Book Co. carries everything from computer manuals to science-fiction and mystery books, as well as magazines.

Hagar Books
2176 W. 41st Ave.
☎*263-9412*
This bookstore has been around for some 30 years.

Little Sisters Book and Art Emporium
1238 Davie St.
☎*669-1753 or 800-567-1662*
Little Sisters Book and Art Emporium is the only bookshop in Western Canada specializing in gay literature as well as essays on subjects such as homosexuality and feminism. It is also a vast bazaar, with products that include humorous greeting cards. For many years, this bookshop has been fighting Canada Customs, which arbitrarily blocks the importation of certain publications deemed to be pornographic. Books by recognized and respected authors such as Marcel Proust have been seized by Canada Customs, which has taken on the role of censor. Some of the same titles bound for regular bookshops have mysteriously escaped seizure by Canada Customs, leading to questions about discrimination.

Librairie Sophia Books
492 W. Hastings St. at Richards St.
☎*684-0484*
Sophia Books specializes in multilingual books and other resources.

Barbara Jo's Books to Cook
1128 Mainland St.
☎*688-6755*
Foodies with a penchant for cooking should check out the cookbooks in this Yaletown shop.

Jewellery

Silver Gallery
1226 Robson St.
☎*681-6884*
The Silver Gallery is the least expensive store for fine-quality Aboriginal jewellery and crafts. Solid silver bracelets, necklaces and rings with gold enamelling can be found at competitive prices. They also sell Indonesian objects, including masks, at affordable prices. Attentive service.

Sports and the Outdoors

Comor Go Play Outside
1918 Fir St.
☎*731-2163*
Everything for outdoor sports, especially cycling and skateboarding. Equipment, clothing, helmets, shoes and more.

Mountain Equipment Co-op
130 W. Broadway Ave.
☎*872-7858*
Mountain Equipment Co-op is a gigantic store that offers everything you need for your outdoor activities. You must be a member to make purchases, but a lifetime membership only costs $5.

Ruddik's Fly Shop
1077 Marine Dr.,
North Vancouver
☎*985-5650*
Ruddik's Fly Shop is a wonderful store for fly-fishers that even inspires newcomers to the sport. There are thousands of different flies for all sorts of fish. The owner will be glad to assist you. They also sell super-light rods, state-of-the-art fishing reels, souvenir clothing as well as fishing-related sculptures and gadgets.

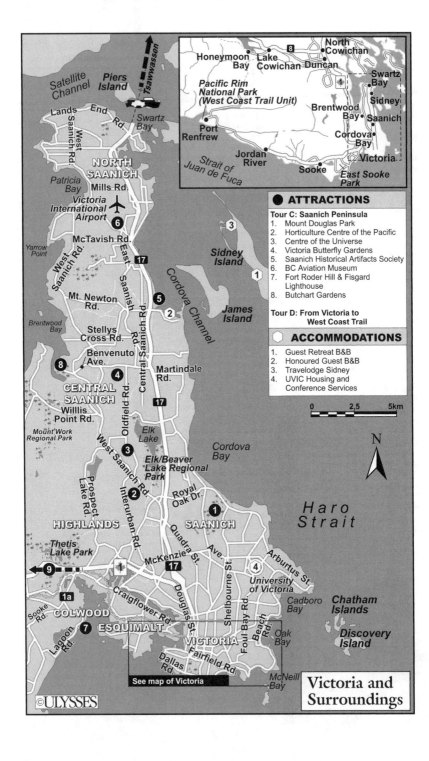

ATTRACTIONS

Tour C: Saanich Peninsula
1. Mount Douglas Park
2. Horticulture Centre of the Pacific
3. Centre of the Universe
4. Victoria Butterfly Gardens
5. Saanich Historical Artifacts Society
6. BC Aviation Museum
7. Fort Roder Hill & Fisgard Lighthouse
8. Butchart Gardens

Tour D: From Victoria to West Coast Trail

ACCOMMODATIONS
1. Guest Retreat B&B
2. Honoured Guest B&B
3. Travelodge Sidney
4. UVIC Housing and Conference Services

0   2,5   5km

N

Victoria and Surroundings

©ULYSSES

Victoria and Surroundings

Is Victoria ★★★
really more English than England, as people often say it is? Well, with high tea, lawn bowling and cricket as local pastimes, there is no denying its characteristic English flavour.

This is still a North American city, however, and along with all the English, it has welcomed large numbers of French Canadians, Chinese, Japanese, Scots, Irish, Germans and Americans.

Located at the southern tip of Vancouver Island, Victoria is the capital of the province and has a population of nearly 300,000 scattered across a large urban area. Its harbour looks out onto the Strait of Juan de Fuca, a natural border with Washington State. Victoria is set against a series of small mountains no higher than 300m in altitude, and its waterfront stretches several kilometres.

When Europeans began moving into the region in the mid-19th century, three Aboriginal groups, the Songhees, the Klallam and the Saanich, were already living here. In 1842, the Hudson's Bay Company established a fur-trading post near the Victoria Harbour.

One year later, aided by the Aboriginal people,

who were given a blanket for every 40 wooden stakes they cut, the company's adventurers built Fort Victoria alongside the seaport.

The fur trade attracted new workers, and with the gold rush of 1858, Victoria developed into a large town, welcoming thousands of miners on their way inland. The city flourished, and its port bustled with activity. In 1862, Victoria was officially incorporated; shortly thereafter, the fort was demolished, making way for real-estate development. The site is now known as Bastion Square, and the former warehouses of the fort

have been transformed into commercial space.

For all those years, Victoria was a colony in its own right, just like British Columbia. The two were united in 1866, and it wasn't until a couple of years later that Victoria became the capital of British Columbia. The design of the parliament buildings was chosen by way of a competition. The winner was a 25-year-old architect named Francis Mawson Rattenbury, who left his mark all over the province. One of his most noteworthy projects was the prestigious Empress Hotel.

The downtown area rises up behind the port, whose

waters are shared by ships, yachts and ferries. Like a railway station surrounded by yards, the port is the focal point; the squares, hotels, museums and parliament buildings are all located nearby. A stroll along the waterfront gives a good sense of how the city has preserved a human dimension in its squares and streets.

Victoria is the seat of the provincial government. Accordingly, the civil service occupies an important place in the local economy, as does tourism. This former colony's British heritage attracts many visitors in search of traditions like afternoon tea at the Empress Hotel; quite a few people come here to purchase tartans as well.

Like the Europeans and the Aboriginals, the Chinese played an important role in the city's development. They came here by the thousands to help build the railroad and settled in the northern part of town. The local Chinatown thus bears the stamp of authenticity, as it bears witness to a not so distant past. Victoria is also the home town of painter Emily Carr, who left her mark on the early 20th century with her scenes of native life on the west coast.

As the capital of an economically powerful province that is currently establishing itself as an economic powerhouse, Victoria has no intention of letting itself be outranked by the federal capital, Ottawa, when it comes to

national politics. British Columbia enjoyed an economic boom in the '80s, and is no longer satisfied to be viewed merely as part of a Canadian region, but rather as an influential member of the Canadian federation. And this political power play is increasingly prominent as the international economy shifts toward Asia and places British Columbia in a strategic position.

Finding Your Way Around

By Plane

Victoria International Airport *(☎250-953-7500)* is located north of Victoria on the Saanich Peninsula, a half-hour's drive from downtown on Highway 17.

Air Canada/Air BC Connector
☎888-247-2262
www.aircanada.ca
Air Canada/Air BC Connector offers 16 flights a day between Vancouver and Victoria airports, as well as 11 flights a day on a seaplane between the ports of Victoria and Vancouver.

Pacific Coastal Airlines
114-1640 Electra Blvd., Sidney
☎(604) 273-8666
☎800-663-2872
This company flies between Victoria and Vancouver and offers special advance-purchase fares.

West Coast Air
$198 return
1000 Wharf St.
☎(250) 388-4521 or
800-347-2222

West Coast Air provides twin otter service between Vancouver and Victoria.

Helijet Airways
$200-$275 return
☎(250) 382-6222 Victoria
☎(604) 273-4688 or
800-665-4354 Vancouver
www.helijet.com
Helijet Airways provides frequent, scheduled helicopter service between the ports of Vancouver and Victoria, as well as between Seattle and Victoria.

Harbour Air
$198 return
950 Wharf St.
☎(604) 274-1277 from Vancouver
☎800-665-0212
This company provides frequent service via seaplane between Vancouver and Victoria.

By Ferry

You can reach Victoria by car by taking a BC Ferry from Tsawwassen, located south of Vancouver on the coast. This ferry *(BC Ferry Corporation; in the summer, every day on the hour from 7am to 10pm; in the winter, every day every other hour from 7am to 9pm;* **☎888-223-3779 in B.C. or** *250-386-3431 from outside the province)* will drop you off at the Swartz Bay terminal in Sidney. From there, take Hwy. 17 South to Victoria (see Tour C: Saanich Peninsula, p 120).

BC Ferries also offers transportation to Victoria from the east coast of Vancouver Island. The ferry sets out from the Horseshoe Bay terminal, northwest of Vancouver, and takes passengers to Nanaimo. From there, follow the signs for the TransCanada Hwy. 1 South, which leads to Victoria, 113km away.

By Bus

Airporter Bus
☎*386-2525*
The Airporter Bus transports passengers between Victoria International Airport and the downtown hotels.

Pacific Coach Lines
☎*385-4411 or 800-661-1725*
Pacific Coach Lines offers shuttles back and forth between Vancouver and Victoria eight times a day (16 times a day during summer).

Laidlaw Coach Lines
$17.50 one way
☎*385-4411*
Buses from Laidlaw Coach Lines runs between Victoria and Nanaimo with stops in the major towns along the way. From Nanaimo, two other routes serve the north up to Part Hardy and the West Coast up to Tofino.

By Car

Car Rentals

If you plan on renting a car, make the necessary arrangements once you arrive in Victoria; this will spare you the expense of bringing the car over on the ferry.

Avis Rent A Car
1001 Douglas St.
☎*386-8468*

Budget Car and Truck Rental
757 Douglas St.
☎*953-5300*

Enterprise Rent-A-Car
2507 Government St.
☎*475-6900*

Hertz
655 Douglas St.
☎*360-2822*

National Car and Truck Rentals
767 Douglas St.
☎*386-1213*

Thrifty Car Rentals
625 Frances Ave.
☎*383-3659*

Roadside Assistance

Totem Towing
day or night
☎*475-3211*

By Public Transportation

You can pick up bus schedules and a map of the public transportation system at **Tourism Victoria** *(812 Wharf St.* ☎*953-2033).*

Public transportation in the greater Victoria area is provided by **BC Transit** (☎*382-6161, www.bctransit.com).*

By Taxi

Blue Bird Cabs
☎*382-4235*

Empress Taxi
☎*381-2222*

Victoria Taxi
☎*383-7111*

Tours

Victoria Harbour Ferry Co.
☎*780-0201*
This company can take you to different places in the harbour.

Practical Information

Area code: **250**

Tourist Information

For any information regarding Victoria and its surroundings, contact:

Tourism Victoria Visitor Information Centre
every day 9am to nightfall
812 Wharf St., V8W 1T3
☎*953-2033*

Saanich Peninsula Chamber of Commerce
9768 3rd St., Sidney
☎*656-0525*

Emergencies

In case of serious emergency, dial ☎**911**

Police

Victoria Police Station
850 Caledonia Ave.
☎*995-7654*

Hospital

Victoria General Hospital
35 Helmcken Rd.
☎*727-4212*

Dentist

Emergency Dental Service of British Columbia
☎*361-8901*

Pharmacies

McGill & Orme
649 Fort St.
☎*384-1195*

Shoppers Drug Mart
corner of Yates and Douglas
☎*381-4321 or 384-0544*

Banks

American Express Travel Choice
1213 Douglas St.
☎*385-8731 or 800-669-3636*

Bank of Nova Scotia
702 Yates St.
☎*953-5400*

Canadian Imperial Bank of Commerce
1175 Douglas St.
☎*356-4211*

TD Canada Trust
1080 Douglas St.
☎356-4000

Royal Bank
1079 Douglas St.
☎356-4500

Currency Exchange

Califorex International
724 Douglas St.
☎(250) 384-6631

Custom House Currency Exchange
815 Wharf St.
☎(250) 389-6007

Money Mart
1720 Douglas St.
☎(250) 386-3535

Post Offices

Canada Post
Station B, 1625 Fort St.
☎595-2552
714 Yates St.
☎953-1352

Exploring

To help you make the most of your visit to Victoria and the Saanich Peninsula, we have outlined four tours:

Tour A: Inner Harbour and Old Town ★★★

Tour B: Scenic Marine Drive ★★

Tour C: Saanich Peninsula ★

Tour D: From Victoria to the West Coast Trail ★★

Downtown Victoria is cramped, which can make parking somewhat difficult. There are a number of public lots where you can pay to park your car.

There are city parking lots *($10/day)* at the 600 block of Fisgard Street, the 700 block of Johnson Street, the 500 block of Yates Street, the 700 block of View Street and the 700 block of Broughton Street. These, as well as metred street parking, are free after 6pm, and all day on Sundays and holidays.

Tour A: Inner Harbour and Old Town

Any tour of Victoria starts at the Inner Harbour, which was the main point of access into the city for decades. Back in the era of tall ships, the merchant marine operating on the Pacific Ocean used to stop here to pick up goods destined for England. Once the railway reached the coast, however, the merchandise was transported across Canada by train, thus reducing the amount of time required to reach the east side of the continent. From that point on, the merchant marine only provided a sea link to Asia.

Head to the **Tourism Victoria Visitor Info Centre** *(812 Wharf St., ☎953-2033 or 800-663-3883, ≈382-6539, www. tourismvictoria.com)*, where you can take in a general view of the Inner Harbour and the buildings alongside it, including the **Empress Hotel ★★** (see p 126) and the **Provincial Legislature Buildings ★** (see p 115). Tourism Victoria occupies a former gas station built in the Art Deco style in 1931. The tower above it is a miniature version of a New York–style skyscraper.

Start your tour by strolling northward along Government Street. You'll pass a series of stone buildings housing bookstores, cafés, antique shops and all sorts of other businesses. At View Street, turn left and walk down the little

pedestrian street to **Bastion Square ★**. The **Bastion Square Festival of the Arts** *(☎413-3144)*, not so much a festival as an open-air craft market, is held here from spring to fall *(Apr Thu-Sun, May to Oct Wed-Sun and holidays 10:30am to 5:30pm)*.

Bastion Square marks the former site of Fort Victoria, constructed by the Hudson's Bay Company in 1843, with the help of hundreds of native people. Twenty years later, the fort was demolished to make way for the city. Today, the site is occupied by public buildings like the **Maritime Museum of British Columbia** *($6; every day 9:30am to 4:30pm; 28 Bastion Sq., ☎385-4222, www.mmbc.bc. ca)*, which highlights great moments in the history of sailing, from the days when tall ships sidled up alongside one another in the harbour, up until the present time.

Walk down Bastion Square, turn right on Wharf Street, then head up the north side of Johnson Street. Go into **Market Square ★**, a series of three-storey brick buildings housing shops and cafés, arranged around an inner courtyard. Built in the 1880s, it once housed hotels and saloons, as well as shops. It's a pleasant place to wander and gets very lively during the jazz, blues and theatre festivals and on the Chinese New Year.

Back on Wharf Street, turn right onto Fisgard Street, and left into the oldest **Chinatown ★** *(west of Government Street, between Pandora and Fisgard St..)* in Canada. Full of brightly coloured shops, its sidewalks are decorated with geometric patterns that form a Chinese character meaning "good fortune." At one time, there were over 150 businesses in Chinatown, as well as three schools, five temples, two churches and a hospital. On your way through

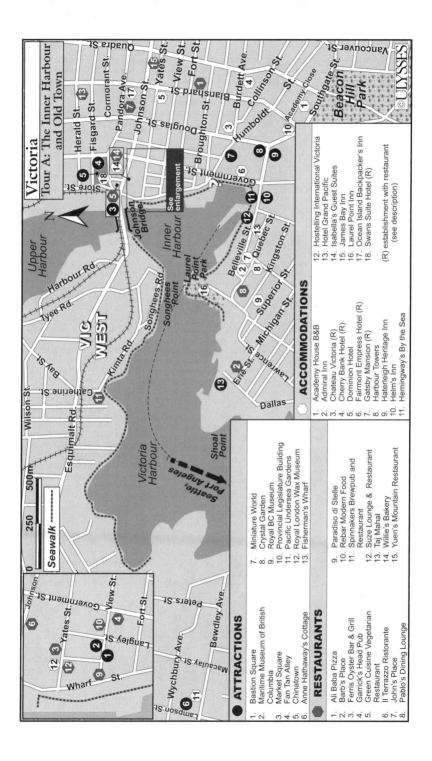

Victoria
Tour A: The Inner Harbour and Old Town

Seawalk ---------

0   250   500m

N

Upper Harbour

Harbour Rd.

Tyee Rd.

VIC WEST

Kimta Rd.

Songhees Rd.

Songhees Point

Wilson St.

Bay St.

Catherine St.

Esquimalt Rd.

Laurel Point Park

Inner Harbour

Johnson Bridge

See enlargement

Belleville St.

Quebec St.

Kingston St.

Superior St.

Michigan St.

Lawrence St.

Erie St.

Dallas

Victoria Harbour

Seattle, Port Angeles

Shoal Point

Beacon Hill Park

Vancouver St.

Quadra St.

Herald St.

Fisgard St.

Cormorant St.

Pandora Ave.

Johnson St.

Yates St.

View St.

Fort St.

Broughton St.

Blanshard St.

Collinson St.

Burdett Ave.

Humboldt St.

Academy Close

Southgate St.

Government St.

Douglas St.

Store St.

© ULYSSES

Enlargement inset
Johnson St.
Government St.
Yates St.
View St.
Fort St.
Langley St.
Wharf St.
Peters St.
Bewdley Ave.
Macaulay St.
Wychbury Ave.
Lampson St.

this neighbourhood, you'll come across the Gate of Harmonious Interest, on Fisgard Street, a symbol of the spirit of cooperation between the Chinese and Canadian communities. **Fan Tan Alley** ★, which runs north-south *(south of Fisgard St.)*, is supposedly the narrowest street in Victoria. People used to come here to buy opium until 1908, when the federal government banned the sale of the drug. Here, you are in the heart of Chinatown.

From Chinatown, turn right on Government Street, retracing your steps to the Inner Harbour. Or, take a short detour to **Victoria West**, home to a popular pub and a growing number of large harbour-side hotels but few attractions. It's a short walk across the Johnson Street Bridge; from there, a pleasant seawalk leads to the West Bay Marina.

From the tourist office, head north on Wharf Street. Cross the Johnson Street Bridge, whose projecting seawall runs alongside the houses and the waterfront, offering a lovely view of the buildings downtown. Farther along, past the Victoria Harbour, you will see the Strait of Juan de Fuca. Stop in at Spinnakers Pub (see

p 129) and wet your whistle while taking in the panoramic view.

The Seawalk runs alongside the houses and the waterfront, offering a lovely view of the buildings downtown. Farther along, past the Victoria Harbour, you will see the Strait of Juan de Fuca. Stop in at Spinnakers Brewpub *(Catherine St.)* and wet your whistle while taking in the panoramic view.

Anne Hathaway's Cottage ★ *($10; every day 10am to 4pm; 429 Lampson St.,* ☎388-4353) is located here, in Victoria West. After crossing the Johnson Street Bridge, turn left on Lampson Street after the sixth traffic light. The Munro Bus, which you can catch at the corner of Douglas and Yates streets, stops at the entrance. This little bit of England is a reconstruction of the birthplace of William Shakespeare and the home of Anne Hathaway, his wife. There are also five additional manor houses, decorated in the same style, where lodging is available (English Inn and Resort). A stroll among these buildings will take you back in time.

West of Victoria West is **Esquimalt**, a small town known mainly for its naval military base and its **CFB Esquimalt Naval & Military Museum** *($2; Mon-Fri 10am to*

3:30pm; ☎363-4312), which has a large collection of military equipment and retraces the history of the base.

Back at the Inner Harbour, make your way to the Fairmont Empress Hotel.

The **Fairmont Empress Hotel** ★★ *(721 Government St.,* ☎384-8111) was built in 1905 for the Canadian Pacific railway company. It was designed by Francis Rattenbury in the Chateau style, just like the Chateau Frontenac in Québec City, only more modern and less romantic. Use the main entrance and cross the lobby, letting yourself be transported back to the 1920s, when the names of influential people found their way into the guest books. Above all, make sure to stop by the Empress for fancy afternoon tea (see p 130), or a curry buffet in the Raj-era Bengal lounge.

At **Miniature World** *($9; mid-May to mid-Jun every day 9am to 7pm, mid-Jun to early Sep every day 8:30am to 9pm, early Sep to mid-Jun 9am to 5pm; Fairmont Empress Hotel, 649 Humboldt St.,* ☎385-9731), you'll see what patience and meticulousness can accomplish: an operational miniature sawmill and other fascinating creations, including two buildings dating back to the end of the 19th century. A sure hit with the kids.

From Miniature World, turn right on Humboldt Street and right again on Douglas Street.

The **Crystal Garden**, by the same architect, is located behind the Empress, at Douglas and Belleville streets. A big glass canopy supported by a visible metal structure, it originally housed a saltwater swimming pool and is now home to a variety of exotic birds and endangered animals.

Fairmont Empress Hotel

Kitty-corner to the Crystal Garden is the **Royal British Columbia Museum ★ ★ ★** *($10; every day 9am to 5pm; IMAX every day 9am to 8pm; museum and IMAX $17.75; 675 Belleville St.,* ☎*356-7226 or 888-447-7977, www.rbcm.gov.bc.ca)*, where you can learn about the history of the city and the various peoples that have inhabited the province. The centrepieces of the collection are a reproduction of Captain Vancouver's ship and a Kwagulth First Nation house. The museum also hosts some interesting temporary exhibitions.

The spectacular First Peoples exhibit begins with some historical artifacts juxtaposed alongside some contemporary art, like that of Musqueam artist Susan Point, to demonstrate the roots and evolution of Northwest Coast art of the type you'll see in galleries, hotels and restaurants during your stay. Throughout the exhibit, there are clear distinctions between coastal and interior peoples, and pre- and post-contact periods. There is a wonderful exhibit of masks and totem poles, arranged by cultural group, with their distinctive elements identified. For example, you'll learn that Haida art is characterized by a carved, raised eyelid line and a concave orbit from the bridge of nose to the temple to the nostril. There are also enormous feast dishes shaped like bears and wolves; magnificent Coast Salish capes, blankets and bags woven with cedar bark; a sound-and-light show explaining the cosmology of Northwest Coast First Nations; more than 100 Haida argillite carvings and countless other items of interest.

In the Modern History exhibit, there are recreations of scenes from the last century of B.C.'s history, including a 1920s rococo-style theatre showing silent films; facades of

Victorian buildings, including a hotel you can walk right into, its woodwork salvaged from a Nanaimo hotel; and a Chinatown street scene. The presentation is attractive and entertaining enough to keep children enthralled. There is also a Natural History exhibit, with models of different landscapes and ecosystems and fascinating pools of local marine animals.

The strange-looking white tower near the Provincial Legislature, at the corner of Belleville and Government streets, is the largest **carillon** in Canada, with 62 bells. Its chimes can be heard every Sunday at 3pm from April to December.

The design for the **Provincial Legislature Buildings ★** *(free tours)* was chosen by way of a competition. The winner was architect Francis Rattenbury, who was just 25 years old at the time and went on to design many other public and privately owned buildings in British Columbia.

Return to the Inner Harbour. Across from the Legislature, the **Pacific Undersea Gardens** *($7.50; Jul and Aug every day 10am to 7pm, Sep to Jun every day 10am to 5pm, Jan and Feb closed Tue and Wed; 490 Belleville St.,* ☎*382-5717)* highlights marine plant and animal life.

Fans of wax museums, like the fabled Madame Tussaud's, are not likely to be disappointed by the **Royal London Wax Museum** *($8.50; Jan 1 to mid-May 9:30am to 5pm, mid-May to early Sep 9am to 7:30pm, early Sep to Dec 31 9:30am to 6pm; 470 Belleville St. on the Inner Harbour,* ☎*388-4461)*. History buffs will see everything from generations of royal families, including all six of Henry VIII's wives (looking strikingly similar), to a gory Plains of Abraham scene, with General Wolfe dying an ago-

nizing death, to a multimedia show dedicated to famous explorers, to a Last Supper scene with the resurrection depicted in lights. In seconds, visitors are taken from the storybook land of Disney to the guillotine in the ghastly chamber of horrors, the obvious highlight of any wax museum. It's Victoria at its cheesiest!

Carry on along the Inner Harbour, past **Laurel Point Park**, where you pick up the pedestrian path. The path continues as far as the Coast Harbourside Hotel and Marina. From there, you must walk along the road *(Kingston Street)* until St. Lawrence Street, where you turn right toward **Fisherman's Wharf ★**. Here you'll find float homes belonging to local fishers, as well as an excellent fish-and-chip shop and a fishmonger. The latter sells herrings at $1 a piece, which you can feed to the more socialized seals in the harbour. Just hold them out over the water until they bite.

When you—and the seals—have had your fill, wander back to the centre of town.

Tour B:
Scenic Marine Drive

This tour leads you along a fabulously scenic coastal road at the bottom of the Saanich Peninsula, by way of detours to a number of important Victoria attractions, located inland. You will pass through the communities of Fairfield, Rockland and Oak Bay. Although this is definitely a driving (or better yet, cycling) tour, it is just minutes from downtown Victoria.

The tour begins at the Ogden Point Breakwater on Dallas Road, near Dock Street. From there, head out along Dallas

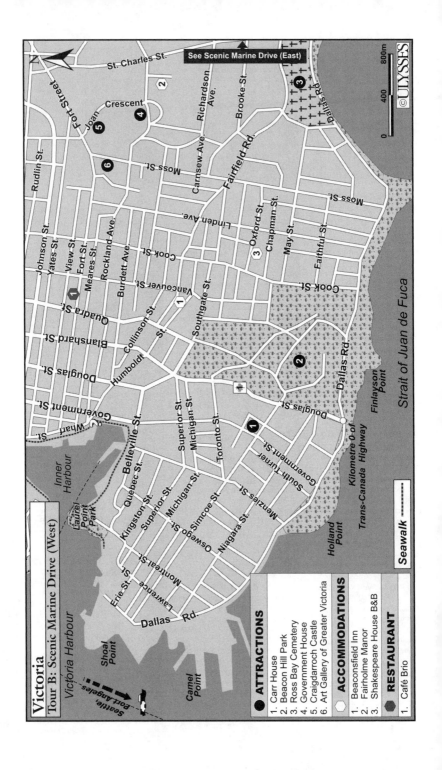

Victoria

Tour B: Scenic Marine Drive (West)

See Scenic Marine Drive (East)

Victoria Harbour

Inner Harbour

Seattle
Port Angeles

Laurel Point Park

Shoal Point

Camel Point

Holland Point

Finlayson Point

Strait of Juan de Fuca

Kilometre 0 of
Trans-Canada Highway

Dallas Rd.

ATTRACTIONS

1. Carr House
2. Beacon Hill Park
3. Ross Bay Cemetery
4. Government House
5. Craigdarroch Castle
6. Art Gallery of Greater Victoria

ACCOMMODATIONS

1. Beaconsfield Inn
2. Fairholme Manor
3. Shakespeare House B&B

RESTAURANT

1. Café Brio

Seawalk --------

© ULYSSES

0   400   800m

St. Charles St.

Fort Street

Joan Crescent

Rudlin St.

Johnson St.
Yates St.
View St.
Fort St.
Meares St.
Rockland Ave.
Burdett Ave.

Quadra St.
Blanshard St.
Douglas St.
Government St.

Collinson St.
Humboldt St.

Vancouver St.
Southgate St.
Cook St.
Linden Ave.

Moss St.
Carnsew Ave.
Fairfield Rd.
Richardson Ave.
Brooke St.
Dallas Rd.

Oxford St.
Chapman St.
May St.
Faithful St.
Moss St.
Cook St.

Wharf St.
Belleville St.
Quebec St.
Kingston St.
Superior St.
Michigan St.
Simcoe St.
Niagara St.
Dallas Rd.

Erie St.
Lawrence St.
Montreal St.
Menzies St.
Oswego St.
Toronto St.
Superior St.
Michigan St.

South Turner St.
Government St.
Douglas St.

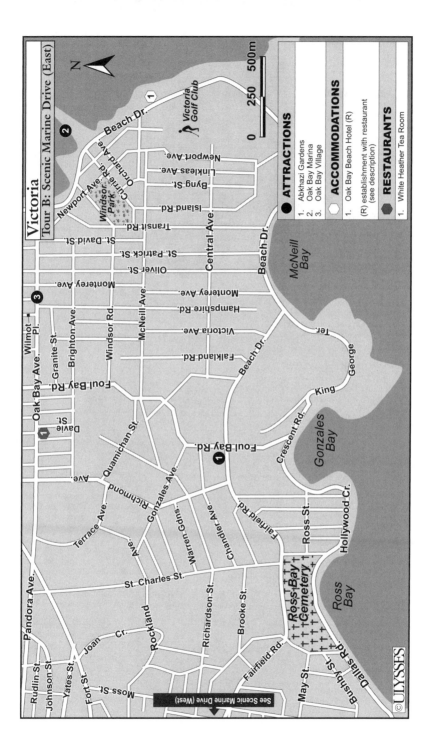

Victoria
Tour B: Scenic Marine Drive (East)

ATTRACTIONS
1. Abkhazi Gardens
2. Oak Bay Marina
3. Oak Bay Village

ACCOMMODATIONS
1. Oak Bay Beach Hotel (R)
(R) establishment with restaurant (see description)

RESTAURANTS
1. White Heather Tea Room

Victoria Golf Club

McNeill Bay

Gonzales Bay

Ross Bay

Ross Bay Cemetery

See Scenic Marine Drive (West)

© ULYSSES

500m
0 250

N

Carr House

Road for a beautiful view of wild and windy Juan de Fuca Strait. Turn left on Government Street, and continue to Simcoe Street.

Here, you are in the Carr family's neighbourhood. Built of wood, **Carr House** ★ (*$5.35; mid-May to mid-Oct every day 10am to 5pm; 207 Government St.,* ☎*383-5843*) was erected in 1864 for the family of Richard Carr. After the American gold rush, the Carrs, who had been living in California, returned to England then came back to North America to set up residence in Victoria. Mr. Carr made a fortune in real estate and owned many pieces of land, both developed and undeveloped, in this residential area. He died in 1888, having outlived his wife by two years. Emily was only 17 at the time. Shortly after, she went first to San Francisco, then London and finally to Paris to study art. She returned to British Columbia around 1910 and began teaching art to the children of Vancouver. She eventually went back to Victoria and followed in her father's footsteps, entering the real-estate business. She also began travelling more along the coast in

order to paint, producing her greatest works in the 1930s.

A unique painter and a reclusive woman, Emily Carr is now recognized across Canada as a great artist who left her stamp on the art world. Be sure to visit the Vancouver Art Gallery (see p 70) to learn more about her art, since the main focus here is her private life. The only original piece of furniture in the house is the bed in which Emily was born in 1871. The house is nevertheless furnished in a style typical of the period. There is a small gift shop on site and a garden, animated by excerpts from Carr's writings. Carr House also distributes maps of the neighbourhood, which show where the family lived at various times.

From Carr House, turn left on Simcoe Street until Douglas Street, where Beacon Hill Park begins.

Beacon Hill Park ★ (*between Douglas and Cook St., facing the Juan de Fuca Strait*) is a peaceful spot where Emily Carr spent many happy days drawing. A public park laid out in 1890, it features a number of trails leading through fields

of wildflowers and landscaped sections. The view of the strait and the Olympic Mountains in the United States is positively magnificent from here. For a reminder of exactly where you are in relation to the rest of Canada, Km 0 of the Trans-Canada Highway lies at the south end of Douglas Street at the corner of Dallas Road.

Carry on along Dallas Road until Memorial Crescent and turn right on Fairfield Road (opposite Stannard Ave.) to the entrance to **Ross Bay Cemetery**. This will take you to the oldest part of the 11ha cemetery, final resting place of many of Victoria's notables, including Emily Carr. Volunteers are often present (*every day mid-May to mid-Sep, 10am to 4pm*) and can provide short tours or self-guided brochures. Tours are regularly scheduled during the tourist season (*$5; Sun 2pm Jul and Aug; tours are indicated "RBC" and start at Bagga Pasta, Fairfield Plaza, 1516 Fairfield Rd.,* ☎*598-8870, www.oldcem.bc.ca*).

From the cemetery, turn left at Charles Street, and left again at Rockland Avenue.

Government House (*1401 Rockland Ave.,* ☎*387-2080*) is another of Victoria's lovely attractions. The house is not open to the public, but its absolutely gorgeous 6ha garden may be visited. There is no admission charge to visit the gardens, which are open every day. If you have even a passing interest in gardens, a look at the rose and herb gardens is worth the visit.

Garden tours are arranged (*$10; one or two per month Wed and/or Sun May to Sep, call for schedule;* ☎*356-5139*).

From the gardens on Rockland Street, head up Joan Crescent to Craigdarroch Castle.

Craigdarroch Castle ★ (*$10; mid-Jun to early Sep every day*

9am to 7pm; winter every day 10am to 4:30pm; 1050 Joan Cr., ☎592-5323) stands at the east end of the downtown area. It was built in 1890 for Robert Dunsmuir, who made a fortune in the coal-mining business. He died before it was completed, but his widow and three children went on to live here. What makes this building interesting, aside from its dimensions, is its decorative woodwork and the view from the fifth floor of the tower. This residence is indicative of the opulent lifestyle enjoyed by the wealthy a century ago.

From the castle, head back to Rockland Street, turn right, and right again on Moss Street.

Both classical and contemporary works are on view at the **Art Gallery of Greater Victoria** ($5; Mon-Sat 10am to 5pm, Thu until 9pm, Sun 1pm to 5pm; 1040 Moss St., ☎384-4101), the city's museum of fine arts. Visitors will find pieces by Emily Carr and by contemporary local and Asian artists. A must for all art lovers. Contact the museum to find out about ongoing exhibitions and activities.

From the gallery, head back down Moss Street until Fairfield Road, and turn left if you're in the mood for another garden visit. If not, take Moss Street all the way back to Dallas Road, and carry on along the coast.

Abkhazi Garden ($7.50; Wed-Sun Mar to late Sep 1pm to 5pm; 1964 Fairfield Rd., ☎598-8096) is a small, suburban garden created by Prince and Princess Nicholas Abkhazi in the 1940s, and tended by the latter until her death in 1994. The garden is naturalistic in style, with rhododendrons, azaleas, lilies and ponds all arranged around rocky outcroppings and trees. Since 2000, it has been run by The Land Conservancy (TLC) of British Columbia, a non-profit organization that is lovingly restoring the garden with the help of dedicated volunteers. A work in progress, the garden is quite small and provides for a very short visit, recommended for serious gardening buffs only. Consider the rather hefty admission fee a contribution to a worthwhile cause.

The Trans-Canada Highway

Mile/Kilometre Zero of the Trans-Canada Highway (TCH), the longest national highway in the world, is indicated by a monument at the corner of Dallas Road and Douglas Street in Victoria. The TCH ends (or begins, depending on your point of view) 7,821km east, in St. John's, in the province of Newfoundland and Labrador. In fact, in front of St. John's city hall, a sign marking the spot declares that "Canada begins right here," so the point of view on the East Coast is pretty clear!

Construction of the TCH began in the summer of 1950, and by the time it was completed in 1970 (the opening ceremonies took place in Rogers Pass, B.C. prior to completion, in 1962), it had cost $1 billion, more than three times the initial estimated cost.

In truth, the highway is neither a single entity, nor does it link the entire country. It needs some help from two ferries (to Victoria and St. John's from the mainland), doesn't quite manage to pass through every Canadian jurisdiction (the Yukon, Northwest Territories and Nunavut are left out), and is in fact two different highways for much of Ontario and Québec. West of Portage la Prairie, Manitoba, it splits into Highway 16, which heads north and ends up in Prince Rupert, B.C., and Highway 1, a southern route that ends up in Victoria.

The TCH's distinctive marker shield is a white maple leaf on a green background.

Take Foul Bay Road back to Marine Drive, known here as Crescent Road. Follow it past the scenic Victoria Golf Club to Oak Bay Marina, a convenient, scenic place for a stop.

From the marina, take Newport Avenue to Oak Bay Avenue. Here, between Monterey and Wilmot, is **Oak Bay Village**, the heart of the community of **Oak Bay** (pop 18,000). Also known as the "Tweed Curtain" in reference to its British heritage, Oak Bay is home to tea rooms, fish-and-chip shops and cafés galore, along with beautiful parks and gardens.

To return to downtown Victoria, take Oak Bay Avenue, which becomes Pandora Avenue, all the way there.

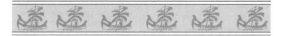

Victoria and Surroundings

Tour C:
Saanich Peninsula

Victoria lies at the southern end of the Saanich Peninsula. The peninsula is first and foremost a suburb, as many people who work in Victoria live here. This region is an unavoidable part of any itinerary involving Vancouver Island and especially Victoria, since the big Swartz Bay Ferry Terminal is located in Sidney, a small town near the tip of the peninsula, 32km from Victoria, accessed via the Patricia Bay Highway.

From downtown, drive south on Douglas Street and turn left on Dallas Road, which follows the shore. This road runs through a number of residential neighbourhoods, changes name a few times (at one point it becomes Beach Drive, then Cadboro Bay Road) and offers some lovely views along the way. Notice the Tudor-style houses and lush, well-tended gardens lining Oak Bay and Cadboro Bay. Once past Cadboro Bay, follow the shore line along Tudor Avenue. Take Arbutus, Ferndale, Barrie and Ash roads to Mount Douglas Park.

At the entrance to **Mount Douglas Park ★★**, turn left on Cedar Hill Road, then right in order to reach the lookout, which offers a 360° view of the Gulf Islands, the Strait of Georgia and Juan de Fuca Strait and the snow-capped peaks along the Canadian and U.S. coast. The colours of the sea and the mountains are most vibrant early in the morning and at the end of the day.

Upon leaving Mount Douglas Park, turn left onto Cordova Bay Road; it follows the shoreline until it becomes Royal Oak Drive, which intersects the Patricia Bay Highway (Hwy. 17) and then West Saanich

Road (Hwy. 17A). These two highways access the east and west sides, respectively, of the Saanich Peninsula and then link in North Saanich by way of Wain Road. You can make this tour in a loop by reversing the order of one of the following two suggested routes, and you can take either tour from the ferry terminal in Swartz Bay by reversing its order.

West Saanich Road

The **Horticulture Centre of the Pacific** (*$5; every day Apr to Oct 8am to 8pm, Nov to Mar 9am to 4:30pm; 505 Quayle Rd., ☎479-6162*) is either a prelude or an encore to a visit to **Butchart Gardens** (see below). Attractions include a winter garden, the Takata Japanese garden and a collection of rhododendrons and dahlias.

If you like science and the stars, head over to the **Centre of the Universe** (*$7; Apr 1 to Oct 31 every day 10am to 6pm, Nov 1 to April 1 Tue-Sun 10am to 6pm; 5071 West Saanich Rd, Little Saanich Mountain, 16km from Victoria, ☎363-8262*), which has one of the biggest telescopes in the world.

The amazing **Victoria Butterfly Gardens** (*$8; mid-Feb to mid-May every day 9:30am to 4:30pm, mid-May to late Sep 9am to 5pm, Oct 9am to 4:30pm; 1461 Benvenuto Ave., ☎652-3822 or 877-722-0272*) are home to all sorts of butterflies, who flutter about freely in a tropical forest setting, accompanying you on your tour. An attractive souvenir shop and a restaurant are also on the premises.

The **Butchart Gardens ★★** (*$10 to $20, depending on the season; call ahead for opening hours; Hwy. 17 N, 800 Benvenuto Ave., ☎652-4422, www.butchartgardens.com*), which cover 26ha, were founded by the family of the same name in 1904. A wide array of flowers, shrubs and

trees flourish in this unique space. Maps are available at the entrance. Fireworks light up the sky on Saturday nights during July and August, and outdoor concerts are held here Monday to Saturday evenings from June to September.

Patricia Bay Highway

The **Saanich Historical Artifacts Society ★** (*Sep to May, every day 9:30am to 12:30pm, Jun to Aug 9:30am to 4:30pm; 7321 Lochside Dr.; ☎652-5522*), located on the outskirts of Victoria, has one of the largest collections of steam engines, tractors and farming equipment in Canada. Of course, you have to be interested in that sort of thing. The museum is halfway between Sidney and Victoria and is easily accessible via Highway 17; head east on Island View Road then north on Lochside Drive and continue to the gate.

Sidney (*Visitor Information Centre; 2295 Ocean Ave.; ☎656-3260*), a small town near the tip of the Saanich Peninsula, has attained a certain level of importance due to the presence of the **Swartz Bay Ferry Terminal**. Among the local attractions are the pretty **Sidney Marine Museum ★** (*admission by donation; May to Oct every day 10am to 4pm, Nov to Apr 11am to 3pm, Jan and Feb Sat and Sun 11am to 3pm; 9801 Seaport Pl., ☎656-1322*), which displays some magnificent whale skeletons and explains the biology and evolution of this animal. At the same location, the **Sidney Historical Museum** (*☎655-6355*), meanwhile, is devoted to the history of Sidney and North Saanich.

The **BC Aviation Museum** (*$5; mid May to mid Sep every day, 10am to 4pm, mid Sep to mid May 11am to 3pm; Victoria International Airport, the big white hangar near the control* *tower, ☎655-3300)* houses a fine collection of World War II airplanes, as well as some more recent models.

Located in the western part of the peninsula in an isolated area, the **Fort Rodd Hill & Fisgard Lighthouse National Historic Site** *($4; Mar 1 to Oct 31 10am to 5:30pm, Nov 1 to Feb 28 9am to 4:30pm; 603 Fort Rodd Hill Rd, follow the Trans-Canada Hwy. and take the Port Renfrew exit, 10km north of Victoria, ☎478-5849)* will delight history buffs. You can walk along the property by the Strait of Georgia. Between 1878 and 1956, the fortifications first defended the British Empire and then independent Canada. Strategically placed, the artillery protected Victoria and Esquimalt, the gateway to Western Canada. As for the Fisgard lighthouse, located on the same site, it was the first lighthouse erected on the West Coast of Canada in the second half of the 19th century. It is still in operation. Pets and bicycles are not allowed on the site.

Tour D: From Victoria to the West Coast Trail

Head north on Douglas Street, which turns into Highway 1A (Old Island Highway) and follow the signs for Sooke. At Colwood, take Highway 14, which becomes Sooke Road near Port Renfrew. You'll pass through the suburbs west of town when you get to Sooke, which lies about 30km from Victoria. At the 17 Mile House restaurant, turn left onto Gillespie Road. This will take you into **East Sooke Regional Park** ★ *(☎478-3344)*, where hiking trails lead through the wild flora by the sea. This is a perfect place for a family outing (see p 122).

Head back to the 14, and turn left toward Port Renfrew. The highway runs alongside beaches and bays. The farther you get from Victoria, the more twists and turns there are in the road. The terrain is mountainous, and the views are spectacular. As you continue west on the 14, you'll notice a change in the landscape; forestry has long been an important source of revenue for the province, and the large valleys in this region have been clear-cut.

Port Renfrew

Port Renfrew is one of two starting points for the **West Coast Trail** ★★★ (the other being Bamfield). This 75km trek is geared towards experienced, intrepid hikers prepared to face unstable weather conditions and widely varied terrain; in fact, it is considered one of the most difficult hiking trails in North America. For more information, contact the Gordon River Information Centre, near Port Renfrew *(☎647-5434)*.

Parks and Beaches

Victoria is surrounded by a host of very different parks and beaches (city beaches, deserted beaches running alongside temperate rain forests, etc.). The West Coast boasts numerous provincial parks, which all feature sandy beaches strewn with piles of driftwood. These parks offer nature lovers a breath of fresh air.

Scenic Marine Drive

There are two beaches in Victoria where families can enjoy a day of sand-castle building and swimming in calm waters.

Willows Beach ★ *(public bathrooms, playground; corner of Estevan Ave. and Beach Dr.)* stretches alongside the chic residential neighbourhood of Oak Bay near a marina and the Oak Bay Beach Hotel.

Cadboro Bay Beach ★ *(public bathrooms, playground; corner of Sinclair Rd. and Beach Dr.)*, a little farther east, is located in the University of Victoria neighbourhood and attracts a young crowd. It looks out onto a bay, with the Chatham Islands and Discovery Island in the distance. The ebb and flow of the tides has transformed the strand at **Beacon Hill Park** ★ (see p 118) into a pebble beach covered with pieces of driftwood.

The summit of **Mount Tolmie** ★★★ *(BC Parks, ☎391-2300)* offers sensational panoramic views of Victoria, Haro Strait, the ocean, and magnificent Mount Baker and the Cascade Range in Washington State (U.S.A.).

Saanich Peninsula

Mount Douglas Park *(Hwy. 17, Royal Oak Dr. Exit; BC Parks, ☎391-2300)*, which covers 10ha and offers access to the sea, is the perfect place for a picnic or a stroll (see p 120).

From Victoria to the West Coast Trail

Goldstream Provincial Park ★★★ *(20min from Victoria by Hwy. 1; BC Parks, ☎391-2300)*, located 17km from Victoria, is one of the major parks in the Victoria area. Picture 600-year-old Douglas firs lining hiking trails leading to Mount Finlayson and past magnificent waterfalls. In November, nature lovers come here to watch coho, chinook and chum salmon make their final voyage, spawn and die in Goldstream River.

The fish are easy to see, as the water is crystal clear. Not to be missed.

The end of the salmon run marks the beginning of another incredible event: the **Eagle Extravaganza**. From December to February, as many as 275 bald eagles per day will visit the estuary during low tide to feed on dead chum salmon. The estuary is off-limits to visitors, but there are viewing platforms, live video cameras and telescopes so that you can observe the feeding eagles from a safe distance. Visitors can also stop by the Nature House to obtain more information on eagles and other birds.

An immense stretch of wilderness (1,422ha), **East Sooke Regional Park** (☎478-3344) is sure to appeal to anyone who likes solitude and tranquility. It is laced with over 50km of trails. At Anderson Cove, you'll find the starting point of a trail leading to Babbington Hill and Mount Macguire, whose summits offer a splendid view of the region. Eagles can be seen swirling about on thermal currents.

Follow the **Galloping Goose Regional Trail** for nearly 60km by bicycle, on horseback or on foot. A former railway line, it runs through some magnificent scenery. You'll spot geese, eagles and even vultures. The trail starts in the heart of Victoria and leads beyond Sooke, and can be picked up at numerous points in between. For more information, call ☎478-3344.

On Highway 14, after Sooke, the waterfront is studded with beaches. **French Beach ★**, a stretch of pebbles and sand lined with logs, has picnicking facilities. It is also wheelchair accessible. A little farther west, still on the 14, lies **China Beach ★ ★**; to get there, you have to take a well laid-out trail down to the base of a cliff

(about 15min). The beach is absolutely magnificent. It is not uncommon to spot a seal, a sea otter or even a grey whale or a killer whale swimming offshore. Just walk a few minutes in either direction to find yourself alone in a little bay. Surfers come here for the waves.

Botanical Beach ★ ★ ★, after Port Renfrew, is a veritable paradise for anyone interested in marine life. When the tide is out you'll discover all sorts of treasures: fish, starfish and various species of marine plant-life are left behind in little tidal pools among the pebbles. To make the most of your visit to the beach, pick up a copy of the *Shore Hiker's Tide Guide* available in Parks Canada interpretive centres.

Pacific Rim National Park *(starting in Port Renfrew)* is a marvellous green space along the ocean front. It is divided into three sections: Long Beach, the Broken Group Islands and the West Coast Trail. For more information on the latter, see p 123.

Outdoor Activities

Cycling

Cycling is a great way to explore Victoria. For information on cycling tours in the city, drop by the **Greater Victoria Cycling Coalition** *(Mon-Fri 3pm to 6pm; 1056A North Park St., off Cook St.,* ☎480-5155). You can also find information on recreational rides on their Web site: *www.gvcc.bc.ca*. Bicycles, including cute-as-a-button tandems, can be rented from the following companies:

Harbour Rentals
816 Government St.
☎995-1661

Cycle BC
950 Wharf St.
☎385-2453

Fishing

As far as deep-sea fishing is concerned, salmon is king. There are five kinds of Pacific salmon: coho, chinook, sockeye, pink and chum. Given this variety, fishing is possible year-round. Of course, you are likely to catch other kinds of fish, such as cod, halibut or snapper. The spawning season for coho, chum, sockeye and pink salmon lasts all summer, while chinook spawns from May to September and in winter in certain regions.

Inner Harbour and Old Town

Those who insist on catching their dinner, be it a sockeye salmon or a 140kg halibut, can arrange a guided fishing charter.

Cuda Marine Adventures
Hotel Grand Pacific, ground level
463 Belleville St.
☎995-2832 or 866-995-2832

From Victoria to the West Coast Trail

Sooke Charter Boat Association
Sooke
☎642-7783 or 888-450-3474
The Sooke Charter Boat Association organizes fishing trips on the ocean and offers a hotel reservation service. The Sooke region is bounded by bays and coves where the rivers empty into the sea.

Sooke Charters
☎642-3888 or 888-775-2659
Sooke Charters provides all the necessary fishing equipment. The rates are very affordable for this sport: $180 for three people (4hrs) or $200 for four.

Golf

Saanich Peninsula

Golf is *the* leisure activity on the Saanich Peninsula. Golfers can try the following courses, listed in order of preference:

Ardmore Golf Course
$25/18 holes
930 Ardmore Dr., Sidney
☎656-4621

Cedar Hill Municipal Golf Course
$34/18 holes
1400 Derby Rd., Saanich
☎595-3103

Arbutus Ridge Golf Club
$50/18 holes
3535 Telegraph Rd., Cobble Hill, 35min north of Victoria
☎743-5000
The Arbutus Ridge Golf Club has an attractive 18-hole course and rents out equipment.

Cordova Bay Golf Course
$54/18 holes
5333 Cordova Bay Rd.
☎658-4444
The Cordova Bay Golf Course also has an attractive 18-hole course with a driving range, a restaurant, a bar and a pro shop.

Hiking

The **Juan de Fuca Marine Trail** *(☎391-2300)* stretches 47km from the south end of Vancouver Island (from China Beach, west of the little village of Jordan River) to Botanical Beach, near Port Renfrew. This trail, inaugurated in 1994 on the occasion of the Commonwealth Games, is geared toward experienced hikers, and, as a safety precaution, anyone planning to take it is advised to leave a detailed description of their itinerary with a friend before setting out.

Note that the northern part of this trail ends at Port Renfrew. Those who want to explore further can extend the hike on the 75km of the **West Coast Trail** that leads to Bamfield. Together, the two paths add up to 122km of trails that require at least a 10-day expedition through the temperate rainforest of the West Coast.

Horseback Riding

Saanich Peninsula

Woodgate Stables
8129 Derrinberg Rd., Saanichton
☎652-0287
Woodgate organizes pleasant outings just 20min north of Victoria.

For more information, contact the Gordon River Information Centre, near Port Renfrew *(☎647-5434)*.

Sea Kayaking

Sea kayaking is a fabulous way to take in some lovely views of Victoria.

Victoria Kayak Tours
950 Wharf St.
☎216-5646
www.kayakvictoria.com
Victoria Kayak Tours can take you on a paddling tour of the Inner Harbour ($69), through Finlayson Fjord to Butchart Gardens ($149), or on several other tours. Guide and owner Cliff Hansen and his staff are knowledgeable about the history of Victoria and can provide plenty of amusing and interesting anecdotes to animate the tour.

Ocean River Sports
1824 Store St.
☎381-4233 or 800-909-4233
Ocean River Sports also arranges custom tours.

Scuba Diving

Saanich Peninsula

David Doubilet, a member of the Cousteau Society and a renowned photographer for *National Geographic*, describes Vancouver Island as "the best cold-water diving destination in the world." The entire coast is a maze of fjords and little islands. Veritable underwater gardens serve as a habitat for over 300 species of aquatic animals.

The Artificial Reef Society maintains some beautiful diving sites in Sidney, north of Victoria. The *Mackenzie*, a 111m destroyer, was sunk so that divers could explore it, and the same was done to the *G.B. Church*, a 53m freighter. **Arrawac Marine Services** *(240 Meadowbrook Rd., ☎479-5098)* organizes dives in the area.

Whale-watching

Inner Harbour and Old Town

At least four species of whales can be found in the waters around Victoria and at least 18 whale-watching companies track their every move. Visitors can go whale-watching aboard an inflatable dinghy or a yacht. Here are two good outfits to try:

Orca Spirit Adventures
$79 3hr tour
☎383-8411 or 888-672-ORCA
offers excursions aboard the *Orca Spirit*, an elegant and extremely comfortable 15m ship equipped with large observation platforms. Transportation from your hotel is available.

Victoria Marine Adventure Centre
950 Wharf St.
☎995-2211
Whale-watching tours are scheduled from April or May to October. Trips are 3hrs long and cost about $75 per adult.

Windsurfing

Scenic Marine Drive

All you have to do is park your car on Dallas Road and plunge into the sea. The scenery is magnificent and the wind, perfect.

Accommodations

Accommodations are somewhat less expensive in Victoria than in Vancouver. Believe it or not, you can actually find a very decent room in high season in Victoria for less than $150—that is, of course, if you don't mind turning your back to the harbour. When booking your reservation, make sure you inquire whether your room will offer a harbour view; be aware that such rooms come at a premium, with rates anywhere

from $30 to $100 higher per night. If you can afford it, however, it's worth the splurge, at least for part of your stay.

The Inner Harbour and Old Town

Ocean Island Backpacker's Inn
$
K, sb, ℜ
791 Pandora Ave.
☎385-1788
www.oceanisland.com
Ocean Island Backpacker's Inn is one of the newest youth hostels to have sprung up in Victoria. Around 100 beds are available in the dormitory and in the double rooms. There's a small, licensed restaurant on-site and Internet access is available.

Hostelling International Victoria
$
sb, K
516 Yates St.
☎385-4511
⇌385-3232
This stone-and-brick building with 108 beds, is located in Old Town, right near the Inner Harbour. Members take precedence in youth hostels, so it can be difficult for non-members to get a bed, especially during the high season. Reservations required.

Dominion Hotel
$$
ℜ
759 Yates St.
☎384-4136 or 800-663-6101
⇌384-5342
www.dominion-hotel.com
The elegant Dominion Hotel has welcomed visitors since 1876. The classic decor of its 101 rooms is sure to please. The pleasant restaurant-bar is located on the main floor.

Cherry Bank Hotel
$$$ bkfst incl.
K, ≡
825 Burdett Ave.
☎385-5380 or 800-998-6688
⇌383-0949
www.bctravel.com/cherrybank.html
The Cherry Bank Hotel B&B is situated in a residential area two blocks from downtown. In keeping with the British ambiance of Victoria, Cherry Bank Inn is a dead ringer for a genuine Victorian English inn, with plenty of cherry-red velvet wallpaper and narrow, labyrinthine corridors sure to bring out the closet claustrophobic in you. While some might find it quaint, others will no doubt find its guestrooms downright dowdy, though a genuine attempt has clearly been made to gussy them up with plants and reasonable facsimiles of canopy beds. Service is friendly and you can't beat the place for quirkiness or price.

Academy House B&B
$$$ bkfst incl.
ℝ
865 Academy Close
☎388-4329 or 877-388-4339
⇌388-5199
www.academyhouse.bc.ca
Academy House B&B is a peaceful establishment located on the border of wonderful Beacon Hill Park. The high ceilings and small balconies add charm.

Isabella's Guest Suites
$$$ bkfst incl.
K
537 Johnson St.
☎381-8414
www.isabellasbb.com
Located above Willie's Bakery (see p 128) in the heart of the Old Town, Isabella's is a real find. There are two very attractive guest suites with fully equipped kitchens, painted in deep colours, tastefully furnished with antiques and contemporary furnishings and featuring hardwood floors. Continental breakfast served at Willie's. Weekly rentals are preferred ($700).

Helm's Inn
$$$
ℜ, ℝ, K, ≡
600 Douglas St.
☎385-5767 or 800-665-4356
⇆385-2221
www.helmsinn.com

All things considered, Helm's Inn is probably the best deal in Victoria. It is located within walking distance of downtown, the museums and the Inner Harbour and has spacious, recently upgraded and pleasantly redecorated rooms and suites, all of them with fully equipped kitchens, as well as laundry facilities. Complimentary in-room continental breakfast and afternoon tea served. A good, affordable choice.

Admiral Inn
$$$ bkfst incl.
ℝ, ⚓
257 Belleville St.
☎388-6267 or 888-823-6472
⇆388-6267
www.admiral.bc.ca

The Admiral Inn is a quiet, family-run establishment located right downtown, a stone's throw from the Inner Harbour. The rooms are very comfortable and the rates reasonable given the central location.

James Bay Inn
$$$
ℜ
270 Government St.
☎384-7151 or 800-836-2649
⇆385-2311
www.jamesbayinn.bc.ca

The recently renovated James Bay Inn is a small, 48-room hotel, located a few minutes' walk from the Legislature and Beacon Hill Park. It was once a retirement home and painter Emily Carr spent the last part of her life here. The rooms are basic and simply furnished with a bed, a television and a small desk. Some of the guestrooms were recently renovated, but the rest are somewhat dowdy. Request a room with a bay window. Heavy packers are forewarned that there is no elevator.

Chateau Victoria
$$$
ℜ, ≈, ☺, K, ℝ
740 Burdett Ave.
☎382-4221 or 800-663-5891
⇆380-1950
www.chateauvictoria.com

Chateau Victoria is an affordable, very pleasant budget option. It's not on the Inner Harbour, but you can see the Empress from some of the standard rooms! Though not huge, the rooms are cheerful enough, with duvets, desks, large TVs and armchairs, all in very good condition. All the standard rooms are located on the second, third and fourth floors, with suites ($$$$), all with balconies, located above. The only downside is that the hotel is located on a slight incline, with a fairly steep approach, possibly representing an access problem for guests with limited mobility. A complimentary city shuttle can help solve that problem, however, based on availability. Complimentary parking.

Harbour Towers Hotel and Suites
$$$$
ℝ, ℜ, ≈, △, ☺, ⚓
345 Quebec St.
☎385-2405 or 800-663-5896
⇆385-4453
www.harbourtowers.com

Harbour Towers is a good choice for those seeking complete comfort, obliging service and a location close to the Inner Harbour at a relatively reasonable rate. All suites have balconies and kitchenettes, while standard rooms on the eighth floor and up offer a harbour view, at a slightly higher rate; some of the latter also have refrigerators. Children are entertained in the Kid Zone, while their parents work out in the fitness centre and relax in the hot tub. Babysitting services are also available.

Swans Suite Hotel
$$$$
ℜ, K
506 Pandora St.
☎361-3310 or 800-668-SWAN
⇆361-3491
www.swanshotel.com

Without question, the Swans Suite Hotel is one of the best places to stay in Victoria, especially if you're travelling in a group. The rooms are actually cozy, two-storey apartments, complete with balconies, that can accommodate several people. Guests will find "real" works of art on the walls, plants, big-screen TVs and a somewhat non-descript, ski-chalet-style decor. The hotel, which dates back to 1913, is located right in the heart of Old Town, steps away from Chinatown and the Inner Harbour. A fun brew pub and a restaurant are on the ground floor.

Gatsby Mansion
$$$$$ bkfst incl.
309 Belleville St.
☎388-9191 or 800-563-9656
⇆920-5651

Under the same ownership as the Ramada Inn and situated right behind it, the Gatsby Mansion offers inn-style lodgings right on the Inner Harbour. There are 10 guestrooms in the main house and another nine in the mansion next door, each individually decorated with antiques and duvets. The location is perfect and the service is professional and polite (including housemaids dressed in black and white!) but the guestrooms (room number 5, with bay windows, king-side bed, balcony and Inner Harbour view, is quite lovely), though pleasant, are not all up to scratch for the price.

The Haterleigh Heritage Inn
$$$$$ bkfst incl.
®
243 Kingston St.
☎*384-9995*
⁼*384-1935*
www.haterleigh.com
This old house, dating from 1901, has been lovingly restored with great attention to detail. A rich past lives on in its magnificent stained-glass windows and antique furnishings. The rooms are decorated in a flowery, over-the-top Victorian style and equipped with whirlpool baths and huge beds.

Hotel Grand Pacific
$$$$$-$$$$$$$
🐾, ℑ, ®, ≈, ☺, △
463 Belleville St.
☎*386-0450 or 800-663-9550*
⁼*380-4475*
www.hotelgrandpacific.com
Located right on the Inner Harbour, its facade bearing more than just a slight resemblance to that of the Empress, the Grand Pacific was built in 1989 and extensively expanded in 2001. The lobby is elegantly done up in marble and chandeliers, and the decor in the standard rooms is rather typical of large hotels, with a nouveau-colonial style and a burgundy-and-green colour scheme. The rooms in the old wing, however, are starting to look a little dated. Each room has a balcony, individually controlled air conditioning, a mini-bar, a feather duvet, as well as the standard accoutrements (hair dryers, iron and coffee makers). Harbour views generally require a $30 supplement. Service is professional and courteous.

🏯 Fairmont Empress Hotel
$$$$$
🐾, ≈, ®, ☺, △, ℜ
721 Government St.
☎*384-8111 or 800-441-1414*
⁼*389-2747*
www.fairmont.com
The Empress is located on the Inner Harbour, adjacent to the museums and the interesting public and commercial areas.

Designed by architect Francis Rattenbury, this luxurious 475-room hotel offers a relaxing atmosphere and a Chateau-style setting and is commonly regarded as *the* place to stay in Victoria. A new wing has been added to the original, quintessentially Victorian building without detracting from its legendary charm. Visitors stop here for afternoon tea or simply to admire the ivy-covered facade. Its three room types, from the standard Fairmont to the slightly larger Deluxe to the harbour-side Premiere, are all lovely and done up in a cranberry, sage or pale-yellow colour scheme. Note that the Premiere rooms (about $100 more than the standard Fairmont rooms) are the only ones that offer a harbour view and that they get booked up first—reserve at least six weeks in advance for a summer stay.

Laurel Point Inn
$$$$$$
≈, △, ℝ, ℜ, ≡, 🐕
680 Montreal St.
☎*386-8721 or 800-663-7667*
⁼*386-9547*
www.laurelpoint.com
The Laurel Point Inn's distinctive building guards the entrance to the Inner Harbour. Its original wing, to the north, dates from 1970, and although its rooms offer the best view of the Inner Harbour, their decor is rather ordinary. The south wing, added in 1989, was designed by well-known architect Arthur Erickson, who also designed the UBC Museum of Anthropology. These spacious rooms are more luxuriously appointed and decorated in natural colours with a rather minimalist approach; those facing the Outer Harbour offer excellent views. They come equipped with decadent marble bathrooms complete with double sinks, soaker tubs, glass walk-in showers, and even mini-TVs and telephones. The grounds are beautifully landscaped, with a pond and a harbour-

side terrace. Sadly, however, despite its many attributes, the service here is not quite as professional, nor as attentive as one would expect of a hotel of this class.

Scenic Marine Drive

UVic Housing, Food and Conference Services
$ bkfst incl.
May 1 to Aug 31
sb, K
Sinclair and Finnerty rds.
☎*721-8395*
⁼*721-8930*
Located on the University of Victoria campus, UVic's 999 dorm-style rooms are open to visitors during the summer months. A number of these were built for the 1994 Commonwealth Games. The rates are based on triple occupancy, but single rooms are also available. The campus lies east of the downtown area on a hill, right near the Cadboro Bay Beach.

Shakespeare House B&B
$$ bkfst incl.
1151 Oxford St.
☎/⁼*388-5546*
www.shakespearehousebb.com
Situated between Beacon Park and the Straight of Juan de Fuca, Shakespeare House B&B offers comfortable rooms. The classic English architecture of the building is interesting.

The Oak Bay Beach Hotel
$$$$ bkfst incl.
ℜ, ℑ
1175 Beach Dr.
☎*598-4556 or 800-668-7758*
⁼*598-6180*
www.oakbaybeachhotel.bc.ca
The Oak Bay Beach Hotel, which has 50 comfortably laid-out rooms, caters to visitors seeking English charm and a pleasant seaside atmosphere. Located on the waterfront in the residential neighbourhood of Oak Bay, it offers an interesting view.

Fairholme Manor
$$$$ bkfst incl.
⊛, ჲ, K, ℜ
638 Rockland Pl.
☎*598-3240 or 877-511-3322*
⇆*598-3299*
www.fairholmemanor.com
Fairholme Manor, an Italianate mansion dating from 1885, was lovingly restored and lavishly decorated by new owners Sylvia and Ross and transformed into one of Victoria's most stunning bed and breakfasts. Its four impeccable guestrooms, all suites, feature high ceilings and ornate moldings, walls painted in heritage colours, hardwood floors accented by Persian carpets, and plush, down-filled armchairs and loveseats; some have bay windows providing a spectacular view of the Olympic Mountains in Washington state. The gardens of Government House (see p 118) surround the place, assuring a verdant, tranquil oasis. The two garden-level suites even have small kitchens, a great idea for those who plan on a self-catering holiday. Located in Rockland, a short drive from downtown.

Beaconsfield Inn
$$$$$ bkfst incl.
ჲ, ⊛
998 Humboldt St.
☎*384-4044 or 888-884-4044*
⇆*384-4052*
www.beaconsfieldinn.com
Located in the heart of Victoria, the Edwardian-era Beaconsfield Inn, listed as a historic monument, combines luxury and sophistication. Guests can enjoy complimentary afternoon tea or a glass of sherry in the library, decorated with leather sofas and Persian carpets and warmed by a gas fire, and feast on a memorable breakfast. Guestrooms are impeccably decorated with antiques, quilts, deep, rich hues or pastels; some feature hardwood floors, others, carpeting. A full breakfast is served, as is an evening glass of sherry, and tea and cookies. Expen-

sive but British ambiance guaranteed.

Saanich Peninsula

Guest Retreat Bed & Breakfast
$$ bkfst incl.
ℜ
2280 Amity Dr., Sidney
☎*656-8073*
⇆*656-8027*
www.guestretreatbb.com
This B&B is located steps away from the beach and has fully equipped apartments with private entrances and lots of closet space. The perfect place for an extended stay. Inquire about the weekly and monthly rates.

Victoria Airport Travelodge
$$$
K, ℜ, ≈, ✖
2280 Beacon Ave., Sidney
☎*656-1176 or 800-578-7878*
⇆*656-7344*
www.airporttravelodge.com
This member of the Travelodge chain offers lovely, comfortable rooms at reasonable rates. The hotel is conveniently located a few minutes from Butchart Gardens, the golf courses, the Swartz Bay BC Ferry terminal and Victoria International Airport.

Honoured Guest Bed & Breakfast
$$$$ bkfst incl.
⊛, ✖, ჲ
8155 Lochside Dr., Saanichton
☎*544-1333*
⇆*544-1330*
www.sidneybc.com/honoured
The sumptuous Honoured Guest Bed & Breakfast is located on the banks of the Cordova Channel, about 15km from Victoria via Highway 17. When the building was erected in 1994, the goal was to make the most of the landscape. The rooms have private entrances, some have whirlpool baths, and all have sweeping views of the sea and Mount Baker. Credit cards are not accepted.

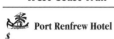
From Victoria to the West Coast Trail

Port Renfrew Hotel
$
✖, sb, ℜ
at the end of Hwy. 14, Parkinson Rd. Port Renfrew
☎*647-5541*
⇆*647-5594*
The Port Renfrew Hotel is located on the village pier, where hikers set out for the West Coast Trail. The rustic rooms are sure to please hikers longing for a dry place to sleep. There are laundry facilities on the premises, as well as a pub that serves hot meals.

Sunny Shores Resort & Marina
$$
≈
5621 Sooke Rd., R.R. #1, Sooke
☎*642-5731 or 888-805-3932*
⇆*642-5737*
www.sunnyshoresresort.com
Sunny Shores has modern rooms with cable television, as well as tent and RV sites. Picnic tables, laundry facilities, a large pool and miniature golf course are all provided. Open year round. Perfect for campers who like fishing. If you have a boat, you can moor it here.

The Arbutus Beach Lodge
$$ bkfst incl.
5 Queesto Dr., Port Renfrew
☎*647-5458*
⇆*647-5552*
www.arbutusbeachlodge.com
The Arbutus Beach Lodge is a very attractive inn set on the beach, snuggled in the renowned West Coast forest. The surroundings are peaceful and the place is so comfortable that you'll feel like extending your stay. Whale-watching and fishing excursions are available upon request.

Victoria and Surroundings

The Seascape Inn Bed & Breakfast
$$$ bkfst incl.
K, ℜ
6435 Sooke Rd., Sooke
☎642-7677 or 888-516-8811
www.sookebandb.com
The Seascape Inn is a lovely place that looks out onto the port. The eggs Benedict are a wonderful way to start off the day, and the owner will even take you crab or salmon fishing if you like.

🌴 The Lighthouse Retreat Bed & Breakfast
$$$ bkfst incl.
K, ℜ, 🐾, ⊛
107 West Coast Rd., Sooke
☎646-2345 or 888-805-4448
www.lighthouseretreat sooke.com
Nestled in the magnificent West Coast forest, this lovely B&B offers bright, airy rooms and a private beach. Contrary to what it's name suggests, however, it is not located in lighthouse.

Arundel Manor Bed & Breakfast
$$$ bkfst incl.
980 Arundel Dr.
☎/≈385-5442
www.arundelmanor.com
You can enjoy a quiet, comfortable stay at the Arundel Manor Bed & Breakfast, a charming house built in 1912. Its three rooms are tastefully decorated, and on the side facing the water, the view is that much more striking. To get there, head north on Highway 1.

Sooke Harbour House
$$$$$ bkfst and picnic lunch incl.
🐾, ⊛, ℜ
1528 Whiffen Spit Rd., Sooke
☎642-3421
≈642-6988
www.sookeharbourhouse. com
Mr. and Mrs. Philip will give you a warm welcome at the Sooke Harbour House, their dream home. It's pricey, but rest assured that staying here will make your trip to Vancouver Island a memorable one.

The 28 exquisite rooms are all equipped with a fireplace and decorated with antiques and works of art. Breakfast is served in your room and lunch in the dining room (see p 131).

Restaurants

Inner Harbour and Old Town

Paradiso di Stelle
$
Bastion Square near Wharf St.
For the best coffee in town, go to Paradiso di Stelle, where the Italian tradition is reflected in your cup. The patio, which has a view of the port, is one of the loveliest in all of Victoria.

Ali Baba Pizza
$
1011 Blanshard St.
☎385-6666
Ali Baba Pizza is a real treat. The generous portions are quarters of 30cm pizzas. The pesto pizza is a must!

Yuen's Mountain Restaurant
$
866 Yates St.
☎382-8812
Yuen's Mountain Restaurant offers the ever-popular deluxe Chinese all-you-can-eat buffet!

California Wrap Bar
$
602 Broughton St.
☎382-9727
Open only during the day, the California Wrap Bar is the perfect place to grab something to go: they prepare wraps (rolled sandwiches) of all kinds and delicious fresh juices. You can also sample these standing at the counter or outside on the sidewalk where four stools surround a small table.

Green Cuisine Vegetarian Restaurant
$-$$
Market Square
560 Johnson St.
☎385-1809
Vegetarians should check out Green Cuisine Vegetarian Restaurant, which is 100% vegetarian (no animal or dairy products). From the salad bar to home-made baked goods to organic coffee, there's something for everyone!

Barb's Place
$-$$
Mar-Oct, 11am to dark
Erie St., Fisherman's Wharf
☎384-6515
What is it about being by the sea that brings on a craving for fried, battered food served in newsprint? Walk, drive, bike or bus (no. 30 from downtown) to Barb's Place for your fix of fish and chips, steamed seafood, or other such treats (veggie fare available). The halibut and chips is very good, grease and all!

🌴 Willie's Bakery
$-$$
537 Johnson St.
☎381-8414
This bustling little bakery is also a little café, cozily laid out between wood floors and brick walls. In addition to muffins and other baked goods (sadly, the croissants are not up to scratch), they serve original, full breakfasts *(Mon-Fri 7am to 11:30am, Sat and Sun 7:30am to noon)*. Soup and sandwiches are served for lunch.

Gatsby Mansion
$ (breakfast/lunch)
$$ (afternoon tea)
309 Belleville St.
☎388-9191
If you've awoken with the sun in your eyes and a taste for a special breakfast, head to the Gatsby Mansion for pancakes and similar delicacies, served in a lovely sunroom, cloyingly decorated with wedding portraits. You can't go wrong here for afternoon tea, either

($21.95, 2pm to 4pm). The scones are scrumptious.

Rebar Modern Food
$$
50 Bastion Square
☎361-9223
If you've had one too many dollops of Devon cream with your afternoon tea and feel the need to redeem yourself with some wholesome, inexpensive food, step into Rebar. The menu at this casual, cheerful spot is vegetarian and vegan, and includes some fish and seafood. Among its popular options is the very comforting monk's curry (oyster mushrooms, Japanese eggplant, tofu in a green curry-coconut sauce) and the almond burger. Rebar has acquired such a reputation over the years that its owners have published their own cookbook! A range of fresh fruit and vegetable juices and wheatgrass drinks is available to set you back on the right track. Open for three meals a day.

Garrick's Head Pub
$$
1140 Government St.
☎384-6835
The sunny patio at Garrick's Head Pub, located on a pedestrian street, is a pleasant place to get together over a local beer. The space may be limited inside, but there is a big-screen TV for sports fans.

Swans Brewpub
$$
506 Pandora Ave.
☎361-3310
Locals claim that Swans Brewpub brews and serves the best beer in North America—visitors might not agree. Nevertheless, they make a good effort and also serve typical pub fare. A good place to meet other travellers. Live music Sunday to Thursday.

 John's Place
$$
723 Pandora Ave.
☎389-0711
An eclectic urban crowd, made up more of locals than tourists, is drawn to the warm decor of John's Place. The copious portions of chicken, seafood and pasta, and cheap prices ensure satisfaction. This place is a must for eggs-Benedict lovers and the place is packed for breakfast on weekends. As for cheesecake, let's just say that you won't be able to resist ordering a slice—even if you're already stuffed!

 Suze Lounge & Restaurant
$$
515 Yates St.
☎383-2829
Suze has a terrific atmosphere. The imaginative and very reasonably priced cuisine includes tasty pizza and pasta, good fish dishes and excellent home-made desserts. The pad Thai is excellent, and a "small" bowl is quite sufficient for most appetites! You can choose one of 18 kinds of martinis or order a Suze, the famous French apéritif for which the place is named. Simply put, the place is a site for sore eyes—highly recommended.

Ferris' Oyster Bar & Grill
$$
536 Yates St.
☎360-1284
The pleasant Ferris Oyster Bar & Grill serves West Coast cuisine and excellent seafood. A good atmosphere for group dining.

Vista 18
$$-$$$$
740 Burdett Ave.,
Chateau Victoria hotel
☎382-9258
You'll get a fabulous view of the Inner Harbour and the mountains beyond seated in a comfy armchair in this 18th-floor restaurant, which is open for breakfast, lunch and din-

ner. The menu includes pasta, steak, tuna, lamb and ostrich...in short, something for everyone. Dishes like the West Coast spinach salad with candied smoked salmon and papaya, pan seared salmon soufflé and the game hen and ostrich medallions testify to something creative occurring in the kitchen. Live jazz on Friday and Saturday nights.

Spinnakers Brewpub & Restaurant
$$$
308 Catherine St.
☎386-2739 or 384-6613
Spinnakers serves beer and food in a laid-back setting, with the house specialties listed on big blackboards. The terrace is very well positioned, beckoning guests to kick back and relax. This popular place radiates a festive, convivial atmosphere.

Taj Mahal
$$$
679 Herald St.
☎383-4662
The Taj Mahal, an Indian restaurant, has an eye-catching exterior. Try the house specialties—lamb biryani and tandoori chicken. An excellent vegetarian menu is also available. Highly recommended.

Pablo's Dining Lounge
$$$-$$$$
Dinner only
225 Quebec St.
☎388-4255
Contrary to what you might think, Pablo's is a French restaurant, though paella is available upon request. Located near the Inner Harbour in an elegant Victorian house. Good, but pricey.

 Café Brio
$$$-$$$$
944 Fort St.
☎383-0009
Lovely Café Brio offers an atmosphere that is at once romantic and very welcoming, with wood tables, cozy booths and bar seating, wide-plank wood floors, subdued lighting

and candlelight, and an eclectic range of framed artwork. The cuisine is Pacific Northwest, with a strong emphasis on local ingredients where possible and a seasonally inspired menu that changes daily. Depending on the day, you might find hearts of romaine salad, lemon and garlic marinated lamb sirloin, seared jumbo Alaskan scallops with Jerusalem artichoke chips, and confit of duck with sugar beet and apple and lentil salad; several pasta selections are always available and accompanying wines are suggested for every item on the menu. The extensive wine list highlights B.C. vintages and offers a selection by the glass and half bottle. A tasting menu, three courses paired with wines, is also available *($39 vegetarian, $52 carnivorous)*. Service is knowledgeable and professional. Highly recommended.

The Fairmont Empress Hotel's Bengal Lounge

$$$$
721 Government St.
☎384-1111
Recapturing the atmosphere of the British Empire of Queen Victoria, the very atmospheric Empress Hotel's Bengal Lounge serves a curry buffet featuring Indian specialties all week, except for Friday and Saturday, when live jazz is offered. The place is tastefully decorated with leather furniture, and guests have lots of elbow room. Stop in for a peek, at least.

Bowman's Rib House

$$$$
825 Burdett Ave.
☎385-5380
Bowman's Rib House offers a wide selection of exquisite meats and fresh fish. The steak here is superb and the honky-tonk piano creates a harmonious atmosphere in the dining room.

Il Terrazzo Ristorante

$$$$
555 Johnson St.
☎361-0028
Il Terrazzo is a popular Italian restaurant with a menu made up mainly of pasta dishes. Creamy sauces flavoured with spices and sweet nuts make for some very interesting taste sensations. The clientele consists of young professionals and tourists. The one sour note is that the wine is kept on a mezzanine where all the heat in the room is concentrated, and is thus served at too warm a temperature.

The Fairmont Empress Hotel's Afternoon Tea

$$$$
721 Government St.
☎384-1111
Tea-lovers get together in the Fairmont Empress Hotel for tea with scones served with different kinds of jam. If you've got a big appetite, stop in for afternoon tea, which comes complete with cucumber and cream-cheese sandwiches. The old wood floors, comfortable furniture, giant teapots and courteous service make for an altogether satisfying experience. Be advised, however, it's very pricey in high season.

Scenic Marine Drive

White Heather Tea Room

$-$$
Tue-Sat 9:30am to 5pm Sun 10am to 4pm
1885 Oak Bay Ave.
☎595-8020
If tea at the Empress is a little rich for your blood, get thee to the White Heather Tea

Room. Agnes, the delightful Scottish owner, serves afternoon tea *(1:30pm to 5pm)* as well as breakfast, Sunday brunch, and light lunches on fine bone china and white linen tablecloths in her small, cheerful tea room. You'll find a variety of loose-leaf teas, homemade jam and Devon cream to slather on your homemade scones, baked daily, as well as Scottish shortbread and oatcakes, pinwheel sandwiches and other goodies. At tea time, choose from "The Wee Tea" *($8.25)*, "The Not So Wee Tea" *($12.75)* or "The Big Muckle Giant Tea" *(for two, $31.95)*. Reservations are recommended for both lunch and tea. Warning: Agnes's Scottish brogue is as addictive as her scones!

The Snug Pub

$$$
1175 Beach Dr.
☎598-4556
The Oak Bay Beach Hotel's pub, known as the Snug, serves local and imported beer and light meals. A quiet, well-kept place, it attracts a rather mature clientele, although a younger crowd flocks to the patio in the summer.

From Victoria to the West Coast Trail

17 Mile House

$$-$$$
5126 Sooke Rd., Sooke
☎642-5942
Located right before the entrance to Sooke Harbour Park, 17 Mile House is actually a pub, though its menu is rather more elaborate than that would suggest. The thoroughly laid-back, cozy atmosphere here makes this just the place to quench your thirst after a day of walking along the waterfront in Sooke. Sunday's seafood platter is particularly popular.

Sooke Harbour House
$$$$
dinner only
1528 Whiffen Spit Rd.
☎*642-3421*
The Sooke Harbour House has been praised to the skies by people from all over the world. The Philips's gourmet cuisine has seduced thousands of palates. The hosts settle for nothing but the best and are masters when it comes to preparing local produce. The dining room, set up inside a country house, offers a view of Sooke Harbour. Enjoy the classic ambiance as you take your seat and look over the menu. The dishes, prepared in the Pacific Northwest style, reveal Japanese and French influences. Vegetarian dishes are available. See also p 128.

Entertainment

Bars and Nightclubs

Swans Brewpub
506 Pandora Ave.
☎*361-3310*
Swans Brewpub is a lively place that serves beer brewed right on the premises. A good place to meet other tourists. Live jazz, blues and Celtic music Sunday to Thursday.

Steamer's Public House
570 Yates St.
☎*381-4340*
Steamer's is a good place to have a drink and kick up your heels to an ever-changing lineup of live musical acts.

The Sticky Wicket Pub
919 Douglas St., Strathcona Hotel
☎*383-7137*
The Sticky Wicket Pub is located inside the Strathcona Hotel, just behind the Empress. This place attracts people of all ages and serves good beer. In nice weather,

everyone heads up to the roof for some fun in the sun and a game of volleyball. At **Legends nightclub**, also in the Strathcona, university students dance to Top 40 hits.

Lucky Bar
517 Yates St.
☎*382-LUCK*
Located next to Suze Lounge and Restaurant (see p 129), Lucky Bar is the spot to catch live music almost every night *(cover around $5)*. It's a cozy spot, with a brick wall festooned with a collection of framed photographs. Sunday night is "Brew and View"— catch a flick, sip a beer.

Hugo's Grill and Brewhouse
619 and 625 Courtney St.
☎*920-4846*
Hugo's is a hip nightspot for a twenty- and thirtysomething crowd that congregates in its attractive post-industrial decor of wood-plank floors, exposed ceiling pipes and plenty of brick. A cozy place to sample a glass of ale or lager, brewed right on the spot.

Cultural Activities

Music

Victoria Jazz Society
☎*388-4423*
www.vicjazz. bc.ca
The Victoria Jazz Society can provide you with information on local jazz and blues shows. The Victoria Jazz Festival takes place from late June to mid-July.

The **Victoria Symphony** *(846 Broughton St.,* ☎*385-9771, www.victoria symphony.bc.ca)* presents both classic and contemporary concerts year-round.

The **Pacific Opera Victoria** *(1316B Government St.,* ☎*382-1641, www.pov.bc.ca)*

stages classic operas like *La Bohème* and *The Marriage of Figaro,* and in an effort to make opera accessible to everyone, there are English sub-titles.

Theatre

Kaleidoscope Theatre
520 Herald St.
☎*383-8124*
www.kaleidoscope.bc.ca
The Kaleidoscope Theatre puts on shows for young audiences.

McPherson Playhouse
3 Centennial Square
☎*386-6121*
www.rmts.bc.ca/ mcpherson
The McPherson Playhouse presents plays and musicals.

Royal Theatre
805 Broughton St.
☎*386-6121*
www.rmts.bc.ca/ royal
All dance and classical-music events are held at the Royal Theatre.

Calendar of Events

Following are some of the major annual events taking place in Victoria and area. For a complete list and specific dates, contact Tourism Victoria.

April

Greater Victoria Performing Arts Festival *(Apr and May, various venues,* ☎*386-9223, www.gvpaf.org)*: a variety of musical performances.

Bastion Square Festival of the Arts *(Apr Fri-Sun, May Thu-Sun, Jun to early Oct Wed-Sun, as well as holidays throughout this season, 10:30am to 5:30pm; Bastion Square, Victoria,* ☎*413-3144)*: outdoor arts-and-crafts sale and music.

Victoria International Walking Festival *(mid-Apr, thoughout the city;* ☎ *380-3949 or 877-488-9255, www.walk victoria.ca)*: seven different scenic walks ranging from 5 to 42km.

UNO Festival *(end Apr to early May; various venues;* ☎ *383-2663, www.victoriafringe. com)*: festival of one-person theatre.

May

Victoria Harbour Festival *(mid to late May; Inner Harbour, Victoria,* ☎ *592-9098)*: a variety of activities centred on the harbour during Victoria Day weekend and U.S. Memorial Day weekend. The annual Swiftsure International Yacht Race takes place during the festival (Juan de Fuca Strait).

Manulife Financial Literary Arts Festival *(mid-May; various Victoria venues,* ☎ *381-6722, www.literaryarts festival.org)*: conversations, readings and interviews with some of the world's finest writers.

Fort Rodd Hill Historical Military Encampment *(mid-May; Fort Rodd Hill National Historic Site,* ☎ *478-5849, www. fortroddhill.com)*: military re-enactments and artifacts reflecting a century of B.C.'s naval and military history (1850s to 1950s).

Victoria Highland Games *(mid-May; Royal Athletic Park, Victoria;* ☎ *598-8961, www. victoriahighlandgames.com)*: traditional Scottish games and entertainment.

Victoria Day Parade *(Victoria Day, third Mon in May; Douglas St., Victoria;* ☎ *382-3111)*: traditional parade, complete with marching bands and floats from Victoria and beyond.

Esquimalt Lantern Festival *(end May; West Bay Walkway;* ☎ *383-8557, www.esquimalt. ca/Recreation)* evening parade of hand-crafted lanterns followed by a dance.

Bastion Square Cycling Grand Prix *(end May; downtown Victoria, Saanich and North Saanich)*: professional cyclists compete on closed-loop circuits on city streets.

June

Oak Bay Tea Party *(early Jun; Oak Bay, Victoria, 388-4457, www.oakbayteaparty.com)*: where else to stage a tea party, but behind the "tweed curtain"?

Victoria Conservatory of Music's Garden Tour: *(☎477-4114)* : eight to 10 of Victoria's finest gardens open their gates to the public.

Summer in the Square *(Jun to Sep; Centennial Square, Victoria)*: local music and dance.

Jazzfest International *(end Jun; various venues in downtown Victoria;* ☎ *388-4423 or 888-671-2112, www.vicjazz. bc.ca)*: more than 50 jazz, blues and world-music performances, both free and ticketed.

Folkfest *(Ship's Point, Inner Harbour, Victoria; end Jun to early Jul;* ☎ *388-4728, www. icafolkfest.com)*: multicultural entertainment, food and festivities.

July

Victoria Symphony Summer Music Festival *(first week of Jul; Christ Church Cathedral;* ☎ *385-6515)*: classical music festival.

Victoria Shakespeare Festival *(mid-Jul to early Aug; Victoria;* ☎ *360-0234, www.islandnet. com/~tinconnu)*

"A Bite of Victoria" Food Festival *(Government House;* ☎ *386-6368, www.tourism victoria.com)*: Victoria's restaurants provide inexpensive samples and musicians and artists provide the entertainment.

Canada Day Fireworks *(Jul 1st; Port Sidney Marina, Sidney)*.

Sidney Days Celebration *(Sancha Hall, Sidney)*: Pancake Breakfast.

Confederation Parade *(Beacon Ave., Sidney)*.

August

Latin Caribbean Music Festival *(Market Square, 560 Johnston St.;* ☎ *361-9433 ext. 212/215, www.vircs.bc.ca/ latinfest.html)*: more than 100 performers from Latin America, the Caribbean and North America.

Victoria Fringe Theatre Festival *(383-2663 or 383-7838, www.victoriafringe.com)*: Your best opportunity to take in some innovative theatre performances.

Symphony Splash *(Inner Harbour, Victoria,* ☎ *385-9771, www.victoriasymphony .bc.ca)*: The Victoria Symphony performs from a barge moored in mid-harbour; a very popular event.

First People's Festival *(Royal British Columbia Museum, Victoria, ☎384-3211, www.tourismvictoria.com)*: a celebration of Aboriginal tradition, art and culture.

Dragon Boat Festival *(Inner Harbour, Victoria, ☎472-BOAT, www.victoriadragonboat.com)*: the highlight of this festival, with ancient Chinese cultural and spiritual roots, involves Dragon Boat races, where paddlers compete in a 650m sprint.

Vancouver Island Brewery Blues Bash *(Victoria, ☎388-4423 or 888-671-2112, www.vicjazz.bc.ca)*: blues and R&B performances staged at various locations.

Central Saanich Days *(Centennial Park, Saanichton.)*

Flower Festival *(Sancha Hall, Sidney).*

September

The Great Canadian Beer Festival *(Victoria Conference Centre, ☎383-2332, www.gcbf.com)*: a tasty celebration of craft brewing.

Saanich Fall Fair *(Saanich Fairground, 1528 Stelly's X Rd., Saanich, ☎652-3314, www.tourismvictoria.com)*: Western Canada's oldest continuous agricultural fair.

Classic Boat Festival *(Labour Day weekend, Inner Harbour)*: masts and woode boats crowd the harbour during this festival.

October

Salmon Run *(mid-Oct; Goldstream Provincial Park, 2930 Trans-Canada Hwy., ☎391-2300, www.goldstreampark.com/salmon.htm)*: see millions of Pacific salmon run upriver to spawn and die.

Ghost Bus Tours *(end Oct; Victoria, ☎598-8870)*: the Old Cemeteries Society organizes a tour of Victoria's favourite "haunts."

Halloween Howl *(Panorama Leisure Centre, Sidney).*

Hallowe'en Bonfire & Fireworks *(Tulista Park, Sidney).*

November

Victoria Christmas Festival *(mid-Nov to early Jan, Victoria)*: decorations and activities throughout the city brighten the city during this festive season.

New Saanich Fair Grounds Arts Fair *(1528 Stelly Rd., Brentwood Bay).*

Christmas Bazaar *(Sancha Hall, Sidney).*

December

Eagle Extravaganza *(mid-Dec to late Feb; Goldstream Provincial Park, ☎478-9414)*: hundreds of bald eagles move into the park to pick over the salmon, which have died after spawning in the Goldstream River (see "Salmon Run," Oct). Visitors can view this magnificent spectacle from an eagle-viewing platform.

Christmas at the Butchart Gardens *(Dec to Jan; ☎652-4422, www.butchartgardens.com)*: Victoria's most famous garden is illuminated by tens of thousands of lights and animated by carollers, children's entertainers, a brass band and food.

Lighted Sailpast *(Sidney Wharf, Tulista Park, Sidney).*

Shopping

Eaton Centre
corner of Douglas and Fort sts
☎381-4012
The enormous Eaton Centre has all sorts of boutiques, shops and restaurants. It is several-storeys high and includes an entire block of buildings.

Market Square
255 Johnson St.
☎386-2441
The Market Square is smaller and more intimate than the Eaton Centre. The shops are smaller and a splendid interior courtyard invites shoppers to linger a while.

Munro's
1108 Government St.
☎382-2464
With its stained-glass windows and 8m ceilings, Munro's is reputed to be the most beautiful bookstore in Canada. Good selection of Canadian, English and American books.

Rogers' Chocolates
913 Government St.
☎384-7021
It is worth stopping in at Rogers' Chocolates to see the shop's lovely early-20th-century decor and pair of Art Nouveau lamps from Italy. Victoria Creams, available in a wide variety of flavours, are the specialty of the house.

The Fish Store
Fisherman's Wharf
☎383-6462
Appropriately named, The Fish Store is a wharf-side spot

for fresh fish, shellfish and smoked salmon, as well as herrings to feed to the seals ($1 each).

Silk Road
1624 Government St.
☎ **704-2688**
This lovely shop carries essential oils and other aromatherapy products as well as tea leaves, gorgeous tea pots and other related items. They also offer tea tastings and a wide range of reasonably priced workshops.

Murchie's Tea
1110 Government St.
☎ **383-3112**
Speaking of tea, Murchie's Tea has been a B.C. institution since 1894, around the time when Grandpa Murchie made a special blend for Queen Victoria. Today you can pick up a variety of unique blends in bulk, as well as a boxes of tea bags such as the delicious, ultra-spicy chai. And of course, you can pick up tea paraphernalia and have a cuppa (or a capuccino, if that's more your style) in the adjoining capuccino bar.

If the quaint British side of Victoria stirs your passion for things antique, you might enjoy a stroll along the stretch of Fort Street between Quadra and Cook streets. Known as **Antique Row**, the area is home to a number of shops selling antiques and curios.

Hill's Native Art
1008 Government St.
☎ **385-3911**
Hill's Native Art sells souvenirs and Aboriginal art in different price ranges. Wide choice of art cards.

Vancouver Island and the Gulf Islands

V ast Vancouver Island stretches over 500km along the West Coast, with its southern tip facing the Olympic Mountains in Washington State (U.S.A.).

The island is split into two distinct regions by a chain of mountains that divides the north from the south. The sea has sculpted the west side, creating big, deep fjords; the shoreline on the east side is much more continuous. Most of the towns and villages on the island lie either on the east coast or along the Strait of Georgia, where the Gulf Islands are located. There is another cluster of these islands in the Johnstone Strait, northeast of Vancouver Island.

The forest and fishing industries have provided several generations with a good source of income in this magnificent region. Thanks to the warm currents of the Pacific, the climate is mild all year round, enhancing the quality of life here.

Once isolated from the mainland, islanders now have access to efficient, modern means of transportation. A number of ferries connect the islands and the mainland every day. This chapter offers an overview of several islands worth exploring. During your

trip, you might be lucky enough to spot a whale, a seal or a sea otter. The BC Ferries' captains have sharp eyes and will let you know if they see anything that might interest you.

To help you make the most of your visit to this part of British Columbia, we have outlined four tours:

Tour A: From Victoria to Nanaimo and the Cowichan Valley ★★

Tour B: From Nanaimo to Tofino ★★★

Tour C: From Comox Valley to Port Hardy ★★

Tour D: The Gulf Islands ★★★

Finding Your Way Around

By Plane

There are regular flights from Vancouver to most towns in this region. Seaplanes transport passengers between the Gulf Islands. The majority of these islands and the municipalities on Vancouver Island are served by the following airlines:

Air Canada
☎*888-AIRCANADA or*
888-227-7368
Vancouver
☎*250-688-5515*
www.aircanada.ca
The AirBC affiliate of this company serves Victoria, Nanaimo, Campbell River, Comox and a number of other municipalities.

Baxter Aviation
Nanaimo
☎*754-1066*
Vancouver
☎*800-661-5599*
www.baxterair.com
Baxter Aviation has a fleet of seaplanes that flies between Vancouver and Nanaimo; it also serves other destinations on the island and on the Sunshine Coast.

Kenmore Air
☎*800-543-9595*
www.kenmoreair.com
and
Harbour Air
☎*604-688-1277 or*
800-665-0212
www.harbour-air.com
Kenmore Air and Harbour Air are small airlines (hydroplanes) that offer direct flights between Vancouver and **Mayne Island**.

By Ferry

Visitors interested in travelling from one island to another have access to a vast network of ferries, that ply back and forth between the islands on a daily basis, and provide transportation to the coast.

BC Ferries
1112 Fort St. Victoria
☎*(250) 386-3431 or*
888-223-3779
≈(250) 381-5452
www.bcferries.com
BC Ferries carries passengers between Vancouver Island

(Swartz Bay or Nanaimo) and the mainland (Horseshoe Bay or Tsawwassen), between Tsawwassen and the Gulf Islands (*reservations required for cars*), between Vancouver Island and the Gulf Islands, and between Campbell River and Quadra and Cortes islands. If you are travelling by car it is a good idea to make reservations in the summertime, or to arrive quite early, to avoid a wait.

If you're going from Port Hardy to the Queen Charlotte Islands or Prince Rupert, you can leave your car on the mainland.

BC Ferries provides service between Little River, on the coast east of Comox, and Powell River, on the Sunshine Coast.

BC Ferries also runs a service which links Port McNeill (☎956-4533) to Sointula and Alert Bay.

Lady Rose Marine Services
Port Alberni
☎*(250) 723-8313 or*
800-663-7192
www.ladyrosemarine.com
Lady Rose Marine crosses Barkley sound and links Port Alberni to Bamfield, north of the West Coast Trail, and Ucluelet, south of Long Beach.

By Bus

Island Coach Lines
700 Douglas St., Victoria
☎*(250) 385-4411 or 388-5248*
www.victoriatours.com
This company offers transportation from Nanaimo to Port Alberni, Ucluelet and Tofino, on the west coast of Vancouver Island.

Greyhound Canada
☎*800-661-8747*
www.greyhound.ca
Greyhound Canada provides a coach service between Nanaimo and downtown Vancouver.

Pacific Coach Lines
700 Douglas St., Victoria
☎*(250) 385-4411 or*
800-661-1725
Vancouver
☎*(604) 662-8074*
www.pacificcoach.com
Pacific Coach Lines operates from downtown Vancouver to downtown Victoria in conjunction with BC Ferries. These buses also serve the Gulf Islands.

Laidlaw Coach Lines
700 Douglas St., Victoria
☎*(250) 385-441 or*
800-318-0818
Laidlaw services Victoria-Nanaimo, Nanaimo-Port Hardy and Nanaimo-Tofino.

By Train

E&N (Via Rail)
Pandora Ave. Victoria
☎*800-561-8630 or*
(250) 953-9000 ext. 5800
www.viarail.ca
E&N provides transportation along the east coast of the island. The major stops on this line are Victoria, Duncan, Nanaimo, Qualicum Beach and Courtenay. The train leaves Victoria at 8:15am from Monday to Saturday and at noon on Sunday.

By Car

Car Rentals

Nanaimo

Budget
☎*800-668-3233 or*
(250) 754-7368
www.budget.ca
Budget will pick you up at the ferry terminal.

National
1602 Northfield Rd.
☎*800-387-4747*
www.nationalvictoria.com

Port Hardy

Budget
4850 Byng Rd.
☎*(250) 949-6442 or*
800-668-3233
www.budget.ca

Gulf Islands

The Gulf Islands are not heavily populated, which is probably why there is no public transportation here. Instead, islanders suggest that pedestrians hitchhike to their destination. The wait is never very long, and the experience will allow you to witness the spirit of cooperation and hospitality that makes the reputation of Gulf Island residents. Note that several lodging establishments offer a shuttle service from the port.

By Taxi

Galiano Island

Go Galiano
☎*(250) 539-0202*

Salt Spring Island

Silver Shadow Taxi
☎*(250) 537-3030*

Salt Spring Taxi
☎*(250) 537-9712*

By Scooter

Pender Island

Otter Bay Marina
$75/4hrs

Salt Spring Island

Marine Drive Car Rental
124 Upper Ganges Rd.
☎*(250) 537-6409 or*
(250) 537-5464

By Car

Car Rental

Pender Island

Local Motion Car Rentals
4539 Bedwell Harbour Rd.
☎*(250) 629-3366 or*
888-850-9900

Salt Spring Island

Marine Drive Car Rental
124 Upper Ganges Rd.
☎*(250) 537-6409 or*
(250) 537-5464

By Bicycle

Although the hilly landscape of the Gulf Islands makes cycling quite a challenge, bicycles are the ideal means of transportation for exploring. Make sure you bring plenty of water and food before taking off on your adventure.

Pender Island

Otter Bay Marina
$35/day

Galiano Island

**Galiano Bicycle Rental &
Repair**
36 Burrill Rd.
☎*(250) 539-9906*

Salt Spring Island

Several hotels on Salt Spring loan or rent bicycles. Since the landscape is flatter here than on the other Gulf Islands, cycling is a fun way of getting around.

Practical
Information

Area Code: **250**

To learn more about Vancouver Island before setting out

on your trip, contact the **Tourism Vancouver Island** *(335 Wesley St., Suite 203, Nanaimo, BC, V9R 2T5,* ☎*754-3500).*

Tourist Information

Tour A: From Victoria to Nanaimo and the Cowichan Valley

Mill Bay-Cobble Hill

Mill Bay Travel Info Centre
☎*743-3566 or 743-5099*

Duncan

Duncan Travel Info Centre
381A Trans-Canada Hwy.,
Duncan, BC, V9L 3R5
☎*746-4636*

Lake Cowichan

**Lake Cowichan Tourism
information Centre**
PO Box 824, Lake Cowichan
☎*749-3244*

Chemainus

**Chemainus Travel
Info Centre**
9758 Willow St., PO Box 1311
Chemainus, BC, V0R 1K0
☎*246-3944 or 246-4701*

Nanaimo

Tourism Nanaimo
Beban House
2290 Bowen Rd., V9T 3K7
☎*756-0106 or*
(800) 663-7337

Tour B: From Nanaimo to Tofino

Qualicum Beach

Oceanside Tourism
174 Railway St., PO Box 374,
Qualicum Beach, BC, V9K 1S9
☎*752-2392*
www.oceansidetourism.com

**Qualicum Beach Travel Info
Centre**
2711 West Island Hwy., BC, V9K 2C4
☎*752-9532*
www.qualicum.bc.ca

Parksville

Parksville Visitor Info Centre
PO Box 99, Parksville, BC, V9P 2G3
☎*248-3613*
www.chamber.parksville.
bc.ca

Port Alberni

**Pacific Rim Tourism
Association**
3100 Kingsway, Port Alberni, BC,
V9Y 3B1
☎*723-7529 or 866-725-7529*
www.pacificrimtourism.ca

**Alberni Valley Visitor Info
Centre**
2533 Redford St. RR2, Suite 215,
Comp 10, Port Alberni, BC, V9Y 7L6
☎*724-6535*

Ucluelet

Ucluelet Travel Info Centre
100 Main St., PO Box 428, Ucluelet,
BC, V0R 3A0
☎*726-4641 or 726-7289*
www.uclueletinfo.com

Tofino

**Tofino Long Beach
Chamber of Commerce**
380 Campbell St., PO Box 249,
Tofino, BC, V0R 2Z0
☎*725-3414*
www.island.net/~tofino

Bamfield

**Bamfield Chamber
of Commerce**
☎*728-3228*

Tour C: From Comox
Valley to Port Hardy

Campbell River

**Campbell River Travel
Info Centre**
1235 Shopper's Row, PO Box 400,
Campbell River, BC, V9W 5B6
☎*287-4636 or 800-463-4386*
www.vquest.com/crchamber

Port McNeill

**Port McNeill Travel
Info Centre**
1626 Beach Dr., PO Box 129
Port McNeill, BC, V0N 2R0
☎*956-3131*
www.portmcneill.net

Port Hardy

Port Hardy Travel Info Centre
7250 Market St., Box 249, Port
Hardy, BC, V0N 2P0
☎*949-7622*
www.ph-chamber.bc.ca

Tour D: The Gulf Islands

Salt Spring Island

**Salt Spring Island
Chamber of Commerce**
121 Lower Ganges Rd., Salt Spring
Island, BC, V8K 2T1
☎*537-5252*
www.saltspringtoday.com

Galiano Island

**Galiano Island Travel
Info Centre**
2590 Sturdies Bay Rd., Box 73,
Galiano, BC, V0N 1P0
☎*539-2233*
www.galianoisland.com

Gabriola Island

**Gabriola Island Chamber of
Commerce**
575 North Rd., Box 249, Gabriola
Island, BC, V0R 1X0
☎*247-9332*
www.gabriolaisland.org

Saturna Island

Contact **Tourism Vancouver
Island** *(see above for address).*

**Quadra Island and
Cortes islands**

Contact the **Campbell River
Tourism Office** *(see above for
address).*

Pender Islands

**Pender Island Chamber
of Commerce**
c/o Pender Island Lumber
3338 Port Washington Rd.
Pender Island, V0N 2M0
☎*888-420-3737*

Exploring

★★

Tour A: From Victoria
to Nanaimo and
the Cowichan Valley

*Head out of downtown Victoria
on Douglas Street and take the
Trans-Canada Highway 1
North toward Duncan and
Nanaimo.*

Travellers driving north from
Victoria will have the chance
to take in the beautiful region
of **South Cowichan**, where
lovely views of Saanich Islet
and the strait that separates
Vancouver Island from the
mainland can be glimpsed all
along the road. The **North
Cowichan** area begins in the
city of Maple Bay. This region
opens right onto the ocean,
and its towns are justifiably
proud of their setting.

Mill Bay-Cobble Hill

This is your first stop in the
region of South Cowichan,
which boasts Mill Bay's large
shopping emporium, the **Mill
Bay Centre** *(Hwy 1, Mill Bay
Rd. exit,* ☎*743-5500)*, comprising some 40 shops, including
grocery stores and clothing
boutiques. Mill Bay Road,
which later turns into
Shawnigan-Mill Bay Road and
then Shawnigan-Cobble Hill
Road, will lead you to Cobble
Hill, a region of parks and
vineyards (see Cowichan
Valley Wines section). Another
attraction in Cobble Hill is

Cowichan Valley Wines ★★★

Just south of the city of Duncan, on a **wine route** open to tourists, lie the vineyards whose wines are among the most renowned on Vancouver Island. Most properties are accessible from Hwy. 1, between Duncan and Victoria. Do not hesitate to pay wine growers a visit: they will be pleased to have you sample their nectars! The entrances are not always easy to find, so look out for particular road-signs (often a bunch of grapes) that will indicate where to make a turn. Those travelling during the low season are advised to call ahead for an appointment.

The Cowichan Valley vineyards have slowly but surely acquired a good reputation. The region's mild climate, sandy beaches and peaceful bays, as well as the beauty of its rural landscapes, have attracted scores of poets and nature lovers. Wine growers from the world over increasingly covet this part of Vancouver Island, and many have managed to set themselves up here. A visit to the following five places is highly recommended: **Vigneti Zanatta**, **Cherry Point Vineyards**, **Blue Grouse Vineyards & Winery**, **Merridale Cider** and **Alderlea Vineyards**.

Vigneti Zanatta *(visits and wine tastings by appoint-* *ment, Sat and Sun 1pm to 4pm; 5039 Marshall Rd., RR3, Duncan,* ☎ *748-2338,* ≈ *748-5684).* The Zanatta family has been producing wine for 40 years. Their vineyard stretches across the horizon, and it has aquired other parcels of land on the hillside over the years. After intensive studies in Italy, Loretta Zanatta developed a personal technique and bouquet. The result: wines made the Italian way, as simply as possible, which respect the flavour of the grape. The Zanatta family receives visitors by appointment, but those who arrive unannounced are also welcome to catch a glimpse of the splendid vineyards.

Cherry Point Vineyards *(every day 11:30am to 6pm; 840 Cherry Point Rd., RR3, Cobble Hill,* ☎ *743-1272,* ≈ *743-1059).* Never has moraine been more welcoming! The 14ha (34 acres) of undulating hills that make up this property are reminiscent of an ancient glacial valley. Cherry Point's success certainly lies in the expertise of the proprietors, Wayne and Helena Ulrich. Since 1990, the couple has been dedicating all of its time and energy to the growth of their grapes in an effort to draw out their intricate flavours. The Ulrichs will be delighted to share their working philosophy with their guests. A new feature:

you can spend the night on the property, as Cherry Point is also a Bed & Breakfast. You can savour a glass of white Pinot while gazing out your bedroom window during a wonderful stay at the farm. A pleasant, worthwhile experience.

Merridale Cider *(Mon to Sat 10:30am to 4:30pm; 1230 Merridale Rd., RR1, Cobble Hill,* ☎ *743-4293)* makes its cider the traditional way. The owner, Al Piggott, grows his own apples in his 6ha (14 acres) orchard. It is, for that matter, the only orchard in Canada exclusively dedicated to the production of cider.

The **Blue Grouse Vineyards** *(by appointment; 4365 Blue Grouse Rd., RR7, Duncan,* ☎ *743-3834,* ≈ *743-9305)* lie in the heart of Cowichan Valley. The owner, Hans Kiltz, offers interested parties a very informative tour of his vineyards. Friendly reception.

Alderlea Vineyards *(Thu to Sun 1pm to 5pm; 1751 Stamps Rd., RR1,* ☎/≈ *746-7122).* Some new cloned vines have been imported from France to increase the production of Pinot Gris, Pinot Noir and Maréchal Foch. After a number of experiments, Roger Dosman, the owner, now knows which grapes adapt best to the island's climate. Happy wine tasting!

Quarry Regional Park ★ (see p 151).

Shawnigan Lake

Approximately 10min on the road heading west from Mill Bay and Cobble Hill lies the lovely village of Shawnigan Lake. This small town's main attribute is, of course, the **lake** of the same name. It is the largest body of water in the region. The other major attraction here is the **Old Kinsol Trestle ★ ★ ★** *(from Shawnigan Lake, take Glen Eagles Rd., turn right on Renfrew Rd. W., then continue on foot for 10min; information: South Cowichan Chamber of Commerce, ☎743-3566)*, one of the longest wooden railway bridges in the world. Built in 1921, it was once used for the transport of copper ore.

Duncan

The **Quw'utsun' Cultural and Conference Centre ★ ★** *($11; early May to late Sep every day 9am to 5pm, Oct to late Apr every day 10am to 5pm; 200 Cowichan Way, ☎877-746-8119 or 746-8119)*, located in Duncan, was founded by the Cowichan First Nation in 1987. It has become a major tourist attraction over the last few years. The centre enables the Cowichan people to introduce others to their culture through interpretive activities and shows, as well as handicraft and art exhibitions. The tour is detailed and most interesting; a beautiful, well-made film, imbued with the spirit of the community, will enthral viewers.

Located near the Trans-Canada Highway and the Cowichan River, the centre is composed of several reconstructions of traditional structures, a restaurant, a café, a gallery and souvenir shop, and a historical interpretive centre that offers a totem-sculpture workshop. The art gallery sells only high quality hand-made

articles, such as baskets, drums, jewellery, knitwear, original or limited edition prints, soapstone sculptures, dolls, blankets, books, as well as wood sculptures inspired by Salish, Nuu Cha Nulth (West Coast) and Kwagulth motifs.

The **Judy Hill Gallery** *(mid-May to late Sep Mon-Fri 9am to 7pm, Sat-Sun 9:30am to 5:30pm; Oct to mid-May Mon-Sat 9:30am to 17:30pm; 22 Station St., ☎746-6663)* boasts the best Aboriginal art collection in the region. This art gallery represents close to 100 artists, all of whom are either painters, sculptors or weavers. Visitors will also find authentic "Cowichan" sweaters here.

The **BC Forest Discovery Centre** *($10; mid-May to early Sep every day 10am to 6pm; early Sep to mid-May every day 10am to 4pm, closed during winter; 2892 Drinkwater, ☎715-1113)* offers rides on a steam locomotive and the chance to get acquainted with Vancouver Island's forest industry. Numerous activities are organized, as are fascinating demonstrations of bygone ways of woodcutting. Situated only 1km north of Duncan via the Trans-Canada Highway.

Maple Bay-Crofton

Located 10min from Duncan via Tzouhalem Road, Maple Bay is bordered by a lovely **bay ★ ★**. This is a paradise for yachting enthusiasts, canoeists and even divers, who can sound the depths Cousteau's team once explored.

A very pretty route leads to Crofton: from Maple Bay, take Herd Road to Osborne Bay Road. Crofton is especially known for being the point of departure of the ferry that travels to Salt Spring Island. Its main tourist attraction is the **Somenos Marsh Wildlife Refuge ★** (see p 151), which

shelters over 200 species of birds.

Lake Cowichan

Lake Cowichan is a small town built on the shores of the lake of the same name. Located 31km east of Duncan, it is easily reached via Hwy. 18. The lake is nicknamed *Kaatza*, which means "the big lake." Thirty kilometres long, it is one of the biggest lakes on the island.

The lovely **Kaatza Station Museum** *(mid-May to mid-Sep every day 9am to 4pm; mid-May to mid-Sep Mon-Fri 9am to 4pm; Saywell Park, South Shore Rd., ☎749-6142)* explains the region's history and the remarkable influence the forest industry has had on the area. Visitors will also see a locomotive dating from 1928, which was once used to transport logs.

Fifty kilometres farther west, via a forest road, are **Carmanah Walbran Park ★ ★ ★** and **Carmanah Pacific Provincial Park ★ ★ ★** *(information at the Cowichan Lake tourist information centre, ☎749-3244)*, magnificent wild expanses encompassing close to 17,000ha of ancient forests where certain trees stand almost 100m tall (see p 151).

★ Chemainus

Chemainus is a small town located about 20km north of Duncan. It owes its existence to the forest industry and probably would have sunk into oblivion had it not been for the ingenuity of its residents. The future looked bleak when the local sawmill shut down, but people here took control of the situation, reopening the facility and creating new jobs. Later, the town organized a big competition, calling upon various artists to cover the

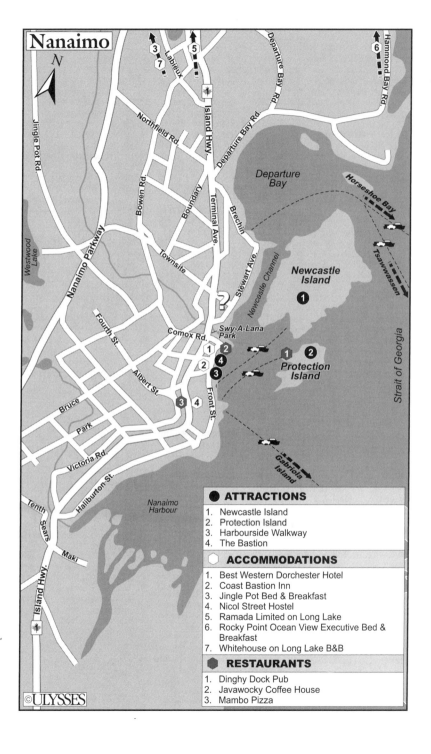

Nanaimo

N

● ATTRACTIONS
1. Newcastle Island
2. Protection Island
3. Harbourside Walkway
4. The Bastion

⬡ ACCOMMODATIONS
1. Best Western Dorchester Hotel
2. Coast Bastion Inn
3. Jingle Pot Bed & Breakfast
4. Nicol Street Hostel
5. Ramada Limited on Long Lake
6. Rocky Point Ocean View Executive Bed & Breakfast
7. Whitehouse on Long Lake B&B

⬡ RESTAURANTS
1. Dinghy Dock Pub
2. Javawocky Coffee House
3. Mambo Pizza

©ULYSSES

walls with murals illustrating the history of Chemainus. The 30 or so murals are worth the trip; it takes about an hour to see them all. The tourist office distributes a map containing a description of each one.

Nanaimo

Nanaimo is an important town because of its link to the coast, where ferries pick up hundreds of tourists headed for this region. It lies 35km from Vancouver, across the Strait of Georgia, and 1h 30min from Victoria by way of the Trans-Canada. Vacationers heading for the northern part of Vancouver Island or for Long Beach, to the west, pass through Nanaimo. This town is much more than just a stopover point, however; its seaport is graced with a pleasant promenade. Furthermore, visitors can easily catch a ferry to **Newcastle Island ★** and **Protection Island ★** to use the outdoor facilities and take in the view of Nanaimo. You can see all the local attractions, including old Nanaimo, on a walking tour.

Upon entering Nanaimo, Hwy. 1 becomes Nicol Street. Turn right on Comox Road and then immediately left on Arena Street, which will take you to Swy-A-Lana Park (you can leave your car there).

Go into the park and turn right when you reach the waterfront, where you'll find **Harbourside Walkway ★★**, a pleasant promenade lined with parks, historic sites and shops.

The Bastion ★ *($1; early Jun to early Sep every day 10:30am to 4:30pm; ☎753-1821)* was built by the Hudson's Bay Company in 1853 in order to protect the new trading post and the local residents. Its construction was supervised by two Quebecers, Jean-Baptiste Fortier and Leon Labine, both employees of the

company. The Bastion never came under attack and was abandoned when the company left in 1862. It was later used as a prison, and has served as a gathering place and a museum since 1910. Daily at noon, watch the cannon-firing, complete with Scottish bagpiping and red-coated Mounties.

The **ferry** *(hourly 9:10am to 11:10pm; ☎753-8244)* for Protection Island departs from the end of **Commercial Inlet**. This little island is more or less a suburb of Nanaimo, with residents commuting to their jobs in town during the week. You can enjoy a refreshing beer and some excellent fish and chips at the island's floating pub (see p 166).

Nanaimo is renowned among scuba divers. The water is at its most beautiful between November and April (see p 156). Many people come here to go bungee jumping as well.

Tour B: From Nanaimo to Tofino

From Hwy. 19, take exit 46 toward Parksville.

Parksville

Parksville is a little town that is resolutely tourism-oriented. Its magnificent **beach ★★★** boasts spectacular tides and will delight any visitor. In August, the Parksville Beach Festival takes place here which includes the **International Sandcastle Competition** *(☎248-3613)*.

Visitors can also stop by **Rho-dodendron Lake**, south of Parksville along Hwy. 19. A forest road will lead you toward a **wild rhododendron reserve** *(☎248-3613)*.

The area is popular with families, with a long, sandy beach, shallow waters and an amusement park that dominates the rather unattractive strip of highway that leads to Parksville's quieter, more attractive sister town of Qualicum Beach (see below).

Qualicum Beach

Lured by the fine weather, many retirees settle in Qualicum Beach. This region gets more hours of sunshine than those farther south. Hwy. 19 is busy around Parksville and Qualicum Beach, whose main attraction is their series of beaches.

Thankfully, Qualicum Beach has been spared the wanton development you'll find in Parksville—a town by-law requiring restaurants to provide table service ensures that you won't find any golden arches here. It is an attractive little town that can be toured in no time and beyond the beach and the shops on Second Avenue, there are a couple of attractions worth your time. The Oceanside region, which comprises Parksville and Qualicum, is home to a number of artisans; pick up a copy of "A Guide to Artists and Studios" from the tourist office and tour to your heart's content!

Included in the guide is the **Old School House Gallery and Art Centre** *(Mon noon to 5pm, Tue-Sat 10am to 5pm, summer Sun noon to 5pm; 122 Fern Rd. W., ☎752-6133)*, which stages monthly exhibits and houses artists' studios and a gift shop, with some lovely arts and crafts created on the island. Occupying a former school (1914-1985) that was converted to its current vocation in 1988, it is operated by a dedicated group of volunteers.

Located about 2km east of Qualicum Beach, the **Milner Gardens and Woodland ★★**

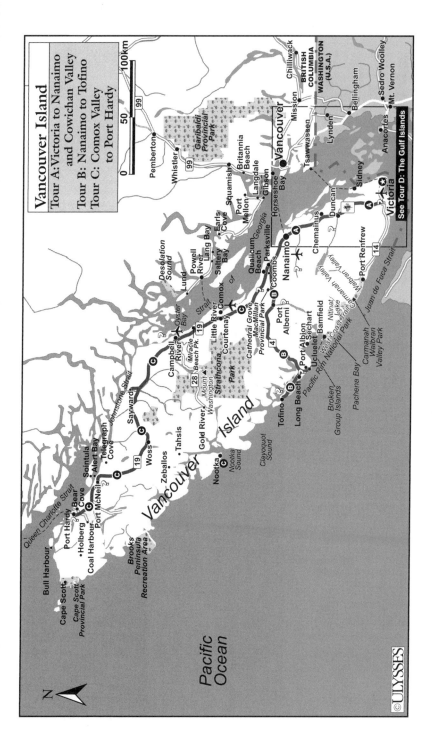

Vancouver Island

Tour A: Victoria to Nanaimo
and Cowichan Valley
Tour B: Nanaimo to Tofino
Tour C: Comox Valley
to Port Hardy

0   50   100km

See Tour D: The Gulf Islands

Pacific
Ocean

N

($10; early Apr to late Oct Thu-Sun and holidays 10am to 5pm, tea room 1pm to 4pm; 2179 West Island Highway, ☎752-6153, www.milner gardens.org) was opened to the public in 2001. Once the estate and garden of philanthropist, businessman and lawyer Ray Milner and his wife Veronica, a gifted artist and gardener who was also a distant relative of the late Diana, Princess of Wales, the estate was given to Malaspina University-College in 1996, two years before Mrs. Milner's death. Horticulture students have a field day in this fabulous 28ha seaside property, which harbours old-growth Douglas firs and cedars, some of which are up to 500 years old, over 60m high and 2m in diameter (ask staff to point out the oldest ones or look for marker no. 6). Interspersed throughout the property are formal gardens, herb gardens and exotic tree species, but the overall impression is that of a very naturalistic, harmonious ensemble. The views of the northern Gulf Islands in the Strait of Georgia are unsurpassed, and the peace and tranquility of the place are broken only by the barking of sea lions or the cry of the many eagles that visit. Prince Charles was impressed enough to sketch this view during his visit with Diana in 1986; Queen Elizabeth and Prince Phillip visited the following year and stayed in the Milner home. Built in the 1930s in a style reminiscent of a Ceylonese tea-plantation house, much of the residence is open to visitors and a tea room has recently been added in the drawing room; refreshments are also available at the gift shop, where they can be enjoyed by the pool—civilized, indeed! Visitors are provided with a self-guided brochure, and assistance is available for mobility-challenged visitors. If you can, visit during the peak of the gorgeous rhododendron

bloom (late Apr to mid-Jun). Even those who don't consider themselves gardening enthusiasts will enjoy a stroll through this magical spot. Call to inquire about special events.

Coombs

On your way west, stop in Coombs, a small community of 400 inhabitants whose **Old Country Market ★** piques the curiosity of passers-by. Built in 1975, this unusual place now lodges a family of goats!

Butterfly World and Gardens ★★ *($7; mid-Mar to late Mar and early May to late Sep every day 10am to 5pm; Apr and Oct every day 10am to 4pm; 1 km west of Coombs via Hwy. 4; 1080 Winchester Rd., ☎248-7026)*. Come visit the foremost artificial butterfly habitat in Canada. A tropical forest has been laid out in a controlled environment in order to allow 80 species of butterflies to flutter about in total freedom. If passing through Coombs, Butterfly World and Gardens is an absolute must.

The route to Port Alberni, passes through **Cathedral Grove MacMillan Provincial Park ★★★** (see p 152)

Port Alberni

Like many towns in British Columbia, Port Alberni owes its existence to the forest industry, fishing and trade. Its harbour is linked to the Pacific by a large canal, putting the town at an advantage as far as shipping is concerned. Port Alberni is also the gateway to the west coast of Vancouver Island. When you reach the top of the mountains surrounding Mount Arrowsmith, at an altitude of nearly 2,000m, you're almost at Port Alberni. Until recently, the range of activities in Port Alberni has been rather lim-

ited, but two new attractions have recently been added.

Alberni Valley Museum *(donations accepted; May to late Sep every day 10am to 5pm, Thu until 8pm; Oct to late Apr Mon-Sat 10am to 5pm, Thu until 8pm; 4225 Wallace St., ☎723-2182)* has an assorted collection of exhibits on the history, culture and art of the region.

The **Steam Train** *($3; weekends mid-May to late Sep, every hour between 11am and 4pm; corner Third Ave. and Argyle St., ☎732-1376)* has rides on a restored two-stroke steam locomotive dating from 1929, which used to transport wood via Port Alberni. In the next few years, the town hopes to extend the ride, which is currently rather short.

Port Alberni is also renowned for its many salmon-fishing spots. Information can be obtained at the tourist office.

Salmon can be found in the local waters. They are born in the rivers, and after spending a good part of their life in the sea, return there to spawn, much to the delight of both commercial and amateur fishers.

Keep left as you enter Port Alberni. Take Port Alberni Highway to Third Avenue, turn left on Argyle Street and then right toward the harbour. The **Harbour Quay** is a pleasant place to have a cup of coffee and inquire about which boats can take you to Pacific Rim National Park for the day. In the middle of the public square, you'll see a fountain adorned with granite sculptures showing the life cycle of the salmon.

The **M.V. Lady Rose** *(call for various rates and operation hours; Harbour Quay, ☎723-8313 or 800-663-7192, www.ladyrosemarine.com)* offers year-round transportation between Port Alberni and

Bamfield, at the north end of the West Coast Trail.

During summer, the **Frances Barkley** carries passengers to and from Ucluelet and the Broken Group Islands, south of Long Beach. All sorts of discoveries await you on these trips; make sure to bring along a camera, a pair of binoculars and a raincoat.

On your way out of the port, turn left on Third Avenue and take Hwy. 4 in the direction of Tofino. This scenic road runs along a mountainside, passing through valleys and beside rivers. At the end, turn right toward Ucluelet.

★
Ucluelet

Located at the south end of Long Beach, Ucluelet is a tiny town whose main street is lined with old wooden houses. In the past, the only way to get here was by boat. The local economy is based on fishing and tourism. Over 200 species of birds can be found around Ucluelet. Migrating grey whales swim in the coves and near the beaches here between the months of March to May, making whale-watching one of the main attractions on the west coast.

At the south end of the village, in **He Tin Kis Park ★★**, there is a wooden walkway leading through a small temperate rain forest beside Terrace Beach. This short walk highlights beauty of this type of vegetation. The walk through the park is now part of the **Wild Pacific Trail**, a 2.7km loop that takes in the **Amphitrite Point Lighthouse ★**, which has stood on the shore since 1908. In those days, this area was known as the "cemetery of the Pacific" because so many ships had run up onto the reefs here. The wreckage of one tall ship still lies at the

bottom of the sea near the point. The Canadian Coast Guard has a shipping checkpoint offshore (*guided tours available during summer*).

This short loop can be walked in well under an hour and is definitely worth your time. A community initiative, the Wild Pacific Trail will be completed in several stages and will eventually join the Long Beach section of Pacific Rim National Park. The second phase of the trail, a 4km loop around Big Beach (end of Matterson Dr.), has recently been added. Heed the signs warning you to keep well off the rocks, as big wave surges are common. Here, views of the Broken Group Islands are magnificent and in spring, you may well catch sight of migrating grey whales and other marine mammals. Keep an eye out for eagles, too.

To get the most out of a walk along this or other trails in the area, book a hike with naturalist and biologist Bill McIntyre (*Long Beach Nature, half-day tour $160/5 pers; ☎ 726-7099*). Bill has a number of different tours available and is an absolutely amazing source of information on the rich waters, land and sky around his home—here's your chance to find out what a "nurse-log" is! He and his wife also run their own B&B (see p 160).

Pacific Rim National Park Reserve, Long Beach Unit

Pacific Rim National Park Reserve, Long Beach Unit (see also p 152), generally simply referred to as Long Beach, begins just outside Ucluelet and takes in the coast until just before Cox Bay, outside of Tofino. Along the way, you'll find nine different trails, all less than 5km long and all well indicated along the Pacific Rim Highway.

Stop by at the **Parks Canada office** (*Easter to Oct; Hwy. 4; ☎ 726-4212*) to pick up a map.

Along the way, you will find the **Wickaninnish Centre** (*free admission; mid-Mar to mid-Oct every day 10:30am to 6pm*), a small interpretive and information centre where you can view films (in English and French) on the natural life of the area. Also on site is the Wickaninnish Restaurant (*mid-Mar to mid-Oct, 11am to 10pm*). Although nobody's raving about the food, it would be difficult to upstage the view.

★
Tofino

Tofino, situated at the northwest end of Long Beach, is a lively town where the many visitors chat about sunsets and the outdoors. Spanish explorers Galiano and Valdes, who discovered this coast in the summer of 1792, named the place after Vincente Tofino, their hydrography professor.

Tofino has a population of just over 1000; during summer, this number quadruples. The town itself is nothing much to look at; vacationers come here to enjoy the sun and sand at Long Beach. The water is rather cold, however. Whale-watching and salmon fishing draw tourists as well.

This town is also an artists' colony. The local painters and sculptors draw much of their inspiration from the unspoiled landscape of the west coast.

Tofino is located on Clayoquot Sound, which is studded by a number of islands and coastal inlets. The area made national headlines in the mid-1980s, when local environmentalists, Aboriginal peoples and townspeople staged a logging blockade—the first in Canada—in protest against the planned commercial logging of old-growth temperate rain forest

The Grey Whale

The grey whale (*Eschrichtius robustus*), summers in the Arctic Ocean and the Bering Strait, where food is plentiful; some stay farther south, around Vancouver Island.

The female grey can weigh up to 40 tonnes and measure between 10 and 15m. The actual colour of the grey whale is pearl grey, but its body generally bears white scars left by the various parasites that cling to its skin.

Almost hunted to extinction in the 19th century, grey whales have been protected for over half a century and the population is no longer at risk.

Grey whales are the only bottom-feeding baleen whales. They swallow a huge quantity of water, which they expel through the baleen, bony fringes that hang in their mouths, retaining only the plankton floating in it.

Just as winter begins to take hold in the north, the whales begin their long migration south to their calving grounds in the calm bays on the Pacific coast of Baja California. They travel a distance of more than 8,000km in no more than five days, never even stopping for food. The whales travel through December and stay until March.

When the migration begins, half of the females are pregnant, having mated with the males the previous winter. Because the gestation period lasts 12 months, the mother has time to return to the mating grounds to give birth.

Most whale sightings occur during the migration north, particularly in March and April. The best place for whale-watching is on the west coast of Vancouver Island; Victoria also offers a great many opportunities.

Every year, close to 19,000 grey whales undertake a 16,000km migratory journey from the Baja peninsula, in Mexico, to the Bering and Chukchi Seas, off Alaska and Siberia. The huge mammals spend the whole summer here consuming the vast schools of krill that abound in these regions.

Several festivities are organized in Tofino to mark the event. See p 157 for whale-watching companies.

There is a day-trip to the only **Hot Springs** on Vancouver Island. The round trip only takes 2hrs and allows you to see some whales and bald eagles. You reach the hot springs after a long boat ride, which lets you off at the start of a 2km path through the woods. A 20min walk through the rain forest leads to the hot springs, which flow into the sea. You can jump from the boiling water into the refreshing seawater. It's great for the circulation, but watch out for the strong ocean currents! Here are the names of a few companies that offer trips to the hot springs:

Chinook Charters
$85
450 Campbell
☎*725-3431 or 800-665-3646*

Sea Trek
$60
441B Campbell
☎*725-4412 or 800-811-9155*

If you want to learn more about the rich (and increasingly rare) rain-forest ecosystem in this temperate region, take a look at the **Rainforest Interpretative Centre** *(free; 451 Main St., ☎725-2560)*. **Friends of Clayoquot Sound** *(corner of Neil St. and First St., ☎725-4218)* is an organization that protects the forests and makes sure companies respect the governmental agreements; if companies do not respect these agreements, the group

on Meares Island, near Tofino. After two decades of protests, an area of some 350,000ha was declared a UNESCO Biosphere Reserve in 2000. Some 110,000ha of this are legally protected as provincial and national parks, as well as ecological reserves, and the remainder consists of buffer areas intended for sustainable development. If you do nothing else while in the area, set aside some time to visit the

giant cedars, spruces, firs and hemlocks on Meares Island; it really is a magical place. A boardwalk trail was built in 1993 by the local First Nations in order to provide access while protecting the soil from trampling.

From mid-March to mid-April, Tofino lives for the **Whale Festival**, a month in which the global grey-whale population passes through the region.

returns to block the logging roads. In a region where an ancient tree can fetch $100,000, it's an uphill battle. You can gain in-depth knowledge about the state of the forest and the organization's activities, and support their commendable efforts by buying a T-shirt or a poster.

Meares Island is one of the Clayoquot Sound islands that has a large area of old-growth forest, ancient trees that were here well before the arrival of the Europeans. To get there, simply go to the Fourth Street Wharf and look for the yellow boat called **Salty** (*$20 round-trip;* ☎ *725-3793*). You can take a long walk on the island among these gigantic 1,000-year-old trees.

The lovely **Tonquin Beach** is a 20min walk from Tofino (*take First Street to the south, turn right on Arnet Road and then right again on Tonquin Road*). If you're not able to go all the way to Long Beach, Tonquin Beach will suffice. It's smaller, but very pretty.

★
Bamfield

Situated on the **Barkley Sound** fjord on Vancouver Island's west coast, **Bamfield** is a charming, rather remote little village that can be reached from **Port Alberni** or **Lake Cowichan** via a network of forest roads that are dusty in summer and muddy in winter. Equip yourselves with a good map, keep your headlights on and always give way to timber trucks, especially those behind you.

The region is a little paradise for outdoor activities and lovers of thousand-year-old forests. Bamfield is also one of the starting points of the famous **West Coast Trail ★ ★ ★**, which cuts through **Pacific Rim National Park ★ ★ ★**. This trail extends over the southeast coast

of Barkley Sound, between the villages of **Bamfield** and **Port Renfrew**. This "Lifesaving Trail," a 77km-long path, was laid out at the turn of the century to help rescue shipwrecked sailors whose vessels frequently crashed against the coast's ominous reefs. These days, the trail attracts hikers from all over the world. Reservations are required and so is a good deal of preparation (see p 154).

Tour C: From Comox Valley to Port Hardy

Denman Island & Hornby Island

To the delight of those who enjoy tranquillity, the tourists who flock to the gulf islands tend to ignore these two magnificent islands in the north.

Great care is taken to safeguard the quality of life on these two islands; the residents don't want rapid, destructive development to take place. This doesn't mean they are against tourists — on the contrary! The inhabitants of these islands enjoy living here and are more than willing to share the natural beauty with you.

Since most tourists head to Hornby to enjoy its magnificent beaches, Denman is the more peaceful of the two islands. Both islands have paved roads allowing beautiful trips by bike or on foot. Bike is definitely the best way to explore the harmonious wilderness of these islands. There are also some sheer cliffs that drop off into the sea, and the view is even more breathtaking when you follow the steep coast by sea kayak. The ferry to Denman Island departs from Buckley Bay, north of Qualicum Beach.

Comox Valley

With a population of 25,000, the Comox Valley is the third largest region on the island after Victoria and Nanaimo. It's also the only place in the province where the ski and golf seasons overlap, allowing you to practise these two sports within the same week if you're in the Okanagan Valley between April and May.

The towns of Cumberland, Comox and Courtenay are unique urban areas located between the glaciers of Strathcona Provincial Park and the east coast of the island. They are idyllic places for golfing and skiing, not to mention kayaking, fishing and mountain biking.

Campbell River

Campbell River is a choice destination for fans of salmon fishing. This sport can be enjoyed here year-round, and five varieties of salmon frequent the local waters. When you get to town, take the time to go to **The Museum at Campbell River ★** (*$5; mid-May to late Sep Mon-Sat 10am to 5pm, Sun noon to 5pm; Oct to mid-May Tue-Sun noon to 5pm; 470 Island Highway, opposite Sequoia Park, Fifth Ave.,* ☎*287-3103 or 287-8043*), which is interesting not only for its elegant architecture but also for its exhibits on Aboriginals and pioneers. Its collection includes a number of artifacts from Campbell River's early days. Furthermore, a significant part of the museum is devoted to Aboriginal engravings, sculpture and jewellery.

On your way into the centre of town, stop for a walk along **Discovery Pier ★** (*Government Wharf*), from which you can admire the Strait of Georgia and the Coast Mountains. At the end, turn right and walk down Shoppers Row, where you can purchase souvenirs, food or basic necessities. The Travel InfoCentre is located on this street as well.

As you leave town, head for Gold River on Hwy. 28. From mid-August to mid-October, you can see the salmon swimming upriver at the **Quinsam Salmon Hatchery ★** *(every day 8am to 4pm; Hwy. 28, ☎287-9564)* on the Campbell River.

Back on Hwy. 28, continue westward to Gold River and Nootka Sound.

Nootka Sound

The Spanish sailed these waters first, in 1774, though it was Captain James Cook who came ashore and claimed the land for England in 1778. You can explore this region, which is steeped in history, by taking a boat tour from Nootka harbour *(call for schedules and fares ☎283-2325).*

Backtrack to Campbell River and head toward Port Hardy on Highland Hwy. 19.

Sayward

When you leave the highway at Sayward Junction, stop at the **Cable Cookhouse ★** *(☎282-3433).* The exterior of this building is made of cables coiled on top of one another. Lumber companies once used these cables to transport wood to the train. More than 2km of cables cover the walls of this restaurant. The forest industry drives the economy of the little town of Sayward. Each July, on **World Championship Logger Sports Day**, lumberjacks come here to demonstrate their skill. This region is best explored by boat. Magnificent Johnstone Strait is dotted with lovely islands and teeming with marine animal life.

★★
Telegraph Cove

This little paradise set back from the eastern shore of Vancouver Island was once the end point of a telegraph line that ran along the coast, hence the name. Later, a wealthy family set up a sawmill on land they had purchased around the little bay. From that point on, time stopped; the little houses have been preserved, and the boardwalk alongside the bay is punctuated with commemorative plaques explaining the major stages in the village's history. Today, vacationers come here to go fishing, scuba diving and whale-watching. If you're lucky, you might catch a glimpse of a seal, an otter or even a whale from the boardwalk.

Be careful along the last kilometre of the road to Telegraph Cove. A local lumber company's trucks haul huge logs along this little secondary road, which leads to Beaver Cove. According to the highway code, these vehicles have the right of way.

Port McNeill

Farther north lies Port McNeill, a town of 2,500 inhabitants. It is the regional centre of three large lumber companies. **North Island Forest Tours ★★** *(free; 5hr tour; Jul and Aug Mon-Fri; North Island Forestry Centre, Port McNeill, ☎956-3844)* will take you into the forest or along the local rivers so that you can see how trees are felled and how the giant trunks are handled. You must reserve a seat and bring along a snack.

Second only to the forest industry, boat touring is very important to the local economy. Visitors to this region can also enjoy wonderful fishing trips and whale-watching excursions in the strait. Native

culture is well represented here, especially in **Sointula** and **Alert Bay**, on the neighbouring islands, which are served by ferries several times a day.

★★
Alert Bay

At the **U'mista Cultural Center ★** *($5; mid-May to early Sep every day 9am to 5pm, early Sep to mid-May Mon-Fri 9am to 5pm; Front St., ☎974-5403),* you can learn about the Potlatch ("to give") ceremony through the history of the U'mista Aboriginal community. Missionaries tried to ban the ceremony; there was even a law forbidding members of the community from dancing, preparing objects for distribution or making public speeches. The ceremony was then held in secret and during bad weather, when the whites couldn't get to the island. A lovely collection of masks and jewellery adorns the walls. Don't miss the **Native Burial Grounds** and the **Memorial Totems ★★**, which testify to the richness of this art.

Port Hardy

Port Hardy, a town of fishers and forest workers, is located at the northeast end of Vancouver Island. There is a wealth of animal life in this region, both in the water and on the land. If you aren't interested in going fishing or whale-watching, treat yourself to a walk through the forest in Cape Scott Park. Visitors en route to Prince Rupert and the Queen Charlotte Islands board the ferry in Port Hardy *(call BC Ferries for schedules and fares, ☎949-6722).*

The **Copper Maker ★** *(free admission; Mon to Sat 9am to 5pm; 114 Copper Way, Fort Rupert, on the outskirts of Port Hardy, ☎949-8491)* is an Aboriginal art gallery and studio, where you'll find totem poles several metres high, some in the process of being made, others waiting to be delivered to buyers. Take the time to watch the artists at work, and ask them to tell you about the symbolism behind their drawings and sculptures.

At the end of Hwy. 19, you'll find the town port, the starting point of a promenade along the waterfront. You can enjoy a pleasant stroll here while taking in the scenery and watching the boats on their way in and out of the harbour.

Tour D: The Gulf Islands

Each of these islands is a different place to commune with nature and enjoy a little seclusion, far from traffic jams. Time is measured here according to the arrival and departure of the ferries. A convivial atmosphere prevails on these little havens of peace, especially at the end of the day, when visitors and islanders mingle at the pub. Surprises await you on each trip — an island straight out of your dreams, perhaps, or the sight of a seal swimming under your kayak — moments that will become lifelong memories.

The Gulf Islands consist of some 200 islands scattered across the Strait of Georgia between the eastern shore of Vancouver Island and the west coast, near the San Juan Islands (U.S.A.).

★★
Gabriola Island

Only 20min or so by ferry from Nanaimo, Gabriola is an island where nature abounds. The best way to visit is to take a slow bike ride around the island. It's a peaceful haven where many Nanaimo residents have taken up permanent residence. For tourists

seeking tranquillity and peaceful landscapes, it's an ideal place to spend a few days.

★
Salt Spring Island

Salt Spring is the largest and most populous of the Gulf Islands. Aboriginals used to come here during summer to catch shellfish, hunt fowl and gather plants. In 1859, the first Europeans settled on the island and began establishing farms and small businesses here. Today, many artists have chosen Salt Spring as their home and place of work. When they aren't practising their art on the street, they welcome the public into their studios. As Vancouver Island is just a short trip from Salt Spring, some residents work in Victoria. The town of Ganges is the commercial hub of the island. A promenade runs alongside its harbour, past a number of shops and through two marinas.

★★
Galiano Island

With just over a tenth of the population of Salt Spring, this island is a quiet, picturesque place. It was named after Dionisio Galiano, the Spanish explorer who first sailed these waters. About 30km long and over 2km wide, Galiano faces northwest on one end and southeast on the other. Its shores afford some lovely views and are dotted with shell beaches.

★
Mayne Island

Mayne Island, Galiano's neighbour to the south, is a quiet place inhabited mainly by retirees. The limited number of tourists makes for a peaceful atmosphere, while the relatively flat terrain is a cyclist's dream. In the mid-19th century, during the gold rush, miners heading from Victoria to the Fraser River used to

stop here before crossing the Strait of Georgia, hence the name Miners Bay. The first Europeans to settle on the island grew apples here, and their vast orchards have survived to this day. A few local buildings bear witness to the arrival of the pioneers. The **St. Mary Magdalene** ★ *(Georgina Point Rd.)* church, built entirely of wood in 1897, merits a visit. Take the opportunity to see the stained-glass windows on Sunday, when the church is open for Mass.

The **Active Pass Lighthouse** ★ *(every day 1pm to 3pm; Georgina Point Rd., ☎539-5286)* has been guiding sailors through these waters since 1885. The original structure, however, was replaced by a new tower in 1940, which was in turn replaced in 1969. The place is easy to get to and is indicated on most maps of the region.

★
Saturna Island

Saturna is possibly the most isolated and least accessible island of all the Gulf Islands, and its residents, who number around 300, are determined to keep it that way. Saturna has very limited facilities, and only two restaurants. Don't let this deter you. Nature lovers will be fascinated by the island's **unusual flora and fauna**, like, for example, the **giant mushrooms** that grow around **Mount Warburton**. Saturna Island also boasts its own vineyard.

Saturna's annual **Canada Day** celebration *(Jul 1)* is a huge lamb roast. It's the island's biggest gathering of the year.

★
Pender Islands

North and South Pender are the second most populated islands after Salt Spring and are joined together by a wooden bridge. They are fairly well

equipped for tourists. Visitors come primarily to cycle or to lounge on the beaches. **Mount Normand** has a good reputation among walkers. From the summit there's an exceptional view of the **San Juan Islands**. The laid-back, bohemian atmosphere is immediately apparent upon arriving, what with all the natural food stores and organic farms. Every Saturday, from May to October, the Driftwood Centre hosts a very colourful **farmer's market** where you'll find good fresh produce.
Pender Island

The north and south Pender islands attract visitors who wish to experience the rhythm of the countryside while en-

joying beaches and lots of outdoor activities. The community of Pender Island is quite active, constantly working on multiple projects, such as community theatre, festivals and arts and crafts. The islands are separated by a narrow canal, which was dug in 1900, and linked by a small bridge. The southern part, less developed, features many hiking trails, including one that leads to the summit of **Mount Norman** and another that reaches the **Beaumont Marine Park**, where you will find a lovely white-sand beach scattered with crushed shells. Most of the population lives on the northern island, in the district of Magic Lake and Trincomali. On the northern

island are **Port Washington**, **Hope Bay** and **Roesland**, with its trails leading to a lake and the ocean.

★★
Quadra Island

Quadra Island has about 4,000 residents. In the summer the number doubles with the influx of tourists drawn here by its exceptional reputation for salmon fishing. Quadra is covered almost entirely by forests. Locals are proud of the lack of crime on their island; politeness and a friendly smile are of the utmost importance. Quadra, like Cortes, is in the northern gulf and is one of the Discovery Islands. It can be reached by a ferry from

Campbell River to **Quathiaski Cove** in less than 10min. Once on the island be sure to visit the **Kwatkiutl Museum and Cultural Centre** (*every day 10am to 6pm;* ☎*285-3111*). This excellent museum of Aboriginal art presents relics that recount the lives of the island's first inhabitants. It is easily the most beautiful museum in the region. **Cape Mudge Lighthouse**, built in 1898, is nearby. Along the beach at the southern tip of the island, **petroglyphs**, drawn by Aboriginals 1000 years ago are revealed at low tide.

On the way to **Heriot Bay**, a small town in the northeast part of the island, you will come across the small BC Ferries terminal. This is where you catch the ferry to Cortes Island. Not far from the dock is lovely little Rebecca Spit Marine Provincial Park.

★
Cortes Island

Cortes Island is located north of the Strait of Georgia, a few nautical miles from Desolation Sound and 45min from Quadra Island by ferry. The ferry ride alone, if the weather is nice, is worth the trip. Once on the island, you will soon realize that services for tourists are very limited. People come here to commune with nature: clear **lagoons** rich in aquatic life, deep **forests** and fine-sand **beaches**. It's a paradise for sea kayaking, cycling and all sorts of excursions. Cortes Island is approximately 25km long and 13km wide. The north end is wild and uninhabited. On the south end, you'll find restaurants, hotels and grocery stores.

Parks and Beaches

Information on B.C. provincial parks is available at:
wlapwww.gov.bc.ca/bcparks

Tour A: From Victoria to Nanaimo and the Cowichan Valley

Quarry Regional Park ★ (*access by Empress Rd. from Shawnigan-Cobble Hill Rd.*). After an hour on the road, you will reach the hill's summit. The **view** from here is magnificent.

Shawnigan Lake Provincial Park (*south of Cobble Hill via Shawnigan-Cobble Hill Rd.,* ☎*743-5332*) is a wonderful place for a picnic and a swim. The sandy shores of the lake are pleasantly shaded. A perfect getaway on a hot summer's day.

Somenos Marsh Wildlife Refuge ★ (*5min north of Duncan via the Trans-Canada Hwy.,* ☎*246-2456*). Over 200 species of migratory birds flock here. A trail made of planks has been laid out in order to limit human impact on the marsh and to avoid disturbing the birds. Don't forget your camera and telephoto lens!

Lake Cowichan (☎*749-3244*), nicknamed Kaatza ("the big lake"), is ideal for sailing, sailboarding, swimming or any other water sport activity.

Carmanah Walbran Park ★★★ and **Carmanah Pacific Provincial Park** ★★★ (*information at the Cowichan Lake tourism information centre,* ☎*749-3244*) are magnificent wild expanses comprising close to 17,000ha of ancient forests that are protected from chainsaws and flourish in the humid

climate of the West Coast. The world's tallest spruces, reaching almost 95m in height, also grow in this region. Moreover, the varied ecosystems and vegetation favour the development of fauna that is every bit as varied, comprising squirrels, mice, raccoons, wolves, eagles and owls.

The parks are situated south of Bamfield, on Vancouver Island's west coast. The most direct route is through Cowichan Lake, but this means taking an unpaved, stony forest road. Make sure to check the condition of your tires before undertaking this 50km journey and bring a detailed map, for roadsigns are decidedly scarce.

A stone's throw from Nanaimo, **Maffeo Sutton Park Morrell Sanctuary** (☎*756-0106 or 800-663-7337*), owned by the Nature Trust of British Columbia, offers 1080ha of more rugged landscape. This park boasts at least 12km of well maintained trails that wind through a magnificent forest of Douglas firs surrounding beautiful Morrell Lake.

Newcastle Island Provincial Park (*take the ferry, May to Oct, from Maffeo Sutton Park, Comox Rd., behind the Civic Arena, Nanaimo,* ☎*391-2300, 756-0106 or 800-663-7337*) is a 306ha island in the Nanaimo harbour. Its shore is studded with beaches, caverns and escarpments. The Coast Salish First Nation lived on this island before its coal-rich subsoil attracted miners here. A Japanese fishing community ran a saltery here for 30 years, up until 1941, when the Canadian government placed the Japanese living and working on the coast into internment camps. The island later became a popular resort after being purchased by Canadian Pacific, which hosted big parties for its employees here. It has been public property since 1955.

Tour B: From Nanaimo to Tofino

Englishman River Falls Pro-vincial Park *(heading west on Hwy. 4 to the intersection of Island Hwy. 19; the park's entrance is easily spotted; ☎391-2300).* This beautiful park lies 16km from the main roads: you will feel like you've reached the edge of the world. This is the perfect place for hiking and picnicking; it is also a fishing enthusiast's paradise as it boasts one of the best trout rivers on the island.

Little Qualicum Falls Provin-cial Park *(right near the village of Coombs, ☎391-2300)* is also a wonderful place for hiking and picnicking. The Little Qualicum River waterfalls create a stunning landscape. What is more, visitors can go swimming in real natural pools in the area surrounding Cameron Lake.

MacMillan Provincial Park - Cathedral Grove ★★ *(east of Coombs, mid-way between Coombs and Port Alberni, along Hwy. 4, ☎391-2300)* is a wonderful, mystical place. The Douglas firs inhabiting this magnificent forest, some of which are over 800 years old, stand almost 80m tall. Hiking on the trails of Cathedral Grove will truly give you the impression of being back in the dinosaur age. It is also indicative of what the first European arrivals encountered on the West Coast. Cathedral Grove was considered a sacred place by Aboriginals. Note that the path is accessi-ble to people with limited mobility. It's level and part is a boardwalk for wheelchairs. A must.

Located 6km east of **Bamfield**, **Pachena Bay ★★★** is a glorious beach in **Pacific Rim National Park**. This beautiful

spot is one you will not soon forget. Camping on the beach is also permitted — and free! Seven day limit.

Pacific Rim National Park, Long Beach Unit ★★★ *(Long Beach information cen-tre, Hwy. 4, ☎726-7721)* This park is trimmed with kilo-metres of deserted beaches running alongside temperate rain forests. The beaches, hiking trails and various facili-ties are clearly indicated and easy to reach. The setting is enchanting, relaxing and stim-ulating at once, as well as being accessible year-round. The beaches are popular with surfing buffs, and **Live to Surf** *(1180 Pacific Rim Hwy., Tofino, ☎725-4464)* rents out surfboards and wetsuits.

Exploring the Tofino area by boat will enable you to un-cover the hidden treasures of the neighbouring islands and bays. If you feel like walking about, you can check out the sulphur springs in the caves or the bears in the forest. **Sea Trek** *(441B Campbell St., Tofino, ☎725-4412 or 800-811-9155)* can arrange an excur-sion for you.

Tour C: From Comox Valley to Port Hardy

Qualicum Beach and **Parksville** are popular for their sandy beaches just off Hwy. 19. The water is ex-tremely shallow, making it safe for children.

Horne Lake Caves Provincial Park *(☎391-2300)* is, in fact, composed of four natural caves and offers a very differ-ent aspect of nature than one would expect to see on Van-couver Island. Situated on the western reach of Horne Lake, via Hwy. 19, just north of Qualicum Lake, the caves are open to the public. Visitors must, however, be in good physical condition, well equipped for spelunking and

have previous experience. These visits are organized by **Riverbend Cave**.

Strathcona Park ★★ *(swim-ming, hiking, fishing and 161 campsites; 59km west of Camp-bell River on Hwy. 28, ☎954-4600)* is the oldest pro-vincial park in British Colum-bia, and the largest on Van-couver Island. Its 210,000ha of forest and fresh water abound in natural treasures, including huge Douglas firs over 90m high. The highest peak on Vancouver Island is found here, the Golden Hinde, it measures 2,220m.

Helliwell Provincial Park *(Hornby Island)* is a little park where you can hike for a day (5km) among the large fir trees and the magnificent coast of Hornby Island. You can admire the crumbling rocks, which the sea has transformed into works of art through thousands of years of erosion.

The **Haig-Brown Kingfisher Creek Heritage Property ★** *(donations accepted; guided tours Jul and Aug every day 1:30pm; 2250 Campbell River Rd., Campbell River, ☎286-6646),* located alongside the Campbell River, is worth a visit. It once belonged to cele-brated Canadian author Roderick Haig-Brown, who fought all his life to protect wild animals and their habitat.

Miracle Beach Park ★ *(28km south of Campbell River, at the intersection of Miracle Beach Rd. and Hwy. 19, ☎391-2300)* is the perfect place for families wishing to enjoy the beach while remaining close to all conveniences.

Cape Scott Provincial Park ★★ *(67km northwest of Port Hardy on Holberg Rd.; register at Port Hardy Chamber of Commerce, ☎949-7622; for all other information, BC Parks, ☎391-2300)* encom-passes 15,070ha of temperate rain forest. Scott was a mer-chant from Bombay (India) who financed all sorts of commercial expeditions. Many ships have run aground on this coast, and a lighthouse was erected in 1960 in order to guide sailors safely along their way. Sandy beaches cover two-thirds of the 64km stretch of waterfront. On the hilly terrain farther inland, you'll find various species of giant trees, such as red cedars and pines. This remote part of Vancouver Island receives up to 500mm of rainfall annually, and is frequently hit by storms. It is best to visit during summertime.

Tour D: The Gulf Islands

Salt Spring Island

Mount Maxwell Provincial Park ★ *(Salt Spring Island, from Fulford-Ganges Rd., take Cranberry Rd., then Mount Maxwell Rd. all the way to the end,* ☎*391-2300)* lies on a mountainside. The lookout is easily accessible, and the view of Vancouver Island and the islands to the south is worth the trip.

Ruckle Provincial Park is the largest park in the Gulf Islands. With its rich history, it is home to the oldest family farm in British Columbia. In addition, there are several hiking trails in the forests and on the coast.

Beddis Beach reveals itself as one of the best beaches on the island. It is a peaceful site, enhanced by a few stretches of fine, white sand.

Galiano Island

Montague Harbour Marine Park ★★ *(on the west side of Galiano Island, 10km from the ferry terminal,* ☎*391-2300)* is a top-notch park featuring a lagoon, a shell beach and an equipped campground. The view of the sunset from the north beach is truly dreamy.

Bluffs Park ★ *(Galiano Island, take Bluff Dr. from Georgeson Bay Rd. or Burrill Rd.)* offers a view from above of aptly named Active Pass, where ferries heading for Swartz Bay (Victoria) and Tsawwassen (Vancouver) cross paths.

Mayne Island

The **Bennet Bay beach** is a very pleasant spot, the best place on Mayne Island to take a walk.

Pender Island

Among the pleasant routes on the Pender Islands, the one that leads from **Mount Normand** to **Beaumont Provincial Park** is undoubtedly the most interesting. Picnic tables and campsites are available in the park, around the beach, so visitors can spend the night.

Outdoor Activities

Bungee Jumping

Tour A: From Victoria to Nanaimo and the Cowichan Valley

If you're looking for some excitement, head to the **Bungy Zone** *(15min south of Nanaimo via Hwy. 1; turn right on Nanaimo River Rd.; Nanaimo;* ☎*716-RUSH or 800-668-7771, www.bungy zone.com)*. The spectacle of thrill-seekers leaping off a bridge over the Nanaimo River has become a local attraction. The first jump costs $100, but if you want more, you only have to pay $35 for each additional jump.

Mountain Biking

Tour B: From Nanaimo to Tofino

A path has been paved along the road that runs between Pacific Rim Park and Ucluelet. It's suitable for cross-country biking, but not mountain biking, since the road is made of asphalt. For bike rentals, enquire at **Raven Tours** (☎*726-7779)*.

Although the region of Tofino only has a few mountain-bike paths, Long Beach is the ideal place to practice this sport. The compact sand on this endless beach insures good tire traction. **Tofino Kite & Bike Shop** *(441-A Campbell,* ☎*725-1221)* rents bikes.

Tour C: From Comox Valley to Port Hardy

Many mountain-bike enthusiasts travel to the Courtenay region, especially **Mount Washington Alpine Rsort** *(Howard Road,* ☎*338-1386)*. Die-hard cyclists will love the Monster Mile Downhill and the Discovery Trail.

Hornby Island and Denman Island make wonderful bike trips. Several mountain-bike paths, especially on Hornby Island, disappear into the central massif of the island. The paths zigzag in the dense forest, and the varied topography of the terrain will delight even hard-to-please sports enthusiasts. Mountain-bike rentals: in Hornby, **Co-op** ☎*335-1121*.

Golf

Tour C: From Comox Valley to Port Hardy

Located in the Comox Valley, **Crown Isle** *($65/18 holes; 399 Clubhouse Dr., Courtenay, ☎703-5050 or 888-338-8439, www.crown-isle.com)* is one of the most beautiful golf courses in the province. Its 18-hole course on its 326ha property has won it many prestigious international awards.

Fishing

Tour C: From Comox Valley to Port Hardy

You can fish at any time, day or night, on **Discovery Pier** *(with valid fishing permit; call for prices; rod rental 7am to 10pm, $3 per hour; 24hrs a day; Government Wharf, Campbell River, ☎286-6199)*, which stretches 150m. This is a popular place to go for a stroll.

Bailey's Charters *($60 an hour; Campbell River, ☎286-3474)* arranges guided salmon and trout fishing trips, which are a terrific way to explore the region's beautiful shoreline.

Calypso Fishing Charters *(384 Simms Rd., Campbell River, ☎888-225-9776, 923-2001 or 923-2067)* offers salmon-fishing excursions in the comfort of a fast boat equipped with a bathroom. Fuel and all fishing gear included. Reservations recommended. Rates: from $75/hr for one or two people, from $85/hr for three to four people, all for a minimum of 5hrs.

Hook & Reel Charters *($70/hr for one or two people, $80/hr for three or four people, for a minimum of 4hrs (taxes included); 16063 Bunny Rd., Campbell River, ☎287-4436)* will take you salmon fishing in the Brown Bay area, 30min north of Campbell River via Hwy. 19.

Tour D: The Gulf Islands

Discovery Charters *(Quathiaski Cove, Quadra Island, ☎285-3146 or 800-668-8054)* is a respected establishment that offers salmon-fishing expeditions. After an exciting day at sea, you can take advantage of one of its many accommodation formulas. The little beach houses on the water are equipped with kitchenettes. Rates: from $199, depending on the formulas and fishing packages.

Hiking

Tour A: From Victoria to Nanaimo and the Cowichan Valley

Nanaimo offers kilometres of nature trails as well as great varieties of outdoor sites. For information concerning organized activities, drop by the first-rate **tourist office** *(Beban House, 2290 Bowen Rd., ☎756-0106 or 800-663-7337)*, which will provide you with all pertinent details as well as excellent maps.

Harbourside Walkway is a paved trail stretching over 4km, starting from the marina in downtown Nanaimo. The trail passes by the Pioneer Plaza shopping centre. Farther along the trail is the Yacht Club, as well as various shops catering to sailors. It is a lovely promenade, at once urban and maritime, as the entire walkway skirts the ocean.

Tour B: From Nanaimo to Tofino

At **Pacific Rim National Park, Long Beach Unit ★★★** *(Long Beach information centre, Hwy. 4, ☎726-4212 or 726-7721)*, you can hike the 2km **rain forest trail ★★★** *(6.4km north of the information centre)*, which runs through a temperate rain forest. Panels explaining the cycles of the forest and providing information on the animal species who live here have been set up along two trails. This park is steeped in history, and a number of trails provide a chronicle of bygone days. It is wise to ask park officials about the risk of encountering animals during your hike. Trails are occasionally closed when there are bears in the vicinity. Note that this is one of nine trails in the area, all signposted on the highway.

The **West Coast Trail ★★★**, part of Pacific Rim National Park *(Ucluelet; ☎726-7721 or 726-4212)*, skirts the southeast coast of **Barkley Sound** between the villages of **Bamfield** and **Port Renfrew**. The "Life-saving Trail," as it has been nicknamed, is a 77km path that was laid out at the turn of the century to help rescue shipwrecked sailors. The trail roughly follows the path of a former telegraph line set up in 1890 along the rugged coastline: 66 ships have run aground in this area known as "Ship Graveyard of the Pacific." The landscape is characterized by sandy beaches and rocky headlands.

The trail runs through a shaded coastal forest where old plantings of spruces, western hemlock spruces and thujas predominate. Some of the tallest and largest trees (over 90m tall) in Canada stand along or near the trail.

Before your departure:

- call or write to the park to request a brochure and read it carefully;

- familiarize yourself with Vancouver Island's southern district and decide in advance whether you will use Bamfield or Port Renfrew as a departure point;

- choose your starting date, whether you will hike the whole trail or get off at Nitinat Lake, and how you will get to and from the trail;

- Take the time to study the route by reading one of the West Coast Trail guides:

  The West Coast Trail & Nitinat Lakes, Sierra Club, Victoria;

  Blisters & Bliss, D. Foster & W. Aitken;

  Pacific Rim Explorer, Bruce Obee, Whitecap Books.

It is important for interested hikers to know that the West Coast Trail can be dangerous: the course is arduous. Injuries and accidents are frequent. The trail is not meant for beginners, but rather, for physically fit and experienced hikers ready to tackle a rugged environment.

Visitors wishing to hike the trail must **reserve ahead of time**; an access permit is required. **Starting dates** are anytime from early May to late September. Call for actual dates.

A non-refundable reservation deposit of $25 is required, plus a $70 Trail fee and a additional $25 ferry fee on the day of the hike. Reservations can be made three months prior to your starting date by calling **Super Natural British Columbia** *(metropolitan Van-*

couver, ☎663-6000, *Canada and United States,* ☎800-435-5622, *www.hellobc.com).*

Groups can be no larger than 10 people, and are issued a permit, which must be put in a visible place on the leader's backpack. Hikers should be experienced and equipped for rainy weather. It is strongly recommended to bring along a portable gas stove and a first-aid kit. Equally important is a good pair of hiking boots; you don't want to be wearing ill-fitting footgear on this type of expedition, when you are completely on your own. Food and water will take up a lot of space in your backpack.

Eagle

Meares Island, which stretches the width of Tofino, is a great place for a 2hr hike among the gigantic, ancient trees of the rain forest. Although the beginning of the path is easy, it becomes much more difficult when the wooden footbridges disappear into the dense greenery. Inquire about the condition of the path with Hugh, the captain of *Salty*, the boat that brings you to the island *($20;* ☎725-3793).

Tour C: From Comox Valley to Port Hardy

Strathcona Provincial Park *(entrance west of Courtenay or Campbell River,* ☎954-4600) has a great variety of hiking paths. You can spend an afternoon or several days in the backcountry.

If your time is limited, take an hour to hike the 1km trail at

Paradise Meadows, which leads to the parking lot of Mount Washington at Forbidden Plateau. Be sure to check the weather conditions before departing, since there can be snow even in July.

Mount Goeffrey Regional Nature Park is located in the middle of Hornby Island. Its paths climb up to the highest point on the island (1,000m), from where you can see an impressive panorama stretching all the way to the snow-capped peaks of Strathcona Park on Vancouver Island.

Cape Scott Provincial Park ★ ★ *(67km northwest of Port Hardy via Holberg Rd.; register at Port Hardy Chamber of Commerce,* ☎949-7622; *for all other information, BC Parks* ☎391-2300) encompasses 15,070ha of temperate rain forest. Hiking trails provide the only means of access to the cape, and it takes a good 8hrs to get there from the parking lot at San Josef Bay.

Sailing

Tour A: From Victoria to Nanaimo and the Cowichan Valley

Herizentm Sailing for Women *(from $250/day; 36 Cutlass Lookout, Nanaimo,* ☎741-1753) is a very special sailing school catering exclusively to women. Also of note is that all the instructors here are women. Herizentm offers full training courses that include some meals, refreshments and accommodations.

Tour D: The Gulf Islands

The **Sailing School on Salt Spring Island** *($759 CYA course, including accommodation for 3 nights; 422 Sky Valley Rd., Salt Spring Island,*

☎537-2741 or 537-2835) offers Sail 'n' Stay packages.

Scuba Diving

Tour A: From Victoria to Nanaimo and the Cowichan Valley

Each year, hundreds of divers flock to the eastern shore of Vancouver Island, lured by the colourful underwater scenery and rich marine life. The Nanaimo region is a wonderful place for this type of sightseeing. Call **Sundown Diving Charters** *(22 Esplanade, Nanaimo, ☎753-1880 or 888-773-3483)* for various packages and pricing.

Tour B: From Nanaimo to Tofino

The **Broken Group Archipelago** in **Pacific Rim National Park** *(information centre, ☎726- 4212)* is a maze of islands, islets, reefs and crags, which lend themselves to interesting diving. All kinds of diving spots can be found here, from easy ones for beginners and others for more seasoned divers to still more challenging ones for experts.

Tour C: From Comox Valley to Port Hardy

Paradise Found Trekking *(☎923-0848 or 800-897-2872)* will take you where the salmon teem on the Campbell River. All the necessary equipment (mask, flippers and wet suit) is provided; all you have to do is let yourself be guided through the scores of salmon, some of which can measure up to 1m long.

Sun Fun Divers *(reservations required; 1697 Beach Dr., Port McNeill, ☎956-2243)* arranges scuba-diving trips in the Telegraph Cove, Alert Bay, Quatsino Narrows and Port

McNeill regions. The water is clearest during the winter months.

Sea Kayaking

Tour A: From Victoria to Nanaimo and the Cowichan Valley

Wild Heart Adventures Sea Kayak Tours *(1560 Brebber Rd., Nanaimo, ☎722-3683)* has been organizing first-rate expeditions all around Vancouver Island since 1990. The one-day or one-week expeditions offered by Wild Heart Adventures are safe, and you need not have experience to participate.

Tour B: From Nanaimo to Tofino

At **Tofino Sea Kayaking** *(320 Main St., Tofino, ☎725-4222 or ☎800-TOFINO-4)*, all excursions begin with a class. Moreover, they are guided by pros who are highly experienced in sea-kayaking and qualified in lifesaving and first aid. Expeditions are organized in Lemmens, on Meares Island and Duffin Passage Islands. Those with enough experience to go solo can also rent a kayak here.

Remote passages *(71 Wharf St., ☎725-3330 or 725-3163)* offers sea-kayaking tours that includes a walk within the old-growth forest on Meares Island *($58/4hrs)* or a shorter sunset trip *($44/2.5hrs)*.

Tour D: The Gulf Islands

T'ai Li Lodge *(Cortes Bay, Cortes Island, ☎935-6749 or 800-939-6644)* is a marine-adventure centre across from the park at Desolation Sound. You can learn to sail and sea kayak in fantastic surroundings with naturalist guides. A pack-

age with accommodation is also available.

Even though you can reach the Broken Islands archipelago easily from Bamfield, kayak excursions from Ucluelet can also be arranged with **Majestic Ocean Kayaking** *(1167 Helen Rd.; ☎800-889-7644 or 726-2868)*. All trips includes gourmet meals.

Salt Spring Island

Sea Otter Kayaking
149 Lower Ganges Rd.
☎**537-5678 or 877-537-5678**
Sea Otter Kayaking offers guided excursions of between 2hrs and six days, courses and equipment rental.

Galiano Island

Galiano Island Sea Kayaking
$45/4hrs
637 Southwind Rd.
☎**888-539-2930**
Guided tours.

Galiano Island & Gulf Island Kayaking
$50/ 3hrs
Montague Marina
☎**539-2442**
Guided tours.

Pender Island

Kayak Pender Island
$45/3 hrs
Otter Bay Marina
☎**629-6939 or 877-683-1746**
Guided tours.

Surfing

Tour B: From Nanaimo to Tofino and the Cowichan Valley

Pacific Rim National Park boasts a magnificent, 45km-long stretch of beach, known as **Long Beach**. Surfers will find unlimited waves, which provide a first-class "ride," cresting at 8m in winter! A surfer's dream. You too can devote yourself to this novel sport by renting equipment and taking courses.

A wetsuit is necessary because the water is very cold!

Here are a few good places in Tofino for rentals and information about necessary precautions:

Storm - The Tofino Surf Shop
444 Cambell
☎*725-3344*

Live to Surf
1180 Pacific Rim Hwy.
☎*725-4464*

Whale-watching

Tour B: From Nanaimo to Tofino

Island West Resort
($425/2pers/6hrs, combined fishing and whale-watching trip; Mar and Apr; 140 Bay St., ☎*726-7515)* as well as **Quest Charters** *(Boat Basin,* ☎*726-7532)* are two of the companies that offer whale-watching excursions departing from Ucluelet.

Chinook Charters *($59; 450 Campbell St., Tofino;* ☎*725-3431 or 800-665-3646)* will take you out to sea to observe grey whales. The best time to go is March to October, when there are large numbers of these sea mammals in the area.

Tour C: From Comox Valley to Port Hardy

Robson Bight Charters *(mid-Jun to Oct 9:30am; Sayward,* ☎*282-3833 or 800-658-0022)* arranges whale-watching tours in the Johnstone Strait. Each year, killer whales use this area as a sort of training ground for the new members of their families. A sight to remember.

Tour D: The Gulf Islands

Galiano Island

Chinook Key Charters
$65/3hrs
departures from Sturdies Bay
☎*539-3388*

Downhill Skiing

Tour C: From Comox Valley to Port Hardy

At the **Mount Washington Ski Resort** *(day pass $45; Howard Rd. or the Strathcona Pkwy.,* ☎*338-1386)*, skiers can enjoy a 360° view encompassing the Coast Mountains and the dozens of islands at the mouth of the Strait of Georgia. The mountain, which is 1,609m high, receives heavy snowfall every year. The ski season starts in December.

Accommodations

Tour A: From Victoria to Nanaimo and the Cowichan Valley

Malahat

 Aerie Resort
$$$$$ bkfst incl.
≡, ≈, ℜ, ◉, △, ℑ
600 Ebedora Lane
☎*743-7115 or 800-518-1933*
⇄*743-4766*
www.aerie.bc.ca
Part of the Relais & Châteaux chain, The Aerie Resort lives up to its slogan "castle in the mountains" with a beautiful, secluded location high atop the Malahat. The furnishings and little extras are lavish, to say the least: most of the standard rooms have a private patio or balcony, and for a

little extra you can have a jacuzzi, fireplace, steam shower, four-poster bed or rich leather sleigh bed. There is an indoor and an outdoor pool, a tennis court and a European spa. Romantic, Gourmet and Pampering packages available.

Cowichan Bay

Oceanfront Grand Resort & Marina
$$$
ℜ, △, ≈
1681 Cowichan Bay Rd.
☎*748-6222 or 800 663-7898*
⇄*748-7122*
www.travellersinnresort. com
Renovated in 2003, the Inn at the Water is a lovely hotel with 56 rooms, each offering a splendid view of the ocean and mountains. A bar and a restaurant also grace the hotel, as do an indoor swimming pool and liquor store. Seaplanes land right in front of the establishment.

Duncan

Falcon Nest Motel
$$
ℜ, K, ≈
5867 Trans-Canada Hwy.
☎*748-8188*
⇄*748-7829*
This is a small, rather antiquated but affordable motel. Moreover, it is conveniently located, just minutes from restaurants on the highway. The proprietor is charming.

Village Green Inn
$$
K, ℜ, ≈, ≡
141 Trans-Canada Hwy.
☎*746-5126 or 800-665-3989*
⇄*746-5126*
The Village Green Inn is the largest hotel in Duncan, providing 80 very comfortable rooms, with kitchenette upon request. The inn is located a short walking distance from downtown boutiques and the Cowichan Native Village. The inn also boasts a bar, a restau-

rant, a liquor store, a swimming pool and a tennis court.

Nanaimo

Nicol Street Hostel
$
sb, K
65 Nicol St.
☎*753-1188*
≈*753-1185*
The friendly, warm atmo-
sphere at the Nicol Street
Hostel makes up for its location on the noisy Trans-
Canada Highway. Located a
few blocks from the centre of
town, the hostel offers its
guests discounts at several
restaurants in Nanaimo. The
most pleasant of Nanaimo's
three hostels.

Rocky Point Executive Bed &
Breakfast
$$ bkfst incl.
≡, ⊛, ℜ
4903 Fillinger Cr.
☎*751-1949 or 888-878-4343*
≈*758-6683*
www.rockypoint.bc.ca
As its name suggests, the
Rocky Point Ocean View Bed
& Breakfast offers a wonderful
view of the Strait of Georgia
and, in clear weather, the
mountains along the coast.
The three rooms are a bit
over-decorated, but the warm
welcome more than compen-
sates for this minor drawback.

Best Western Dorchester
Hotel
$$
ℜ
70 Church St.
☎*754-6835 or 800-661-2449*
≈*754-2638*
www.dorchesternanaimo.
com
The Best Western Dorchester
has 65 simply decorated,
comfortable rooms that offer a
lovely view of the port of
Nanaimo. The layout is the
same at the other Best West-
erns in this region. A safe bet.

Jingle Pot Bed &
Breakfast
$$ bkfst incl.
△, ≡, 🐾, ℜ, ℝ
4321 Jingle Pot Rd.
☎*758-5149 or 888-834-0599*
≈*751-0724*
www.jinglepot.com
Run by a sailor named Captain
Ivan, The Jingle Pot Bed &
Breakfast has two rooms,
which have been fitted out in a
luxurious fashion to ensure
that guests enjoy a pleasant
stay. If you're planning on
going boating, the captain can
give you some good advice.

Whitehouse on Longloake
B&B
$$ bkfst incl.
⊛, 🐾
231 Ferntree Pl.
☎*756-1185 or 877-956-1185*
≈*756-3985*
Located just 10min from the
centre of town on the shore
of Long Lake, Whitehouse on
Longlake B&B has its own
private beach. The ideal spot
for families, this facility is close
to many hiking and biking
paths.

Ramada on Long Lake
$$$
⊘, 🐾, ⊛, △, ℝ
4700 North Island Hwy
☎*758-1144 or 800-565-1144*
≈*758-5832*
www.ramadananaimo.com
Enjoy a relaxing stay on the
shores of Long Lake, north of
Nanaimo. All rooms face the
water, and guests have access
to a private beach as well as a
fitness centre. Only a stone's
throw from BC Ferries' De-
parture Bay harbour.

Coast Bastion Inn
$$$$
ℜ, △, ≡, ≈, 🐾, ⊛, ⊘
11 Bastion St.
☎*753-6601 or 800-663-1144*
≈*753-4155*
www.coasthotels.com
This is a luxurious hotel whose
179 rooms all benefit from
magnificent views of the re-
gion. Some are even equipped
with whirlpool baths. The
hotel boasts a beauty salon, a

chocolate shop, a restaurant
and a pub.

Tour B: From Nanaimo
to Tofino

Parksville

Paradise Sea-Shell Motel
and RV Park
$ - RV park
$$ bkfst incl. - motel
K
411 West Island Hwy
Motel
☎*248-6171 or 877-337-3529*
RV park
☎*248-6612*
≈*248-9347*
The Paradise Sea-Shell Motel
and RV Park is located close to
the big Parksville beach. Those
with an RV can reserve a spot
and benefit from the same
amenities offered to motel
guests: access to the beach
and the colossal Paradise
Adventure Mini-Golf (impossible to miss with its castle and
giant shoe).

The Maclure House Inn
$$-$$$ bkfst incl.
1015 East Island Hwy.
☎*248-3470*
≈*248-5162*
www.maclurehouse.com
The coziness of an English pub
permeates this inn and restaurant with a view of the ocean,
built in the half-timbered
Tudor style in 1921. Rudyard
Kipling is reputed to have
stayed here, in what are today
warm, cozy, Victorian-style
rooms with an authentic, old-
fashioned cachet. The rooms
are an excellent deal at this
price, but keep in mind that
they are located above the
restaurant so getting to sleep
early might be a problem.
Also, reserve well in advance,
particularly for the ocean-view
rooms. Check in before
4:30pm and you'll be treated
to a light afternoon tea.

Tigh-na-Mara Resort Hotel
$$$$
⊛, K, 🐾, ≈, ℜ, ☺, ℑ
1095 East Island Hwy.
☎**248-2072 or 800-663-7373**
⇌**248-4140**
www.tigh-na-mara.com
Nestled in the trees near the beach, this resort is a good option for families. There are one- and two-bedroom log cottages in the forest, condo units with a view of the ocean (unit B, the least expensive) and balconies, as well as studios. Unfortunately, its cozy, inexpensive lodge units recently burnt down, but there are plans to rebuild, so call to inquire. Weekly rates available. This is an interesting option for an easy beach holiday with the kids.

Qualicum Beach

Quatna Manor Bed & Breakfast
$$ bkfst incl.
sb/pb
512 Quatna Rd.
☎**752-6685**
⇌**752-8385**
*www.wcbbia.com/pages/
quatna.html*
The Quatna Manor Bed & Breakfast is definitely a place to keep in mind. The friendly reception you will receive from hosts Bill and Betty will make your stay at their Tudor-style home that much more pleasant. A hearty breakfast is served in the dining room. Bill is retired from the air force. His job required a great deal of travelling, and his stories make for memorable breakfast conversation.

Casa Grande Inn
$$$
K, ℝ, ⊛
3080 West Island Hwy.
☎**752-4400 or 888-720-2272**
⇌**752-4401**
www.casagrandeinn.com
Why on earth Qualicum Beach needed a motel with a New Mexico–style name and design, we don't know. Nevertheless, this brand-spanking new motel offers tidy rooms, all with balconies and many

with an ocean view. If this is the type of accommodation you're looking for, you can't go wrong here.

Qualicum Heritage Inn
$$$
ℝ, ℜ
427 College Rd.
☎**752-9262 or 800-663-7306**
*www.qualicumheritageinn.
com*
A boarding school for boys until 1970, the Qualicum Heritage Inn was established in 1935 in a faux-Tudor half-timbered building. In keeping with the slightly kitschy medieval theme that remains, the interior is rather dark and somber, but don't let that put you off: the guestrooms are comfortable and rather attractive. Those that were recently renovated have pine furnishings and are decorated in pastels or richer hues, and some have balconies and ocean views. If you make it past the suit of armour in the lobby, it's a very acceptable choice.

Hollyford Bed and Breakfast
$$$$ bkfst incl.
ℑ
106 Hoylake Rd. E.
☎**752-8101 or 877-6559**
www.hollyford.ca
Jim and Marjorie's lovely cottage has an extension built onto it, where all of their sound-proofed, attractively decorated guestrooms are located. They are endowed with antiques and reproductions, poster beds, quality linens, duvets, bathrobes, deep soaker tubs and individual thermostats for maximum comfort, and provide access to a tiny outside seating area. A full breakfast is served at individual tables in the dining room. Jim is an avid collector of Canadiana, and he and Marjorie are wonderful sources of information on their region. An excellent choice, if a bit pricey.

Port Alberni

Personal Touch Hostel
$
K, sb
4908 Burde St.
☎**723-2484**
⇌**723-8602**
The Personal Touch Hostel is run by an Aboriginal family. The place isn't that pretty, but you can get a good night's sleep here and the prices are unbeatable.

Coast Hospitality Inn
$$$
≡, 🐾, ≈
3835 Redford St.
☎**728-8111 or 800-663-1144**
⇌**723-0088**
www.coasthotels.com
The Coast Hospitality Inn is located right in the middle of Port Alberni. The hotel boasts approximately 50, recently upgraded, very comfortable and relatively luxurious rooms. It is particularly favoured by business people. There is a decent restaurant on the ground floor and a lively pub in the basement.

Ucluelet

Ucluelet Campground
$
🐾
early Apr to late Sep
260 Seaplane Base Rd.
☎**726-4355**
Located within walking distance of Ucluelet. Reservations required.

West Coast Motel
$$
K, ≈, ☺
247 Hemlock St.
☎**726-7732**
⇌**726-4662**
While it's a much better choice than the similarly priced and singularly unpleasant Ucluelet Hotel, don't expect a warm welcome at the West Coast Motel. Nevertheless, the rooms are large and clean and some have a full kitchenette. French is spoken.

Ocean's Edge Bed and Breakfast
$$
855 Barkley Cr.
☎726-7099
⇌726-7090
www.oceansedge.bc.ca
Bill and Susan offer three comfortable, immaculate rooms on the ground floor of their cliff-side home, all of which allow direct access, via sliding glass doors, to the beach below. Bill, a biologist and former naturalist with the Pacific Rim National Park, is a gold mine of information on the area and leads wonderfully informative walking tours. A good choice at a good price.

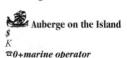 Canadian Princess Resort
$$$-$$$$
sb/pb
mid-Mar to late Sep
Peninsula Rd.
☎598-3366 or 800-663-7090
⇌726 7121
www.canadianprincess.com
This is a ship that sailed the waters along the coast for nearly 40 years, and is now permanently moored at the Ucluelet pier. It has 26 rooms, which are claustrophobically small and don't have a lot of extras, but offer a pleasant nautical atmosphere. There are also attraction motel-style rooms onshore, by the boat. Fishing charters are organized. There is a bar and restaurant on the ship and service is genuinely pleasant.

Tauca Lea by the Sea
$$$$$
K, ◉, ℑ, ℛ
☎726-4625, 800-979-9303 or 888-252-4454
www.taucalearesort.com
Understated, rustic elegance is the name of the game at Tauca Lea by the Sea, a new resort (2000), located on what is technically a tiny island off Ucluelet. These blue-shingled cottages house 33 privately owned one- and two-bedroom suites that are rented to the public. Each offers a view of the beach and

is fully equipped and beautifully designed with handcrafted wood furnishings, a mixture of terra cotta flooring and beige carpeting and cathedral ceilings (in the two-bedroom unit)—an earthy, tasteful West Coast vibe. The reception area houses an art gallery and there's a good, similarly designed restaurant (see p 167) on-site. Affordable off-season rates.

A Snug Harbour Inn
$$$$$ bkfst incl.
◉, ℑ
460 Marine Dr.
☎726-2686 or 888-936-5222
www.awesomeview.com
Rhyming couple Sue and Drew warmly welcome guests to their blue-shingled home on a bluff with a truly "awesome view" of the ocean. You can admire it all from four luxurious, fully equipped guestrooms, complete with sumptuous linens, balconies, robes and a heated bathroom floor; a cottage was recently added to the main house. Soak up the rugged coastal scenery as you soak in the outdoor hot tub, then dry off in the cozy great room, where a telescope lets you spy on the bald eagles that often visit. A path leads down to the private, rocky beach. Feel free to arrive by helicopter, if you so desire, as there is a landing pad on the property. A little pricey, but a true delight if your budget allows.

Tofino and Long Beach

C&N Backpackers
$
K
241 Campbell St.
☎725-2288
www.cnnbackpackers.com
There are numerous youth hostels in the Tofino region. The most recent addition is the C&N Backpackers, which opened in August 1999.

There are also some pleasant youth hostels outside Tofino on two neighbouring islands

situated in a breathtaking natural setting.

Auberge on the Island
$
K
☎0+marine operator

Vargas Island Inn & Hostel
$
K
☎725-3309
Both Auberge On The Island and Vargas Island Inn & Hostel offer dormitory-style accommodation in the middle of the magnificent temperate tropical forest.

Wilp Gybuu (Wolf House)
$$ bkfst incl.
ℑ
311 Leighton Way
☎725-2330
www.tofinobedandbreakfast.com
There is a peaceful, soothing, artistic feeling to Wendy and Ralph's home, located just a short walk from the centre of town. Wilp Gybuu offers three guestrooms, all simply but pleasantly furnished and equipped with showers and attractive linens; two have private entrances. A full breakfast is served in a dining room with a lovely view of Clayoquot Sound, and guests have access to their own pantry. Children 12 years and older welcome. Allergy-sufferers, be forewarned: cats in residence.

BriMar
$$$ bkfst incl.
ℑ, ℛ
1375 Thornberg Cr.
☎725-3410 or 800-714-9373
BriMar, named for its absentee owners Brian and Mark, is now tended by an easygoing, affable couple with a penchant for offering good food and a good laugh. That, and the three attractive, richly furnished rooms, with hardwood floors, sleigh beds, clawfoot tub (in the loft), and robes, ensures an enjoyable stay in

this lovely, beach-side home. Children 12 years and over welcome.

Tombolo Sweet
$$$-$$$$
☎(604) 823-7134
www.frankisland.com
Looking for something a bit different? How about waiting until the tide is out and taking a short walk from Chesterman Beach to a tiny, private island called Frank. There, hidden in the trees, or hugging the rocky coast, you'll find Tombolo Sweet and Tombolo Studio. Tony and Carol Mulder, who own half the island, have designed, built and decorated them *au naturel*, with plenty of wood, colourful artwork and linens, and other necessities (note, however, that there's no electricity). The studio, which accommodates four and was completed in 2002, is lined with windows and affords a breathtaking view of nothing but rocks and sea. Reserve four to six months in advance for July and August. Sweet indeed...

Inn at Tough City
$$$-$$$$
ॐ, ⊛, ⚔
350 Main St.
☎725-2021 or 877-725-2021
www.toughcity.com
If you prefer to lodge right in the centre of Tofino rather than at one of the many beach-side establishments—and, frankly, that would be a shame—the Inn at Tough City is a promising option. Housed in a restored industrial brick building right on the harbour, the inn offers eight guestrooms with wood floors, decorated in rich colours, many with balconies and soaker tubs. The lobby is festooned with 1950s memorabilia and the place boasts plenty of wonderful stained glass, which seems a tad out of place, here in the Wild West...

Pacific Sands
$$$$
K, ॐ
☎725-3322 or 800-565-2322
⇄725-3155
www.pacificsands.com
This family-oriented resort dates from 1973 and its overwhelmingly ordinary-looking suites and cottages are showing their age. Nevertheless, they have complete kitchens and the price is good for the area. The lighthouse suites, which have were recently renovated, are the coziest. Note that there are no telephones in the guestrooms. Pacific Sands is located on Cox Bay, prime surfing and sand-dollar-collecting territory.

Best Western Tin Wis Resort Lodge
$$$$
⊙, *K, ॐ, ℜ*
1119 Pacific Rim Hwy.
☎725-4445 or 800-661-9995
⇄725-4447
www.tinwis.com
The Best Western Tin Wis Resort Lodge is a large hotel run by Tla-O-Qui-Aht First Nations people. The guest rooms are rather ordinary looking, but offers all the comforts you would expect from a Best Western. The plants and wooden decorative elements blend harmoniously with the immediate surroundings.

Chesterman's Beach Bed & Breakfast
$$$$
ॐ, ℜ
1345 Chesterman's Beach Rd.
☎/⇄725-3726
www.island.net/~surfsand
Picture a shingled house on a beach lined with lush vegetation with the setting sun reflecting off the water; that's what awaits you at the heavenly Chesterman's Beach Bed & Breakfast. A simple walk on the beach every day is all you need to enjoy a satisfying vacation here. Three units with private entrance are available. The Lookout suite is particularly cozy and romantic.

Despite its name, breakfast is no longer offered.

Long Beach Lodge Resort
$$$$$
ℜ, ॐ, ⚔
1441 Pacific Rim Hwy.
☎725-2442 or 877-844-7873
⇄725-2402
www.longbeachlodgeresort.com
Long Beach Lodge Resort, a shingled, gabled low-rise that opened in 2002, blends right into the coastline scenery and looks completely unassuming from the outside. But step inside and marvel at just about everything. Common areas feature impressive First Nations masks, prints and carvings, which are available for purchase. Guestrooms face either the forest or the beach, the latter offering balconies, plenty of windows and fireplaces. They are decorated in soothing sage green and other earthy shades and are furnished with custom-designed Douglas fir furniture and cozied up by luxury linens with a thread count as high as the nightly rate. Bathrooms feature Chinese-slate floors and deep soaker tubs that communicate with the main room. Easily the hippest digs around and frankly, this is where you *really* want to stay.

The Wickaninnish Inn
$$$$$
⊛, ॐ, ✿, ℜ, △
Osprey Lane, Chesterman Beach
☎725-3100 or 800-333-4604
⇄725-3110
www.wickinn.com
The Wickaninnish Inn is a superb, high-class hotel set deep in the country, at the foot of an escarpment, with a fantastic view of Chesterman Beach. The rooms are comfortable and very well decorated. The hotel's restaurant, The Pointe (see p 167), is set up in a glassed-in, octogonal room offering a breathtaking 240-degree view of the sea.

Bamfield

Bamfield Inn
$$
ℜ
Bamfield Inlet
☎728-3354
⇆728-3446
The Bamfield Inn offers a lovely view of the port, boasts a good restaurant and organizes salmon-fishing and whale-watching excursions. There are washing machines on the premises.

Tide's Inn B&B
$$ bkfst incl.
sb
22 South Bamfield Rd.
☎728-3376
www.tidesinntofino.com
Tide's Inn B&B is a wonderful facility located by the ocean. The rooms and breakfasts are impeccable. The friendly owners will lend you their kayaks, and you can also travel along the first few kilometres of the West Coast Trail nearby.

Bamfield Trails Motel Hook & Web Pub
$$$
226 Frigate Rd.
☎728-3231
The Bamfield Trails Motel Hook & Web Pub is located right in the heart of the village, a few minutes from the port and services. The rooms are rather antiquated but relatively comfortable. A laundromat on the ground floor is at guests' disposal, as is a lively pub.

Tour C: From Comox Valley to Port Hardy

Courtenay

Comox Lake Hostel
$
K, sb
4787 Lake Trail Rd.,
☎338-1914
www3.telus.net/hostel
The Comox Kale Hostel is perfectly situated on a 4ha property about 12km west of Courtenay. With Strathcona

Provincial Park nearby, this charming setting has many hiking and mountain-bike paths as well as some enchanting spots to go swimming. This B&B is suitable for those who enjoy the great outdoors since it's a long way from civilization.

Greystone Manor B&B
$$ bkfst incl.
4014 Haas Rd.
☎338-1422
www.greystonemanorbb. com
Built in 1918, Grey-stone Manor B&B offers incredible views of the enormous mountains along the Sunshine Coast. A gigantic English-style garden enhances the beauty of the premises. The rooms are attractively designed and your hosts will tell you about the attractions to visit in the valley.

Coast Westerly Hotel
$$$
ℜ, ⌂, ≈, ✖, ☺
1590 Cliffe Ave.
☎338-7741 or 800-668-7797
⇆338-5442
www.coasthotels.com
The Coast Westerly Hotel is situated right in the heart of Comox Valley, close to golf courses, beaches and the Mount Washington ski resort. The Coast Westerly Hotel is a vast establishment with 108 luxurious rooms, some of which offer beautiful views of the area.

Kingfisher Oceanside Resort & Spa
$$$
≈, ☺, ⊛, ⌂, ℜ, ℑ, K, ✪
4330 South Island Hwy.
☎338-1323 or 800-663-7929
⇆338-0058
www.kingfisherspa.com
Kingfisher Oceanside Resort & Spa is located slightly south of Courtenay by the water's edge. It's a comfortable establishment that specializes in health retreats, offering a wide range of services (massages, mud baths, algae masks, sauna, and the like). It also has tennis courts, and guests can use the kayaks.

Comox Valley

Alpine House B&B
$$ bkfst incl
sb/pb
263 Alpine St.
☎339-6181 or 877-339-6181
⇆339-4892
www.alpinehousebb.com
Alpine House B&B is situated directly in front of the hospital on a residential street in Comox. A great place for families, it has suites with several rooms.

Campbell River

Edgewater Motel
$$
✖, K
4073 South Island Hwy. near Oyster Bay
☎/⇆923-5421
www.edgewatermotel.ca
As its name suggests, the pretty little Edgewater Motel is located on the waterfront. The rooms are decent for the price, and you can prepare meals in them — a real plus if you're on a tight budget.

The Haig-Brown House
$$ bkfst incl.
sb/pb
2250 Campbell River Rd., Hwy. 28, Golf River Hwy.
☎286-6646
⇆286-6694
The Haig-Brown House once belonged to Roderick Haig-Brown, renowned for both his writing and his efforts to protect the environment. Literary workshops are held on the estate, which is now a provincial heritage property. This spectacular place lies on the banks of the Campbell River. The rooms are simply decorated in old-fashioned style, and the walls of the study are lined with books. The dining room is bathed in natural light. The house and guest rooms are minded by Kevin Brown, who has a passion for both literature and the history of the Haig-Brown estate.

Best Western Austrian Chalet
$$$
🐾, ℜ, △, ≈
462 South Island Hwy.
☎*923-4231 or 800-667-7207*
⇌*923-2840*
www.vquest.com/austrian
The Best Western Austrian
Chalet is an attractive hotel
overhanging Discovery Pas-
sage. It offers its guests a spec-
tacular view of the ocean and
mountains. Completely reno-
vated in 1996, the Austrian
Chalet has all the amenities,
making it a first-class establish-
ment.

Telegraph Cove

🛶 **Telegraph Cove Resorts**
$ campsite
$$ cabin
K, 🐾, ℜ
☎*928-3131 or 800-200-4665*
⇌*928-3105*
www.telegraphcoveresort.
com
The Telegraph Cove Resorts
welcome visitors from May to
October. The campground,
equipped with basic facilities, is
somewhat bare, but the view
of the bay makes up for that.
The cabins blend into the
picturesque setting. The service is friendly, and you'll feel
as if you're at some sort of
summer camp. If you have to
spend a few days in the northern part of the island, Telegraph Cove is a thoroughly
pleasant place to visit.

Port Hardy

Many travellers passing
through town on their way to
Prince Rupert arrive to Port
Hardy's Bed and Breakfasts
late and leave early, which
would explain why local residents make so little fuss about
renting rooms to visitors in
need of a place to stay.

Mrs. P's Bed & Breakfast
$$ bkfst incl.
sb, 🐾
8737 Telco St.
☎*949-9526*
Hosts Herma and Frank will
give you a warm welcome at

Mrs. P's Bed & Breakfast,
which has two soberly deco-
rated rooms in the basement.
The place is located within
walking distance of the har-
bour and a number of restau-
rants.

North Shore Inn
$$
ℜ
7370 Market St.
☎*949-8500*
⇌*949-8516*
The North Shore Inn over-
looks the ocean, as do all its
rooms. The hotel is located
right in the middle of Port
Hardy and about 10min from
the ferry terminal, whence
guests can participate in fishing, scuba-diving and
whale-watching excursions
organized by the establishment.

Glen Lyon Inn & Suites
$$
🐾, ⊙, K, ℜ
6435 Hardy Bay Rd.
☎*949-7115 or 877-949-7115*
⇌*949-7415*
www.glenlyoninn.com
Close to the BC Ferries termi-
nal, the Glen Lyon Inn is a
good hotel, offering rooms
with a view of the ocean and
excellent breakfasts. In fact,
locals claim the Glen Lyon Inn
serves the best breakfasts in
town.

Seagate Hotel
$$
ℜ
8600 Granville St.
☎*949-6348*
⇌*949-6347*
The Seagate Hotel is located a
stone's throw from the town
pier. All of the rooms are
sparingly decorated, and the
view makes those facing the
port much more attractive.

Tour D: The Gulf Islands

The Gulf Islands are covered
with **bed and breakfasts** of all
types. Though these places
are generally quite expensive,

you are unlikely to hear any
complaints from the guests.

Galiano Island

Dionisio Point and **Montague
Harbour** (☎*539-2115*) offers
campsites with lovely views of
the coast. Note that Dionisio
Point Park is only accessible by
boat.

🛶 **La Berengerie**
$$ bkfst incl.
sb/pb, ℜ
Montague Harbour Rd.
☎*539-5392*
At La Berengerie, which has
four rooms, guests enjoy a
relaxing atmosphere in the
woods. Huguette Benger has
been running the place since
1983. Originally from the
South of France, Madame
Benger came to Galiano on a
vacation and decided to stay.
Take the time to chat with
her; she'll be delighted to tell
you all about the island. Break-
fast is served in a large dining
room. La Berengerie is closed
from November to March.

🛶 **Mount Galiano Eagle's
Nest Bed & Breakfast**
$$ bkfst incl.
2-720 Active Pass Dr.
☎*539-2567*
The Eagle's Nest is located
right on one of the most
beautiful waterfront properties
of the Discovery Islands. The
house is splendid and the view
of the ocean is spectacular. If
you haven't got a car, don't
worry; they can pick you up at
the ferry dock.

Serenity by the Sea
$$$
K, ❄, ℝ, ✪, pb/sb
225 Serenity Lane
☎*800-944-2655*
www.serenitybythesea.com
A small, peaceful oasis over-
looking the ocean, Serenity by
the Sea offers retreats focused
on self-discovery through
creativity. Accessories such as
therapeutic chairs and exercise
balls, as well as massage treat-
ments, are available to guests.

In addition, yoga sessions are held every morning. With an unusual architectural style that creates intimate spaces, the rooms and cabins all have a view of the ocean and a private balcony. On site, there are also beautiful gardens, a small stream and a popular cliff-side pool.

The Bellhouse Inn
$$$ bkfst incl.
®
29 Farmhouse Rd.
☎*539-5667 or 800-970-7464*
www.bellhouseinn.com
A historical home that was converted into an inn in 1925, the Bellhouse Inn, surrounded with pastures, sheep and majestic fruit-bearing trees, is located on a 2.4-hectare farm. Facing the Active Pass, a passageway for ferries and whales, and offering direct access to the beach, the inn is a fascinating sea-observation site. The establishment features four comfortable, antique-furnished rooms, three of which have a balcony overlooking the ocean. Sheep's wool is also found in the rooms thanks to cozy comforters, and a welcoming homemade sherry is offered upon your arrival.

Galiano Inn
$$$$$ bkfst incl.
®, ⌦, ◐, ℜ, ◠
134 Madrona Dr.
☎*539-3388 or 877-530-3939*
www.galianoinn.com
Situated near the bridge, the elegant Galiano Inn offers 10 spacious rooms with Mediterranean-inspired decor. Each room features a fireplace and a balcony or terrace with a view of the ocean and the Active Pass, where guests can observe the comings and goings of ferries and whales. Facing the inn is a garden leading to a small beach. The establishment's spa and wellness retreat was due to be up and running at press time; it will offer a wide array of treatments, from acupressure to massage therapy. There is

also a small art gallery where interesting works by local artists are displayed. In addition, the site includes the irresistible Atrevida restaurant, one of the best on the Gulf Islands (see p 169).

Salt Spring Island

In addition to the official campgrounds listed below, several hotels on Salt Spring offer a few campsites on their property. Contact the tourism office for more information.

Ruckle Provincial Park
Beaver Point, south of de Salt Spring
☎*877-559-2115*

Lakeside Gardens Resort
1450 North End Rd., St. Mary's Lake
☎*537-5773*

Cedar Beach Resort
1136 North End Rd.
☎*537-2205*

Salt Spring Island Hostel
$-$$
640 Cusheon Lake Rd.
☎*537-4149*
www.beacom.com/ssihostel
This establishment offers numerous lodging options, such as private family rooms, tree houses, tepees, gypsy caravans and, at lesser cost, dormitories. The inn is located in the heart of the forest. Two short hikes of about 30min lead to Cusheon Lake, where you can swim, and to Beddis Beach.

Spindrift
$$$
✖, *K*, ⌦, ℝ
225 Welbury Point Dr.
☎*537-5311*
www.spindriftsaltspring island.com
The Spindrift, located on a peninsula bordered by two white-sand beaches, offers adults a peaceful ambiance in harmony with nature. Its six cabins, equipped with kitchenettes and fireplaces, provide views of the ocean. Here, the luxury of big hotel chains is put

aside (shower only, no television or telephone) so that you can fully enjoy the unique experience of living among white-tailed deer, seals and otters.

Seabreeze Inne
$$$
🐾
101 Bittancourt Rd.
☎*537-4145 or 800-434-4112*
www.seabreezeinne.com
The Seabreeze Inne is a very comfortable, reasonably priced motel. Downtown Ganges is a short drive away. The manager offers a wealth of information for tourists. The establishment features an outdoor whirlpool tub, a gazebo and a terrace where guests can use the equipment to grill and barbecue. The Seabreeze Inne's mission is to become the top family establishment on Salt Spring. To explore the island, bicycles are available to guests and scooters can be rented.

Beach House Bed and Breakfast
$$$$ bkfst incl.
🐾, ⌦
369 Isabella Point Rd.
☎*653-2040*
The Beach House is one of the rare bed and breakfasts on the beach at Salt Spring. In fact, from the French doors of your room, which also serve as a private entrance, it is just a few steps to the waterfront. The rooms offer impeccable comfort and original decor. Breakfasts too, have their own quality and charm. A whirlpool tub overlooking the ocean and Fulford Harbour, as well as a campfire site, are available to guests. Keep this one in mind.

Salt Spring Spa Resort
$$$$
®, *K*, ⌦, ℝ, ◐
1460 North Beach Rd.
☎*537-4111 or 800-665-0039*
⚏*537-2939*
www.saltspringspa.com
The Salt Spring Spa Resort offers spacious, sunny cabins with a view of the ocean or

the forest. In addition to being fully equipped, each cabin features a whirlpool tub. For its wide array of treatments and body care, the Salt Spring Spa Resort uses healing minerals waters that come from the island. The establishment also loans bicycles, rowboats and crab cages. Adults only.

Quarrystone House B&B
$$$$ bkfst incl.
⊛, ℑ
1340 Sunset Dr.
☎537-5980 or 866-537-5980
⇌*537-5937*
www.quarrystone.com
Overlooking Stonecutters Bay, the Quarrystone House offers a breathtaking view from high atop a cliff. This inn, located in the heart of the countryside, is surrounded with fruit trees, sheep-dotted pastures and a pony that is quite popular with children. Short pedestrian trails criss-cross the property through gardens and undergrowth. The decor in the house and rooms, filled with antiques, simply exudes country charm. The rooms are bright and cozy.

Hastings House
$$$$$ bkfst incl.
≡, K, ℑ, ℝ, ⊙, ℜ
160 Upper Ganges Rd.
☎537-2362 or 800-661-9255
⇌*537-5333*
www.hastingshouse.com
A Sussex-style manor and several historical buildings stand on the majestic, peaceful domain that is Hastings House. The main buildings dominate a cliff that plunges into Ganges Harbour, and all around, pastures, orchards and gardens are accessible to those who wish to stroll about. Hastings House offers solemn, charming suites and cabins and relaxing treatments in its new health spa. Unfortunately, the rooms are rather conventional and do not reach the level of quality and luxury that one might expect from such an establishment.

Mayne Island

Oceanwood Country Inn
$$$$$ bkfst incl.
⊛, ℜ, ℝ, ℑ
630 Dinner Bay Rd.
☎539-5074
⇌*539-3002*
www.oceanwood.com
This is another great spot on Mayne Island. This elegant English-style country inn offers pleasantly decorated rooms, most equipped with a fireplace. Visit the Fern Room and the Rose Room – they won't disappoint! The food is deliciously prepared. A stay at this exquisite establishment is sure to leave you with fond memories.

Pender Islands

It is possible to camp at **Prior Centennial Provincial Park** *(North Pender, ☎800-689-9025)*. The campground is located in the middle of a forest, and Medicine and Hamilton beaches are easily accessible.

Hummingbird Hollow Bed & Breakfast
$$ bkfst incl.
ℝ
RR 2, 36125 Galleon Way
☎629-6392
www.gulfislands.com/birdsong
Peaceful Hummingbird Hollow, surrounded with a forest, is a cozy, friendly place to escape to. Here, a lush natural setting is offered to guests, and the establishment, located on the lakeshore, generously loans boats (rowboats and canoes). In the gardens leading to the lake, you will find a hammock and a gazebo, which are available to vacationers. An impressive number of deer wander the site; curious and used to the presence of humans, they will probably even come and greet you! The two rooms are comfortable and feature a terrace and private sunroom.

Eatenton House Bed & Breakfast
$$$ bkfst incl.
4705 Scarff Rd., R.R. 1
☎629-8355
Eatenton House Bed & Breakfast promises a rejuvenating stay in a totally natural setting. The cosy rooms have antique furniture and there's a fireplace in the living-room. Noteworthy are the delicious breakfasts, the outdoor whirlpool as well as the spectacular view of the mountains and ocean.

Alice's Shangri-La Oceanfront Bed and Breakfast
$$$$ bkfst incl.
✂, ⊛, ℑ, ℝ
5909 Pirate's Rd.
☎629-3433 or 877-629-6555
www.alicesoceanfrontbnb.com
From high atop its cliff, Alice's B&B offers a warm welcome and an exceptional 360-degree view of the ocean and nearby islands. The three rooms feature an intimate terrace where you'll find a whirlpool tub, a barbecue and everything you need to enjoy a meal. Note to Trekkies: one of the rooms is entirely decorated à la *Star Trek*! The common living room, for its part, features a pool table, an authentic player piano, a fireplace and a mini-bar. You can explore the surroundings by taking shorts walks in the forest.

Saturna Island

East Point Resort
$$-$$$
✂, K
187 East Point Rd.
☎539-2975
www.gulfislands.com/eastpointresort
The East Point Resort provides natural surroundings with exclusive access to a smooth sandy beach. Visitors can choose from six small, luxurious and attractively decorated cottages. No credit cards.

Quadra Island

Whiskey Point Resort Motel
$$$
⋈, *K,* ≈
725 Quathiaski Cove
☎*285-2201 or 800-622-5311*
www.whiskeypoint.com
The hotel is located just across from the ferry dock and dominates the whole bay of Quathiaski Cove. The rooms are very comfortable, well equipped for extended stays, and have kitchenettes. There is also a massage and relaxation facility. The manager is very friendly and will tell you about all the best places to visit. Show him your Ulysses guide – you're sure to be well received.

April Point Resort & Marina
$$$$$
⋈, *☄, ℜ*
May to Oct
903 April Point Rd.
☎*285-2222 or 800-663-7090*
⇋*285-2411*
www.aprilpoint.com
The April Point is a luxury establishment for lovers of salmon fishing, nature and gourmet food. If you feel like going for a ride, the hotel can lend you a bicycle.

Cortes Island

Gorge Harbour Marina Resort
$ camping
$$ units
ℜ, ℝ
follow signs from the ferry
☎*935-6433*
⇋*935-6402*
http://oberon.ark.com/~gorge har/
Cortes's big resort has approximately 40 RV sites, campsites as well as rustic, yet comfortable, rooms. Services include a good restaurant, motor-boat rental, fishing expeditions, fishing permits, marine charts as well as camping equipment. This is a very calm and well maintained place where deer-sightings are not uncommon.

Hollyhock
prices vary depending on the packages, fb
ℜ
from the Cortes ferry follow signs to Smelt Bay and Hollyhock; the road is winding, so be careful not to end up in Squirrel Cove; approximately 18km from the ferry
☎*935-6576 or 800-933-6339*
⇋*935-6424*
www.hollyhock.bc.ca
Hollyhock is a "new age" retreat. You can choose to stay in either a tent or a room, both of which take advantage of the surrounding wilderness. Hollyhock offers a variety of relaxation packages that will allow you to re-energize.

Restaurants

Tour A: From Victoria to Nanaimo and the Cowichan Valley

Nanaimo

Javawocky Coffee House
$
8-90 Front St.
Pioneer Waterfront Plaza
☎*753-1688*
Located on the seawall, the Javawocky Coffee House serves a wide assortment of coffee and light meals and offers a view of the Nanaimo port and the crowd strolling about there.

Mambo Pizza
$
16 Victoria Cr.
☎*753-6667*
The pizza at Mambo Pizza's pizza is the antithesis of the frozen product. With a crust thinner than a plate, it's bursting with home-made flavour and freshness. Open until 1am.

Dinghy Dock Pub
$$
May to mid-Oct, 11am to 11pm, midnight Fri and Sat
no. 8 Pirate's Plank Protection Island
☎*753-2373*
At this floating pub, which is attached to the Protection Island pier, you can enjoy a good local beer while observing the comings and goings in the Nanaimo harbour. The fish & chips are succulent. To get to the island, take the ferry from Commercial Inlet *(every hour from 9:10am to 11pm)*.

Tour B: From Nanaimo to Tofino

Qualicum Beach

Shady Rest
$$
3109 West Island Hwy.
☎*752-9111*
This casual, beach-side pub and restaurant serves up an inspired, pub-style menu, heavily weighted toward fish and seafood. If you're there for lunch, the fresh, tasty halibut burger might be just the ticket. Landlubbers needn't worry, as there's plenty for them, including some interesting salads.

Beach House Restaurant-Cafe
$$-$$$
2775 West Island Hwy.
☎*752-9626*
You've come all this way to be close to the ocean—it would be a shame not to soak in the view while you dine. This unpretentious seaside spot offers the best view in town, and it's even better from the patio. Unfortunately, the interior, all pink walls and plants, could use some TLC, but you've come for the lovely sea view, haven't you? The food is pretty good too, with local fish and seafood specialties, pasta, sandwiches and burgers, as well as some Austrian specialties that reflect the chef/owner's origins.

Ucluelet

Blueberries Cafe & Cappuccino Bar
$$
1627B Peninsula Rd.
☎726-7751
Blueberries Cafe & Cappuccino Bar serves great dishes, such as chicken curry or scrumptious fettuccini with fresh seafood. And then there's the delectable blueberry deserts — with a cappuccino of course!

Matterson House
$$-$$$
1682 Peninsula Rd.
☎726-2200
People come to the Matterson House, located on the main street, in one of the oldest homes in Ucluelet (1931), all day long. Don't hesitate to order salmon here; it's very fresh. There's also good Mexican-style dishes, fish—and non-fish burgers, and excellent chowder. Patio.

Boat Basin
$$$$
Tauca Lea by the Sea, 1911 Harbour Dr.
☎726-4644
Located in the Tauca Lea by the Sea resort and furnished in the same tastefully understated fashion as its studios, with Northwest Coast First Nations art, handcrafted wooden tables and an open kitchen, the Boat Basin is a lovely, sophisticated spot to sample a cornucopia of imaginatively prepared local products from land and sea. For nibblers, there is also a tapas menu and a less-expensive lounge and patio menu, as well as a selection of thin-crust pizzas. A seat on the patio, by the waters of Barkley Sound, and the friendly, professional service, are just what the doctor ordered.

Long Beach

Wickaninnish Restaurant
$$-$$$
1943 Peninsula Rd.
☎726-7706
Set on a big rock overlooking the beach, the Wickaninnish Restaurant offers a spectacular view of the Pacific Ocean that is unmatched by any other restaurant in the area, except of course **The Pointe** (see below), with which is should not be confused. The menu is made up of seafood dishes. The pasta with smoked salmon is particularly tasty but to be honest, the view is the real attraction. Under the same ownership as the Canadian Princess Resort (see p 160), the restaurant can be reached via shuttle bus from the resort.

The Pointe Restaurant
$$$
Wickaninnish Inn, Osprey Lane at Chesterman Beach
☎725-3100 or 800-333-4604
This high-class restaurant is built against a crag and offers a superb view of Chesterman Beach. The Pointe Restaurant as well as the On-The- Rocks Bar are set up in a glass-walled, octogonal room with a stunning 240° view of the ocean. The chef prepares excellent, quintessentially West Coast, locally influenced cuisine composed of farm and organic ingredients. An excellent choice.

Tofino

Breakers
$
131 First St.
☎725-2558
Breakers does the impossible: it serves up quality food in no time at all. On hot summer nights, there's often a long line waiting for the best ice cream cone in Tofino.

Common Loaf Bake Shop
$
180 First St.
☎725-3915
The Common Loaf Bake Shop offers a vast selection of breads and pastries freshly baked every morning. It also serves salads and a variety of sandwiches, served up in a log cabin with a warm atmosphere. Curry seems to be the favourite flavour here. Notice the collection of masks at the entrance.

Rain Coast Café
$
101-120 Fourth St.
☎725-2215
The Rain Coast Café offers unique, alternative fare. The very colourful dishes pay homage to the world's various cuisines. Reservations recommended.

Surfside Pizza
$
☎725-2882
The address is unnecessary as Surfside only delivers. A good place to order from should you suffer from hunger pangs in your hotel room.

The Loft Restaurant
$$
346 Campbell St.
☎725-4241
The Loft Restaurant serves West Coast cuisine. Excellent seafood and pasta dishes.

Blue Heron Dining Room
$$$-$$$$
634 Campbell St.
☎725-3277
The Blue Heron Dining Room is a spacious 90- seat restaurant enjoyed by families and tourists alike. The menu features regional specialties. This restaurant offers unobstructed views of the port, Clayoquot Sound and Meares Island.

Schooner Restaurant
$$$$
331 Campbell St.
☎725-3444
The Schooner Restaurant is a classic. It serves seafood and

British Columbian wines. An inviting place, it has been decorated to look like a ship's hold and deck. The soft lighting creates a relaxing comfortable atmosphere. Open for breakfast, lunch and dinner.

Café Pamplona
$$$$
closed Dec and Jan
1084 Pacific Rim Hwy.
☎**725-1237**
Located at the entrance to the Tofino Botanical Gardens, Café Pamplona offers delicious cuisine redolent with the flavour of the herbs tended in its kitchen garden. A few dark-wood tables on a terracotta floor, high ceilings, displays by local artists, a library, a piano and a few tables outside complete the picture. Its two chefs, both formerly at The Pointe (see p 167), have created a menu that is brief and to the point, stressing fresh island products, such as Dungeness crab, wild Pacific salmon and local oysters. We savoured every mouthful of the herb-crusted Pacific halibut with wild-rice sauté and orange tarragon sauce. The café is also open for breakfast and lunch. In short, the only thing missing is a sea view. Both the set menu and the main courses are a good value.

Tour C: From Comox Valley to Port Hardy

Comox Valley

The Bar None Cafe
$-$$
244 Fourth St., Courtenay
☎**334-3112**
Vegetarian cuisine has no limits at the Bar None Cafe. Have a seat on the magnificent patio and taste one of its many sandwiches or simply a cappuccino (made from organic coffee beans of course!)

Orbitz Pizza
$-$$
corner First St. and Fitzgerald Ave. Courtenay
☎**338-7970**
Orbitz Pizza makes the best pizza in the valley and serves it up in a hip decor.

Atlas Cafe
$$-$$$
250 Sixth St. Courtenay
☎**338-9838**
The Atlas Cafe serves up a variety of dishes from the four corners of the globe, such as Italy, Mexico, Greece and Japan. The refined cuisine here is delectable.

Campbell River

Tomeli's Fish & Chip Bistro
$$
151 G Dogwood St.
☎**286-0814**
Tomeli's Fish & Chip Bistro is a family-style restaurant that serves up fried cod and halibut. You won't go hungry here.

The Seasons Bistro
$$$
261 Island Hwy.
☎**286-1131**
The Seasons Bistro has an original menu featuring seafood pasta. This place attracts both locals and tourists, and jazz lovers in particular.

Port Hardy

Cheekers Roadhouse
$$-$$$
8600 Granville St.
☎**949-6348**
The Seagate Hotel Restaurant has a wide-ranging menu. While enjoying a view of the harbour, you will dine alongside local residents, including fishers fresh from a day at sea.

Tour D: The Gulf Islands

Galiano Island

Grand Central Emporium
$-$$
2740 Sturdies Bay Rd.
☎**539-9885**
Housed in one of the island's oldest buildings, the Grand Central Emporium, built entirely of wood, presents a fun and refreshing menu. The covered terrace welcomes diners in a simple, casual atmosphere. On the menu, you'll find the famous smoked-meat sandwich, for which the ingredients come directly from Montréal. There are also other culinary specialities, such as the curry chicken burger. During the summer months, the establishment presents jazz shows on Saturday nights.

Hummingbird Pub
$-$$
47 Sturdies Bay Rd.
☎**539-5472**
In a laid-back atmosphere, the Hummingbird Pub serves simple, delicious cuisine that highlights seafood. The pleasant terrace is the ideal spot to feel the pulse of the island and its inhabitants, who come here with family or friends. Affordable prices and personalized service make the Hummingbird Pub a much-appreciated spot for both travellers and residents!

La Berengerie
$$
Montague Harbour Rd.
☎**539-5392**
La Berengerie has a four-course menu with a choice of fish, meat or vegetarian dish. The dining room, located on the ground floor of a bed and breakfast, is furnished with antiques. Candlelight makes the atmosphere that much more inviting. Owner Huguette Benger prepares the delicious meals herself. During the day, her son's restaurant, **La Bohème**, serves vegetarian

dishes on the terrace overlooking the garden.

Atrevida
$$$
Galiano Inn, 134 Madrona Dr.
☎*539-3388 or 877-530-3939*
Diners who wish to dress
their best and experience the
languorous island way of life
should definitely enjoy a meal
at Atrevida. With a masterful
touch, the French chef con-
cocts refined, delicious dishes
with top-quality ingredients to
compose a cuisine that is
classical yet open to various
influences. For instance, fish,
meat and poultry dishes,
among others, are accompa-
nied with orange slices, figs
and couscous. The establish-
ment's wonderful view of the
ocean and the melancholic airs
played by the pianist add to
the restaurant's stylish atmo-
sphere.

Salt Spring Island

Tree House Café
$-$$
near Mouat's, on the Ganges Har-
bour dock, Salt Spring
☎*537-5379*
In a small courtyard lined with
trees and ivy, the enchanting
Tree House Café offers cuisine that is based on local
products, often organic, in
generous portions at affordable prices. The menu is brief
but quite varied and features
mouth-watering dishes that
will please both meat-eaters
and vegetarians. Among others, you will find a dish composed of smoked salmon with
Camembert in phyllo, lamb
stew, Thai curry, pesto pizza
and burgers. The Tree House
Café also features a take-out
counter with several dishes,
sauces and soups. Come night
time, it is the setting for jazz,
blues and folk concerts high-
lighting local artists (see
p 170).

The Oystercatcher Seafood Bar & Grill
$$-$$$
near Mouat's, on the Ganges Harbour dock, Salt Spring
☎*537-5041*
The Oystercatcher, a culinary
and social landmark for both
residents and visitors, is a very
lively spot. Thanks to its huge
building, it combines several
distinct ambiances: romantic,
family, etc. This harbour-side
establishment, where you can
admire one of the most beautiful views of Ganges, specializes in seafood. The menu
features classic dishes such as
grilled salmon, fish 'n' chips
and crab cakes, and the high-
quality homemade beer is a
perfect accompaniment. In
addition, service is efficient and
courteous.

The Currant Café
$$$
on the Ganges Harbour dock, Salt
Spring Island
☎*537-5747*
The lovely Currant Café
draws its inspiration from the
land and sea that surround it.
Here, fresh local products are
guaranteed (fish, poultry,
lamb, vegetables), and several
are also certified organic or
handmade, such as bread and
cheese. The menu varies from
day to day, season to season,
and is composed of a selection
of vegetarian, fish, seafood and
meat dishes. The cuisine is
international, served in healthy
portions, and is as delicious as
it is imaginative.

Vesuvius Inn Neighbourhood Pub
$$$
805 Vesuvius Bay Rd., Ganges
☎*537-2312*
Vesuvius has a fairly varied
menu but specializes in West
Coast cuisine. Try the Saturday and Sunday brunch,
served until 3pm.

House Piccolo
$$$$
108 Hereford Ave., Ganges
☎*537-1844*
House Piccolo is an elegant
restaurant whose menu features Mediterranean and Scandinavian flavours. The cuisine
is very sophisticated and very
tasty. Be careful, the bill adds
up quickly. The restaurant is a
member of *La Chaîne des
Rôtisseurs*.

Pender Islands

That Little Coffee Place
$
5827 Schooner Way
☎*629-3080*
What a charming café! Tiny,
with a loveseat and a terrace,
That Little Coffee Place offers
coffee and tea, as well as an
array of pastries, in a most
friendly ambiance. There is
also an Internet station for
clients *($2/15min)*.

Pistou Grill
$$$
Driftwood Centre, 4605 Bedwell
Harbour Rd.
☎*629-3131*
The Pistou Grill is a casual and
trendy bistro whose decor is a
reflection of the French-Cana-
dian duo that owns the place.
The mouth-watering menu
features, among others, a dish
of grilled salmon topped with
an orange, ginger, maple and
chilli marinade, and a
rosemary-lamb dish accompa-
nied with black-olive tapen-
ade. Unfortunately, the un-
even, rather cold service takes
a little of the charm away from
this lovely culinary experience.

Islanders Restaurant
$$$-$$$$
1325 MacKinnon Rd.
☎*629-3929*
Without a doubt the best
eatery in Pender Island, Island-
ers Restaurant offers a lively
ambiance and a colourful
decor. The enthusiastic staff is
visibly happy to serve its
guests, and the owner often
leaves the kitchen to make
sure that diners are all satis-

fied. In addition, there is a magnificent view of the ocean and an ever-changing exhibit of works by local artists. On the menu, you will find a delicious appetizer of mussels (all the way from the Atlantic!) in a creamy sauce of white wine and *sambuca*, as well as several crêpe and fish dishes, and even a dish composed of musk-ox meat with cranberries.

Quadra Island

Heriot Bay Inn and Marina
$$
mid-May to mid-Sep every day, mid-Sep to mid-May Sat only
just across from the ferry terminal
☎*285-3322*
The restaurant has a very friendly atmosphere and a lovely view of the harbour. In the summer, you can eat on the terrace. The house specialties are seafood, steak and home-made pies. A good spot.

Tsa-Kwa-Luten Lodge
$$$-$$$$
May to Sep every day
Lighthouse, Quadra Island
☎*285-2042*
Reservations recommended. The site is truly spectacular, providing an unobstructed view of Discovery Passage, and it's not unusual to see eagles flying overhead. Regional specialties with a native influence are served here; try the excellent snapper burger. The wine list is extensive. In the summer, you can enjoy some barbecued salmon on the big outdoor terrace.

April Point Lodge & Fishing Resort
$$$-$$$$
900 April Point Rd.
☎*285-2222 or 800-663-7090*
For breakfast, lunch and dinner, the restaurant at this impressive resort serves meals that easily meet gourmets' high expectations. The wine list is equally impressive.

Cortes Island

The Old Floathouse Restaurant
$$-$$$
early May to late Sep
Whaletown, follow the signs from the ferry terminal Gorge Harbour Marina Resort
☎*935-6631*
in winter
☎*935-6433*
The Old Floathouse Restaurant is one of the rare good restaurants on the island. It also benefits from a superb location on a magnificent property.

Entertainment

Bars and Nightclubs

Tour D: The Gulf Islands

Galiano Island

The Hummingbird Pub
$
every day until 12:30am
47 Sturdies Bay Rd. Galiano Island
☎*539-5472*
This is a friendly place where tourists and locals mingle over a good beer and a plate of fries.

Salt Spring Island

Tree House Café
near Mouat's, on the Ganges Harbour dock
☎*537-5379*
On summer nights, the Tree House Café's lush courtyard is transformed into a stage for local artists who present jazz, blues and folk concerts. Once a week, clients can also get their 15 minutes of fame by playing an instrument to accompany the musicians! The establishment offers excellent micro-brewed beer.

Moby's Marine Pub
120 Upper Ganges Rd.
☎*537-5559*
A lively atmosphere reigns at Moby's when shows, such as jazz concerts, are presented. Located at the marina, the pub features a pleasant terrace and a complete menu composed of fish and seafood dishes. There is also a good selection of beer, including several local brands.

Calendar of Events

January

Polar Bear Swim
Salt Spring Island
☎*866-830-1113*
www.northcentralisland. com
On January 1, hundreds of people rush into the ocean for an annual icy dip.

February

Chinese New Year
in the streets of Nanaimo
☎*753-1821*
www.nanaimo.museum.bc. ca

March

Pacific Rim Whale Festival
Ucluelet/Tofino
☎*726-7742*

Winter Film Fest
Paramont Theatre, Port Alberni
☎*724-3412*

Upper Island Music Festival
Beban Park Social Centre
☎*756-5200*

April

Arts & Crafts Show
Woodgrove Centre
☎*390-2721*

Antique Show
Woodgrove Centre
☎*390-2721*

May

Ballroom Dance Competitions
Beban Park Social Centre
☎*756-5200*

Fishing Derby
Silva Bay
☎*247-8807*

June to September

Fresh-food market on Saturdays, craft market on Sundays (*Salt Spring Island*).

July

Nanaimo Marine Festival
downtown
☎*753-7223*

International Bathtub Races
at the port of Nanaimo
☎*753-7223*

International Sandcastle Competition
Parksville Beach
☎*954-3999*

August

Fringe Theatre Festival
☎*753-8528*

Fulford Music Festival
Salt Spring Island

World Croquet Championship
☎*248-6171 or*
Parksville Chamber of
Commerce
☎*248-3613*

Kidfest
Parksville Community Park
☎*248-3252*

September

Vintage Car Rally
between Victoria and Nanaimo
☎*754-8141*

Crab Fest
Parksville Community Hall
☎*752-6263*

October

Oktoberfest
Beban Park Social Centre
☎*756-5200*

Wood Carving Show
Beban Park Social Centre
☎*756-5200*

Shopping

Tour A: From Victoria to Nanaimo and the Cowichan Valley

Nanaimo

Nanaimo is truly a city of shopping centres. The shops here are really nothing special aside from their incredible variety. **Rutherford Mall** *(Mon to Thu 9:30am to 5:30pm, Wed-Fri 9:30am to 9pm, Sat 9:30am to 5:30pm, Sun 11am to 5pm; on North Island Hwy., close to Long Lake, at Rutherford Rd.,* ☎*758-8111)* is a good example, with over 60 establishments, including department stores as well as clothing boutiques, jewellers, booksellers, restaurants, etc.

Tour B: From Nanaimo to Tofino

Qualicum Beach

There are a number of artisan studios in the area, including those at the **Old School House Gallery and Art Centre** (see p 142). Another good stop is **Smithford's** *(164 Second Ave.,* ☎ *752-3400)*, whose motto is "Don't need it, we got it." It is full of whimsical items, garden accessories, and other fun stuff.

Ucluelet

Du Quah Gallery
1971 Peninsula Rd.
☎*726-7223*
The Du Quah Gallery exhibits Aboriginal art. It is worth the trip just to see the building, which looks like a Longhouse (a traditional Aboriginal cedar building).

Tofino

Eagle Aerie Gallery
350 Campbell St.
☎*725-3235*
The Eagle Aerie Gallery was built by the Aboriginal artist Roy Henry Vickers. The artist's world-renowned paintings, inspired from his life, are exhibited here. The smell of weathered wood emanates from the walls of the gallery. A must-see.

The House of Himwitsa
300 Main St.
☎*725-2017*
The House of Himwitsa is an art gallery that displays drawings, paintings, sculptures and silver and gold jewellery. Ask about the legends referred to in these pieces and the symbolism employed by the artists.

Tour C: From Qualicum Beach to Port Hardy

Campbell River

Tyee Plaza
1309 Shoppers Row, behind the Travel InfoCentre
☎*286-0418*
The Tyee Plaza has a covered walkway and 24 stores and restaurants of all different sorts. If you are in a rush or looking for a shopping mall, this is the place to go.

Port Hardy

Copper Maker
114 Copper Way
☎949-8491
The Copper Maker displays the works of a number of Aboriginal artists. Masks, pottery and symbolic jewellery can all be purchased here. These articles might seem expensive, but the prices are lower than in the bigger cities.

Tour D: The Gulf Islands

Salt Spring Island

Home Hardware
106 Fulford Rd.
☎537-5551
Home Hardware is well stocked with all the necessary supplies for camping and outdoor activities.

Ganges Village Market
374 Lower Ganges Rd., Ganges
The Ganges Village Market sells all kinds of groceries. There's also a bakery and a delicatessen.

Everlasting Summer
194 MacLennan Dr.
☎653-9418
Everlasting Summer specializes in dried-flower bouquets and aromatic plant cultivation. Don't miss the beautiful, romantic, rose garden where weddings are often held.

Each Saturday from April to October is Salt Spring's famous **Market in the Park** *(Centennial Park, ☎537-4448)*. Visitors can get acquainted with the island's craftspeople and farmers, who bring much colour and vitality to the market. A wide variety of high-quality local products is displayed here.

Galiano Island

Galiano Island Books
76 Madrona Dr.
☎539-3340
This small, surprisingly well-stocked bookshop, has welcomed several famous Canadian authors; indeed, many of them choose Galiano Island Books to launch their latest work. There is also a children's section, used books and artist's material.

Bill Boyd Ceramics
86 Ganner Dr.
☎539-2692
www.billboydceramics.com
Bill Boyd's ceramics, created through an unusual technique, are as intriguing as they are spectacular: during the fabrication process, crystals form at random on the piece. Works that are for sale are displayed in the workshop, and the artist himself can answer visitors' questions.

Pender Islands

During the summer months, Pender Island's craftspeople and farmers meet on Saturdays from 9am to noon at the **Farmer's Market** *(weekly market)*. This is a great opportunity to get to know the community's top-quality work.

Mayne Island

If you need supplies for camping or hiking, stop in at **Miners Trading Post** *(☎539-2214)*, in the town of **Fernhill**. You can also pick up venison or beef for a tasty barbecue at the **Arbutus Deer Farm** *(☎539-2301)*.

Quadra Island

Heriot Bay Consignment Shop
West Rd., not far from the ferry dock
☎285-3217
You'll find absolutely everything at the Heriot Bay Consignment Shop and have a lot of fun in this second-hand store while you're at it.

Whale

Southern British Columbia

T his region, which
borders on the United States, is characterized by a
blend of the urban and the undeveloped.

T he Vancouver area, for
example, resembles a big
American city, though it is set
against a backdrop of green
mountains and blue sea; here,
you will find both wilderness
and civilization. The Okanagan
Valley is home to countless
orchards and some of the best
wineries in the county.

A s one majestic landscape
succeeds another, your
eyes will be dazzled by the
sea, the everlasting snows and
the spring colours, which
appear very early in this region.

C ommuning with nature is a
memorable experience of
any trip in southern British
Columbia. The waters that
wash the deserted beaches
beckon you to relax and let
your mind wander. Stately
trees stand guard over tranquil
areas untouched by the forestry industry. Dotted with
national and provincial parks,
which lie stretched across

the loveliest parts of the province, this region has an extremely varied landscape, with
everything from perpetual
snows to desert valleys to
rivers teeming with fish.

A trip to southern British
Columbia offers a chance
to explore towns and parks
set between the sea and the
sky and meet people from a
wide range of cultures. We
have outlined five tours

through four large areas
whose character and appearance range from one extreme
to the other: Southwestern
British Columbia, the High
Country, Kootenay Country
and the Okanagan-
Similkameen.

The tours are as follows:

**Tour A: The Sunshine
Coast ★★**

**Tour B: Coast Montain Circle
Tour ★★**

**Tour C: The Thompson River
as Far as Revelstoke ★**

**Tour D: Okanagan-
Thompson ★★★**

Trout

Tour E: Kootenay Country ★★

Finding Your Way Around

By Plane

A number of airlines serve the various parts of the province.

Air BC
Kamloops, Kelowna, Penticton, Vernon, Powell River
in Vancouver
☎(604) 643-5600 or
800-663-3721

Central Mountain Air
Kamloops, Kelowna
☎800-865-8585
book through Air BC
www.cmair.bc.ca

West Jet
Kelona
☎888-937-8538 or
8000-538-5696
www.westjet.com

By Car

Every highway in southern British Columbia is more spectacular than the last. One of these is the Trans-Canada (Hwy. 1), which runs east-west across mountains, rivers, canyons and desert valleys.

The Trans-Canada provides an easy route eastward out of Vancouver, although the traffic is always fairly heavy. The road leads to Calgary, running along the Fraser River, the Thompson River and Lake Shuswap at different points along the way. Another option is to take Hwy. 7 (the continuation of Broadway Ave.) out of downtown Vancouver, along the north bank of the Fraser River. If you're pressed for time, you can take the Coquihalla Highway (Hwy. 5),

which runs between Hope and Kamloops. This is a toll highway, the only one in the province and is faster than the Fraser Canyon (4hrs from Vancouver to Kamloops), yet not as attractive.

The spectacular Sea to Sky Highway (99) will take you up into northern British Columbia; simply cross the Lions Gate Bridge and follow the signs for Whistler and Squamish.

By Train

Once extremely busy, railway stations only see a few regular trains nowadays. The *Canadian* still crosses the Rockies, running along mountainsides and through numerous tunnels. From North Vancouver, you can take a train that skirts northward around Howe Sound, passing through Squamish and Whistler along the way and offering passengers a chance to contemplate the landscape.

BC Rail
1311 W. First St., North Vancouver
☎(604) 984-5246 or
800-663-8238
www.bcrail.com
Serves the towns in the northern part of the province by way of the Whistler resort area.

Via Rail Canada
1150 Station St., Vancouver
☎888-842-7245
www.viarail.ca
Via Rail Canada serves the following towns: Port Coquitlam, Matsqui, Chilliwack, Hope, Boston Bar, Ashcroft, Kamloops and several other communities in the northeastern part of the province.

By Bus

Greyhound Lines of Canada
Pacific Central Station, 1150 Station St., Vancouver
☎800-661-8747
www.greyhound.ca

Maverick Coach Lines
Pacific Central Station, 1150 Station St., Vancouver
☎(604) 940-8727 or
800-667-6301
www.maverickcoachlines. bc.ab
Caters mainly to skiers going to Whistler for the day, but also serves other towns along Hwy. 99.

Whistler Transit System
☎(604) 932-4020
www.whistler.com/transit/

By Ferry

To reach the Sunshine Coast, you must take a ferry from the coast or from Vancouver Island.

BC Ferries
1112 Fort St., Victoria
☎(250) 386-3431 *Victoria*
☎888-223-3779
www.bcferries.bc.ca

Practical Information

The area code is **604** in the Lower Mainland (Vancouver and suburbs). In the rest of the province *(north of Whistler, east of Hope, the islands)* the area code is **250**.

In case of serious emergency, dial ☎911

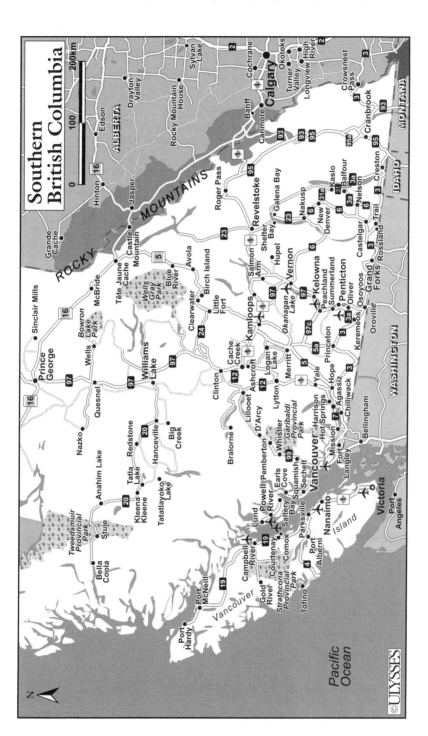

Southern
British Columbia

Tourist Information

Tour A: The Sunshine Coast

**Vancouver,
Coast and Mountains**
250-1508 W. Second Ave., Vancouver
☎*(604) 739-9011 or
800-667-3306
www.coastandmountains.
bc.ca*

Gibsons InfoCentre
900 Gibsons Way, Unit 21, Gibsons
☎*(604) 886-2325
www.gibsonschamber.com*

Powell River Visitors Bureau
4690 Marine Ave., Powell River
☎*(604) 485-4701 or
877-817-8669
www.discoverpowellriver.
com*

Tour B: Coast Mountain Circle Tour

**Vancouver,
Coast and Mountains**
250-1508 W. Second Ave., Vancouver
☎*(604)739-9011 or
800-667-3306
www.coastandmountains.
bc.ca*

**Squamish & Howe Sound
Chamber of Commerce**
37950 Cleveland Ave., Squamish
☎*(604) 892-9244
www.squamishchamber. bc.ca*

Whistler Travel InfoCentre
2097 Lake Placid Rd., Whistler
☎*(604) 932-5528
www.bcadventure.com*

**Whistler Activity
and Information Center**
4010 Whistler Way, Whistler, BC
☎*(604) 932-2394, ext 2
www.tourismwhistler.com*

Lytton Travel InfoCentre
400 Fraser St., Lytton
☎*(250) 455-2523
www.lytton.org*

Hope Travel InfoCentre
919 Water Ave., Hope
☎*(604) 869-2021
www.hopechamber.bc.ca*

**Harrison Hot Springs Travel
InfoCentre**
499 Hot Springs Rd., Harrison Hot
Springs
☎*(604) 796-3425
www.harrison.ca*

Tour C: The Thompson River as Far as Revelstoke

**Thompson–Okanagan
Tourism Association**
1332 Water St., Kelowna
☎*800-567-2275
www.thompsonokanagan.
com*

Kamloops Visitor InfoCentre
1290 West Trans-Canada Hwy.,
Kamloops
☎*(250) 374-3377 or
800-662-1994
www.adventurekamloops.
com*

Revelstoke Travel InfoCentre
204 Campbell Ave., Revelstoke
☎*(250) 837-5345 or
800-487-1493*

Revelstoke City Hall
216 Mackenzie Ave., Revelstoke
☎*(250) 837-2161
www.cityofrevelstoke.com*

Tour D: Okanagan Valley

**Thompson–Okanagan
Tourism Association**
see above

Princeton Travel InfoCentre
57 route 3E, Princeton
☎*(250) 295-3103*

Osoyoos Visitor InfoCentre
9912 Hwy. 3, Osoyoos, BC
☎*(250) 495-7142 or
888-676-9667*

**Penticton and Wine Country
Visitor Information Centre**
888 Westminster Ave. W., Penticton
☎*(250) 492-4103 or
800-663-5052*

Kelowna Travel InfoCentre
544 Harvey Ave.
☎*(250) 861-1515
www.tourismkelowna.org*

Vernon Tourism
701 Highway 97
☎*(250) 542-1415 or
800-665-0795
www.vernontourism.com*

**Merritt & District Chamber of
Commerce**
2185B Voght St.
☎*(250) 378-5634 or
877-330-3377
www.merritt-chamber.bc.ca*

Tour E: Kootenay Country

Tourism Rockies
P.O. Box 10, 1905 Warren Ave.,
Kimberley
☎*(250) 427-4838
www.bcrockies.com*

**Nakusp and District Chamber
of Commerce**
92 6th Ave. NW, Nakusp
☎*(250)265-4234 or
800-909-8819*

Nelson Visitor InfoCentre
225 Hall St., Nelson
☎*(250) 352-3433 or
877-663-5706
www.discoverynelson.com*

Rossland Tourist Information
intersection of Hwy. 3B and Hwy. 22,
located at the Rossland Museum
☎*(250) 362-7722*

Kimberley Visitor InfoCentre
115 Gerry Sorrensen Way, Kimberley
☎*(250) 427-3666*

Cranbrook Visitor InfoCentre
2279 Cranbrook St. N., Cranbrooks
☎*(250) 426-5914*

Internet

It is usually easy to connect to the Web at a terminal in one of the municipal libraries. In some cases, such as in the Okanagan Valley, you can use the internet for one hour a day free of charge.

Some Internet terminals have also been set up in a few youth hostels.

Exploring

British Columbia is exceptional in many respects, first of all because it has something to offer all manner of tourists, whether they're travelling by car or hiking. The southern part of the province is a large territory, which is flat in certain places and then suddenly very hilly in others. The construction of the railroad blazed a trail for the highways, each of which is more spectacular than the last.

Tour A:
The Sunshine Coast

Most people get to the Sunshine Coast by boat. There are no roads linking Vancouver to these resort towns; the daily comings and goings are dictated by the ferry schedule. As a result, the mentality here is completely different. The towns that have grown up along this coast benefit from the sea and what it yields. The Sunshine Coast runs along the Strait of Georgia, and is surrounded by Desolation Sound to the north, the Coast Mountains to the east and Howe Sound farther south.

Langdale

It takes 40min to reach Langdale, a small port city at the southern tip of the Sunshine Coast. Ferries shuttle back and forth several times a day, but you have to arrive at the Horseshoe Bay terminal at least an hour early for some weekend departures. **Horseshoe Bay** lies 20km northwest of Vancouver. With **BC Ferries** *(information: 7am to 10pm; Vancouver: ☎888-223-3779, ☎888-223-3779; B.C. Only, Victoria: ☎250-386-3431)* You

can save up to 15% on the price of your ticket if you return by way of Vancouver Island instead of opting for a round-trip. Ask for the Sunshine Coast Circlepac.

During the ferry ride, your notion of distance will change; the time required to get from point A to point B can no longer be measured in the same way. Let yourself be carried away; just sit back and contemplate the view between the sea and the mountains.

The Coast Salish First Nation were the first people to inhabit the coast. The Squamish and Sechelt lived in the present-day Gibsons region. Europeans first sailed these waters in the 1790s, but it wasn't until Captain Richards came here in 1859 and 1860 that a record was made of all the bays, coves, islands and sounds.

★
Gibsons

Visitors to Gibsons are sure to recognize the site of *The Beachcombers*, a Canadian Broadcasting Corporation (CBC) television series that was shot here for close to 20 years and broadcast in over 40 countries. On the way from Langdale to Gibsons, stop off at **Molly's Reach** (see p 221) to take a look at the photographs of the actors from the popular television show and to explore the little shops and restaurants along **Molly's Lane ★**. More recently Gibsons became Castle Rock for the film *Needful Things*, based on a Steven King novel.

A visit to the **Sunshine Coast Maritime Museum ★** *(at the end of Molly's Lane, ☎604-886-4114)* is a must. You will be greeted by a charming woman who will inspire you with her passion for the local marine life.

The Sunshine Coast has been developed in a thin strip alongside the forest. The area abounds in plant and animal life—orchids and wild roses, deer and black bears. River otters and beavers can be found near the coast, while sea-lions and seals swim about farther offshore.

Sechelt

To get to **Sechelt**, take Hwy. 101 northward. The landscape is rather dreary, but its beauty is soon enhanced by the sea and the islands. Sechelt is an important administrative centre for the Aboriginal community. At the **House of Hewhiwus** *(5555 Hwy. 101, beside the tourist office)*, you'll find a theatre, an art gallery and a souvenir shop. Members of the community can tell you about Aboriginal art, each piece of which is associated with a legend.

The Sunshine Coast is best explored aboard a boat on one of the neighbouring waterways. Turn right on Wharf Road and go to Government Wharf. **Sunshine Coast Tours ★** *($55; every day 10:30am to 4:30pm; ☎604-885-0351 or 800-870-9055)* arranges outings on Sechelt Inlet, as far as the Skookumchuck Rapids, aimed at familiarizing visitors with the local marine life. A salmon barbecue is served on the shore, and a you'll enjoy a ride on the Skookumchuck ("strong waters") Rapids at high tide, when the water is over 3m higher. If you simply want to take a look at the rapids, go to Egmont; to get there, keep right before Earls Cove on the road to Powell River. The parking lot is nearly 4km from the viewing area.

Pender Harbour

Still heading toward Earls Cove, you will pass alongside **Pender Harbour**, whose series of little islands is a

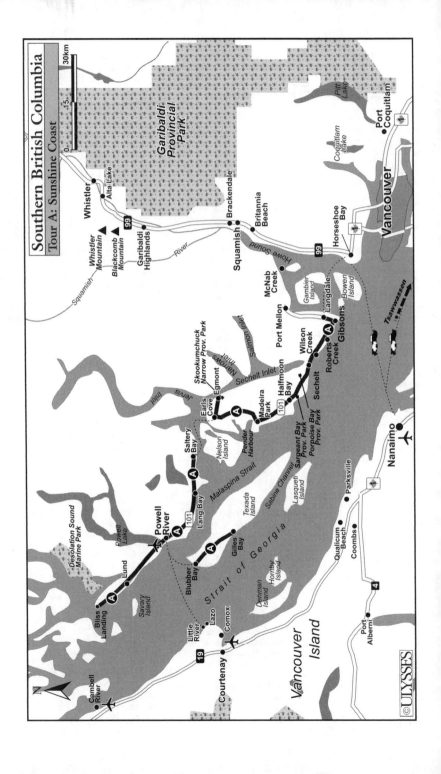

fisher's dream come true. Easily accessible by both land and water, this place is popular with salmon fishers. **Lowe's Resort** (☎604-883-2456) arranges fishing, scuba-diving and sightseeing excursions.

The Sunshine Coast is divided in two. A ferry will take you from Earls Cove to Saltery Bay, offering yet another opportunity to take in British Columbia's splendid scenery.

★
Powell River

Powell River, an important waterfront town, boasts magnificent sunsets over Vancouver Island and the islands in the Strait of Georgia. The spotlight is on outdoor activities in this region, since the temperate climate is conducive to year-round fun and games. Forestry plays an important role in the local economy, but visitors come here for the lakes, the woods, the wildlife and the views.

After a walk in the mountains or along the waterfront, the most beautiful views of the Strait of Georgia will be forever etched in your mind. Visitors to this region enjoy a host of water sports 12 months a year. There are activities to suit every budget, and all of them are immediately accessible.

The limpid water lures scuba-diving buffs here every year, especially during winter. In **Saltery Bay Provincial Park ★**, a bronze statue of a mermaid lies hidden away among the ocean's treasures at a depth of 20m.

Texada Island

Located in the Strait of Georgia, not far from Powell River, Texada Island was once an important mining centre where, in 1880, iron was exploited. The island now attracts only nature lovers

who explore it either on foot, by bicycle or by scuba diving. Since the services on the island are very limited, you are advised to come as equipped as possible and with a specific plan so that you're not left "stranded" without knowing what to do.

★★
Savary Island

Savary Island is one of the Northern Gulf Islands. It is accessible by taxi-boat from Powell River. The distance of the crossing is about 20km. It is nicknamed British Columbia's Hawaii and Pleasure Island, due to its **white sand beaches ★★★** and **crystal-clear water**, making swimming a pleasure. Large numbers of **eagles** visit the island and **seal** colonies frequent the shores. Activities practised on Savary Island are walking, cycling, swimming and sunbathing. It truly is *the* summer destination. Don't think about bringing your car; the island is very small *(8km long and 1km wide)*, and there are no roads. A bicycle is therefore an indispensable means of transportation here.

★★
Lund

Lund, located at the beginning (or the end, depending on what direction you're heading in) of Hwy. 101, is the gateway to marvellous **Desolation Sound ★★**, a marine life sanctuary easily accessible by canoe or kayak. The town port is magnificent, with its old hotel, its adjoining shops and its wooden promenade, which skirts round the bay. Imagine a typical fishing village and your harbour will undoubtedly be filled with the fishing boats moored here. In terms of activities, there is much to choose from here, from fishing and whale-watching trips to snorkelling and kayaking.

You can take the ferry from Powell River to Vancouver Island or backtrack to Langdale and return to Vancouver by way of Horseshoe Bay.

Tour B: Coast Mountain Circle Tours

Magnificent panoramic views abound all along the coast. Whether you are travelling by car, by train or aboard a ferry, a succession of fjords, mountains, forests and scenic viewpoints will unfold before you. The Sea to Sky Highway is a winding road used by many visitors who come to Whistler for sporting vacations in both winter and summer. Forestry and tourism are the two mainsprings of this vast region's economy. Beautiful **Furry Creek** golf course, renowned throughout the province and even the country, attracts experienced golfers all summer. The challenge is to keep yourself from being distracted by the enchanting landscape. The first stop on the 99, coming from Vancouver, is Britannia Beach.

★
Britannia Beach

For nearly a century, **Britannia Beach** was an important mining town where thousands of tonnes of copper were extracted. It has been transformed into a giant museum where visitors can learn how the mines operated from the turn of the century to the early 1970s, when they shut down. A train ride through the tunnels will take you back to another era, while a guide explains and demonstrates the various drilling techniques that were used as the machinery became more and more advanced. The tour ends at the mill, where the ore was cleaned. The **B.C. Museum of Mining ★** *($12.95; early May*

Southern British Columbia

to mid-Oct every day 9am to 4:30pm, mid-Oct to Nov 30 and Feb to early May Mon-Fri 10am to 4:30pm; ☎604-896-2233 or 800-896-4044).

Hwy. 99 runs alongside Howe Sound to Squamish. For many years, the only means of getting to the town from the south was by boat; some communities still rely on ferries to reach the coast farther north.

Squamish

Located at the north end of Howe Sound, Squamish owes its existence to the forest industry, which still helps support the local economy. You can see the forestry workers in action in the woods, at the sawmill or in the sorting yard, where gigantic machines put blocks of wood in place. At the entrance from Squamish, you'll be intrigued by the big, black rock face, known as The Chiefs, that descends steeply to the edge of the road. If you like rock climbing, you can tackle it with a guide. The **Soo Coalition for Sustainable Forests** ★ *(4hr walk in the woods $20; dryland sort tour $5; saw-mill tour $5 with own car, $10 without car; reservations required; ☎604-892-9766)* is an organization that works toward preserving both the forest and the jobs related to the industry. It arranges tours of the forest and the lumber yard in order to educate the public on this subject.

Windsurfers come to Squamish, whose name means "mother of the wind," for the wind that sweeps down the sound and then shifts inland. Mountain-climbing is also becoming more popular in this region. The place to go is **Stawamus Chief Mountain**. The trails leading to this granite monolith will take you to places where you can watch the mountain climbers. For more information, contact

the **Squamish & Howe Sound District Chamber of Commerce** *(☎604-892-9244).*

Hwy. 99 heads inland and runs alongside Garibaldi Park on its way through the valley that leads to Whistler.

Brackendale

Drawn by a mysterious force, every winter salmon make their way back from the Pacific Ocean to the Squamish and Cheakamus Rivers to spawn and die. Not far behind are the thousands of **bald eagles** that choose the small town of Brackendale as their winter residence. They feed on the decomposing salmon washed up along the river.

Only 70km north of Vancouver by the Sea to Sky Highway (Hwy. 99), the small Aboriginal community of Waiwecum, now called Brackendale, is actually a suburb of Squamish. It has recently been recognized as the most significant gathering site for bald eagles in the world, ahead of the Chilkat Bald Eagle Reserve in Alaska. Eagles are everywhere: on the trees, on the roofs of houses and along the road. This unique phenomenon draws over 2,000 amateur naturalists every weekend (From December to January). Eagles can be viewed from the "Eagle Run" on Goverment Road *(Exit Hwy. 99 at Mamquam Rd. and head north on Government Rd.).*

Every year, a census of the eagles is organized by the **Brackendale Art Gallery,** which exhibits paintings and sculptures, some very fine work. Also in the summer, **Brennan Park Leisure Centre** ensures a good time for both young and old alike. There are also **five provincial parks**, all along the Sea to Sky Highway, that offer the chance to participate in all sorts of outdoor activities.

For more information about the Brackendale eagles, contact the **Squamish & Howe Sound Visitor Info Centre** open all year, or the **Brackendale Art Gallery** *(noon to 10pm Sat, Sun and holidays; ☎604-898-3333).*

Some Advice: This region is inhabited by many black and grizzly bears. Be very careful. Bears may sometimes seem peaceful and harmless but they can be very dangerous.

★★
Whistler

Whistler attracts skiers, golfers, hikers, sailors and snowboarders from all over the world. An impressive hotel complex graces the little village at the foot of Blackcomb and Whistler Mountains. Other amenities at this internationally renowned resort include restaurants, shops, sports facilities and a convention centre. Whistler is popular in summer and winter alike, and each season offers its own assortment of activities.

For several years now, it has been rated among the top North American wintersports resorts. Besides the big hotels, more and more condominiums are being built and stores have multiplied. To allow visitors to get around more easily, a shuttle service around the village has been instituted. Of course, the shops are mostly geared towards tourists but many are also for residents; there are shopping centres and large grocery stores. This encourages people to buy condos as secondary residences and benefits Whistler's economy.

In the early 1960s, a group of adventurers wanted this area to host the 1968 Winter Olympics and created Garibaldi Park for that purpose. Although their hopes for the Olympics did not come through, they did not give up

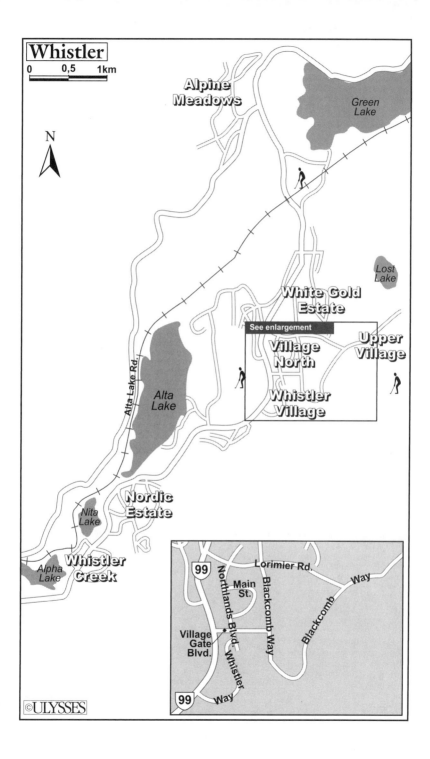

on the idea of turning the valley into a huge ski resort. The population of Whistler increased tenfold in 20 years, and in the year 1993 alone over a million people enjoyed the outdoors here.

Whistler receives, on average, nearly 1000cm of snow each year, and the temperature hovers around -5°C during the winter months. For details about the host of activities available here, refer to the "Outdoor Activities" section (see p 204).

Whistler hosts all sorts of events throughout the year, including a men's World Cup downhill competition, World Cup acrobatic skiing, gay skiers' week and a jazz festival.

Take the time to walk through the hotel village at the foot of the mountains and soak up the festive, relaxed atmosphere. Everything has its price here, and enjoying yourself can be quite expensive.

Outside of the little village, at the edge of the Whistler area, lies Function Junction, a small-scale industrial centre.

Pemberton

The pretty little town of Pemberton is nestled in a hollow in impressive Mount Currie. This little farming area has rapidly gained a serious reputation among outdoor enthusiasts. There is an infinite number of hiking trails around the town which lead to small mountain lakes and spectacular glaciers. If you have a vehicle with sufficient ground clearance, you can also venture onto B.C. Forest Service roads. Rough campsites have been set up next to the road, and there's access to lovely little fishing spots with an abundance of trout.

In the winter, snowmobilers head to the **Pemberton Ice**

Cap ★ ★ ★ (see "Outdoor Activities", p 209).

Lillooet

During the Gold Rush, Lillooet was the most important place in British Columbia, considered Mile 0 of the Gold Rush Trail to Caribou Country. Miners and tradespeople came to this wild territory and took this dangerous route with the sole objective of making their fortune. Now Lillooet is a peaceful community of 2,000 inhabitants and is mostly known its natural beauty. In the summer, people come for the fishing and the camping. The dry, warm climate attracts tourists from neighbouring regions who are sometimes exasperated by the rain, even in the summer. You can reach Lillooet by the Duffey Lake Road (Hwy. 99), past Whistler and Pemberton.

The tourist office in the town museum, beside the totem poles, can provide you with information on the best fishing spots and how to get to magnificent **Seton Lake** ★ ★ ★. It is impossible to miss if you're coming from the north.

From Lillooet you can travel north on Hwy. 12 to the intersection with the Trans-Canada, which you can take south a few kilometres to Cache Creek and the road to Ashcroft (see p 184); or you can take Hwy. 12 south to Lytton.

Lytton

Lytton, the rafting capital of the province, marks the point at which the Thompson flows into the Fraser. Here again, the scenery is breathtaking. The valleys are desert-like, with low, dense vegetation. Those interested in running the rapids can rely solely on paddles or opt for motorized canoes.

Yale

Three major historical events contributed to the development of Yale: the growth of the fur trade, the gold rush and the construction of the railway. The town also marks the beginning of the Fraser Canyon, so buckle your seatbelts and keep your eyes wide open.

The **Alexandria Bridge** spans the Fraser at a striking point along the river that is only accessible by foot. The bridge is no longer part of the road system, but you can enjoy some splendid views of the Fraser from its promenade. A sign alongside the Trans-Canada Highway shows the way.

Hell's Gate ★ *($11;* *604-867-9277)* owes its name to Simon Fraser, the first European to navigate this river. For a while, even the salmon had trouble making their way through this gorge, which had narrowed as a result of major landslides. The current was so strong that the fish couldn't swim upriver to spawn. To solve the problem, a pass was cleared. A cablecar will take you down to the water's edge, 152m below.

★
Hope

Hope, located at the confluence of the Coquihalla, Fraser and Nicolum Rivers, marks the gateway to the Fraser Canyon. The Hudson's Bay Company established a fur-trading post named Fort Hope on this site in 1848; 10 years later, prospectors lured by the discovery of gold would stock up on supplies here.

The **Kettle Valley Railway** left a significant mark on the Hope region. Five tunnels known as the **Othello-Quintette Tunnels** were bored through walls of granite so that trains could cross the Coquihalla canyon.

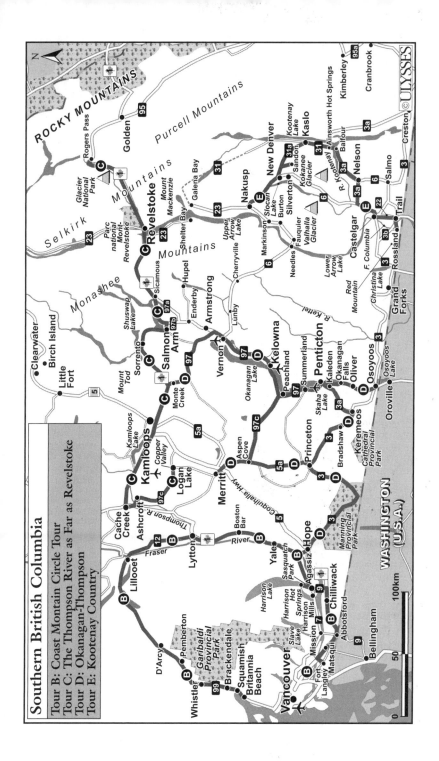

Southern British Columbia

Tour B: Coast Montain Circle Tour
Tour C: The Thompson River as Far as Revelstoke
Tour D: Okanagan-Thompson
Tour E: Kootenay Country

N

ROCKY MOUNTAINS

Purcell Mountains

Rogers Pass
Golden
95

Glacier National Park
Revelstoke
Mount Mackenzie
Galena Bay
Shelter Bay
23
31

Parc national Mont-Revelstoke
23

Selkirk
Mountains
Monashee
Mountains

Clearwater
Birch Island
Little Fort
5
Mount Tod
Shuswap Lake
Sicamous
97a
97b
Salmon Arm
Sorrento
Enderby
Hupel
Armstrong
Lumby
Cherryville

Nakusp
New Denver
Sandon
31a
31
Kaslo
Kootenay Lake
Ainsworth Hot Springs
Kimberley
95a
Cranbrook

Burton
Silverton
Slocan Lake
Markinson
Fauquier
Needles
Valhalla Glacier
6
Lower Arrow Lake

Kokanee Glacier
Balfour
3a
Nelson
3a
6
Salmo
3
Creston

Castelgar
E
22
Trail

Upper Arrow Lake
23
6

Red Mountain
F. Columbia
3b
Rossland
3
Grand Forks

Christina Lake
Washington (U.S.A.)

Kamloops Lake
Copper Valley
Kamloops
Logan Lake
97c
5a
Monte Creek

Vernon
97
Kelowna
D
Peachland
Okanagan Lake
97c
Summerland
97
Penticton
Skaha Lake
Kaleden
3a
Okanagan Falls
Oliver
Osoyoos
D
Osoyoos Lake
Oroville

Cache Creek
Ashcroft
12
Lillooet
Fraser
Lytton
Thompson R.
Boston Bar
River
5
Yale
Merritt
Coquihalla Hwy.
Aspen Cove
5a
Princeton
Bradshaw
3
Keremeos
Cathedral Provincial Park

D'Arcy
Pemberton
Garibaldi Provincial Park
Brackendale
Squamish
Britannia Beach
Whistler
99

Harrison Lake
Sasquatch Park
Harrison Hot Springs
Harrison Mills
Slave Lake
Mission
Agassiz
9
7
Chilliwack
Abbotsford
Matsqui
Bellingham
9
Hope
Manning Provincial Park
3

Vancouver
Fort Langley

100km
50
0

© ULYSSES

Like other sections of this railroad, fallen debris and avalanches got the better of the tracks.

A visit to this magnificent linear park will give you an appreciation for the genius of those who built the railway and a chance to admire the majestic landscape looming up in front of it. Hollywood even picked this spot as a setting for the films *First Blood* and *Shoot to Kill*.

Take Wallace Street from downtown Hope, turn right on Sixth Ave., then left on Kawkawa Lake Road; after crossing a bridge and a set of railroad tracks, turn right on Othello Road. The entrance to the parking lot will be on your right. Don't forget to bring a camera.

A local chainsaw sculptor creates impressive pieces that delight visitors and residents alike. It all started when sculptor Pete Ryan transformed the trunk of a large tree in Memorial Park into an eagle with a salmon in its claws. Ever since, a number of his works, covering a variety of themes, have come to adorn downtown Hope.

If you'd like to take in a bird's-eye view of the region, go to the Hope airport and take a ride in a glider (see "Outdoor Activities", p 204).

From Hope travellers have several options. One is to hop on the Trans-Canada west and drive directly to Vancouver (150km). A more leisurely route, Hwy. 7 west, leads to Harrison Hot Springs and Mission, described below. Finally, travellers can push east through Manning Provincial Park (see p 187) to Princeton and Tour D (see p 187), in the beautiful Okanagan Valley, via Hwy. 3 east.

★ Harrison Hot Springs

The Harrison Hot Springs are located at the southern end of Harrison Lake. The Coast Salish First Nation used to come to here to soak in the warm mineral water, which supposedly has curative powers. Gold prospectors discovered the springs in 1858, when a storm on Lake Harrison forced them to return to shore and they happened to step into the warm water. The lake is surrounded by successive mountains peaks that stand out against the sky, making for a spectacular setting.

The indoor **Harrison Hot Springs Public Pool ★** *($7.25; Mon-Thu 9am to 9pm Fri 9am to 10pm Sat 8am to 10pm Sun 8am to 9pm; at the intersection of Hot Springs Rd. and Lilloet Ave., ☎604-796-2244)* offers access to the springs. In addition to running the public pool, the Harrison Hotel has acquired rights to the springs. Every year in September and October, sand-castle enthusiasts flock to the beaches on Harrison Lake, with impressive results. The road, which runs alongside the lake, leads to **Sasquatch Provincial Park** (see p 203).

Mission

Xá:ytem LongHouse Interpretive Centre *(35087 Lougheed Hwy., 3km east of Mission; donations accepted, ☎604-820-9725)*. This First Nations archaeological site was discovered in 1990. *Xa:ytem* (pronounced *HAY-tum*) is an Aboriginal word designating a boulder on a plateau on the Fraser River. According to geologists, the rock was deposited there by shifting glaciers. The Sto:lo First Nation, who have inhabited this region for more than 4,000 years, explain the boulder's presence by saying that it is what became of three chiefs who had

committed a sin. Hundreds of relics have been found in this area, including tools and weapons made of stone. These articles are displayed in the centre, which has Sto:lo guides.

From Mission, take the bridge across the Fraser to Abbots Ford, then get on the Trans-Canada (Hwy. 11) to Langley.

Fort Langley

Fort Langley National Historic Site ★ *($5; Mar to Oct every day 10am to 5pm Nov to late Feb Mon-Fri 10am to 5pm; Exit 66 North of the Trans-Canada, towards Fort Langley, at the intersection of Mavis and Royal Sts.; ☎604-513-4777)*. Fort Langley was erected in 1827, 4km downriver from its present location, on the south bank of the Fraser. It was moved in 1839, only to be ravaged by fire the following year. The Hudson's Bay Company used the fort to store furs that were to be shipped out to Europe.

On November 19, 1858, British Columbia's status was officially proclaimed here, marking the end of the Hudson's Bay Company's control over the territory. Of the 16 buildings that once stood inside the palisade, only the warehouse remains. Erected around 1840, it is the oldest European-style structure on the west side of the Rockies. Six other buildings, as well as the palisade itself, have been reconstructed in order to acquaint the public with that era.

Tour C: The Thompson River as far as Revelstoke

Ashcroft

Ashcroft lies a few kilometres east of Hwy. 1. In 1860, gold prospectors heading north set out from here. You can go back to the Trans-Canada I East and make your way to Kamloops, passing through Cache Creek on the way in order to skirt Kamloops Lake and see the ginseng fields (see below). We recommend taking Hwy. 97C to Logan Lake and the Copper Valley mine. As you make your way through a magnificent desert valley, you'll see the **Sundance Guest Ranch** (see p 213 for details on staying there), which looks out over the Thompson River. Ever since the 1950s, this ranch has been sending visitors off on horseback rides across thousands of hectares of fields. Like most ranches in the region, it was once the home of stockbreeders.

Highland Valley Copper ★ ★ *(free admission; May to Sep Mon-Fri two tours per day; tours last 2hrs, call first to book;* ☎*250-523-3507)* is one of the largest open-cut copper mines in the world. The industrial machinery and the equipment used to transport the ore are gigantic. Though you can't tour the mine, you'll notice its lunar landscape from the highway.

Continue driving east. When you reach the Coquihalla Highway (5), head for Kamloops.

Kamloops

Kamloops (pop. 78,000), the hub of inland British Columbia, is a major stopover point. The local economy is driven chiefly by the forestry and tourism industries, with mining and stock-breeding playing subsidiary roles.

The Kamloops area offers many interesting vacation opportunities. The stunning natural surroundings and favourable climate cater to outdoor enthusiasts. Stroll about the city; it has great restaurants and movie theatres and the tourist centre can offer

information on golf, skiing, fishing and many other seasonal outdoor activities.

Culture also plays an important role in Kamloops. The **Kamloops Symphony Orchestra** *(335 Victoria St.,* ☎*250-372-5000)*, the **Western Canada Theatre Company** *(1025 Lorne St.,* ☎*250-372-3216)*, the **Sagebrush Theatre** *(*☎*250-374-5483)* and the **Kamloops Museum and Archives** *(Tue-Sat 9:30am to 4:30pm; 207 Seymour St.;* ☎*250-828-3576)* are all very active.

In 2002, the **2141**, or the *Spirit of Kamloops ($12.50; Jun to Sep Fri-Sun 9:30am and 11:30am departures, Fri and Sat 7:30pm; 510 Lorne St.,* ☎*250-374-2141)*, started taking passengers again after a lengthy period of restoration. Built in 1912, the *2141* is one of just a few remaining operational steam engines in the world. She rode the rails on short lines in Alberta and Saskatchewan before retiring in 1958, and was then sold to the City of Kamloops in 1961. Kamloops Heritage Railway now operates the rumbling and hissing engine, as it sets out on tours from the east end of the town centre. Perfect for train aficionados and children, tours include a mock train heist by famed Kamloops outlaw Billy Miner.

An activity that underlines the importance of the rivers in British Columbia is a cruise aboard the *Wanda-Sue,* which sails along the Thompson River through bare mountains. First Nations, trappers, gold prospectors, lumberjacks and railway workers all travelled by boat before the railway lines and roads were laid here. The *Wanda-Sue ★* sets out from the **Old Kamloops Yacht Club** *($13.50; Apr to Sep; the trip lasts two hours; 1140 River St., near Tenth Ave.,* ☎*250-374-7447)*.

West of Kamloops, ginseng crops lie hidden in fields beneath big pieces of black cloth. Large farms produce this root, which is highly coveted by Asians for the health benefits it is supposed to procure. The variety grown here, known as American ginseng, was discovered in eastern Canada several hundred years ago by Aboriginal people, who made potions with it. At the **Sunmore Company** *(925 McGill Place,* ☎*250-374-3017)*, you can drop in and learn about ginseng farming in North America and how local methods differ from those employed in Asia.

Secwepemc Museum & Native Heritage Park *($6; Jun to Aug Mon-Fri 8:30am to 8pm; Sat, Sun and Holidays 10am to 8pm, Sep to May Mon-Fri 8:30am to 4:30pm; 335 Yellowhead Hwy.,* ☎*250-828-9801)* is located on the Kamloops First Nations reserve east of town (take the Jasper exit on the Trans-Canada Hwy.).

This museum gives you an opportunity to discover the culture of the Shuswaps, Kamloops's First Nations people. An exhibit has been set up outside on a 4.8ha area along the Thompson River. It allows visitors to understand their way of life. A small village has been restored, and the Shuswaps' hunting, fishing and agricultural methods are presented. Costumed animators recreate the First Nationsnspirit of the region.

Leave Kamloops and head towards Revelstoke on the Trans-Canada, which runs alongside the water, beaches, mountains and golf courses. Gorges become narrower and narrower and the heart of the Rockies appears on the horizon. The vegetation is much more luxuriant here, with blue-grey sage brush giving way to mighty trees.

Salmon Arm

There are two reasons that might warrant a stop in Salmon Arm: houseboats and salmon. The town itself, the commercial centre for communities on the shores of vast Shuswap Lake, is mainly an uninteresting stretch of businesses along the Trans-Canada Highway. Turn left on Ross Street to reach the more appealing Harbourfront Drive, on Shuswap Lake.

The lake, renowned for its warmth, is popular with vacationers looking to wile away some time on the beach, or even better, aboard a houseboat. Nearby Sicamous is the self-proclaimed houseboat capital of Canada, and boats can be rented from a number of operators there and in Salmon Arm, including **Twin Anchors Houseboats** *($2,560/3 nights, 15-person sleeping capacity, reservations required; Apr to Sep; 101 Martin St., Sicamous, ☎800-663-4026).* The boats are large and comfortable, and as well equipped as hotel rooms, with hot tubs and fireplaces.

A less expensive activity can be enjoyed every fall, when a dramatic Darwinian struggle occurs in the Adams River, just west of Salmon Arm. In October, chinook, coho, pink and sockeye salmon return to the place of their birth in October from the Pacific Ocean, to spawn and then die. **Roderick Haig-Brown Provincial Park** *(50km west of Salmon Arm, 8km northeast of Trans-Canada junction at Squilax; ☎250-851-3000)* was created to conserve and protect spawning beds and is the best spot to view the impressive natural show.

Every four years, the dominant race of Adams sockeye salmon makes a run that dwarfs all others, and the river teems with around two million crimson fish. As one local says,

"you could walk across the river on salmon." Toward the end of October, birdwatchers will be impressed with the eagles and waterfowl that gather to ravage the fish carcasses, while bears emerge from the forests to enjoy an easy feed. The next big sockeye run will occur in 2006, but the magnificent display is worth seeing each fall.

Continue east along the Trans-Canada Hwy. to reach Revelstoke.

★★
Revelstoke

The history of Revelstoke is closely linked to the construction of the transcontinental railway, when many Italians came here to apply their expertise in building tunnels. To this day, the town's 9,000 residents rely mainly on the railroad for their income. Tourism and the production of electricity also play important roles in the economy of this magnificent town.

Revelstoke is a century-old town that has managed to retain its charm. Numerous Queen Anne, Victorian, Art Deco and neoclassical buildings here bear witness to days gone by. Pick up a copy of the **Heritage Walking & Driving Tour ★** at the Revelstoke Museum (see below) or at the **Travel Info Centre** (see p 176).

The **Revelstoke Railway Museum ★** *($6; Jul and Aug every day 9am to 8pm; May, Jun and Sep every day 9am to 5pm; Apr and Oct Mon-Sat 1pm to 5pm; Nov Mon-Fri 9am to 5pm; Dec, Jan, Feb and Mar Mon-Fri 1pm to 5pm; 719 Track St., ☎250-837-6060 or 877-837-6060)* focuses on the construction of the railway across the Rockies and the history of Revelstoke. The exhibit features railway artefacts, photos from the

local archives and, most importantly, a 1940s locomotive and a company director's personal railway car, built in 1929.

At the **Revelstoke Dam ★** *(free admission; May to mid-Sep every day 9am to 5pm; closed mid-Sep to May although group visits are permitted during the low season; take Hwy. 23 North, ☎250-837-6211),* you can learn about the production of hydroelectricity and visit a number of rooms, as well as the dam itself, an impressive concrete structure.

Hiking enthusiasts will be thrilled by all the outdoor excursions to be enjoyed in this area (see p 205).

Revelstoke is a crossroads between the Rockies and the Kootenays, to the south. If you plan on continuing east to Alberta, stay on the Trans-Canada to Golden, Field and Lake Louise (see **The Rocky Mountains**, p 265). We recommend driving down into the Kootenays, which are lesser known than the Rockies, but equally fascinating. Before heading south, however, continue until you reach **Rogers Pass ★ ★**, named after the engineer who discovered it in 1881. This valley was originally supposed to serve as a passage between the east and the west, but after a number of catastrophes, during which avalanches claimed the lives of hundreds of people, the Canadian Pacific Railway company decided to build a tunnel instead. At the **Rogers Pass Discovery Centre ★** *(free with $3 park entrance fee; ☎250-814-5233),* located an hour from Revelstoke ins Glacier National Park, visitors can learn about the epic history of the railway. A trail that runs along the former tracks will take you past the ruins of a railway station destroyed in an avalanche.

Back in Revelstoke, cross the town bridge and head toward Shelter Bay on Hwy. 23 South in order to take the free ferry (every day 6pm to 11:30am) and continue southward to Nakusp (see Tour E, p 198). Get your camera ready during the trip across Upper Arrow Lake (30min), because you're in for some splendid views of the Kootenays. Recent cutbacks have resulted in long waits to board the ferry on holiday weekends. Take this route during the week if you can.

Tour D: Okanagan Valley

This tour starts in Hope. See p 182.

All sorts of natural treasures await discovery in this part of British Columbia. With its stretches of water and blanket of fruit trees, the Okanagan Valley, which runs north-south, is one of the most beautiful areas in the province. Okanagan wines have won a number of prizes; the orchards feed a good portion of the country; and the lakes and mountains are a dream come true for sporty types. The climate is conducive to a wide variety of activities: the winters, mild in town and snowy in the mountains, can be enjoyed by all. In the spring, the fruit trees are in bloom, while in summer and fall, a day of fruit-picking is often followed by a dip in one of the many lakes.

Head east on Hwy. 3 to Princeton.

Located 45min from Hope, **Manning Provincial Park ★★** attracts hundreds of visitors each season. Twice the size of Cathedral Park, it covers 60,000ha of wilderness, where you'll find all sorts of treasures (see Parks and

Beaches, p 202, and Hiking, p 206).

Princeton

Princeton is situated not far from the Cascade Mountains, where the Tulameen and Similkameen Rivers converge. Founded in 1883 by a cowboy who discovered gold, this **Granite City** has experienced its share of Gold Rush fever. The 2,000 miners and prospectors left behind some traces from those bygone days, some of which are still around today. Although there's little gold left in the rivers you will find salloons and old-style shops. With its two rivers, Princeton is a favourable spot for sports such as **kayaking**, **canoeing** and **rafting**. Its many lakes are visited by a wide variety of birds. Cycling is also a pleasant way of discovering the surrounding area and performing some spectacular feats on the nearby Trans Canada Trail.

American researchers come to the **Princeton Museum and Archives ★** *(Jul to Sep Tue-Fri 10am-6pm Sat and Sun 11am to 3pm, Oct to Jun Sat and Sun 11am to 3pm or by appointment, ☎250-295-7588, home ☎250-295-3918)* to study its impressive collection of fossils. You'll get caught up in curator Margaret Stoneberg's enthusiasm as she tells you about the pieces and how they bear witness to the region's history. Due to underfunding, the fossils pile up without being properly displayed, but it is nevertheless amazing to see how much the museum holds.

As you continue eastward on Hwy. 3, you will be leaving the vast Okanagan-Similkameen region and heading into the southwestern part of the province, back to the confluence of the Fraser and Coquihalla Rivers.

Keremeos

Keremeos is the **kingdom of fruit**. This is why this small town, abundantly stocked with mini-markets is nicknamed the "fruit-stand capital of the world." All along the road, shops compete for the freshest fruit, the best display of farm products and to have the best decor. The apple pyramids are delightful, as are the gigantic ones made with pumkins around Hallowe'en.

In Keremeos, history is recounted at the **Historic Grist Mill ★** *(May to Oct every day 9am to 5pm; RR1, Upper Bench Rd., ☎250-499-2888)*, founded in 1877 to produce flour for local First Nations people, cowboys and miners. The water mill, equipment and original buildings have been restored and are now a British Columbia Heritage Site.

Cathedral Provincial Park ★★ covers 33,000ha of mountains, lakes, valleys, wildlife and flowers. It is criss-crossed by trails that everyone can enjoy, since most cover fairly level terrain and are suitable for a variety of fitness levels. Furthermore, almost all of the bears in this region were driven off by the cowboys decades ago. A cozy lodge accommodates visitors wishing to stay in the park (see Parks and Beaches, p 204, and Hiking, p 206).

At the park exit, get back on Hwy. 3, which will take you to Osoyoos.

Osoyoos

Osoyoos lies at the bottom of the valley, flanked on one side by Osoyoos Lake and on the other by verdant slopes decked with orchards. It is located next to the U.S. border, in an arid climate more reminiscent of a Southwestern desert, or even southern Italy, than a Canadian town. The main attraction here is the exceptionally warm lake, where you can enjoy a variety of water sports during summer.

On your way into town on Hwy. 3 from the east, take a look at **Spotted Lake ★**. A natural phenomenon causes white rings to form on the surface of this lake, whose waters contain high levels of mineral salts. The lake, a sacred First Nations Site, was recently purchased by the government and given to the Okanagan Nation. By June, the lake has dried up, but circular mineral deposits remain on the cracked clay.

Osoyoos's main street is crowded with lousy motels, which detract from the beauty of the setting. The public parks on the west side are worth visiting, however, especially at the end of the day when the sun lights up the valley.

A tiny **desert ★★★**, made up of suge and antelope brush grasslonds, pokes its toe into the Southern Okanagan Valley. It is an amazing sight in this part of Canada, and is the only one in the country. The unique wildlife and vegetation here bear witness to nature's endless store of surprises.

Without irrigation, this valley would still be a desert and the orchards and vineyards would not have been able to thrive and bear fruit each year. The mini-desert is part of the same desert that begins in Baja California, Mexico and the state of Chihuahua before crossing the western United States.

The **Nk'mip Desert and Heritage Centre ★** *($7; Apr to Oct every day, summer 9am to 8pm, Sep and Oct 9am to 5pm; 1000 Rancher Creek Rd., off of 45th St. at east end of town, ☎250-495-7901 or 888-495-8555)*, which opened in 2002, is one of two focal points for exploring the desert. It is a

cultural as well as a natural site, with interpretive tours providing a First Nations perspective on the landscape of the Osoyoos First Nation. Self-guided trails wind through 20ha of sage grasslands and ponderosa pine forests. Exhibits in the interpretive centre explore the history of the Okanagan people and the Osoyoos First Nation, as well as the natural history of desert fauna like snakes and scorpions. There is a village area with a reconstructed pithouse, *tulemate* teepee and sweathouse.

For a strictly natural perspective, The **Desert Centre** *($6; Apr to Oct every day 10am to 3pm, Night tour $5, Jul and Aug every Fri, adv. booking and payment required; 3km north of Osoyoos, off of 146th Ave., ☎250-495-2470 or 877-899-0897, www.desert.org)* heightens awareness about the fragility of this particular ecosystem. The area is home to one of the largest intensities of species at risk in Canada. Footbridges cross a 2km trail along the rattlesnake's habitat. The explanations of the biologist-guide will teach you about the complexity of life in this world without water. It is fascinating to learn how desert animals and vegetation can survive here.

★★★
The Wine Route

The Thompson Okanagan region offers a memorable opportunity to discover a completely original wine route. The landscape in particular is unique; the parched hills and valleys aren't the colour and shape that you would expect when touring vineyards. Vines flourish in this climate and everything possible has been done to make the most of the region, and the results of these efforts have been fruitful.

Two aspects of wine-producing distinguish the region. The most recent, which is being developed in the Similkameen Valley, is associated with farm cultivation and expansion of the fertile soil. The other, more traditional aspect in the large Okanagan Valley, is related to a proud heritage of wine growing since the 1800s. This valley has similar characteristics to renowned German wine-producing areas. The presence of four lakes (Skaha, Osoyoos, Vaseux and Okanagan) creates a climate that is perfectly suited to producing great wines.

British Columbia puts considerable effort into promoting the quality of its wines. In the early 1980s, poor quality vines were removed. Through the perseverance of the government and wine growers, the **Chardonnay**, **Pinot Noir**, **Merlot** and **Gewurztraminer**, to name a few, all established undeniable reputations. In 1990, there was a need to create quality standards, and, as a result, the Vintners Quality Alliance started putting its mark on bottles, "**VQA**," to certify high-quality wine from British Columbia.

Of course, festivals are organized throughout the region. The **Annual Spring Okanagan Wine Festival** takes place during the first five days in May. There are scores of outings, picnics, meals well doused in the fruit of the vine, and dances, not to mention educational wine-tasting sessions for beginners.

The other big wine event is the **Annual Fall Okanagan Wine Festival**, which takes place during the first 10 days of October every year. Most of the Valley's 50 plus wineries participate and, as well as sampling all sorts of red, white sparkling and ice wines, you can try other delicacies, such as roast pigeon, baked salmon and chocolate specialties, all

Region's Best-Known Wines

hite Wines

uxerrois
eminiscent of Alsatian wine, slightly fruity.

Bacchus
Another wine similar to Alsatian wine, but drier.

Chardonnay
Very popular. Neither too dry nor too sweet. Served as an aperitif or with meals.

Chasselas
This wine takes its inspiration from the Swiss Alps and has an aroma of apples and lemons.

Gewurztraminer
With a slightly spicy aftertaste, this wine, as its homonym in Alsatian indicates, is served with fish and seafood.

Reisling
The climate is favourable to the cultivation of this grape which is quite dry and has a flowery, honey-like aroma.

Pinot Blanc
This white wine has become famous in British Columbia. It's taste, which is both dry and fruity, and its rich body make it worthy of its ancestor born in France in the 14th century.

Red Wines

Cabernet Sauvignon
Classified in the Bordeaux category, it has good body and is fragrant.

Chancellor
A fruity wine whose flavour has hints of strawberries and cherries.

Merlot
Another wine in the Bordeaux family – sweet, with a rich berry flavour.

Pinot Noir
A spicy, smooth wine with a plum and black-cherry flavour.

Southern British Columbia

presented and prepared with great care. Advance reservations are recommended. For information call ☎*(250) 861-6654, www.owfs.com.*

The clearly indicated wine route offers pleasant trips, among farms and orchards along Highway 97, revealing first-class views of Okanagan Lake at every turn.

This mouth-watering trail of discovery goes from Osoyoos to Salmon Arm each vineyard vies to offer the best reception and most elegant presentation to attract people. Wines are available to sample. Medals, international awards and anything attesting to a wine's quality cover the walls of shops. Even if it costs five

dollars to try a few drops of ultra sweet ice wine, a specialty of the region made from grapes that are picked frozen at the beginning of winter, curious wine-lovers are happy to oblige.

The list of wineries is long and interesting. Over the short distance of 200km, there are more than 50 establishments, with new ones opening to the public. Some are active throughout the year, but a few are open to visitors only during the tourist season. Call ahead before planning a wine-tasting trip.

For more information on the wine route, touring the vineyards and the wine festivals, contact the **B.C. Wine Infor-**

mation Centre *(888 Westminster Ave., Penticton,* ☎*250-494-9772 or 800-663-5052, www.bcwineinfo.com)* or the Okanagan-Thompson Tourism Association (see p 176).

The wine route runs through the vast Okanagan region. North of Osoyoos and south of Oliver, you'll come across **Domaine Combret ★** *(32057-131st Rd. 13, Oliver,* ☎*250-498-8878 or 866-837-7647)*. In 1995, the *Office International de la Vigne et du Vin*, based in Burgundy, France, awarded this French-owned vineyard the highest international distinction for its Chardonnay. Its Reisling also won a prize in 1995. You must call beforehand for a tour of the premises, as the wine growers spend a good part of

Vineyards Open to the Public

The letters and numbers in the following vineyard addresses are a local reference system – if you ask for directions, area residents will understand "RR 1, S58, C10," for example. In any case the wine route is well charted and every winery is clearly marked by a sign on the main road. Telephone before your tour for exact directions and to be sure that the vineyards of interest to you are open.

Cawston (just east of Keremeos on Hwy. 3)
Crowsnest Vineyards: Surprise Dr., RR1, S18, C18, ☎499-5129, www.crowsnestvineyards.com

Kelowna
Calona Vineyards: 1125 Richter St., ☎762-9144 or 888-246-4472
Cedarcreek Estate Winery: 5445 Lakeshore Rd., ☎764-8866
Gray Monk Estate Winery: 1055 Camp Rd., Okanagan Centre (north of Kelowna off of Hwy. 97), ☎766-3168 or 800-663-4205, www.graymonk.com
House of Rose Vineyards: 2270 Garner Rd., RR5, ☎765-0802
Mount Boucherie Estate Winery: 829 Douglas Rd., ☎769-8803, www.mtboucherie.bc.ca
Pinot Reach Cellars: 1670 Dehart Rd., ☎764-0078
Sandhill Wines: 1125 Richter St., ☎762-3332
St. Hubertus Estate Winery: 5225 Lakeshore Rd., ☎764-7888, www.st-hubertus.bc.ca
Summerhill Estate Winery: 4870 Chute Lake Rd., ☎764-8000 or 800-667-3538

Naramata
Elephant Island Orchard Wines: 2370 Aikens Loop, RR1, ☎496-5522, www.elephantislandwine.com
Kettle Valley Winery: 2988 Hayman Rd., ☎496-5898
Lake Breeze Vineyards: 930 Sammet Rd., ☎496-5659
Lang Vineyards: 2493 Gammon Rd., RR1, S11, C55, ☎496-5987
Nichol Vineyards: 1285 Smethurst Rd., RR1, S14, C13, ☎496-5962
Red Rooster Winery: 910 Debeck Rd., ☎496-4041

Okanagan Falls
Blue Mountain Vineyards & Cellars: open by appointment only
Allendale Rd., RR1, S3, C4, ☎497-8244, www.bluemountainwinery.com
Hawthorn Mountain Vineyards: Green Lake Rd., ☎497-8267, www.hmvineyard.com
Stag's Hollow Winery: 2215 Sun Valley Way, RR1, S3, C36, ☎497-6162
Wild Goose Vineyards: Sun Valley Way, RR1, S3, C11, ☎497-8919, www.wildgoosewinery.com

Oliver
Black Hills Estate Winery: 30880 Black Sage Rd., RR2, S52, C22, ☎498-0666
Burrowing Owl Vineyards: 100 Burrowing Owl Place, RR1, S52, C20, ☎498-0620 or 877-498-0620
Carriage House: 32764 Black Sage Rd., ☎498-8818
Domaine Combret: 32057 13 Rd., ☎498-8878 or 866-837-7647, www.combretwine.com
Fairview Cellars: 13147-334th St., ☎498-2211
Gehringer Brothers Estate Winery: Road 8, RR1, S23, C4, ☎498-3537 or 800-784-6304
Gersighel Wineberg: 29690 Hwy 97, RR1, S40, C20, ☎495-3319
Hester Creek Estate Winery: 13163-326th Ave., ☎498-4435, www.hestercreek.com
Inniskillin Okanagan Vineyards: Road 11, RR1, S24, C5, ☎498-6411, www.inniskillin.com
Jackson-Triggs Vintners: 38691-97th St., ☎866-589-4637, www.jacksontriggswinery.com
Silver Sage Winery: 32032-87th St., Road 9, ☎498-0310, www.silversagewinery.com

Oliver (continued)
Tinhorn Creek Vineyards: Road 7, RR1, S58, C10, ☎498-3743, www.tinhorn.com
Vincor International: Hwy. 97, ☎498-4981

Osoyoos
Nk'mip Cellars: 1400 Rancher Creek Rd., ☎495-2985

Peachland
Hainle Vineyards Estate Winery: 5355 Trepanier Bench Rd., RR2, S27A, C6, ☎767-2525 or 800-767-3109, www.hainle.com

Penticton
Benchland Vineyards: 170 Upper Bench Rd., ☎770-1733
Hillside Estate Winery: 1350 Naramata Rd., ☎493-6274, www.hillsideestate.com
La Frenz Winery: 740 Naramata Rd., ☎492-6690, www.lafrenzwinery.bc.ca
Poplar Grove: 1060 Poplar Grove Rd., ☎492-4575

Salmon Arm
Larch Hills: 110 Timms Rd., ☎832-0155, www.larchhillswinery.bc.ca

Summerland
Scherzinger Vineyards: 7311 Fiske Rd., ☎494-8815
Sumac Ridge Estate Winery: 17403 Hwy. 97, ☎494-0451, www.sumacridge.com
Thornhaven Estate Winery: 6816 Andrew, RR2, S68, C15, ☎494-7778

Vernon
Bella Vista Vineyards: 3111 Agnew Rd., ☎558-0770

Westbank
Mission Hill Family Estate: 1730 Mission Hill Rd., ☎768-7611, www.missionhillwinery.com
Quail's Gate Estate Winery: 3303 Boucherie Rd., ☎769-4451, www.quailsgate.com
Slamka Cellars: 2815 Ourtoland Rd., ☎769-0404, www.slamka.bc.ca

Southern British Columbia

the day outside among the vines during the grape-picking season. Originally from the south of France, the Combrets come from a long line of vintners. Stop by and sample some wine.

Take Hwy. 97 toward Penticton. Alternatively, you can continue east on Hwy. 3 to Grand Forks (see p 200).

Kaleden

Tucked away atop a mountain near **Kaleden** is the **Dominion Radio Astrophysical Observatory ★** *(Jul and Aug, Sun 2pm to 5pm, ☎250-493-7505)*, run by the Canadian National Research Council. If you're looking for a star, this place can help you find it.

★
Penticton

Penticton lies between Okanagan Lake, to the north, and Skaha Lake, to the south. The town has nearly 30,000 inhabitants and boasts a dry, temperate climate. Tourism is the mainspring of Penticton's economy. The area's First Nations named the site *Pentak-tin*, meaning "the place where you stay forever." A beach lined with trees and a pedestrian walkway run along the north end of town. The dry landscape, outlined by the curves of the sandy shoreline, contrasts with the vineyards and orchards. People come to Penticton for the outdoor activities, fine dining and local *joie de vivre.*

Take Main Street to Lakeshore Drive, turn left and stop in front of the **SS Sicamous** *($4; early Sep to end Oct every day 9am to 6pm; Nov to mid-Dec Mon-Fri 10am to 4pm; mid-Jan to Mar Mon-Fri 10am to 4pm; early Mar to mid-Jun every day 9am to 6pm; mid-Jun to Sep every day 9am to 9pm; ☎250-492-0403)*, a survivor of a bygone era. This paddleboat was once the principal means of transportation on Okanagan Lake. Built in Ontario in 1914 and assembled here, it was in service for over 20 years before being hauled

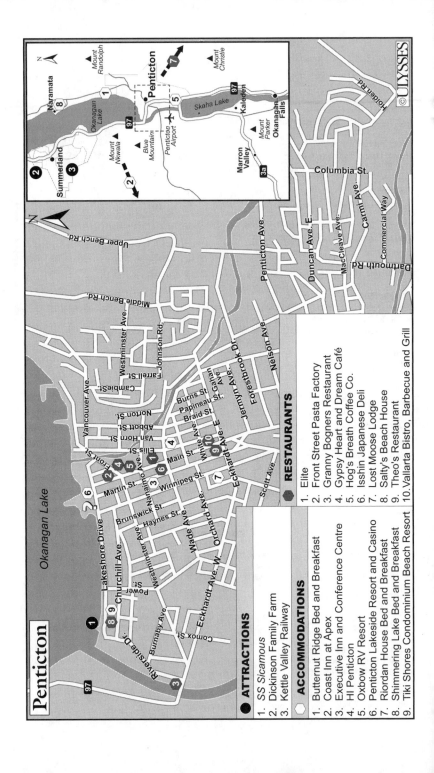

Penticton

Okanagan Lake

ATTRACTIONS
1. SS Sicamous
2. Dickinson Family Farm
3. Kettle Valley Railway

ACCOMMODATIONS
1. Butternut Ridge Bed and Breakfast
2. Coast Inn at Apex
3. Executive Inn and Conference Centre
4. HI Penticton
5. Oxbow RV Resort
6. Penticton Lakeside Resort and Casino
7. Riordan House Bed and Breakfast
8. Shimmering Lake Bed and Breakfast
9. Tiki Shores Condominium Beach Resort

RESTAURANTS
1. Elite
2. Front Street Pasta Factory
3. Granny Bogners Restaurant
4. Gypsy Heart and Dream Café
5. Hog's Breath Coffee Co.
6. Isshin Japanese Deli
7. Lost Moose Lodge
8. Salty's Beach House
9. Theo's Restaurant
10. Vallarta Bistro, Barbecue and Grill

© ULYSSES

up onto the beach and turned into a museum.

Penticton hosts a major sporting event, the **World Cup Ironman Triathlon**, a swimming, cycling and running race. Athletes from all over the world take part in the Ironman, and many of them live in Penticton while awaiting the next competition. They train here, and it is not uncommon to see them cycling or running along the highway. The triathlon takes place in August, at the beginning of the fruit-picking season. For further information contact the **Ironman Office** (☎250-490-8787) or see Mike Barrett, the owner of the **Hog's Breath Coffee Co.** (202 Main St., ☎250-493-7800), who has competed in numerous triathlons. Athletes often congregate at this café.

A visit to an orchard is a must, especially in the heart of summer, during the fruit-picking season. Not only is the fruit plentiful, but more importantly it's delicious. From July to late September, the region is covered with fruit trees bursting with scent and colour. The **Dickinson Family Farm** (turn left onto Jones Flat Rd. from Hwy. 97 North, then right onto Bentley Rd. 19208, ☎250-494-0300) invites visitors to stroll through its rows of fruit trees. You can purchase fruit (apples, pears, etc.) and fruit-based products on the premises. For a real treat, try the peach butter and the freshly pressed apple juice.

Head out of Penticton on Lakeshore Drive and take the 97 north toward Summerland.

An outing in the mountains along the former route of the **Kettle Valley Railway ★★** offers another perspective of the Okanagan Valley. Laid at the turn of the 20th century, these tracks connected Nelson, in the east, to Hope, in the west, thus providing a link

between the coast and the hinterland, where tonnes of ore, and later fruits, were being extracted. Mother Nature was a major obstacle throughout the railway's short existence; fallen debris, avalanches and snowstorms made the tracks impossible to use, and the line was abandoned. The $20 million cost of building the railway was never recovered.

The rails have been removed and you can follow the trail on foot, by bicycle or on horseback. The railtrail runs through Penticton on the east shore of Okanagan Lake, the terrain is a gradual 2% descent from Chute Lake into Penticton. Enjoy the view of Okanagan Lake, the orchards and vineyards, tunnels and trestles. For a pleasant outing, contact **Kettle Valley Trails Tours & Shuttle** ($23; Penticton pick-up 9:15 a.m, ☎250-496-5220) to shuttle you to Chute Lake, and enjoy a downhill ride. To take the uphill ride, start on Main Street at the Hogs Breath in downtown Penticton, and follow Front Street up Vancouver Hill. Turn left on Vancouver Place. The trail begins at the end of the street. Cross over the newly constructed Randolph Draw Bridge. The trail crosses Naramata Road at **Hillside Estate Winery** (1350 Naramata Rd., ☎250-493-6274), where you might want to stop for a tour and tasting or lunch on the patio. Some 6km from the winery there is a dip in the trail which crosses Naramata Creek. After 5.6km you will pass through the Little Tunnel Viewpoint. Make noise as you walk to drive off any rattlesnakes, black bears or cougars, and carry plenty of water. For a KVR map, stop at the **Visitor Information Centre** (888 Westminster Ave. W.; ☎800-663-5052). You'll enjoy a direct view of Okanagan Lake along the way.

On the west shore, in Summerland, a part of the track is now used by the Summerland Steam Train. Head toward Summer-land on Hwy. 97 North, turn left on Solly Road and follow the signs for the **Prairie Valley Station of the Kettle Valley Steam Railway** ($15; 2 trips/day 10:30am and 1:30pm; mid-May to Jul Sat, Sun and Mon, early Jul to early Sep Thu-Mon, early Sep to mid-Oct Sat-Mon; ☎250-494-8422 or 877-494-8424). Maps for both areas are available at the Penticton tourist office on Westminster Avenue.

Here is the perfect family activity on a scorching summer day when it's so hot that the lake seems like it could boil: float down the canal with the current on an innertube. The canal connects Okanagan Lake and Skoaha Lake on the other side of Penticton. **Coyote Cruises** ($10/inner tube and return transportation; mid-Jun to mid-Oct every day 9am to 8pm215 Riverside Dr., ☎250-492-2115) rents inner tubes and provides bus transfers. The "descent" lasts about 2hrs and is incredibly refreshing!

Stay on the 97 North, which leads through the towns of **Summerland** and **Peachland** on the way to **Kelowna**. This stretch of road runs along a mountainside and Okanagan Lake, and is lined with orchards, wineries and rest areas.

★
Kelowna

Kelowna, the largest city in inland British Columbia, has a population of more than 1000,000. Its economy is driven by forestry, fruit farming, wine-making, manufacturing and, as of more recently, a number of hi-tech industries as well. Tourism is also important to Kelowna, and the town has a lot to offer its many visitors.

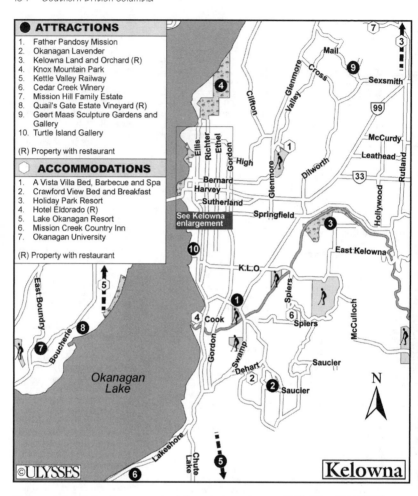

ATTRACTIONS

1. Father Pandosy Mission
2. Okanagan Lavender
3. Kelowna Land and Orchard (R)
4. Knox Mountain Park
5. Kettle Valley Railway
6. Cedar Creek Winery
7. Mission Hill Family Estate
8. Quail's Gate Estate Vineyard (R)
9. Geert Maas Sculpture Gardens and Gallery
10. Turtle Island Gallery

(R) Property with restaurant

ACCOMMODATIONS

1. A Vista Villa Bed, Barbecue and Spa
2. Crawford View Bed and Breakfast
3. Holiday Park Resort
4. Hotel Eldorado (R)
5. Lake Okanagan Resort
6. Mission Creek Country Inn
7. Okanagan University

(R) Property with restaurant

Okanagan Lake

©ULYSSES

Kelowna

The beautiful sandy beaches that border Okanagan Lake draw more and more tourists every year. You can lounge under a beautiful summer sky, organize a family picnic, or simply admire the scenery.

Kelowna is the heart and mind of the Okanagan Valley. It was here that a French Oblate by the name of Father Charles Pandosy set up the first Catholic mission in the hinterland of British Columbia in 1859. He introduced apple and grape growing into the Okanagan Valley and was thus largely responsible for its becoming a

major fruit-producing region.

The **Father Pandosy Mission** *(May to early Oct, every day; on 3685 Benvoulin Rd., at the corner of Casorso Rd., ☎250-860-8369)*, which has been listed as a provincial historic site since 1983, includes a church and a number of farm buildings, as well as a school, a home and a store.

On the other side of Mission Creek from the mission in south Kelowna, **Okanagan Lavender** *(Jul and Aug Thu-Sun 10am to 3pm, Jun and Sep Thu-Mon 10am to 4pm; 4380*

Takla Rd., ☎764-77950) has 27 different varieties of lavender on a pretty acreage. The country store has fragrant products made out of organic lavender such as jellies, teas and bath salts.

North of the lavender farm at the east end of K.L.O. Road, **Kelowna Land and Orchard** *($5.25; May to Sep every day 11am to 3pm, Oct every day 11am to 1pm; 3002 Dunster Rd., ☎250-763-1091)* offers tours of a working orchard, with an antique yellow tractor carting visitors between the

Kelowna
enlargement

N

Roanoak
Walrod
Jones
Royal View
Bay
Recreation
Crowley
Sunset
Bailey
Weddel
Gaston
Waterfront Park
Vaughn
Clement
Coronation
Oganakan Lake
Cawston
Wilson
St Paul
Smith
Fuller
Doyle
Bertram
Stockwell
Richter
Martin
Ethel
Graham
Gordon
Water
Lawson
Queensway
Ellis
Bernard
City Park
Lawrence
Leon
Harvey
Pandosy
Saucier
Laurier
Dehart
Borden
Floating Bridge
Rowcliffe
Sutherland
Abbott
Elliot
©ULYSSES
Burne
Cadder

● ATTRACTIONS	○ ACCOMMODATIONS	⬡ RESTAURANTS
1. Kelowna Museum 2. Orchard Museum and Wine Museum 3. Ogopogo 4. Kelowna Art Gallery 5. Bronze Rooster Gallery 6. Art Ark	1. Abbot House Bed and Breakfast 2. Chinook Motel 3. The Grand Okanagan 4. Kelowna Samesun Motel Hostel	1. Bean Scene Coffee House 2. Christopher's 3. de Montreuil's 4. Fresco 5. La Bussola 6. Mekong 7. Yamas Taverna

lines of apple trees. The best part…fruit samples.

Back in the town centre, there are a number of museums in close proximity. The **Kelowna Museum** *(donations accepted; Tue-Sat 10am to 5pm; 470 Queensway Ave., ☎250-763-2417, www.kelownamuseum. ca)* has collections and exhibits with a regional bent—the more intriguing being the First Nations artefacts—and less interesting international displays. A few blocks south is the **Laurel Packinghouse** *(1304 Ellis St.)*, a heritage building that houses both the **Orchard Museum** *(donations accepted; Tue-Sat 10am to 5pm; ☎763-0433)* and **Wine Museum** *(donations accepted; Mon-Sat 10am to 5pm, Sun 12pm to 5pm; ☎250-868-9272)*. The Orchard Museum explores the transformation of the Okanagan Valley from cattle range to fruit mecca with displays on packing, processing and preserving. The Wine Museum looks at wine production from the Etruscans, Greeks and Chinese to the local scene, with exhibits and artefacts chronicling the valley's grape revolution. The self-guided tour ends with a wine tasting.

The statue of the monster **Ogopogo** *(Waterfront Walkway, near downtown)*, whose native name is Nha-a-itk, has drawn international media attention to Kelowna. Aboriginals were so dependent on Okanagan Lake and wanted to take such good care of it that they were afraid to anger Ogopogo, the lake god. He is said to look like a snake, be a cousin of the Loch Ness Monster and some claim

to have spotted him. Both Canadian and Japanese television programs have featured the subject.

Kelowna boasts several scenic parks. One of these is **Knox Mountain Park**, where you'll find a magnificent viewing area. You might even catch a glimpse of Ogopogo. To get to the park, take Ellis Street north out of downtown.

Like Penticton, Kelowna is located along the **Kettle Valley Railway**; which runs some 480km between the communities of Midway and Hope. The Myra Canyon access, a lovely part of the trail, with 18 trestles and two tunnels, is just a short drive from Kelowna. This section of the trail is also part of the Trans Canada Trail. The 12km Myra Canyon section can be walked or cycled by the whole family. After strolling down Bernard Street and the beaches on Okanagan Lake for a little while, get back in your car and take Pandosy Street. Turn left (eastward) on KLO Road, which becomes McCulloch, watch for the signs to the KVR Myra Canyon access. Parking is available at the end of the road.

It takes about 20min to reach the first wooden bridge, which stretches through a section of the **Myra Canyon ★★**. If you enjoy walking, you'll love this excursion. **Tourism Kelowna** *(544 Harvey Ave., ☎861-1515)* can help you plan your way. Cyclists can pedal about to their heart's

content; the more adventurous can spend a day riding to Penticton.

Almost all of the wine produced in British Columbia comes from the Okanagan region (see **The Wine Route**, p 188). Over the past few years, local wines have won a number of international prizes. There are three vineyards along Lakeshore Road, south of Kelowna, including the **CedarCreek Winery** *(5445 Lakeshore Rd., ☎250-764-8866 or ☎800-730-9463, www.cedarcreek.bc.ca)*, which, like its competitors in the region, produces both white and red wines. It is located on a pretty hill surrounded by vines and looking out onto Okanagan Lake. A free tour of the premises will give you a chance to sample some of the wines; the chardonnay is particularly noteworthy. You can also purchase a few bottles while you're there and enjoy lunch on their patio.

More wine is to be tasted by taking the floating bridge over Okanagan Lake to Westbank to find **Mission Hill Family Estate ★★★** *($5 tour and tasting, call ahead; Jul to late Sep every day 10am to 7pm, Oct to late Jun every day 10am to 5pm; 1730 Mission Hill Rd., access via Boucherie Rd. off of Hwy. 97, ☎250-768-6411, www.missionhill winery.com)*, the one winery in the valley that must be visited. The 2001 *Canadian Winery of the Year* is an impressive and beautiful facility perched on a hill with a view of the lake. The grounds are immaculate, with tiered green lawns, a Tuscan pillared courtyard, outdoor amphitheatre and 12-storey bell tower with four bronze bells that were cast in Annecy, France. It's an absolutely beautiful place and a world-class winery.

Mission Hill Family Estate

Tours commence with a slick, unnecessary propaganda film featuring the winery's founder, Anthony von Mandl. From there it gets interesting, with a visit to the vast cellars full of U.S. and French-made oak barrels, and of course, the wine tasting.

Just a hop away from Mission Hill, **Quail's Gate Estate Winery** *($5 tour and tasting, call ahead; early May to end Jun and early Sep to mid-Oct every day 11am to 3pm, end Jun to early Sep every day 11am to 4pm; 3303 Boucherie Rd., ☎250-769-4451, www.quailsgate.com)* has an interesting tour that takes you into the vineyard to try grapes right off the vines. The cabin that houses the wine shop was constructed by the first non-native pioneers in the valley in 1873, and was the first building on the west side of Kelowna. Tours end with a super-sweet shot of Riesling icewine in a chocolate cup. There is also a popular restaurant here (see p 225).

As far as culture is concerned, the visual arts are of great importance in Kelowna as can be seen by the large number of galleries in the town centres.

The **Kelowna Art Gallery** *(Tue-Sat 10am to 5pm, Thu 10am to 9pm, Sun 1pm to 4pm; 1315 Water Str., ☎250-762-2226)* presents local artists and encourages work by students in the region, but also plays host to international exhibitions. The **Geert Maas Sculpture Gardens and Gallery** *(250 Reynolds Rd., ☎250-860-7012)* exhibits bronze sculptures that are worth the trip. Maas is an artist and sculptor who has provided works to collectors from 20 countries. He meets people by appointment, but the gallery is open from May to October. And if you're really a sculpture enthusiast, the **Bronze Rooster Gallery** *(559 Lawrence Ave., ☎250-868-*

2533) has many of these, as well as paintings by Canadian artists.

The tour wouldn't be complete without a stop at the **Turtle Island Gallery** *(2950 Pandosy St., ☎250-717-8235)*, which has an impressive collection of works by local First Nations artists. Downtown's **Art Ark** *(135-1295 Cannery Ln., ☎250-862-5080 or 888-813-5080)* is a vast studio-style gallery of painting, sculpture, photography and pottery, featuring work by both regional and national artists. Gary Nylander's exquisite black-and-white photography is a highlight.

Music and theatre also share in the prestige: **Kelowna Community Theatre** *(Water St. and Doyle Ave., ☎250-763-9018)* is home to **The Sunshine Theatre Company** *(☎250-763-4025)* Kelowna's community theatre, which regularly presents interesting plays and the **Okanagan Symphony Orchestra** *(☎250-763-7544)* which offers a complete and highly diverse season of programming every year. In addition, the **Rotary Centre for the Arts** *(☎250-717-5304)*, just west of the Laurel Packinghouse, was almost completed at the time of publication, and will be home to theatre, visual arts, music and festivals.

Vernon

Get back on the 97 North and continue on to Vernon, which is set amidst three lakes. The town started out modestly in the 1860s, when Cornelius O'Keefe established a ranch here. The northern part of Vernon is an important stockbreeding area. Stop by the **Historic O'Keefe Ranch** *($7; every day May to Oct; 12km north of Vernon on Hwy. 97, ☎250-542-7868)*, where you'll find the original ranch house, wooden church and ranching equipment. Forestry and agriculture play

greater economic roles here than in Kelowna and Penticton, where tourism is more important.

Hwy. 97 North intersects the Trans-Canada at Monte Creek, east of Kamloops (see Tour C, p 185). You can also reach the 1 from the 97A, which leads to Sicamous, west of Revelstoke (see Tour C, p 186). Otherwise, backtrack to Kelowna and take Hwy. 97C to Merritt.

Merritt

Merritt lies in a region with over 150 lakes, surrounded by mountains and pastures where tens of thousands of heads of cattle can be seen grazing. If you'd like to step back in time to the days when cowboys met here to talk and live it up, head downtown to the **Coldwater Hotel**, built in 1908, or over to the **Quilchena Hotel**, located 23km northeast of Merritt on the 5A.

From Merritt, take Hwy. 5 north to Kamloops (see Tour C, p 185) or south to Princeton (see p 187). Another option is to take Hwy. 8 northwest to Spences Bridge, where you can get on the Trans-Canada (Hwy. 1) south to Lytton (see Tour B, p 182).

Tour E: Kootenay Country

This tour can be picked up from Revelstoke (see Tour C, p 186), or from Osoyoos (see Tour D, p 187), in which case its order must be reversed.

Located off the beaten tourist track, this region is a gold mine for visitors with a taste for mountains, lakes, history and chance encounters. Once again, the landscape is one of the major attractions; this is British Columbia, after all! Because this region is under-appreciated, it remains virtually unspoiled, making it that much more interesting to explore.

Located in the southeast part of the province, the Kootenays are a series of mountains (the Rockies, the Purcells, the Selkirks and the Monashees) stretching from the north to the south. The great Columbia River runs through this region, creating the vast body of water known as the Arrow Lakes on its way. Natural resources such as forests and mines have played a major role in the region's development. A number of towns bear witness to the different stages in the Kootenays' history.

Nakusp

Before setting off across the Kootenays, you might want to stop at Nakusp's **Leland Hotel** *(Fourth Ave.)*, located on the shores of upper Arrow Lake. You can sit on the terrace and have a bite to eat while taking in the scenery. During the mining boom, hundreds of prospectors flooded into Nakusp.

If sulphurous hot springs are your cup of tea, then you will be interested to know that there are two of them on the road that heads north to the pier of the Galena Bay ferry. You can also camp at these two places for about $20.

The **Nakusp Hot Springs** *($5.75; 12km north of Nakusp,* ☎*800-909-8819)* are nestled in the rolling valley behind Nakusp, quite a distance from Upper Arrow Lake. The old, round building adds a certain charm to the facility, which is somewhat overridden with tourists.

The **Halcyon Hot Springs** *($9; 32km north of Nakusp,* ☎*250-265-3554 or 888-689-4699)* directly face Upper Arrow Lake and offer an endless view of the snow-capped peaks on

the opposite shore. Relax while admiring the incredible panorama.

New Denver

New Denver was the gateway to silver country at the turn of the century, when there was an abundant supply of the metal in this region. The history of that era is presented at the **Silvery Slocan Museum** *(mid-May to mid-Oct Sat and Sun 10am to 4pm; Jul and Aug every day; 206 6th Ave.,* ☎*250-358-2201).*

When Canada declared war on Japan during the Second World War, Japanese residents of British Columbia were interned in camps in a number of towns in this region, including New Denver and Sandon. To learn more about their experience, stop in at the **Nikkei Internment Memorial Centre** *($4; May to Oct, every day 9am to 5pm; by appt. during winter; 306 Josephine St.,* ☎*250-358-7288).*

Take Hwy. 31A in the direction of Kaslo, and stop at Sandon, the former capital of Canada's silver mines.

★★
Sandon

At the turn of the century, 5,000 people lived and worked in Sandon. By 1930, the price of silver had dropped and the mine had been exhausted, prompting an exodus from the town. During World War II, Sandon became an internment centre for Japanese who had been living on the coast. Shortly after the war, it became a ghost town once again, and a number of buildings were destroyed by fire and floods. Today, visitors can admire what remains of a number of old buildings, as well as the first hydroelectric power plant constructed in the Canadian West, the Silversmith Powerhouse which still produces electricity. **Tours** are

available every day *(donations accepted; Apr to end-Oct 10am to 4pm;* ☎*250-358-2247)*

A 12km road, negotiable with an all-purpose vehicle, leads from Sandon to the Idaho Lookout, where you can take in a view of the Kokanee and Valhalla glaciers.

Get back on Hwy. 31A and continue on to Kaslo.

Kaslo

Kaslo was built on the hills on the west shore of Kootenay Lake during the heyday of silver mining. A walk along the waterfront and a visit to the town hall will give you a glimpse of how beautiful the setting is. At the beginning of the century, people used to come here by paddle-boat. For nearly 60 years, up until 1957, the *SS Moyie* shuttled passengers back and forth across Kootenay Lake for Canadian Pacific. The boat has since been transformed into a museum *($5; every day mid-May to end Oct 9:30 to 5pm; 324 Front St.,* ☎*250-353-2525).*

At **Ainsworth Hot Springs** ★ *(swimsuit and towel rentals available year-round, every day;* ☎*250-229-4212 or 800-668-1171, www.hotnaturally. com)*, which is located in an enchanting setting along the shore to the south, bathers can alternate between very cold and very warm water. The swimming pool overlooks Kootenay Lake and the valley which is brilliant at sunset. The U-shaped cave studded with stalactites, the humidity and the almost total absence of light will transport you to another world. The temperature rises as you near the springs at the back of the cave, reaching as high as 40°C.

Take Hwy. 31 south. At Balfour, take Hwy. 3A to Nelson.

★ ★
Nelson

Make sure to park your car as soon as possible and explore this magnificent town on foot. Located at the southern end of the West Arm of Kootenay Lake, Nelson lies on the west flank of the Selkirk Mountains. In 1867, during the silver boom, miners set up camp here, working together to build hotels, homes and public facilities. Numerous buildings now bear witness to the town's prosperous past. Nelson has managed to continue its economic growth, thanks to light industry, tourism and the civil service.

The Visitor Info Centre distributes two small pamphlets that will guide you through over 350 historic buildings. The town's elegant architecture makes walking here a real pleasure. Classical, Queen Anne and Victorian buildings proudly line the streets. The stained-glass windows of the **Nelson Congregational Church ★** (at the corner of Stanley and Silica Streets), the Chateau-style **City Hall ★** (502 Vernon St.), the group of buildings on **Baker Street** and above all the Italian-style **Fire Station ★** (919 Ward St.) are eloquent reminders of the opulence of the silver mining era. For a more detailed history of Nelson, the **Nelson Museum** ($2; May to Oct

City Hall

Mon-Sat 1pm to 6pm, off season Mon-Sat 1pm to 4pm, 402 Anderson St., follow Hwy. 3A east of the town centre, ☎250-352-9813) has displays on local First Nations, explorers, miners, traders and settlers.

Its lovely architecture is not the only thing that sets Nelson apart from other inland towns in British Columbia. Dubbed the "best small arts town in Canada," Nelson is home to many local artists, musicians and craftspeople. The resulting creative atmosphere is appealing, and Nelson's streets are crawling with travellers who arrive out of curiosity, and end up staying to ski, hike or just hang out. Unlike in many small towns in Western Canada, a purple mohawk or long dreadlocks won't garner you a second look in Nelson.

You will find a number of art galleries here, many of which are integrated into restaurants, so you can contemplate works of art while looking over the menu. This setup is known as the **Artwalk**, which enables artists to exhibit their work in participating businesses each year. For further information, contact the **Nelson and District Arts Council** (☎250-352-2402).

The **Nelson Brewing Company ★** (512 Latimer St., by appointment Thu 3:30pm; ☎250-352-3582) was founded in 1893, and still produces beer for the local and regional market. The company has occupied the same Victorian building since 1899.

Old **Streetcar no. 23** of the **Nelson Electric Tramway Company** ($2; mid-May to end May Sat and Sun, end May to early Sep every day, early Sep to mid-Oct Sat and Sun noon to 6pm; ☎250-352-7672 or 250-352-3971) has been put back into service and carries passengers 1km through Lakeside Park, near the town bridge.

At the intersection of Ward and Vernon Streets, head for Hwy. 3A, which will take you to Castlegar.

Castlegar

Castlegar lies at the confluence of the Columbia and Kootenay rivers and downtown area, which is located north of the highway, is easily missed. While crossing the bridge in the direction of the airport, you'll see a suspended bridge built by the Doukhobors; turn left for a closer look.

Back on the highway, go uphill, then turn right to reach the **Doukhobor Museum ★** ($4; May to Sep every day 10am to 6pm, ☎250-365-6622). Fleeing persecution in Russia, the Doukhobors emigrated to Canada in 1898. They wanted to live according to their own rules rather than those of the State; for example, they were against participation in any war. They established communities on the prairies and farmed the land, adhering to their traditional way of life and gradually developing towns and setting up industries. One group, led by Peter Verigin, left the prairies for British Columbia and took up residence in the Castlegar area. After the economic crisis of 1929 and the death of Verigin, the community diminished, but their descendants have taken up the task of telling visitors about their ancestors.

After exiting the museum or tomb, take Hwy. 3 in the direction of Grand Forks, then turn onto the 3B in order to reach

Rossland. You can take the 22 there as well, but the 3 and the 3B are worth the detour.

★ Rossland

Rossland is a picturesque little turn-of-the-century town that thrived during the gold rush and has managed to retain its charm. Located inside the crater of a former volcano, at an altitude of 1,023m above sea level, it attracts skiers and people who simply enjoy being in the mountains. Nancy Greene Provincial Park, named after the 1968 Olympic champion, a native of Rossland, boasts several majestic peaks. Red Mountain, renowned for its high-quality powder, is a world-class resort. Skier Kerrin Lee-Gartner, who won the gold medal in the 1992 Olympic Games, is also from Rossland.

All of the gold was mined from this region long before these Olympic skiers arrived. In 1890, a prospector discovered a large vein of gold here. The news spread, and hundreds of adventurers came to try their luck, resulting in a gold rush. Numerous hotels, offices and theatres were built, and Rossland flourished. Then came the crash of 1929, which hit the town hard; that same year, a major fire destroyed part of the town centre.

Rossland was on the decline; the famous **Le Roi** mine closed down, and the future did not look bright. Visitors can learn about the history of the gold rush at the **Le Roi Mine ★** and the **Rossland Historical Museum** *($8 for mine tour and museum, $4 for museum; mid-May to mid-Sep, every day 9am to 5pm; tours 9:30am to 3:30pm at the intersection of the 3B and the 22; take Columbia Ave. east of the downtown area, ☎250-362-7722 or 888-443-7444),* which features an audiovisual

presentation and a collection of objects from that era. The **Ski Hall of Fame**, located in the same building, highlights the careers of Nancy Greene and Kerrin Lee-Gartner.

Rossland's yellow gold has been replaced by the "white gold" on the slopes, which attracts thousands of skiers here every year. (See Red Mountain, p 209).

Trail

The neighbouring town of Trail came to Rossland's rescue in a way. This large mining town has been transforming the ore from Rossland's mines since 1896. Cominco, a large metallurgical company, employs a sizeable portion of the local population to this day.

Get back on Hwy. 3 and head west for Grand Forks. This pleasant road runs alongside Christina Lake on its way across the southern part of the Monashee Mountains. You can also continue east on Highway 3 to reach Creston and the East Kootenays. There is a time change around Creston, so set your watch ahead one hour.

Grand Forks

Grand Forks lies at the confluence of the Kettle and North Fork Rivers. Numerous artifacts have been found here, indicating that First Nations people once lived in this area. The first Europeans to come to this valley regularly were trappers working for the Hudson's Bay Company. The region later developed around the mining industry, but a drop in the price of copper in 1919 thwarted the community's growth. Thanks to farming and forestry, Grand Forks is once again a thriving town.

Keep heading west on Hwy. 3.

Starting in Grand Forks, the landscape becomes desert-like again. The road leads through some lovely valleys, but the

real highlight of the trip comes when you enter the **Okanagan Valley** from the east. The town of Osoyoos (see p 187) and Osoyoos Lake are visible several hundred metres below.

Creston

This small, isolated town (pop. 5,000) lies in a pretty valley on the eastern side of the towering Salmo-Creston summit. First inhabited by the Kutenai (meaning "water people") First Nation, non-native prospectors began passing through the area in the 1860s. The first settler decided to stay for good in 1883, and later arrivals would foster a way of life centred on mining. Today, forestry and agriculture (including strawberry, alfalfa and canola crops) are the major economic stimulants.

The **Creston Valley Wildlife Area ★★** *($3; May to mid-Oct 9am to 4pm; to the right after descent into Creston Valley, ☎250-402-6906, www.crestonwildlife.ca)* is certainly worth stopping at. The internationally acclaimed conservation area is a 7,000ha active wetland, with yellow-headed blackbirds, western painted turtles and spotted frogs. More than 265 species of nesting and migratory birds can be viewed here. For just $5, you can take an excellent one-hour guided canoe tour of the marshes.

Continue east on Hwy. 3 to Cranbrook.

Cranbrook

Conveniently located between the Okanagan Valley and Calgary, Cranbrook is situated on the plains between the Purcell and Rocky Mountains. The discovery of gold, and then the subsequent arrival of the Canadian Pacific Railway in 1898, made the community the region's main trading area. The town is still the service centre for the East Kootenays, and is home to more than 20,000 people, but it is marred by an unsightly stretch of motels and fast-food outlets. You are likely to find yourself here halfway through a long drive, so you'll be pleased to know that there a couple of sites of interest.

The **Canadian Museum of Rail Travel** (*$11.95 deluxe tour; Apr to mid-Oct every day 10am to 6pm, mid-Oct to Apr Tue-Sat noon to 5pm; 57 Van Horne St. South, off Hwy. 3 in town, ☎250-489-3918*) is noteworthy, with the recently reconstructed Royal Alexandra Hall (an example of early 20th-century railway hotel architecture), a museum with exhibitions reliving the glory days of rail travel and 28 restored locomotives and cars.

Fort Steele Heritage Town ★★ (*$8.50; Jun to Aug every day 9:30am to 8pm, May, Sep and Oct 9:30am to 5:30pm; on Hwy. 93/95, ☎250-426-7352*) is a wonderful reconstructed boomtown with 58 buildings, about 10km north of Cranbrook. The original community emerged with the gold rush, and due to strife with the local Kootenay First Nation, the Northwest Mounted Police sent Inspector Sam Steele to build the barracks that became known as Fort Steele. The decision to take the railroad through Cranbrook instead of Fort Steele in 1898 sealed the town's fate, and by the end of World War II the population had dwindled to a measly 50.

An old steam train or horse-drawn wagon can toot you around, as costumed interpreters recreate the atmosphere of the Old West. For a fright, visit the dentist's office—you'll never complain about having to get a filling again. Call ahead for details on the musical variety shows at the **Wild Horse Theatre**.

From Cranbrook, take Hwy. 95A north for 31km to Kimberley

Kimberley

Kimberley is a small ski town fortunately situated in elegant, natural beauty. The town developed around the Sullivan Mine, a source of lead, silver and zinc, which was extracted by the Cominco company up until the mine's depletion and closure in December 2001.

Everyone knew well in advance that Kimberley's mineral resources would not last forever, and in 1973 the regrettable decision was made to transform Kimberley into the "Bavarian City of the Rockies," complete with a moustached mascot named Happy Hans, accordionists and a ridiculously large cuckoo clock. In a word it's…odd, but keep tongue firmly planted in cheek and remember that the best restaurants in the region can be found here, and the many visitors who arrive for outdoor activities like golf, skiing and hiking don't seem to be complaining.

The town is centred around the **Platzl**, a Bavarian-style town common with restaurants and shops. Yodelling blasts out of speakers and the above-mentioned cuckoo clock goes off sporadically as those interested plug in 25 cents.

The **Visitor Info Centre** (see p 176) lies just north of the Platzl, and the **Bavarian City Mining Railway (BCMR)** (*$7; Jul and Aug every day, Jun and Sep Sat and Sun; ☎250-427-3922*) departs from the building. The 9km, 1hr trip visits the Sullivan Mine surface facilities as guides recount the history of the area. The **Sullivan Mine Interpretive Centre** is right beside the Info Centre, and consists of a 1920s miner's residence,

Kimberley's first schoolhouse and information on the mine.

The **Kimberley Alpine Resort** (see p 209) is situated at the north end of Gerry Sorrensen Way and is undergoing extensive construction.

Parks

Tour A:
The Sunshine Coast

Southern British Columbia

Porpoise Bay Provincial Park (*☎604-689-9025*), northeast of Sechelt, is a sylvan park that offers nature interpretation programs with naturalists. One of the most pleasant sand beaches in the area is at Porpoise Bay. You can go for a swim under the watchful eye of a lifeguard. It's a perfect spot for the family.

Divers will be pleased to learn about the **HMCS Chaudiere**, a warship that was sunk at Kunechin Point in order to create an artificial reef. The park has 84 campsites. Reservations are accepted (*☎800-689-9025, www.discover camping.ca*); during the summer they are recommended. Payment is made in cash upon arrival.

Sargeant Bay Provincial Park (*☎604-689-9025*) is located 7km west of Sechelt, on the Sunshine Coast. The area offers infinite sailing and kayaking possibilities. Sargeant Bay is famous for its rich marine life. You can get to the park by car on Hwy. 101, or by boat. A picnic area has been set up at the entrance to the park.

The **Skookumchuck Rapids of Skookumchuck Narrows Provincial Park ★★★** (*☎800-870-9055*) are definitely one of the Sunshine Coast's most spectacular features. When the tides change, the sea water rushes into the Skookumchuck Narrows Canyon as if it were a great funnel. Skookumchuck is a Chinook word that means "powerful water." The significance of the word is clear when you see the rapids with your own eyes. To get there, go north on Hwy. 101 past Sechelt and Pender Harbour to the Egmont exit, 1km from the ferry terminal at Earl's Cove. Continue on Egmont Road until you reach the parking lot of Skookumchuck Narrows Provincial Park.

From here, a trail will lead you to the rapids. Bring good shoes, since it will take 30min to reach the site. These are considered to be among the **biggest rapids in the world**. If you're lucky, you'll see some kayakers literally surfing the waves.

Saltery Bay Provincial Park *(north of the Saltery Bay terminal, 42 campsites, beaches, scuba diving, &; B.C. Parks, Garibaldi/Sunshine Coast District, ☎604-689-9025 or 800-689-9025)* is an outstanding place to go scuba diving; a bronze mermaid awaits you underwater, and you have a good chance of spotting a killer whale, a seal or a sea-lion.

Shelter Point Regional Park *(Powell River Regional District, 5776 Marine Ave., Powell River, ☎604-486-7228)* is located on the southwest coast of Texada Island, approximately 20km from the Blubber Bay ferries. There's a campground here, with washrooms and showers, and a shelter where you can prepare food. This is a place for isolation, fishing and communion with nature. Dogs are allowed in the park.

Jedediah Island Marine Provincial Park *(☎604-689-9025 or 800-689-9025)* is an island

between Lasqueti Island and Texada Island, in the Strait of Georgia. The island was acquired by coastal residents in 1995, who made it into a park. There are thousand-year-old trees and major bird colonies. This magnificent wild area is only accessible by boat.

Desolation Sound Marine Park ★ ★ *(north of Lund, accessible by boat; campsites, hiking, kayaking, swimming, fishing, scuba diving, potable water, toilets; B.C. Parks at Tenedos Bay, Sechelt Area Supervisor, ☎604-885-9019)* is popular with ocean lovers, who come here to observe the animal life inhabiting these warm waters. More and more people are coming here to go sea kayaking, something even novices can enjoy.

Manning Provincial Park ★ ★ *(tourist information: summer, every day 8:30am to 4:30pm; winter, Mon-Fri 8:30am to 4:30pm; ☎250-840-8836)* is located on the boundary of the southwestern part of the province and the huge Thomson Okanagan region. It lies 225km from Vancouver, making it a popular getaway for city-dwellers in search of vast green spaces. The park is home to a resort as well as cabins, chalets and campsites.

Tour B: Coast Mountain Circle Tour

Alice Lake, Brandywine Falls, Garibaldi, Porteau Cove and Shannon Falls are the provincial parks located around Squamish. Here, you can camp, fish, swim, kayak, canoe, climb, walk or even do some mountain-biking. Call ☎800-689-9025 for information.

Shannon Falls Provincial Park *(☎604-689-9025)*, along Hwy. 99 toward Squamish, is the site of one of the most impressive waterfalls in

Canada. It's practically impossible to see the origin of the falls since they're so incredibly high. The pure clear water of Shannon Creek was once used by Carling O'Keefe breweries, until they gave the land to the provincial government. The park has trails all around the falls and picnic areas.

Porteau Cove Provincial Park *(☎604-689-9025)* is located some 20km north of Horseshoe Bay, on the east coast of Howe Sound, between Gambier and Bowen Island. The waters contain a number of sunken shipwrecks to the delight of the many scuba divers that come here. One example is an old mine-sweeper from World War II.

Stawamus Chief Provincial Park *(☎604-689-9025)* is located almost right after Shannon Falls Provincial Park, in the direction of Squamish on Hwy. 99 (Sea to Sky). The park is renowned for its rock-climbing and hiking. The view from the summit of The Chief is truly magnificent. The park is open all year and has 15 campsites. Reservations are not accepted.

Alice Lake Provincial Park *(☎604-689-9025, to reserve a campsite: ☎800-689-9025)* is 13km north of Squamish around the lake of the same name (Alice Lake) and has 88 campsites. It's a very popular park, especially in the middle of summer when the weather is really hot. Tourists and children flock to the beach to cool off. There are showers and many hiking trails.

Brandywine Falls Provincial Park *(☎604-689-9025)* is a small park, with 15 campsites, 47km north of Squamish. The many waterfalls and vertiginous peaks make this area a photographer's paradise. Daisy Lake and the splendid mountains of Garibaldi Park are not far from here.

Vast **Garibaldi Provincial Park ★ ★** *(information Garibaldi/Sunshine District, Brackendale; 10km north of Squamish, ☎604-689-9025),* which covers 195,000ha, is extremely popular with hikers during summertime. Hwy. 99 runs along the west side of the park, offering access to the various trails.

In the Whistler valley, near the village, there are five lakes where you can go swimming, windsurfing, canoeing and sailing. Here are two of them:

At little **Alpha Lake** *(at the traffic light at Whistler Creekside, turn left on Lake Placid Rd. and continue until you reach the beach),* you can enjoy a picnic, rent a canoe or play tennis or volleyball.

Alta Lake *(north of Whistler Creekside on Hwy. 99; turn left on Alta Vista Rd. and right on Alpine Crescent, then keep left until the end of the road to reach Lakeside Park)* attracts windsurfers. Sailboard rentals are available here, along with canoes and kayaks.

Joffre Lakes Provincial Park *(Pemberton Chamber of Commerce, ☎604-689-9025)* is located about 20km from Pemberton. It's a superb mountain park where you'll find three turquoise lakes and vertiginous summits covered by an enormous glacier. The trail is in good condition but be prepared to climb the steeper slopes. Watch out for mosquitoes in July. Reservations are not accepted.

Birkenhead Lake Provincial Park *(☎604-689-9025)* is 55km northeast of Pemberton, reached by an access road at D'Arcy. The park is equipped with campsites and a boat-launching ramp. Deer, moose and bears are not rare sights in this lovely mountain park. The lake offers great trout fishing too. The park is open from May to September.

The **Sasquatch Provincial Park** *(beach, playground, boat-launching ramp; Cultus Lake, ☎604-689-9025)* lies tucked away in the mountains by Harrison Lake. You can camp, and beaches have been laid out so that visitors can spend a pleasant day here enjoying one of the lakes. According to a Coast Salish Aboriginal legend, the Sasquatch is half-man, half-beast and lives in the woods. To this day, some Aboriginals claim to have seen the creature around Harrison Lake.

Kilby Provincial Park *(☎604-689-9025, campsite reservations: ☎800-689-9025)* is a lovely park on the banks of the Fraser River, only 29km northwest of Chilliwack. It is known for being peaceful and for the abundance of birds of prey such as eagles and owls. You can plan a picnic or spend a few days at one of the 38 campsites. Don't miss the **General Store Museum**. This grocery store from the beginning of the 1900s will make you feel like you're back in pioneer days. The park is open all year.

Chilliwack Lake Provincial Park *(☎604-689-9025, campsite reservations: ☎800- 689-9025)* is located 64km southeast of Chilliwack. It can be reached by a well-maintained gravel road that is accessible from the Trans-Canada Highway (Hwy. 1). This park offers many services and activities: large beaches, campsites, etc. It is mostly frequented by people who live in the area. So, expect many families, children and Jet Skis. It is open from May to October.

Cultus Lake Provincial Park *(☎604-689-9025, campsite reservations: ☎800-689-9025)* is 656ha in size and is located 13km south of Chilliwack on the Trans-Canada Highway. There are four campgrounds with showers, washrooms, and firewood. Due to its prox-

imity to the Fraser Valley's urban centres, this park is literally stormed by campers when the weather is nice, and, therefore, its campgrounds, Fraser Creek (80 sites); Delta Grove (58 sites); Entrance Bay (52 sites) and Maple Bay (106 sites) are almost always full on weekends.

Golden Ears Provincial Park *(☎604-689-9025, campsite reservations: ☎800-689-9025)* is located in the coastal mountain chain, not far from the small town of Maple Ridge, only 41 kilometres east of Vancouver by Hwy. 7 from Haney or Albion. There are two campgrounds near Alouette Lake with washrooms and showers. The first, Alouette, has 205 campsites and the other, Gold Creek, has 138. Fishing and hiking are the activities of choice. The park is unusual in that it allows horseback riding. You can go for a ride by contacting the ranches at the park's entrance.

Tour C: The Thompson River as Far as Revelstoke

There are five municipal parks in the Kamloops area where various tournaments and competitions are held. You can go for a walk and catch a football or softball game, a cricket or tennis match or a golf tournament.

Riverside Park, a swath of green space between Landsdowne Street and the Thompson River, offers a meandering trail along the river that is just a short walk from downtown. In July and August there is live music here every night at 7pm.

Kamloops Wildlife Park *($8; end-Jun to early Sep every day 8am to 8:30pm, early Sep to end Jun every day 8am to 4:30pm; 9077 Trans-Canada, ☎250-573-3242)* is a zoo where both young and old can observe animals in their natural habitat. You'll see bears, of course, but also Siberian tigers and wolves.

You can explore the woods on scores of paths in **Mount Revelstoke ★ ★** and **Glacier ★ ★ National Parks** *(for maps, information and regulations, contact Parks Canada in Revelstoke, ☎250-837-7500).* The level of difficulty varies; some trails run past centuries-old trees or lead to the tops of mountains, affording splendid panoramic views.

Tour D: Okanagan Valley

Cathedral Provincial Park ★ ★ *(no dogs, no mountain bikes; for detailed maps and information, contact the BC Parks District Manager; Box 399, Summerland, B.C. V0H 1Z0, ☎250-494-6500)* is located 30km southwest of Keremeos, in the southern part of the province, right alongside the U.S. border. There are two distinct kinds of vegetation here—the temperate forest and the plant growth characteristic of the arid Okanagan region. At low altitudes, Douglas firs dominate the landscape, giving way to spruce and heather higher up. Deer, mountain goats and wild sheep sometimes venture out near the turquoise-coloured lakes.

Okanagan Mountain Provincial Park *(☎250-494-6500)* is about 16km south of Kelowna and is accessed by Lakeshore Road as it winds along Lake Okanagan. It features 10,000ha of wilderness that can only be explored on foot, by bike or on horseback. There are a number of hiking trails (some of which are extremely difficult), beaches, campsites and a dock for boats. There is a handful of smaller lakes at the park's centre.

Knox Mountain Park lies in the north end of Kelowna and offers a beautiful view of Okanagan Lake, whose waters are supposedly inhabited by a monster named Ogopogo. To get there from downtown, head 2km north on Ellis Street.

Kalamalka Provincial Park *(a few kilometres south of Vernon, ☎800-689-9025)* is a pretty wooded area with a beach and the perfect spot to spend an afternoon or a day. *National Geographic* ranks Kalamalka Lake as one of the 10 most beautiful lakes in the world — and as soon as you see its turquoise blue water, you will know why. Kalamalka means "lake of many colours" in the Aboriginal language. People come here to stroll on its many hiking trails, go mountain biking or simply relax by the water's edge. Don't forget your bathing suit!

Tour E: Kootenay Country

Kokanee Glacier Provincial Park ★ ★ *(West Kootenay, Nelson, ☎250-689-9025)* has about 85km of hiking trails of average difficulty. The park is accessible from a number of different places.

Outdoor Activities

Canoeing

Tour A: The Sunshine Coast

A canoe trip is a must, especially if you're dying to discover a series of lakes and are up for portaging. The **Powell**

Forest Canoe Route ★, a tour of eight lakes, takes four days. For more information, contact the **Sunshine Coast Forest District Office** *(☎604-485-0700).*

Flying

Tour B: Coast Mountain Circle Tour

Gliding enthusiasts have claimed the sky over Hope as their flying space. A westerly wind sweeps down the Fraser River Valley and up the big mountains around Hope, enabling the aircraft to stay in the air for hours. For a fee, you can accompany a pilot aboard an engineless plane. At Exit 165 on Hwy. 1, west of Hope, follow the sign for the airport; turn left at Old Yale, just before the viaduct, and continue until you reach the red and white building of the **Vancouver Soaring Association** *(☎604-869-7211).*

Bird-watching

Tour B: Coast Mountain Circle Tour

See Brackendale, p 180

Tour D: Thompson-Okanagan

If you like birds, don't miss Vaseaux Lake at the **Federal Migratory Bird Sanctuary**, 10km south of Okanagan Falls on Rte. 97. Don't forget your binoculars.

Haynes Point Provincial Park *(Summerland, ☎250-494-6500),* located on Osoyoos Lake, features a new bird-watching boardwalk and blind. Watch for marsh-wrens, white-throated swifts and red-winged blackbirds; on occasion turkey vultures are spotted high above the valley.

Fishing

Tour C: Thompson River as far as Revelstroke

Kamloops is nicknamed "fly fishing capital of the world." With its 200 lakes less than an hour's drive away, you don't have to go far to reel in a prize catch. Some of the most popular lakes are Roche Lake, Lac Le Jeune, Crystal Lake and Tunkwa Lake. For tourists guides, licences or any other information, contact **Gordon Honey's** (*☎250-828-1286*).

Tour D: Thompson-Okanagan

All around Merritt, the **Nicola Valley** offers an abundance of **lakes**, around 150, true to the local proverb (a lake a day as long as you stay) and is a paradise for fishing. Information is available at the many shops that sell mandatory fishing permits.

Golf

Tour B: Coast Mountain Circle Tour

Furry Creek Golf & Country Club (*150 Country Club Rd., Furry Creek; Club House ☎604-896-2224 or 888-922-9462*). Located on the east shore of Howe Sound, Furry Creek is 48km north of Vancouver by Hwy. 99 (Sea to Sky Highway) and 66km south of Whistler. The landscape is fabulous. With the sea and mountains having such a hypnotizing effect, golfers have a hard time

concentrating. The restaurant serves West Coast meals and has glass walls through which you can see magnificent views of the surrounding greenery.

People come to Whistler Valley from May to October to play golf in spectacular surroundings. The greens fees vary greatly from one club to the next. At the **Whistler Golf Club** (*$70-$160; May to Oct; take the Village Gate Blvd., turn right at Whistler Way and go under the 99, ☎604-932-3280 or 800-376-1777*) you'll discover a magnificent, winding golf course set against the steep cliffs of the mountains. The **Pemberton Valley Golf and Country Club** (*$45; May to Oct; ☎604-894-6197 or 800-390-4653*), in Pemberton, 23km north of Whistler, is just as beautiful as the clubs in Whistler but much less expensive.

Tour C: The Thompson River as Far as Revelstoke

Kamloops has at least six 18-hole, and a few nine-hole golf courses:

Dunes at Kamloops
652 Dunes Dr., Kamloops
☎(250) 579-3300

Rivershore Golf Club
$56
Mar to Oct
South Thompson River, Kamloops
☎250-573-4622 or 866-886-4653
Rivershore Golf Club is an 18-hole course developed by Robert Trent Jones, Sr. located alongside the Thompson River. It goes without saying that the view is exceptional.

Tour D: Okanagan Valley

The Okanagan Valley has been called a **Golf Mecca** for the quality of its courses and tournaments. Pleasant temperatures, views of the vineyards, as well as some worthwhile **Stay & Golf** packages, all

serve to encourage ever-increasing numbers of golfers.

There are more than 50 golf courses in the province's hinterland, most located near the towns of **Penticton**, **Kelowna** and **Vernon**. In the Kelowna area alone, there are 16 courses. The terrain varies greatly depending on whether you're playing in the north, amidst wooded mountains, or in the desert-like south, which is scattered with sagebush.

Gallaghers Canyon Golf & Country Club (*$95; 4320 Gallagher's Dr. W., ☎250-861-4240*) This 18-hole course designed by Bill Robinson and Les Furber is sure to please golfers seeking a challenge. As the name indicates, it is built in a forest hollow along Gallaghers Canyon; it goes without saying that the view is spectacular.

The newest course is The **Bear at the Okanagan Golf Club** (*3200 Via Centrale, Kelowna, ☎250-765-5955*), an 18-holes, par 72 course (*$85 green fees*). The Okanagan Golf Club is also home to the **Quail Course**, designed by Les Furber.

There are other prestigious golf courses in this region; for complete information about the establishments or rates contact the **Tourism Kelowna** (see p 176)

Hiking

Tour A: The Sunshine Coast

Inland Lake Park, located 12km north of Powell River, has been specially designed to enable people in wheelchairs to enjoy nature. The lake is 13km in circumference. Campsites have been laid out, and a few log houses are reserved for people with limited mobility. The picnic tables and swimming docks have been built with wheelchair-users in mind. The premier of British Columbia awarded the forest ministry a medal for the layout of this park.

The pride of the northern Sunshine Coast, the new **Sunshine Coast Trail** is a 180km stretch of scenic terrain that begins in Saltery Bay, east of Powell River, and runs north to Sarah Point (Lund). The trails is an ideal challenge for seasoned hikers, but with some 20 access points along the way, hikers can do the entire trail or just sections of it depending on time and ability. There are over 20 campsites along the way as well as more comfortable lodgings. Trail guides and maps are available from the **Powell River Visitors Bureau** *(☎604-485-4701)* and more information is available on ***www.sunshinecoast-trail.com***. Expect some breathtaking coastal views.

Manning Provincial Park (see p 202) is located on the boundary of the southwestern part of the province and the huge Okanagan-Similkameen region. It is popular with Vancouverites in search of vast green spaces. The magnificent mountains and valleys are crisscrossed by hiking trails.

Tour B: Coast Mountain Circle Tour

Except for the built-up area around Whistler, **Garibaldi Provincial Park** *(information Garibaldi/Sunshine District, Brackendale; 10km north of Squamish, ☎604-898-3678)* is a huge stretch of untouched wilderness. Hiking here is a magical experience, especially when you reach Garibaldi Lake, whose turquoise waters contrast with the blue of the glacier in the background. The trails cover long distances, so you have to bring along food,

as well as clothing for different temperatures.

A series of hiking trails runs all the way up **Whistler Mountain** *(☎604-932-3434 or 800-766-0449)* and **Blackcomb Mountain** *(☎604-932-3141, www.whistler-blackcomb.com)*. From atop Whistler, you can see Black Tusk, a black sugar-loaf 2315m high.

Tour C: The Thompson River as Far as Revelstoke

There are opportunities for all sorts of walks and hikes for all levels around Kamloops. Excursions can last from 1 to 7hrs. The hike up **Mount Peter and Paul** follows a somewhat difficult route but the view from the summit is ample reward for the 7hrs of walking. You have to call the **Indian Band Office** *(☎250-828-9700)* to get authorization you must fill in a permit in person at Aboriginal reserve *(7:30am to 1:30pm; 355 Yellowhead Hwy.)*. The **Paul Lake Provincial Park** trail takes you to Paul Lake Road. It's an easy and pleasant walk that takes between 1.5 and 2hrs.

Mountain goat

At **Mount Revelstoke National Park ★★** *($5, covers both Mount Revelstoke and Glacier; permit required for entry into the park; outside Revelstoke, east of the bridge on the Trans-Canada, InfoLine ☎250-837-7500)*, you have to drive 24km up to the summit of the mountain, where you'll find a

trail and a number of picnic areas.

There are a number of trails in **Glacier National Park** *(east of Revelstoke; for maps, information and regulations, contact Parks Canada in Revelstoke, ☎250-837-7500)*, which enable you to view flourishing plant and animal life up close. There are varying levels of difficulty; some trails run past centuries-old trees or climb to the tops of mountains, offering views of the neighbouring peaks.

Tour D: Thompson-Okanagan

The entrance to **Cathedral Provincial Park** *(for detailed maps and information, BC Parks District Manager, Box 399, Summerland, B.C. V0H 1Z0, ☎250-494-6500; www.gov.bc.ca/bc.parks; no dogs, no mountain bikes)* is located near Kere-meos, on Hwy. 3. Some of the trails here extend more than 15km, and require a day of hiking, on average. At the summit, the trails are shorter and crisscross hilly terrain teeming with plant and animal life. You can ride to the top in an all-purpose vehicle; to reserve a seat, call the **Cathedral Lakes Lodge** *(☎888-255-4453, www.cathedral-lakes-lodge.com)*.

For a hike that takes only an hour but is incredibly beautiful, go to **Kalamalka Provincial Park** (see p 204), a few kilometres from Vernon. The short trail leads right up to a little hill that steeply drops off into wonderful Kalamalka Lake.

Tour E: Kootenay Country

Kokanee Glacier Provincial Park *(for maps, contact the BC Parks Kootenay West Area Office, Nelson, ☎250-825-3500)* has about 85km of hiking trails. The Gibson Lake Loop Trail is an easy, 2.5km,

1hr return trip that offers lovely views of surrounding peaks, old mine workings, flowers in season and sub-alpine vegetation. There is also good fishing along the trail

Mountain Biking

Tour E: Kootenay Country

Rossland, in Kootenay Country, is the self-proclaimed mountain-bike capital of British Columbia – with good reason, it would seem. Long trails of varying levels of difficulty make this place accessible to anyone with an interest in the sport. Former railway lines, cross-country trails and wood-cutting paths all converge near the centre of town. The terrain is far from flat; this is a very mountainous region. You can pick up a map of the trails at the local **Visitor Info Centre** (☎250-326-5666) or at any of the bike rental centres.

Mountain Climbing

Tour B: Coast Mountain Circle Tour

Mountain climbing is becoming more popular in the Sea to Sky region. The place to go is **Stawamus Chief Mountain**. The trails leading to this granite monolith also lead to spots where you can watch the mountain climbers. For more information, contact the **Squamish & Howe Sound Chamber of Commerce** (☎604-892-9244, see p 176)

Tour D: Okanagan Valley

One of North America's top climbing areas, the **Skaha Bluffs** attract climbers from around the world. The bluffs

are a collection of gneissic cliffs on the east side of Skaha Lake overlooking Penticton and are the sunniest climb in all of Canada. There are approximately 60 crags and hundreds of routes accessible from the Loop Trail, which is 8km long and takes about three hours to complete. There is an extremely steep set of stairs leading to it. Climbers and non-climbers alike enjoy the spring wildflowers, unique plants, views of wildlife, and stunning vistas along the hike. For year-round guiding or instructional services, contact **Skaha Rock Adventures** (☎250-493-1765). To access the Bluffs from downtown Penticton, drive along Main Street toward Skaha Lake. Turn left on Lee Avenue. Cross South Main Street to Crescent Hill Road. Turn right on Valleyview Road and drive slowly through this residential area. Toward the end, the road narrows. Keep to the right and continue on to the Braesyde Farm parking area ($6/day). Maps are available at the Visitors Information Centre (888 Westminster Ave. W., ☎800-663-5052).

The Penticton region is renowned among North American mountain climbers for its wide assortment of rock walls. Many of these surfaces measure a single rope's length, and the level of difficulty can vary greatly. For information on Skaha Bluffs or other areas, contact Ray Keetch of **Ray's Sports Den** (101-399 Main St., no. 100, Penticton, V2A 5B7, ☎250-493-1216) or **Penicton and Wine Country Camber of Commerce** (see p 176).

For climbing and hiking enthusiasts, **Wild Horse Canyon**, at the end of Lakeshore Road, in Okanagan Mountain Provincial Park approximately 16km southwest of Kelowna, offers extraordinary views of the surrounding area. The same is true of **Gallaghers Canyon**, which is more easily accessi-

ble, just next to the golf course.

Rafting

Tour B: Coast Mountain Circle Tour

Hundreds of adventurers come to the gorges of the Fraser and Thompson Rivers each year to brave the tumultuous waters in small groups. Many packages are available to visitors wishing to travel downriver on inflatable rafts, including those offered by **Kumsheen Raft Adventures** (Lytton ☎250-455-2296 or 800-663-6667).

Scuba Diving

Tour A: The Sunshine Coast

Porpoise Bay Charters (7629 Inlet Dr., Sechelt, ☎604-885-5950 or 800-665-3483) will fill your tanks if you are a certified diver, if not, you can join their team which goes to **Porpoise Bay Provincial Park** to dive around the **HMCS Chaudiere**, a warship that was sunk at Kunechin Point to create a natural reef.

Skiing and Heli-skiing

Tour B: Coast Mountain Circle Tour

The Whistler ski resort is considered one of the best in North America, with an annual snowfall of 9m and a 1,600m vertical drop. There are two mountains to choose from: **Whistler Mountain** and

45min north of Kamloops, on Todd Mountain; ☎250-578-7222 or 888-578-8369) resort has recently undergone major renovations and now offers more accommodations and restaurants.

Olympic champion Nancy Greene welcomes visitors to Sun Peaks Resort where they offer complete ski programs. (45min NE of Kamloops, 3150 Creekside Way, ☎800-807-3257).

Located 6km south of downtown on Airport Way, **Powder Springs** (Revelstoke ☎250-837-515 or 800-991-4455) is a family resort renowned for its high-quality powder. It is also fully equipped with ski lifts, dining facilities, a ski school and an equipment rental centre. Under new management, the resort has new run and has widened existing ones.

Mount Revelstoke National Park (☎250-837-7500, see Parks, p 204, or Hiking, p 206) covers an immense stretch of virgin snow set against a backdrop of white peaks. This is a good place for cross-country skiing, since a number of longer trails have been laid out with shelters.

The immense skiing area at **Glacier National Park** (☎250-837-7500) (see Parks, p 204) is perfect for those in search of adventure and quality powder. Because of the steep slopes and risk of avalanches, visitors are required to obtain a permit in order to ski here.

Heli-skiing and cat-skiing are available in this region; they attract a large number of skiers in search of unexplored terrain, far from ski lifts and artificial snow. This region receives record snowfall; in fact, Environment Canada has set up a centre here in order to measure the levels of precipitation. A number of outfits, including **Cat Powder Skiing Inc.** (☎250-

Blackcomb Mountain

Blackcomb Mountain (hotel reservations, ☎604-932-4222 or 888-403-4727; from Vancouver ☎604-685-3650; from the U.S. ☎800-634-9622). The skiing here is extraordinary, and the facilities ultramodern – but mind your budget! You will understand why prices are so high upon seeing hordes of Japanese and American tourists monopolize the hotels and intermediate ski runs.

Whistler and Blackcomb Mountains together make up the largest skiing area in Canada. These world-class, twin ski playgrounds are blessed with heavy snowfalls and boast enough hotels to house a city's entire population. This top-of-the-range ski metropolis also offers the possibility of gliding through pristine powder and, weather permitting, you will find yourself swooshing through an incredibly beautiful alpine landscape.

Whistler Mountain ($51; from Vancouver, Hwy. 99 heading north for 130km, information ☎604-932-3434, ski conditions ☎604-932-4191) is the elder of the two resorts. Experts, powderhounds and skijumpers will all flock to Peak Chair, the chair lift that leads to the top of Whistler Mountain. From its summit, diehard skiers and snowboarders have access to a ski area composed of blue (intermediate) and

expert (black diamond and double-diamond) trails, covered in deep fleecy snow.

Blackcomb Mountain ($48; in Whistler; from Vancouver, Hwy. 99 heading north for 130km; information ☎604-932-3141, ski conditions ☎604-932-4211) is the "stalwart" skiing mecca of ski buffs in North America. For years now, a fierce debate has been waged by skiers over which of the two mountains (Whistler or Blackcomb) is the best. One thing is certain, Blackcomb wins first place for its vertical drop of 1,609m. Check out the glacier at Blackcomb – it is truly magnificent!

If you're looking for a thrill, you can hop aboard a helicopter and set off for vast stretches of virgin powder. Contact **Whistler Heli-Skiing Ltd.** ($450, three rides up, lunch, guide; ☎604-932-4105).

Mountain Heli Sports (4340 Sundial Cr., Whistler, ☎604-932-2070) is a very versatile agency, offering not only flights over mountains and Vancouver, but heli-skiing as well.

Tyax Heli-Skiing (☎604-932-7007) is a very well-known agency in Whistler for heli-skiing.

Tour C: The Thompson River as Far as Revelstoke

Albeit smaller than Whistler, the **Sun Peaks** (day pass $54;

837-5151 or 800-991-4455) and **Selkirk Tangiers Heli-Skiing Ltd.** *(☎800- 663-7080 or 250-837-5378)* offer package deals.

Tour D: Okanagan Valley

The Okanagan Valley is one of the places where, in April, you can ski in the morning and play golf in the afternoon. For skiing, **Silver Star Mountain Resort** *($55; ☎250-542-0224 or 800-663-4431, www.silver starmtn.com)* is a mountain situated less than 30min from Vernon. It offers 84 runs and gets more than 6m of snow annually.

You can go downhill skiing all over this region. The major resorts are the **Apex Resort**, near Penticton, **Big White Ski Resort** near Kelownaand the **Silver Star Mountain Resort** near Vernon. They offer cross-country skiing, dog sledding, snowmobile tours, skating and tubing.

Skiing in the Okanagan, which already has a good reputation, is now enjoying a new boom with the creation of **Big White Ski Resort** *(☎800-663-2772 or 250-765-8888)*. The Schumann family has invested $45 million in the site. With 5 to 6m of snow falling here every year, the powder on these slopes is referred to as "champagne powder", and makes for fine skiing.

Two hours from Kelowna and 1hr from Penticton, **Mount Baldy** has been offering affordable skiing on pleasant powder-covered slopes for 25 years.

Tour E: Kootenay Country

Kokanee Glacier is a provincial park located 21km northeast of Nelson on Hwy. 3A. The road is gravel for 16 of the 21km and is not maintained in winter, when the only way to reach the park is

on cross-country skis or by helicopter. Visitors are strongly advised to obtain specialized equipment for this type of excursion. The Kalso Kake Cabin can accommodate up to 12 people. Due to high demand a lottery is held each October.

Whitewater Ski Resort *(☎250-354-4944 or 800-666-9420)* lies a few minutes south of Nelson on Hwy. 6. This resort is the perfect place to spend a day skiing, whether you're an expert or just starting out.

Red Mountain, located 5min from Rossland, is one of the main centres of economic activity in this region. In the past, miners used to work the mountain; today, it is a playground for skiers. Granite Mountain, renowned for its deep, fluffy powder, is also part of this resort. Opposite Red Mountain, **BlackJack Cross Country Trails** consists of 50km of cross-country ski trails of all different levels of difficulty. **Red Mountain Resorts Inc**. *(☎250-362-7384, reservations ☎800-663-0105)*.

Kimberley Alpine Resort *(☎250-427-4881)* offers majestic views of the Rocky Mountains on a nice little hill. The summit is 1,982m and the mountain receives an average snowfall of 400m. Like many of the ski resorts in B.C., the area is undergoing a scurry of construction and renovation, and will likely continue to expand over the next few years.

Snowmobiling

Tour B: Coast Mountain Circle Tour

The **Pemberton Ice Cap** has the biggest snowmobiling site

in British Columbia. It's in an extraordinary alpine zone among the glaciers and sharp peaks of the coastal chain. The season begins early in December and ends at the end of May. It's important to be informed about the snow conditions before heading out to the mountains. Avalanches occur very frequently. It's also important to travel in groups and to have adequate survival equipment with you.

Windsurfing

Tour B: Coast Mountain Circle Tour

Windsurfers come to **Squamish** (see p 180) for the constant winds that sweep down the sound and then head inland. For information, contact the **Squamish & Howe Sound District Chamber of Commerce** *(☎604-892-9244)*.

Alta Lake *(north of Whistler Creekside on Hwy. 99; turn left on Alta Vista Rd. and right on Alpine Crescent, then keep left until the end of the road to reach Lakeside Park)* attracts windsurfers. This little lake is located in an enchanting setting, which offers lovely panoramic views of Whistler and Blackcomb.

Tour E: Kootenay Country

Lakeside Park, to the right of the bridge on the way into Nelson, offers access to Kootenay Lake. During summer, you can swim and windsurf here to your heart's content.

Accommodations

Tour A:
The Sunshine Coast

Gibsons

Bonniebrook Lodge & RV Campground
$ for camping
$$$ for rooms bkfst incl.
⊛, ℛ
9.4km west on Gower Point Rd. follow directions from Hwy. 101
☎*(604) 886-2887 or*
877-290-9916
⇋*886-8853*
www.bonniebrook.com
A 35min ferry ride from Horseshoe Bay, Bonniebrook is a calm, pleasant place with easy access to the water. Extensive renovations were recently completed.

Langdale Heights RV Resort
$
⚑
2170 Port Mellon Hwy.
☎/⇋*(604) 886-2182*
Langdale Heights is located just 4.5km from the Langdale ferry terminal. It offers RV connections, even for telephones and cable TV! There are also spots for campers with tents. The unusual thing about Langdale Heights is that it has a magnificent nine-hole golf course, which is free for clients.

The Maritimer Bed & Breakfast
$$ bkfst incl.
521 S. Fletcher Rd.
☎*(604) 886-0664 or*
877-886-0664
Run by Gerry and Noreen Tretick, The Maritimer Bed and Breakfast overlooks the town and the marina. The charming scenery, friendly hosts and cozy atmosphere are sure to please. A private suite in the attic includes a

sundeck. On the ground floor, there is a large room decorated with antique furniture and works of art by Noreen; a beautiful quilt graces one of the walls. Breakfast, served on the terrace, which looks right out onto the bay.

Sechelt

Bella Beach Inn
$$
ℛ
from Vancouver, take the Horseshoe Bay ferry to Langdale, continue north on Hwy. 101 to Davies Bay
☎*(604) 885-7191 or*
800-665-1925
⇋*(604) 885-3794*
www.bellabeachinn.com
This spot is considered one of the most beautiful places to stay on the Sunshine Coast. You can enjoy magnificent sunsets right from your window. The rooms are very pretty and extremely comfortable, and visitors have almost immediate access to the beach. The hotel has a sushi restaurant.

Powell River

Willingdon Beach Municipal Campsite
$
4845 Marine Ave
☎*(604) 485-2242*
Here is a campsite in a lovely park not far from the water. The sites are well maintained and showers are free. It's right near a playground.

Oceanside Campground & Cabins
$ for campsites
$$ for cabins
8063 Hwy. 101
☎*(604) 485-2435 or*
888-889-2435
www.oceansidepark.com
This is an excellent spot for families. The campsites overlook the sea and are not far from downtown Powell River. There's a big playground and a games room for children and a water park with slides. Recre-

ational vehicles are accepted and it's open all year.

Beacon B&B and Spa
$$ bkfst incl.
◎
3750 Marine Ave.
☎*(604) 485-5563*
877-485-5563
⇋*(604) 485-9450*
www.beaconbb.com
Your hosts, Shirley and Roger Randall, will make you feel right at home. What's more, they will take great pleasure in telling you all about their part of the country. The Beacon faces west and looks out onto the sea, so you can enjoy the sunset while taking a bath, no less! The simply laid-out rooms each have fully equipped bathrooms. Breakfast includes a special treat: blueberry pancakes. Children 12 and up.

Beach Gardens Resort & Marina
$$
△, ⚑, ☺
7074 Westminster Ave.
☎*(604) 485-6267 or*
800-663-7070
⇋*(604) 485-2343*
www.beachgardens.com
All the rooms are on the water's edge and offer spectacular views of the coast. A fitness centre top off the list of facilities. The resort also has a beer and wine store.

The Coast Town Centre Hotel
$$$
≡, ℛ, ⚑
4660 Joyce Ave.
☎*(604) 485-3000 or*
800-663-1144
⇋*(604) 485-3031*
The Coast Town Centre is near Town Centre Mall, a large shopping centre in the heart of Powell River. The rooms are impeccable and spacious, and the hotel is equipped with a fitness centre. They also organize salmon-fishing excursions. Gulf and fishing packages are available.

Accommodations   211

Texada Island

The Retreat
$$
ℝ, *K*
Gillies Bay
☎*(604) 486-7360*
The Retreat is in a very iso-
lated area right near Shelter
Point Regional Park. The
Retreat offers fantastic views of
the Strait of Georgia and
Vancouver Island from its
balconies. There are seven
units with kitchens for ex-
tended visits and seven RV
sites.

Lund

Lund Hotel
$$$
ℜ
at the end of Hwy. 101
☎*(604) 414-0474*
A relaxing atmosphere prevails
at the century-old Lund Hotel,
which opens onto the bay.
The peaceful location and
view of the boats coming and
going more than compensate
for the motel-style rooms.

Tour B: The Sea to Sky Highway – Fraser River Loop

Whistler

The village of Whistler is
scattered with restaurants,
hotels, apartments and bed &
breakfasts. There is a reservation service to help you take
your pick: **Whistler Resort**
☎*(604) 932-4222*
☎*(604) 664-5625 Vancouver*
☎*800-944-7853*

Whistler International Hostel
$
sb, △
5678 Alta Lake Rd.
☎*(604) 932-5492*
⇒*(604) 932-4687*
www.hihostels.bc.ca
Whistler International Hostel
has 32 beds and a fun vacation
ambiance. Discount for
Hostelling International members.

Shoestring Lodge
$-$$
pb/sb, ℜ
1km north of the village to the right
on Nancy Greene Dr.
☎*(604) 932-3338 or*
877-551-4954
⇒*(604) 932-8347*
www.shoestringlodge.com
The Shoestring Lodge is one
of the least expensive places
to stay in Whistler. Its low
rates make it very popular, so
reservations are imperative.
The rooms include beds,
televisions and small bathrooms; the decor is as neutral
as can be. The youthful atmosphere will make you feel as if
you're at a university summer
camp where the students just
want to have fun—and that's
pretty much what this place is.
The pub is known for its excellent evening entertainment
(see p 227).

Stancliff House B&B
$$ bkfst incl
⊛
3333 Panorama Ridge
☎*(604) 932-2393*
⇒*(604) 932-7577*
Stancliff House B&B is one of
the most reasonably priced
B&Bs in the area. The view of
the surrounding mountains is
beautiful and the breakfasts are
excellent. The home is near
the centre of Whistler, but
away from the hustle and
bustle.

Tantalus Lodge
$$-$$$$$$
≈, △, ≡, *K*, ℜ, 🐾
4200 Whistler Way
☎*(604) 932-4146 or*
888-633-4046
⇒*(604) 932-2405*
www.tantaluslodge.com
Tantalus Lodge is situated near
golfing and not far from the
slopes. Its 76 condominiums
are spacious and fully
equipped. Tennis and volley-
ball courts extend the range of
the town's activities.

Chalet Beau Sejour
$$$ bkfst incl.
⊛
7414 Ambassador Cr.
White Gold Estate
☎*(604) 938-4966*
⇒*(604) 938-6296*
***www.beausejourwhistler.
com***
The Chalet Beau Sejour, run
by Sue and Hal, is a big, inviting house set on a mountainside. You can take in a lovely
view of the valley and the
mountains while eating the
copious breakfast Sue loves to
prepare. A tour guide, she
knows the region like the back
of her hand; don't hesitate to
ask her what to see and do.

Holiday Inn
$$$-$$$$
ℜ, ♥, ⊛, *K*, 🍴
4295 Blackcomb Way
☎*(604) 938-0876 or*
800-229-3188
⇒*(604) 938-9943*
www.whistlerhi.com
The Holiday Inn is located
right near the two mountains.
Every room has a fireplace and
a kitchenette; some have
balconies. All the comforts of a
well-equipped hotel are of-
fered, including a very sophisti-
cated fitness centre.

Listel Whistler Hotel
$$$$$$
🐾, ≈, ≡, △, ℜ
4121 Village Green
☎*(604) 932-1133 or*
800-663-5472
⇒*(604) 932-8383*
www.listelhotel.com
The Listel Whistler Hotel is
located in the heart of the
village, so you don't have to
look far to find some place to
eat or entertain yourself. The
simple layout of the rooms
makes for a comfortable stay.

Southern British Columbia

Fairmont Chateau Whistler Resort
$$$$$$
☉, 🐾, ≈, ◉, △, ℜ, ✪, ℑ, =
4599 Chateau Blvd.
☎*(604) 938-8000*
☎*800-606-8244 or*
800-441-1414
⇻*(604) 938-2291*
www.fairmont.com
The luxurious Fairmont Chateau Whistler Resort lies at the foot of the slopes of Blackcomb Mountain. It resembles a smaller version of Whistler Village, fully equipped to meet all your dining and entertainment needs and to ensure that your stay is relaxing.

Westbrook Whistler
$$$$$$
△, ℜ, K, ◉, ≈, ℑ
4340 Sundial Cr.
at the foot of the lifts
☎*(604) 932-2321 or*
800-661-2321
⇻*(604) 932-7152*
www.whistler.net/westbrook
The Westbrook Whistler has attractive rooms, some with kitchenettes, and beautiful suites with fireplaces. The staff even organizes receptions for newlyweds. Golf packages are available.

Pan Pacific Lodge
$$$$$$
=, K, ≈, △, ✪, ℑ
4320 Sundial Cr.
☎*(604) 905-2999 or*
888-905-9995
⇻*(604) 905-2995*
www.panpac.com
The Pan Pacific Lodge is inspired by the old hotels of the Rockies, and the establishment blends in well with the countryside. Built in the middle of town at the foot of the gondolas that go to the summits of Whistler and Blackcomb, it is difficult to find a better situated or a more luxurious hotel.

Pemberton

Hitching Post Motel
$$
K
Portage Rd., Mount Currie
30min north of Whistler on Hwy. 99
☎*(604) 894-6276 or*
866-894-6276
Hitching Post Motel offers rooms with kitchenettes in a calm spot with beautiful views of Mount Currie.

Log House Bed & Breakfast
$$$ *bkfst incl.*
◉
1357 Elmwood Dr.
☎*(604) 894-6000 or*
800-894-6002
⇻*(604) 894-6000*
Log House Bed & Breakfast is close to everything, is non-smoking and has seven attractive, spacious rooms with all the comforts you could ask for, including a TV and a whirlpool.

Lillooet

Cayoosh Creek Campground
$
early Apr to late Oct
Hwy. 99
☎*(604) 256-4180 or*
877-748-2628
www.cayooshcampground.com
Cayoosh Creek Campground has been set up along a 500m stretch of the Fraser River. The campground offers showers, a beach and a volleyball court, all right near downtown. Warning: there's not much shade.

4 Pines Motel
$-$$
ℝ, =, K
108 Eighth Ave.
☎*(604) 256-4247 or*
800-753-2576
⇻*(604) 256-4120*
www.4pinesmotel.com
4 Pines Motel is located in downtown Lillooet, across from the tourist office. The rooms are well equipped with air conditioning, kitchenettes and satellite television.

Hope

Manning Provincial Park
$
Coldspring, Hampton and Mule Deer: reservations are not accepted. Lightening Lake: reservations only.
☎*(604) 689-9025 or*
800-689-9025
☎*(250) 840-8822 or*
800-330-3321
www.discovercamping.ca
Manning Provincial Park lies on the boundary of the southwestern part of the province and the huge Okanagan-Similkameen region, 225km from Vancouver. City-dwellers come here by the thousands to enjoy all sorts of sports, the most popular being hiking and mountain biking and cross-country skiing in the winter. During summer, you can drive up to Cascade Lookout to take in the view. In addition to several campgrounds, there is a lodge, cabins, chalets and a resort on site (*$$-$$$$*).

Simon's On Fraser
$$ *bkfst incl.*
690 Fraser St.
☎*(604) 869-2562*
Simon's On Fraser, a pretty little Victorian style house adjacent to Memorial Park, has simply decorated, cozy rooms. The house is adorned with woodwork and has been completely repainted in bright colours.

Harrison Hot Springs

Sasquatch Provincial Park
$ *for four people*
Cultus Lake
☎*(604)689-9025 or*
800-689-9025
At Sasquatch Provincial Park, you choose your own campsite and a park employee passes by to collect payment. Hidden in the mountains near Harrison Lake, this park has three campgrounds (177 sites), which welcome nature lovers every year. According to a Coast Salish legend, the Sasquatch is half-man, half-beast and lives in the woods. To this day, some Aboriginal

people claim to have seen the creature around Harrison Lake.

Bigfoot Campgrounds
$
670 Hot Springs Rd.
☎*(604) 696-9767*
Bigfoot Campgrounds is a large, 5ha park that offers all the comforts and has a grocery store, minigolf and video games. There are also cabins available.

Glenco Motel & RV Park
$ camping
$$ room
K, ≡
259 Hot Springs Rd., downtown
☎*(604) 796-2574*
Glenco Motel & RV Park offers motel accommodations and campsites.

🌴 Harrison Heritage House and Kottage
$$-$$$ bkfst incl.
312 Lillooet Ave.
☎*(604) 796-9552*
www.bbharison.com
Jo-Anne and Dennis Sandve will give you a warm welcome at their pretty house, located one street away from the beach and the public pool. Jo-Anne makes her own preserves. Certain rooms have whirlpools and fireplaces.

🌴 Harrison Hot Springs Resort & Spa
$$$-$$$$
🐾, ☉, ≈, ℜ, ⌂
100 Esplanade
☎*(604) 796-2244 or*
800-663-2266
⇥*(604) 796-3682*
www.harrisonresort.com
The Harrison Hot Springs Hotel offers the benefits of the lake and the mountain. It is also the only hotel with access to the mineral springs; it's a fun place where visitors get a sense of well-being. Outdoor heated pools, golf, dancing, children's playground and more. Pets are permitted in cottages only.

Little House on the Lake Bed & Breakfeast Lodge
$$$$ bkfst incl.
⊛, ℑ
6305 Rockwell Dr.
☎*(604) 796-2186 or*
800-939-1116
⇥*(604) 796-3251*
www.littlehouseonthelake.com
The Little House on the Lake is a superb log house set on the east shore of the lake. This is an extremely comfortable place to relax and enjoy water sports like sailing and kayaking.

Tour C: The Thompson River as Far as Revelstoke

Ashcroft

🚣 Sundance Guest Ranch
$$$$ fb
ℜ, ≡, ≈
Highland Valley Rd.
☎*(250) 453-2422 or*
(250) 453-2554
⇥*(250) 453-9356*
www.sundance-ranch.com
Run by former clients, the Sundance Guest Ranch will take you back to a bygone era when cowboys roamed freely on horseback across as yet unexplored regions. The cost covers a stay of at least one day. Guests have access to a living room, where they can bring their drinks; there is a separate living room just for children.

Kamloops

Kamloops Old Courthouse Hostel
$
K, sb, ≡
7 West Seymore
☎*(250) 828-7991*
⇥*(250) 828-2442*
The Kamloops Hostel, is located in the old Provincial Law Courts building, which dates from 1909. The dining room is located in the courtroom where the original witness stands and seats for

the judge and jury have all been preserved.

Joyce's Bed & Breakfast
$$ bkfst incl.
≡, pb/sb
49 W. Nicola St.
☎*(250) 374-1417 or*
800-215-1417
Located steps away from the centre of town, Joyce's Bed and Breakfast is a turn-of-the-century house with big balconies that offer a view of the surrounding scenery. You've got to be a cat-lover to stay here, since the house has two feline residents. Although you'll find little to inspire you indoors, the armchairs on the huge balcony beckon travel-weary visitors to relax and enjoy the view of Kamloops. The three rooms are decent, and given the price and location, it's worth making an effort.

Lazy River Bed and Breakfast
$$ bkfst incl.
≡, ☉, ℑ
1701 Old Ferry Rd., Monte Creek
take Exit 396 off the Trans-Canada Hwy.
☎*(250) 573-3444*
⇥*(250) 573-4762*
www.bbexpo.com/lazyriver
The eight rooms at Lazy River have a country feel, and the South Thompson River winds its way peacefully by this modern, angular home. Rooms are tastefully decorated, with hardwood floors, local artwork, custom-made wood furniture and views of the river. There is access to a boat launch nearby, and this part of the river is popular with those looking to catch themselves some dinner.

Courtesy Inn Motel
$$
≡, 🐾, ⊛, K, ≈, ℝ, ✪
1773 Trans-Canada Hwy.
☎*(250) 372-8533 or*
800-372-8533
⇥*(250) 374-2877*
www.courtesymotel.kamloops.com
If you're looking for budget lodging, you could do much

Southern British Columbia

Plaza Heritage Hotel

worse than the Courtesy Inn Motel. You certainly won't be blown away, but the 45 rooms are comfy enough, and if you're just passing through Kamloops, it's conveniently located on the Trans-Canada Highway. Unfortunately, the highway noise infiltrates, so if you're a light sleeper try somewhere else.

Park Place Bed and Breakfast
$$ bkfst incl.
≡, ≈
720 Yates Rd.
☎(250) 554-2179
⇌(250) 554-2678
Trevor and Lynn Bentz have welcomed visitors to their Westsyde home along the North Thompson River for more than a dozen years, and despite the bed-and-breakfast explosion that has occurred since then, they can still fill their three cozy rooms. They are extremely considerate hosts, and their house's proximity to the river makes for a great stay. Come in autumn to watch chinook salmon swim up the river to spawn right outside your bedroom window.

Best Western Kamloops
$$-$$$
≈, ⊛, △, ⊘, ℜ
1250 Rogers Way
**☎(250) 828-6660 or
800-665-6674**
⇌(250) 828-6698
Located right near the Trans-Canada Highway on the way into town, the Best Western Kamloops Towne Lodge is a very comfortable, classic-style hotel that offers some splendid views of Kamloops and the Thompson River. You can also enjoy the scenery from one of the nearby motels, which vary only in price.

Plaza Heritage Hotel
$$$
≡, 🐾, ℜ
405 Victoria St.
**☎(250) 377-8075 or
877-977-5292**
⇌(250) 377-8076
www.plazaheritagehotel.com
The Plaza Hotel is a pleasant surprise in the heart of Kamloops. It's hard to tell from the outside the extent to which 1999 restorations have returned the old building to its heyday of the 1920s. The warm heritage style guestrooms—with antiques, colourful duvets, and some with four-poster beds and claw foot bathtubs—are

gorgeous. The elevator is interesting…it's more than 70 years old.

Coast Canadian Inn
$$$$
≡, ⊘, ℜ, ≈, △, ✪
339 St. Paul St.
**☎(250) 372-5201 or
800-663-1144**
⇌(250) 372-9363
This Kamloops hotel is conveniently located one block from Victoria Street in the centre of town. There are 98 clean rooms, and while on the whole it's not an inspiring place, there are no surprises. There is a good pub with live music downstairs (see p 227).

South Thompson Inn Guest Ranch and Conference Centre
$$$$-$$$$$
≡, ⊘, 🐴, ℜ, ⊛, ℑ, K, ≈, ℝ, ✪
RR2, Site 12, Comp 25, take Exit 390 (Lafarge Rd.) off the Trans-Canada Hwy.
**☎(250) 573-2853 or
800-797-7713**
⇌(250) 573-2853
www.stigr.com
A 20-minute drive east from Kamloops along the Thompson River leads to this green-and-white Kentucky-style inn, with its 55 uniquely decorated rooms and ranch-like atmosphere. Polished hardwood floors, patios looking out on the river and bright country linens are part of the package, and the tranquil setting might make you happy you chose to stay outside of the town limits.

Salmon Arm

KOA Campground
$
🐾, sb, ≈, ✪
381 Hwy. 97B
☎(250) 832-6489
⇌(250) 832-1178
www.koa.com
There are 70 sites with full RV hook-ups (six for tenters) at KOA's forested tract of land at the eastern edge of Salmon Arm. It's a good facility with a games room, pool table and general store for campers.

Best Western Villager West Motor Inn
$$ bkfst incl.
⊛, *K,* ≈
61-10th St. SW
☎*(250) 832-9793 or*
800-528-1234
Best Western Villager West Motor Inn has rooms for non-smokers, a heated indoor pool, a whirlpool. They also organize cruises on Shuswap Lake.

Prestige Harbourfront Resort and Convention Centre
$$$-$$$$
≡, ⊛, ℜ, ☉, *K,* ≈, ✪
251 Harbourfont Dr. NE
☎*(250) 833-5800 or*
877-737-8443
⇥*(250) 833-5858*
www.prestigeinn.com
The Prestige is a new yellow and brick-tiled resort on the marshy flat lands of Lake Shuswap. There's a Tuscan feel to it all, and you can pop down to the lobby for anything from a manicure to a cappuccino. Rooms are fairly standard. Golf and ski packages are available.

Revelstoke

Samesun Hostel
$
sb
400 Second St.
☎*(250) 837-4050*
⇥*(250) 837-6410*
www.samesun.com
The Samesun has 56 dorm beds in a convenient location in the centre of town. Laundry and Internet services are available, private rooms can be had for around $40 per night, and you can rent a bicycle for $20 per day.

Powder Springs Inn
$
≡, ☉, ℜ, *K,* ℝ
200 Third St. West
☎*(250) 837-5151 or*
800-991-4455
⇥*(250) 837-5711*
www.catpowder.com
Well, Powder Springs certainly isn't going to win any prizes for interior decorating. The green decor with awful red

and blue blinds is terrible, but the town centre location and great price will appeal to travellers on a budget. They offer ski and stay packages at Powder Springs Resort for a ridiculous $29.

Green Gables Loft Bed and Breakfast
$$ bkfst incl.
≡, ℝ
503 Third St. East
☎*(250) 814-0185 or*
877-263-4783
⇥*(250) 814-0186*
Gundy Baty's green-gabled house is close to the town centre and allows for a homey stay while in Revelstoke. The charming Royal Suite has a four-poster bed and gold-and-bordeaux decor. The cream-coloured Garden Suite opens on to the backyard with a fountain and two-person hammock. Bikes and a kayak are available to guests, and you can practice your German or French with Gundy.

Griffin Lake Mountain Lodge Bed and Breakfast
$$-$$$ bkfst incl.
ℜ
7776 Trans-Canada Hwy., 27km west of Revelstoke
☎*(250) 837-7475 or*
877-603-2827
⇥*(250) 837-7476*
www.griffinlakelodge.com
There are beautiful views of Mount English, Griffin Mountain, and of course, Griffin Lake, from this lodge-like establishment. The air is crisp here outside of the summer months, and the smell of woodstoves and the rustic decor—including snowshoes on the walls and a high-beamed common area—add to the ambiance. There are five rooms for guests to use as a starting point for a number of outdoor activities; hiking trails are accessible and canoes are available free of charge.

Best Western Wayside Inn
$$-$$$
≡, 🐾, ≈, ⊛, △, ℜ
1901 Laforme Blvd.
☎*(250) 837-6161 or*
800-663-5307
⇥*(250) 837-5460*
The Best Western Wayside Inn, on the north side of the Trans-Canada, is not only close to everything, but offers the added attraction of a pastoral setting with views of Revelstoke and the Columbia River.

Coast Hillcrest Resort Hotel
$$$
≡, ☉, 🐾, ≈, ℝ, ✪, ℜ, △
turn right off the Trans-Canada Hwy. west of Revelstoke
☎*(250) 837-3322 or*
800-663-1144
⇥*(250) 837-3340*
www.coasthotels.com
The chateau-style Coast Hillcrest has 75 rooms and five specialty suites, many with balconies looking out on Mount Begbie Glacier from its spot in the Selkirk Mountains. It's a fine facility with lots of amenities, comfortable rooms and a calm alpine location.

Glacier House Resort
$$$
≡, ⊛, ☉, ℑ, ≈, ✪, ℜ, △
take Westsyde Rd. 7km north of Revelstoke
☎*(250) 837-9594 or*
877-837-9594
⇥*(250) 837-9592*
www.glacierhouse.com
Across from the Revelstoke Dam (see p 186) Mount Revelstoke and Mount Begbie Glacier, the Glacier House Resort is an oversized pine-wood cabin in the wilderness. Rooms are standard enough, but the setting is wonderful. Keep your eyes peeled for moose or black bear as you have breakfast on the patio. Columbia Mountain Adventures operate out of the resort, and offer a variety of tours and rentals.

Tour D:
Okanagan-Valley

Cathedral Provincial Park

Cathedral Lakes Lodge
$$$$$ all incl.
Slocan Park
☎*(250) 492-1606 or*
888-255-4453
*www.cathedral-lakes-
lodge.com*
Cathedral Lakes Lodge has 10
rooms and 6 small cottages.
The road to the top of the
mountain is only open to the
lodge's all-terrain vehicle, so
you have to leave your car on
Ashnola River Road in the
lodge's base camp. If you go
by foot, it will take you more
than 5hrs to reach the lodge.
There is a two-night minimum
stay. Do not forget to reserve
your seat in the vehicle. Turn
left 4.8km west of Keremeos,
cross over the covered bridge
and drive along Ashnola River
Road for 20.8km. If you plan
on taking the bus, you have to
call the lodge ahead of time to
make arrangements for some-
one to pick you up. All this
might seem complicated, but
once you reach the top,
you're sure to be enchanted
by the mountain goats, marmots and flowers, not to
mention glaciers stretching as
far as the eye can see. Canoes
and rowboats are available
and the lodge has a fireplace
and a bar.

Osoyoos

Cabana Beach Campground
$
early May to mid-Sep
2231 Lakeshore Dr.
☎*(250) 495-7705*
www.cabanabeach.com
Cabana Beach Campground
has facilities for recreational
vehicles and all the necessary
services as well as access to
the beach. Animals are not
allowed from July 1 to August
15.

Lake Osoyoos Guest House
$$ bkfst incl.
K
5809 Oleander Dr.
☎*(250) 495-3297 or*
800-671-8711
⇔*(250) 495-5310*
*www.lakeosoyoosguest
house.com*
At the Lake Osoyoos Guest
House, Sofia Grasso cooks up
breakfast in her huge kitchen
while guests sip freshly
squeezed juice at the edge of
Osoyoos Lake. Guests have
use of a pedalboat to enjoy
the lake and the changing
colours of the valley as the day
wears on.

**Villa Blanca Bed and
Breakfast**
$$ bkfst incl.
ℝ, ☼
23640 Deerfoot Rd., RR1, Site 52,
Comp. 11
☎*(250) 495-5334*
⇔*(250) 495-5314*
Nature lovers will love Villa
Blanca. The white and green-
trimmed house overlooks the
parched Okanagan Valley,
Osoyoos Lake and Washing-
ton State from its spot at the
foot of Anarchist Mountain,
about 10km east of town on
Highway 3. The establishment
takes full advantage of the
region's unique ecosystem,
with white-tailed deer nibbling
on the hosts' flowerbeds, owls
hooting at night and the rare
white-headed woodpecker
poking around in the trees.
The two modern-style
guestrooms and suite are
immaculate, and breakfast is
ordered off a menu.

Bella Bella Motel
$$
K, ≈
close to Hwy.3
☎*888-495-6751*
The Bella Bella Motel has
14 rooms in a calm setting that
is well-suited to families. Free
coffee is served, and there are
picnic areas with tables and
barbecues. It also has its own
private sandy beach.

Holiday Inn Sunspree Resort
$$$$
K, ≈, ☺, ℜ, ≡
Rte. 3
☎*(250) 495-7223 or*
877-786-7773
www.holidayinosoyoos.com
The Holiday Inn Sunspree
Resort is a luxury establish-
ment that offers lakeside con-
dominiums. It has a private
beach, indoor pool, gym,
conference rooms, restaurant,
golf packages and more.
There are also large suites for
families.

Kaleden

**Deer Path Lookout Bed
and Breakfast**
$$$ bkfst incl.
≡, 🍴, ≈
150 Saddlehorn Dr., 17km south of
Penticton off of Hwy. 97
☎*(250) 497-6833 or*
877-497-8999
www.deerpathlookout.bc.ca
This Santa Fe-style hilltop
abode has four excellent guest
suites. The ground floor
rooms feature great nutmeg-
coloured stamped concrete
floors, while the upstairs has
lovely maple hardwood. Each
suite has French doors and
cream-coloured styling, and is
full of beautiful First Nations
and local artwork. The furniture is locally made, aside for a
few antique pieces from Quebec. The sunny hilltop setting
only improves on what is
already a gorgeous place.

Penticton

HI-Penticton
$
464 Ellis St., Penticton
☎*(250) 492-3992*
⇔*(250)492-8755*
www.hihostels.ca
HI-Peniaction has room for 52
people in dormitory and
double rooms. Kitchen and
lounge.

Oxbow RV Resort
$

198 Skaha Place
☎(250) 770-8147
↝(250) 770-8145
www.oxbow-rv-resort.com
Situated on Skaha Lake at the
south end of Penticton's
"strip," this camping facility has
full hook-ups for RVs, cable
television, a laundromat,
washrooms and showers.
Eight of the sites are left for
travellers with tents, but reservations are needed well in
advance for summer months.

Riordan House Bed and Breakfast
$$ bkfst incl.
sb, ≡
689 Winnipeg St.
☎/↝(250) 493-5997
www.icontext.com/riordan
The Riordan House Bed and
Breakfast is an Arts and Crafts
style house built in 1920. Its
owners, John and Donna
Ortiz, have decorated it with
antiques. Their little dog, Dust,
will give you a loud welcome,
but his bark is bigger than his
bite. Children 13 and older
are welcome. No smoking

Butternut Ridge Bed and Breakfast
$$ bkfst incl.
≡
1080 Three Mile Rd.
☎(250) 490-3640 or
877-990-3650
↝(250) 490-3670
Bob and Maggie Handfield are
excellent hosts, and their
home is well situated amongst
vineyards and orchards. Their
three guest rooms are decorated in the Arts and Crafts
style, with comfortable beds
and serene views of Okanagan
Lake or the mountains to the
east. Bob is an excellent cook
(his breakfast burritos are
fantastic), and there are complimentary bikes and a free lift
to the **Kettle Valley Railway**
(see p 196) available if desired.

Shimmering Lake Bed and Breakfast
$$-$$$ bkfst incl.
≡
1015 Hyde Rd., RR1, S6, C4,
Naramata
☎(250) 496-5050
↝(250) 496-5051
The appropriately named
Shimmering Lake Bed and
Breakfast (Okanagan Lake
really does shimmer from
Naramata), offers two
guestrooms and one suite on
a pretty 5ha property in the
heart of wine and fruit country. Rooms have private entrances, the large hardwood
patio looks out on the lake and
a private beach is just a short
walk away.

Executive Inn and Conference Centre Penticton
$$-$$$
K, ≡, ℜ, ☺, ≈, 🐾, ⊛, bp, ℑ. △
333 Martin St., downtown
not far from the beach
☎(250) 492-3600 or
800-665-2221
↝(250) 492-3601
The Executive Inn and Conference Centre Penticton has
101 rooms, each with its own
character, for family vacations,
honeymoons or business trips.
Jacuzzies in some rooms,
health club with saunas, restaurant, golf and ski packages.
Newly renovated.

Tiki Shores Condominium Beach Resort
$$$
⊛, ≈, ℜ, K
914 Lakeshore Dr.
☎(250) 492-8769 or
866-492-8769
↝(250) 492-8160
www.tikishores.com
This motel is located steps
away from the beach on
Okanagan Lake, near the
tourist office and a number of
restaurants.

Coast Inn at Apex
$$$-$$$$
Nov to Apr
≡, ℜ, ℑ, K, ℝ, ✪
1000 Strayhorse Rd.
☎(250) 292-8126 or
888-252-4454
↝(250) 292-8127
www.coasthotels.com
The chateau-style Coast Inn
sits at the bottom of Apex
Mountain and is ideal for skiers
and snowboarders looking for
a ski-in, ski-out facility. There
are 90 rooms here, including
the standard variety, studios
and lofts that can accommo-
date up to six people. Apex
Mountain Resort, with restau-
rants, pubs and shopping, is
metres from the front doors.

Penticton Lakeside Resort and Casino
$$$$
≡, ☺, ℜ, ⊛, K, ≈, ℝ, △, ✪
21 Lakeshore Dr. West
☎(250) 493-8221 or
800-663-9400
↝(250) 493-0607
www.pentictonlakeside
resort.com
All of the amenities are here
for those who need them,
wrapped up nicely with a
grand view of Okanagan Lake
from room balconies. The
tasteful Tuscan-style lobby
extends to a casino for those
who want to try to win back
the substantial amount of
money needed for a room,
although it will be immaculate.
Golf and ski packages are
available, and boats and per-
sonal motorcraft are docked
out back if you want to hit the
water.

Summerland

The Illahie Beach
$
north of Penticton on Hwy. 97
☎(250) 494-0800
The Illahie Beach campground
welcomes vacationers from
April to October. The beaches
and views of the Okanagan
Valley make for a heavenly
setting. The site offers 170
campsites, free showers,
laundry, pay phone and a
convenience store.

Peachland

Log Home Bed and Breakfast
$$-$$$ bkfst incl.
5146 MacKinnon Rd.
☎/⇰*(250) 767-9698*
www.loghome.bb.com
Priska and Ulrich Laux are extremely proud of the log home they have built along a forested back road, and rightfully so. It's a bright and sunny mountainside dwelling built out of massive douglas fir logs. There are two country-style guestrooms and a wood and cream-coloured common room with an impressive 10m ceiling. This place is not for those who cherish privacy however, as you will share the common area with your hosts. The home is unmarked and tricky to find, so call ahead for reservations and directions.

Kelowna

Kelowna Samesun Motel Hostel
$
K, ≡
245 Harvey Ave.
☎/⇰*763-9814*
☎*877-562-2783*
www.samesun.com
Kelowna's youth hostel, the Kelowna Samesun Motel Hostel, is located in the centre of town and can accommodate 24 people in its dormitories.

Abbot House Bed and Breakfast
$$ bkfst incl.
≡, ⊗, 🐾, bp/sb, K
1763 Abbot St.
☎*(250) 763-6373*
This heritage home is well situated; it's about 300m from the town centre and lakefront, but is still hidden by trees in a fairly quiet neighbourhood. Mill Creek runs through the backyard, and the rooms' hardwood floors, yellow walls and eclectic furniture are appealing.

🛶 Crawford View Bed and Breakfast
$$ bkfst incl.
≈, ≡, ℝ
810 Crawford Rd.
☎*(250) 764-1140*
⇰*(250) 764-2892*
The Crawford View Bed and Breakfast overlooks the valley and Okanagan Lake. You will be enchanted by your hosts, Fred and Gaby Geismayr, as well as by the beautiful surroundings. The wooden house is surrounded by an apple orchard, a tennis court and a swimming pool. At the end of September, the Geismayrs are busy picking apples, but all the activity simply adds to the charm of the place.

Mission Creek Country Inn
$$ bkfst incl.
⊗, sb
3652 Spiers Rd.
☎/⇰*860-6108*
☎*877-860-1909*
Built in 1909, Mission Creek is a Cape Cod-style, cedar-shingled heritage home with four bedrooms. The inn sits on a 14.5ha sheep farm, and interpretive programs are offered to spinners and weavers, students learning English and retirees. The inside is thinly furnished in the Arts and Crafts style. The inn is located along a quiet road in southern Kelowna.

Okanagan University
$$
3180 College Way
☎*(250) 470-6055 or 877-589-6073*
⇰*(250) 470-6051*
In summer, you can rent a room or an apartment with up to four rooms at Okanagan University.

Chinook Motel
$$
≡, K
1864 Gordon Dr.
☎*(250) 763-3657 or 888-493-8893*
⇰*(250) 868-8893*
The Chinook Motel is ideally located near everything, in-

cluding the beach and the town centre. The facility offers typical motel comfort with no surprises.

Holiday Park Resort
$$$
S1-415 Commonwealth Rd.
north of the city
☎*(250) 766-4255 or 800-752-9678*
Holiday Park Resort offers comfort and luxury in a lovely natural setting on the waterfront. Health, golf and wine festival packages are offered at reasonable prices.

🚣 Hotel Eldorado
$$$-$$$$
≡, 🐾, ℛ, ⊛
500 Cook Rd.
☎*(250) 763-7500*
⇰*(250) 861-4779*
www.hoteleldorado kelowna.com
Take Lakeshore Drive south to find the unassuming Hotel Eldorado, tucked away by the lake. It doesn't look like much with a sign reminiscent of a 1940s Florida motel, but the inside is splendid, with 20 rooms individually decorated with antiques. The original Eldorado Arms was built as a ranch house, but due to demand from cowboys was turned into a hotel. It was moved to its present location in the 1980s and floated up Okanagan Lake on a barge. Views of the lake are lovely, and there is a fantastic restaurant on the premises (see p 225).

A Vista Bella Bed, Barbecue and Spa
$$$$-$$$$$ half bd.
≡, ⊗, ℜ, K, ≈, ℝ
962 Ryder Ave.
☎*(250) 762-7837*
⇰*(250) 762-7167*
www.avistavilla.com
This much-lauded spa has four incredibly designed rooms with European stylings on a hillside in northern Kelowna. Guests are pampered here, with a complimentary dinner every night, spa services and beds with custom-made goose down duvets. The

Regal Suite has a double-sided fireplace that not only keeps you warm in bed, but also opens onto the bathroom's double whirlpool tub. The only drawback is that it's a couples-only establishment, so singles miss out on all the finery.

Lake Okanagan Resort
$$$$$
ℜ, ≈ , ☉ , *K*, ≡
2751 Westside Rd.
☎*(250) 769-3511 or*
800-663-3273
⇒(250) 769-6665
www.lakeokanagan.com
Lake Okanagan Resort is located right on the lake and offers a complete luxury service to ensure a pleasant vacation. Golf, skiing, swimming, tennis, hiking and horseback riding are all offered. Families can take advantage of rooms, condos or cottages and there are even activities for kids. After a wonderful day outdoors you can sample one of their fine dinners to music.

The Grand Okanagan Lakefront Resort and Conference Centre
$$$$$
ℜ, ≈, ≡ , ☉, ✈
1310 Water St.
☎*(250) 763-4500 or*
800-465-4651
www.grandokanagan.com
The motto of The Grand Okanagan is "Simply Grand," which is a sign of what awaits: a luxurious stay on the waterfront, elegant rooms and exquisite cuisine. Staff members are courteous and the many activities are all associated with the exceptional natural setting and take place around the lake, beaches, golf courses and vineyards. There are also many dining options close by.

Vernon

Dutch's Tent & Trailer Court
$
15408 Kalamalka Rd.
☎*(250) 545-1023*
Dutch's Tent & Trailer Court rents campsites near a little creek only 5min from Vernon's main beach.

Lodged Inn/Vernon Hostel
$
3201 Pleasant Valley Rd.
☎*(250) 549-3742 or*
888-737-9427
www.lodgedinn.com
Located in an old home dating from 1894, Lodged Inn/Vernon Hostel is one of the loveliest youth hostels around. You really feel at home here, and the centre of town is only minutes away. The owner, who loves the great outdoors (climbing, mountain biking, canoeing, skiing, etc.), will give you some great tips.

Richmond House 1894 B&B
$$ bkfst incl.
⊛, ≡
4008 Pleasant Valley Rd.
☎*/⇒(250) 549-1767*
www.richmondhousebandb.com
Richmond House 1894 B&B is an old Victorian-style home that has been completely restored. Its modern jacuzzi blends well with the antique furniture in the other rooms and the tasty breakfast leaves no one hungry.

Merritt

A.P. Guest Ranch
$$ bkfst incl.
ℜ
Rte. 5A
☎*(250) 378-6520 or*
(250) 378-3492
The A.P. Guest Ranch, where both the landscape and the decor are Old West style offers simple rooms in their lodge. Offered are all the activities of a ranch in addition to horse rides on trails with

exclusive views, fishing, snow-mobile excursions and skiing. Quite an experience. The restaurant is open in the evenings. All inclusive ranch and horseback-riding packages available.

Quilchena Hotel
$$-$$$
sb/pb, ℜ
Apr to Oct
23 km northeast of Merritt on Hwy. 5A North
☎*(250) 378-2611*
⇒(250) 378-6091
www.quilchena.com
The historic Quilchena Hotel, located in the heart of ranch country, harkens back to the days when cowboys relaxed around the dinner table. The place is furnished with antiques. Bikes for rent.

Southern British Columbia

Tour E: Kootenay Country

Ainsworth Hot Springs

Ainsworth Hot Springs Resort
$$$
≈, ℜ, ≡
Hwy. 31
☎*(250) 229-4212*
☎*(800) 668-1171*
⇒229-5600
The Ainsworth Hot Springs Resort is part of the facilities surrounding the caves. Guests have free access to the caves, and can get passes for friends. Sauna in the caves with naturally warm water and ice-cold pool.

Nelson

Dancing Bear Inn
$
sb
171 Baker St.
☎*(250) 352-7573*
⇒(250) 352-9818
www.dancingbearinn.com
Nelson's HI establishment sets the bar high for affordable accommodation in the region, and for hostels everywhere. It's more like an inn, with

charming locally made furniture and a sunny and vibrant common room that is often full of international travellers. Private rooms are also available. In 2001, the Dancing Bear Inn won Hostelling International's award for the most outstanding hostel in Canada.

Nelson Tourist Park
$
🐾
mid-Apr to mid-Oct
90 High St.
☎(250) 352-7618 or
(250) 357-2152 off-season
The City Tourist Park is a 35-site campground located in downtown Nelson, within walking distance of the major local attractions and restaurants. At the end of the day, head over to neighbouring Gyro Park to take in the view of the town and Kootenay Lake.

The Heritage Inn
$$ bkfst incl.
ℜ
422 Vernon St.
☎(250) 352-5331 or
877-568-0888
⇌(250) 352-5214
www.heritageinn.org
The Heritage Inn was established in 1898, when the Hume brothers decided to build a grand hotel. Over the years, the building has been modified with each new owner. In 1980, major renovations breathed new life into the old place. The walls of the rooms and corridors are covered with photographs capturing the highlights of Nelson's history.

Inn the Garden Bed & Breakfast
$$ bkfst incl.
sb/pb, K, ℑ, ℝ
408 Victoria St.
☎(250) 352-3226 or
800-596-2337
⇌(250) 352-3284
www.innthegarden.com
This charming Victorian house, renovated by owners Lynda Stevens and Jerry Van Veen, lies steps away from the main street. They also have a three-bedroom guesthouse. The couple's warm welcome will make your stay in Nelson that much more pleasant. Ask them to tell you about the town's architectural heritage: it is one of their passions.

Nelson Guesthouse
$$-$$$ bkfst incl.
🐾, ⊛, ℑ
2109 Fort Sheppard Dr.
☎/⇌(250) 354-0198
☎888-215-2500
www.nelsonguesthouse.com
From the top of the hill overlooking Nelson, the cedar Nelson Guesthouse has two charming rooms and a suite decorated with Asian commodities and wicker furniture. It's a warm and tasteful atmosphere, and very feng shui, feeling much like a charming Japanese inn. Unfortunately, breakfast is of the do-it-yourself variety.

Rossland

🚢 Ram's Head Inn
$$$ bkfst incl.
△, ℝ
at the foot of the slopes
on Red Mountain Rd.
☎(250) 362-9577 or
877-267-4323
⇌(250) 362-5681
www.ramshead.bc.ca
An inviting house owned by Tauna and Greg Butler, the Ram's Head Inn feels like a home away from home. The fireplace, woodwork, simple decor and pleasant smells wafting out of the kitchen create a pleasant, informal atmosphere.

Hotel Uplander
$$$
≡, *K*, 🐾, △, ☺, ⊛, ℜ
1919 Columbia St.
☎/⇌(250) 362-7375
☎800-667-8741
www.uplanderhotel.com
The Hotel Uplander is a full-service property situated right in the centre of town. A shuttle service brings you to the Red Mountain ski slopes. The hotel offers ski and golf packages depending on the season.

A comfortable, quality establishment.

Cranbrook

Singing Pines Bed and Breakfast
$$-$$$
≡, ℑ, ℝ, ☻
5180 Kennedy Rd., just north of Cranbrook off of Hwy. 95A
☎(250) 426-5959 or
800-863-4969
This little green home nestled in pine trees has three rooms decorated in what can best be described as a cowboy motif. It's a quiet spot with a view of the Rocky Mountain Trench as it runs between the Columbia and Rocky Mountains. Rooms are cheerful, and there's an antique piano in the common room for those who wish to tickle the ivories. Ermine, the proprietors' beautiful white dog, keeps a friendly watch over the premises.

Kimberley

Samesun Hostel
$ bkfst incl.
≡, *sb*, ☻
275 Spokane St.
☎(250) 427-7191
⇌(250) 427-7095
www.samesun.com
There are 58 beds available at the Samesun Hostel, located in the back corner of the **Platzl** (see p 201). The price is right, even if the walls are a strange lime green colour. It's a good place to make friends that are in town to take advantage of Kimberley's many outdoor activities, and there's a do-it-yourself pancake breakfast available. The downside or upside, depending on your point of view, is that the hostel is overtop a happening nightspot (see p 227).

Purcell-Rocky Mountain Condo Hotel
$$-$$$

ॐ, K, ℝ, △, ✪
follow signs from the town centre to the ski resort
☎/⇌*427-5385*
☎*800-434-3936*
www.purcellrocky.com
Don't be too discouraged by the pseudo-Bavarian front and the brown-carpeted, ratty hallways—the rooms at this hotel are more tasteful than you'd think, with wooden bed frames and local artwork. It's great for skiers, with a chairlift running right up the mountain beside the hotel.

Restaurants

Tour A: The Sunshine Coast

Gibsons

Daily Roast
$
Mon-Fri 5am to 6pm
Sat 6:30am to 16pm
Sun 8:30am to 4pm
5547 Wharf Rd.
☎*(604) 885-4345*
The Daily Roast is a good café with the best coffee in the area; the espresso is excellent. It also sells cookies and home-made muffins.

Lighthouse Marine Pub
$
just after Porpoise Bay Rd.
on the waterfront
☎*(604) 885-4949*
Great hamburgers and good beer. Friendly, lively atmosphere. During your meal, you can watch hydroplanes taking off. A liquor store (beer and wine) is integrated into the pub.

 Molly's Reach Restaurant
$$
647 School Rd.
☎*(604) 886-9710*
Gibsons became famous throughout the world as the setting for *The Beachcombers*, a Canadian Broadcasting Corporation (CBC) television series. The show was produced for close to 20 years and broadcast in over 40 countries. Molly's Reach Restaurant is the place where all the characters met; it appeared in every episode. The walls of the restaurant are decorated with photos from the series. The environment is always lively and enjoyable and the food is good. If you go to Gibsons you must to go to Molly's Reach.

Sechelt

Poseidon Restaurant
$$
closed Mon, Sun-dinner only
Davis Bay, on Hwy. 101
☎*(604) 885-6046*
The Poseidon Restaurant is a good Greek restaurant that also serves pasta, steak and seafood.

Tour B: The Sea to Sky Highway – Fraser River Loop

Squamish

Midway Restaurant
$-$$
40330 Tantalus Way
in the Best Western
☎*(604) 898-4874*
Midway Restaurant offers home-style food in a friendly, lively environment.

Lotus Gardens
$$
38180 Cleveland Ave.
☎*(604) 892-5853*
Lotus Gardens is a Chinese restaurant with a long, detailed menu, with many different chicken, pork, fish and vegeta-ble dishes. You can also get your meal to take out.

Squamish Valley Golf & Country Club
$$$
2458 Mamquam Rd.
☎*(604) 898-9521 or*
(604) 898-9691
Squamish Valley Golf & Country Club's restaurant serves breakfast, lunch and supper and offers daily specials. The staff is friendly and it's open all year, as is their Sport Bar & Grill.

Whistler

 The Roundhouse
$$
Nov to Jun, 7:30am to 3pm
at the top of the Whistler Village Gondola
☎*(604) 932-3434*
If you want to be among the first to ski the slopes in the morning, head to Pika's for breakfast; it is worth getting up early the day after a storm.

Trattoria di Umberto
$$-$$$
4417 Sundial Place
near Blackcomb Way
on the ground floor
of the Mountainside Lodge
☎*(604) 932-5858*
At the Trattoria di Umberto, you'll find pasta as well as meat and fish dishes and a homey atmosphere.

Zeuski's
$$$
Town Plaza
☎*(604) 932-6009*
Zeuski's is a Greek-mediterranean restaurant. Tzatziki, hummus and souvlaki are served and the prices are very reasonable for Whistler.

Black's Pub & Restaurant
$$$
below Whistler and Blackcomb Mountains
☎*(604) 932-6408 or*
(604) 932-6945
Black's Pub & Restaurant serves breakfast, lunch and dinner for the whole family in a friendly atmosphere. The

views are exceptional and it has one of the best beer selections in Whistler.

Città Bistro
$$$$
every day 11am to 1am
Whistler Village Square
☎(604) 932-4177
Located in the heart of the village, Città Bistro has an elaborate menu with selections ranging from salads to pita pizzas. This is the perfect place to sample one of the local beers. In both winter and summer, a pleasant mix of locals and tourists makes for an extremely inviting atmosphere. Now offers a more formal dinner menu.

Thai One On
$$$$
every day, dinner only
in the Le Chamois hotel
at the foot of the Blackcomb Mountain slopes
☎(604) 932-4822
As may be gathered by its name, Thai One On serves Thai food, with its wonderful blend of coconut milk and hot peppers.

Monk's Grill
$$$$
4555 Blackcomb Way
at the foot of Blackcomb
☎(604) 932-9677
Monk's Grill is great for an après-ski dinner. On the menu are specialty steaks and Alberta prime rib as well as fresh fish, sea food and pasta dishes.

Araxi Restaurant & Bar
$$$$
Whistler Village
☎(604) 938-3337
Featuring Pacific Northwest cuisine with French and Italian influences Araxi is the restaurant of choice on the Pacific coast. It specializes in fresh local seafood prime Canadian beef and locally grown organic produce. The wine cellar is renowned as are the head chef and pastry chef. Fully

renovated bar and patio in summer.

Pemberton

The Pony Expresso
$$$
1426 Portage Rd.
☎(604) 894-5700
The Pony Expresso specializes in fresh seafood.

Harrison Hot Springs

Kitami
$$$
318 Hot Springs Rd.
☎(604) 796-2728
Kitami is a Japanese restaurant that invites you to enjoy a meal in one of their Tatami Rooms or at the sushi bar.

Black Forest Restaurant
$$$
180 Esplanade Ave.
☎(604) 796-9343
The Black Forest Restaurant is an Alsatian-style restaurant with flowery windows. The food, including schnitzel, Chateaubriand and fresh pasta, has a European flavour. They also serve B.C. salmon. The wine list is extensive. It's open year round in the evening, but only in the summer for lunch.

Copper Room
$$$$
100 Esplanade
☎(604) 796-2244 or 800-663-2266
The restaurant at the Harrison Hot Spring Hotel offers dinners that are a gastronomical

delight accompanied by music and dancing. They serve meats and fish.

Tour C: The Thompson River as Far as Revelstoke

Kamloops

Zack's
$
377 Victoria St.
☎(250) 374-6487
Saloon-style Zack's is the token funky place for coffee in Kamloops. Always full, there are bagels, toast and cinnamon buns for breakfast, and sandwiches, samosas and baked goods for lunch. The usual array of coffees and teas is available.

Swiss Pastries
$
Tue-Sat 8am to 5pm
359 Victoria St.
☎(250) 372-2625
This simple café is always full of locals tasting a variety of sandwich combinations for lunch, or desserts like black forest cake and Grand Marnier almond loaf. There is a noisy espresso machine pouring out lattes and cappuccinos, and some Swiss specialties like buendnerfleisch are also available.

Hot House Bistro
$$
438 Victoria St.
☎(250) 374-4604
The Hot House Bistro is a fantastic restaurant. From the Guatemalan fabrics on the walls to the strawberry-orange vinaigrette on the salad, this is the one place in Kamloops you simply must eat at, whether it's lunch on the Victoria Street patio or dinner in the dining room. Cuisine is Mexican and international, and the service is friendly. Try the enchiladas, but careful, they may bite back.

Taka Japanese Restaurant
$$
270-1210 Summit Dr.
☎(250) 828-0806
Seemingly endless pasta and seafood dishes can become tiresome, so Kamloops residents frequent this small Japanese restaurant, unfortunately located in a shopping mall near the university. Take out is popular, and the variety much appreciated.

La Cucina Ristorante
$$-$$$
229 Victoria St.
☎(250) 372-7711
This small Italian eatery with a red neon sign and green-and-white chequered tablecloths features a menu of individual pizzas, pasta and chicken dishes. The pasta lunches for around $8 are a good deal.

Mino's Greek Souvlaki
$$-$$$
262 Tranquille Rd.
☎(250) 376-2010
Take the bridge north over the river to find this gem of a café under familiar blue Greek lettering. It's an intimate place, and don't let the poor decor turn you away. Souvlaki, moussaka, steaks and seafood are the staples, and as an added bonus, there are belly dancers on weekends.

Nick of Thyme
$$$
Tue-Sat, lunch and dinner
474 Tranquille Rd.
☎(250) 376-5555
The pink walls probably have to go, but the food is recommended at this popular restaurant. Gourmet pasta and seafood dishes—like sesame and ginger crusted tiger prawns—are offered, and there is live music on Fridays and Saturdays.

Ric's Mediterranean Grill
$$$-$$$$
Mon-Fri 11am to 11pm, Sat and Sun 4pm to 11pm
227 Victoria St.
☎(250) 372-7771
Ric's is the Kamloops fine dining option, with its romanti-

cally lit dining room and original artwork reminiscent of an Italian villa. The menu is huge, with plates like grilled Tuscan jumbo prawns and scallops and toasted coconut chicken. The grilled New Zealand spring lamb chops with Sicilian roasted potatoes are lovely.

The Old Steak and Fish House
$$$-$$$$
172 Battle St.
☎(250) 374-3227
This dining room feels a bit like a boat's deck, and as the name would imply, a variety of seafood and beef dishes are available. Wild B.C. halibut and premium ahi tuna are available inside, or on a garden patio overlooking the city. The wine list is extensive.

Revelstoke

Frontier Restaurant
$
every day 5am to 10pm
at the intersection of the Trans-Canada Hwy. and the 23
☎(250) 837-5119
At the Frontier Restaurant, you can put away a big breakfast in a typically western setting.

🍃 Woolsey Creek Café
$$-$$$
212 Mackenzie Ave.
☎(250) 837-5500
A café with burgundy walls and blues guitar emanating from speakers, Woolsey Creek adds some much-needed charm to Revelstoke dining. Mountaineering trendy types come here to sip cocktails or chow down on vegetarian dishes. You can still get a great steak though, and you might as well wash it down with a pint of locally brewed High Country Kölsch. If you're not hungry, this is still a good place to just have a drink and hang out.

Black Forest
$$-$$$
5min west of Revelstoke on the Trans-Canada Hwy.
☎(250) 837-3495
The Black Forest is a Bavarian-style restaurant that serves Canadian and European cuisine. Top billing on the menu goes to cheese and fish. The setting and view of Mount Albert are enchanting.

Tour D: Okanagan-Similkameen

Osoyoos

Indiana's Café
$
7am to 2pm, closed Mon
7414 Hwy.97
☎(250) 495-2575
For breakfast and lunch, locals recommend this small, yellow-walled café with a Mexican feel to it. Prices are certainly affordable, with $6 omelettes in the morning and an assortment of burgers and wraps for midday.

Campo Marina Café and Restaurant
$$$
Tue-Sun, dinner
5907 Main St.
☎(250) 495-7650
Campo Marina is an Italian bistro with yellow walls and chequered tablecloths. It's a local favourite for dinner, with a long pasta menu including rigatoni, linguini, fettuccine, gnocchi, lasagne and cannelloni. Veal, snapper and chicken dishes also have their place. Take a breath mint as you leave—the chef loves his garlic.

Penticton

Hog's Breath Coffee Co.
$
202 Main St.
☎(250) 493-7800
The Hog's Breath is the perfect place to start off your day with a good cup of coffee, and even more importantly, some peach muffins (in season):

you'll love them! If you're looking for outdoors destinations, the owner, Mike Barrett, will gladly offer some suggestions.

Gypsy Heart and Dream Café
$-$$
Tue-Sun
74 Front St.
☎*(250) 490-9012*
Funky, eclectic—whatever you want to call it—the tablecloths are colourful and the choices for vegetarians extensive at this Front Street café/gift shop. There are often live performances to accompany your panini sandwich or wrap, and bright, imported commodities are everywhere. It's a bohemian crowd, which is perfect after a day of being surrounded by the overgroomed beach set.

Isshin Japanese Deli
$-$$
Mon-Sat
101-401 Main St.
☎*(250) 770-1141*
Craving sushi? Isshin is a cozy, wooden deli that was voted *Best New Restaurant in 2002* by *Okanagan Life Magazine*. Tempura, sashimi and noodle dishes are also on the menu. The restaurant is popular with locals for takeout, so grab some good Japanese fare and head for the lake.

The Elite
$-$$
340 Main St.
☎*(250) 492-3051*
The Elite has been open for 75 years, so they're probably doing something right. This is a good place for a $5 bacon-and-egg breakfast, or an unpretentious but hearty lunch or dinner. The décor is 1950s diner-style, with vinyl booths and old-school metal napkin dispensers on the tables.

Front Street Pasta Factory
$$
75 Front St.
☎*(250) 493-5666*
The Front Street Pasta Factory offers a lively, pleasant family

atmosphere with good pasta and service. Reservations recommended.

Lost Moose Lodge
$$
8min. from the centre of Penticton
Beaverdell Rd.
☎*(250) 490-0526*
Lost Moose Lodge offers music, spectacular views and good barbecued food.

Vallarta Bistro, Barbecue and Grill
$$-$$$
610 Main St.
☎*(250) 492-5610*
This *casa* has a great menu of authentic Mexican cuisine, excellent ambiance, a long wine list and great *al fresco* seating. The food is fresh and tasty—everything is made daily from scratch—and includes fajitas, quesadillas and enchiladas. From the food, to the Mexican music, to the sun flowered tablecloths, so much is done well here. *Fantastico*.

Granny Bogners Restaurant
$$$
closed Mon.
302 Eckhardt Ave. W.
☎*(250) 493-2711*
This magnificent Tudor house was built in 1912 for a local doctor. In 1976, Hans and Angela Strobel converted it into a restaurant, where they serve fine French, German and Austrian cuisine made with local produce.

Theo's Restaurant
$$$
687 Main St.
☎*(250) 492-4019*
Fine Greek cuisine and a relaxed atmosphere make for a pleasant meal at this extremely popular spot.

Salty's Beach House
$$$$
998 Lakeshore Dr.
☎*(250) 493-5001*
Seafood fans will find their favourite foods at Salty's Beach House. Make sure to come

here at lunchtime so you can enjoy the view of Okanagan Lake from the terrace. The pirate-ship decor gives the place a festive atmosphere.

Kelowna

Bean Scene Coffee House
$
274 Bernard Ave.
☎*(250) 763-1814*
Unfortunately, Kelowna has a high proportion of Kens and Barbies, and this is the decidedly non-Starbucks haven for their antitheses. Comfortable armchairs, cool music and information on the local underground music and arts scene make it popular with those looking for coffee or an organic green tea smoothie. Baked goods are available to munch on.

La Bussola Restaurant
$$-$$$
234 Leon Ave.
right near City Park
☎*(250) 763-3110*
La Bussola Restaurant is famous for the quality of its food and the pleasant, intimate setting. Since 1974 Franco and Lauretta have been welcoming clients and delighting them with their Italian food. Reservations are recommended.

Mekong
$$$
1030 Harvey
☎*(250) 763-2238*
Mekong serves refined Chinese and Szechwan cuisine in its luxurious dining room.

Christopher's
$$$
242 Lawrence Ave.
right near city Park
☎*(250) 861-3464*
Christopher's is one of the best restaurants in Kelowna. Open every day, the ambiance is elegant and the service is very friendly. Reservations recommended.

The Yamas Taverna
$$$
1630 Ellis St.
downtown
☎(250) 763-5823
The Yamas Taverna is a
Greek restaurant *par excellence*. White and blue, and
abundantly flowered, this
restaurant assures clients an
excellent evening with a Mediterranean flavour. You won't
be disappointed, especially on
Saturday nights when they
feature belly dancing.

The El
$$$-$$$$
500 Cook Rd.
☎(250) 763-7500
As the sun sets on Okanagan
Lake, the candles are lit at this
wonderful restaurant at Hotel
Eldorado. The dining room is
long, narrow and intimate, and
there isn't a bad view in the
house. You can be extravagant
with a $37 rack of lamb, or
more reasonable with a $16
chicken alfredo or pizza. The
jumbo shrimp and sun dried
tomato linguine is sublime.

Old Vines Patio
$$$-$$$$
May to Oct, every day, 11am to
dusk
3303 Boucherie Rd., Quail's Gate
Vineyard
☎(250) 769-4451
Old Vines Patio is an outdoor
dining room on Quail's Gate
Estate Vineyard with fantastic
views of the Okanagan Valley,
a flowered setting and cedar
decor to blend in with the
rows of vines. Pasta, seafood
and steaks are on the menu,
while there are small plates
available at more reasonable
prices, and perfect for trying
out some wine-food combinations. Grant de Montreuil is
the well-respected chef in
charge of the kitchen, and also
operates de Montreil's and the
Teahouse at Kelowna Land
and Orchard (see below).

Fresco
$$$-$$$$
1560 Water St.
☎(250) 868-8805
Fresco is a fine dining option
with exposed brick and concrete walls and an open
kitchen. The atmosphere is
great, and the food, care of
chef Rodney Butters, renowned. Steaks and seafood
are prominent.

The Teahouse at Kelowna Land and Orchard
$$$-$$$$
lunch and dinner
3002 Dunster Rd.
☎(250) 712-9404
The Teahouse is a sunny,
hardwood-floored dining
room that has been voted
Most Romantic by *Okanagan
Life Magazine*. There's a reason for that, with long windows overlooking the finest
Okanagan orchards. Scrumptious entrees like saffron
poached halibut and pistachio
crusted chicken breast are
served.

De Montreuil's
$$$-$$$$
high season dinner only, off-
season lunch and dinner
368 Bernard Ave.
☎(250) 860-5508
Grant de Montreuil calls his
work Cascadian Cuisine for its
use of fresh, locally grown and
organic products. His bistro at
the town centre is warm,
decorated with red and orange and hardwood floors,
while the wine list is extensive.
You can try fresh coho salmon
broiled and glazed with
Okanagan lavender jelly, or
perhaps pan roast Fraser Valley duck breast with blackberry and roast *cipoline* onion
confit. Lunch is offered in the
off-season from the same
kitchen, but at a third of the
price of dinner.

Vernon

Johnny Appleseeds Juice Bar & Cafe
$
3018 30th Ave.
☎(250) 542-7712
Johnny Appleseeds Juice Bar &
Cafe serves excellent fresh
juice concoctions, such as the
Eye Opener, which combines
orange, pineapple and apple
juice. Coffee and delicious light
fare are also served.

Hang Chou Restaurant
$-$$
3007 30th Ave.
☎(250) 545-9195
The Chinese buffet at Hang
Chow Restaurant is a good
choice when you're famished.

Eclectic Med on Main
$$$-$$$$
100-3117 32nd St.
☎(250) 558-4646
This warm Mediterranean
restaurant at the centre of
town is a favourite of locals
and critics alike. Influences are
varied, with a number of
pastas and fusion-style dishes
like Tuscan tuna.

Merritt

Coldwater Hotel
$$
restaurant 7:30am to 9pm
saloon to 2am
at the corner of Quilchena and
Voght
☎(250) 378-5711
Both the restaurant and the
saloon in the Coldwater Hotel
have always been popular
with local cowboys. The food
is somewhat heavy, but the
prices are right. The rooms
can be rented nightly or the
week.

Best Western
$$
4025 Walters St.
☎(250) 378-4253
Best Western offers service
inside or on the terrace. Elegant country-style atmosphere. Sunday brunch and
prime ribs on Fridays.

Tour E:
Kootenay Country

Nelson

Sidewinders
$
696 Baker St.
(250) 352-4621
Situated at the north end of Baker Street, Sidewinders offers the best coffee in the area. Grab a latté or *chai* tea and head for the sidewalk seating to join Nelsonites hunched over their chessboards. Fresh sandwiches and baked goods are on the menu.

All Seasons Café
$$$
dinner 5pm to 10pm
620 Herridge Lane, behind Baker St.
(250) 352-0101
The All Seasons Café is not to be missed. It lies hidden beneath the trees, so its terrace is bathed in shade. The soups might surprise you a bit – apple and broccoli (in season) is one example. The menu is determined by the season and what's available in the area, with lots of space accorded to the fine wines of British Columbia. The friendly, efficient service, elegant decor and quality cuisine make for an altogether satisfying meal. The walls are adorned with works of art.

Mazatlan
$$$
198 Baker St.
(250) 352-1388
The food's wonderful, the atmosphere festive and the ambiance authentic, but the service is frustratingly inattentive. If you can handle being ignored though, the Mexican dishes here are fantastic, and the live music and warm light bouncing off brick walls are appealing. Tacos, enchiladas, tamales and burritos are all here, as are a number of imported tequilas.

Rossland

Many quaint cafes line Columbia Street in the heart of Rossland. The population doubles in December when the slopes open, giving the town a festive, ski-resort atmosphere. Sunshine Cafe and Bean There offer light fare and hearty breakfasts.

Clancy's Cappucino
$
breakfast and lunch
2040 Columbia
(250) 362-5273

Sunshine Cafe
$
breakfast and lunch
2116 Columbia
(250) 362-5070

Olive Oyl's
$$-$$$
Tue-Sun
2067 Columbia
(250) 262-5322
Olive Oyl's cuisine is best described as contemporary or fusion cuisine, combining several different culinary trends. Its offerings include pasta, pizza and enormous brunches, all meticulously prepared and presented.

Flying Steamshovel Inn
$$$
Washington St., corner Second Ave.
(250) 362-7323
With its green wall and his oak wood, Flying Steamshovel Inn parlour in a saloon atmosphere. The menu includes big, fat sandwiches, pasta, salads and, of course, a good selection of beer on tap.

Mountain Gypsy Cafe
$$$$
every day
lunch Tue-Fri
2167 Washington St.
(250) 362-3342
Mountain Gypsy Cafe offers a unique variety of eclectic dishes.

Cranbrook

Max's Café
$
301 Victoria Ave.
(250) 439-3538
Located between the interior of B.C. and Calgary, Cranbrook makes a convenient lunch stop for many travellers, and this sunny café is a good choice. Counter-service sandwiches, wraps and desserts, as well as a number of fresh salads and baked goods are available.

Kimberley

Snowdrift Café
$
110 Spokane St.
(250) 427-2001
The decor needs some work at this hole-in-the-wall café in the Platzl, but it's popular for its simple fare. How simple? You can get a peanut butter and jam sandwich. It's a good choice for vegetarians, with meatless chili, pizza and lasagna on the menu.

Gasthaus am Platzl
$$-$$$$
240 Spokane St.
(250) 427-4851
Canadian, international and Austrian cuisine is served at this undeniably cheesy restaurant. The Bavarian shtick is poured on fairly thick, with frocked *fraulines* serving dinner, but the proprietors are, in fact, Austrian. The steaks and prime rib are great (the portions are huge) and there's Warsteiner Pilsner on tap, as well as a long wine list. Look for the Bavarian building front on the Platzl, curiously decorated with a picture of the Last Supper.

Entertainment

Bars and Nightclubs

Tour A: Sunshine Coast

Whistler

Cinnamon Bear Bar
4050 Whistler Way,
in the Delta Hotel
☎(604) 932-1982
The relaxed atmosphere at the Cinnamon Bear Bar attracts sporty types of all ages.

The Boot Pub
1km north of the village on the right, on Nancy Greene Dr.
☎(604) 932-3338
At the Boot Pub, located in the Shoestring Lodge hotel, live musicians play Reggea & Blues to an enthusiastic clientele.

Tommy Africa's
Gateway Dr.
☎(604) 932-6090
Young dance music fans get together at Tommy Africa's. Line-ups are common due to its popularity.

Tour C: The Thompson River as Far as Revelstoke

Kamloops

Duffy's
179 Pacific Way
☎(250) 372-5453
Just north of the Visitor's Centre, Duffy's is a popular pub and sports bar. It's been voted the best pub in Kamloops for the last five years.

Sgt O'Flaherty's
339 St. Paul St.
☎(250) 372-5201
Sgt O'Flaherty's, located in the Coast Canadian Inn, is a great place for a cold pint and live folk, country and rock music.

Tour D: Thompson-Okanagan

Penticton

Old Barley Mill Pub
2460 Skaha Lake Rd.
☎(250) 493-8000
This pub is popular with both young and old and has a hearty selection of ales, pilsners and stouts. If you're looking for an athletic event, there are various televisions locked on the sports channels.

Kelowna

Doc Willoughby's
353 Bernard Ave.
☎(250) 868-8288
Doc's hops on weekends with young Kelownans, while during the week it's a quieter spot to grab a cold one. There's a large patio facing Bernard Avenue.

Splash's
275 Leon Ave.
☎(250) 762-2956
This is a popular two-storey nightclub that is generally crawling with Kelowna's young, tanned and preened. On Wednesdays the second floor features a rock, alternative and hip-hop DJ that brings out an entirely different crowd.

Tour E: Kootenay Country

Nelson

The Royal Bar and Grill
330 Baker St.
☎(250) 352-1202
The Royal gets packed on weekends, when there is a live band. Admission at such times is usually around $5, and some great music gets played here, from rock to ska to reggae.

Mike's Place
422 Vernon St.
☎(250) 352-5331
Mike's Place is a huge pub with three levels in the Heritage Inn. It can get busy on any day of the week.

Kimberley

Ozone Pub
275 Spokane St.
☎(250) 427-7191
This pub in the Samesun Hostel is likely the only place really worth venturing out for a drink for in Kimberley or Cranbrook. It gets hopping, and the nomadic outdoorsy types and international crowd add some welcome energy.

Calendar of Events

February

Kamloops Festival of Performing Arts
☎(250) 374-3491
Kamloops celebrates its artists, musicians and actors with a month of performances at various venues throughout town. If you're here in February or early March, you will certainly be able to catch a show.

July

Kamloops Cattle Drive
☎800-288-5850
www.cattledrive.bc.ca
Every July, participants arrive from around the world for a five-day cattle drive on horseback from Nicola Ranch to the open range near Kamloops. Events include a parade, banquet and wind-up dance.

Kimberley JulyFest
☎(250) 427-3666
Kimberley's annual celebration of all-things Bavarian occurs in mid-July each year. Enjoy German beer, music and dance, and of course, stick around for the Kimberley International Old Time Accordion Championships.

Nelson StreetFest
☎(250) 352-7188
www.streetfest.bc.ca
Nelson's Baker Street is closed off for three days each July to allow for performers and vendors to take over the streets.

August

Salmon Arm Roots and Blues Festival
Salmon Arm Fair Grounds
☎*(250) 833-4096*
For the last 10 years, the Salmon Arm Fair Grounds have rocked to the blues each August. Canadian and international performers take the stage during the three-day concert.

September

Pentastic Hot Jazz Festival
☎*(250) 770-3494*
www.pentasticjazz.com
Jazz lovers will want to take note that for three days in September, Penticton plays host to world-class jazz bands at venues throughout the town.

October

Okanagan Wine Festival
☎*(250) 861-6654*
www.owfs.com

Kelowna's famous **Wine Festivals** *(☎250-861-6654)* are held every spring, summer and fall and winter (ice wine) and the **BC Wine Label Awards** are held in October at the **Wine Museum** *(☎250-868-0441)*.

December

Lighted Boat Parade for Christmas
Gibsons Harbour
☎*(604) 886-8500*

Shopping

Tour B: Coast Mountain Circle Tour

Squamish

Vertical Reality Sports Store
38154 Second Ave.
☎*(604) 892-8248*
Vertical Reality Sports Store sells and rents mountain bikes, offers guided tours, gives advice on rock-climbing and will even take you there.

Whistler

Just south of the little village,on the outskirts Whistler, lies **Function Junction**, a small commercial and light industrial area of sorts. You won't find just any industries here, however!

Blackcomb Cold Beer & Wine Store
in the Glacier Lodge, across from Fairmont Chateau Whistler
☎*(604) 932-9795*
Blackcomb Cold Beer & Wine Store has a large selection of B.C. wines. Helpful and courteous staff.

The Wright Choice Catering
12-1370 Alpha Lake Rd.
☎*(604) 905-0444*
The Wright Choice Catering will make supper for you. Every day you can pick up something different such as *focaccia*, pizza, grilled vegetables and chicken. They also prepare complete picnics, ready to take out.

Little Mountain Bakery
7-1212 Alpha Lake Rd., Function Junction
☎*(604) 932-4220*
Little Mountain Bakery sells bread, pastries and sweets.

Mountains Blooms
Market Place
☎*(604) 932-2599 or 877-932-2599*
Mountains Blooms has a wonderful selection of fresh flowers and bouquets for special occasions. You can also have flowers sent anywhere in the world.

All Seasons Spa
Fairmont Chateau Whistler
☎*(604) 938-2086*
Will help you relax and recuperate in grand style.

Whistler Sailing & Water Sports Centre Ltd
Lakeside & Wayside Parks Alta Lake
☎*(604) 932-7245*
Whistler Sailing & Water Sports Centre Ltd has all the necessities for sailing and water sports.

Adele-Campbell Fine Art Gallery
4050 Whister Way, close to the entrance of the Delta Whistler Resort
☎*(604) 938-0887*
Adele-Campbell Fine Art Gallery exhibits works by renowned artists from B.C. and throughout Canada.

Plaza Galleries
22-4314 Main St.
☎*(604) 938-6233*
Plaza Galleries present works by both, local and international artists in the region.

The Grove Gallery
Delta Whistler Resort
☎*(604) 932-3517*
The Grove Gallery offers landscapes of Whistler and the mountains.

Whistler Inuit Gallery
4599 Chateau Blvd., Westin Resort and Spa
☎*(604) 938-3366*
Whistler Inuit Gallery exhibits very attractive wood, bone, marble and bronze pieces by Aboriginal sculptors.

Harrison Hot Springs

Curiosities
160 Lillooet Ave.
☎*(604) 796-9431*
Curiosities, as the name suggests, sells souvenirs, toys for children, T-shirts and other vacation clothing.

A Question of Balance
80 Hot Springs Rd.
☎*(604) 796-9622*
A Question of Balance is an art gallery created by Canadian craftspeople. The knitting, sewing, ceramics and blown glass are beautiful and interesting.

Harrison Watersports
The Esplanade
☎*(604) 796-2244, ext 299*
Harrison Watersports rents Jet Skis and organizes rides.

Crafts & Things Market
☎*(604) 796-2171*
From March to November, Harrison Hot Springs hosts a number of markets; call for dates and times.

Tour C: The Thompson River as Far as Revelstoke

Kamloops

Farmer's Markets
☎*(250) 573-3981*
Delightful food markets are organized from May to October. Saturday markets are located at 200 block-St Paul Street, Wednesday markets are at the corner of Third Avenue and Victoria Street.

At Second Glance Used Books
246 Victoria St.
☎*(250) 377-8411*
This used bookstore on Kamloops's busiest street is a good spot to pick up an old classic.

Castles and Cottages Antiques
118 Victoria St.
☎*(250) 374-6704*
Castles and Cottages is in a red brick heritage building at the west end of Victoria Street. The collection of antiques is rather disorderly, but some treasures may be hiding in here.

Tour D: Thompson-Okanagan

Kelowna

Far West Factory Outlet
230-2469 Hwy. 97
☎*(250) 860-9010*
The Far West Factory Outlet sells comfortable, light clothing by major name brands.

Valhalla Pure Outfitters
453 Bernard Ave., downtown
☎*(250) 763-9696*
Valhalla Pure Outfitters is a popular local manufacturer that specializes in clothing.

Mosaïc Books and Coffee
411 Bernard Ave.
☎*(250) 736-4418*
Mosaïc Books and Coffee carries a good selection of maps for excursions and books.

Penticton

Front Street
Colourful Front Street branches off of Main Street. just before it runs into Lake Okanagan, and consists of a number of gift and craft oriented shops in pretty little brick buildings.

The Bookshop
242 Main St.
☎*(250) 492-6661*
The Bookshop's claim to fame is that it's the largest second-hand bookstore in Western Canada.

The Lloyd Gallery
598 Main St.
☎*(250) 492-4484*
The Lloyd Gallery has an extensive collection by Okanagan artists. Penticton painter Jennifer Garant's colourful work is especially worth seeing.

The Lane
675 Main St.
☎*(250) 493-9221*
This is the place for a less expensive memento of your trip through the Okanagan, with reasonably priced ceramics, crafts and artwork up for grabs under an open walkway off Main Street.

Tour E: Kootenay Country

Nelson

Craft Connection Cooperative
441 Baker St.
☎*(250) 352-3006*
Nelson has been dubbed "the best small arts town in Canada," so a stop at this cooperative is certainly in order, even to just browse through the creative efforts of local artisans.

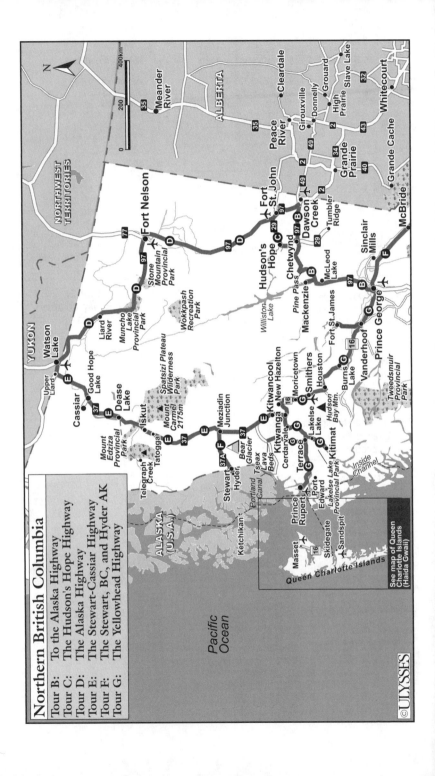

Northern British Columbia

Tour B: To the Alaska Highway
Tour C: The Hudson's Hope Highway
Tour D: The Alaska Highway
Tour E: The Stewart-Cassiar Highway
Tour F: The Stewart, BC, and Hyder AK
Tour G: The Yellowhead Highway

© ULYSSES

See map of Queen
Charlotte Islands
(Haida Gwaii)

Pacific
Ocean

Queen Charlotte Islands
(Haida Gwaii)

ALASKA
(U.S.A.)

YUKON

NORTHWEST
TERRITORIES

ALBERTA

Northern British Columbia

British Columbia has long been renowned for its exceptional and varied range of outdoor activities.

If you have a taste for adventure and exploring, or if you simply love nature, you will be repeatedly delighted and surprised by the unspoiled, little known northern part of the province.

Eighty percent of this territory is studded with mountains, many of which are perpetually covered with snow or glaciers. The lakes, which collect the run-off from the glaciers, are almost iridescent, while the forests are among the most renowned in the world. These enchanting surroundings offer endless possibilities for outdoor activities — just let your imagination run wild.

Two distinct regions make up northern British Columbia, the North by Northwest and the Peace River-Alaska Highway regions; together, they account for 50% of the province's total area. Despite their isolated location, a number of towns are fully equipped to welcome tourists with campgrounds, hotels and restaurants that offer amenities comparable to those found in big cities.

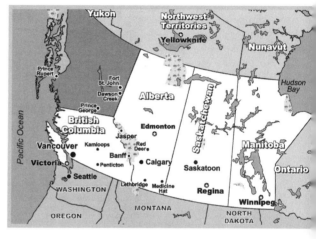

Only three major roads lead through these vast northern spaces. The Stewart-Cassiar Highway (Hwy. 37), to the west, passes through the heart of the North by Northwest region. The Alaska Highway, in the east, starts at Dawson Creek. And finally, the Yellowhead Highway (Hwy. 16) runs along the southern part of these two regions, all the way to the shores of the Pacific, where visitors can set out for the Queen Charlotte Islands.

The starting point of any visit to northern British Columbia is the city of Prince George. From there north, the summer days grow noticeably longer. This phenomenon becomes more and more evident the farther north you go. The summertime sky never darkens completely, and depending on where you find yourself, you might even see the midnight sun. Near the province's border with the Yukon, along the 60th parallel, the summer sky always has a trace of light even in the dead of night, and the northern lights, or aurora borealis, are a common sight during the long winter months.

Summer is characterized by long sunny days with temperatures often higher than in the south. The winters are long. In the northwest, where the snowfall is very heavy, the weather is relatively mild, despite sub-zero Celsius temperatures. In the northeast, the climate is continental, with less snow and severe, dry cold.

Contrary to popular belief, the cost of living in the country is by no means less expensive than in big cities. Farming and stockbreeding are not carried out on a major scale in northern British Columbia, nor are any raw materials processed here; as a result, food, fuel, hotels, etc. are all 50% to 100% more expensive, depending on where you are. As far as telephone calls are concerned, keep in mind that phone booths are quite rare, and can only be found near parks and in towns and villages.

A trip to northern British Columbia offers a chance to take in some of the most beautiful scenery in Canada. To help you make the most of your trip, we have outlined seven tours:

Tour A: The Gold Rush Trail and the Cariboo Mountains ★★

Tour B: To the Alaska Highway ★★

Tour C: The Hudson's Hope Route ★★

Tour D: The Alaska Highway ★★★

Tour E: The Stewart-Cassiar Highway ★★★

Tour F: To Stewart, BC and Hyder, AK ★★★

Tour G: The Yellowhead Highway ★★★

Tour H: The Queen Charlotte Islands (Haida Gwaii) ★★★

Finding Your Way Around

By Car

Tour A: The Gold Rush Trail and the Cariboo Mountains

This tour forms a straight line between Prince George and William's Lake, a distance of about 200km. Starting at Quesnel, the halfway point, the Cariboo Mountains are about a 100km jaunt to the east.

This region sprung up over 100 years ago. Before heading off into the remote regions, gold diggers stopped in the towns of the Fraser River Plateau (William's Lake and Quesnel) to stock up on provisions and gear for the tough job ahead.

Hwy. 97 heads southward between Prince George and William's Lake. At the halfway point, just a few kilometres north of Quesnel, Hwy. 26 branches off to the east towards the old mining towns of Bowron Lake Provincial Park – a paradise for canoeists.

Tour B: To the Alaska Highway

Hwy. 97 leads from Prince George to Dawson Creek,

Km/mile 0 of the Alaska Highway. The region has developed mostly around the lumber and hydroelectric industries. It is quite common to come across bears and moose here, particularly in the provincial parks, which have well laid-out campsites. Halfway through the tour, you will reach the turnoff for Hwy. 39, which leads to Mackenzie, another 29km away. Since the 39 is a dead-end, you'll have to backtrack to pick up the 97 again. Crossing Pine Pass, you'll see the first foothills of the Rockies and discover how truly immense the forest is. About 100km past Powder King, the ski resort, lies the town of Chetwynd. From there, you can reach Tumbler Ridge, but you will have to double back to the 97 again to complete the tour.

Tour C: The Hudson's Hope Route

Another way of getting to the Alaska Highway from Prince George is to take the 29 North, which leads to the village of Hudson's Hope and intersects with the Alaska Highway at Km 86.

Tour D: The Alaska Highway

This tour covers the part of the Alaska Highway that runs through British Columbia. It starts at Km/mile 0, in Dawson Creek, and leads to the town of Watson Lake, a little over a 1,000km away, just over the province's border with the Yukon. The first town you will pass through is Fort St. John, followed by Fort Nelson and the Stone Mountain, Muncho Lake and Liard Hot Springs Provincial Parks.

When the Alaska Highway was first being laid, distances were gauged in miles. Since Canada adopted the metric system in the 1970s, the Canadian portion of this legendary highway has been officially measured in terms of kilometres as well. Even today, however, it is not uncommon to come across road maps and government brochures with distances still labelled in miles. Furthermore, in deference to tradition (and American influence), the entire road is studded with commemorative milestones showing no metric equivalents.

Like tour C, Tour D ends at Watson Lake, in the Yukon. Visitors can combine Tours C and D into a single big loop, since the Stewart-Cassiar Highway and the Alaska Highway intersect at Junction 37, at mile 649 of the Alaska Highway, not far from Watson Lake.

Road Conditions

Dawson Creek:
☎*800-663-4997*

Fort Nelson:
☎*(250) 774-7447 or (250) 774-6956*

Tour E: The Stewart-Cassiar Highway

Visitors usually take this tour from south to north, starting at Kitwanga. On the left, 169km from Kitwanga, Hwy. 37A branches off toward Stewart and Hyder, Alaska (see "Tour E," below). You will head north on Hwy. 37 for the entire tour, which covers a little under 600km. The road passes numerous little towns along the way, including Tatogga, Iskut, Dease Lake, Good Hope Lake and Upper Liard (Yukon). Once you've arrived at Dease Lake, it is worth taking the time to visit Telegraph Creek, 129km away; a well-marked, well-maintained dirt road leads there.

Tour F: To Stewart, BC and Hyder, AK

This tour starts at Meziadin Junction, along the Stewart-

Cassiar Highway (see Tour D, above); turn right onto Hwy. 37 A, commonly known as Glacier Highway. The town of Stewart lies 65km away, while the village of Hyder, Alaska lies 2km farther, on the road that runs alongside the Portland Canal.

Tour G: The Yellowhead Highway

This tour will take you from the town of McBride, in eastern British Columbia, to Prince Rupert, on the coast, about 1,000km away. The Yellowhead Highway runs through an impressive variety of landscapes (mountains, plains and plateaux), as well as several sizeable towns, including Prince George, Smithers, Terrace and Prince Rupert.

Road conditions

Prince Rupert:
☎*800-663-4997*

Tour H: The Queen Charlotte Islands (Haida Gwaii)

All the local villages are linked by a single 120km road, Hwy. 16.

By Plane

Tour B: To the Alaska Highway

Prince George

The airport is located a few kilometres east of downtown and is accessible by way of the Yellowhead Bridge to the north and the Simon Fraser Bridge to the south (☎*963-2400*). The airport is served by **Air Canada Regional Airlines** (☎*888-247-2262, www.aircanada .ca*), **Berry Air** (☎*250-563-7788*) and **Westjet** (☎*800-538-5696, www.westjet. com*).

Tour D: The Alaska Highway

Dawson Creek

Dawson Creek Municipal Airport, south of town, is accessible by way of Hwy. 2. It is served daily by **Hawkair** (☎*800-487-1216, www. hawkair.ca*) and **Central Mountain Air** (☎*888-865-8585, www. cmair.bc.ca*); regional flights are offered by **Kenn Borek Air** (☎*782-5561, www.borekair.com*).

Fort St. John

The airport (☎*787-7170*) is 10km from town, on the road to Cecil Lake, along 100th Ave. It is served by **Air Canada Jazz** (☎*888-247-2262, www.aircanada.ca*) and **Peace Air** (☎*800-563-3060, www.peaceair.net*).

Fort Nelson

The airport (☎*250-774-2069*) is 10km from downtown via Airport Rd. Served by **Air Canada Jazz** (see above) et **Central Mountain Air** (see above).

Watson Lake (Yukon)

The airport is 13km from downtown; take the Campbell Highway north. It is served by **Alkan Air** (*in Whitehorse* ☎*867-668-2107, www.alkan air.com*), the Yukon's main airline, and **Central Mountain Air** (see above).

Tour G: The Yellowhead Highway

Smithers

The airport is on Hwy. 16, 10km west of Smithers (☎*250-847-3664*). It is served by **Central Mountain Air** and **Air Canada Jazz** (see above).

Prince Rupert

The airport (☎*250-624-6274*) is on Digby Island; transportation is provided by a small municipal ferry (*$11 one-way*) at the end of Hwy. 16, at the southwest end of Prince Rupert. The airport is served by **Hawkair Aviation Services** (*☎800-487-1216, www. hawkair.net*).

Tour H:
The Queen Charlotte
Islands (Haida Gwaii)

There is an airport in Masset, on the northern part of Graham Island, and another in Sandspit, on Moresby Island. Both are clearly indicated. These airports are served by **Northern Thunderbird Air** (*☎250-963-9611 or 866-232-9211, www.ntair.ca*) and **Air Canada Jazz** (see above).

By Bus

Greyhound (*☎800-661-8747, www.greyhound.ca*) serves the communities covered in this chapter. Below, you'll find the address and telephone number of local bus stations.

Tour A: The Gold Rush
Trail and The Cariboo
Mountains

Quesnel
365 Kinchant St.
☎*(250) 992-2231*

William's Lake
215 Donald Rd.
☎*(250) 398-7733*

Tour B:
To the Alaska Highway

Prince George
at the corner of 12th and Victoria Sts.
☎*(250) 564-5454*

Tour D:
The Alaska Highway

Dawson Creek
1201 Alaska Ave.
☎*(250) 782-3131*

Fort St. John
10355 101st Ave.
☎*785-6695*

Fort Nelson
5031 51st Ave., West Fort Nelson
☎*(250) 774-6322*

Watson Lake (Yukon)
at the corner of the Campbell and Alaska Highways
☎*(867) 536-2606*

Tour E: The Stewart-
Cassiar Highway

Stewart
Seaport Limousine
516 Railway St.
☎*(250) 636-2622*

Tour G:
The Yellowhead Highway

Smithers
on Hwy. 16, a couple of blocks from the Travel InfoCentre
☎*(250) 847-2204*

Prince Rupert
at the corner of Third Ave. and Sixth St.
☎*(250) 624-5090*

By Train

Tour G:
The Yellowhead Highway

Smithers

The train station is on Railway Ave., not far from downtown (*☎800-561-8630*). Tickets must be purchased through a travel agent: **Mackenzie Travel** (*☎250-847-2979*); **Uniglobe Priority Travel** (*☎250-847-4314*).

Prince Rupert

Via Rail
on Waterfront Ave.
☎*888-842-7245*
www.viarail.ca

By Ferry

Tour G:
The Yellowhead Highway

Prince Rupert

BC Ferries
west end of Second Ave. (Hwy. 16) in Fairview
☎*(250) 386-3431 or 888-223-3779*
www.bcferries.com

Tour H:
The Queen Charlotte
Islands (Haida Gwaii)

To get to this archipelago, you must take either a plane or a ferry to Graham Island, the largest and most populous of the 150 islands. **BC Ferries** (see above) reservations are strongly recommended, especially during summer. A small ferry shuttles back and forth between Skidegate Landing, on Graham Island, and Alliford Bay, on Moresby Island, the second largest of the Queen Charlotte Islands.

Practical
Information

The area code in Northern British Columbia and in Hyder, Alaska is **250**. In Watson Lake, Yukon, the area code is **867**.

Tourist Information

Northern British Columbia Tourism Association
☎*561-0432 ou 800-663-8843*
⇒*561-0450*
850 River Rd., Prince George
www.northernbctravel.com

Tour A: The Gold Rush Trail and the Cariboo Mountains

Quesnel
Mon-Sat 9am to 6pm
405 Barlow St.
☎992-8716
visitorinfo@cityquesnel.bc.ca

Tour B: To the Alaska Highway

Prince George
Mon-Sat 8:30am to 5pm
1198 Victoria St
☎562-3700 or 800-668-7646
www.tourismpg.bc.ca

Mackenzie
The tourist office is only open from mid-May to mid-Sep *(at the intersection of Hwy. 39 and 97, 29km from downtown* ☎750-4497, 977-5459 or 877-622-5360; *www.mackenzie chamber.bc.ca)*; during the rest of the year, you can obtain information from the **Chamber of Commerce** *(86 Centennial St.,* ☎997-5459).

Chetwynd
early May to late Oct everyday 9am to 5pm
5400 North Access Rd
☎788-1943
☎401-4100 *(off-season)*
www.gochetwynd.com

Dawson Creek
early May to late Sep everyday 8am to 7pm, early Oct to late Apr Tue-Sat, 9am to 5pm
900 Alaska Hwy
☎782-9595 ou 866-645-3022
www.tourismdawsoncreek. com

Tour C: The Hudson's Hope Route

Hudson's Hope
mid-May to mid-Sep everyday 8:30am to 8pm
opposite the museum and the church
☎783-9154
☎783-9901 *(off-season)*
http://dist.hudsons-hope.bc. ca

Tour D: The Alaska Highway

Fort St. John
mid-May to early Sep Mon-Fri 8am to 8pm, Sat and Sun 8am to 6pm; early Sep to mid-May Mon-Fri 9am to 5pm
9923 96th Ave., just across from a 50m derrick
☎785-3033
www.fortstjohnchamber. com

Fort Nelson
summer everyday 8am to 8pm
west end of the downtown area, inside the recreation centre
☎774-2541

Watson Lake (Yukon)
early May to mid-Sep, everyday 8am to 8pm
at the junction of the Alaska and Campbell Highways
☎(867) 536-7469
www.touryukon.com

Tour E: The Stewart-Cassiar Highway

Dease Lake
Hwy. 37
☎771-3900
www.stikine.net

Kitwanga
mid-May to mid-Sep everyday
Valley Rd.
☎866-417-3737
www.stewartcassiar.ca

Tour F: To Stewart, BC and Hyder, AK

Stewart
222 5th Ave.
☎636-9224

Hyder
in the Hyder Community Building on Main St.
☎636-9148

Tour G: The Yellowhead Highway

Prince Rupert
everyday 9am to 5pm
First Ave., at McBride Ave., adjoining the Museum of Northern British Columbia, Suite 100, 215 Cow Bay Rd.
☎624-5637 or 800-667-1994
www.tourismprincerupert. com

McBride
mid-May to mid-Sep, everyday 9am to 5pm
in a railway car (the sculpture of a family of grizzlies at the entrance makes it easy to spot)
☎569-3366

Vanderhoof
downtown, Burrard St.
☎567-2124

Burns Lake
Chambre of Commerce
540 Hwy. 16
☎692-3773

Houston
along the highway; you'll spot the fishing pole from far away
☎845-7640

Smithers
at the intersection of Hwy. 16 and Main St.
☎847-5072 or 800-542-6673

New Hazelton
intersection of Hwy. 16 and 62
☎842-6071 *(May to Sep)*
☎842-6571 *(Sep to Apr)*

Terrace
mid-May to mid-Sep everyday 9am to 8pm, mid-Sep to mid-May Mon-Fri 9am to 4:30pm
4511 Keith Ave.
☎635-2063 or 800-499-1637
www.terracetourism.com

Kitimat
2109 Forest Ave.
☎632-6294 or 800-664-6554
www.haisla.net

Northern British Columbia

Tour H:
The Queen Charlotte
Islands (Haida Gwaii)

To properly plan a stay in Queen Charlotte Islands (*Haida Gwaii* means "Land of the Haida" in the Aboriginal language), it is best to contact tourism offices.

Queen Charlotte City
Visitor InfoCentre
3320 Wharf St.
☎559-8316

Gwaii Haanas
☎559-8818

Masset
open in summer only
in a small trailer on the south edge of the village
☎626-3982
www.massetbc.com

Exploring

★★

Tour A: The Gold Rush Trail and the Cariboo Mountains

This tour extends from the north to the south between Prince George and William's Lake. Some typical tourist attractions are found east of Quesnel via Hwy. 26. For those who want to explore a little deeper, we suggest going farther south of William's Lake to discover the splendour of Well's Gray Provincial Park. Another option is to take the bumpy road that heads west from William's Lake. It leads to Bella Coola and the only seaport between Prince Rupert and Vancouver Island. This much longer, rougher trip will delight those who like to stray from the beaten path. As for breath-taking scenery, your only problem will be deciding

which one of the infinite number of views to take in.

★★★
Quesnel

Located 188km south of Prince George, it takes a little more than 30min to reach Quesnel. Its tree-lined streets and flowers, as well as its location at the confluence of two rivers, make it the most beautiful town in the region.

Like many other towns in the area, Quesnel lived through the 19th-century Gold Rush. Gold diggers stocked up on foodstuffs and survival gear in Quesnel before heading off to look for those famous nuggets in the distant valleys, which is how Quesnel got its nickname "Gold Pan City."

Today, the forest industry has replaced the mining industry as the economic engine for the region. More than 2,000 families rely on it for their livelihood.

Quesnel is a departure point for various excursions. If you only have a few days to spend in this region, concentrate on Quesnel and choose among the wide range of activities it has to offer: canoeing, rafting, a visit to a reconstructed mining town or a paper mill. During the third week of July, Billy Barker Days celebrates the historical heritage of the town. The theme, of course, is based on the Gold Rush. There are activities for the entire family.

Quesnel & District Museum *($2; 405 Barlow St., ☎992-9580)* also houses the tourist information centre, which makes for a practical and pleasurable visit. The permanent collection exhibits everyday items that the pioneers used in the fields, mines and in the home more than a century ago.

Pinnacles Park *(on the outskirts of the west side of town; follow the directions)* is a spectacular – and free – tourist attraction. A 20min walk through the evergreen forest leads to a group of sandy hills called "hoodoos." They are unusual earth-tone vertical formations whose origin dates back some 12 million years when they were formed by the erosion of several layers of volcanic ash. Today, only the strongest layers remain intact. They proudly thrust up into the sky.

Quesnel has three pulp and paper mills that can be visited by calling beforehand.

Quesnel River Pulp
1000 Finning Rd.
☎992-8919
www.daishowa.bc.ca

Cariboo Pulp & Paper
North Star Rd.
☎992-0200
everyday

West Fraser Mills
1250 Brownmiller
☎992-9244

Barkerville ★★★ *($7.25, mid-Jun to early Sep; free admission, early Sep to mid-Jun; 25km east of Quesnel; ☎994-3302 ext 29, www.barkerville. com)* sprung up out of nowhere in 1862 when Billy Barker discovered gold in William's Creek. During the eight years that followed, 100,000 people came here to try their luck, making Barkerville the largest town west of Chicago and north of San Francisco.

Unfortunately, the reserves were completely exhausted. Today, the town is a protected historic site where more than 125 buildings have been restored to their original frontier-town look. The result is striking: saloon, hotel, post office, printer and blacksmith. Everything here is a perfect illusion. Illusion you say? There are even a few gold prospectors that still pan the bottom of the river that flows through the region.

Just 30km from Barkerville, the **Bowron Lake Provincial Park ★ ★ ★** is famous for one particular activity: canoeing (see p 253). As soon as you see all the boats mounted on the cars flocking to Quesnel, you realize that the mountains are a world-renowned attraction for vacationers.

Wells Gray Provincial Park *(via 100 Mile House on Clearwater, ☎851-3000)* is the second largest park in the province. There is a great range of possible activities, such as canoeing, hiking or fishing (one-day or week-long excursions). The park is also famous for its many mesmerizing waterfalls.

Tour B:
To the Alaska Highway

This tour starts in the town of Prince George. You can reach Km/mile 0 of the Alaska Highway, in Dawson Creek, by taking Hwy. 97, which crosses the Rocky Mountains. The itinerary suggested below leads through pleasant wooded areas strewn with lakes.

★ ★
Prince George

Prince George (pop. 70,000) considers itself the capital of northern British Columbia. As any map will tell you, however, it actually lies in the centre of the province. Its geographic location has made it a hub not only for the railway, but also for road transport, since it lies at the intersection of Hwy. 16, which runs the width of the province, and Hwy. 97, which runs the length.

Prince George is 800km north of Vancouver, about an hour's flight or a 10hr drive along the Trans-Canada and Hwy. 97 North. The town's history is linked to two rivers, the Nechako and the Fraser. By the beginning of 19th century, trappers and *coureurs des bois* were using these waterways to reach the vast territories of the north. Before long, they saw that the region was rich in wolves, minks, muskrats, foxes, etc. Fur-trading posts thus began to spring up along the banks of the two rivers.

In 1807, the first building, Fort George, was erected. In 1821, it was taken over by the Hudson's Bay Company. In 1908, when the Grand Trunk Pacific Railway (GTR) was constructed, Fort George was slated to become an important distribution centre for the transcontinental railroad. All of these major changes led to a considerable growth in population, and it became necessary to develop a second residential area, known as South Fort George.

The GTR finally began operating in the region in 1914. A second area, Prince George, had to be developed to accommodate the flood of new arrivals. Now the third largest city in British Columbia, Prince George derives most of its income from forestry. It is home to no fewer than 15 sawmills and three pulp and paper mills. The climate is continental — warm and dry in the summer and cold in the winter.

The **Fraser Fort George Regional Museum ★ ★** *($6.50; mid-May to mid-Sep, every day 10am to 5pm; mid-Sep to mid-May, Tue-Sun noon to 5pm; at the end of 20th Ave., ☎562-1612)* stands on the very site where Fort George was erected in 1807. The museum is an excellent place to learn about the history of Prince George, from the ar-

rival of Alexander Mackenzie and the beginning of the fur trade to the introduction and development of the forest industry. The museum's Northwood Gallery, a sure hit with young children, presents an exhibit on the region's flora and fauna. Along the Fraser River lies the **Railway & Forestry Museum ★ ★** *($6; mid-May to Sep, every day 9am to 5pm Oct 10am to 4pm; 850 River Rd, ☎563-7351, www.pgrfm.bc.ca)*, which will take you back in time to the days when the railroad was new and modern woodcutting techniques had yet to be developed.

If you enjoy and appreciate Aboriginal art, make sure to stop at the **Prince George Native Art Gallery** *(Tue-Fri 9am to 5pm, Sat 10am to 4pm; 1600 Third Ave., ☎614-7726, www.pgnfe.com)*. This private gallery displays a wide array of art, including carvings, prints and jewellery.

For a short walk or a picnic, head to the **Cottonwood Island Nature Park ★ ★**, which covers 33ha along the Nechako River, right near downtown. It has an interesting wildlife-observation area, where you can watch foxes, beavers and eagles.

Connaught Hill Park ★, located in the centre of town, offers a 360° view of Prince George and its surroundings. To get there, take Queensway southward, then turn right on Connaught Drive and right again on Caine.

Forestry is the mainspring of Prince George's economy, so it is not surprising that three factories are open to the public. **Canadian Forest Products ★ ★** *(PG Pulpmill Road, ☎563-0161)* offers free tours of its facilities. A bus takes visitors to cutting and replanting areas. At the **Northwood Pulp & Timber and North Central Plywoods ★ ★**

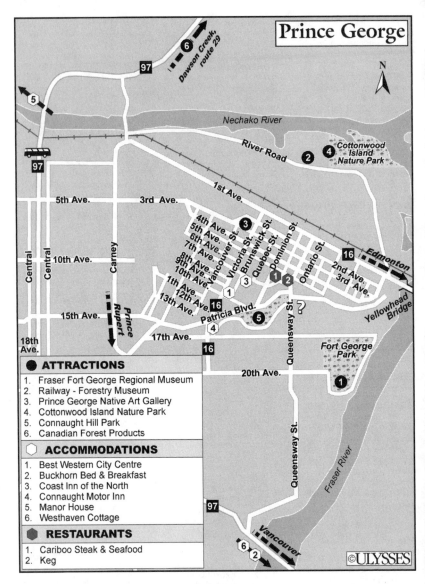

(mid-May to Sep; reservations recommended, ☎561-5700), everything is very modern, from the greenhouse where the next generation of trees is nurtured to the sawmill where the trunks are cut up. The third factory, owned by Northwood, is supposedly the "greenest" in Canada. It produces pulp and paper, as well

as construction materials. Visitors will learn how paper, chipboard and plywood are made. As the tour involves a long walk, partly on uneven terrain, it is recommended to wear closed, flat shoes and pants.

Mackenzie

A small, ultra-modern community, Mackenzie is a typical boom town. It was built in 1966, following the construction of the Peace River dam. Less than a year after the first stone was laid, hundreds of workers arrived in the area,

Dawson Creek

N

ATTRACTIONS

1. Northern Alberta Railway Park, Station Museum, Dawson Creek Art Gallery
2. Mile 0 Post

ACCOMMODATIONS

1. Alaska Hotel (R)
2. George Dawson Inn
3. Ramada Dawson Creek

(R) establishment with restaurant
(see description)

©ULYSSES

which was completely undeveloped at the time. Today, with a population of 5,200, Mackenzie has become a village of superlatives, boasting the largest artificial lake on the continent, **Williston Lake**, a byproduct of the dam, as well as the **world's biggest tree-chipper**, which was used to

clear a passage through the forest back when the town was founded.

Chetwynd

This little town was once known as Little Prairie, but its name was changed in honour of Railway Minister Ralph

Chetwynd, who pioneered rail transport in northern British Columbia. Today, Chetwynd is a prosperous working-class town. It was constructed to the north of one of the largest coal deposits in the world. Natural gas and the forest industry have further strengthened the local economy. A simple walk down the street reveals how important forestry is here; Chetwynd is the self-proclaimed **world capital of chainsaw sculpture**, and carved animals adorn the tops of buildings all over town.

★
Dawson Creek

Dawson Creek was named after Dr. George Dawson, a geologist who, in 1879, discovered that the surrounding plains were ideal for agriculture. He might have thought that Dawson Creek would become a farming capital, but he probably never suspected that oil and natural gas would be discovered here.

The other major turning-point in Dawson Creek's history took place in 1942, when the town became Km/mile 0 of the Alaska Highway. Today, nearly 30,000 tourists from all over the world come to Dawson Creek to start their journey northward.

The **Station Museum** ★ and the **Dawson Creek Art Gallery** ★ are part of the **Northern Alberta Railway Park (NAR)** ★★. You can't miss the NAR, with its immense grain elevator, which was renovated in 1931 and stands at the corner of Alaska Avenue and Eighth Street.

The **Station Museum** ★ *(Jun to end Aug, every day 8am to 7pm; Sep to end May, Tue-Sat 10am to noon and 1pm to 5pm; 900 Alaska Ave.; ☎782-9595)* traces the history of the Alaska Highway, as well as that of the area's first inhabitants. The collection on display includes the largest mammoth tusk ever found in the Canadian West, as well as a number of dinosaur bones.

Inside the grain elevator, the **Dawson Creek Art Gallery** *(Sep to May, Tue-Sat 10am to noon and 1pm to 5pm; Jun to*

Aug, every day 9am to 5pm; ☎782-2601) displays handicrafts and works by local artists; it also hosts travelling exhibitions.

Right beside the NAR Park, you'll spot a sign — surely the most photographed one in the province — indicating the starting point of the Alaska Highway. The legendary **Mile 0 Post**, also worth a picture, is located downtown.

If you'd like to sample the local produce, stop at the **Dawson Creek Farmer's Market** *(Sat 8am to 3pm; ☎782-8928)*, which is held near the NAR Park, just behind the sign for the Alaska Highway.

Tour C: The Hudson's Hope Route

This tour is an alternate route from Prince George to Dawson Creek. Simply take Hwy. 29 from Chetwynd.

Hudson's Hope

This area was first explored in 1793 by Alexander Mackenzie. In 1805, a fur-trading post was set up here. Nowadays, Hudson's Hope is known mainly for its hydroelectric complexes, one of which was built in the 1960s (WAC Bennett), the other slightly more recently (Peace Canyon).

The tourist office is located right near **St. Peter's United Church** ★, a charming old wooden building. Also nearby is the **Hudson's Hope Museum** *(mid May to mid Sep Mon-Sun 9:30am to 5:30pm, mid Sep to early Oct Sat and Sun only; 9510 Beattie Dr.; ☎783-5735)*, which displays fossils, some of dinosaurs, and various artifacts from the area.

Of course, the major points of interest in Hudson's Hope are

the **WAC Bennett** ★★ *(mid May to early Sep, every day 10am to 6pm, bus tours 10:30am to 4:30pm; early Sep to early May, Mon-Fri 10am to 5pm, bus tour 1:30pm; phone for reservations in winter; about 20km west of Hudson's Hope, ☎783-5000)* and **Peace Canyon** ★★ *(mid-May to early Sep, every day 8am to 4pm; mid-Sep to May, Mon-Fri 8am to 4pm; phone for reservations in winter; 7km south of Hudson's Hope, ☎783-9943)* hydroelectric facilities. Free tours are available at both. The WAC Bennett dam is the largest structure in the world, a hodgepodge of stone and concrete that fills in a natural valley. Its reservoir, Williston Lake, is the largest artificial lake on the planet!

Tour D: The Alaska Highway

This tour starts at Km/mile 0 of the highway, in Dawson Creek (see above), and ends at kilometre 1011/mile 632, in Watson Lake, in the Yukon. The entire road is paved and well-maintained. Before setting out, though, make sure that your car's engine and tires are in good condition, since there aren't very many repair shops along the way. A lot of roadwork is carried out during summer, and the resulting dust makes driving conditions more difficult. You are therefore better off leaving your lights on at all times. In summer as in winter, it is always wise to check the road conditions before setting out by calling ☎867-667-8215 or *www.dot.state.ak.us*

The Alaska Highway started out as a war measure. The Americans, who initiated the project, wanted to create a communication route that would permit the transport of military equipment, provisions

Isn't it tempting to hop in one of these canoes
and explore the waterways of the Rockies? - *Tibor Bognar*

Grain silos and railroads are part of the classic Prairie landscape.
- *Walter Bibikow*

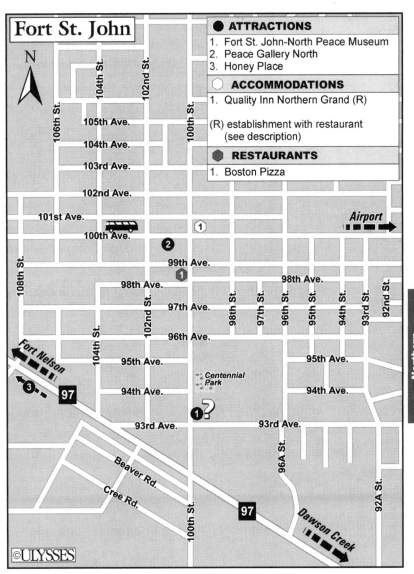

Fort St. John

N

● ATTRACTIONS

1. Fort St. John-North Peace Museum
2. Peace Gallery North
3. Honey Place

○ ACCOMMODATIONS

1. Quality Inn Northern Grand (R)

(R) establishment with restaurant
   (see description)

● RESTAURANTS

1. Boston Pizza

Northern British Columbia

and troops by land to Alaska. Construction started in March 1942, in the village of Dawson Creek, which had only 600 inhabitants at the time. Within a few weeks, over 10,000 people, mostly military workers, had flooded into the area.

Over 11,000 American soldiers and engineers, 6,000 civilian workers and 7,000 machines and tractors of all manner were required to clear a passage through thousands of kilometres of wilderness. The cost of this gargantuan project, which stretched 2,436km and included 133

bridges, came to $140 million (CAD). Even today, the building of the Alaska Highway is viewed as a feat of engineering on a par with the Panamá Canal. The Canadian section was given to Canada by the United States in 1946 and remained under military supervision until 1964.

Today, this extraordinary highway is a vital social and economic link for all northern towns. It also offers tourists from all over the world unhoped-for access to the majestic landscapes of this region. The Alaska Highway celebrated its 60th anniversary in 2002.

★
Fort St. John

kilometre 75.6/mile 47

Fort St. John is the largest community on the British-Columbian section of the Alaska Highway. A prosperous, modern little town of about 16,000, it has a highly diversified economy. Agriculture plays a significant role here, as there are 800 farms in the area, but petroleum and natural gas are the main sources of income. It is not without good reason that Fort St. John calls itself the energy capital of British Columbia.

In keeping with this oil community's industrial calling, the tourist office is located near a 50m-high derrick, just steps away from the downtown area. In the same building, the **Fort St. John-North Peace Museum ★** *($3; Mon-Sat 9am to 5pm; 9323 100th St., ☎787-0430)* deals with the history and prehistoric past of the Fort St. John region, with a collection of nearly 6,000 objects, including some fossils and bones. The **Peace Gallery North** *(Mon-Sat 10am to 5pm; 1005 100th Ave., in the cultural centre, ☎787-0993)* exhibits a large number of works by local artists. **The Honey Place ★** *(early May to end Sep, Mon-Sat 9am to 5:30pm, Tue-Sat 9am to 5pm; tours; kilometre 67.2/mile 42 of the Alaska Highway, ☎785-4808)* arranges guided tours of the world's largest glassed-in hive, offering visitors a chance to observe, first-hand, the marvellous spectacle of bees making honey.

Fort Nelson

kilometre 454.3/mile 283

This small industrial town has fewer than 4,000 inhabitants. Its history has been linked to the fur trade since 1805. In 1922, the town was connected to Fort St. John by the Godsell Trail, thus ending its isolation. In those years, Fort Nelson was home to only 200 Aboriginals and a handful of whites. Later, after the Alaska Highway was constructed, the town grew considerably when service stations, hotels and restaurants set up business here. It officially became a municipality in 1987.

History lovers will enjoy a visit to the **Fort Nelson Heritage Museum ★** *($3; mid-May to Sep, every day 8:30am to 7:30pm; opposite the tourist office, downtown, ☎774-3536)*.

★★★
Stone Mountain
Provincial Park

kilometre 627/mile 392

The entrance to **Stone Mountain Provincial Park** *(BC Parks, ☎787-3411)* is located at the highest point on the Alaska Highway, at an altitude of 1,267m. It covers 25,691ha of rocky peaks, geological formations and lakes, and is home to the largest variety of animal life in northern British Columbia. There are large numbers of moose here, as well as deer, beavers, black bears, grizzlies and wolves, not to mention the hundreds of caribou, which can often be seen near the road. Visitors unaccustomed to walking in the mountains in northern latitudes are advised not to venture too high. The climatic conditions can change rapidly, and the temperature can drop more than 10° in a few hours. It snows quite often on these peaks, even in the middle of summer.

★★★
Northern Rocky
Mountain Park

Northern Rocky Mountains Park is a provincial park connected to Stone Mountain *(BC Parks, ☎787-3411)*. Only accessible by foot or on horseback, this 37,800ha stretch of wilderness is not a place for inexperienced hikers. Simply getting there is an expedition. The most well-known trail leads from Mac-Donald Creek to Wokkpash Valley, covering a distance of 70km on foot or 50km by four-wheel-drive vehicle, with a 1,200m change in altitude. It requires at least seven days of walking. Beware of flash floods on rainy days.

★★★
Muncho Lake
Provincial Park

kilometre 729/mile 456

Muncho Lake *(BC Parks, ☎787-3411)* is one of the loveliest provincial parks in Canada and definitely one of the highlights on the British Columbian portion of the Alaska Highway. It encompasses 88,416ha of bare, jagged mountains around magnificent Muncho Lake, which stretches 12km. Like all parks in the region, it owes its existence to the Alaska Highway. Large numbers of beavers, black bears, grizzlies, wolves and mountain goats make their home here, while the magnificent plant-life includes a variety of orchids. There are almost no trails in the park, so the best way to explore it is along the Alaska Highway.

★★
Liard Hot Springs
Provincial Park

kilometre 764.7/mile 477.7

Liard Hot Springs Provincial Park *(BC Parks, ☎776-7000)* is the most popular place for travellers to stop. Here, you can relax in natural pools fed by 49°C hot springs. The microclimate created by the high temperature of the water, which remains constant in summer and winter alike, has enabled a unique assortment of plants to thrive here. Giant ferns and a profusion of carnivorous plants give the area a slightly tropical feel.

★★★
Watson Lake
(Yukon)

kilometre 1021/mile 612.9

The Alaska Highway tour comes to an end at Watson Lake, in the Yukon. Around 1897, an Englishman by the name of Frank Watson set out from Edmonton to lead the adventurous life of a gold-digger in Dawson City. After passing through regions that hadn't even been mapped yet, he ended up on the banks of the Liard River. He decided to stop his travels there and take up residence on the shores of the lake that now bears his name. The construction of a military airport in 1941 and the laying of the Alaska Highway the following year enabled Watson Lake to develop into a real town. It is now a transportation, communication and supply hub for the neighbouring communities, as well as for the mining and forest industries.

A visit to the **Alaska Highway Interpretive Centre ★★** (*at the intersection of the Alaska and Campbell Highways; mid-May to mid-Sep every day 8am to 8pm; ☎867-536-7469 or 536-7827 off-season*) is a must for anyone interested in the history of the Alaska Highway. The epic story of the famous highway comes to life through a slide show and photographs. The **Alaska Highway Signpost Forest ★★★** is far and away the main attraction in Watson Lake. It is a collection of over 37,450 signs from the world

over, placed on the posts by the tourists themselves. Some of them are highly original. You can create your own sign when planning your trip, or have one made for you on the spot for a few dollars.

Tour E: The Stewart-Cassiar Highway

This tour usually starts in Kitwanga (43km south of Hazelton on Hwy. 16, but travellers who have taken the Alaska Highway can set out from Watson Lake instead. You can actually combine Tours D and E into one big loop, as the two highways intersect at **Junction 37**, at kilometre 1038/mile 649 of the Alaska Highway, a few kilometres from Watson Lake.

Completed in 1972, the Stewart-Cassiar Highway (37) meets all highway standards and can thus be used at any time of the year. Three large sections of the road are unpaved, however, and get dusty in dry, hot weather and muddy in the rain, making driving conditions difficult from time to time. For this reason, the Ministry of Transportation recommends keeping your lights on at all times. Although you are better off driving this road with a car with high ground clearance or with an all-terrain four-wheel-drive vehicle, you can get by with a conventional automobile.

The Stewart-Cassiar Highway is the trucking route used to bring supplies to communities in the northern part of the province and beyond. While the trip is a bit shorter than the Alaska Highway, the scenery is equally magnificent.

★
Kitwanga

Kitwanga, which has just under 1,500 inhabitants, is the first community you'll come across on your way south. Known mainly for its historic past, it is home to **Kitwanga Fort National Historic Site ★** near the junction of Hwys 16 and 37, and Battle Hill, setting of a battle between Aboriginals over 200 years ago. The site is open year-round and is located near the video club that doubles as the local tourist office.

If you'd like to see some beautiful **totem poles ★**, make a quick stop at the **Gitwangak Indian Reserve** (*shortly before the village of Kitwanga, just after the intersection of Hwys. 16 and 37*); a whole series of them is lined up opposite **St. Paul's Anglican Church ★**, built in 1893.

★
Kitwancool

This little Gitksan village is known chiefly for its **totem poles ★**. The oldest one, **Hole-in-the-Ice**, dates back nearly 140 years.

Meziadin Junction

Meziadin Junction, located 170km from Kitwanga, is the starting point for the excursion to **Stewart, BC and Hyder, AK ★★★**. See Tour F, p 243.

★★★
Spatsizi Plateau
Wilderness Park

The Spatsizi Plateau Wilderness Park is only for real adventurers (*on Tattoga Lake, not far from Iskut, on Hwy. 37, 361km north of the intersection of Hwy. 16 and 37, in Kitwanga. Take Ealue Lake Road for 22km. Cross the Klappan River to the BC Rail dirt road, which leads 114km*

Northern British Columbia

to the southwest end of the park. Never set out on an excursion here without calling BC Parks beforehand, ☎*847-7320).* The plateau stretches across 656,785ha of wilderness, and is accessible by foot, by boat or by hydroplane.

Spatsizi means "red goat" in the language of the Tahltan First Nation. The name was inspired by the scarlet-coloured mountains, whose soil is rich in iron oxide. The park is in fact located on a plateau, at a nearly steady altitude of about 1,800m. The highest peak in the park is Mount Will (2,500m), in the Skeena Mountain chain.

This region's dry, continental climate is characterized by cold winters with only light snowfall and summers with an average temperature of 20°C and little rainfall. These weather conditions have enabled a large number of animals, including caribou, grizzlies, beavers, and nearly 140 bird species, to make their home here.

Iskut

Iskut is a small community of 300 people, mostly Aboriginal. In the heart of the reserve, you will find a service centre — that is, a gas station, a post office and a grocery store *(Iskut Lake Co-op, Hwy 37 N.;*

☎*234-3241).* Iskut's most distinguishing feature is its surrounding **countryside ★★**, which is positively magnificent, especially when it is decked out in autumn colours. In the fall, it is not uncommon to see wolves crossing the highway at nightfall.

★★★
Mount Edziza
Provincial Park

Mount Edziza Provincial Park covers 230,000ha in the northwest part of the province, west of the Iskut River and south of the Stikine River. It is most notable for its volcanic sites, the most spectacular in all of Canada.

Some Advice Before Taking the
Stewart Cassiar and Alaska Highways

Most of the northern highways in British Columbia are paved. Some portions of the Stewart Cassiar Highway and the Alaska Highway however, are gravel. Flat tires are common so it is important to check your spare tire. Bring along an antiflat spray as tire repair workshops are relatively uncommon. Ensure that your vehicle is in good working order before heading out. A tow to the nearest town and waiting around for parts from Vancouver will cost you a lot of time and money.

Fill up your gas tank whenever you can since gas stations are rare. Take a 25-litre jerry can just to be sure.

Don't forget to buckle up and keep your headlights on

at all times for better visibility on the sometimes dusty, long straight stretches.

The Weather
and the Highway

You've probably figured out that winters are cold in this part of the province, but not many people know that the summers in northern B.C. are sunny and often very hot. The temperature can fall below -50°C in January, but can easily reach 35°C in July.

Choosing the right clothes for the seasons is essential. In summer: cotton is the material of choice and a basic wardrobe consists of shorts, long-sleeve shirts, t-shirts, sweaters and sturdy shoes. Sandals are good to have if you're driving for long

periods. If you will be stopping in the mountains bring a windbreaker, a hat and sunscreen. The effects of the sun can be easy to forget in this northern region, they are just as harmful, however. Be aware that it can also snow, even during the summer, and, although snowfalls tend to be brief, it's better to be prepared.

During the winter it's best to dress in layers; this provides the best insulation, rather than wearing a big coat. Don't forget gloves, a hat, good boots and blankets. A breakdown or flat can turn out to be a survival test ending in tragedy if you're not travelling! Happy travelling!

Mount Edziza (2,787m), the highest peak in the park, is a perfect example of a volcanic formation. The eruption that created this impressive basalt cone occurred nearly four million years ago. The lava from Mount Edziza flowed almost 65km. Afterward, numerous little eruptions took place, creating about 30 more cones, including the perfectly symmetrical Eve cone.

Like many parks in northern British Columbia, Mount Edziza Provincial Park is very hard to reach and offers no services. Only experienced, well-equipped hikers can get there safely. Although the temperature can climb as high as 30°C during summer, it can snow at any time of the year here. *(To plan a trip, call BC Parks, ☎771-4591, at Dease Lake).*

Dease Lake

With 750 inhabitants, Dease Lake is the largest community on the Stewart-Cassiar Highway (Hwy. 37). It is the self-proclaimed jade capital of the world, due to the large number of quarries around the village. Lovely handcrafted sculptures are available in the many shops along the highway. Dease Lake is also an important industrial centre and a hub for government services.

Above all, this is a place to enjoy outdoor activities. Vast **Dease Lake ★★**, 47km long, is ideal for trout and pike fishing, as well as being the point of departure for plane and horseback rides in Mount Edziza Provincial Park and the Spatsizi Plateau Wilderness Park.

★★★
Telegraph Creek

It is worth going to Telegraph Creek, if only for the pleasure of driving there. Laid in 1922, the winding road leads

through some splendid scenery. The village at the end beckons visitors back in time to the pioneer era.

To get there, go to the end of Boulder St., Dease Lake's main street. The road that leads to Telegraph Creek, 119km away, is well maintained but rather narrow, making it extremely ill-suited to large vehicles and trailers. All along the way, you'll enjoy **unforgettable views ★★** of Tuya River, the Grand Canyon of the Stikine, the Tahltan-Stikine lava beds, etc. The village itself, a small community of 450 people, makes a striking first impression. While its **period buildings ★** give it a quaint look, it is fully equipped to accommodate the needs of tourists (gas station, repair shop, restaurant, hotel, etc.). For information about tourist activities in the area, head to the **Stikine RiverSong** *(café, inn, grocery store and information office; ☎235-3196).*

Good Hope Lake

This little Aboriginal village (pop. 100) is of interest mainly for its magnificent **crystal-clear lake ★★★**.

Tour F: To Stewart, BC and Hyder, AK

★★★
The Road to Stewart

This tour starts at Meziadin Junction (see p 243), along the Stewart-Cassiar Highway. Head west on Hwy. 37A, aptly nicknamed Glacier Highway. You will notice a major change in the scenery along the way. The mountains, with their snow- and glacier-capped peaks, look more and more imposing the closer you get.

Exactly 23km from Meziadin Junction, around a bend in the road, you will be greeted by the spectacular sight of **Bear Glacier ★★★**, which rises in all its azure-coloured splendour out of the milky waters of Strohn Lake at the same level as the road! Nineteen kilometres farther, you'll reach Stewart, a frontier town located just 2km from the little village of Hyder, Alaska. Both communities lie at the end of the 145km-long **Portland Canal ★★★**, the fourth deepest fjord in the world. In addition to forming a natural border between Canada and the United States, this narrow stretch of water gives Stewart direct access to the sea, making this little town of 1000 people the most northerly ice-free port in Canada.

The setting is simply magnificent. The town is surrounded on all sides by towering, glacier-studded mountains. In the summer, the mild temperature is governed by the occasionally damp Pacific climate, while heavy snowfall is common in the winter (over 20m total).

Stewart

Stewart boasts a large number of period buildings, such as the **Fire Hall** (1910), located on Fourth St., and the **Stone Storehouse**, on the Canadian-U.S. border. The latter was erected by the U.S. army in 1896 and originally served as a prison.

★★
Hyder, Alaska

Hyder (pop. 70) considers itself the most friendly ghost town in Alaska. This little community is known mainly for its three pubs, open 23hrs a day, and its duty-free shops. Keep in mind that although there is no customs office between the two countries here, the border still exists, and ignorance of the law is no excuse. It is best to respect all regulations concerning limits on tax-free merchandise. The tourist office and the **museum ★★**, which exhibits documents related to Hyder's history, are located in the **Hyder Community Building** *(Main St., ☎636-9148)*.

Fifteen minutes past Hyder lies **Fish Creek ★★★**, the most important spawning area for **pink salmon** in all of Alaska *(Jul to Sep)*. Dozens of **black bears** and **grizzlies** come here to feast on the fish, which are easy to catch after their long, exhausting journey. A platform has been set up so that tourists can observe this gripping spectacle. Caution: Keep a good distance from the bears. Don't be fooled by their friendly, clumsy appearance; they are unpredictable by nature, and can run as fast as 55km/h!

The same road leads to **Salmon Glacier ★★★**, the world's fifth largest glacier. The road is very narrow in places, making it unsuitable for large vehicles. Watch out for ruts and large rocks. The road is closed from November to June. For a worry-free trip, call **Seaport Limousine** *(guided minibus tours; ☎636-2622)*. In clear weather, the view of the glacier is breathtaking.

Tour G:
The Yellowhead Highway

The Yellowhead is an impressive highway that starts in Winnipeg, Manitoba, runs through Saskatchewan and Alberta, and ends at Prince Rupert. This tour covers the section between McBride, in eastern British Columbia and Prince Rupert, about 1000km away in the westernmost part of the province. The incredibly varied scenery along the way includes high mountains, canyons, valleys and dense

forests. This tour provides an excellent overview of the geology and topography of British Columbia.

McBride

This little working-class community of 719 people is sustained by the forest industry. It lies in a pleasant setting at the foot of the Rockies, on the banks of the Fraser River. We recommend walking up to the **Tear Mountain overlook ★★★**, which offers an unimpeded view of the region.

★★
Prince George

See "Tour B: To the Alaska Highway," p 237.

Vanderhoof

Vanderhoof is a small farming community with a population of just over 4,000. The town is surrounded by lakes renowned for trout fishing.

Fort St. James

Fort St. James, a little town of 2,000 inhabitants, lies about 60km from Vanderhoof via Hwy. 27. Its main claim to fame is **Fort St. James National Historic Site ★★** *($4; every day mid-May to end Sep 9am to 5pm; ☎996-7191)*, an authentic trading post established by the Hudson's Bay Company in 1896. Actors in period dress recreate the atmosphere of bygone days.

Burns Lake

There's no doubt that Burns Lake is a perfect place for **fishing**. The carved wooden fish at the entrance to town is a clear indication of what kind of atmosphere you'll find here. The local mottos are "3,000 Miles of Fishing" and "The Land of a Thousand Lakes." Fishers flock here for the lake trout, salmon and pike. However, knowing where exactly

to cast your line can prove quite difficult if you're not familiar with the region, given the maze of dirt roads.

Burns Lake Museum *(donations accepted; early Jun to end Aug Mon to Fri 10am to 4pm Hwy. 16 West, Burns Lake, ☎692-3773)* is a small historical museum that relates the origins of Burns Lake and the pioneering spirit of the first settlers. There's also a collection of old tools and equipment that belonged to the area's first lumberjacks.

Houston

Houston, like Burns Lake, has clearly identified its summertime vocation: **fishing**. Not just any fishing, though; Houston is the self-proclaimed world steelhead capital. This famous sea trout is among the noblest of fish. Fishing buffs will be encouraged by the sight of the world's largest fly rod (20m) at the entrance of the tourist office, which also distributes a guide to the good fishing spots.

★★
Smithers

Smithers is a pretty, pleasant town with unique **architecture ★★**. The mountain setting, dominated by glacier-capped **Hudson Bay Mountain ★★★**, is splendid. Since its reconstruction in 1979, the town has taken on the look of a Swiss village. For this reason, many Europeans, lured by the local atmosphere and way of life, are among the town's 5000 residents. The **Ski Smithers ★★** *(553m vertical drop, 35 runs, ☎800-665-4299 or 847-2058)* ski area, which looks out over the valley, has powdery conditions from November on. A few metres away from the tourist office, the **Bulkley Valley Museum ★★** *(donations accepted, mid-May to mid-Sep every day 10am to 5pm; mid-Sep to mid-May Mon-Sat 10am* to 5pm; in the Central Park Building at the corner of Main and Hwy. 16, ☎847-5322) exhibits objects used by the pioneers and photographs from the local archives. The Central Park Building also houses the **Smithers Art Gallery** (☎847-3898). Another interesting place to visit is **Driftwood Canyon Provincial Park ★★**, a major fossil site in this region. The tourist office can provide you with a map so you don't lose your way. On the weekend preceding Labour Day weekend, Smithers hosts the **Bulkley Valley Fall Fair ★★★**, one of the largest agricultural fairs in British Columbia.

★★
Moricetown Canyon and Falls

Along the Bulkley River, 40km west of Smithers on Aboriginal land, there is a fishing area known as **Moricetown Canyon**, which has been frequented by Aboriginals for centuries. Today, the Aboriginal people still use the same fishing methods as their ancestors. Using long poles with hooks on them, they catch onto the salmon, then trap them in nets as they swim upstream. This is a very popular place to take pictures.

★★
Hazelton

Hazelton is the largest of three villages, the other two being South Hazelton and New Hazelton. Inhabited mainly by Aboriginal people (pop. 8,000), these three communities date back to the late 19th century, when the Hudson's Bay Company established a fur-trading post in the area (1868). The main attraction here is the **'Ksan Historical Village and Museum ★★★** ($2, tours $10; Apr to Sep every day 9am to 6pm; call for winter schedule; 7km from Hwy. 16, just after Hazelton, ☎842-5544), a replica of a

Gitksan village, where visitors can watch artists at work.

Terrace

Terrace is one of the larger towns on the Yellowhead Highway (Hwy. 16). It lies on the banks of the magnificent Skeena River, the second largest river in the province after the Fraser, and is surrounded by the Coast Mountains. Terrace is typical of a community dedicated to work, in that little effort has been put into making the town pretty and inviting. The surrounding **scenery ★★★**, on the other hand, is splendid.

Check out the **Heritage Park Museum ★★** (summer every day 10am to 6pm; Kerby St., ☎635-4546) which deals with the history of the pioneers. There are a number of period buildings here, including a hotel, a barn, a theatre and six log cabins. Most date from 1910.

★★★
Tseax Lava Beds

Off Hwy. 16 and north of Terrace on Kalum Lake Drive, are the **Tseax Lava Beds**, the only natural site of its kind in Canada. Here, you'll find a number of **volcanic craters** and a stretch of lava 3km wide and 18km long. According to experts, the last eruptions took place about 350 years ago, which, on a geological scale, equates to a few minutes. Turquoise-coloured water has reappeared on the surface, adding a bit of colour to this lunar landscape. Right beside the lava beds is the **Nisga'a Memorial Lava Bed Park**, founded in memory of the 2,000 Nisga'a people who perished during the last eruption. With a little luck, you'll spot a Kermodei bear. The sight of one of these creatures, which belong to the same family as the black bear, but have a pure white coat, can

make for a truly unforgettable visit.

★★
Lakelse Lake Provincial Park

Located on Hwy. 37 halfway between Terrace and Kitimat, **Lakelse Lake Provincial Park** is the perfect spot for those looking to relax. On the shores of the magnificent lake for which the park is named, you'll find a splendid **sandy beach ★★**. A number of picnic areas have been laid out here, along with hiking trails and a campground.

Kitimat

Visitors interested in both industry and nature will find a combination of the two in the little town of Kitimat (pop. 11,300), less than an hour from Terrace. Kitimat is an industrial town in the true sense of the term. It was established in the mid-1950s to accommodate workers from the **Alcan** (☎639-8259) aluminum smelter, the **Eurocan Pulp** (☎639-3597) paper mill and the **Methanex** (☎639-9292) petrochemical plant, which together employed over two thirds of the population. All three companies offer free guided tours of their facilities, but reservations are required. Those interested in local history can stop at the **Centennial Museum** (Jun to Aug Mon to Sat 10am to 5pm Sep to May Mon to Fri 10am to 5pm, Sat 12pm to 5pm; 293 City Centre, ☎632-8950), which exhibits Aboriginal artifacts found in the area. Although the surrounding mountains make Kitimat seem landlocked, the town is actually a port with direct access to the Pacific by way of the **Douglas Channel ★★★**. Salmon pass through this natural fjord on their way to the ocean's tributaries, making Kitimat a popular fishing spot.

★★★
From Terrace
to Prince Rupert

The 132km stretch of highway between Terrace and Prince Rupert is undoubtedly one of the loveliest in Canada. The road follows the magnificent **Skeena River ★★★** almost curve for curve as it peacefully weaves its way between the **Coast Mountains ★★★**. On fine days, the **scenery ★★★** is extraordinary. Rest and picnic areas have been laid out all along the way.

★★★
Prince Rupert

The landscape changes radically near Prince Rupert. Huge hills covered with vegetation typical of the Pacific coast (large cedars, spruce trees) stretch as far as the eye can see. There is water everywhere, and although you will feel surrounded by lakes, what you see is actually the ocean creeping inland. A look at a map reveals that there are thousands of islands and fjords in this region. In fact, the town of Prince Rupert itself is located on an island, Kaien Island, 140km south of Ketchikan (Alaska). Prince Rupert is the most northerly point serviced by BC Ferries, and an important terminal for

ferries from Alaska (Alaska Marine Highway).

The **scenery ★★** is quite simply superb; mountains blanketed by dense forest encircle the town, and a splendid **natural harbour ★★**, the second largest in the Canadian West, will remind you that you have reached the coast. The history of Prince Rupert dates back to 1905, when engineers from the Grand Trunk Pacific Railway (GTPR), the transcontinental railroad, came here to look into the possibility of ending the line here. Over 19,000km of possible routes were studied before it was decided that the railroad would in fact run alongside the Skeena River. Charles Hays, president of the GTPR, held a contest to christen the new terminus. The name Prince Rupert was chosen from nearly 12,000 entries, in honour of the explorer and first head of the Hudson's Bay Company, a cousin of Charles II of England.

Today, Prince Rupert (pop. 14,600) is a lovely, prosperous community unlike any other town in northern British Columbia. You won't find any concrete or garish neon signs here; instead, you will be greeted by opulent-looking **Victorian architecture ★★**, large, pleasant streets, lovely

shops and numerous restaurants reflecting a cosmopolitan atmosphere.

The interesting **Museum of Northern British Columbia ★★** *($5; Jun to Aug Mon-Sat 9am to 8pm, Sun 9am to 5pm; Sep to May Mon-Sat 9am to 5pm; 100 1st Ave. W.; ☎624-3207)* displays various artifacts, as well as magnificent works of art and jewellery, which serve as proof that Aboriginal people have been living in this region for over 5,000 years. The gift shop, located inside the museum, features a vast selection of books on indigenous art, as well as displaying crafts and paintings.

Boat trips ★★ to **archeological sites** can be arranged at the tourist office. Space is limited and reservations are required.

The small seaside **Kwinitsa Station** *(summer only)* was built in 1911. It is one of 400 identical stations along the Grand Trunk Pacific Railway, the transcontinental line from Winnipeg to Prince Rupert. If you head north on Sixth Ave., you will see signs for the **Seaplane Base ★★**, one of the largest of its kind in Canada. The continuous spectacle of the aircraft taking off and landing has something hypnotic about it, and makes for lovely photographs.

The picturesque neighbourhood of **Cow Bay ★★★**,

Cow Bay

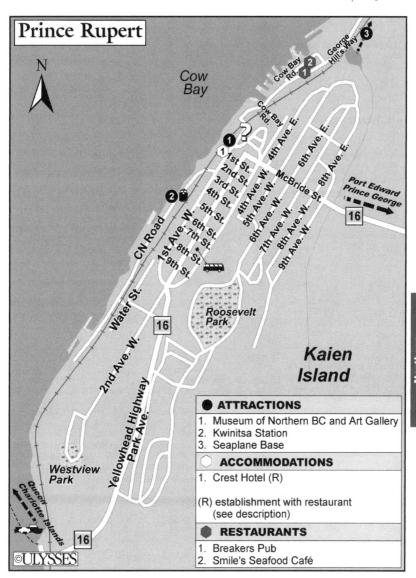

Prince Rupert

N

Cow
Bay

Cow Bay Rd.

George Hills Way

Cow Bay Rd.

4th Ave. E.

6th Ave. E.

8th Ave. E.

Port Edward
Prince George

1st St.
2nd St.
3rd St.
4th St.
5th St.
6th St.
7th St.
8th St.
9th St.

4th Ave. W.
5th Ave. W.
6th Ave. W.
7th Ave. W.
8th Ave. W.
9th Ave. W.

McBride St.

1st Ave. W.

CN Road

Water St.

16

16

Roosevelt
Park

Kaien
Island

2nd Ave. W.

Yellowhead Highway
Park Ave.

Westview
Park

Queen Charlotte Islands

16

©ULYSSES

● ATTRACTIONS

1. Museum of Northern BC and Art Gallery
2. Kwinitsa Station
3. Seaplane Base

◻ ACCOMMODATIONS

1. Crest Hotel (R)

(R) establishment with restaurant
    (see description)

● RESTAURANTS

1. Breakers Pub
2. Smile's Seafood Café

Northern
British Columbia

built on piles and overlooking a pretty sailing harbour, is a must-see. All sorts of shops, cafes and restaurants are clustered together in a colourful seaside setting. The **Seafest** takes place on the second weekend in June. Paraders march through the streets at 11am on Saturday, and sporting activities are held all weekend.

About 15km from Prince Rupert, in the little village of Port Edward, you will find the **North Pacific Cannery Village Museum ★ ★** *($10; May to end Sep every day 9am to 6pm; 1889 Skeena Dr., ☎628-3538),* a former salmon canning factory built over 100 years ago. During summer, actor David Boyce puts on a show that traces the history of the Skeena River and salmon fishing, which has been the mainspring of the regional economy for over a century now.

Some 40km northeast of Prince Rupert is the **Khutzey-Mateen Grizzly Bear Sanctuary**, the only such place in Canada. This rugged 44,300ha coastal ecosystem is a Provincial Park that is accessible only by boat. Visitation is by permit only. Terrace District Office *(BC Parks; ☎683-6530)*

Tour H: The Queen Charlotte Islands (Haida Gwaii)

However you choose to get to the islands, once there you'll discover an atmosphere and landscape that are truly beyond compare. Though the 5,000 islanders are very modest about their little piece of paradise, they actually go out of their way to attract and welcome visitors from the world over. The archipelago consists of 150 islands of various sizes. Almost all of the urban areas are located on the largest one, **Graham Island**, to the north. **Moresby Island** is the second most populous. Here, you'll find two villages, Sandspit and Alliford Bay, as well as the amazing Gwaii Haanas National Park.

The Queen Charlotte Islands lie about 770km, as the crow flies, from Vancouver. Because they are located so far west, the sun rises and sets at different times here than on the mainland. Although the islands are known for their wet climate, the more populated eastern coasts receive only slightly more rainfall than Vancouver (1,250mm). The precipitation on the western coasts, however, reaches record levels (4,500mm). The jagged relief of the Queen Charlotte and San Christoval Mountains has always protected the east coast from the westerly storms.

Despite the weather, the Haidas, who already inhabited the archipelago, established living areas on the west coast some 10,000 years ago. The Haidas are known to this day for their high-quality handicrafts and beautiful works of art.

Because the islands are so isolated, services are limited here. There are only two automated-teller machines on the archipelago, one in Masset and the other in Queen Charlotte City.

Skidegate

This is the first place you'll see if you take the ferry to the Queen Charlotte Islands, since the landing stage is located at the edge of the village. Skidegate is a small Haida community of 470 inhabitants, located on the beach in the heart of **Roonay Bay ★★★**.

While you're here, make sure to visit the internationally renowned **Queen Charlotte Islands Museum ★★★** *(Tue-Fri 10am to 5pm, Sat and Sun 1pm to 5pm, closed Mon; ☎559-4643)*, devoted exclusively to articles made by the Haidas over the ages, up until the present day. All modes of expression are represented here: everything from totem poles, sculptures and drawings to fabrics and basketry, not to mention jewellery made with precious metals. The shop boasts an impressive but pricey selection of books and quality souvenirs.

Balance Rock, the area's most unusual sight, lies 1km away in the opposite direction (north). As its name indicates, it is a boulder balanced on a pretty pebbly **beach ★★**. You can't miss it.

★★
Queen Charlotte City

Located 4km south of Skidegate, Queen Charlotte

City is a pleasant coastal village with 1,100 inhabitants. The atmosphere is very relaxed here, and the streets are filled with young people during the summer season. This is the jumping-off point for sea-kayak expeditions.

Right before Queen Charlotte City, on your way from Skidegate, you'll see **Joy's Island Jewellers**, a souvenir shop that doubles as the archipelago's official **tourist office**. There is not much to do in town. The islands' greatest attractions are the sea, the forest, the fauna (there are eagles everywhere) and the coasts, where you will discover traces of the Haida Nation.

The **Gwaii Haanas National Park ★★★** *($10, reservations recommended; ☎800-435-5622 or 604-435-5622)* cannot be reached by land. This park, located at the southern tip of the archipelago, is home to many unusual sights, each more remarkable than the last. First, there is **Hot Springs Island ★★★**, a paradise for anyone who enjoys a good soak. Then there's **Laskeek Bay ★★★**, frequented by dolphins and whales. **Ninstints ★★★**, a former Haida village on the tip of the island of Sgan Gwaii, is a UNESCO World Heritage Site. Here, you will find the largest collection of totem poles and Aboriginal-built structures in the Queen Charlotte Islands. There is something unreal and mystical about the location itself.

Sandspit

A village of lumberjacks, Sandspit (pop. 740), like Gwaii Haanas National Park, is located on Moresby Island. It has the second largest airport on the archipelago, after Masset's. The ferry shuttles back and forth between Queen Charlotte City and Moresby Island several times a

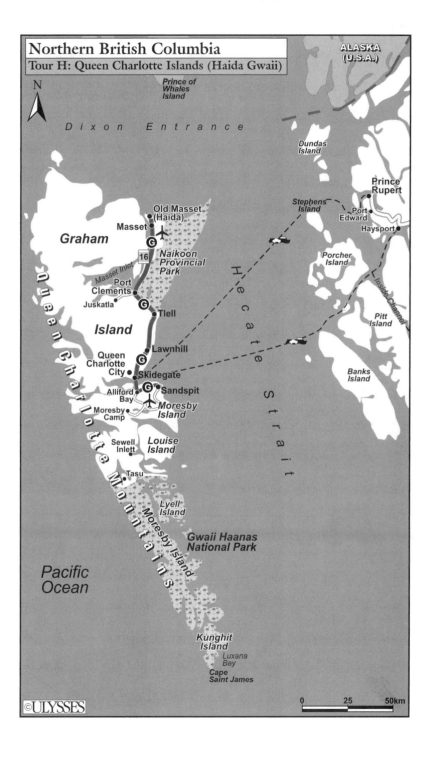

Northern British Columbia
Tour H: Queen Charlotte Islands (Haida Gwaii)

N

ALASKA
(U.S.A.)

Prince of
Whales
Island

Dixon   Entrance

Dundas
Island

Stephens
Island

Prince
Rupert

Port
Edward

Haysport

Old Masset
(Haida)

Masset

Graham

G

16

Naikoon
Provincial
Park

Porcher
Island

Masset Inlet

Port
Clements

Juskatla

G

Tlell

Island

H
e
c
a
t
e

Pitt
Island

Inside Channel

Lawnhill

G

Queen
Charlotte
City

G

Skidegate

Banks
Island

S
t
r
a
i
t

Alliford
Bay

G

Sandspit

Moresby
Camp

Moresby
Island

Sewell
Inlett

Louise
Island

Tasu

Lyell
Island

Moresby Island

Gwaii Haanas
National Park

Pacific
Ocean

Queen Charlotte Mountains

Kunghit
Island

Luxana
Bay

Cape
Saint James

©ULYSSES

0   25   50km

day. The fare is inexpensive, and the crossing only takes a few minutes.

Tlell

This pretty little rural village (pop. 150) lies 43km north of Skidegate along the lovely **Tlell River**, which is popular with fishing buffs.

Port Clements

Port Clements is a community of 450 people, most of whom derive their income from fishing or the forest industry. The big draw here used to be the incredible **Golden Spruce** , at least until the 300-year-old, 50m-high tree was deliberately destroyed in January of 1997. A malefactor armed with a chainsaw committed this senseless act as a protest against what he called "university-trained professionals". He was arrested and claimed he meant no disrespect to the Haida. The fact remains, however, that a piece of Haida legend and culture, not to mention a biological treasure, is no more. The Golden Spruce was the only tree known to exhibit the golden pigmentation instead of the typical green foliage, the result of a mysterious genetic mutation.

Masset

Masset is the most important town on the Queen Charlotte Islands, with a population of 1,400 people. Since 1971, life here has been shaped to some extent by the local Canadian Forces base. Along with Queen Charlotte City and Sandspit, Masset is one of the few towns on the archipelago with a **tourist office**. It has all of the services one would expect to find in a large town, including an airport, restaurants, an auto-repair shop, a hospital, etc.

Old Masset

Old Masset, also known as Haida, is a Haida village of 630 inhabitants, which faces onto peaceful **Masset Sound**. It is best to go straight to the local tourist office, where you can learn the addresses of the resident artists. You'll find many works of art at **Haida Arts and Jewellery** *(every day 11am to 5pm during summer; 387 Eagle;* ☎*626-5560)*, a shop with traditional architecture. The two totem poles at its entrance make it easy to spot.

★★★
Naikoon Provincial Park

Naikoon is one of the islands' treasures. You can get there from the highway in Masset, or through Tlell, where the park headquarters are located *(BC Parks,* ☎*557-4390)*. The former option, through McIntyre Bay, is the most spectacular. The road runs along **South Beach ★★**, an extraordinary 15km stretch of sand, through a dense, damp and mossy forest. It ends at Agate Beach, where the park campground is located. **Agate Beach ★★** lies at the foot of **Tow Hill ★★**, a 109m-high rock that is home to a number of bald eagles. The view **★★★** from the top is phenomenal (30min on foot). After Tow Hill, the beach continues, becoming **North Beach ★★★** for 10km. The park is also known for its lengthy hiking trails, which can be a real adventure. A good example is the one at **East Beach ★★★**, which covers 89km along an endless beach, through forests and across tidewaters.

Outdoor Activities

Birdwatching

These vast northern spaces abound with birds. Most notably, the Queen Charlotte Islands are home to the largest concentration of peregrine falcons in North America. Great herons and bald eagles, furthermore, are as common a sight around local villages as pigeons are in the big cities to the south.

Fishing

Northern British Columbia is a fishing paradise, for trout as well as the king of fish, salmon. The latter can be caught either in the region's rivers or in the sea. Don't forget to obtain a permit beforehand.

Tour A: The Gold Rush Trail and the Cariboo Mountains

The region of Quesnel conceals many idyllic spots for fly-fishing. Fishpot Lake, 125km west of Quesnel, is one of these places. For more information, go to the tourist information office (see p 235).

Salmon

Tour G:
The Yellowhead Highway

There are a number of well-known spots, like **Burns Lake**, whose town slogans say it all: "3,000 Miles of Fishing" and "The Land of a Thousand Lakes." The Chamber of Commerce is a mine of information for fishing buffs.

As in Burns Lake, life in **Houston** centres around fishing during the summer – and not just any kind of fishing; the town is the self-proclaimed steelhead capital of the world. The tourist office can show you where you have the best chances of catching this famous sea trout.

Around **Smithers**, the Bulkhead River is teeming with steelhead and salmon. **Kitimat** is also renowned for fishing, for it is here that salmon swim up the Douglas Channel, a natural fjord, to the ocean's tributaries. A wealth of information is available at the tourist office.

Tour H: The Queen
Charlotte Islands
(HaidaGwaii)

The Queen Charlotte archipelago is ideal for deep-sea fishing, as it is home to the Chinook salmon, aptly nicknamed the "King" because of its size (up to 40 kg). For further information, contact **Queen Charlotte Adventures** *(320 Warf St., ☎559-8990 or 800-668-4288)*.

Hiking

Hiking is far and away the top activity in northern British Columbia. It enables visitors to appreciate the region's enchanting, unspoiled wilderness at close range. There are so many provincial and national parks here that even the most

demanding outdoor enthusiast will have a hard time choosing between them. Those not to be missed include Stone Mountain, Wokkpash Recreation Area, Muncho Lake, Liard Hot Springs, the Spatsizi Plateau Wilderness Park, Mount Edziza and the Tseax Lava Beds.

Tour A: Gold Rush Trail
and the Cariboo
Mountains

At **Barkerville**, a network of trails follows the paths taken by the gold diggers. The wilderness is still relatively untouched and the flora and fauna are breathtaking. There are old cabins, once inhabited by gold diggers, along the path. The proposed tours take one day, but it is also possible to camp overnight and return the next day. A trail pass is available at the information office at the entrance to the historic town of Barkerville.

★★★
Tweedsmuir
Provincial Park

Tweedsmuir is the largest park in British Columbia. The best way to get here is via Hwy. 20, which meets the West Coast at William's Lake. After driving 360km, you finally arrive at this paradise of lakes, greenery and mountains. This heaven on earth can be explored by foot, thanks to a network of trails. Excursions can range from a few hours up to a month.

One of the most impressive attractions has to be **Hunlen Falls**. Fed by Turner Lake, this waterfall is 260m high (more than four times the height of Niagara Falls). A 16.4km path leads to a great observation point. Set aside an entire day for this trip. The hilly terrain offers a 2,000m climb for experienced hikers. To get there, follow the directions along Hwy. 20.

Alexander Mackenzie Trail is a 420km trip. It follows the last leg of the journey that Alexander Mackenzie made over several months in 1793 before he became the first Englishman to view the West Coast of North America from this latitude. The 80km section (five to seven days) that crosses Tweedsmuir Park probably offers the most impressive panoramic views. Those interested in making the entire trip, which begins near Quesnel and ends at Bella Coola, can obtain more information from the **Alexander Mackenzie Trail Association** *(PO Box 425, Station A, Kelowna, BC, V1Y 7P1)*

Rafting

Tour A: The Gold Rush
Trail and the Cariboo
Mountains

Big Canyon Rafting *($90; May to mid-Sep;120 Lindsay St., ☎992-RAFT)* offers rides of several hours on the tumultuous Quesnel River.

Canoeing

Tour A: The Gold Rush
Trail and the Cariboo
Mountains

A canoe trip through six connected lakes between Kidney Lake and Turner Lake can be made in **Tweedsmuir Provincial Park** *($8, vehicle entry fee)*. The six short portages offer breathtaking views. Several beaches are scattered along the 15km journey. Canoe rentals available on site *(☎398-4414)*.

You can have one of the most beautiful canoe trips in the

world at **Bowron Lake Provincial Park** *($50; ☎800-435-5622)* There are some 115km of lakes, rivers and short portages, all framed by 2,500m mountains. It's a memorable experience that you'll want to repeat – even before your first day has ended.

All camping equipment and canoe rentals are available at **Becker's Lodge** *(Bowron Lake Rd.; ☎992-8864)*. Stock up on supplies at Quesnel before leaving, and plan seven days for this epic journey among the moose and eagles.

Kayaking

Tour G: The Queen Charlotte Islands (Haida Gwaii)

Gwaii Haanas National Park offers some excellent sea kayaking. Excursions are organized by **Queen Charlotte Adventures** *(Queen Charlotte City, ☎559-8990 or 800-668-4288)* and by **Moresby Explorers** *(469 Alliford Bay Sandspit, ☎637-2215 or 800-806-7633)*.

Adventure packages

Tour G: The Queen Charlotte Islands (Haida Gwaii)

To organize excursions, the best place is without a doubt **Queen Charlotte Adventures** *(3207 Wharf St., ☎559-8990 or 800-668-4288, ⇌559-8983)*. It offers tours of the Gwaii Haanas National Park by motorboat, sailboat or sea kayak.

Cross-Country Skiing and Snowshoeing

During winter, snow takes over the landscape. Cross-country skiing and snowshoeing can be enjoyed just about everywhere.

Downhill Skiing

Tour B: To the Alaska Highway

Powder King *($35/per day, credit cards not accepted; ☎962-5899)*, a smaller resort than Ski Smithers (see below),

located between Prince George and Dawson Creek, boasts excellent snow coverage.

Tour G: The Yellowhead Highway

Ski Smithers *($35/per day; ☎250-847-2058 or 800-665-4299)* on **Hudson Bay Mountain** has a 533m vertical drop and 18 runs and offers powdery conditions beginning in November. It is the largest ski area in the northern part of the province.

Accommodations

Tour A: The Gold Rush Trail and the Cariboo Mountains

Quesnel

Gold Pan Motel
$
≡, ℝ, *K*
855 Front St.
☎992-2107 or 800-295-4334
⇌992-1125
The Gold Pan Motel is located in the middle of Quesnel. It has the comfort typical of a mid-priced facility.

Ramada
$$ bkfst incl.
≡, ℝ, ≈, *K,* 🐾
383 St. Laurent Ave.
☎992-5575 or 800-663-1581
⇌992-2254
www.ramada.ca
There are other motels in the mid-price range. The Ramada Inn is peaceful.

Barkerville

Many camping grounds are located near the historic town of Barkerville. Adjacent to Bakerville 1860s goldrush town, more than 160 campsites are available. For reservations, call ☎800-689-9025.

Barkerville's two bed and breakfasts are the only lodging available in the town. Be sure to reserve well in advance. The turn-of-the-century ambience is wonderfully recreated at both of these B&Bs. The decor is splendid and the staff is courteous, the St. George in particular.

Kelly House
$$ bkfst incl.
☎/≈994-3328
☎994-3312 off season

St. George Hotel
$$$ bkfst incl.
Hwy 26
☎994-0008 or 888-246-7690
≈994-0008
www.cariboo.net.com/ stgeorge

For less expensive alternatives, a group of mid-range hotels are located in the town next to Wells.

White Cap Motor Inn
$ camping
$$ room
K, ⊛
Ski Hill Rd.
☎994-3489 or 800-377-2028
≈994-3426
The White Cap Motor Inn offers decent, though haphazardly decorated, rooms. The Swiss staff speaks German and is very welcoming.

Bowron Lake Provincial park

The accommodations here include campsites *($10-$20)*, cabins *($15)* and luxurious cottages *($50-$150)*.

Becker's Lodge Resort
$$$
ℜ , *K*
Bowron Lake Rd.
May to Sep, Dec to Mar
☎992-8864 or 800-808-4761
≈992-8893
www.beckers.bc.ca
Becker's Lodge has magnificent log cabins. The wealthy German owner also has a chain of bakeries in Europe. With his firm handshake,

cowboy hat and theatrical personality, everyone who meets Lother agrees: he is definitely a colourful character! The facilities that he built are beautiful and blend nicely with the countryside. The luxurious cottages are cosy and exquisitely designed. Camping available.

Tour B:
To the Alaska Highway

Prince George

The Buckhorn Bed & Breakfast
$ bkfst incl.
🏍, *K*
14900 Buckhorn Place
☎888-933-8555
≈963-8884
www.pgonline.com/bnb/ buckhorn.html
The Buckhorn is located at the southern edge of Prince George, 1km east of Hwy. 97 and 13km south of the Fraser Bridge. A charming Victorian house, it has two bedrooms, each with a queen-size bed, a single bed and an adjoining bathroom.

Best Western City Centre
$$$
≡, ≈, △, ⊙, ℜ
910 Victoria St.
☎563-1267 or 800-528-1234
≈563-9904
www.bestwesternbc.com
The newly renovated Best Western provides accommodations in the heart of Prince George. Its 53 rooms are clean and pleasant.

Connaught Motor Inn
$$
≈, ℜ, ℜ, ≡ 🏍
1550 Victoria St.
☎800-663-6620
☎/≈562-4441
Located downtown, the Connaught Motor Inn is right near all sorts of shops and services. It is a large, comfortable motel with a swimming pool and 98 rooms, each

equipped with cable television and a refrigerator.

Westhaven Cottage by the Lake
$$
23357 Fyfe Rd.
☎964-0180
South of Prince George, is this heavenly place set in the heart of nature. This charming cottage offers a splendid view of the lake. Guests have access to a private beach and hiking and cross-country ski trails.

The Manor House
$$
⊛, *K*, 🔥
8384 Toombs Dr.
☎562-9255
≈562-8255
"Elegant" is the word that best describes the Manor House, located northwest of town on the banks of the Nechako River. This immense place lives up to its name. The executive suites are equipped with a gas fireplace, a bathroom, a kitchenette and a private entrance (in some cases).

Coast Inn of the North
$$$
ℜ, 🐕, ≈, ⊙, △
770 Brunswick St.
☎563-0121 or 800-663-1144
≈563-1948
www.coasthotels.com
If you like urban comfort, try the Coast Inn of the North, also located downtown. A modern, 152-room hotel, it boasts a swimming pool, sauna, workout room, nightclub, pub, shop, etc.

Mackenzie

Alexander Mackenzie Hotel
$$
🏍, *K*, ℜ, △
403 Mackenzie Blvd.
☎997-3266
≈997-4675
As far as accommodations in Mackenzie are concerned, the 99-room Alexander Mackenzie Hotel is hard to beat. This modern, luxurious place is like an oasis in the midst of the

region's vast stretches of wilderness. It is located right in the centre of town, just a few steps away from Williston Lake, and includes a shopping centre with 37 stores. The rooms are spacious and some have a kitchenette.

Chetwynd

Country Squire Inn
$$
△, ℝ, 🐾, ℜ
5317 South Access Rd.
☎788-2276
⇌788-3018
Similar to the Stagecoach in style, the Country Squire Inn is a full-comfort modern hotel, complete with refrigerators in every room, satellite television, a laundry, an ice machine, a sauna and a whirlpool.

Stagecoach Inn
$$
△, K, ℝ, ℜ, 🐾, ≡
5413 South Access Rd.
☎788-9666 or 800-663-2744
⇌788-3418
Chetwynd's main street is studded with quality motels. The Stagecoach Inn is situated in the heart of the village, close to all the local services. It has a restaurant, a sauna and 55 rooms, some with a kitchen. The modern, spacious rooms are equipped with a television and movie channels.

Dawson Creek

 **The Alaska Hotel**
$
sb, ℝ
10209-10213 10th St.
☎782-7998
⇌782-6277
The Alaska Hotel is the symbol of Dawson Creek just as the Eiffel Tower is that of Paris. It would be hard to miss this white building with green trim, built in 1928, with "Alaska" written in capital letters on its facade. The

rooms have not lost their old-fashioned charm, and the bathrooms for some are on the landing. Restaurant (see p 261), Pub (see p 263).

Ramada Dawson Creek
$$ bkfst incl.
🔷, 🐾
1748 Alaska Ave.
☎782-8595 or 800-663-2749
⇌782-9657
www.ramada.ca
The Ramada is located at the intersection of the Alaska Highway and Hart Highway, just after the Pioneer Village. It's a very comfortable hotel and rooms are equipped with mini refrigerators.

George Dawson Inn
$$ bkfst incl.
≡, 🔷, 🐾, ℜ
11705 Eighth St.
☎782-9151 or 800-663-2745
⇌782-1617
www.georgedawsoninn.bc.ca
Somewhat different in style, the George Dawson Inn is a large modern hotel with 80 spacious, well-equipped rooms. Luxury suites are also available. The inn has a tavern and a restaurant as well.

Tour C: The Hudson's Hope Route

Hudson's Hope

Sportsman's Inn
$
ℜ, K, 🐾, ≡
10501 Cartier Ave.
☎783-5523 or 877-783-5520
⇌783-5511
The Sportsman's Inn is well-suited to long stays, as 37 of its 50 rooms are equipped with kitchenettes. The hotel also includes a bar and a restaurant. All sorts of information of interest to fishing buffs is provided free of charge.

Tour D: The Alaska Highway

Fort St. John

Quality Inn Northern Grand
$$$
🔷, 🐾, ≈, ⊚, △, ℜ
9830 100th Ave.
☎787-0521 or 800-663-8312
⇌787-2648
www.choicehotels.ca
The Pioneer Inn, located in the centre of town, just 8km from the airport, is the last luxury hotel on the British-Columbian portion of the Alaska Highway. It has a bar, a restaurant, an indoor pool, a sauna and a whirlpool. The large, well-equipped rooms have cable television with sports and movie channels.

Mile 72 Alaska Highway

Shepherd's Inn
$
ℜ, 🐾
Mile 72 Alaska Hwy.
☎827-3676
The Shepherd's Inn is located 45km north of Fort St. John. You'll find comfortable, rustic rooms here, as well as a small restaurant that serves home-made meals.

Pink Mountain

🔷 **Mai's Kitchen**
$$
Mile 143 of the Alaska Hwy.
☎772-3215
Mai's is a peaceful place to spend the night. The rooms are rustic and you can sample some of their home-made bread. There is a service station here as well.

Fort Nelson

Travelodge Fort Nelson
$$
🐾, ≡, △, ℜ, 🔷
4711 50th Ave. S.
☎774-3911 or 800-578-7875
⇌774-3730
With its almost "city-style" level of comfort, the Coach House

Inn is far and away the best hotel in Fort Nelson. It is located in the centre of town, on the west service road of the Alaska Highway, and offers 70 spacious, air-conditioned rooms. Guests enjoy the use of a sauna, a bar and two restaurants.

Muncho Lake Provincial Park

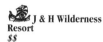 **J & H Wilderness Resort**
$$
May to Sep
ℜ
Mile 463 of the Alaska Hwy.
☎*776-3453*
⇄*776-3454*
The J & H Wilderness Resort is the ultimate northern motel. Its eight little rustic-style rooms lie just steps away from magnificent Muncho Lake. The rooms have no telephone or television, but nothing beats the feeling of spending the night in such heavenly surroundings. Camping also available.

Northern Rockies Lodge
$$
🐾, ℜ
Mile 462 of the Alaska Hwy.
☎*776-3481 or 800-663-5269*
⇄*776-3482*
www.northern-rockies-lodge.com
The Northern Rockies Lodge is becoming better known in Europe than in Canada. The owners, a brush pilot named Urs and his wife Marianne, attract many visitors from Germany, their native country. It is not uncommon to find charter buses parked in front of this 40-unit hotel, located just a stone's throw from the lake. Some of the rooms are motel-style, others cottage-style.

Liard Hot Springs Provincial Park

 **Liard River Lodge**
$$
ℜ
Km 801/mile 496 of the Alaska Hwy.
☎*776-7349*
⇄*776-7340*
Located on the Alaska Highway, just opposite the entrance to Liard Hot Springs Provincial Park, the Liard River Lodge is an establishment built in the purest northern style. An immense, two-storey log "cabin," it has 12 rooms, a restaurant, a souvenir shop and a gas station. Camping is also available.

Watson Lake (Yukon)

Big Horn Hotel
$$
🐾, ⊛, K
on the west side of the Alaska Hwy., downtown
☎*(867)536-2020*
⇄*(867) 536-2021*
With its trailer-style architecture, the Big Horn Hotel is not exactly attractive from the outside. Nevertheless, the place has 29 spacious, luxurious and comfortable rooms (some equipped with a kitchenette and a whirlpool), whose elaborate decor is worth a look. The rates, moreover, are reasonable for the area.

Watson Lake Hotel
$$
🐾, ℜ, K
downtown, right near the Signpost Forest, on the east side of the Alaska Hwy.
☎*(867) 536-7781*
⇄*(867) 536-7563*
The Watson Lake Hotel is the best known place to stay in town. Watson Lake's oldest hotel, it has typical Yukon architecture, with massive beams and log walls. The 48 rooms are extremely comfortable. There is a coffee shop, a restaurant and a bar.

Belvedere Motor Hotel
$$$
🐾, ℜ, ≡, ⊛
on the west side of the Alaska Hwy., downtown
☎*(867) 536-7712*
⇄*(867) 536-7563*
The Belvedere Motor Hotel is located right near the Big Horn Hotel & Tavern, to which it bears certain similarities. Unlike its competitor, however, it also offers rooms with a waterbed and houses a travel agency, a magazine and souvenir shop and a hairdressing salon.

Tour E: The Stewart-Cassiar Highway

Meziadin Junction

Meziadin Lake Provincial Park
$
🐾
May to Oct
Meziadin Junction
☎*847-7320*
Meziadin Lake Provincial Park has 62 campsites for tents and motorhomes, a picnic area and a beach. It's a pleasant spot if you like fishing. Cash only.

Iskut

Trappers Souvenirs
$$
7km north of Iskut; radiomobile 2M3 520, Mehaus Channel
Trappers Souvenirs is a souvenir shop that rents out a log cabin at a modest price.

Red Goat Lodge
$/hostel
$/camping
$$/B&B
🐾
3.2km south of Iskut
☎/⇄*234-3261*
☎*888-733-4628*
www.karo-ent.com/redgoat.htm
The Red Goat Lodge is the local YHA hostel. It looks out onto pretty Eddontenajon Lake. It lies adjacent to a campground, which is truly

first-rate, considering its isolated location here in the wild. Dormitory rooms are all that is available for the moment. This is a popular place, so it is wise to make reservations. Kitchen, coin laundry, tv lounge, canoes.

Dease Lake

Northway Motor Inn
$$
K, ℜ, 🐾
downtown on Boulder Ave.
☎*771-5341*
⇄*771-5342*
The Northway Motor Inn has 46 spacious, comfortable units, most of which have a kitchen equipped with a dishwasher. Monthly rates are available as well. A restaurant, which is open May to Oct, and a coffee shop lie a short walk away.

Telegraph Creek

 **Stikine River Song Lodge**
$$
🐾*, K*
on Stikine Ave.
☎/⇄*235-3196*
www.stikineriversong.com
Set up inside an historic building, the Stikine Riversong is a cafe, an eight-room inn and a grocery store rolled into one. The rooms are somewhat basic but nonetheless very pleasant. This is the only place of its kind in Telegraph Creek, so it is wise to make reservations in order to avoid any unpleasant surprises.

Tour F: To Stewart, BC and Hyder, AK

Stewart

King Edward Hotel & Motel
$$
ℜ, *K*, ≡
right in the centre of the village, at the corner of Fifth and Columbia Sts.
☎*636-2244 or 800-633-3126*
⇄*636-9160*
www.kingedwardhotel.com
The King Edward Hotel & Motel is the best hotel in Stewart. It has 50 comfortable, well-equipped units, some with a complete kitchen for longer stays. There is also a café and a fully licenced seafood restaurant on the premises.

Hyder, Alaska

Sealaska Inn & Camp Run-A-Muck
$
ℜ
on Premier Ave.
☎*636-9006 or 888-393-1199*
⇄*636-9003*
www.sealaskainn.com
The Sealaska Inn is a pleasant place located over a pub. The atmosphere is lively, and can get noisy, especially on weekends, so you might have a hard time falling asleep some nights.

Tour G: The Yellowhead Highway

Prince George

See "Tour B ; To the Alaska Highway p 255"

Vanderhoof

Grand Trunk Inn
$$
ℜ, *K*, 🐾
2351 Church Ave.
☎*567-3188 or 877-567-3188*
⇄*567-3056*
The Grand Trunk Inn lies in the centre of town, one block

north of Hwy. 16. It is one of the larger hotels in Vanderhoof, with 32 units, some of which include a kitchen. The rooms are simple but comfortable. A hairdressing salon, a pub and a restaurant are all located on the premises.

Fort St. James

 **The Stuart Lodge**
$$
K, 🐾
Stone Bay Rd.
☎/⇄*996-7917*
The Stuart Lodge is set on 24ha of land on the shores of Stuart Lake, 5km north of Fort St. James. In addition to offering a view of the lake, its six charming little cottages are fully equipped, complete with a barbecue and a television. Small motorboats are also available for rent.

Smithers

Berg's Valley Tours Bed & Breakfast
$$ bkfst incl.
3924 13th Ave.
☎*847-5925 or 888-847-5925*
⇄*847-5945*
Berg's Valley Tours Bed & Breakfast is perfect for active types, as the owners, David and Beverley, offer guided hikes in the mountains, including a trip in an all-terrain vehicle and a snack, as well as skiing packages and guided driving tours of the region.

Hazelton

Ksan Campground
$
near the Ksan Historic Indian Village Museum
☎*842-5544*
The Ksan Campground is an extremely well-equipped and well-maintained campground. It can accommodate large motorhomes. There are trails around the site for walks. A small tourist shop has been set up at the campground.

Terrace

Mount Layton Hotsprings Resort
$$
ℜ
22km south of Terrace via Hwy. 37
☎*798-2214 or 800-663-3862*
⇌*798-2478*
www.kurtknoll.com/hot springs.html
With its water slides and swimming pools filled by natural hot springs, the Mount Layton Hotsprings Resort, located just 15min from Terrace, is a fantastic place to stay during summertime. Its 22 rooms are comfortable and well-equipped.

Coast Inn of the West
$$$
🐾, ℜ
4620 Lakelse Ave.
☎*638-8141 or 800-663-1144*
⇌*638-8999*
www.coasthotels.com
A big hotel for a big town, the Coast Inn of the West is impeccable but expensive. It has 58 luxurious rooms with nothing lacking.

Kitimat

City Centre Motel
$$
K
480 City Centre
☎*632-4848 or 800-663-3391*
⇌*632-5300*
The City Centre Motel is right in the centre of town, near all the local services. The comfortable, spacious rooms are equipped with kitchenettes. This is definitely one of the best deals in town.

Prince Rupert

Crest Hotel
$$$
☺, 🐾, ℜ, △
222 First Ave. W
☎*624-6771*
⇌*627-7666*
www.cresthotel.bc.ca
The Crest Hotel boasts the best view in town, since it is located alongside a cliff overlooking the port. The rooms are worthy of the finest luxury

hotel, and the service is impeccable. You really get your money's worth here. The Crest also has two excellent restaurants. All of these things combined make it one of the finest hotels in the North by Northwest region.

Tour H: The Queen Charlotte Islands (HaidaGwaii)

Queen Charlotte City

🦐 Spruce Point Lodge
$$ bkfst incl.
609 Sixth Ave.
☎/⇌*559-8234*
The pretty Spruce Point Lodge has very simple, yet very comfortable, rooms, each with a bathroom, a television, and its own private entrance. There is a common terrace with a view of magnificent Hecate Strait. Mary, the owner, keeps up to date on everything that's going on in the region, and knows a lot about the various companies that organize outdoor activities and adventures.

Sea Raven
$$
K, 🐾, ℜ, ℝ, ≈
3301 Third Ave.
☎*559-4423 or 800-665-9606*
⇌*559-8617*
www.searaven.com
The Sea Raven is a comfortable, modern hotel. Some of the rooms offer a view of the sea. The seafood restaurant adjoining the hotel is excellent.

Sandspit

Moresby Island Guest House
$$
385 Alliford Bay Rd.
☎*637-5300 or*
(604) 894-6466
⇌*637-5300*
www.moresbyisland-bnb. com
The Moresby Island Guest House is located on magnificent Shingle Bay, close to the airport, shops, restaurants and

beaches. The 10 rooms are clean and comfortable and big enough for families. There is a common kitchen that can be used to prepare breakfast.

Seaport Bed & Breakfast
$ bkfst incl.
K
371 Alliford Bay Rd.
☎*637-5698*
⇌*637-5697*
Just a stone's throw away from the airport, the Seaport Bed & Breakfast has two cottages, actually trailers, with a view of the bay. Each one is equipped with a kitchenette. Credit cards are not accepted, but you won't find better value for your money on Moresby Island.

Sandspit Inn
$$
K
Airport Rd.
☎*637-5334*
⇌*637-5334*
The Sandspit Inn is a modern 35-unit hotel located right near the Sandspit airport and has a large business clientele.

Tlell

Tlell River House
$$
🐾, ℜ
Beitush Rd.
☎*557-4211 or 800-667-8906*
⇌*557-4622*
This inn is hidden away in the woods, in a pleasant setting alongside the Tlell River and Hecate Strait. The rooms are simple and comfortable, and the restaurant serves quality food.

Port Clements

Golden Spruce Motel
$$
🐾, 🍴
2 Grouse St.
☎*557-4325 or 877-801-4653*
⇌*557-4502*
The Golden Spruce is one of the few hotels in the Port Clements area offering 12 very simple units. There is also

a coin laundry on the premises.

Masset

Alaska View Lodge
$$ bkfst incl.
sb/pb
at the entrance of Naikoon Provincial Park, midway between Masset and Tow Hill
☎*626-3333 or 800-661-0019*
≈*626-3303*
www.alaskaviewlodge.com
The Alaska View Lodge boasts a privileged site at the edge of the renowned Pacific forest, alongside South Beach, a magnificent 10km stretch of sand. The owners, Eliane, from Paris, and her husband Charly, from Bern (Switzerland), have created an "Old World" atmosphere for their guests. The Alaska View Lodge is an excellent choice for visitors looking to step out of their element into truly heavenly surroundings.

Singing Surf Inn
$$
K, ℜ
1504 Old Beach Rd.
☎*626-3318 or 888-592-8886*
≈*626-5204*
www.singingsurfinn.com
Located on the way into town, the Singing Surf Inn is a veritable institution in Masset. The newly renovated comfortable rooms are equipped with satellite television, and some offer a view of the port. The hotel also has a souvenir shop, a bar and a restaurant.

Naikoon Provincial Park

At **Naikoon Provincial Park** *(B.C. Parks,* ☎*847-7320)* there are two campgrounds: one at **Agate Beach** with 43 sites, west of Tow Hill, and the other at **Misty Meadows**, with around 30 sites. They both have washrooms, drinking water and firewood. They are often full during the summer but don't worry, wilderness camping is allowed in the park. There are three shelters to protect against bad weather,

where you can also do a bit of cooking. They are at **Cape Ball**, **Ocanda** and **Fife Point**. There are no stores around the park, the closest supplies are in Masset, 30km away.

Restaurants

Tour A: The Gold Rush Trail and the Cariboo Mountains

Quesnel

Granville's Coffee
$
383 Reid St.
☎*992-3667*
Granville's Coffee is a cute little place to stop for an expertly prepared coffee. The decor is brightened up by wood panelling and jute coffee bags covering the ceiling. They serve delectable sandwiches as well as scrumptious desserts.

Mr Mikes
$$-$$$
450 Reid St.
☎*992-7742*
With its fireplace, sitting imposingly in the middle of the dining room, Mr Mikes resembles a chalet. The hamburgers are great and the service is impeccable.

Savata's
$$$
240 Reid St.
☎*992-9453*
Savata's cooks up steaks to perfection according to the customer's taste. The antique furnishings and the subdued lighting give this place a privileged status in Quesnel. Don't miss the salad bar – it offers a great selection.

Tour B: To the Alaska Highway

Prince George

Cariboo Steak & Seafood
$$$-$$$$
Mon-Fri
1165 Fifth Ave.
☎*564-1220*
If you're tired of gobbling down hamburgers, try the Cariboo Steak & Seafood, which serves very good steak and has a large all-you-can-eat buffet at lunchtime.

The Keg
$$$
582 George St.
☎*563-1768*
Another excellent place for steak is The Keg, a member of the well-known chain. In fact, steak is the specialty of the house, and is prepared in a number of ways. You can have yours served with seafood if you like.

Mackenzie

The Alexander Mackenzie Hotel
$$
403 Mackenzie Blvd.
☎*997-6549*
The Alexander Mackenzie is *the* place to eat in town. The menu lists a variety of hamburgers, as well as chicken and a good choice of salads.

Chetwynd

 Stagecoach Inn
$$
5413 South Access
☎*788-9666*
In the heart of the village, the Stagecoach Inn has a small, family-style restaurant. You won't find gourmet cuisine here, but the food is of good quality.

The Swiss Inn Restaurant
$$-$$$
downtown on Hwy. 97, 800m east of the traffic light
☎*788-2566*
The Swiss Inn Restaurant serves Swiss German-style cuisine. The menu lists dishes like schnitzel, as well as typical North American fare, such as pizza, steak and seafood.

Dawson Creek

 Alaska Restaurant
$$$
10209 10th St.
☎*782-7040*
The Alaska Restaurant, a multi-coloured building dating back to 1928, with the word "Alaska" written in orange letters on its facade, is easy to spot from a distance. The "antique and rustic" decor is pleasant, and the food, high-quality. The impressive wine list is especially noteworthy.

Tour C: The Hudson's Hope Route

Hudson's Hope

Sportsman's Inn
$$
10501 Beattie Ave.
☎*783-5523*
The restaurant of the Sportsman's Inn is without a doubt the best place to eat in Hudson's Hope. This is a family-style place with a traditional menu.

Tour D: The Alaska Highway

Fort St. John

Boston Pizza
$$$
9824 100th St.
☎*787-0455*
As indicated by its name, Boston Pizza serves a wide selection of pizza. The menu

also lists spicy ribs, pasta dishes, steaks and sandwiches.

White Spot Restaurant
$$$
9830 100th Ave.
☎*261-6961*
This restaurant, located at the Northern Grand Quality Inn, downtown, has a varied menu and serves generous portions.

Fort Nelson

Coach House Restaurant
$$$
4711 50th Ave. S
☎*774-3911*
The restaurant at the Travelodge, a traditional stopping place for travellers on the Alaska Highway, is always very busy during summer. It serves a variety of dishes and even has a special menu for children. An all-you-can-eat buffet is served on Sundays 10am to 2pm.

Muncho Lake Provincial Park

 **The Northern Rockies Lodge**
$$$-$$$$
Mile 462 of the Alaska Hwy.
☎*776-3481*
The Northern Rockies Lodge serves hamburgers, as well as German dishes. You won't go wrong ordering the sausages and sauerkraut. Close your eyes and let your imagination transport you to Alsace or Germany. German beer is available on tap here – of course!

Liard Hot Springs Provincial Park

 Liard River Lodge
$$$
Km 801/mile 497 of the Alaska Hwy.
☎*776-7349*
The Liard Hot Springs Provincial Park, just opposite the entrance to the park, serves tasty, copious breakfasts.

Tour E: The Stewart-Cassiar Highway

Iskut

Tenajohn Motel
$$
in the centre of the village, along Hwy. 37
☎*234-3141*
The restaurant of the Tenajohn Motel serves a variety of dishes including hamburgers and salads.

Dease Lake

Northway
$$
on Boulder Ave., downtown
☎*771-4114*
With its big green roof, Northway is the easiest restaurant to find in town. The menu lists soups and sandwiches.

Telegraph Creek

 Stikine Riversong
$$
on Stikine Ave.
☎*235-3196*
Located in an historic building, this is a small bistro (as well as an inn and a grocery store). It has a good reputation, and is the one place in Telegraph Creek where you can enjoy a good meal.

Tour F: To Stewart, BC and Hyder, AK

Stewart

King Edward Restaurant
$$
at the corner of Fifth and Columbia Sts., in the heart of the village
☎*636-2244*
The King Edward is a perpetually busy cafeteria, where truckers, miners and tourists start arriving early for breakfast.

Northern British Columbia

Tour G:
The Yellowhead Highway

Prince George

See "Tour B: To the Alaska Highway, p 260."

Smithers

 **Aspen Restaurant**
$$$
west of town on Hwy. 16, inside the Aspen Motor Inn
☎*847-4551*
The Aspen, which serves good, fresh seafood, is highly reputed in Smithers.

Terrace

White Spot
$$$
4620 Lakelse Ave.
☎*638-7977*
The White Spot is located in the same building as the Coast Inn of the West. It is one of a chain of restaurants in the province, known for their sandwiches, salads and burgers.

Lakelse Lake Lodge
$$$
on Hwy. 37, halfway between Terrace and Kitimat
☎*798-9541*
The owner, Emmanuel, a Frenchman from the Basque Country, prepares light dishes using local game, trout and salmon. The atmosphere is pleasant and convivial.

Kitimat

The Chalet Restaurant
$$$$
852 Tsimshian
☎*632-2662*
The Chalet offers a varied menu, in keeping with Kitimat's cosmopolitan character. It serves generous breakfasts in the morning.

Prince Rupert

 Breakers Pub
$$$
117 George Hill's Way
☎*624-5990*
The Breakers Pub, located in the pretty neighbourhood of Cow Bay, serves excellent fish and chips and well prepared fish dishes on a lovely terrace with a view of the port. This is a very pleasant place to spend the afternoon. A wide choice of draft beer is also available.

Smile's Seafood Café
$$$
in the heart of the Cow Bay area
☎*624-3072*
Smile's is the most highly reputed place in town for seafood and fish, with good reason. The portions are generous, and the prices relatively modest.

The Crest Motor Hotel
$$$
222 First Ave.
☎*624-6771*
The Crest Motor Hotel has two good restaurants. The first, something like a snack-bar, serves tasty sandwiches, while the other, more classic in style, prepares delicious and very elaborate dishes.

Tour H: The Queen
Charlotte Islands
(Haida Gwaii)

Queen Charlotte City

Sea Raven Restaurant
$$$
3301 Third Ave.
☎*559-4423*
The Sea Raven is a very good seafood restaurant with a varied menu. The daily special is always well-prepared.

The Oceana
$$$
Third Ave.
☎*559-8683*
The Oceana is a top-notch Chinese restaurant with a pretty view of the strait. The

dishes are well-prepared and served in generous portions.

Tlell

Tlell River House
$$$
Beltush Rd.
☎*557-4211*
The Tlell River House serves gourmet North American dishes. It is one of the finest restaurants on the island. Watch out, though: the prices add up quickly!

Masset

 **Singing Surf Inn
Restaurant**
$$
1504 Old Beach Rd.
☎*626-3318*
The Singing Surf Inn restaurant is an institution in Masset. You won't find gourmet cuisine here, but the setting and the view are pleasant.

Entertainment

Bars and Nightclubs

Wide open spaces are, of course, a big part of travelling in Northern British Columbia. Nevertheless, after a long day of exploring, there is nothing like relaxing to some music with a nice cold drink, at least for some anyhow. The bar situation is limited at best, depending of course on where you end up; danceclubs are nonexistant.

There are, however, friendly local bars, usually attached to a hotel or restaurant. Those attached to hotels are often called lounges, and are the gathering spots of local townspeople. It is not uncommon to find yourself in a discussion with a gold-digger, trapper or fisher at these places.

Tour B:
To the Alaska Highway

Dawson Creek

Alaska Hotel
10209 10th St.
☎*782-2625*
The best pub in town, where
rock, country and blues are
played all weekend long, is
located in the lobby of the
Alaska Hotel.

Tour D:
The Alaska Highway

Watson Lake (Yukon)

1940s Canteen Show
every day at 8pm, Jun to Aug
behind the signpost forest
☎*(867) 536-7781*
The musical revue 1940s
Canteen Show takes you back
to the days of the construction
of the Alaska Highway.

Cultural Activities

Tour B:
To the Alaska Highway

Prince George

Prince George is the cultural
capital of the north. It has its
own symphony orchestra and
many theatre companies.
Shows are only presented in
the winter. When the weather
is nice people tend to prefer
outdoor activities.

**Prince George Symphony
Orchestra**
*performance season from Sep
to May*
☎*562-0800*
www.pgso.com
Call for program information.

**Prince George Theatre
Workshop**
*performance season from Sep
to May*
☎*563-8401*
www.pgtw.bc.ca
The Prince George Theatre
Workshop has been active in
Prince George for 30 years. It

offers comedy, drama and
classic theatre productions.

Theatre NorthWest
118-101 North Tabor Blvd.
☎*563-6969*
www.theatrenorthwest.com
Theatre NorthWest is a professional theatre company
offering quality plays with both
Canadian and international
performers. Contact the company for program details.

Calendar of Events

February

The **Prince George Iceman**
*(Prince George, ☎564-1552,
www.jumbe.com/pgiceman.
htm)*, is a series of events
including an 8km cross-country ski run, over 10km on foot,
then 5km of ice skating and
finally, an 800m swim.

Mardi Gras of Winter *(Prince
George, ☎564-3737, www.
city.pg.bc.ca/wintercities/events.
html)* is an important winter
celebration with over a hundred organized events.

March

Prince George Music Festival
(www.pgmusicfestival.com)
features all the big names in
the Prince George music
scene. Organ, brass, string
instruments and singing.

May

Northern Children's Festival
*(Prince George, ☎562 4882,
www.princegeorge.com/cncf/)*
is an impressive event devoted
to childhood. Thousands of
families head to Fort George
Park for performances by
international artists. Entrance is
free.

Mile 0 Celebration *(third
week, Dawson Creek, ☎782-
5804)*

June

The **Prince George Rodeo**
*(Exhibition Grounds, Prince
George)* is really worth the trip,
particularly if you've never
been to a rodeo. You can also
attend an air show put on by
parachutists, as well as square-
dancing and country-music
shows.

Hudson's Hope Rodeo *(first
week, Hudson's Hope, ☎783-
9901)*

July

Mackenzie, Pouce Coupe,
Hudson's Hope, Fort St. John
and Fort Nelson all host
Canada Day celebrations on
the First.

If you are so inclined, you can
participate in the **Prince
George Triathlon** *(Prince
George, ☎964-3936)*, a competition that consists of a 1.5km
swim, a 40km bicycle race and
a 10km run.

August

**Word's Invitational Gold
Panning Championships** *(first
week of August)* Try your hand
at gold panning, play a bame
of Bingo, enjoy a barbecue or
just saunter on the markets
and enjoy the parade.

International Food Festival
(Prince George, ☎563-4096).
At this festival you can sample
specialties from all over the
world. Delicious!

Prince George Exhibition
(Prince George, ☎563-4096) is
a big event in this city. It's an
agricultural and food fair also
touching on the home and
gardening. The lumberjack
show is always a big hit with
kids.

Rodeo, Fall Fair Stampede
*(second week, Dawson
Creek,☎782-9595)*

Riverboat Days *(first week of
August; Terrace; ☎635-4997)*.

**Northern
British Columbia**

Salmon barbecue, fireworks, slingers race, bed race and parade.

October

Oktoberfest is an important tradition in Prince George's German community. You can dance to the sounds of "oompah-pah" music or just enjoy the beer.

Shopping

Tour B:
To the Alaska Highway

Dawson Creek

Make sure to stop at the **Dawson Creek Farmer's**

Market *(Sat 8am to 3pm)* to sample the local produce. It is located near the NAR Park, right behind the sign for the Alaska Highway.

Tour D:
The Alaska Highway

From early May to early October there are **farmer's markets** every Saturday in Chetwynd and Fort St. John.

Tour H: The Queen
Charlotte Islands
(Haida Gwaii)

Tlell

Sitka Studio *(at the end of Richardson Rd.,* ☎*557-4241)* is a small craft and art gallery open every day. It also has books.

Old Masset

Haida Arts and Jewellery *(every day 11am to 5pm)*, with its traditional architecture and two totem poles marking the entrance, offers a fine selection of art.

Grizzly bear

The Rocky Mountains

In Canada, the term

"Rockies" designates a chain of high Pacific mountains reaching elevations of between 3,000 and 4,000m. These mountains consist of crystalline and metamorphous rock that has been thrust upwards by collision between the Pacific tectonic plate and the North American continental plate, and then later carved out and eroded by glaciers.

The mountain chain runs east-west along the border between Alberta and British Columbia, and covers the Yukon territory. This vast region, which stretches more than 22,000km², is known the world over for its natural beauty and welcomes some six million visitors each year. Exceptional mountain scenery, wild rivers sure to thrill whitewater rafting enthusiasts, still lakes whose waters vary from emerald green to turquoise blue, parks abounding in all sorts of wildlife, world-renowned ski centres and quality resort hotels all come together to make for an unforgettable vacation.

Geography

The history of the Rockies begins about 600 million years ago, when a deep sea covered the area where the mountains now stand. Bit by bit, layers of sediment, including clay shale, silt-laden rocks, sand and conglomerates from the erosion of the Canadian Shield to the east, accumulated at the bottom of this sea. These sedimentary layers were up to 20km deep in some places, and under the pressure of their own weight they crystallized to form a rocky platform. This explains the presence of marine fossils like shells and seaweed in many cliff faces; the Burgess Shale in Yoho National Park, declared a UNESCO World Heritage Site in 1981, is one of the most important fossil sites in the world with the fossilized remains of some 140 species. About 160 million years ago, following a shift of the tectonic plates, the earth's forces began to exert a tremendous amount of pressure on the sedimentary rock, compressing, folding and pushing it upward until it finally broke apart. The western chains emerged first (Yoho and Kootenay National Parks) and then the principal chains (the highest including the immense ice fields and Mount Robson, the highest point in the Rockies at 3,954m) straddling the Continental Divide, the line that separates the drainage basins of North America. A few million years later, the chains next to the prairies emerged, and then, after a final terrestrial upheaval, the rolling foothills of the Rockies. The effect of the earth's forces on this ancient platform of sedimentary rock are evident everywhere. The rippling of the rock can be seen on mountain faces; when the movement has resulted in the rock forming an "A" geologists refer to it as "anticlinal", and when it forms a "U", as "synclinal".

Of course, the Rocky Mountains were further shaped by other forces. The next step was the extreme erosion caused by constant battering by wind, rain, snow and ice, and by freezing and thawing.

Initially, water was the most important factor in the transformation of the Rockies' strata. One need only consider that 7,500km^3 of water fall on Earth each year to imagine the enormous destructive potential of the waterways that would result from that much rain. A constant flow of water can erode even the hardest rock, acting like sandpaper. The grains of sand broken loose from the rock and transported by the torrential waters of mountain streams scrape the rocky bottom; gradually polishing the surface and infiltrating crevices. These slowly get bigger and bigger until huge pieces of rock break off or enormous cavities are hollowed out like those in the Maligne River Canyon, which are called "potholes". When the rock is of a more crumbly variety, or even water soluble like limestone, the rain and snow easily carve out deep fissures. The mountains finally lost their primitive look thanks to this slow but unrelenting erosion, as the water eventually worked its way through several layers of rock, forming deep V-shaped valleys.

Glaciers

About two million years ago, during the first ice age, a huge, moving ice field covered more than one-fifth of the surface of the earth, through which only the highest summits of the Rockies emerged. The ice receded and advanced over this region a total of three times.

The glaciers and their runoff radically changed the landscape of the Rockies, breaking off the upper portions of the rock along the edges, and reshaping the rock over which they advanced. Contrary to the water, which bored deep into the earth, the glaciers altered the mountains in depth and width, creating huge U-shaped valleys known as glacial troughs. The icefields region is an excellent example of this, with its wide, steep-sided valleys. The bigger the glacier the more destructive it was to the mountain and the deeper and wider the valley it created. In the icefield region, visitors will see what are termed suspended valleys, which result from the erosion caused by a small glacier that attaches itself to a larger mass of ice. The valley left behind by the smaller glacier is not nearly as deep as the one left by the larger glacier, and appears to be suspended once the ice has melted; an example is the Maligne Valley, which is suspended 120m above the Athabasca Valley.

Flora

The forests of the Rocky Mountains are essentially made up of **lodgepole pine**. Natives used these trees to build tepees because they grow very straight, are fairly tall and have little foliage. Ironically, forest fires guarantee the trees' survival. Heat causes the resin in the pine cones to melt slowly, releasing the seeds that are held within. The seeds are then dispersed by the wind, and the forest essentially rises from its own ashes. If such fires were completely eliminated, the lodgepole pines would get old

and the forest would be taken over by other vegetation and die, which would in turn force out the moose. From time to time, therefore, Parks Canada sets controlled fires, and the burnt-out trunks of lodgepole pine are a common sight along the roads.

The **aspen** is the most common broad-leaved tree in the forests of the Rocky Mountains. Its trunk is white and its leaves round. The slightest breeze makes the leaves tremble, and for this is it often called a trembling aspen.

The **Englemann spruce** is found at high altitudes, near the tree line. It is the first tree to grow at these altitudes on the gravel of ancient moraines. This tree has a long lifespan; some near the Athabasca glacier are more than 700 years old. It generally has a twisted trunk due to strong winds that sweep across the mountainsides. In valleys, the spruce can measure up to 20m.

The **Douglas fir**, found north of Jasper, grows in forests at the bottom of the valleys of the Rockies.

The wildflower season does not last very long in alpine regions. The flowering time, production of seeds and reproduction are a veritable race against the clock during the few short weeks of summer. Their perennial nature, however, helps them to survive. In fact, perennial plants store everything they need for new shoots, leaves and flowers in their roots and rhizomes or in the previous year's bulb. Before the snow has even melted, they are ready to emerge from the earth. The secret of alpine zone flowers lies in the fact that they remain dormant all winter and then take full advantage of the humidity and strong sunshine of summer.

The **western anemone** is a common sight in mountainous zones. Though it is not common to see it in bloom, it is easy to spot in summer, when its stem has a downy covering. Towards the end of summer, the seeds, with their long, feather-like appendages, are carried off by the wind, assuring the reproduction of the flower.

Heather has also adapted well to the rigours of the alpine zone. Its hardy leaves help it to store energy and spare it from having to produce new leaves every year. Among the many types of heather common to this region are **pink heather**, which has little red flowers, **yellow heather** with white flowers and yellow sepals, and **purple heather** with white, bell-shaped flowers and reddish-brown sepals. Purple heather resembles a cushiony sponge and grows at the tree line on mountain slopes long ago abandoned by glaciers.

The **Indian paintbrush** varies from pale yellow to vibrant red. This flower is easy to spot since it is actually its leaves that are coloured, while the flower lies tucked among the upper folds of the stem.

The **bluebell** is a tiny blue flower that grows close to the ground in gravel or sand near water.

Fauna

The **black bear** is the smallest bear in North America. As its name suggests, it is usually black, although there are some with dark brown fur. Its head is quite high and the line between its shoulders and its hindquarters is much straighter than on a grizzly. The male weighs between 170 and 350 kg and can grow to up to 168 cm long and 97 cm at the withers. The female is one-third smaller. These bears are

found in dense forests at lower altitudes and in clearings. They are mammals and feed on roots, wild berries and leaves.

The **grizzly**'s colouring varies between black and blond and its fur often appears to be greying, hence its name. Larger and heavier than its cousin the black bear, the grizzly measures 110 cm at the withers, and up to 2 m when standing on its hind legs. Its average weight is about 200 kg, though some have been known to weigh up to 450 kg. The grizzly can be distinguished from the black bear by the large hump at its shoulders. This hump is actually the muscle mass of its imposing front paws. Its hindquarters are also lower than its shoulders, and it carries its head fairly low. Despite these differences, it is often difficult to tell a young grizzly from a black bear. Take extreme caution if you encounter a bear, as these animals are unpredictable and can be very dangerous.

Cougars (also called pumas or mountains lions) are the largest of the Felidae, or cat family, that inhabit the Rockies and Kananaskis Country, where about one hundred have been counted. These large cats weigh from 72 to 103 kg (45 kg for females), and when hungry can attack pet dogs

and even humans. Unfortunately, these nocturnal felines can rarely be spotted.

Lynxes are also members of the cat family, but are much smaller than pumas, weighing about 11 kg. Their bob tails and pointed ears topped with little tufts of longer fur make them easy to identify. Also nocturnal, they are hard to spot.

Cervidae: The Rockies are a veritable paradise for these animals, which can be seen in great numbers. It is not uncommon to spot **moose**, those huge mammals that can weigh up to 500 kg and whose characteristic antlers are large and impressive. **Mule-deer**, **white-tailed deer**, **mountain caribou** and **moose** can often be spotted along the highways.

Bighorn sheep are not cervidae, but rather horned ungulates, or hoofed animals. The difference between these two families is that ungulates do not lose their horns every year, but rather keep them for their whole life. Bighorn sheep are easy to spot thanks to their curved horns. They are a common sight along the road. They are quite tame and will readily approach people in the hopes of being fed. Under no circumstances should you give them any food since they will quickly develop the bad habit of approaching people and thus run the risk of being killed by the many cars that travel park roads.

Mountain goats also belong to the horned ungulate family. Their numbers are low, and they are rarely

Black bear

spotted, except in alpine areas. They are recognizable by their long white fur and two small, black pointed horns. They are very timid and will not tolerate being approached.

Coyote

Wolves, **coyotes** and **foxes** can also be seen in the parks, especially in the forests of Kananaskis Country.

Birds: The **bald eagle**, **golden eagle**, **great-horned owl** and several **falcon** species are among the birds of prey found in the Rockies.

Ptarmigans resemble chickens. Their colouring changes with seasons, varying between a white-speckled brown in the summer to snowy white in the winter. **Grouse** are also common.

Two other noteworthy, though sometimes annoying, birds are the **grey jay** and **Clark's nutcracker**, who won't hesitate to swipe the food right off your plate the minute you decide to have a picnic in the forest. Clark's nutcracker has grey breast plumage, black and white wings and a relatively long beak. The grey jay's plumage is dark and its beak much shorter.

Lastly, two types of pesky insects abound during certain seasons in the Rockies. First the **mosquito**, of which there are no less than 28 different species, all equally exasperating to human beings. Arm yourself for an encounter with these critters, either with insect repellent or mosquito

netting. Between the months of April and June, another insect, the **Anderson tick**, makes life in the Rockies more of an adventure. These should be avoided but not to the point of panic (on the rare occasions when it is carrying Rocky Mountain fever it can cause death). The tick is found in the dry grassy parts of the Rockies. Regularly check your clothes and yourself if you are walking in these areas in the spring. If you find one, slowly remove it (burning it does not work) and see a doctor at the first sign of headache, numbness or pain.

History

The presence of human beings in this area goes back some 11,000 years, but the arrival of the first whites dates from the era of the fur trade, towards the middle of the 18th century. The Stoney Aboriginals, who knew the region well, served as guides to these new arrivals, showing them mountain passes that would play an important role in the fur trade.

No less than 80° of longitude separate the most easterly point of Newfoundland and the Queen Charlotte Islands in the west. This immense territory, however, had only about four million inhabitants by 1850. To overcome the threat posed by the American giant to the south, which was richer and more populous, and following political and economic crises in 1837 under the government of William Mackenzie, a desire emerged to establish a more efficient organization in the form of Canadian Confederation, eventually leading to the 1867 vote on the British North America Act. This new Canadian state, which went from

colony to British Dominion, consisted originally of four provinces, Ontario, Québec, Nova Scotia and New Brunswick, all located in the east. Therefore, when the United States purchased Alaska from Russia for seven million dollars in March of 1867, British Columbia found itself in a precarious position, hemmed in on two sides by the United States. Furthermore, British Columbia was cut off geographically from the Canadian Confederation, such that when delegates from this province wanted to get to Ottawa they first had to travel to San Francisco by boat and then take the new transcontinental train line through Chicago to Toronto. Before Canada could be united, therefore, British Columbia demanded an end to this isolation and the construction of a road connecting the province with the rest of the Confederation. To its great surprise, the Macdonald government offered even more, the construction of a railway! Linking the Maritime provinces in the east to Victoria was indeed a prodigious feat and certainly an unprecedented technological and financial challenge for such a young and sparsely populated country. Transportation creates commerce, and such a vast nation clearly could not grow and prosper without relying on modern modes of communication. It had to establish commercial stability despite the harsh realities of winter, which slowed and occasionally immobilized ground and maritime transportation, thereby isolating entire regions of this huge country.

The economy of the Rocky Mountains took off following the construction of the railway, as prospectors, alpinists, geologists and all sorts of visitors joined the railway agents, participating in some of the most memorable moments in the region's history.

Economy

"If we can't export the scenery, we'll import the tourists!" This statement by William C. Van Horne, vice-president of the Canadian Pacific Railway, pretty well sums up the situation. The economy of the Canadian Rockies, in the five national parks of Alberta and British Columbia, relies almost solely on tourism. The preservation of these areas is assured by their status as national parks, which also guarantees the complete absence of any type of development, be it mining or forestry related. In fact, coal, copper, lead and silver mines (see Silver City, p 278) as well as ochre deposits (see Paint Pots, p 287) were abandoned and villages were moved in order to return the mountains to their original state and to stop human industry from marring all this natural beauty.

Finding Your Way Around

Getting to the Rockies

Very reasonable fees are charged to gain access to the national parks of the Canadian Rockies, and these must be paid at the entrance gate of each park *($5 for one day, $35 per year)*.

Up until recently the fees only applied to cars entering the parks, but from now on every person must pay an individual fee. This allows Parks Canada to earn extra revenue from travellers arriving by foot, bike, train or bus, which contributes to maintaining park facilities.

Parks Canada also charges travellers wishing to practise certain activities (excursions of more than one day, rock-climbing, interpretive activities...) and for the use of certain facilities, like hot springs.

A complete list of the fees for each year is available at park entrance, at the parks' information centres (see addresses and telephone numbers below) or by calling ☎800-651-7959.

By Plane

Most people fly into the airports in Calgary, Edmonton or Vancouver and then drive to the national and provincial parks.

By Bus

Tour A: Banff National Park

The **Bus Station** *(☎762-6767 or 800-661-8747)*, located on the way into Banff on Mount Norquay Road, at the corner of Gopher Road, is used by **Greyhound** *(☎800-661-8747, www.greyhound.com)* and **Brewster Transportation and Tours** *(☎403-762-6767 or 800-661-1152, www.brewster.ca)*. This latter company takes care of local transportation and organizes trips to the icefields and Jasper.

Tour C: Jasper National Park

The **Greyhound Bus Station** *(☎780-852-3926)* is located right in the middle of Jasper, on Connaught Drive. **Heritage Cabs** *(☎780-852-5558)* serves the area and **Jasper Taxi** (780-852-3600).

By Train

Tour A: Banff National Park

The **Rocky Mountaineer Train Station** is right next to the bus station on Railway Drive.

Taxis are available for the trip downtown.

Legion Taxi
☎*(403) 762-3353*

Mountain Taxi and Tours
☎*(403) 762-3351*

Taxi Taxi and Tours
☎*(403) 762-3111*

Banff Taxi and Tours and Limousine
☎*(403) 762-4444*

Tour C: Jasper National Park

Via
☎*800-561-8630*
www.viarail.ca
The train station is located next to the Greyhound bus terminal.

By Car

Because of the hemmed-in location of the Rockies, driving is the most practical means of transportation here. The roads throughout this mountainous region are generally in good condition considering the winds, snow and ice that quickly deteriorate infrastructure. Driving along these winding roads does, however, require extra attention and caution, especially in winter. Be sure to stop regularly to rest and, of course, to admire the spectacular scenery. Also, beware of animals crossing roads.

It is important to check road conditions before heading off in the winter, as heavy snowfalls often lead to road closures. Furthermore, your car should also be equipped with snow tires, studded tires or in some cases chains. Generally, however, the major arteries are open year-round, while secondary roads are often used as cross-country ski trails in the winter.

For information on road conditions, you can call:

Banff National Park

The Alberta Motor Association (AMA)
☎(780) 471-6056
www.trans.gov.ab.ca

Jasper National Park

Weather service
☎(780) 852-3185

Park Road Report
☎(780) 852-4444

Yoho National Park

Tourist office
☎(250) 343-6100

Kootenay National Park

Park Office
☎(250) 347-9615

This kind of information is also available at the entrance gates of the national parks and in all local offices of Parks Canada.

This chapter is divided into five tours:

Tour A: Banff National Park ★★★

Tour B: The Icefields Parkway ★★★

Tour C: Jasper National Park ★★★

Tour D: Yoho and Kootenay National Parks ★★

Tour E: Kananaskis Country ★★

Tour A: Banff National Park

Banff National Park is the most well-known and visited of Canadian parks. It is incredibly beautiful, but its renown also makes it one of the busiest parks, overrun with visitors from all over the world. Its main town, Banff, has grown as a result of tourism and is home to a large number of

shops, hotels and restaurants of all different types.

This tour starts in the small town of Canmore, located only about 20km from the entrance to the park, then leads to Banff on the Trans-Canada Highway or on the Bow Valley Parkway (Hwy 1A), which runs parallel to the former. The tour weaves its way around Banff town site and ends up in the village of Lake Louise, known the world over for its exquisite, shimmering, emerald-green lake.

Tour B: The Icefields Parkway

This tour starts in the village of Lake Louise and snakes its way through Banff National Park on Hwy. 93. It allows you to discover some of the highest summits of the Canadian Rockies before ending up in the immense Columbia Icefield. Stunning landscapes line the whole route, and by stopping at the various lookout points along the way you'll find yourself journeying through the geological history of these mountains and valleys and reliving the experiences of the adventurers who discovered this region. The focal point of this tour is the Athabasca Glacier, at the entrance to Jasper National Park. With the proper equipment and an understanding of safety techniques for hiking on ice, adventurers can set off from the Columbia Icefields information centre to conquer the Athabasca, Dome and Stutfield glaciers.

Tour C: Jasper National Park

This tour explores the surroundings of Jasper, the central point of the national park of the same name, before heading northeast on Hwy. 16

to the small town of Hinton, located about 30km from the entrance to Jasper National Park.

Tour D: Kootenay and Yoho National Parks

Sometimes referred to as the Golden Triangle, this tour starts out from Castle Mountain in Banff National Park, then heads down Hwy. 93, which passes through Kootenay National Park to Radium Hot Springs. The tour then heads back up the valley of the Columbia River towards Golden and then on to Lake Louise through Yoho National Park.

Tour E: Kananaskis Country

Due to its extensive facilities for travellers, Canmore is the obvious focal point of this tour. It is therefore from this little town that you will discover Kananaskis Country. Though its mountainous scenery is slightly less spectacular than that of the Rocky Mountain national parks, this region nevertheless offers nature lovers beautiful hiking trails without the hordes of tourists that invade Banff and Jasper.

Practical Information

The parks in the Rocky Mountains straddle two Canadian provinces, Alberta and British Columbia, which have two different area codes.

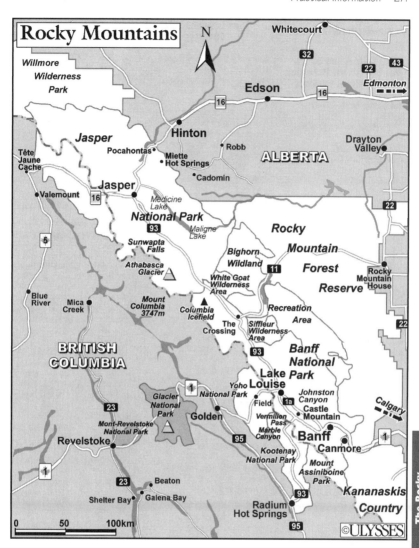

Rocky Mountains

N

Willmore Wilderness Park

Whitecourt

32

22 43

Edmonton

Edson

16

Hinton

Jasper

Pocahontas
Robb

Miette Hot Springs

Drayton Valley

ALBERTA

Tête Jaune Cache

Cadomin

Jasper

Valemount

16

Medicine Lake

22

National Park

93

Maligne Lake

Rocky

Sunwapta Falls

Bighorn Wildland

Mountain

Athabasca Glacier

White Goat Wilderness Area

11

Forest

Rocky Mountain House

5

Blue River

Mica Creek

Mount Columbia 3747m

Columbia Icefield

The Crossing

Siffleur Wilderness Area

Reserve

Recreation Area

22

BRITISH COLUMBIA

93

Banff National Park

Lake Louise

Yoho National Park

Johnston Canyon

Calgary

Glacier National Park

Field

1a

Castle Mountain

Golden

Vermilion Pass

Mont-Revelstoke National Park

23

95

Marble Canyon

Banff

1

Revelstoke

Kootenay National Park

Canmore

Mount Assiniboine Park

Kananaskis

1

23

Beaton

Shelter Bay

Galena Bay

93

Radium Hot Springs

Country

95

0   50   100km

©ULYSSES

The Rocky Mountains

The area code is ☎403 for Alberta, except for Jasper, which is ☎780, and ☎250 for British Columbia.

Parks Canada Offices

Information about the different parks and regions is available

through the offices of Parks Canada (www.parks canada.gc.ca) and the tourist information offices.

Banff National Park
224 Banff Ave., Box 900
Banff, Alberta, T0L 0C0
☎(403) 762-1550

Jasper National Park
607 Connaught Drive, Box 10
Jasper, Alberta, T0E 1E0
☎(780) 852-6176

Kootenay National Park
Box 220, Radium Hot Springs
BC, V0A 1M0
☎(250) 347-9615

Tourist Information

Tour A and B:
Banff National Park and
The Icefields Parkway

Banff/Lake Louise Tourism Bureau
224 Banff Ave., PO Box 1298, Banff, AB, T1L 1B3
☎*(403) 762-8421*
www.banfflakelouise.com

Lake Louise Visitor Information Centre
Samson Mall, PO Box 213, Lake Louise, AB, T0L 1E0
☎*(403) 522-3833*
www.lakelouise.com

Tour C:
Jasper National Park

Jasper Tourism & Commerce
500 Connaught Dr. or 409 Patricia St., Jasper, AB, T0E 1E0
☎*(780) 852-3858 or (780) 852-6176*
www.jaspercanadianrockies. com

Ski Jasper
PO Box 98, Jasper, AB, T0E 1E0
☎*(780) 852-5247 or 800-473-8135*
www.skijaspercanada.com

Tour D: Kootenay and
Yoho National Parks

Radium Hot Springs Chamber of Commerce
PO Box 225, Radium Hot Springs, BC, V0A 1M0
☎*(250) 347-9331*
www.rhs.bc.ca

Golden and District Chamber of Commerce and Travel Information Centre
500-10th Avenue North, Golden, BC, V0A 1H0
☎*(250) 344-7125 or 800-622-4653*

Field
at the entrance of town
☎*(250) 343-6783*

Tour E:Kananaskis
Country

Kananaskis Country Head Office
Suite 200, 3115 12th St. NE., Calgary, AB, T2E 7J2
☎*(403) 297-3362*
This office offers basic information only: for more detailed information contact the Barrier Lake Information Centre (see below).

Tourism Canmore
2801 Bow Valley Trail, Canmore, AB, T1W 2B3
☎*866-226-6673*
www.tourismcanmore.com

Bow Valley Provincial Park Office
PO Box 280, Exshaw, AB, T0L 2C0, (located near the town of Seebe)
☎*(403) 673-3663*

Peter Lougheed Provincial Park Visitor Information Centre
PO Box 130, Kananaskis, AB, T0L 2H0, (located 3.6 km from Kananaskis Trail, Hwy. 40)
☎*(403) 591-6322*

Barrier Lake Information Centre
PO Box 280, Exshaw, AB, T0L 2C0, (Hwy. 40, 7km south of the Trans Canada Hwy.)
☎*(403) 673-3985*

Elbow Valley Information Centre
☎*(403) 949-4261*

Internet

Tour A: Banff National
Park

Cyber Web Café *($8/hr, $5/hr after 9:30pm; every day 10am to midnight; 215 Banff Ave., basement of Sundance Mall,* ☎ *762-9226).*

Tour B:
Jasper National Park

The two places in Jasper where you can connect to the Internet are across from each

other. **Soft Rock Internet Cafe** *(8$/hr; 632 Connaught,* ☎*852-5850)* also offers light snacks (see p 316). **More Than Mail** *($6/hr; 620 Connaught Dr.,* ☎ *780-852-3151)* is a store that also offers fax, telephone and postal services.

Exploring

Tour A:
Banff National Park

The history of the **Canadian Pacific** railway is inextricably linked to that of the national parks of the Rocky Mountains. In November of 1883, three workmen abandoned the railway construction site in the Bow Valley and headed towards Banff in search of gold. When they reached Sulphur Mountain, however, brothers William and Tom McCardell and Frank McCabe discovered sulphur hot springs instead. They took a concession in order to turn a profit with the springs, but were unable to counter the various land rights disputes that followed. The series of events drew the attention of the federal government, which sent out an agent to control the concession. The renown of these hot springs had already spread from railway workers to the vice-president of Canadian Pacific, who came here in 1885 and declared that the springs were certainly worth a million dollars. Realizing the enormous economic potential of the Sulphur Mountain hot springs, which were already known as **Cave and Basin**, the federal government quickly purchased the rights to the concession from the three workers and consolidated its property rights on the site by creating a nature reserve the

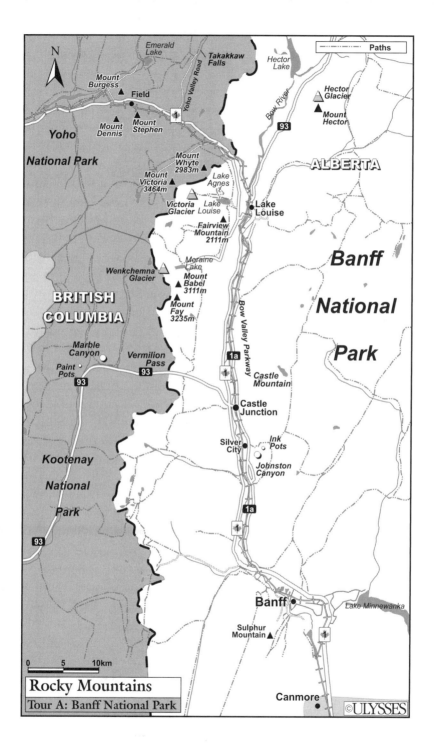

Rocky Mountains
Tour A: Banff National Park

©ULYSSES

same year. Two years later, in 1887, the reserve became the first national park in Canada and was named Rockies Park, and then Banff National Park. In those days there was no need to protect the still abundant wildlife, and the mindset of government was not yet preoccupied with the preservation of natural areas. On the contrary, the government's main concern was to find an economically exploitable site with which to replenish the state coffers, in need of a boost after the construction of the railroad. To complement the springs which were already in vogue with wealthy tourists in search of spa treatments, tourist facilities and luxury hotels were built. Thus was born the town of Banff, today a world-class tourist mecca.

★★★
Banff Townsite

At first glance, Banff looks like a small town made up essentially of hotels, motels, souvenir shops and restaurants all lined up along Banff Avenue. The town has much more to offer, however. The best spot to start your visit of Banff is at the **Banff/Lake Louise Tourism Bureau** (see p 272). If you are visiting Banff in the summer, you can pick up a calendar of events for the Banff Arts Festival. The offices of Parks Canada are located in the same building.

A bit farther along Banff Avenue, stop in at the **Natural History Museum** ★ *($1.50; Jun to Sep 10am to 5pm; 108 Banff Ave., ☎403-762-4652)*. This museum retraces the history of the Rockies and displays various rocks, fossils and dinosaur tracks, as well as several plant species that

you're likely to encounter while hiking.

The view down Banff Avenue ends on the other side of the bridge, at the famous **Cascade Gardens** and the administrative offices of the park. The park itself offers a wonderful view of Cascade Mountain.

The **Whyte Museum of the Canadian Rockies** ★★★ *($6; every day 10am to 5pm; 111 Bear St., ☎403-762-2291)* relates the history of the Canadian Rockies. You'll discover archaeological findings from ancient Kootenay and Stoney Aboriginal settlements, including clothing, tools and jewellery. Museum-goers will also learn the history of certain local heros and famous explorers like Bill Peyto, as well as that of the railway and the town of Banff. Personal objects and clothing that once belonged to notable local figures are exhibited. The

---

● ATTRACTIONS

1.	Natural History Museum	7.	Banff Upper Hot Springs
2.	Cascade Gardens	8.	Banff Gondola
3.	Whyte Museum of the Canadian Rockies	9.	Bow River Falls
4.	Banff Public Library	10.	Banff Centre
5.	Luxton Museum	11.	Hoodoos Lookout
6.	Cave and Basin		

○ ACCOMMODATIONS

1.	Banff Alpine Centre Hostel	16.	King Edward Hotel
2.	Banff Caribou Lodge	17.	Mount Royal Hotel
3.	Banff Rocky Mountain Resort	18.	Norquay's Timberline Inn
4.	Banff Voyager Inn	19.	Pension Tannanhof
5.	Bow View Motor Lodge	20.	Red Carpet Inn
6.	Brewster's Mountain Lodge	21.	Rimrock Resort Hotel
7.	Cascade Court Bed and Breakfast	22.	Rundle Stone Lodge (R)
8.	Douglas Fir Resort & Chalets	23.	Traveller's Inn
9.	Fairmont Banff Spring Hotel	24.	Tunnel Mountain I
10.	Global Village Backpackers	25.	Tunnel Mountain II
11.	High Country Inn	26.	Tunnel Mountain Resort
12.	Holiday Lodge	27.	Tunnel Mountain Trailer Campground
13.	Homestead Inn	28.	Two Jack Lake Campgrounds
14.	Inns of Banff, Swiss Village and Rundle Manor		
15.	Johnston Canyon Campground	(R)	establishment with restaurant (see description)

● RESTAURANTS

1.	Balkan Restaurant	8.	Magpie & Stump
2.	Barpa Bill's Souvlaki	9.	Rose and Crown
3.	Beaujolais	10.	Saltlik
4.	Caboose	11.	St. James Gate
5.	Grizzly House Fondue Dining	12.	Sukiyaki House
6.	Joe BTFSPLK's	13.	Sunfood Café
7.	Korean Restaurant	14.	Ticino

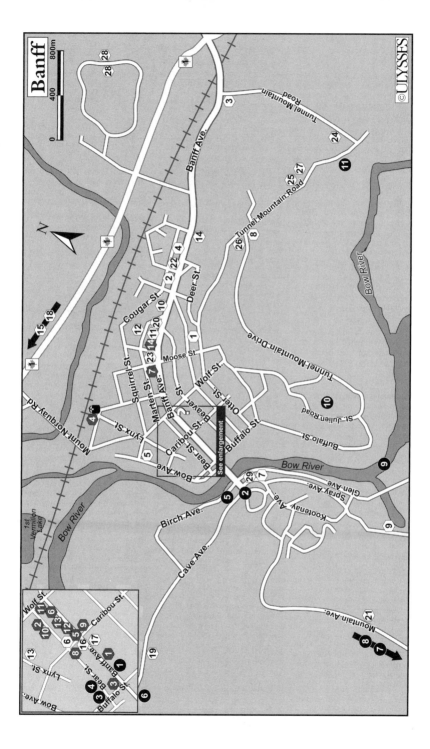

Banff

0 400 800m

N

© ULYSSES

museum also houses a painting gallery and extensive archives, in case you want to know more about the region. Right next to the Whyte Museum is the **Banff Public Library** *(Mon-Thu 11am to 6pm, Fri 10am to 6pm, Sat 11am to 6pm, Sun 1pm to 5pm, closed Sun from late May to early Sep; 101 Bear Ave., corner Buffalo St., ☎403-762-2661).*

The **Luxton Museum** ★★ *($6; Jun to Oct 10am to 6pm, mid-Oct to Jun 1pm to 5pm; 1 Birch Ave., on the other side of the Bow River Bridge, ☎403-762-2388)* is dedicated to the lives of the aboriginal peoples of the northern plains and the Canadian Rockies. Their way of life, rituals and hunting techniques are explained, and various tools they used are displayed. The museum is accessible to the disabled, and guided tours are available but must be arranged by calling the museum ahead of time.

Cave and Basin ★★★ *($4; mid-May to end Sep every day 9am to 6pm; Oct to mid-May Mon-Fri 11am to 4pm, Sat-Sun 9:30am to 5pm; at the end of Cave Ave., ☎403-762-1556)* is now a national historic site. These springs were the origin of the vast network of Canadian national parks (see p 272). However, despite extremely costly renovations to the basins in 1984, the pool has been closed for security reasons since 1992. The sulphur content of the water actually deteriorates the cement, and the pool's paving is badly damaged in some places. You can still visit the cave into which three Canadian Pacific workers descended in search of the springs, and smell the distinctive odour of sulphurous gas, caused by bacteria that oxydize the sulphates in the water before it spurts out of the earth. The original basin is still there, but swimming is no longer permitted. If you watch the water, you'll see the

Why is the Water Hot?

By penetrating into fissures in the rock, water makes its way under the western slope of Sulphur Mountain, absorbing calcium, sulphur and other minerals along the way.

At a certain depth, the heat of the earth's centre warms the water as it is being forced up by pressure through a fault in the northeastern slope of the mountain.

As the water flows up to the surface, the calcium settles around the source in pale-coloured layers that eventually harden into rock, called "tufa".

These formations can be seen on the mountainside, at the small exterior spring 20m from the entrance to the facilities.

sulphur gas bubbling to the surface, while at the bottom of the basin you can see depressions appearing in the sand caused by this same gas (this is most obvious in the centre of the basin). In the theatre you can take in a short film on Banff National Park and the history of the hot springs and their purchase by the government for only $900.

You'll learn that the McCardell brothers and Frank McCabe were not actually the first to discover the springs, Assiniboine Aboriginals were already familiar with their therapeutic powers. European explorers had also already spoken of them. However, the three Canadian Pacific workers, knowing a good thing when they saw it, were the first to try to gain exclusive rights over the springs and the government simply followed suit.

If you want to experience the sensation of Sulphur Mountain's waters (how rapturous it is to soak in them after a long day of hiking!), head up Moun-

tain Avenue, at the foot of the mountain, to **Banff Upper Hot Spring** ★★★ *($7.50 mid-May to mid-Oct every day 9am to 11pm; $5.50 mid-Oct to mid-May Sun-Thu 10am to 10pm, Fri-Sat 10am to 11pm; bathing suit and towel rentals available; up from Mountain Ave., ☎403-762-1515 or 800-767-1611).* The establishment includes a hot water bath (40°C) for soaking and a warm pool (27°C) for swimming. There are change rooms available as well as restaurants and boutiques.

The Pleiades Massage Therapy and Spa which is located in the bathhouse, offers massage, reflexology, reiki, shiatsu, body treatment and aromatherapy wraps to name a few. It is recommended to reserve in advance.

Aboriginal people and early visitors alike believed in the curative powers of sulphurous waters, which were thought to improve one's health and even to cure skin problems. Though the water's curative powers are contested these days, there is no denying their calming effect on body and soul.

If you haven't got the energy to hike up to the top of the mountain, you can take the **Banff Gondola** *($20; open until sundown; at the end of Mountain Ave., at the far end edge of the Upper Hot Springs parking lot, ☎403-762-2523).* The panoramic view of Banff, Mount Rundle, the Bow Valley, the Aylmer and the Cascade Mountains is superb. The gondola starts out at an altitude of 1,583m and climbs to 2,281m. Be sure to bring along warm clothes, as it can be cold at the summit.

The **Fairmont Banff Springs ★★★** *(405 Spray Ave.)* is also worth a look. After visiting the springs at Cave and Basin, William Cornelius Van Horne, vice-president of the Canadian Pacific railway company, decided to have a hotel built to accommodate the tourists who would soon be flocking to the hot springs. Construction began in 1887, and the hotel opened its doors in June 1888. Although the cost of the project had already reached $250,000, the railway company launched a promotional campaign to attract wealthy visitors from all over the world. By the beginning of the century, Banff had become so well known that the Banff Springs Hotel was one of the busiest hotels in North America. More space was needed, so a new wing was built in 1903. It was separated from the original building by a small wooden bridge in case of fire. A year later a tower was built at the end of each wing. Even though this immense hotel welcomed 22,000 guests in 1911, the facilities again proved too small for the forever increasing demand. Construction was thus begun on a central tower. The building was finally completed as it stands today in 1928. The

Tudor style interior layout, as well as the tapestries, paintings and furniture in the common rooms, are all original. If you decide to stay at the Fairmont Banff Springs (see p 303) you may run into the ghost of Sam McAuley, the bellboy who helps guests who have lost their keys, or that of the unlucky young bride who died the day of her wedding when she fell down the stairs and now supposedly haunts the corridors of the hotel.

Heading downhill from the Banff Springs Hotel, you can stop a while at a pretty lookout point over **Bow River Falls**.

The **Banff Centre** *(107 Tunnel Mountain Dr., ☎403-762-6300, 403-762-6100, 403-762-6180 or 800-565-9989, www.banffcentre.ab.ca),* created in 1933, is the home of the Banff Centre of the Arts. More commonly known as the Banff Centre since 1978, this renowned cultural centre hosts the **Banff Arts Festival** *(☎403-762-6301 or 800-413-8368)* in the month of August. The festival attracts numerous artists and involves presentations of dance, opera, jazz and theatre. The centre also offers courses in classical and jazz ballet, theatre, music, photography and pottery. Finally, each year the centre organizes an international mountain film festival. There is a sports centre inside the complex as well.

Around Banff

Hoodoos Lookout *(take Tunnel Mountain Rd. west at the south end of Banff Ave.)* is just outside of the Banff townsite. The Hoodoos aren't as striking as those to be found in Central Alberta's Badlands, but they are worth a quick look. Like gigantic stalagmites, the windswept pillars of sand, silt, gravel and dissolved limestone stand like sentinels out of the

forest. It's a brief 5min walk up to the lookout.

The **Ski Banff@Norquay** (see p 299) was the first one created in Banff National Park. This 2,522-metre mountain was named in honour of John Norquay, their premier of Manitoba. In the winter, a cablecar carries passengers to the summit to admire the magnificent scenery of the Bow River Valley, as well as of the town of Banff.

By following the Lake Minnewanka road, you'll soon come upon the vestiges of the former mining town of **Bankhead ★**. The disappearance of this small town is linked to the creation of Banff National Park. In fact, Bankhead, a product of the coal mining activity in the area, had to be completely dismantled because all forms of mining and forestry development are prohibited in national parks. Today a trail leads around the few remaining foundations and slag heaps, visible in the distance. Back on the road, 200m higher up on the right, are the remains of the church steps. The pleasant **Upper Bankhead** site, a bit farther along on the left, has been equipped with picnic tables and small firepits.

Twenty-two kilometres long and two kilometres wide, **Lake Minnewanka ★★** is now the biggest lake in Banff National Park, but this expanse of water is not completely natural. Its name means "lake of the water spirit". These days it is one of the few lakes in the park where motor boats are permitted. Originally, the area was occupied by Stoney Aboriginal encampments. Because of the difficulties involved with diving in alpine waters and the scattering of vestiges that can be seen here, this lake is popular with scuba divers. Guided walks are given Tuesdays, Thursdays and

Saturdays at 2pm. Besides taking a guided boat-tour with **Minnewanka Boat Tours** (see p 296), you can fish on the lake if you first obtain the appropriate permit from Parks Canada, and skating is possible in the winter. A 16-kilometre hiking trail leads to the far end of the lake. At the **Aylmer Lookout Viewpoint** you will probably spot some of the mountain goats who frequent the area.

★★
Bow Valley Parkway

To get from Banff to Lake Louise, take the Bow Valley Parkway (Hwy 1A), which is a much more picturesque route than the Trans-Canada. About 140 million years ago, mountains emerged from an ancient sea as a result of pressure from the earth's strata. Flowing from the mountains, the Bow River was born, littering the plains to the east with sediment. Forty million years later, the foothills rose from the plains and threatened to prevent the river from following its course. However, even when rocks got in its path, the river managed to continue its route, sweeping away the rocky debris. This continual erosion resulted in the formation of a steep-sided V-shaped valley.

At the beginning of the ice age, about a million years ago, the riverbed of the Bow was taken over by moving ice. The glacier transformed the steep sides of the valley, which took on the shape of a U. As the last glacier receded, it left behind the debris it had been carrying, and the meltwater formed a torrential river which tumbled down the valley. Meltwater no longer feeds the Bow, which can barely make it through the debris left behind by the glaciers. Weaving its way along the mountains, the Bow Valley Parkway affords some exquisite views of the Bow River. It is important to

drive slowly as animals often approach the road at sunrise and sunset.

A stop at beautiful **Johnston Canyon ★★★**, located on the right-hand side about 20km beyond Banff, is a must. A small dirt trail has been cleared through the canyon, where you can behold the devastating effect even a small torrent of water can have on all kinds of rock. The first waterfall, called the Upper Falls, is only 1.1km along the trail, and the path there is easy, though a bit slippery in spots. The second, called the Lower Falls lies another 1.6km farther. This canyon is a veritable bird sanctuary, you might spot some dippers, who live in the canyon year-round and like to dive into the icy waters in search of insect larvae. Black swifts build their nests in the shady hollows of the canyon. They arrive in mid-June and stay until the beginning of fall, long enough to raise their young before heading back south to the warmth of the tropics. Beyond both these falls, you can see what are called the "shimmering walls". A sign explains the phenomenon, which results from the combination of several varieties of algae saturated with minerals. When the sun hits the wall the effect is spectacular. The second waterfalls are the highest in the canyon. The trail continues for another three kilometres to the **Ink Pots**, formed by seven cold springs, in different shades of blue and green. The Ink Pots trail is 5.8km long.

The abandoned town of **Silver City** lies farther up the Bow Valley Parkway, on the left. Silver, copper and lead were discovered in the area in 1883. Prospectors arrived two years later, but the mineral deposits were quickly exhausted and ultimately the town was abandoned. In its glory days, this little city had some 175 buildings and sev-

eral hotels, but just vestiges of these remain.

★★★
Lake Louise

Jewel of the Canadian Rockies, Lake Louise is known the world over thanks to its small, still, emerald-green lake. Few natural sites in Canada can boast as much success: this little place welcomes and average of about six million visitors a year! The public's fancy with this spot is nothing new, and visitors today owe its rediscovery (not discovery, since this area was already well known to aboriginal people) to Tom Wilson, a railway surveyor for Canadian Pacific. In 1882, while working near the Pipestone River, Tom Wilson heard the rumbling of an avalanche coming from the Victoria Glacier. He proceeded to ask a Stoney Aboriginal named Nimrod to lead him to the "Lake of the Little Fishes", which is what the local native people called the lake. Struck by the colour of the water, Tom Wilson renamed the lake "Emerald Lake". Well aware of how beautiful the site was, the railway company erected a first building on the shores of the lake and at the foot of the glacier in 1890. This construction was completely destroyed by fire and rebuilt in 1909; it could accommodate about 500 people. At the time, rooms at the Chateau Lake Louise were rented for four dollars. To transport the numerous visitors already eager to view the scenery, construction of a railway line was undertaken. Up until 1926, when a road was finished, all of the tourists arrived by train at the Laggan station, located 6km from the lake. From there, guests of the Chateau Lake Louise were brought to the hotel in a horse-drawn trolley.

Today, you can reach the lake by car, but finding a place to

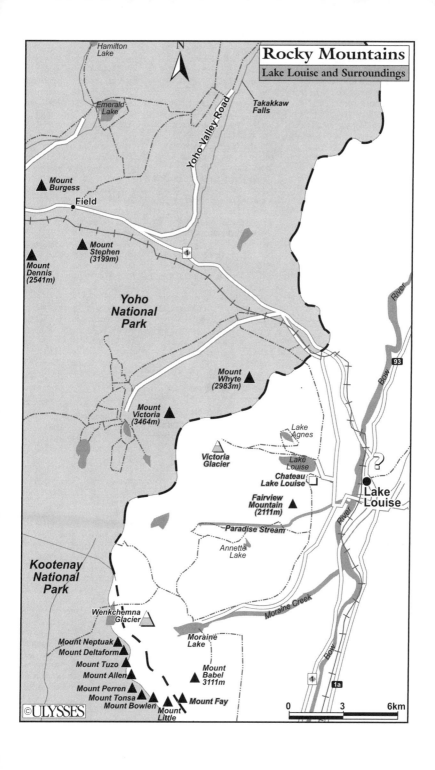

park here can be a real challenge. Stroll quietly around the lake or climb the mountain along the network of little trails radiating out from the lake's shore for a magnificent view of the Victoria Glacier, the lake and the glacial valley. Reaching **Lake Agnes** requires extra effort, but the **view ★★★** of **Victoria** (3,464m), **White** (2,983m), **Fairview** (2,111m), **Babel** (3,111m) and **Fay** (3,235m) **Mountains** is well worth the exertion.

If you aren't up to such a climb, you can always take the **Lake Louise SightSeeing Gondola** (*$18.95; May 9am to 4pm, Jun and Sep 8:30pm to 6pm, Jul-Aug 8am to 6pm; ☎403-522-3555*), which transports you to an altitude of 2,089m in just 10 minutes.

Though the present-day **Fairmont Chateau Lake Louise ★★** (*111 Lake Louise Dr.*) has nothing to do with the original construction, it remains an attraction in itself. This vast hotel can accommodate 700 visitors. Besides restaurants, the hotel houses a small shopping arcade with boutiques selling all kinds of souvenirs.

In the centre of the village of Lake Louise, the Samson Mall houses the **tourist information office** (*☎403-522-3833*) and the offices of Parks Canada. Souvenir shops, photo shops, bookstores and a few cafés and restaurants, all busy with visitors, are located next door. Be careful, as prices tend to be a bit high; you are better off bringing along lots of film so that you won't have to stock up here.

★★★
Moraine Lake

When heading to Lake Louise, you will come to a turnoff for Moraine Lake on the left. This narrow, winding road weaves its way along the mountain for about 10km before reaching

Moraine Lake, which was immortalized on the old Canadian $20 bill. Though much smaller than Lake Louise, Moraine Lake is no less spectacular. Inaccessible in the winter, the lake often remains frozen until the month of June. Don't arrive unprepared for the cool temperatures, even in the summer. Bring a sweater and a wind-breaker if you plan to stroll along the shores. The valley of Moraine Lake, known as the "valley of the 10 peaks", was created by the **Wenkchemna Glacier**, which is still melting. The 10 summits were originally known by the Assiniboine words for the numbers one to 10, but many have since been renamed, and only the appellation Wenkchemna remains. The Moraine Lake Lodge, on the shore of the lake, has a restaurant and a small café (see p 316) where you can warm up.

Tour B:
The Icefields Parkway

The route through the icefields follows Hwy. 93 from Lake Louise for 230km to the Continental Divide, which is covered by glaciers, before ending up in Jasper. This wide, well-paved road is one of the busiest in the Rockies during the summer, with a speed limit of 90km per hour. It runs through some incredibly majestic scenery.

The **Hector Lake ★★** lookout on the left, 17km from Lake Louise, offers a great view of both the lake and Mount Hector. The lake is fed by meltwater from the Balfour Glacier and the Waputik Icefields.

One kilometre before **Mosquito Creek**, you can clearly see the Crowfoot Glacier from the road. Photographs reproduced on information

panels by the road show just how much the glacier has melted in recent years. A bit farther along you can stop to take in the magnificent view of Bow Lake, and then visit little **Num-Ti-Jah Lodge** ("Num-Ti-Jah" is a Stoney Indian name that means "pine marten"), built in 1922 by a mountain guide named Jimmy Simpson. At the time, there was no road leading this far, and all the building materials had to be hauled in on horseback. One of Simpson's descendants has since converted the place into a hotel and cleared a road for guests. Since all the tour buses stop here, the administration of the **Num-Ti-Jah Lodge** (see p 306) has decided in an effort to protect the privacy of its clientele, that only people with reservations for the night should be permitted to enter the building. It is therefore preferable to limit your tour to the outside of the chalet; otherwise you may receive a rather gruff welcome.

Bow Summit ★★ (2,609m) lies at the highest point of the Icefields Parkway and on the continental divide for the waters of the Bow and Mistayac rivers. At this point the vegetation changes drastically, giving way almost completely to sub-alpine plant-life. By the side of the road, there is a rest area that overlooks **Peyto Lake** (pronounced Pee-Toh). You can take a hike through an area of alpine vegetation, and if the weather is right, you can admire a lovely little lake. Western anemones (*Anemone Occidentalis*) line the trail, as do various types of heather and very pretty Indian paintbrush. Bring a good sweater and a jacket for this walk to protect yourself from the wind and the cool temperatures at this altitude. Originally from the region of Kent in England, Bill Peyto is one of the most well-known local characters. During your trip through Banff

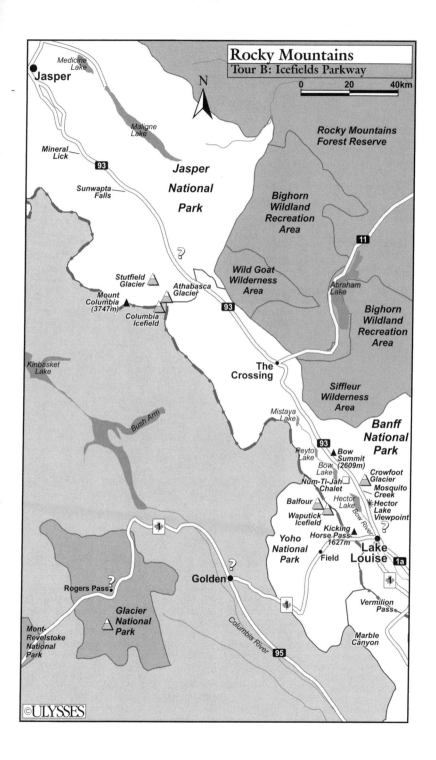

Geological Terms for Mountain Terrain

Suspended valley: A valley whose floor is higher than that of the valley towards which it leads.

Glacial cirque: A crescent-shaped basin formed in a mountainous region by the erosive action of ice. When two cirques meet they form a ridge.

Crevasse: A deep crack or fissure in the top layer of a glacier. Transversal crevasses fracture the ice from one side to the other and are commonly seen when the glacier covers a steep uphill section of a mountain. Marginal crevasses are found on the edge of glaciers and result from friction with the mountainside. Longitudinal crevasses are found at the extremities of the glacier.

Sérac: Series of crevasses where the glacier overhangs a cliff or covers a steep slope. As the glacier continues to advance, the crevasses at the base of the cliff will close up while others will open farther up.

Ogive: The colour of a glacier is not uniform, but actually contains stripes of white and grey. The lighter and paler areas are called ogives and result from the crevasses of a sérac which, when they open in summer, gather dust and silt and, when they open in winter, collect snow and air pockets.

Moraine: Glacial deposits (mix of silt, sand, gravel and rock debris carried by a glacier). As the glacier retreats, it deposits masses of rocky debris at its sides. These are called lateral moraines when the debris comes from the neighbouring faces and frontal moraine when the deposits are at the end of the glacier.

Névé or firn: Mass of hardened, porous snow that attaches to the glacier.

Glacial trough: A U-shaped valley carved out by a glacier.

Icecap: A convex-shaped, thick mass of ice that covers an area of land. Several glaciers can branch off from one icecap, as is the case in the Columbia Icefields.

Alpine glacier: Smaller glaciers located in high-altitude valleys that resemble long tongues of ice and do not originate from icecaps. The Angel Glacier on Mount Edith Cavell is a good example.

Glacial nest: Small glaciers that form on rocky cliffs and appear suspended.

National Park, you will certainly encounter his image, complete with cocked hat, pipe and piercing gaze. Peyto arrived in Canada at the age of 18, and settled in the Rockies where he became one of the most celebrated trappers, prospectors and mountain guides. He enjoyed stopping off at Bow Summit to admire the little lake down below, which was named in his memory. Curiously, the colour of

this lake varies considerably depending on the season. With the first signs of spring it brightens to a marvellous metallic blue, which becomes paler and paler as more and more sediment mixes with the water.

At the intersection of Hwy. 93 and 11, called **The Crossing**, you'll find a few souvenir shops, a hotel and some restaurants. Make sure your gas

tank is full since there are no other gas stations before Jasper. This region was once inhabited by Kootenay Aboriginals who were forced to the western slopes by Peigan Aboriginals armed with guns thanks to white merchants from the southeastern Rockies. Fearing that the Kootenay would eventually arm themselves, the Peigans blocked the way of white explorers who were attempting to cross the pass, and thus kept their enemies completely isolated.

About 30km farther along, at the **Weeping Wall** lookout, you can see several waterfalls cascading over the cliffs of **Mount Cirrus** as the ice melts. In the winter, the falls freeze, forming a spectacular wall of ice, to the delight of ice-climbers.

The **Castleguard Cave** is located 117km from Jasper. A network of underwater caves, the longest in Canada, extends over 20km under the Columbia Icefield. Because of frequent flooding and the inherent dangers of spelunking, you must have authorization from Parks Canada to enter the caves.

The **Parker Ridge** ★★ trail, just 3km farther, makes for a wonderful outing. About 2.5km long, it leads up to the ridge, where, if you're lucky, you may spot some mountain goats. It also offers a great view of the Saskatchewan Glacier. Both the vegetation and the temperature change as you pass from the subalpine to the alpine zone. Warm clothing and a pair of gloves are a good idea.

At the **Sunwapta Pass** you can admire the grandiose scenery which marks the dividing line between Banff and Jasper National Parks. At 2,035m, this is the highest pass along the Icefields Parkway, after Bow Summit.

The **Athabasca Glacier** ★★★ and the **Columbia Icefield** are the focal points of the icefields tour. At the Athabasca Glacier, information panels show the impressive retreat of the glacier over the years. Those who wish to explore the ice on foot should beware of crevasses, which can be up to 40m deep. There are 30,000 on the Athabasca Glacier, some

hidden under thin layers of snow or ice. Those without sufficient experience climbing on glaciers or lacking the proper equipment are better off with a ticket aboard the **Snocoach Tour** *($27.95; May to mid-Oct, every day; tour leaves every 15min; tickets sold at the Brewster counter, near the tourist information centre, ☎877-423-7433)*. These specially equipped buses take people out onto the glacier. Once there, passengers can get off the bus to explore specific areas, determined to be safe by the staff of **Brewster Transportation** (see p 269). The Brewster Transportation company was created in 1900 by two Banff businessmen, brothers Jim and Bill Brewster. The company has continuously contributed to the expansion of tourism in the Banff National Park area, even building a few hotels. Today the prosperous enterprise offers millions of travellers the opportunity to get around the national parks and more importantly, to explore the magnificent Athabasca Glacier up close.

The **Stutfield Glacier** ★★ lookout provides a view of one of the six huge glaciers fed by the Columbia Icefield, which continues one kilometre into the valley.

About 3km farther, on the west side, are several avalanche corridors, some of which come right up to the road. Generally, however, park rangers trigger avalanches before the thick layers of snow become dangerous.

Fifty-five kilometres before Jasper, the **Sunwapta Falls** ★★★ and canyon provide a good example of how water can work away at limestone. The countryside offers some typical examples of suspended valleys, which result when smaller glaciers attach themselves to larger ones. The valley left by the

larger glacier is much deeper, and the shallower, smaller one appears suspended. Several hiking trails have been cleared, one of which leads to the base of the Sunwapta Falls. Be careful while hiking as this is one of the prime habitats of bears and moose in the park.

Seventeen kilometres farther, heading to Jasper, you'll come to an area called the **Mineral Lick**, where mountain goats often come to lick the mineral-rich soil.

The trail leading to the 25m high **Athabasca Falls** ★★, located seven kilometres farther along, takes about an hour to hike. The concrete structure built there is an unfortunate addition to the natural surroundings, but heavy traffic in the area would have otherwise destroyed the fragile vegetation. Furthermore, some careless types have suffered accidents because they got too close to the edge of the canyon. Travellers are therefore reminded not to go beyond the barriers; doing so could be fatal.

Tour C:
Jasper National Park

★★
Jasper and Surroundings

The town of Jasper takes its name from an old fur-trading post, founded in 1811 by William Henry of the Northwest Company. Jasper is a small town of just 4,000 residents which owes its tourist development to its geographic location and the train station built here in 1911. When the Icefields Parkway was opened in 1940, the number of visitors who wanted to discover the region's majestic scenery just kept growing. Although this area is a major tourist draw, Jasper remains a

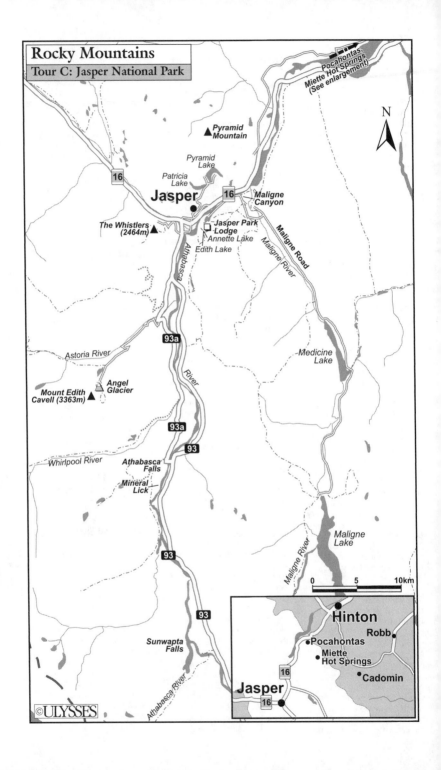

Rocky Mountains
Tour C: Jasper National Park

N

Pocahontas;
Miette Hot Springs
(See enlargement)

▲ Pyramid
Mountain

Pyramid
Lake

Patricia
Lake

16

Jasper

16

Maligne
Canyon

The Whistlers ▲
(2464m)

Jasper Park
Lodge
Annette Lake
Edith Lake

Maligne River

Maligne Road

Athabasca

93a

Astoria River

Medicine
Lake

Mount Edith
Cavell (3363m) ▲

△ Angel
Glacier

River

93a

93

Whirlpool River

Athabasca
Falls

Mineral
Lick

Maligne
Lake

93

Maligne River

0   5   10km

93

Sunwapta
Falls

Hinton

Robb

• Pocahontas
Miette
Hot Springs

Athabasca River

16

• Cadomin

Jasper

16

©ULYSSES

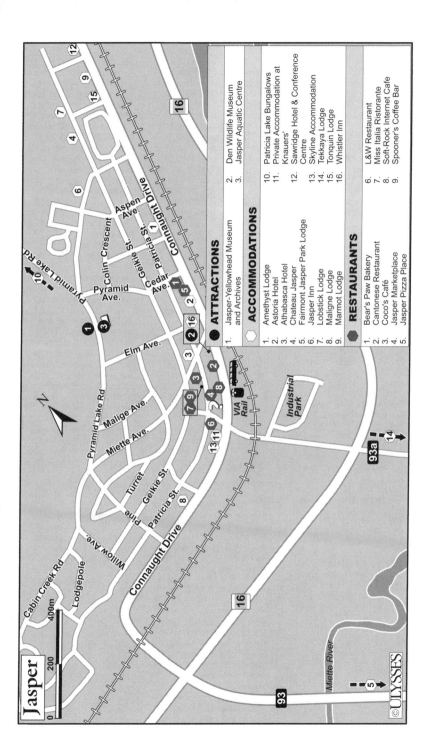

Jasper

● ATTRACTIONS

1. Jasper-Yellowhead Museum and Archives
2. Den Wildlife Museum
3. Jasper Aquatic Centre

◇ ACCOMMODATIONS

1. Amethyst Lodge
2. Astoria Hotel
3. Athabasca Hotel
4. Chateau Jasper
5. Fairmont Jasper Park Lodge
6. Jasper Inn
7. Lobstick Lodge
8. Maligne Lodge
9. Marmot Lodge
10. Patricia Lake Bungalows
11. Private Accommodation at Knauers'
12. Sawridge Hotel & Conference Centre
13. Skyline Accommodation
14. Tekkaya Lodge
15. Tonquin Lodge
16. Whistler Inn

⬡ RESTAURANTS

1. Bear's Paw Bakery
2. Cantonese Restaurant
3. Coco's Café
4. Jasper Marketplace
5. Jasper Pizza Place
6. L&W Restaurant
7. Miss Italia Ristorante
8. Soft-Rock Internet Cafe
9. Spooner's Coffee Bar

© ULYSSES

decidedly more tranquil and less commercial spot than Banff. This doesn't prevent hotel prices from being just as exorbitant as elsewhere in the Rockies, however.

A good place to start your visit of Jasper and its surroundings is at the **Information Centre** *(500 Connaught Dr.)*, where you can pick up maps of the region. The office Parks Canada office is in the train/bus station *(607 Connaught Dr.)*.

The **Jasper-Yellowhead Museum and Archives ★** *($3.50; mid-May to early Sep, every day 10am to 9pm; early Sep to mid-Oct, every day 10am to 5pm; winter, Thu-Sun 10am to 5pm; 400 Pyramid Lake Rd., facing the Aquatic Centre, ☎780-852-3013)* tells the story of the region's earliest First Nations inhabitants, as well as mountain guides and other legendary characters from this area.

The **Den Wildlife Museum ★** *($3; every day 9am to 10pm; at the corner of Connaught Dr. and Miette St., inside the Whistler Inn, ☎780-852-3361)* exhibits a collection of stuffed and mounted animals from the region.

The **Jasper Aquatic Centre** *($6.25 Jul-Aug; $5 Sep to Jun; 401 Pyramid Lake Rd., ☎780-852-3663)* and the **Jasper Activity Centre** *(on Pyramid Ave., near the Aquatic Centre, ☎780-852-3381)* are both open to visitors who want to go for a swim, take a sauna or shower, or play tennis or racquetball (reservation recommended). During the month of August, a rodeo contest is organized inside the Jasper Activity Centre (ask at the tourist information office for dates).

Mount Edith Cavell ★ ★ ★ is 3,363m high. To get there, take the southern exit for Jasper and follow the signs for the Marmot ski hill. Turn right,

then left, and you'll come to a narrow road, which leads to one of the most lofty summits in the area. The road snakes through the forest for about 20km before coming to a parking lot. Several hiking trails have been cleared to allow visitors to enjoy a better view of this majestic mountain, as well as its suspended glacier, the **Angel Glacier**. The mountain is named after Edith Louisa Cavell, a British nurse who became known in World War I for her refusal to leave her post near Brussels so that she could continue caring for the wounded in two camps. Arrested for spying by the Germans and accused of having helped Allied prisoners escape, she was shot on October 12th, 1915. To commemorate this woman's exceptional courage, the government of Canada decided to name the most impressive mountain in the Athabasca Valley after the martyred nurse. Previous to this, Mount Edith Cavell had been known by many other names. Native people called it "the white ghost", while travellers who used it as a reference point called it "the mountain of the Great Crossing", then "the Duke", "Mount Fitzhugh" and finally "Mount Geikie". No name had stuck, however, until the government decided to call it Mount Edith Cavell.

In just a few minutes, the **Jasper Tramway ★ ★** *($18; mid-Apr to late Oct; take the southern exit for Jasper and follow the signs for Whistler's Mountain, ☎780-852-3093)* whisks you up some 2,277m and deposits you on the northern face of **Whistler's Mountain**. You'll find a restaurant and souvenir shop at the arrival point, while a small trail covers the last few metres up to the summit (2,470m). The view is outstanding.

The road to Maligne Lake follows the valley of the river of the same name for 46km.

Because of the tight curves of this winding road and the many animals which cross it, the speed limit is 60km per hour. Before reaching the lake, the road passes by one of the most beautiful resorts in Canada, the **Jasper Park Lodge**, run by Canadian Pacific. You can have a picnic, go boating or take a swim in one of the two pretty little lakes, **Annette** and **Edith**, right next to this facility. Ten thousand years ago, as the glacier was retreating out of this valley, two immense blocks of ice broke free and remained in place amidst the moraines and other debris left by the glaciers. As they melted they formed these two small lakes. Lake Agnes has a beach.

Maligne Canyon ★ ★ ★ lies at the beginning of Maligne Road. Hiking trails have been cleared so that visitors may admire this spectacular narrow gorge abounding with cascades, fossils and potholes sculpted by the turbulent waters. Several bridges span the canyon. The first offers a view of the falls; the second, of the effect of ice on rock; and the third, of the deepest point (51m) of the gorge.

Dominated by the Maligne and Colin chains, **Medicine Lake ★** looks like any other lake in the summer, but come October it disappears completely. In the spring, you'll find nothing but a tiny stream flowing slowly along the muddy lake-bottom. The depth of this lake can vary 20m over one year, a phenomenon aboriginal people attributed to a reprimand by a medicine man. It is actually due to the presence of an underwater river which has worked its way through the limestone and reappears in the Maligne River. When the glaciers melt in the summer, the underground network of rivers becomes insufficient to drain the water, which thus rises to the surface and forms a lake. The bottom of Medicine Lake consists of dolines (shallow, funnel-shaped holes) filled with gravel, through which the water flows. The short lower trail offers a good view of these.

Maligne Lake ★ ★ is one of the prettiest lakes in the Rockies. Water activities like boating, fishing and canoeing are possible here, and a short trail runs along part of the shore. The chalet on the shore houses a souvenir shop, a restaurant-café and the offices of a tour company that organizes trips to little **Spirit Island**, the ideal vantage point for admiring the surrounding mountain tops.

The road (Hwy. 16) that heads east to Edmonton crosses the entire Athabasca Valley. A large herd of moose grazes in this part of the valley, and the animals can often be spotted between the intersection of Maligne Road and the old town of Pocahontas, near Miette Hot Springs.

By continuing on the road to Hinton, you'll soon reach the hottest springs in all of the parks in the Rockies, **Miette Hot Springs**. The sulphurous water gushes forth at 57°C and has to be cooled down to 39°C for the baths. A paved path follows Sulphur Stream past the water purification station to the old pool, built out of logs in 1938; the trail finally ends at one of three hot springs beside the stream. Several hiking trails have been cleared in the area for those who wish to explore the back country and admire the splendid scenery.

The ruins of the town of **Pocahontas**, abandoned in 1921, lie at the turn-off for the road to Miette Hot Springs. Bit by bit, nature has reclaimed the remains of the buildings. Pocahontas was originally the name of a Native American princess. When coal was discovered here in 1908, a concession was established, and the region was exploited extensively. Full of hope, residents named the town after the famous Virginia coal basin, Pocahontas, the headquarters of the company. When the mines shut down in 1921, many buildings were dismantled and transported to other towns.

Hwy. 16 West, the Yellowhead Highway, links Jasper with Mount Robson Provincial Park, 26km away in British Columbia. It traverses the main chains of the Rockies, affording some magnificent panoramic vistas. The road runs through Yellowhead Pass, along the Continental Divide.

To reach **Patricia** and **Pyramid** lakes, located only seven kilometres from Jasper, you have to take Cedar Avenue from Connaught Drive in downtown Jasper. This road becomes Pyramid Avenue and leads to Pyramid Lake. This is an ideal spot for a walk or a picnic. You can go swimming or canoeing in the lake.

Tour D: Kootenay and Yoho National Parks

★ ★
Kootenay National Park

Although less popular with the public than Banff and Jasper, Kootenay National Park nevertheless boasts beautiful, majestic landscapes and is just as interesting to visit as its more touristy neighbours. It contains two large valleys, the humid Vermillion River Valley and the drier Kootenay River Valley; the contrast is striking. The park owes its existence to a bold attempt to lay a road between the Windermere region and the province of Alberta. In 1905, Randolphe Bruce, a businessman from the town of Invermere who became lieutenant governor of British Columbia, decided to turn a profit with the local orchards. To accomplish this end, he had to be able to transport produce to other parts of the country, hence the necessity of laying a road between isolated Windermere and the cities to the east. Bruce was so influential that construction began in 1911. A number of obstacles presented themselves, and the audacious project soon proved too costly for the province to finance alone. The 22km of road, born of a bitter struggle between man and nature, ended up leading nowhere, and the enterprise was abandoned. Refusing to admit defeat, Bruce turned to the federal government, which agreed to help in return for the property alongside the road; thus was born Kootenay National Park in 1922.

To reach Kootenay National Park from Banff, take the Trans-Canada to Castle Mountain Junction. Hwy. 93, on the left, runs the entire length of the park.

Vermilion Pass, at the entrance of Kootenay Park, marks the Continental Divide; from this point on, rivers in Banff Park and points east flow to the east, while those in Kootenay Park flow west and empty into the Pacific.

A few kilometres farther lies **Marble Canyon ★ ★**. Marble Canyon is very narrow, but you'll find a lovely waterfall at the end of the trail there. Several bridges span the gorge, and the erosion caused by torrential waters makes for some amazing scenery. Five hundred metres to the right, past the canyon, you'll find a trail leading to the famous **Paint Pots ★ ★**. These ochre deposits are created by subterranean springs which cause iron oxide to rise to the surface. Native people used this

substance as paint. They
would clean the ochre, mix it
with water, and mould it into
little loaves, which they would
bake in a fire. They would
then ground it into a fine powder and mix it with fish oil.
They could use the final product to paint their bodies or
decorate their tepees and
clothing. According to the
Aboriginals, a great animal
spirit and a thunder spirit lived
in the streams. Sometimes
they would hear a melody
coming from here, other
times battle songs; in their
minds, this meant that the
spirits were speaking to them.
For these natives, the ochre
was the symbol of spirits,
legends and important customs, while the first whites to
come here saw it as an opportunity to make money. At the
beginning of the century, the
ochre was extracted by hand
and then sent to Calgary to be
used as a coloring for paint.
You can still see a few rem-
nants of this era, including
machines, tools and even a
few piles of ochre, which
were left behind when the
area was made into a national
park and all work here came
to a halt.

One of the best places in the
park for elk- and moose-
watching is the **Animal Lick**, a
mineral-rich salt marsh. The
best time to go is early in the
morning or at dusk. Viewing
areas have been laid out along
the road so that you can admire the scenery. The view is
particularly lovely from the
**Kootenay Valley
Viewpoint ★★**, located at
the park exit.

Upon arriving at Radium Hot
Springs, right after the tunnel,
you will see a parking lot on
your left. You can get out of
your car and take a look at the
limestone cliffs, which have
been stained red by iron oxide.

Radium Hot Springs

This little town, located at the
entrance to the park, is surprisingly nondescript. You can,
however, take a dip in the
pool at the **Radium Hot
Pools ★★** *($6.25; at the
entrance of Kootenay Park,
☎250-347-9485 or 800-347-
9704)*, whose warm waters
are apparently renowned for
their therapeutic virtues.
Whether or not you believe
these claims, which have yet
to be backed by any medical
evidence, a soak in these
38°C non-sulphurous waters
is definitely very relaxing.

*South of Radium Hot Springs,
Hwy. 95 continues south
through the British Columbia
Rockies meeting up with Hwy.
3 from Crowsnest Pass. This
alternative route is one way of
getting to Southern Alberta*

Invermere

Invermere is a service town
for the surrounding cottage
country, which Albertans and
British Columbians escape to
on weekends. Picturesque
Windermere Lake ★, really a
widening of the Columbia
River, is popular with boaters.

The **Windermere Valley Pioneer Museum** *($2; Jul and
Aug Tue-Sat 9:30am to
5:30pm, Jun and Sep Mon-Fri
1pm to 4pm; 622 3rd St.,
☎250-342-9769)* with its collection of memorabilia is yet
another place to immerse
yourself in those pioneer days.

Eighteen kilometres west of
Invermere is **Panorama Resort**, a ski hill and hotel with a
variety of lodging options.

Fairmont Hot Springs

This tiny town exists almost
exclusively as a tourist centre
for the hot springs. There is
golf, skiing and great scenery.
The **hot springs** *(every day
8am to 10pm; ☎800-663-
4979)*, located at the resort of
the same name are free if you

are staying at the resort and
$9 (day pass) otherwise.

*Continuing east of Hwy. 3
towards the Alberta border,
there is good downhill skiing in
Fernie.*

*Alternatively, continue your
tour north from Radium Hot
Springs by heading up Hwy.
95, which runs along the floor
of the Columbia River Valley, to
the little town of Golden. The
scenery along this road is quite
pretty, with the foothills of the
Rockies on one side and the
Purcell Mountains on the other.
From Golden the Trans-
Canada Highway continues on
to Revelstoke, about 150 kilometres west of the edge of the
Rocky Mountain parks.*

★★
Yoho National Park

As in all the other parks in the
Rockies, you must pay an
entrance fee *($6 for one day,
$42 a year)* if you wish to stay
here. This fee does not apply if
you are simply passing through
the park.

About 5km from the park
entrance, on the right, you'll
find a trail leading to **Wapta
Falls**, on the **Kicking Horse
River**, thus named when
adventurer James Hector
suffered the painful misfortune
of being kicked in the chest by
his horse here in 1858. The
river is a very popular place to
go rafting. The falls are 30m
high, and the trail leading to
them is fairly short and easy.

A little farther along, you'll find
another trail leading to the
Hoodoos, natural rock formations created by erosion. The
trail, which starts at the Hoodoo Creek campground, is
very steep but only 3.2km
long and offers an excellent
view of the Hoodoos.

A small road offers access to
the **Natural Bridge**, sculpted
by the torrential waters of
Kicking Horse River. There
were falls here before, but the

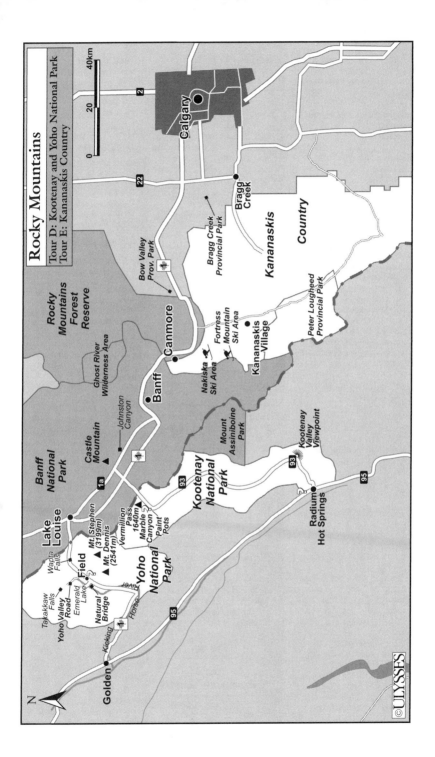

Rocky Mountains

Tour D: Kootenay and Yoho National Park
Tour E: Kananaskis Country

0   20   40km

N

Calgary

Bragg Creek

Bow Valley
Prov. Park

Rocky
Mountains
Forest
Reserve

Ghost River
Wilderness Area

Canmore

Banff

Johnston
Canyon

Castle
Mountain

Banff National
Park

Kananaskis   Country

Bragg Creek
Provincial Park

Fortress
Mountain
Ski Area

Nakiska
Ski Area

Kananaskis
Village

Peter Lougheed
Provincial Park

Mount
Assiniboine
Park

Kootenay Valley
Viewpoint

Kootenay
National
Park

Radium
Hot Springs

Lake
Louise

Mt. Stephen
(3199m)

Mt. Dennis
(2541m)

Vermillion
Pass
1640m

Marble
Canyon

Paint
Pots

Wapta
Falls

Takakkaw
Falls

Yoho Valley
Road

Emerald
Lake

Natural
Bridge

Field

Yoho
National
Park

Golden

Horse

Kicking

River

© ULYSSES

water, full of sand and gravel, acted like sandpaper, gradually wearing its way into the rock and creating the formation we see now. This spot also offers a splendid view of **Mount Stephen** (3,149m) and **Mount Dennis** (2,541m).

Hiking to **Emerald Lake ★★** has become a tradition here in Yoho National Park. A short trail (5.2km) takes you around the lake. You can then visit **Hamilton Falls**. Picnic areas have been laid out near the lake. Thanks to a small canoe-rental outfit, you can also enjoy some time on the water. There is a small souvenir shop beside the boat-launching ramp.

The park's tourist office is located in Field, 33km east of the park entrance. During summer, visitors can learn more about the Yoho Valley by taking part in any number of interpretive activities. There are 400km of hiking trails leading through the valley deep into the heart of the region. Maps of these trails, as well as of those reserved for mountain bikes, are available at the **tourist office** *(May and Jun 9am to 5pm, Jul and Aug 9am to 7pm, Sep to May 9am to 7pm; on the way into town, ☎250-343-6783)* in **Field**.

You can also purchase a topographical map of the park for $13 from the **Friends of Yoho** *(☎250-343-6364)*. If you plan on staying more than a day here, you must register at the Parks Canada office, located in the same place. You can climb some of the mountains, but a special permit is required to scale Mount Stephen because fossils have been discovered in the area you must pass through to reach the top.

You can buy some provisions at the little **Siding General Store and Cafe** *(every day 9am to 9pm, in summer 8am to 10pm; on Stephen Ave., beside*

the post office; ☎250-343-6462) in Field.

You must be accompanied by a guide to visit the **Burgess Shale ★★★**. In 1886, a paleontologist discovered several large trilobite beds on Mount Stephen, near Field. Since the Rockies were once covered by an ocean, all of these fossils were beautifully preserved by a thick layer of marine sediment. The invaluable fossil beds on Mount Burgess, beside Mount Stephen, were pushed to the surface by the geological upheavals that led to the emergence of the Rockies. You'll need to set aside an entire day to visit the Burgess Shale, since the trip there and back involves a 20km hike and only guided hikes are allowed. To enlist the services of a guide, contact the park offices *(☎250-343-6783)* or the **Yoho Burgess Shale Foundation** *(☎250-343-3006)* several days in advance.

A few kilometres past Field, **Yoho Valley Road** branches off to the left, toward **Takakaw Falls**. On the way, you can stop at the **Upper Spiral Tunnel Viewpoint ★★** to admire the advanced technology the engineers working for the railway company had to employ in order to lay a dependable line across this hilly terrain. The small road twists and turns for 13km, leading to a wonderful scenic viewpoint from which you can contemplate the Yoho and Kicking Horse Rivers. It comes to a dead end at the **Takakaw Falls ★★** (254m), which are among the highest falls in Canada.

Tour E: Kananaskis Country

When Captain John Palliser led a British scientific expedition here from 1857 and

1860, the numerous lakes and rivers he found led him to christen the region Kananaskis, which means "gathering of the waters". Located 90km from Calgary, this region covers more than 4,000km², including the **Bow Valley**, **Bragg Creek** and **Peter Lougheed** provincial parks. Because of its proximity to Calgary, its beautiful scenery and the huge variety of outdoor activities that can be enjoyed here, it soon became one of the most popular destinations in the province, first with Albertans and then with visitors from all over the world.

No matter what season it is, Kananaskis Country has a great deal to offer. During summer, it is a veritable paradise for outdoor enthusiasts, who can play both golf and tennis here, or go horseback riding, mountain biking, kayaking, river rafting, fishing or hiking. With its 250km of paved roads and 460km of marked trails, this region is easier to explore than any other in Alberta. In winter, the trails are used for cross-country skiing and snowmobiling. Visitors can also go downhill skiing at Fortress Mountain or at Nakiska, speed down the toboggan runs, go skating on one of the region's many lakes or try dogsledding.

★ Canmore

Canmore is a paradise for lovers of the great outdoors. It has the greatest concentration of Canadian mountaineers who have participated in expeditions to the Himalayas. Canmore is a unique training ground for mountaineers and it is also the place for fly-fishing enthusiasts. An idyllic spot for mountain biking, the town hosted the mountain-biking World Cup from 1998 to 2000. Due to its enchanting location and its recreational activities, it's one of the most rapidly developing towns in the country.

The name Canmore comes from the Gaelic *Ceann mor*, which means "big head". The name was given as a nickname to the Scottish king Malcolm III, son of Duncan I, who became king in 1054 and established his place in history by killing the usurper Macbeth.

After searching for the most practical route for the railway to the west, Canadian Pacific chose to go through the Bow Valley. It was decided that the supply station for the project would be placed at the entrance to the Rockies, and thus was born the town of Canmore. Coal deposits found here later were mined until July 13th, 1979.

This quiet little town of about 11,000 experienced its finest hour yet during the 1988 Winter Olympics. The cross-country, nordic combined and biathlon events were held here, along with the disabled cross-country skiing demonstration event. Since the games, the facilities at the **Canmore Nordic Centre** *(every day 9am to 5:30pm; from the centre of town head up Main St., turn right on 8th Ave. and right to cross the Bow River. Turn left and head up Rundle Dr., then turn left again on Three Sisters Dr. Take Spray Lake Rd. to the right and continue straight. The parking lot of the centre is located farther up on the right,* ☎403-678-2400) have been used for other international events like the World Cup of Skiing in 1995. In summer the cross-country trails become walking and mountain biking trails. Dogs are permitted between April 11th and October 30th if they are on a leash. Bears are common in the region in the summer, so be extra careful.

By continuing beyond the Canmore Nordic Centre, you'll come upon two small lakes called **Grassi Lakes**. To

reach them, head up Three Sisters Drive and turn right on Spray Lakes Road. Turn left at the turn-off near the artificial lake called the Reservoir, then left again on the first small dirt road. The starting point for a hiking trail begins a bit farther along. The lakes are named after Lawrence Grassi, an Italian immigrant who worked as a miner and cleared the trail to the lakes. A short walk climbs quickly up to Grassi Falls and then on to the crystal-clear lakes. A great view of Canmore and the Bow Valley can be had from this spot. Good walking shoes are necessary. The Canmore area is also well known for its dog-sled races, which take place annually in January.

Marvellously well situated at the entrance to Banff National Park and at the gateway to Kananaskis Country, Canmore welcomes many visitors each year, but it is often easier to find better accommodations here than in Banff. Nevertheless, it is a good idea to reserve your room well in advance.

The main attraction of this small town, besides the Canmore Nordic Centre, is its exceptional location and the many outdoor activities possible. Besides skiing, dog-sledding, ice-climbing, heli-skiing, snowmobile trips and ice fishing in the winter, summer activities include parasailing, hang-gliding, hiking, mountain biking, rock-climbing, canoeing, and the list goes on... All sorts of useful addresses can be found in the Outdoor Activities section of this chapter

The **Canmore Centennial Museum** *(free admission; late May to early Sep Tue-Sun 10am to 5pm; early Sep to late May Mon-Fri noon to 4pm, call ahead for off season weekend operating hours; 801 7th Ave.,* ☎403-678-2462) is a tiny little museum that retraces the

town's mining history. It also has a section on the 1988 Winter Olympics.

The **Canmore Recreation Centre** *(every day 6am to 10pm; 1900 8th Ave.,* ☎403-678-5597) organizes all sorts of summer activities for children. The facilities include a municipal pool, a sports centre and an exercise centre.

Maps pertaining to these activities are available at the **Barrier Lake Information Centre** (see p 272), where you'll also find the torch from the Calgary Olympics. It was carried all over Canada for three months, and then used to light the Olympic flame in Calgary on February 13, 1988. Eight events (downhill, slalom and giant slalom) were held in the Kananaskis region, on Mount Allan, in Nakiska.

★★
Kananaskis Valley

The **Nakiska Ski Resort** *(near Kananaskis Village,* ☎403-591-7777 or 800-258-7669) was designed specifically for the Olympic Games, at the same time as the Kananaskis Village hotel complex. It boasts top-notch, modern facilities and excellent runs.

Kananaskis Village consists mainly of a central square surrounded by two luxurious hotels. It was designed to be the leading resort in this region. Its construction was funded by the Alberta Heritage Savings Trust and a number of private investors. The village was officially opened on December 20, 1987. It has a post office, located beside the **tourist information centre** *(summer every day 9am to 9pm; winter Mon-Fri 9am to 5pm)*, as well as a sauna and a hot tub *($2; every day 9am to 8pm)*, both of which are open to the general public. The Lodge at Kananaskis houses a shopping arcade complete with souvenir and clothing shops, cafés and restaurants.

The **Kananaskis Golf Club** leaves absolutely nothing to be desired. Its fabulous 36-hole course stretches along the narrow Kananaskis River valley at the foot of **Mount Lorette** and **Mount Kidd**.

The **Fortress Mountain Ski Resort** *(turn right at Fortress Junction,* ☎*403-591-7108 or 800-258-7669)* is less popular than Nakiska, but nevertheless has some good runs. Furthermore, snowfall is heavy here on the Continental Divide, at the edge of Peter Lougheed Provincial Park.

The tourist office in **Peter Lougheed Provincial Park** *(near the two Kananaskis Lakes)* features an interactive presentation that provides all sorts of information on local flora, fauna, geography, geology and climatic phenomena. Mount Lougheed and the park were named after two well-known members of the Lougheed family. Born in Ontario, the honorable Sir James Lougheed (1854-1925) became a very prominent lawyer in both his home province and in Alberta, particularly in Calgary, where he was Canadian Pacific's legal advisor. He was named to the senate in 1889, led the Conservative Party from 1906 to 1921 and finally became a minister. The park owes its existence to his grandson, the honorable Peter Lougheed (1928-), who was elected Premier of Alberta on August 30, 1971. You can pick up a listing of the numerous interpretive programs offered here at the tourist office.

Right near the tourist office, you'll find **William Watson Lodge**, a centre for the elderly and those with disabilities which offers a view of **Lower Kananaskis Lake**. At the end of the road leading to **Upper Kananaskis Lake**, turn left and

drive a few kilometres farther to **Interlakes**, where you can take in a magnificent view. The **Smith-Dorrien Trail**, a gravel road stretching 64km, leads back to Canmore. Although parts of it have been deeply rutted by rain and snow, the road is wide and you'll have it almost all to yourself. There are no service stations along the way. This is a beautiful area that seems completely cut off from the rest of the world. The road comes to an end at Grassi Falls in Canmore.

Outdoor Activities

The Canadian Rockies, which cover an area of over 22,000km², are a paradise for anyone who appreciates mountain landscapes and clean air, enjoys having lots of space to roam and takes pleasure in outdoor activities like hiking, mountain climbing, horseback riding, canoeing, river rafting, golf and cross-country and downhill skiing. Because this region has been set aside as a series of national parks, it has not been marred by the unbridled construction of ski resorts and chalets, which do not always blend harmoniously with the landscape. Consequently, although the Rockies welcome six million visitors annually, you don't have to go far off the beaten track to enjoy some quiet moments that will remain with you forever.

Climate

The cool winds that characterize the Rockies might make you forget the dangers of the sun, which in mountain regions, are very real. Be sure to prepare yourself with a good sunscreen, a hat and sunglasses. When hiking in the

mountains the combination of the physical exertion, the sun and the changing weather conditions can often lead to hypothermia, which can ultimately be fatal. The best way to avoid these problems is to dress properly.

Clothing

An excursion in the mountains requires careful planning. Whether you plan on visiting the Rockies in winter or summer, it is important to always bring along warm and comfortable clothing.

During the winter, do not forget to bring along warm long underwear that allows your skin to breathe, natural wool or synthetic fleece sweaters, a few good pairs of socks, a jacket and pants that are windproof, gloves, a scarf and a hat.

If you plan on doing any cross-country skiing, remember that it is always better to wear layers instead of one heavy jacket which will prove too warm when you make the least exertion, but not warm enough when you stop to rest. A small backpack is a good idea for carrying some food, an extra sweater and a pair of socks in case your feet get wet. Never stop to rest in wet clothes, bring along a change of clothes instead.

The same precautions should be taken in summer. Temperatures are much lower at higher altitudes, and the smallest wind can significantly lower temperatures. Furthermore, climatic changes occur quickly in the mountains. Be sure to dress properly when heading out on an excursion, a good sweater and windbreaker are a good idea, even in summer. An ear warmer and gloves might also come in handy. Rain is common, so bring along a water-resistant jacket. Finally, with proper footwear, including a good pair of socks and a solid pair of hiking boots, you'll be ready to tackle the most spectacular trails of the region.

Hiking

Hiking is probably the most popular outdoor activity in the region's national parks, which are crisscrossed by trails suitable for everyone from novices to experts. Environment Canada's park service puts out free brochures on some of the wonderful hiking trips to be enjoyed in the Rockies; these are available at the tourist information offices in Banff, Lake Louise and Jasper. You can pick up a map of the hiking trails in Kootenay National Park for one dollar at the Parks Canada offices located at each entrance of the park. Keep in mind that if you plan on spending several days in the heart of one of these parks, you must register with Parks Canada, specifying your itinerary and the length of your stay.

Banff

The relatively easy **Cave and Basin Trail** (6.8km) leads to the historic site of the same name, offering some lovely views of the Bow River along the way. It starts at Banff Centre, on St. Julian Road. Follow the Bow River trail to the falls and walk alongside the water. Go over the Banff Avenue bridge and turn right on Cave Avenue. The trail leads to the parking lot of the Cave and Basin hot springs. Return the way you came.

The **Stoney Squaw** trail is definitely worth a visit. The excursion departs from the parking lot at Mount-Norquay ski station. The path climbs 1,880m and the 5km course takes about 2hrs to complete.

The path is relatively easy to hike and it offers magnificent views of Mount Cascade.

Those looking for a challenge will enjoy the 6km of steep hills leading up to the summit of **Mount Rundle** (3,000m). The trail zigzags in the valley before arriving at the end of the forest and then continuing up the mountain. For quite a ways, the passage is barely wider than a few metres, with sheer cliffs on both sides. The view of Spray River and Mount Sulphur is arresting. Be sure to bring warm clothing as winter snowstorms can rage even in June. The trail begins after the bridge that crosses Spray River near the golf club. Follow the edge of the woods on the right-hand side after the bridge. Plan for at least 6hrs of hiking, and make sure you have good knees!

The continuation of the Cave and Basin trail, the **Sundance Canyon Trail** (13.6 km), is even easier. Go past the Cave and Basin building and head back down toward the Bow River. The well-marked trail runs alongside Sundance Creek, climbing up to the canyon and then making a loop, giving you a chance to see a little more of the landscape.

The **Sulphur Mountain Trail** is a little more difficult than the two mentioned above because it involves a significant change in altitude. It starts near the base station of the Sulphur Mountain Gondola, then winds its way up the mountain, offering a magnificent, panoramic view of the Bow River valley.

The trail leading to the **Vermilion Lakes** starts at the Banff Centre, although there are all sorts of other ways to get there. Follow the Tunnel Mountain Trail, which leads to the Bow River falls. Take Buffalo Street, then, a little farther along on the left, the

trail that runs along the river. Cross the Banff Avenue bridge, then walk along the banks of the Bow River. You will come to the canoe rental service on Bow Avenue. The first of the three Vermilion Lakes lies just over the railroad tracks. Continue your tour along Vermilion Lakes Drive. The area around these swampy lakes is wonderful for bird-watching. This hike is a bit long, but very easy. You can also reach the Vermilion Lakes by canoe, starting from the Bow River.

This guide would not be complete if it didn't mention the hiking trail that leads to the summit of **Cascade Mountain**. The departure is from the parking lot at Mount Norquay Ski Centre on the other side of the Trans-Canada Highway. This 18km trail is even more exhausting than that of Mount Rundle. On the other hand, it has the most beautiful panoramic view of Banff and Bow Valley. The snow always melts late in the year on the shady side of Cascade Mountain. For this reason, the trail only opens, at the earliest, at the beginning of July.

If you would like to take part in a longer excursion organized by professionals, you can contact one of the following outfits: **White Mountain Adventures** *(provides transportation and free guides for hiking at Sunshine Meadows; Canmore;* ☎*403-678-4099 or 800-408-0005)* and **Canadian Active Experience** *(*☎*403-678-3336)*. Reservations required.

Lake Louise

To reach **Lake Agnes and the Big Beehives**, start out at the Chateau Lake Louise and walk along the lakeside promenade. On the right, you will see a little trail leading up the mountain through the forest. This will take you to Mirror Lake (2.7km) and Agnes Lake

Respect the Mountain!

As a hiker, it is important to realize your role in preserving and respecting the fragility of the ecosystem and to comprehend your impact on your surroundings. Here are a few guidelines:

First of all, stay on the trails even if they are covered in snow or mud in order to protect the ground vegetation and avoid widening the trail.

Unless you're heading off on a long trek, wear lightweight hiking boots, they do less damage to vegetation. When in a group in alpine regions, spread out and walk on rocks as much as possible to avoid damaging vegetation.

It is just as important to protect waterways, bodies of water and the ground water when in mountainous regions. When digging back-country latrines, place them at least 30 metres from all water sources, and cover everything (paper included) with earth.

Never clean yourself in lakes or streams.

At campsites dispose of waste water only in designated areas.

The water in mountain regions is not always potable and therefore should be boiled for at least 10 minutes before drinking.

Never leave any garbage behind. Bags for this are provided at Parks Canada offices.

Certain types of flowers are endangered, so do not pick anything.

Leave everything as you find it, that way those that follow can enjoy the beauty of nature as you did.

For safety reasons, always keep your dog on a leash, or leave it at home. Dogs that roam free have a tendency to wander off and chase wild animals. They have even been known to chase down bears and then take refuge with their masters.

Finally, if you are exploring the Rockies on horseback, remember that only trails set aside for these animals may be followed.

(3.6km). When you get to Agnes Lake, which lies 365m higher than Lake Louise, you will find a small café set up inside a cabin, where you can regain your strength over a cup of tea or hot chocolate before continuing your ascent to the Big Beehives. The trail runs alongside little Agnes Lake then climbs steeply for 140m to the Little Beehives. The Big Beehives lie another 30m uphill. Your efforts will be richly rewarded by a superb view of Lake Louise and its valley.

You can also set out on an excursion to the **Plain of the Six Glaciers** from the Chateau Lake Louise. Walk along the lakeside promenade and,

instead of taking the trail that branches off toward Agnes Lake, keep following the shoreline. The trail runs near some moraines (masses of rocks deposited by glaciers), then comes to an end 5.5km from the starting point near a small cabin where you can have a light meal or a hot drink. From there, you can climb 1.3km farther to the magnificent viewpoint at Abbot Pass and Death Trap.

Immediately to the left after the parking lot at Moraine Lake is a trail leading to the **Consolation Lakes**. This trail, which is only three kilometres long and requires little effort, affords some magnificent panoramic views of the Tem-

ple Mountains and the Ten Peaks. Visitors are advised to wear good walking shoes for this outing, since the trail is scattered with moraines and large rocks.

For a view of Moraine Lake and the Ten Peaks, which are depicted on the old Canadian $20 bill, take the **Moraine Lakeshore Trail**, a short path that leads all the way to the far end of the lake.

Jasper National Park and Surroundings

The **Old Fort Point trail** is easy to climb and is suitable for all ages and fitness levels. The trail takes about an hour to complete. You can admire the mountain peaks in the area, the zigzagging Athabasca River and the small town of Jasper. To get there, take Hwy. 93A to south of Jasper and then turn left after Hwy. 16.

The **Path of the Glacier Trail** (1.5 km) starts near the parking lot at Mount Edith Cavell and leads to a small lake formed by the run-off from the glacier. You can admire the glacier suspended above you and ponder the dramatic impact glaciers have had on the vegetation and topography of these mountain valleys.

To reach the **Cavell Meadow Trail and Peak** from the parking lot at Mount Edith Cavell, walk up the trail on the left, which will take you opposite the Angel Glacier. You won't have to look hard to spot marmots and pikas along the way. Upon reaching the forest, the trail climbs steeply up to a clear-cut zone. You can already see the Angel Glacier from here; in fact, it appears to be very close. You can keep going to Cavell Meadow Park, since the trail winds its way farther and farther up. The last 500m are the most demanding, but your efforts will be richly rewarded by a magnificent view.

The **Maligne Lake Trail** is a short lakeside trail that starts at the second parking lot near the chalet, where you can purchase drinks and souvenirs. Only 3.2km and easy enough to be enjoyed by the most inexperienced hiker, it leads to the Schäffer Viewpoint, which was named after Mary Schäffer, the first woman to explore the valley. After the viewpoint, the trail leads into the forest, where you'll find "potholes" created by the glaciers, then heads back to the chalet.

The trail to **Mona and Lorraine Lakes** is also short, relatively easy and extremely

pleasant. It leads through a forest of lodgepole pine to the two charming little lakes.

To reach the trail that skirts **Patricia Lake**, take the road to Pyramid Lake as far as the parking lot for the stables. This short (4.8km), easy hike makes for a charming excursion. The trail starts out by climbing gently through the forest, then heads back down to the south shore of the lake. It then winds its way down to a small valley frequented by deer, moose and beavers, as well as by a large number of birds. It is best to come here in the early morning or late afternoon, when the temperature is cool and the animals come out of the forest to feed in the fields and quench their thirst at watering holes. Trivia buffs might be interested to know that Patricia Lake was named after the daughter of the Duke of Connaught, Canada's Governor General from 1911 to 1914.

Mountain Biking

Mountain bikes are permitted on certain trails. Always keep in mind that there might be people or bears around each bend. We also recommend limiting your speed on downhill stretches.

Banff National Park

You won't have any trouble renting a bicycle in Banff, since you can do so at a number of hotels. **Bactrax** *(from $8/hr for a mountain bike and $6/hr for a city bike, $30/day; every day 8am to 8pm; 225 Bear St.; ☎403-762-8177)* organizes mountain-bike trips in the Banff area (each package includes a bicycle, a helmet, transportation to the point of departure, refreshments and the services of a guide).

Jasper National Park

The Jasper area is crisscrossed by bike trails.

A nine-kilometre trail leads from the parking lot opposite the Jasper Aquatic Centre to **Mina Lake** and **Riley Lake**. The pitch is fairly steep until you reach the firebreak road leading to Cabin Lake. Cross this road and continue to Mina Lake. Three and a half kilometres farther along, another trail branches off toward Riley Lake. To return to Jasper, take Pyramid Lake Road.

The **Saturday Night Lake Loop** starts at the Cabin Creek West parking lot and climbs gently for 24.6km, offering a view of the Miette and Athabasca Valleys. Past Caledonia Lake, it winds through the forest to the High Lakes, where the grade becomes steeper. It then leads to Saturday Night Lake and Cabin Lake. From there, follow the firebreak road to Pyramid Lake Road, which will take you back to Jasper.

The **Athabasca River Trail** (25km) starts at the Old Fort Point parking lot, near Jasper Park Lodge. For the first 10km of the trail after the lodge's golf course, you will have to climb some fairly steep slopes, especially as you approach the Maligne Canyon. Bicycles are forbidden between the first and fifth bridges of the canyon trail, so you have to take Maligne Road for this part of the trip. After the fifth bridge, turn left and ride alongside the Athabasca River on trail 7. If you don't want to go back the way you came, take Hwy. 16.

Like the Athabasca River Trail, the **Valley of the Five Lakes Trail** and the **Wabasso Lake Trail** both start at the Old Fort Point parking lot. Trails 1, 1A and 9 begin here. The trip, which covers 11.2km, is quite easy up until the first lake in the valley, although a few spots are a bit rocky. At the first lake, the trail splits in two; take the path on the left, since it offers the best view of the lakes. The two trails merge into one again near a pond at the turn-off for Wabasso Lake. Pick up Hwy. 93, unless you want to go to Wabasso Lake, in which case you have to take trail 9 (19.3 km), to the left of the pond. Head back to Jasper on the Icefields Parkway.

You have to drive to the parking lot at Celestine Lake, which marks the beginning of the trail (48km). A gravel road leads to the **Snake Indian Falls**, 22km away. About one kilometre farther, the road turns into a small trail that leads to Rock Lake.

Mountain Bike Rentals

Freewheel Cycle
$8/hr, $24/day
618 Patricia St., Jasper
☎*(780) 852-3898*
Freewheel Cycle rents out quality mountain bikes. You can also have repairs done here.

On-Line Sport & Tackle
$15/half-day, $20/day
600 Patricia St., Jasper
☎*(780) 852-3630*
At On-Line Sport & Tackle you'll find bikes, helmets and maps of bike paths.

The Kananaskis Region

Canmore is a mountain biker's dream come true, with challenging trails and breathtaking views. From 1998 to 2000, the **Canmore Nordic Centre** *(1988 Olympic Way, ☎403-678-2400)* hosted the Mountain Biking World Cup, which challenged the best in the world. Beginners can take a lesson at the centre and then enjoy the rolling double track, while advanced bikers will fall in love with the sinuous single track and screaming downhill tracks on both sides of the valley. Stop in at any bike shop in town to find out

where the best trails are. The **Banff Trail** is a 40km path that goes right up to the Banff Springs golf course before returning to Canmore.

Trail Sports
Canmore Nordic Center
☎*(780) 678-6764*

The **Georgetown Trail** is relatively flat and joins the Bow River near Georgetown, formerly a mining town.

Fishing

Fishing permits are required in all Canadian national parks. You can obtain one at any of the parks' administrative or tourist information offices, from park rangers and at some boat rental outfits. Visitors under the age of 16 do not need permits if they are accompanied by a permit-holder. The waters are teeming with rainbow and brown trout, char and pike. There are a number of rules to follow. You can obtain a copy of the regulations concerning sport fishing in the region's national parks through any Parks Canada office. Fishing is permitted year-round in the Bow River, but is only legal during very specific periods on some lakes. For more information on these dates, contact Parks Canada.

Tour A: Banff National Park

Monod Sports
129 Banff Ave.
☎*(403)762-4571*
Monod Sports specializes in fly fishing; guided excursions include equipment.

Minnewanka Boat Tours
mid-May to early Oct
on the landing stage at the entrance to Minnewanka Lake
☎*(403) 762-3473*

Tour C: Jasper National Park

Maligne Tours
from $185 per person
627 Patricia St., Jasper
☎*(780) 852-3370*
Maligne Tours offers guided fishing trips, with meals and equipment included. Reservations required.

On-Line Sport & Tackle
$149 half a day
$189 full day incl. lunch
600 Patricia St., Jasper
☎*(780) 852-3630*

Tour E: The Kananaskis Region

Banff Fishing Unlimited
Canmore
☎*(403) 762-4936*
Banff Fishing Unlimited provides professional guides, who can direct you to the best spots. Equipment is included in the price.

Mountain Fly Fishers
102-512 Bow Valley Trail, Canmore
☎*(403)678-9522 or*
800-450-9664
Mountain Fly Fishers arranges fly-fishing trips that last several days. Prices vary according to the length of the trip.

Rafting

The rivers running through the Rockies have a lot to offer thrill-seekers. Whether it's your first time out or you already have some rafting experience, you'll find all sorts of interesting challenges here.

The most popular places to go rafting in the Banff area are **Kicking Horse River** and **Lower Canyon**. A few words of advice: wear a bathing suit and closed running shoes that you don't mind getting wet, dress very warmly (heavy wool and a windbreaker) and bring along a towel and a change of clothes for the end of the day.

Tour A and D: Banff, Kootenay and Yoho National Parks

Hydra River Guides
$90 plus tax
closed Oct to Nov
211 Bear St.,Banff
☎*(403)762-4554 or 800-684-8888*
Hydra River Guides offers day trips in Upper Canyon on Kicking Horse River. The rate includes transportation and a BBQ lunch or dinner. Advance booking is required.

Wild Water Adventures
mi-May to mid-Sep
Lake Louise and Banff
☎*(403) 522-2211 or 800-647-4444*
Wild Water Adventures offers half-day ($72), full day ($99) and two-day packages.

Rocky Mountain Raft Tours
mid-May to late Sep
$26/hr
Banff
☎*(403) 762-3632*
Canoe rentals are also offered.

Glacier Raft Company
late May to late Aug
$89 per day
$55 half-day
☎*(403) 762-4347 Banff*
☎*(250) 344-6521 Golden BC*
The Glacier Raft Company organizes trips down the Kicking Horse River. There is a special rate *($110, tax included)* for the **Kicking Horse Challenge**, which is a slightly wilder ride than the others.

Wet'n'Wild Adventure
mid-May to early Sep
$83 and up
Golden, BC
☎*(250) 344-6546 or 800-668-9119*
Wet'n'Wild Adventure offers trips from Golden, Lake Louise and Banff. A half-day on the Kicking Horse River will cost $55. Those wishing to spend several days on the water can take advantage of some interesting package deals

($160 per person). A minimum number of passengers is required, however.

Alpine Rafting Company
late Apr to early Sep
$60-$110
Golden, BC
☎*(250) 344-6778 or 800-599-5299*
The Alpine Rafting Company has a variety of packages for novice and experienced rafters down the Kicking Horse River.

Kootenay River Runners
$85-$123 incl. lunch
Edgewater, BC
☎*(250) 347-9210 or 800-599-4399*
☎*(403) 762-5385 Banff*
The Kootenay River Runners offers voyageur canoe trips, which add a historical dimension to the Columbia River and its abundant wildlife-viewing opportunities.

Jasper National Park

Whitewater Rafting
early May to early Oct
$42 to $58
Jasper
☎*(780) 852-7238 or 800-557-7238*
Whitewater Rafting has a counter in **Jasper Park Lodge** (☎*780-852-6091*), and another at the **Alpine Petro Canada** gas station *(711 Connaught Dr.,* ☎*780-852-3114)*. This company organizes trips down the Athabasca, Maligne and Sunwapta Rivers.

Maligne River Adventures
$45 and up
627 Patricia St., Jasper
☎*(780) 852-3370 or 866-625-4463*
Maligne River Adventures, in addition to other excursions, offers an interesting three-day trip down the Kakwa River for $450 *(May and Jun)*. Some experience is required, since these are class IV rapids, and are thus rather difficult to negotiate.

All outfitters in Jasper offer trips for novices and children who would like to try rafting

on slower moving rapids: **Jasper Raft Tours** *($46, children $16; Jasper,* ☎*780-852-2665 or 888-553-5628)*

Horseback Riding

Horseback riding is a pleasant way to explore the more remote parts of the parks in the Rockies. A number of trails have been set aside for riders and their mounts. If you would like to ride your own horse, you must inform the agents at one of the Parks Canada offices and obtain a map of the bridle paths.

Tour A: Banff National Park

Warner Guiding and Outfitting *(Banff,* ☎*403-762-4551, or 800-661-8352)* offers short, easy rides of one, two or three hours, as well as real expeditions. Three days of riding in Mystic Valley will cost about $540, and a six-day wildlife interpretation trip, $1,200. In all, there are over fifteen excursions to choose from, with something for everyone, whether you're a camping buff or prefer staying in lodges. All of these outings, of course, are led by professional guides who can tell you anything you might like to know about the flora, fauna and geological characteristics of the areas you will be riding through.

The **Brewster Lake Louise Stables** *($35/day; Lake Louise,* ☎*403-762-5454 or 800-691-5085)* are located right beside the Chateau Lake Louise.

Tour C: Jasper National Park

Pyramid Stables *($26/hr, $45/2hrs, $65/3hrs; May to Oct; near Patricia Lake, 4km from Jasper heading toward*

Pyramid Lake, ☎ *780-852-7433)* arranges short pony rides for small children and longer outings for adults.

Skyline Trail Rides *(from $25; Jasper Park Lodge, Jasper,* ☎ *780-852-4215 or 888-852-7787, in winter* ☎ *780-865-4021).*

Paragliding

This activity is forbidden in the national parks in the Rockies but is permitted in Kananaskis Country. **Paraglide Canada** *(Apr to Oct; 6857 Hwy. 6 East, Vernon,* ☎ *250-503-1962)* offers one-day courses *($180)* and tandem flights *($150)* appropriate for beginners, as well as other packages. Equipment sales.

Golden Mountain Adventures *(☎403-344-4650 or 800-433-9533)* offers paragliding packages near Mount Stephen.

Golf

Tour A: Banff National Park

Canmore Golf & Curling Club
$25 for 9 holes
$38 for 18
$40 for equipment rental
☎*(403) 678-5959*
Equipment can be rented on the premises.

Banff Springs Hotel
☎*(403) 762-6801*
The Banff Springs Hotel has a magnificent 18-hole course set in enchantingly beautiful surroundings.

Tour C: Jasper National Park

Jasper Park Lodge
☎*(780) 852-3301*
There is a lovely golf course near the Jasper Park Lodge. Reservations can be made at the front desk of the lodge.

Tour D: Kootenay and Yoho National Parks

The Columbia River Valley is a veritable paradise for golfers, with more courses than you can count. We have only indicated a few below; for a more exhaustive list, pick up the golfing brochure at the tourist office in Radium Hot Springs.

Golden Golf & Country Club
$49.50/18 holes
Golden
☎*866-727-7222*
The magnificent golf course at the Golden Golf & Country Club is surrounded by grandiose landscapes. It lies alongside the Trans-Canada Highway, near the Columbia River, between the Rockies and the Purcell Mountains.

Way-Lyn Ranch Golf Course
$22/18 holes
Hwy. 95A, S.S.3, site 19-4
Cranbrook
☎*(250) 427-2825*
The nine-hole Way-Lyn Ranch Golf Course is located between the towns of Cranbrook and Kimberley.

Trickle Creek
$99/18 holes
Kimberley
☎*(250) 427-5171 or 888-874-2553*
Trickle Creek is an 18-hole golf course. Reservations recommended.

The two golf courses at **The Radium Resort** *($45; Radium Hot Springs,* ☎*250-347-9311 or 800-667-6444)* and the **Springs Golf Course** *($69)* are three of the loveliest golf courses in British Columbia.

Tour E: The Kananaskis Region

Canmore Gulf and Curling Club
$25/9 holes
$38/18 holes
☎*(403) 678-5959*
Equipment rental ($40).

Kananaskis Country Golf Course
Mar to Oct
$70/18 holes
Kananaskis Village
☎*(403) 591-7154 or 877-591-2525*
Kananaskis Country Golf Course has two excellent 18-hole golf courses located south of the Trans-Canada Highway via Hwy. 40.

SilverTip
$140 Thu-Sun
$120 Mon-Wed
1000 SilverTip Trail, Canmore
☎*(403) 591-7272 or 877-877-5444*
Silvertip was built in 1998 on the sunny side of the Bow River valley. Each hole of this adventurous golf course snakes up and down the mountainside, with great views of the countryside. Experts, get out your clubs!

Downhill Skiing

It is impossible to look at the Rockies without imagining the hours of pleasure you'll have tearing down the endless slopes. Able to satisfy the most demanding skiers, the resorts here offer a variety of beautifully maintained trails covering all levels of difficulty and excellent skiing conditions. The ski season generally starts around October and can continue into May.

Tour A: Banff National Park

Ski Banff@Norquay
$49 full-day pass
on Norquay Rd., Banff
☎*(403)762-4421*
Ski Banff@Norquay was one of the first ski resorts in North America. It takes just 10 minutes to drive here from downtown Banff. For ski conditions, call ☎(403) 762-4421. The resort has both a ski school and a rental shop.

Sunshine Village
$60 full day
8 km west of Banff, Banff
☎*(403) 760-6500 or*
800-661-1676
Sunshine Village is a beautiful ski resort located at an altitude of 2,700m on the Continental Divide between the provinces of Alberta and British Columbia. This resort has the advantage of being located above the tree line and thus gets lots of sun. Dial ☎(403) 277-SNOW for ski conditions. Ski rentals available.

Lake Louise
$59/day
Lake Louise
☎*(403) 522-3555*
Lake Louise has the largest ski resort in Canada, covering four mountainsides and offering skiers over 50 different runs. Both downhill and cross-country equipment are available for rent here. For ski conditions, call ☎(403) 762-4766.

Tour C: Jasper National Park

Marmot Basin
$52 full day
take Hwy. 93 toward Banff then turn right on 93A to get to the resort, Jasper
☎*(780) 852-3816*
☎*(780) 488-5909 for ski conditions*
Marmot Basin is located about 20 minutes by car from downtown Jasper. Ski rentals available.

Tour D: Kootenay and Yoho National Parks

Kimberley Alpine Resort
$49 full day
Kimberley
☎*(250) 427-4881 or*
800-258-7669
The Kimberley Ski Resort is the only real attraction in Kimberley, an amazing little Bavarian village. It has some decent trails that are perfect for family skiing.

Kicking Horse Mountain Resort
$49 per day
1500 Kicking Horse Way, Golden
☎*(250) 439-5400 or*
866-754-5425
Formerly Whitetooth, Kicking Horse Mountain Resort, Canada's newest ski resort opened in winter 2000. It has a vertical drop of 1,250m. There are ski resorts at the base of the mountain.

Panorama Resort
$49
Panorama
☎*800-663-2929*
Panorama Resort Ski Hill boasts a vertical rise of 1,300m with glade and bowl skiing in the Purcell Mountains.

Tour E: Kananaskis Country

Nakiska
$46 day
P.O. Box 1988, Kananaskis Village
☎*(403)591-7777 or*
800-258-7669
Nakiska hosted the men's and women's downhill, slalom and combination events during the 1988 Winter Olympics. Built specifically for that purpose, along with Kananaskis Village, this resort boasts excellent, modern infrastructure and top-notch trails. Downhill and cross-country equipment are both available for rent here.

Fortress Mountain
$34 day
take Hwy. 40, past Kananaskis Village, and turn right at Fortress Junction, Kananaski Village
☎*(403) 256-8473 or*
(403) 244-6665
for ski conditions
Fortress Mountain, located on the Continental Divide, at the edge of Peter Lougheed Provincial Park, is less popular than Nakiska but nevertheless has some very interesting runs.

Cross-Country Skiing

There are countless cross-country trails in the parks of the Rockies, whose tourist information offices distribute maps of the major trails around the towns of Banff and Jasper and the village of Lake Louise.

Canmore Nordic Centre
1988 Olympic Way, ste. 100
Canmore
☎*(403) 678-2400*
The Canmore Nordic Centre, which hosted the cross-country events of the 1988 Winter Olympics, deserves special mention for its magnificent network of trails.

Heli-Skiing

Heli-skiing is an extraordinary experience for top-notch skiers longing for untouched stretches of powder. The calmness and immensity of the surroundings are striking and you can take in panoramic views that could once be enjoyed only by mountain climbers. Prices for this type of excursion vary greatly, depending on where the helicopter takes you. We therefore recommend shopping around a bit.

The Rocky Mountains

Assiniboine Heli Tours
125 Railway Ave., Canmore
☎*(403) 678-5459*
Assiniboine Heli Tours organizes group outings to the peaks around Banff, Lake Louise and Whistler, as well as the Purcell, Selkirk and Chilcotin Mountains.

Canadian Mountain Holidays
Banff
☎*(403) 762-7100 or*
800-661-0252
Canadian Mountain Holidays has been in operation for 30 years, and the quality of the service leaves nothing to be desired. You can choose from a wide variety of excursions ranging from one to several days in length. Professional guides escort visitors to Mount Revelstoke, Valemount, the Monashees and the Cariboos.

Selkirk Tangiers Helicopter Skiing
Jan to mid-Apr
Revelstoke
☎*(250) 837-5378*
for British Columbia
☎*800-663-7080*
Selkirk Tangiers Helicopter Skiing offers day- and week-long excursions in the Selkirk and Monashee Mountains.

R.K. Heli-ski Panorama
Dec to Apr
reservation counters, in the Banff Springs Hotel, and the Chateau Lake Louise and in downtown Banff at R&R Sports
☎*(250) 342-3889 or*
800-661-6060
R.K. Heli-ski Panorama arranges guided excursions for intermediate and advanced skiers in the Purcell Mountains in British Columbia.

Mountain Climbing

Tour A: Banff National Park

Yamnuska Summit Centre
200, 50 Lincoln Park, Canmore
☎*(403) 678-4164*
www.yamnuska.com
Yamnuska is both the name of the climbing school and the name of the first mountain you see as you leave Calgary. The school offers a range of climbing courses, from glacier climbing, to mountain survival-training, to anything that has to do with mountaineering in general, whether by foot, skis or snow board. It's the most renowned school of its kind in the country, and its professionalism is impeccable.

Alpine Club of Canada
Indian Flats Road
4.5km east of Canmore
☎*(403) 678-3200*
Alpine Club of Canada is also for mountain lovers since it has a wide range of expeditions, from the first great climb, to an easy afternoon climb. The possibilities are endless, and the prices accommodate all budgets. One of the most interesting excursions involves passing the night in one of many huts belonging to the association.

Tour C: Jasper National Park

Peter Amann of Mountain Guiding and Schools offers mountaineering lessons for novices and experienced climbers alike *(from $150 for 2 days, Jasper,* ☎*780-852-3237).*

Dogsledding

Tour A: Banff National Park

Kingmik Expeditions Dog Sled Tours
Lake Louise
☎*(250) 344-5298*
897-919-7779
Kingmik Expeditions Dog Sled Tours has a variety of packages ranging from half-hour tours to five-day expeditions.

Tour D: Kootenay and Yoho National Park

Golden Mountain Adventures (see p 298) also offers dogsledding trips.

Tour E: Kananaskis Country

Snowy Owl Sled Dog Tours
$80/2hrs
$295/8-10hrs
Canmore, AB
☎*(403) 678-4369 or*
888-311-6874
Snowy Owl Sled Dog Tours specializes in dogsledding and ice-fishing trips.

Howling Dog Tours
Canmore
☎*(403) 678-9588 or*
977-DOG-SLED
Howling Dog Tours offers 2-hr or 3.5-hr trips from Canmore or Banff as well as other options.

Snowmobiling

Tour A: Banff National Park

Challenge Snowmobile Tours
Canmore
☎*(403) 678-2628 or*
800-892-3429
The guides at Challenge Snowmobile Tours are all

instructors. Some tours last several days and offer a chance to explore some of the region's back country. Nights are spent in back-country cabins.

Tour D: Kootenay and Yoho National Parks

The **Golden Snowmobile Club** *(Box 167, Golden, BC, V0A 1H0; ☎250-344-6012)* arranges outings in the Golden area. You will be supplied with a map of the various trails.

Accommodations

Tour A: Banff National Park

Banff

Banff is a tourist town whose population doubles in summer, when, needless to say, the prices also double.

A list of private homes that receive paying guests is provided at the tourist information office located at 224 Banff Avenue. You may obtain this list by writing to the Banff/Lake Louise Tourism Bureau (see p 272).

It is impossible to reserve a campsite in advance in the park, which has a policy of first come, first served, unless you are leading a fairly large group, in which case you should contact the Parks Canada offices in Banff.

Campsites generally cost between $13 and $16, according to the location and the facilities at the site. We advise you to arrive early to choose your spot. In the high season, the Banff campgrounds are literally overrun with hordes of tourists. It is forbidden to pitch your tent outside the area set aside for this purpose. Camping at unauthorized sites is strictly prohibited, for reasons of safety and also to preserve the natural environment of the park.

Tunnel Mountain Trailer Campground
$
on Tunnel Mountain Rd. near the Banff Youth Hostel
Tunnel mountain Trailer Campground has more than 300 spaces set up exclusively for trailers.

Tunnel Mountain 1 and 2
$
mid-May to end Sep
on Tunnel Mountain Rd near the Banff Youth Hostel
Tunnel Mountain 1 and 2 has about 840 spaces for trailers and for tents. There are toilets on the site for the campers.

Two Jack Lake Campgrounds
$
end May to mid-Sep
take the road going to Lake Minnewanka then head toward Two Jack Lake
☎(403) 762-1759
The Two Jack Lake Campgrounds are located on either side of the road that runs alongside Two Jack Lake. There are showers at the campground near the water. The other campground, deeper in the forest, offers a more basic level of comfort. It is easier to find spaces at these two campgrounds than at those in Banff.

Johnston Canyon Campground
$
early Jun to mid-Sep
on Hwy. 1A, toward Lake Louise, a little before the Castle Mountain crossroads
☎(403)762-1581
Set in the forest, the Johnston Canyon Campground is much less busy than the other campgrounds. Set up for trailers and tents, it offers about 100 places.

YWCA
$-$$
102 Spray Ave.
☎*(403)762-3560 or 800-813-4138*
≈*(403) 762-2606*
www.ywcabanff.ab.ca
The YWCA offers a very basic level of comfort. You must bring your own sleeping-bag if you want to sleep in a dormitory. Private rooms are also available. Otherwise, for about $79, you can rent a private room with a bathroom. Very near the centre of town.

Banff Alpine Centre Hostel
$-$$
801 Coyote Dr. (Tunnel Mountain Rd.)
☎*(403)762-4122*
≈*(403) 253-6503*
www.hihostels.ca
Banff International Youth Hostel remains the cheapest solution, but it is often full. It is essential to reserve well in advance or else to arrive early. This friendly youth hostel is only about 20 minutes' walk from the centre of town. It offers a warm welcome, and the desk staff will be pleased to help you organize river rafting and other outdoor activities. Private and family rooms available ($$)

Global Village Backpackers
$-$$
bp/sb
449 Banff Ave.
☎*(403) 762-5521*
≈*(403) 762-0385*
www.globalbackpackers.com
This new hostel has a variety of rooms, from dorms to semi-private chambers to well-equipped hotel rooms. Banff is a notorious party town for travellers and international hotel staff, and this place can be pretty raucous come weekends. Still, it's a good price, and if you're feeling sociable, you'll probably have a great time with all of the international guests. The ground floor has a pool table, kitchen, Internet kiosk and video games.

Holiday Lodge
$$ bkfst incl.
♨

311 Marten St.
☎(403) 762-3648
www.banffholidaylodge.com
Holiday Lodge has five clean and relatively comfortable rooms and two cabins. This old restored house, located in the centre of town, offers good and copious breakfasts.

Cascade Court Bed and Breakfast
$$-$$$ bkfst incl.
2 Cascade Court
☎(403) 762-2956
≈(403) 762-5653
www.tarchuk.com
Just a 5min walk from the Banff Springs Hotel, Cascade Court sits in a ritzy cul-de-sac. The cedar-shingled Victorian contemporary home has two large rooms with modern styles. It's a tidy place, with few decorations, and the choice of one queen or two twin beds. The sitting area for guests is great; there's a small library and a skylight with a perfect view of slanted Rundle Mountain.

King Edward Hotel
$$-$$$
137 Banff Ave.
☎(403) 762-2202 or
800-344-4332
≈(403) 670-0876
www.banffkingedwardhotel.
com
The King Edward Hotel, open since 1904, has a good location at the centre of the action in Banff. It's by no means charming, but many people will be happy with the great price and location. Rooms are fairly bare, but standard enough, and you have the choice between queen, king and twin beds. There is one family room with one king bed and two twins. Security is certainly solid—you need a key to get up the elevator.

Pension Tannanhof
$$$ bkfst incl.
121 Cave Ave
☎(403) 762-4636 or
877-999-5011
≈(403) 762-5660
www.pensiontannenhof.com
Tannanhof Pension has eight rooms and two suites located in a lovely, big house. Some rooms have cable television and private baths, while others share a bathroom. Each of the two suites has a bathroom with tub and shower, a fireplace and a sofa-bed for two extra people. Breakfast is German-style with a choice of four dishes.

Homestead Inn
$$$
217 Lynx St.
☎(403) 762-4471 or
800-661-1021
≈(403) 762-8877
www.homesteadinnbanff.
com
The Homestead Inn is located in the heart of Banff, but not on busy Banff Avenue, which is an advantage in itself. Tastefully decorated rooms and large beds.

Red Carpet Inn
$$$
≡, 🐕
425 Banff Ave.
☎(403) 762-4184 or
800-563-4609
≈(403) 762-4894
The Red Carpet Inn offers simply decorated, lovely rooms. Enjoy a good night's sleep on the soft mattresses.

Banff Voyager Inn
$$$
△, ≈, ℜ
555 Banff Ave., Banff
☎(403)762-3301 or
800-879-1991
≈(403) 762-4131 or
(403) 760-7775
Banff Voyager Inn has comfortable rooms, some with mountain views.

High Country Inn
$$$$
△, ℑ, ≈
419 Banff Ave.
☎(403) 762-2236 or
800-293-5142
≈(403) 762-5084
www.banffhighcountryinn.
com
Located on Banff's main drag, this inn has big, comfortable, spacious rooms with balconies. Furnishings are very ordinary, however, and detract from the beauty of the setting.

Brewster's Mountain Lodge
$$$$
△, ℜ
208 Caribou St.
☎(403) 762-2900 or
888-762-2900
www.brewsteradventures.
com
Brewster's Mountain Lodge features spacious rooms with a mountain decor including cosy log furniture. It is centrally located and a good place to organize your trip from as they offer many touring options.

Traveller's Inn
$$$$
△, ℜ
401 Banff Ave.
☎(403) 762-4401 or
877-886-6660
≈(403) 762-5905
www.banfftravellersinn.
com
Most rooms at the hotel have small balconies that offer fine mountain views. Rooms are simply decorated, big and cosy. The hotel has a small restaurant that serves breakfast, as well as heated underground parking, an advantage in the winter. During the ski season, guests have the use of lockers for skis and boots, as well as a small store for the rental and repair of winter sports equipment.

Rundle Stone Lodge
$$$$
ℜ, ≈, ⊛
537 Banff Ave.
☎(403) 762-2201 or
800-661-8630
⇄(403) 762-4501
www.rundlestone.com
Rundle Stone Lodge occupies a handsome building along Banff's main street. In the part of the building located along Banff Avenue, the rooms are attractive and spacious, each with a balcony. Some also have whirlpool baths. The hotel offers its guests a covered, heated parking area in the winter. Rooms for disabled travellers are available on the ground floor.

Bow View Motor Lodge
$$$$
ℑ ≈, ℜ
228 Bow Ave.
☎(403)762-2261 or
800-661-1565
⇄(403) 762-8093
www.bowview.com
The Bow View Motor Lodge has the immense advantage of being located next to the Bow River and far from noisy Banff Avenue. Only a five minute walk from the centre of town, this charming hotel provides comfortable rooms; those facing the river have balconies. The restaurant, pretty and peaceful, welcomes guests for breakfast.

Norquay's Timberline Inn
$$$$ for rooms
$$$$$ for cabins
ℜ
a little before the entrance to Banff north of the Trans-Canada Hwy. and near Mount Norquay
☎(403) 762-2281 or
877-762-2281
⇄(403) 762-8331
www.banfftimberline.com
Norquay's Timberline Inn offers views of Mount Norquay from its lower-priced rooms, and views of the valley and city of Banff from the others. Though the higher-priced rooms have prettier views, they do unfortunately also overlook the Trans-Canada. There are two

very peaceful cabins available on the Mount Norquay side in the middle of the forest, that accommodate six people.

Douglas Fir Resort & Chalets
$$$$-rooms
$$$$$-chalet
≈, ⊛, △, ℑ, K, ☺
525 Tunnel Mountain Road
☎(403) 762-5591 or
800-661-9267
⇄(403) 762-8774
Toll free fax
⇄800-267-8774
www.douglasfir.com
The recently renovated Douglas Fir Resort & Chalets has 133 rooms and fully equipped cottages (fridge, stove, fireplace, etc) that are ideal for families. Their pleasant layout makes them feel like apartments. The resort offers an incredible view of Mount Rundle and you can take advantage of the squash courts, pool and indoor waterslides.

Inns of Banff, Swiss Village and Rundle Manor
$$$$ Swiss Village
$$$$$ Rundle Manor
$$$$$ Inns of Banff
ℜ ℑ 🐾, K, ≈
600 Banff Ave.
☎(403) 762-4581 or
800-661-1272
⇄(403) 762-2434
www.innsofbanff.com
These three hotels are really one big hotel, with a common reservation service. Depending on your budget, you have the choice of three distinct buildings. Inns of Banff, the most luxurious, has 180 very spacious rooms, each facing a small terrace. The Swiss Village has a little more character

and fits the setting much better. The rooms, however are a bit expensive at $185 and are less comfortable. Finally, Rundle Manor is the most rustic of the three but lacks charm. The Rundle's units have small kitchens, living rooms and one or two separate bedrooms. Pets are allowed. This is a safe bet for family travellers. Guests at the Rundle Manor and Swiss Village have access to the facilities of the Inns of Banff.

Mount Royal Hotel
$$$$$ bkfst incl.
△, ≈, ☺, ℜ
138 Banff Ave
mid-May to early Sep
☎(403) 762-3331 or
800-267-3035
⇄(403) 762-8938
www.mountroyalhotel.com
Mount Royal Hotel, right in the centre of town not far from the tourist information centre, rents comfortable rooms.

🚢 Fairmont Banff Springs Hotel
$$$$$
☺, △, 🐾, ℜ, ≈, ✪
Spray Ave.
☎(403) 762-2211 or
800-441-1414
⇄(403) 762-4447
www.fairmont.com
Banff Springs Hotel is the biggest hotel in Banff. Overlooking the town, this five-star hotel, which once belonged to the Canadian Pacific chain, offers 770 luxurious

Fairmont Banff Springs Hotel

The Rocky Mountains

rooms in an atmosphere reminiscent of an old Scottish castle. The hotel was designed by architect Price, to whom is also credited Windsor Station in Montréal and the Château Frontenac in Quebec City. Besides typical turn-of-the-century chateau style, old-fashioned furnishings and superb views from every window, the hotel offers its guests bowling, tennis courts, a pool, a sauna, a large whirlpool bath, and a massage room. You can also stroll and shop in the more than 50 shops in the hotel. Golfers will be delighted to find a superb 27-hole course, designed by architect Stanley Thompson, on the grounds.

Rimrock Resort Hotel
$$$$$
☺, ☻, ≡, ℜ, ≈, △
100 Mountain Ave.
☎*(403) 762-3365 or*
800-661-1587
≈*(403) 762-4132*
www.rimrockresort.com
From afar, the Rimrock Resort Hotel stands out majestically from the mountainside much like the Banff Springs does. The rooms are equally well appointed though more modern. The various categories of rooms are based on the views they offer, the best view is of the Bow and Spray Valleys. The hotel is right across the street from the Upper Hot Springs.

Tunnel Mountain Resort
$$$$$ per chalet
△, ≈, ℜ, ☺, K
intersection of Tunnel Mountain Rd. and Tunnel Mountain Dr.
☎*(403) 762-4515 or*
800-661-1859
≈*(403) 762-5183*
www.tunnelmountain.com
Tunnel Mountain Chalets offers fully-equipped cottages and condo-style units with kitchens, fireplaces and patios. This is a great option for families and for those looking to save some money by avoiding eating out. The interiors are standard, but clean and very

comfortable. The larger units can sleep up to eight people.

Banff Rocky Mountain Resort
$$$$$
ℜ, △, ℜ, ⊛, ≈, ☺
at the entrance to the town
1029 Banff Ave.
☎*(403) 762-5531 or*
800-661-9563
≈*(403) 762-5166*
www.rockymountainresort.
com
Banff Rocky Mountain Resort is an ideal spot if you are travelling as a family in Banff National Park. The delightful little chalets are warm and very well equipped. On the ground floor is a bathroom with shower, a very functional kitchen facing a living room and dining room with a fireplace while upstairs are two bedrooms and another bathroom. These apartments also have small private terraces. Near the main building are picnic and barbecue areas as well as lounge chairs where you can lie in the sun.

Banff Caribou Lodge
$$$$$
ℜ, △, ☺
521 Banff Ave.
☎*(403) 762-5887 or*
800-563-8764
≈*(403) 760-8287*
www.banffcaribou
properties.com
Caribou Lodge is another Banff Avenue hotel offering comfortable, spacious rooms. A rustic western decor of varnished wood characterizes the reception area and guest rooms.

Between Banff
and Lake Louise

Johnston Canyon Resort
$$$-$$$$$
🐾, ℜ, K, ℜ
from Banff, take the Trans-Canada Hwy to the Bow Valley exit then take Hwy 1A , the Bow Valley Parkway
☎*(403) 762-2971 or*
888-378-1720
≈*(403) 762-0868*
www.johnstoncanyon.com
Johnston Canyon Resort constitutes a group of small log

cabins right in the middle of the forest. The absolute calm is suitable for retreats. Some cabins offer a basic level of comfort, while others are fully equipped and have kitchens, sitting rooms and fireplaces. The biggest cabin can accommodate four people comfortably. A small grocery store, offering a basic range of products, is part of this tourism complex, as is a café and restaurant.

Near Silver City

Castle Mountain Campground
$
on your right, just after Silver City
☎*(403) 762-1550*
≈*(403) 762-3880*
No reservation is required to spend the night here. You have to register yourself at the campground entrance, by placing your payment in one of the envelopes provided and dropping it into the payment box.

Castle Mountain Wilderness Hostel
$
27 km from Banff on Hwy 1A at the Castle Junction crossroads across from Castle Mountain Village
for reservations, call the Calgary reservations office
☎*(403) 521-8421 or*
866-762-4122
≈*(403) 522-2253*
Castle Mountain Youth Hostel occupies a small building with two dormitories and a common room set around a big fireplace. The atmosphere is very pleasant.

Castle Mountain Chalets
$$$$$
K, ⊛
Lake Louise
☎*(403) 522-2783 or*
(403) 762-3868
www.castlemountain.com
Castle Mountain Village is a superb collection of 20 small log cabins located at Castle Junction on Hwy. 1A. Each cabin can accommodate four people, and some can house up to eight. A small grocery

store provides everyday products. The interiors of the cabins are very comfortable and seem intended to make you feel at ease. The one and two bedroom chalet have kitchens that are fully equipped and include microwave ovens and dishwashers. The main bathrooms have whirlpool baths. A roaring fire in the fireplace and the VCRs provided in the newer cabins constitute the perfect remedy for those cold mountain evenings. A very good choice.

Lake Louise

Lake Louise Campground
$
for information, contact the Lake Louise Visitor Centre
☎*(403) 522-3833*
leaving the Trans-Canada Hwy turn left at the main Lake Louise intersection and continue straight then cross the railroad and turn left on Fairview, the campground is at the end of the road
As everywhere in Lake Louise, there are few places available, making it important to arrive early. Reservations are not accepted. The Bow River cuts through the campground.

Lake Louise Inn
$$$$
🛏, ≈, ℜ
210 Village Rd.
☎*(403) 522-3791 or 800-661-9237*
⇥*(403) 522-2018*
www.lakelouiseinn.com
Lake Louise Inn is located in the village of Lake Louise. The hotel offers very comfortable, warmly decorated rooms.

 Deer Lodge
$$$$
ℜ, ⌂
near the lake, on the right before reaching the Chateau Lake Louise
☎*(403) 522-3747 or 800-661-1595*
⇥*(403) 522-3883*
Deer Lodge is a very handsome and comfortable hotel. Rooms are spacious and tastefully decorated. The atmosphere is very pleasant.

Mountaineer Lodge
$$$$
⌂
101 Village Rd.
☎*(403) 522-3844*
⇥*(403) 522-3902*
www.mountaineerlodge. com
Located in the village of Lake Louise, the Mountaineer Lodge has 78 rather simply furnished rooms.

Baker Creek Chalets
$$$$
ℜ, K, ⌺
☎*(403) 522-3761*
⇥*(403) 522-2270*
www.bakercreek.com
Located just 10min south of Lake Louise, next to the Bow Valley Parkway, Baker Creek Chalets offer guests several charming log cabins equipped with all the necessary conveniences, such as a stove and fridge. Cabins are available for groups of any size. In addition to its proximity to the Lake Louise Ski Resort and a wide array of hiking trails, this peaceful haven will allow you to relax in the surrounding countryside.

Skoki Lodge
$$$$$
open mid-Dec to Apr and Jun to Sep
⌂
reached by an 11-km trail (hike, ride, or ski) from the Lake Louise ski slopes
☎*(403) 522-3555*
⇥*(403) 522-2095*
www.skokilodge.com
All meals are included in the price of the room.

Paradise Lodge & Bungalows
$$$$$
K, ℝ
on your right, just after the Lake Moraine cutoff
☎*(403) 522-3595*
⇥*(403) 522-3987*
www.paradaselodge.com
Paradise Lodge & Bungalows is a complex with 21 small log bungalows and 24 luxury suites. It should be noted that rooms do not have telephones.

Moraine Lake Lodge
$$$$$
Jun to Oct
ℜ
☎*(403) 522-3733*
⇥*(403) 522-3719*
www.morainelake.com
Moraine Lake Lodge is located at the edge of Lake Moraine. Rooms do not have phones or televisions. The setting is magnificent but packed with tourists at all times, detracting from its tranquillity.

Post Hotel
$$$$$
≈, ℜ
☎*(403) 522-3989 or 800-661-1586*
⇥*(403) 522-3966*
www.posthotel.com
The magnificent Post Hotel is part of the Relais et Châteaux chain. Everything at this elegant establishment, from the rooms to the grounds, is tastefully and carefully laid out. The restaurant is exquisite and the staff, friendly. If you can afford the extra cost and are looking to treat yourself, then this is the best place in Lake Louise.

Fairmont Chateau Lake Louise
$$$$$
⊙, ≈, ℜ, ⌂
111 Lake Louise Dr.
☎*(403) 522-3511 or 800-257-7544*
⇥*(403) 522-3834*
Chateau Lake Louise is one of the best-known hotels in the region. Built originally in 1890, the hotel burned to the ground in 1892 and was rebuilt the following year. Another fire devastated parts of it in 1924. Since then, it has been expanded and embellished almost continuously. Today, this vast hotel, which once belonged to the Canadian Pacific Chain, has 511 rooms with space for more than 1,300 guests, and a staff of nearly 725 to look after your every need. Perched by the turquoise waters of Lake Louise, facing the Victoria Glacier, the hotel boasts a divine setting.

Tour B:
The Icefields Parkway

Between Lake Louise and the Icefields Parkway

Athabasca Falls Youth Hostel
$
32km south of Jasper, Sky Tram Rd.
Closed Tue Oct to Apr
**☎(780) 852-3215 or
877-852-0781
≈(780) 852-5560
www.bihostels.ca**
In keeping with the rustic decor, this hostel has no running water, but it does have electricity and a kitchen. It is situated next to Athabasca Falls. Cyclists and hikers will appreciate this hostel's great location.

Wilcox Creek Campground
Columbia Icefield Campground
$
a few kilometres from the Columbia Icefield
These two campgrounds are equipped with the basics. You have to register yourself.

Rampart Creek Campground
$
end Jun to early Sep
a few kilometres from the intersection of Hwys 11 and 93
The entrance to the campground is unguarded. You must register yourself, and leave the payment for your stay in an envelope.

Mount Kerkeslin Campground
$
Mount Kerkeslin Campground is located 35km south of Jasper.

Honeymoon Lake Campground
$
mid-May to Nov
51 km south of Jasper and 52 km north of the Columbia Icefield interpretive centre
With the Sunwapta falls close by, this campground promises you a fine view of the Athabasca Valley.

Waterfowl Lake Campground
$
end Jun to mid-Sep.
above Lake Mistaya, just after the Mount Chephren lookout
As everywhere in the parks, it is first come, first served. Reservations are not possible unless you are a group. If that is the case, call the Parks Canada offices in Banff.

Rampart Creek Wilderness Hostel
$
closure dates may apply, call for details
near the campground of the same name on Hwy 93
**☎(403) 521-8421 or
866-762-4155
≈(403) 762-3441
www.bihostels.ca**
Rampart Creek Youth Hostel comes off as a little rustic, but it is very well situated for hikers and cyclists visiting the glaciers.

Beauty Creek Youth Hostel
$
partial closure Oct to Apr
$50 deposit require
87km from Jasper and 17km north of the Columbia Icefield interpretation centre
**☎(403) 852-3215 or
877-852-0781
≈(403) 852-5560
www.bihostels.ca**
A day's pedalling from Jasper, this is a good spot for cyclists. The level of comfort is basic, but the atmosphere is pleasant. Moreover, you can take a side trip to beautiful Stanley Falls, located close by.

Jonas Creek Campground
$
mid-May to Nov
77km south of Jasper and 9km north of the Beauty Creek Youth Hostel

Mosquito Creek Wilderness Hostel
$
△
on Hwy 93, a few kilometres after Lake Hector
**☎(403) 521-8421 or
866-762-4122
www.bihostels.com**
Mosquito Creek Youth Hostel offers a very basic level of comfort, with no running water or electricity. There is however a wood-fired sauna. Lodging is in mixed dormitories and private rooms.

The Crossing
$$
△, ℜ
at the crossroads of Hwys 93 and 11, 80 km from Lake Louise
**☎(403) 761-7000 or
800-387-8103
≈(403) 761-7006**
The Crossing is a good place to stop along the Icefields Parkway.

Columbia Icefield Chalet
$$$$
open May to mid-Oct
ℜ
Icefields Parkway
at the foot of the Athabasca Glacier
**☎877-423-7433
≈877-766-7433
www.brewster.ca/attractions**
The Columbia Icefield Chalet, with its terrific location, boasts equally terrific views. If you can afford the extra $20 opt for the glacier-view rooms. All rooms are fairly standard, with queen-sized beds and large bathrooms. You are staying here for the setting, after all.

Num-Ti-Jah Lodge
$$$$$
△, ℜ
on the shore of Bow Lake
about 35 km from Lake Louise
**☎(403) 522-2167
≈(403) 522-2425 or
(403) 762-3441
www.num-ti-jah.com**
Num-Ti-Jah Lodge was built by Jimmy Simpson, a famous mountain guide and trapper from the region. Jimmy Simpson's two daughters also have a place in the history of the Rockies. Peg and Mary

became world-class figure skaters in their time and made numerous tours of Canada and the United States. The name Num-Ti-Jah comes from a Stoney Aboriginal word for pine marten. The spot is popular with tourists, for Bow Lake is one of the most beautiful in the region.

Tour C:
Jasper National Park

Jasper

Jasper Home Accommodation Association
$-$$
www.stayinjasper.com
The Jasper Home Accommodation Association is a group of private homes, each offering up to three bedrooms. The prices and inspections are regulated by Parks Canada, which insures certain quality standards. A good, reasonably priced alternative for those who want more than an anonymous hotel room.

Athabasca Hotel
$$-$$$
sb/pb, ℜ
510 Patricia St.
☎*(780) 852-3386 or*
877-542-8422
⇄*(780) 852-4955*
www.athabascahotel.com
Athabasca Hotel is located right in the centre of Jasper, half a block from the Via Rail station and the Brewster and Greyhound bus terminal. Decorated in old English style, the rooms are not very big, but they are appealing. The least expensive are near a central bathroom, but the others have their own facilities. Neither flashy nor luxurious, this hotel is quite adequate, and the rooms are pleasant. This is the cheapest place to stay in Jasper, so you'll have to reserve in advance. The hotel does not have an elevator.

Astoria Hotel
$$$$
ℜ, ℑ
404 Connaught Dr.
☎*(403) 852-3351 or*
800-661-7343
⇄*(403) 852-5472*
www.astoriahotel.com
The Astoria Hotel has the character and charm of a small European hotel. The attractively designed building faces the busiest street in Jasper in the centre of town. Built in 1920, it's one of the oldest building in Jasper.

🏕 Tekara Lodge
$$$$/cabin
K, ℑ, ℜ
early May to mid-Oct
1km south of Jasper
☎*(780) 852-3058 or*
888-404-4540
⇄*852-4636*
Tekkara Lodge is located in an idyllic spot near the banks of the Miette and Athabasca Rivers. The furnishings are luxurious and spacious, and include a fireplace and a kitchenette. Open your window and let yourself be lulled by the streams that flow down the glaciers at your door.

Marmot Lodge
$$$$
🐾, ℑ, ≈, ℜ, *K*
86 Connaught Dr. at the Jasper east exit, toward Edmonton
☎*(780) 852-4471 or*
888-852-7737
⇄*(780) 852-3280*
Marmot Lodge offers very attractive rooms at what are considered reasonable prices in Jasper. The rooms are decorated in bright colours and old photographs hang on the walls, for a change from the normal decor. A terrace with tables has been set up in front of the pool, and this is a good spot for sunbathing. The decor, the friendly staff and the scenery all contribute to making this hotel a very pleasant place. It provides the best quality-to-price ratio in town.

Maligne Lodge
$$$$
≈, *K*, ℜ, △, ⊛, ℑ
900 Connaught Dr.
leaving Jasper toward Banff
☎*(403) 852-3143 or*
800-661-1315
⇄*(403) 852-4789*
www.malignelodge.com
Maligne Lodge offers 98 very comfortable rooms and suites, some of them with fireplaces and whirlpool baths.

Whistler's Inn
$$$$
≡, ℜ, △
☎*(403) 852-3361 or*
800-282-9919
⇄*(403) 852-4993*
www.whistlersinn.com
Renovations and upgrades have transformed the old Pyramid Hotel into the Whistler Inn. There is a steam room and an outdoor, rooftop hot tub. Each of the rooms, whose decor is standard but very tasteful, offers a view of the surroundings. Parking and ski lockers.

Patricia Lake Bungalows
$$$$
early May to mid-Oct.
K
5km north by Patricia Lake Road
☎*(403) 852-3560 or*
888-499-6848
⇄*(403) 952-4060*
The Patricia Lake Bungalows are located in an idyllic setting in the mountains facing a pretty lake. The discreetly decorated individual bungalows are all cosy, and the kitchenettes make you feel at home. Just a stone's throw from outdoor activity areas.

Tonquin Inn
$$$$
ℑ, ≈, 🐾, △, *K*, ℜ, ≡
at the east entrance to Jasper
100 Juniper St.
☎*(403) 852-4987 or*
800-661-1315
⇄*(403) 852-4413*
www.tonquininn.com
The newer wing is laid out around the pool, providing all rooms direct access to it. The rooms in the old wing are less attractive and resemble motel

rooms, though they do provide an adequate level of comfort. We suggest, nevertheless, that you request a room in the new wing when reserving your room.

Amethyst Lodge
$$$$
≡, ℜ
200 Connaught Dr.
☎*(780) 852-3394 or 888-852-7737*
⇟*(780) 852-5198*
www.mtn-park-lodges.com
Amethyst Lodge is a luxurious hotel whose exterior is not aesthetically pleasing, but its rooms are spacious and comfortable. Good location.

Jasper Inn
$$$$$
△, ℜ, ≈, K
98 Geikie St.
☎*(780) 852-4461 or 800-661-1933*
⇟*(780) 852-5916*
www.jasperinn.com
Jasper Inn offers spacious, attractive, comfortable rooms, some of them equipped with kitchenettes.

Fairmont Jasper Park Lodge
$$$$$
☼, ✚, ≈, ℜ, ℝ, ☺, △
☎*(780) 852-3301 or 800-441-1414*
⇟*(780) 852-5107*
www.fairmont.com
Jasper Park Lodge constitutes beyond a doubt the most beautiful hotel complex in the whole Jasper area. Once part of the Canadian Pacific chain, the Jasper Park Lodge has attractive, spacious, comfortable rooms. It was built in 1921 by the Grand Trunk Railway Company to compete with Canadian Pacific's Banff Springs Hotel. The staff are very professional, attentive and friendly. A whole range of activities are organized for guests. These include horseback riding and river rafting. You will also find one of the finest golf courses in Canada, several tennis courts, a big pool, a sports centre, and

canoes, sailboards and bicycles for rent in the summer, plus ski equipment in the winter. Several hiking trails criss-cross the site, among them a very pleasant 3.8-kilometre trail alongside Lake Beauvert. Whether you're staying in a room in the main building or in a small chalet, you are assured of comfort and tranquility. Each year, The Fairmont Jasper Park Lodge organizes theme events, and hotel guests are invited to participate. Some weekends may be dedicated to the mountains and relaxation, with yoga and aerobics classes as well as water gymnastics and visits to the sauna; while another weekend may be set aside for the wine tastings of Beaujolais Nouveau; other activities are organized for New Year's. Ask for the activities leaflet for more information.

Lobstick Lodge
$$$$$
≡, K, △, ℜ, ≈
96 Geikie St.
☎*(780) 852-4431 or 888-852-7737*
⇟*(780) 852-4142*
www.lobsticklodge.com
Lobstick Lodge is located some distance from town, but it's a fine, quality hotel.

Sawridge Hotel & Conference Centre
$$$$$
☼, ≈, ℜ, ≡, △
82 Connaught Dr.
☎*(780) 852-5111 or 800-661-6427*
⇟*(780) 852-5942*
www.sawridge.com/jasper
Sawridge Hotel offers big, warmly decorated rooms.

Chateau Jasper
$$$$$
≡, ≈, ℜ
☎*(780) 852-5644 or 800-661-9323*
⇟*(780) 852-4860*
www.chateaujasper.com
Chateau Jasper offers comfortable, very attractive rooms.

Outside Jasper

Mount Edith Cavell Youth Hostel
$
mid-Jun to mid-Oct
26km south of Jasper take Hwy. 93A and then go 13km up the winding road leading to Mount Edith Cavell
☎*(403) 852-3215 or 877-852-0781*
⇟*(780) 852-5560*
www.hihostels.ca
Mount Edith Cavell Youth Hostel constitutes a genuine high mountain refuge, without water or electricity. It is built on one of the most beautiful mountains near Mount Edith Cavell. Take warm clothing and a good sleeping bag, for you are in a high mountain area, and the temperatures are unpredictable. If you enjoy tranquillity and beautiful walks, you will be in paradise here.

Wapiti Campground
$
mid-Jun to early Sep
4km from Jasper
Wapiti Campground, with its 366 sites welcomes trailers and tents. Water, electricity and toilets are available.

Whistler Campground
$
open early May to mid-Oct
2.5 km south of Jasper take Hwy 93 then turn on the road leading to the Whistler Mountain ski lift taking the first left for the campground
Whistler Campground, with its 781 sites, has facilities for both trailers and tents. Water, showers and electricity are available. You can also find firewood on the site. The maximum stay at the campsite is 15 days. To reserve, call the Parks Canada office in Jasper (see p 271).

Jasper International Youth Hostel

$

7 km west of Jasper taking the Skytram road

☎(403) 852-3215 or 877-852-5560

⇌(780) 852-5560

www.hihostels.ca

Jasper International Youth Hostel is quite a comfortable establishment. It is a few minutes' walk from the summer gondola that goes to the top of Whistler Mountain, where there is a superb view over the Athabasca Valley. Reserve well in advance. Family rooms are available.

Maligne Canyon Hostel

$$

closed Wed in winter, Oct to Apr

11km east of Jasper on the Maligne Lake road

☎(403) 852-3215 or 877-852-781

⇌(780) 852-5560

www.hihostels.com

Maligne Canyon Youth Hostel comes across as the ideal spot for anyone who likes hiking and other outdoor activities. The Skyline hiking trail begins right near the hostel, leading experienced hikers through Alpine scenery. The hike takes two or three days, but the superb view over the Jasper valley is a good reward for your efforts. Also located near the hostel, the Maligne River canyon offers some fine rapids and waterfalls photo opportunities. Do not hesitate to talk with the manager of the hostel: he is an expert on local fauna and conducts research for Jasper National Park.

Pine Bungalow Cabins

$$

☉, *K*

on Hwy. 16, near the Jasper golf course

☎(780) 852-3491

⇌(780) 852-3432

Pine Bungalow Cabins fit the category of a motel. The cabins are fully equipped, and some even have fireplaces, but furnishings are very modest and in rather poor taste.

All the same, it is one of Jasper's cheapest places to stay.

Jasper House Bungalows

$$$

K, ℜ

a few kilometres south of Jasper on Icefields Parkway at the foot of Whistler's Mountain.

☎(780) 852-4535

⇌(780) 852-5335

www.jasperhouse.com

Jasper House consists of a group of little chalet-style log cabins built along the Athabasca River. Comfortable and quiet, the rooms are big and well equipped.

Alpine Village

$$$

☉, *K, ℜ*

2km south of Jasper near the cutoff for Mount Whistler

☎(403) 852-3285

www.alpinevillagejasper.com

Alpine Village is an attractive group of comfortable little wood cabins. Facing the Athabasca River, the spot is calm and peaceful. If possible, ask for one of the cabins facing the river directly: these are the most pleasant. Reserve far in advance, as early as January for the summer.

Becker's Chalets

$$$ per cabin

☉, *K, ℜ*

on Icefields Parkway, Hwy 93 South, 5km south of Jasper

☎(780) 852-3779

⇌(780) 852-7202

www.beckerschalets.com

Becker's Chalets, also located along the Athabasca River, are comfortable and well equipped. You will also find a laundromat.

Pyramid Lake Resort

$$$$

☉, ℜ

From the town, follow Pyramid Lake Rd. to Patricia and Pyramid Lake.

☎(403) 852-4900 or (403) 852-3536

☎888-852-4900

⇌(403) 852-7007

www.pyramidlakeresort.com

Pyramid Lake Resort offers simple but comfortable rooms facing Pyramid Lake, where you can enjoy your favourite nautical activities. Rentals of motorboats, canoes, and water-skis are available at the hotel.

Miette Hot Springs

Miette Hot Spring Bungalows

$-$$

K, ℜ

next to the Miette Hot Springs Jasper East

☎(780) 866-3750 or (780) 866-3760 in the off-season

☎(780) 852-4039

⇌(780) 866-2214

Miette Hot Spring Bungalows offers accommodations in bungalows and a motel. The motel rooms are rather ordinary, but those in the bungalows offer good quality.

Pocahontas Bungalows

$$ per cabin

🛏, *K, ≈*

on Hwy. 16, near Punchbowl Falls

☎(780) 866-3732 or 800-843-3372

⇌(780) 866-3777

Pocahontas Bungalows is a small group of cabins located at the entrance to Jasper National Park, on the road leading to Miette Hot Springs. The least expensive cabins do not have kitchenettes.

The Rocky Mountains

Outside Hinton

Suite Dreams B&B
$$$ bkfst incl
⊛, ℑ
when you arrive at the junction with the 40N, turn right toward the south, then immediately left onto William's Road
☎*(780) 865-8855*
www.suitedream.com
Located a few kilometres before Hinton, Suite Dreams B&B is a superb Victorian-style home that has four magnificently decorated bedrooms. Reserve early during the summer season.

Overlander Mountain Lodge
$$$$
ℜ, K, ≡
2km to the left after leaving Jasper National Park toward Hinton
☎*(780) 866-2330*
⇰*(780) 866-2332*
www.overlandermountain lodge.com
The Overlander Mountain Lodge has several charming cabins. This establishment is rendered more pleasant by the fact that it is set in a much calmer area than the outskirts of Jasper, and the surrounding scenery is truly exquisite. This place stands out from the majority of motel-style establishments in this town. Reservations should be made far in advance, as Hinton is a common alternative to lodging in Jasper.

Tour D: Kootenay and Yoho National Parks

From Castle Junction to Radium Hot Springs

Kootenay Park Lodge
$$
mid-May to late Sep
✖, ℜ, ℝ
on Hwy 93 heading south 42km from Castle Junction
☎*(403) 762-9196*
in the off-season, Calgary:
☎/⇰*(403) 283-7482*
www.kootenayparklodge.com
Kootenay Park Lodge rents 10 small log cabins clinging to the steep slopes of the mountains of Kootenay National Park. On site you will find a small store offering sandwiches and everyday items.

Radium Hot Springs

Surprisingly, accommodations in Radium Hot Springs consist essentially of very ordinary motel rooms. All along the town's main drag you will find motel fronts that rival each other in ugliness. The region is popular with visitors, however, so here are a few suggestions.

Redstreak
$
Off Hwy 93/95, 2km off Redstreak Rd.
Located a short distance from the road before you arrive in Radium, Redstreak has 242 campsites and is the least expensive campground in the area. Reservations not accepted.

Canyon RV Resort
$
✖, ☎
5012 Sinclair Creek Rd.
☎*(250) 347-9564*
⇰*(250) 347-9501*
www.canyonrv.com
Canyon Camp is an attractive campground with many spaces for trailers and tents along Sinclair Creek. The spots shaded by numerous

trees confer a pleasing atmosphere on this campground.

Chalet Europe
$$ bkfst incl.
☺, ✖, ℑ, K
☎*(250) 347-9305 or
888-428-9998*
⇰*(250) 347-9306*
www.chaleteurope.com
The Chalet offers several rooms with balconies, modestly furnished but comfortable. Perched above the little town of Radium Hot Springs, this big Savoy chalet-style house offers an interesting view of the valley below.

Radium Resort
$$ bkfst incl. (off-season)
≡, ☺, ℜ, K, ≈, ℝ, △, ✪
8100 Golf Course Road
☎*(250) 347-9311*
⇰*(250) 347-6299*
www.radiumresort.com
The Radium Resort saw a big upswing in business in 2002, when a new general manager came in and dropped rates to $89 per night. It's great to see a resort that prices itself honestly, and the value here is refreshing. There are lots of perks like an onsite golf course. It's a good choice for families and offers all of the amenities. While the brown carpets are certainly questionable, the large staff is very friendly and helpful.

Motel Tyrol
$$
≈, K
5016 Highway 93
☎*(250) 347-9402 or
888-881-1188*
⇰*(250) 347-6363*
www.moteltyrol.com
Motel Tyrol offers adequate, modestly furnished rooms. The terrace by the pool is pleasant.

Misty River Lodge
$$
≡, K, ✖
5036 Hwy 93
☎/⇰*(250) 347-9912*
Misty River Lodge is a B&B youth hostel. The rooms offer a decent level of comfort. The bathrooms are spacious and

very clean. Without a doubt, the best motel in town.

Radium Hot Springs Lodge
$$$
𝕽, ≈, △, 🐾
facing the Radium Hot Springs thermal pool
☎(250) 347-9341 or 888-222-9341
⇌(250) 347-9342
www.radiumhotsprings lodge.com
Radium Hot Springs Lodge has large, extremely ordinary, though modestly furnished, rooms. It's restaurant tries to be chic but serves over-priced food of average quality. All the same, the hotel does have the advantage of being well located and can be considered among the few good spots in Radium Lodge.

Nipika Lodge and Touring Centre
$$$-$$$$
🐾, 🎿, △, ✿
4968 Timbervale Place
☎(250) 342-6516 or 877-647-4525
⇌(250) 342-0516
www.nipika.com
Nipika, meaning "the place people go" in the language of the local Kootenay First Nations, is a beautiful, steadily developing collection of pinewood cabins in a forest off the highway through Kootenay National Park. While officially in the Invermere Forest District along the Kootenay River, the facility is actually about 30km north of Radium, and is accessible by a poorly marked old logging trail called Settler Road. It's rustic and appealing with timber-framed cabins, a lodge, an awe-inspiring setting and 50km of groomed cross-country ski trails in the winter. You will be "roughing it" here, with pots, pans and plates available, but little else. That being said, there's still a wood-framed hot tub and sauna, and the rooms are lovely.

Fairmont Hot Springs

Fairmont Hot Springs Resort
$$$$
≈, 𝕽, △, 𝕽, 🎿
on Hwy. 93-95
near the Fairmont ski hills
☎(250) 345-6311 or 800-663-4979
⇌(250) 345-6616
www.fairmonthotsprings. com
Fairmont Hot Springs Resort is a magnificent resort, wonderfully laid out, offering special spa, ski and golf packages. Hotel guests can also take advantage of tennis courts and a two superb 18-hole golf course. Guests have unlimited access to the hot springs. This establishment also has a vast adjacent RV park *($30)*. Reservations required.

Invermere

Delphine Lodge
$$ bkfst incl.
pb/sb, 🐾
Main St., Wilmer
☎(250) 342-6851 or 877-342-6869
⇌(250) 342-6110
The Delphine Lodge is actually in Wilmer, 5km from Invermere. Though the rooms are a bit small, they and the lodge are packed with lovely antiques and rustic furniture. Handmade quilts, a pretty garden, a fireplace and various special little touches make this historic inn (1890s) a cosy favourite. Non-smoking. Only small pets (check ahead).

Best Western Invermere Inn
$$$ bkfst incl.
≈, ⊙, 🐾, 𝕽, ℝ
1310 Seventh Ave.
☎(250) 342-9246 or 800-661-8911
⇌(250) 342-6079
www.invermereinn.com
The Best Western Invermere Inn has a good location at the centre of town, just a 5min walk from Windermere Lake and an appealing beach.

Rooms are fairly typical and both king and queen-sized beds are available. There is both a restaurant and pub onsite.

Panorama Resort
$$$$
≈, 𝕽, △, ⊙
18 km west of Invermere
☎(250) 342-6941 or 800-663-2929
⇌(250) 3442-3395
www.panoramaresort.com
Panorama Resort offers standard hotel rooms, quite nice, as well as equipped condo-style units, which are particularly handy if you are here to ski, downhill or cross-country. Besides skiing they offer tennis, horseback riding and golf. Pleasant family atmosphere.

Yoho National Park

Monarch & Kicking Horse
$
early May to mid-Oct
toilets, showers at Kicking Horse
☎(205) 343-6387
Monarch and Kicking Horse are located a few kilometres east of Field. No reservations accepted.

Emerald Lake Lodge
$$$$$
🎿, 𝕽
☎(403) 609-6150 or 800-663-6336
⇌(403)609-6158
www.emeraldlakelodge.com
Emerald Lake Lodge, in Yoho National Park, was built by Canadian Pacific in the 1920s and today is an exquisite mountain hideaway. The central lodge built of hand-hewn timber is the hub of activity, while guests stay in one of 24 cabins. Each features a fieldstone fireplace, willow-branch chairs, a down duvet, a private balcony and terrific lake views. Just 40km from Lake Louise.

The Rocky Mountains

Golden and Surroundings

Whispering Spruce Campground and RV Park
$

open mid-Apr to mid-Oct
🐾, ☎

1422 Golden View Rd.
☎*(250) 344-6680*
Whispering Spruce Campground and RV Park has 135 spaces for tents and trailers. Arrive early to reserve your place.

Golden Municipal Campground
$
🐾

1407 S. Ninth St.
☎*(250) 344-5412*
⇔*(250) 344-6577*
Golden Municipal Campground has 70 spaces for tents and trailers. The campground is situated next to tennis courts and a pool.

Columbia Valley Lodge
$$ bkfst incl.
on Hwy 95 a few kilometres south of Golden
☎*(250) 348-2508 or 800-311-5008*
⇔*(250)348-2505*
www.columbiavalleylodge. com
Columbia Valley Lodge has 12 rustic rooms. It resembles a mountain refuge with a basic level of comfort, but it is nonetheless completely adequate. This is a good stopping point for cyclists travelling around the area.

McLaren Lodge
$$ bkfst incl.
above Hwy 95 leaving Golden toward Yoho National Park
☎*(250) 344-6133 or 800-668-9119*
⇔*(250) 344-7650*
www.wetnwild.bc.ca
McLaren Lodge is an interesting spot in Golden for nature-lovers. The owners organize river rafting excursions. Rooms are rather small and have a pleasant old-fashioned air. This spot has the best quality-to-price ratio in Golden.

Golden Rim Motor Inn
$$
ℜ, 🐾, ≈, △, ≡, *K*
☎*(250) 344-2216*
⇔*(250) 344-6673*
Golden Rim Motor Inn has ordinary motel-style rooms.

Prestige Inn
$$$
🐾, *K*, ®, ≈, ℜ, ☺
1049 Trans-Canada Hwy
☎*(250) 344-7990*
⇔*(250) 344-7902*
www.prestigeinn.com
Prestige Inn is Golden's best hotel. Rooms are quite spacious, and bathrooms are well equipped.

Tour E:
Kananaskis Country

Eau Claire Campground
$
just north of Fortress Junction near the Fortress Mountain
☎*(403) 591-7226*
www.kananaskiscamping. com
Eau Claire Campground is a small campground situated right in the forest. Dress warmly, as the nights are cool in this spot. No reservations accepted.

Mount Kidd RV Park
$
🐾, △
on Hwy 40, a few kilometres south of Kananaskis Village
☎*(403) 591-7700*
www.mountkiddrv.com
Mount Kidd RV Park has a surprising set-up. Located at the edge of the river in a forested area, it is definitely the most pleasant campground in the region. Guests also have the use of tennis courts or can head off on any of the many hiking trails in the area. Be sure to reserve ahead (groups especially) at this popular spot.

Kananaskis Interlakes Campgrounds
$
leaving Upper Kananaskis Lake, go left and follow the road, a few kilometres to Interlakes
☎*(403) 591-7226*
www.kananaskiscamping. com
Kananaskis Interlakes Campgrounds offers a superb vista over the lakes and forest. There is a no-reservations, first-come first-served policy here.

Kananaskis Village

Kananaskis Wilderness Hostel
$
along the road leading to the central square of Kananaskis Village
☎*(403) 762-4122 or 866-762-4122*
⇔*(403) 762-3441*
www.hihostels.ca
Kananaskis Wilderness Hostel is a pleasant little hostel that is almost always crowded. Do not wait to the last minute to reserve, or you will be disappointed. The common room, in front of the fireplace, is a pleasant spot to recover from the day's activities.

🚣 The Delta Lodge at Kananaskis
$$$$-$$$$$
🐾, ℜ, ≈, △, ®, ☺
on the central square of Kananaskis Village
☎*(403) 591-7711 or 888-244-8666*
⇔*(403) 591-7770*
The Delta Lodge has 250 spacious, intimate rooms of great comfort, and advance reservations are recommended year-round. Also included in the facilities is the Signature Club which offers 70 comfortable rooms and is very pleasant thanks to the friendly staff.

Canmore

Two campgrounds have been set up for trailers and tents less than 10km from Canmore on the way from Calgary. The **Bow River Campground** *(early*

May to end Sep, reservations accepted; 4km west of Dead Man's Flats along Hwy 1; ☎403-673-2163) and the **Three Sisters Campground** *(mid-Apr to end Nov, reservations not accepted; in Dead Man's Flats)* each charge about $17 per site.

Alpine Club of Canada
$
4.5km east of Canmore on Hwy. 1A
☎*(403) 678-3200*
⇄*(403) 678-3224*
The Alpine Club of Canada offers an interesting alternative for nature lovers who want to sleep "in the great outdoors." This association has dorm-style accommodation, not only near Canmore, but also in several areas of the Rocky Mountains. You can even combine hiking tours with accommodation.

Restwell Trailer Park
$ camping
$$$ cabins
🛖
across Hwy 1A and the railway line near Policeman Creek
☎*(403) 678-5111*
www.restwelltrailerpark. com
Restwell Trailer Park has 247 spaces for trailers and tents, as well as cabins *($125)*. Electricity, toilets, showers and water are available. Reservations accepted.

Rocky Mountain Ski Lodge
$$
K
1711 Mountain Ave.
☎*(403) 678-5445 or*
800-665-6111
⇄*(403) 678-6484*
www.rockymtnskilodge.com
Rocky Mountain Ski Lodge faces a pleasant little garden. Rooms are clean and spacious. Units with living-rooms, fireplaces, and fully equipped kitchens start at $130.

Riverview and Main Bed and Breakfast
$$-$$$ bkfst incl.
98 Main St.
☎*(403) 678-9777*
www.riverviewandmain. com
This bed and breakfast has a great location on the south end of Main Street, just a hop away from shops and restaurants. There are two appealing country-style rooms and a suite complete with pinewood beds. The queen-bedded guest room is lovely, with burgundy walls and wicker furniture. The views of the Rundle Range are pretty good too, and there is a public tennis court just behind the house.

Lady MacDonald Country Inn
$$-$$$$$ bkfst incl.
🐎, ⊛
1201 Bow Valley Trail
☎*(403) 678-3665 or*
800-567-3919
⇄*(403) 678-9714*
www.ladymacdonald.com
Lady MacDonald Country Inn is a magnificent little inn established in a very pretty house. Twelve elegantly decorated rooms are placed at guests' disposal. Some rooms have been specially equipped to receive disabled travellers; others are spread over two floors to welcome families of four. The superb "Three Sisters Room" offers a magnificent view of the Rundle Range and Three Sisters mountains, as well as a fireplace and a whirlpool bath.

Ambleside Lodge
$$$ bkfst incl.
123A Rundle Dr.
☎*(403) 678-3976*
⇄*(403) 678-39169*
www.amblesidelodge.com
Ambleside Lodge welcomes you to a large and handsome residence in the style of a Savoyard chalet just a few minutes from the centre of town. The big and friendly common room is graced with a beautiful fireplace. Some rooms have private baths.

Georgetown Inn
$$$ bkfst incl.
⊛
1101 Bow Valley Trail
☎*(403) 678-3439 or*
800-657-5955
⇄*(403) 678-6909*
Georgetown Inn has resolutely gone for an old-fashioned British ambiance. Rooms are comfortable, and some are equipped with whirlpool baths. Breakfast, which you can take in the Three Sisters dining room, is included in the price of your room. The fireplace, the old books and the reproductions hung on the walls give this place a warm atmosphere.

Rundle Mountain Lodge
$$$
≈, *K ($10 extra)*
1723 Mountain Ave.
☎*(403) 678-5322 or*
800-661-1610
⇄*(403) 678-5813*
www.rundlemountain.com
Rundle Mountain Lodge is a motel modelled on Savoy-style chalets. It has 61 rooms that are in keeping with this type of establishment.

Quality Resort/Chateau Canmore
$$$$
≡, ⊛, ☺, 🐎, ≈, ℝ, ❂, ℜ, ◌
1720 Bow Valley Trail
☎*(403) 678-6699 or*
800-261-8551
⇄*(403) 678-6954*
www.chateaucanmore.com
The Quality Resort is a handsome hotel on Canmore's Bow Valley Trail with a long list of amenities for travellers. There's a spa for beauty treatments and massages, a basketball and tennis court that is flooded in winter to create a skating rink and a lobby complete with a trickling water fountain and pine furniture. Ask for a room on the north side of the hotel as the south side faces the railway tracks.

The Rocky Mountains

Four Points Sheraton
$$$$-$$$$$

≡, ☉, 🐾, ℛ, ℑ, ✿

1 Silver Tip Trail

☎ *(403) 609-4702 or*
888-609-4422

🖷 *(403) 609-0008*

www.fourpointscanmore.
com

The Four Points Sheraton gets a fifth point for being one of the few major hotels that isn't situated on Canmore's noisy train tracks. It is located just off the Trans-Canada, but far enough into the woods to make it a quiet setting. There are 99 rooms including 19 loft-style suites with fridges and microwaves. The traditional rooms are fairly standard, but have good views of the Rockies. Internet access is available in every room.

🍁 Paintbox Lodge
$$$$$ bkfst incl.

ℑ

629 10th St.

☎ *(403) 678-2463 or*
888-678-6100

www.creekhouse.com

The newly opened and impeccable Paintbox Lodge is run by Gail and Greg of the Creek House. They certainly know what they're doing, and if you have a deep wallet, definitely spend a night or two here. It's all timber frame elegance, with five upscale lodge-style suites with fireplaces and comfy beds. The style is, well, perfect, and all the little things are taken care of, such as breakfast vouchers to **Chez François** (see p 319) and fancy shampoos in the bathroom.

🍁 Bear and Bison Inn
$$$$ bkfst incl.

≡, ◉, ✿

705 Benchlands Trail

☎ *(403) 678-2058*

🖷 *(403) 678-2086*

www.bearandbison
inn.com

Summer 2002 was the first season for the Bear and Bison, and it was just a start, because this place is fantastic. A lot of thought has been put into this very

high-end establishment by proprietors Lonny and Fiona Middleton. All 10 rooms were built on one side of the inn, allowing for views of the Three Sisters from every pillow and tub in the house. Guest rooms have three themes: historic travellers, Canadiana and the classy honeymoon suites featuring canopied beds. Breakfast is gourmet, and packed lunches are provided for those heading out to the mountains. Lonny can apparently turn 24 hours into 28, as he made each room's beautiful bed by hand, while holding down a full-time job. Yes, it's expensive. It's also very, very good.

🍁 The Creek House
$$$$$ bkfst incl.

701 Mallard Alley

☎ *(403) 678-2463 or*
888-678-6100

🖷 *(403) 678-8721*

www.creekhouse.com

The Creek House is one of the most beautiful places to spend the night in Canmore and all of the Rockies. Gail and Greg of the Paintbox Lodge bought and completely renovated this old house on the edge of the Policeman's Creek, from where you can see the Three Sisters. The decor in the rooms is impeccable. An artist made some magnificent murals, such as the one in the stairwell. At the end of 1999, Greg added the final touch — a rooftop jacuzzi!

Restaurants

Tour A:
Banff National Park

Banff

Barpa Bill's Souvlaki
$

223 Bear St.

☎ *(403) 762-0377*

Barpa Bill's is a tiny counter-service Greek spot beside Banff's movie theatre. It's a hidden treasure (the entrance is shared with a laundromat), but if you're craving a souvlaki pita or Greek salad, this is the place to go. There's not much room inside (maybe half a dozen chairs), so take your eats to one of Banff's parks, weather permitting, and make a picnic out of it.

Sunfood Café
$-$$

215 Banff Ave., Sundance Mall, Second Floor

☎ *(403) 760-3933*

The Sunfood Café is a must visit for vegetarians and vegans in this carnivorous province, with entrées like teriyaki tofu steak and portabella mushroom pasta. The pasta is made fresh, the rice is organic and there's even some organic wine from Italy. The décor is simple, with sunflowers prominent. Chef Christian Lendi is in love with vegetarian cuisine, and if you're lucky, you might hear his Chilean wife tickling the ivories over dinner. There's only room for 17 people in here, so if you're with a group you should probably call ahead for a reservation.

St. James Gate
$$
205 Wolf St.
☎(403) 762-9355

Ireland makes its mark on the menu of St. James Gate, with dishes like steak, Guinness and mushroom pie and Jameson's Whiskey strip steak. The food is hearty and well priced for Banff, and the pseudo-Celtic atmosphere is warm. Give the Irish stew with buttermilk dumplings a go. There is often live music here in the weekends, and it's a pretty good place to go out for a pint. *Fáilte!*

Joe BTFSPLK's
$$
closed Nov
221 Banff Ave.
facing the tourist information centre
☎(403) 762-5529

Joe BTFSPLK's (pronounced bi-tif'-spliks) is a small restaurant with 1950s decor and good hamburgers. You'll learn that Joe BTFSPLK was a strange comic book character who walked around with a cloud above his head causing disasters wherever he went. It seems the only way today to avoid annoyances (such as spending too much money) may be to come to this little restaurant, very popular with locals for the burgers, fries, salads, chicken fingers and milkshakes. The restaurant also serves breakfasts for under $6.

Rose and Crown
$$
upstairs at 202 Banff Ave.
☎(403) 762-2121

Rose and Crown prepares light meals consisting essentially English pub food, hamburgers, chicken wings and *nachos*. In the evening, the spot becomes a bar with musicians.

Balkan Restaurant
$$
120 Banff Ave.
☎(403) 762-3454

Balkan Restaurant is Banff's Greek restaurant. The blue and white decor with fake vines and grape clusters, recalls the Mediterranean. The main dishes are good, although they are unimaginative and often show North American influences. The staff seems overworked and is not always very pleasant.

The Saltlik
$$-$$$$
221 Bear St.
☎(403) 762-2467

The Saltlik is a trendy steakhouse for meat lovers that opened its doors in 2001. You can go for beef tenderloin, blue cheese Californian cut New York steak, peppercorn New York strip loin, barbecued ribs and the like. The second-floor dining room has colourful artwork and a large fireplace and patio. A cheesy Canadian Mountie welcomes you to the main floor pub.

The Pines
$$-$$$$
bkfst 7am to 10:30am, dinner from 5:30pm
537 Banff Ave.
☎(403) 760-6690

There aren't that many really good dining options in Banff, but you could do much worse than The Pines. The dining room feels a bit empty, but the country styling and unfinished antique furniture is attractive. The food is really good, with Canadian content prevalent both on the menu and the wine list. You can have Atlantic lobster, B.C. salmon, or perhaps a peppered ostrich steak. If it's available when you're here, start with a bowl of the venison soup. Wow.

Silver Dragon Restaurant
$$$
211 Banff Ave.
☎(403) 762-3939

Silver Dragon Restaurant offers adequate Chinese cuisine. They also deliver.

Magpie & Stump
$$$
203 Cariboo St.
☎(403) 762-4067

Magpie & Stump serves Mexican dishes accompanied with refried beans, Spanish rice, salads, sour cream and salsa. Its classy decor gives it a distinguished ambience.

Sukiyaki House
$$$
upstairs at 211 Banff Ave.
☎(403) 762-2002

Sukiyaki House offers excellent Japanese cuisine at affordable prices. The sushi is perfect, and the staff is very courteous. The impersonal decor, however, leaves a bit to be desired.

Ticino
$$$
415 Banff Ave.
☎(403) 762-3848

Ticino serves pretty good Italian and Swiss cuisine as well as fondues. The decor is very ordinary, and the music tends to be too loud.

Caboose
$$$-$$$$
corner of Elk St. and Lynx St.
☎(403) 762-3622 or
(403) 762-2102

Caboose is one of Banff's better eateries. The fish dishes, trout or salmon, are excellent, or you may prefer the lobster with steak, American style, or perhaps the crab. This is a favourite with regular visitors.

Grizzly House Fondue Dining
$$$$
207 Banff Ave.
☎(403) 762-4055

Grizzly House specializes in fondue and big, tender, juicy steaks. The western decor is a bit corny, but your attention will quickly be diverted by your delicious meal.

Le Beaujolais
$$$$
212 Buffalo St.
☎*(403) 762-2712*
Le Beaujolais prepares excellent French cuisine. The dining room is very elegant and the staff is highly attentive. The British Columbia salmon is a true delicacy. The best food in Banff.

Lake Louise

Lake Louise Grill & Bar
$$$
in Samson Mall, in the centre of Lake Louise village
☎*(403) 522-3879*
Lake Louise Grill & Bar serves Chinese food and traditional American cuisine in lacklustre fashion.

Moraine Lake Lodge
$$$$
at the edge of Moraine Lake
☎*(403) 522-3733*
The Moraine Lake Lodge has a restaurant where you can enjoy good meals while contemplating the superb view over the lake and the Ten Peaks which stretch before your eyes.

Deer Lodge Restaurant
$$$$
near the lake on the right before the Chateau Lake Louise
☎*(403) 522-3747*
Deer Lodge Restaurant is an attractive restaurant with somewhat rustic decor. The food is excellent.

Fairview Dining Room
$$$$
Chateau Lake Louise
☎*(403) 522-3511*
The Edelweiss Dining Room offers delicious Canadian cuisine with an international flavour in very elegant surroundings with a view over the lake. Reservations are recommended.

Post Hotel
$$$$
at the edge of the Pipestone River near the youth hostel
☎*(403) 522-3989*
Post Hotel houses an excellent restaurant recognized by the Relais et Châteaux association. Reservations are necessary, for this is one of the best dining rooms in Lake Louise. The setting of the hotel is enchanting.

Tour B:
The Icefields Parkway

This tour crosses a sparsely populated area, and restaurants are few and far between. There are nonetheless a few little cafés that serve light meals.

Num-Ti-Jah Lodge
$-$$$$
early Dec to mid-Oct
at the edge of Bow Lake about 35 km from Lake Louise
☎*(403) 522-2167*
The gift shop at the Num-Ti-Jah Lodge sells sandwiches, muffins and cakes. You can warm up in this little café with tea or other hot beverages. This spot is popular with tourists and is often crowded. The dining room offers a formal three-course set menu, specializing in Venison.

The Crossing
$$
mid-Mar to end Oct
at the junction of Hwys 93 and 11 80km from Lake Louise
☎*(403) 761-7000*
The Crossing houses a fairly large cafeteria with light meals where just about every traveller seems to stop. As a result, it is very crowded, with long line-ups.

Tour C:
Jasper National Park

Jasper

Bear's Paw Bakery
$
Cedar Ave., near Connaught Dr.
☎*(780) 852-3233*
Bear's Paw Bakery makes buns and other treats at the crack of dawn. It also serves good coffee and juice. A good place for breakfast or a snack after hiking.

Coco's Café
$
608 Patricia St.
☎*(780) 852-4550*
Coco's Café is a little spot that serves bagels, sandwiches and cheesecake.

Spooner's Coffee Bar
$
610 Patricia St.
☎*(780) 852-4046*
Light meals and freshly squeezed juices are served at Spooner's Coffee Bar. The café has a good selection of teas. The view over the nearby mountains and the young atmosphere combine to make this a very pleasant spot.

Jasper Marketplace
$
627 Patricia St.
☎*(780) 852-9676*
The Jasper Marketplace is a pleasant place to have a snack any time of day. Healthy, quality food.

Soft Rock Internet Cafe
$-$$
every day
633 Connaught Dr.
☎*(780) 852-5850*
The Soft Rock Internet Cafe is much more than simply a place to send a few E-mails. It serves up enormous breakfasts all day long.

Miss Italia Ristorante
$$
610 Patricia St.
upstairs at the Centre Mall
☎*(780) 852-4002*
Miss Italia Ristorante offers decent Italian cooking. The staff is friendly and attentive.

Cantonese Restaurant
$$
across from the bus terminal on Connaught Dr.
☎*(780) 852-3559*
Cantonese Restaurant serves Szechwan and Cantonese dishes in a typically Chinese decor.

Jasper Pizza Place
$$
402 Connaught Drive
☎*(780) 852-3225*
Jasper Pizza Place serves up a good selection of pizzas cooked in a conventional oven. Many original combinations are offered: spinach and feta cheese, Mexican with jalapeños…

L&W Restaurant
$$-$$$
corner Hazel Ave. and Patricia St.
☎*(780) 852-4114*
The L&W Restaurant is a family-style restaurant that serves steaks, spaghetti and other dishes in a beautiful dining room filled with plants.

Beauvert Dining Room
$$$
in Jasper Park Lodge
at the northern approach to Jasper
☎*(780) 852-3301*
Beauvert Dining Room is a rather fancy restaurant. The French cuisine on offer is excellent. One of the best restaurants in Jasper.

Jasper Inn Restaurant
$$$$
Jasper Inn, 98 Geikie St.
☎*(780) 852-3232*
Jasper Inn Restaurant serves up excellent fish and seafood. This is a very popular spot.

Anthony's Restaurant
$$$$
Amethyst Lodge, 200 Connaught Dr.
☎*(780) 852-3394*
The Amethyst Dining Room has been fully renovated and now offers its traditional menu in a pleasant atmosphere.

Outside Jasper

Becker's Chalet Restaurant
$$$$
on Icefield Parkway, 5km south of Jasper
☎*(780) 852-3535*
Becker's Chalet Restaurant, located at the edge of the Athabasca River, serves perfectly decent traditional cooking. Unfortunately, the decor is rather impersonal.

Hinton and Surroundings

Ranchers
$$
in the Hill Shopping Centre
☎*(780) 865-9785*
Ranchers prepares all sorts of pizzas. This spot is generally quite busy.

Fireside Lounge
$$
in the Holiday Inn
☎*(780) 865-3321*
Fireside Dining Room is the best and most attractive restaurant in Hinton.

Greentree Café
$$-$$$
in the Holiday Inn
☎*(780) 865-3321*
Greentree Café prepares delicious and copious breakfasts at unbeatable prices.

Overlander Mountain Lodge
$$$$
in the Overlander Mountain Lodge, 2km past the toll booths leaving Jasper National Park heading toward Hinton go left toward the hotel
☎*(780) 866-2330*
The Overlander Mountain Lodge's attractive restaurant serves excellent food. The menu changes daily, but if you have the opportunity, give in to temptation and savour

some trout stuffed fish or their specialty lamb.

Tour D: Kootenay and Yoho National Parks

Kootenay Park Lodge Restaurant
$$$
mid-May to late Sep, every day 8am to 10am, noon to 2pm and 6pm to 8:30pm
on Hwy 93 heading south 42km from Castle Junction
☎*(403) 762-9196*
Kootenay Park Lodge Restaurant offers light meals in simple surroundings. Isolated amidst grandiose scenery, you may want to finish your meal with a stroll through the surrounding countryside.

Radium Hot Springs and Surroundings

Melting Pot Eatery
$$$
Apr to end Oct, every day end Oct to early Apr, closed Mon-Tue
4935 Hwy 93
☎*(250) 347-9848*
Silver Garden Restaurant offers excellent fusion food.

Mountain Flowers Dining Room
$$$
on Hwy 93-95, near the Fairmont ski hill
☎*(250) 345-6311 or 800-663-4979*
The newly renovated restaurant at the Fairmont Hot Springs Resort will satisfy the most demanding customers. Its healthy food is excellent, and the Roman Style decor is pleasant.

Invermere

 Strands
$$$-$$$$
818 12th St.
☎*(250) 342-6344*
Delightful Strands is the most reliable place to dine in Invermere. It really is an excellent establishment in a historic village home with four inti-

The Rocky Mountains

mate country-style dining rooms, stained glass and oak panelling. The place has a reputation, so make a reservation as the four dining areas fill up fast in the summer. The cuisine by chef Anthony Wood includes fusion-style dishes like Polynesian prawns and chicken, Madagascar pepper steak and pheasant shitake. Of course, the menu changes regularly, but one constant, and a brilliant constant at that, is the chicken Oscar. Order this chicken breast filled with crab in a mustard cream sauce and you won't be sorry. Three-course early bird dinner specials (a steal at $13.95) are offered between 5pm and 6pm.

Yoho National Park

Emerald Lake Lodge
$$$$
Box 10 Field
☎*(250) 343-6321*
Emerald Lake Lodge boasts one of the finest dining rooms in the Canadian Rockies. They serve Rocky Mountain Cuisine, a blend of the fine meals once served in CPR dining cars, the hearty fare once enjoyed by mountain guides and local ingredients like berries and wild game. The exceptional surroundings are sure to make your meal memorable.

Golden

As you cross the city, you will pass several fast-food restaurants.

Golden Village Inn
$$
on the Trans-Canada Hwy at the entrance to Golden
☎*(250) 439-1188*
There is a restaurant in the Golden Village Inn. The building, perched on a hill, is relatively uncrowded, and the food is adequate.

ABC Restaurant
$$
1049 Trans-Canada Hwy, in the Prestige Inn
☎*(250) 344-7661*
The restaurant at the Prestige Inn encompasses the best of traditional cuisine in Golden.

Golden Rim Motor Inn
$$$
1416 Golden View Rd.
☎*(250) 344-5056*
Golden Rim Motor Inn houses a gloomy little restaurant which prepares simple, traditional items.

Tour E:
Kananaskis Country

Bistro Wild Flower
$$$$
in the Kananaskis Mountain Lodge in the centre of the village
☎*(403) 591-7500*
The Kananaskis Inn Restaurant has a simple but warm decor. The menu is interesting, and the food is quite good.

Mount Engadine Lodge
$$$$
Spray Lakes Rd.
☎*(403) 678-2880*
Mount Engadine Lodge offers an interesting *table d'hôte*. The European-style cuisine is delicious.

Canmore

Bella Crusta
$
Mon-Sat 10am to 8pm
902 Sixth Ave.
☎*(403) 609-3366*
Unpretentious to say the least, Bella Crusta has two simple tables inside for sitting and munching on slices of pizza and sandwiches on foccaccia bread. It's good for a light lunch or evening snack, and during the summer, there's outdoor seating. Check out the amusing reproduction of Michelangelo's *Creation of Man* from the Sistine Chapel, with God handing Adam a slice of pizza.

Village Bistro
$
Tue-Sun 7am to 5pm
718 10th St.
☎*(403) 678-3747*
The Village Bistro is a light-filled little place with affordable counter breakfast and lunch service. There are *croque monsieurs*, eggs, bagels and a long list of coffees, as well as baked goods and croissants. The owner's friendly service makes the place even more appealing. Soups and sandwiches are available throughout the day.

The Grizzly Paw
$-$$
622 Main St.
☎*(403) 678-9983*
The Grizzly Paw is an award-winning pinewood brewpub on Canmore's strip. Its burgers, pastas, sandwiches, pizzas and salads are popular for lunch. It's affordable and pretty popular, and there are pub snacks like potato skins, nachos and foccaccia cheese bread. There's also a good selection of draught beer on tap.

Summit Café
$-$$
102-1001 Cougar Creek Dr.
☎*(403) 609-2120*
The Summit Café is the place for substantial breakfasts like *huevos rancheros* and the usual egg deals, while for dinner the place transforms into a Mexican *casa*. Enchiladas, fajitas, tacos and tostados are served with Mexican rice, black beans, tortilla chips and red-hot salsa. The walls feature bright colours, with an Aztec sun featured on one. During the day there's counter service, while in the evening a server will bring your margaritas to the table for you.

Crazyweed Kitchen
$-$$
2-626 Eighth St.
☎*(403) 609-2530*
Crazy is an appropriate name for this café on a weekday lunch hour, when it's more or

less impossible to get a seat. It's popular for a reason with original dishes like Thai red seafood curry on jasmine rice and smoked salmon quesadillas. It can get a bit loud with its long lunch counter and open kitchen, but the good food makes up for it. There are also a few outdoor seats.

 Zona's
$$
710 Ninth St.
☎*(403) 609-2000*
Zona's is the classiest, and the most original, restaurant in town. The menu is terrific, with North American, Thai, Indian and Mexican influences, while the setting is inviting. A deejay in the corner spins mellow tunes, and the Chinese lanterns on tables and romantic lighting add to the package. The house specialty is a great Moroccan molasses lamb curry, and if it's offered the night you're there, make sure to go for a bowl of the hearty and spicy miso soup. Zona's is also a happening nightspot, with locals often coming for martinis or beers on Thursday nights.

The Sherwood House
$$-$$$
Mon-Fri 4pm to 11pm, Sat and Sun 9am to 11pm
838 Eighth St.
☎*(403) 678-5211*
The Sherwood House dining room is an attractive pine log and stained glass refectory. The menu is a mix of Canadiana and international dishes like lamb vindaloo. On the higher end you can gorge on bison rib steak, venison scallops Béarnaise or chicken korma. For the budget conscious, there are pizzas and pastas. There's a great pub here too, with a patio that's packed throughout the summer.

Santa Lucia
$$-$$$
closed Tue
714 8th St.
☎*(403) 678-3414*
Santa Lucia is a small Italian restaurant with a family atmosphere. The *gnocchis* are excellent. They also deliver.

Chez François
$$$
adjacent to the Best Western Green Gables Inn, Hwy 1A
☎*(403) 678-6111*
Chez François is probably the best place to eat in Canmore. The chef, who comes from Québec, offers excellent French cuisine and a warm atmosphere in his restaurant.

 Sinclairs
$$$$
637 8th St.
☎*(403) 678-5370*
Sinclairs offers good food in a warm ambiance enhanced by a fireplace. Reservations are recommended in high season, for the restaurant is often full. The restaurant also offers an excellent selection of teas, a rarity around here.

Entertainment

Bars and Nightclubs

Tour A: Banff National Park

Banff

The primarily tourism-driven existence of the small town of Banff has lead to the opening of several establishments aimed at entertaining visitors. There is something here for everyone.

Banff Springs Hotel
Spray Ave.
☎*(403) 762-6860*
The Banff Springs Hotel has a number of entertainment

options, depending on what you're looking for. Dancing is possible in the Alhamber Restaurant. Those in search of something more soothing can spend the evening in the Rundle Lounge where live classical piano music is presented.

Outabounds
137 Banff Ave.
☎*(403) 762-8454*
This dark basement watering hole is popular with Banff's young army of tourism staff. As a result, it's a great place to meet people from all over the world and shake it up a bit to a spinning DJ or some hip-hop. There's a marginal cover charge on weekends.

Rose and Crown
202 Banff Ave.
☎*(403) 762-2121*
The Rose and Crown combines the western motif with classic English pub decor. There is a dance floor, and live bands often play here. You can also try your hand at a game of darts or pool.

Wild Bill's Legendary Saloon
upstairs at 201 Banff Ave.
☎*(403) 762-0333*
If you prefer kicking up your heels in a real "western" setting, pull on your jeans and cowboy boots, grab your Stetson and saddle up for Wild Bill's Legendary Saloon. With a bit of luck, a friendly cowboy may just show you how to dance the two-step.

Barbary Coast
upstairs at 119 Banff Ave.
☎*(403) 762-4616*
The Barbary Coast is a pleasant, friendly spot.

King Eddy's Billiards
upstairs at 137 Banff Ave.
☎*(403) 762-4629*
Pool fans hang out at King Eddy's Billiards.

The Rocky Mountains

Buffalo Paddock Lounge and Pub
124 Banff Ave.
☎*(403) 762-3331*
The Buffalo Paddock Lounge and Pub is a huge, slightly noisy bar in the basement of the Mount Royal Hotel.

Bumper's Loft Lounge at Bumper's Beef House Restaurant
603 Banff Ave.
☎*(403) 762-2622*
Bumper's Loft Lounge often shows short skiing films and plays traditional and folk music.

Cultural Activities

Banff Centre
107 Tunnel Mountain Dr.
☎*(403) 762-6180 or 800-565-9989*
www.banffcentre.ab.ca
A cultural centre of some repute, the Banff Centre is the central spot for classical and jazz ballet, theatre, music, photography and pottery, and organizes some renowned festivals (see below).

Festivals and Events

In July and August, the Banff Centre hosts the **Banff Arts Festival** *(☎403-762-6301)* with events and performances from across a broad spectrum of the arts, including Aboriginal arts, cultural journalism, dance, music, new media, opera, theatre and the visual arts.

Canadian literature enthusiasts will also certainly want to be in town in October for **Wordfest** *(☎403-762-6301 or 800-413-8368)*, the Banff-Calgary International Writers Festival. It is Alberta's hottest literary event and the third-largest festival of its kind in Canada. More that 50 writers make their appearances over five days in both Banff and Calgary.

Finally, the busy Banff Centre also puts on the **Banff Moun-**

tain Film Festival *(☎403-762-6301 or 800-413-8368)* the first weekend in November. The international competition features the world's best films on mountain and adventure subjects.

Lake Louise

Nights out are considerably more laid back in the town of Lake Louise. There are however two favourites that are sure to please night owls.

The charming little **Explorer's Lounge** is located in the **Lake Louise Inn** *(Village Rd., ☎403-522-3791)*. This is a pleasant spot to have a drink and listen to some music. Simple dishes are also served.

Glacier Saloon
Chateau Lake Louise
☎*(403) 522-3511*
The Glacier Saloon generally attracts a young, sporting crowd.

Tour C:
Jasper National Park

Jasper

There are two good spots for those in search of the latest tunes. They are **Pete's on Patricia** *(upstairs at 614 Patricia St., ☎780-852-6262)* and the **Atha-B Pub** *(Athabasca Hotel, 510 Patricia St., ☎780-852-3386)*, which each have a dance floor, the latest music and a bar. **Tent City** *(in the basement of the Jasper Park Lodge, ☎780-852-3301)* is a good choice for sports fans.

Nick's Bar
Juniper St. between Connaught Dr. and Geikie St.
☎*(780) 852-4966*
Nick's Bar shows acrobatic skiing movies on a large screen – the stuff of dreams for those who wish they could tear down the slopes on two skis. A few light dishes are also served here. A pianist provides

the musical entertainment some evenings.

Those in search of an English-style pub have two choices: the **Whistler Inn** *(105 Miette Ave., ☎780-852-3361)* is great for a pint and a game of darts or pool (a warm fireplace makes for a cozy atmosphere), while **Champs** *(Sawridge Hotel, 82 Connaught Dr., ☎780-852-5111)* offers a similar type of diversion with dart boards and pool tables.

Buckles Saloon
at the west end of Connaught Dr.
☎*(780) 852-7074*
The decor is in keeping with Canada's wild west. Country music fans can dine on beer, hamburgers and sandwiches.

Tour D : Kootenay and Yoho National Parks

Golden
Map Trapper Neighbourhood Pub
1205 9th St. S.
☎*(250) 344-6661*

Radium

Horsethief Pub & Eatery
7538 Main St. E.
☎*(250) 347-6400*

Shopping

Tour A:
Banff National Park

Banff

Banff's main drag is lined with souvenir shops, sports stores and clothing stores of all kinds. When it comes to shopping the landscape is dotted with jewellery, souvenirs, essentials, sporting goods and t-shirts.

Hudson's Bay Company
125 Banff Ave.
☎(403) 762-5525
The Hudson's Bay Company is owned by the oldest clothing manufacturer in Canada, established in 1670, and still sells clothes, along with souvenirs, cosmetics and much more.

The Shirt Company
200 Banff Ave.
☎(403) 762-2624
The Shirt Company as its name suggest, sells t-shirts for all tastes and sizes.

Monod Sports
129 Banff Ave.
☎(403) 762-4571
Monod Sports is the place for all of your outdoor needs. You'll find a good selection of hiking boots, all sorts of camping accessories as well as clothing.

Roots Canada
227 Banff Ave.
☎(403) 762-9434
Known throughout Canada for their quality leather goods, Roots Canada sells shoes, purses, handbags and beautiful leather jackets, as well as comfortable clothing.

Orca Canada
121 Banff Ave.
☎(403) 762-2888
Orca Canada jewellers is a good place for gift ideas. Many pieces found here, and in other jewellers in the region, contain "ammolite", a fossilized rock found in Alberta. Though it can be expensive, it does make a typically Albertan gift.

A Bit of Banff
120 Banff Ave.
☎(403) 762-4996
A Bit of Banff sells every kind of souvenir imaginable from postcards to posters, picture books on the Rockies, and native masks, as well as native-style soapstone carvings. Be careful, however, as these carvings tend to be overpriced here.

Luxton Museum Shop
Luxton Museum on the Plains Indian, 1 Birch Ave.
☎(403) 762-2388
The Luxton Museum Shop is a small souvenir shop that sells First Nations artwork as well as books on the subject.

Chocolaterie Bernard Callebaut
111 Banff Ave.
☎(403) 762-4106
The Chocolaterie Bernard Callebaut is a favourite of Belgian chocolate lovers. The truffles are excellent.

Mountain Magic Sportswear and Equipment
224 Bear St.
☎(403) 762-2591
Mountain Magic Sportswear and Equipment is the multi-storey emporium for all the gear you might need to explore the Rockies. There's a climbing wall, inline skates, kayaks, bikes and pretty much anything else you can think of.

Hemp and Company
101-230 Bear St.
☎(403) 760-4402
Hemp and Company offers durable hemp clothing as only Banff can…it's upscale stuff like fancy cardigans and skirts. That being said, you can still get seeds and soap here.

Canada House
201 Bear St.
☎(403) 762-3757
Canada House is very pricey, but the store has lovely Canadian and First Nations' painting, sculpture and glasswork and is very browser friendly. Along the same line are the **Quest Gallery** and **Very Canada** (*105 Banff Ave.*, **☎**403-762-2722*), two side-by-side craft shops. The Quest Gallery is higher end, while Very Canada has some less interesting, but also less expensive, items for sale.

Lake Louise and Surroundings

Moraine Lake Trading
early Jun to early Oct
Moraine Lake Lodge
☎(403) 522-2749
Moraine Lake Trading is a small boutique where you'll find pieces of artwork made by Aboriginal artists as well as some of the world's finest imports.

Woodruff and Blum Booksellers
Samson Mall, Lake Louise, **☎(403) 522-3842**
Woodruff and Blum Booksellers have an excellent selection of both souvenir photography books and practical books on hiking trails in the region, rock-climbing, fishing and canoeing. They also sell postcards, compact discs, posters and topographical maps.

Tour C: Jasper National Park

Jasper

Maligne Lake Books
Beauvert Promenade, Jasper Park Lodge
☎(780) 852-4779
Maligne Lake Books sells beautiful books of photography, newspapers and novels.

Exposures Keith Allen Photography
Building 54, Stan Wright Industrial Park
☎(780) 852-5325
Exposures Keith Allen Photography does custom framing and has a large stock of black-and-white and colour photographs of the area dating the 1940s on, including unedited shots of Marilyn Monroe from the making of *River of No Return*, which was filmed in Jasper.

The Rocky Mountains

Film Lab
Beauvert Promenade, Jasper Park Lodge
☎(780) 852-4099
Besides photo-developing services, Film Lab also offers professional photography services.

Jasper Originals
15 Jasper Park Lodge St., Jasper Park Lodge
☎(780) 852-5378
Jasper Originals sells interesting pieces of art in the form of paintings, sculptures, pottery and jewellery that make lovely souvenirs.

Jasper Camera and Gifts
412 Connaught Dr.
☎(780) 852-3165
Jasper Camera and Gifts has a good selection of books on the Rockies. You will also find Crabtree & Evelyn products here. The shop sells binoculars, so that you can observe the wildlife up-close when adventuring in the mountains, and also develops film.

The Liquor Hut
Jasper Market Place, Patricia St. and Hazel Ave.
☎(780) 852-3152
The Liquor Hut stocks a fine selection of wines and spirits.

Surroundings of Jasper

Sunwapta Falls Resort Gift Shop
53km south of Jasper, on the Icefields Parkway
☎(780) 852-4852
The Sunwapta Falls Resort Gift Shop sells native artwork like blankets, moccasins and soapstone carvings. The jewellery section of the boutique includes jade, lapis-lazuli and "ammolite" pieces.

Bighorn sheeps

Calgary

Calgary is a thriving
metropolis of concrete and steel, and a western city through and through

Set against the Rocky Mountains to the west and prairie ranchlands to the east, this young, prosperous city flourished during the oil booms of the 1940's, 1950's and 1970's but its nickname, Cowtown, tells a different story. Before the oil, there were cowboys and gentlemen, and Calgary originally grew thanks to a handful of wealthy ranching families.

The area now known as Calgary first attracted the attention of hunters and traders after the disappearance of the buffalo in the 1860s. Whisky traders arrived from the United States, generally causing havoc with their illicit trade. This brought the North West Mounted Police, and in 1875, after building Fort Macleod, they headed north and built a fort at the confluence of the Bow and Elbow Rivers. It was named Calgary, which in Gaelic means "clear, running water." The first settlers came with the railroad, when the Canadian Pacific Railway decided the line would cross the mountains at Kicking Horse Pass. The station was built in 1883 and the town site laid out; just nine years later, Calgary was incorporated as a city. Tragically, a

fire razed most of it in 1886, prompting city planners to draw up a by-law stipulating that all new buildings had to be constructed out of sandstone. Calgary thus took on a grand look of permanence that is still in evidence today.

Next came ranching. Overgrazed lands in the United States and an open grazing policy north of the border drew many ranchers to the fertile plains around Calgary. Wealthy English and American investors soon bought up land near Calgary, and once again Calgary boomed. The beginning of the 20th century was a time of population growth and expansion, only slightly jarred by World War I. Oil was the

next big ticket. Crude oil was discovered in Turner Valley in 1914 and Calgary was on its way to becoming a modern city. Starting in the 1950's, and for the next 30 years, the population soared and construction boomed. As the global energy crisis pushed oil prices up, world corporations moved their headquarters to Calgary, and though the oil was extracted elsewhere, the deals were made here.

Thirty years ago, Robert Kroetsch, an Alberta storyteller, novelist, poet and critic, called Calgary a city that dreams of cattle, oil, money and women. Cattle, money and oil are still top concerns of many of the local residents, and as the city matures, issues like the arts, culture and the environment have also gained importance. Quality of life is a top priority here: urban parks, cycling paths and a glacier-fed river make the outdoors very accessible. The city gives much to its residents, and the residents give back. In 1988, they were both rewarded when Calgary hosted the Winter Olympic Winter Games. After suffering a drop in oil prices, the city flourished once again.

Finding Your Way Around

By Car

The majority of Calgary's streets are numbered, and the city is divided into four quadrants, NE, NW, SE and SW. This may seem extremely unimaginative on the part of city-planners, but it makes it easy for just about anyone to find their way around. Avenues run east-west and streets run north-south. **Centre Street** divides the city between east and west, while the Bow River is the dividing line between north and south. The TransCanada Highway runs through the city, where it is known as 16th Ave. N. Many of the major arteries through the city have much more imaginative names; not only are they not numbered but they are called trails, an appellation that reflects their original use. These are **Macleod Trail**, which runs south from downtown (ultimately leading to Fort Macleod, hence its name); **Deerfoot Trail** which runs north-south through the city and is part of Highway 2;

and **Crowchild Trail** which heads northwest and joins **Bow Trail** before becoming Highway 1A.

Calgary's "Motel Village" is located along 16th Ave. NW between 18th St. NW and 22nd St. NW.

Car Rentals

National Car Rental
Airport
☎*(403) 221-1692*
Northeast
2335 78th Ave. NE
☎*(403) 250-1396*
Southeast
114 Fifth Ave. SE
☎*(403) 263-6386*
www.nationalcar.com

Budget
Airport
Downtown
140 Sixth Ave. SE
☎*(403) 226-1550*
☎*800-267-0505*
www.budget.ca

Avis
Airport
☎*(403) 221-1700*
Downtown
211 Sixth Ave. SW
☎*(403) 269-6166*
☎*800-879-2847*
www.avis.com

Thrifty
Airport
☎*(403) 221-1961*
Downtown
123 Fifth Ave. SE
☎*(403) 262-4400*
☎*800-367-2277*
www.thrifty.com

Discount
Airport
☎*(403) 299-1222*
Downtown
240 Ninth Ave. SW
☎*(403) 299-1224*
☎*888-412-3733*
www.discountcar.com

Hertz
Airport
☎*(403) 221-1676*
Downtown
Bay Store, 227 Sixth Ave. SW
☎*(403) 221-1300*
☎*800-263-0600*
www.hertz.com

Dollar
Airport
☎*(403) 221-1888*
www.dollar.com

By Plane

Calgary International Airport is located northeast of downtown Calgary. It is Canada's fourth-largest airport and houses a whole slew of facilities and services. It features restaurants, an information centre, hotel courtesy phones, major car rental counters, currency exchange and a tour bus operator.

Air Canada, Canadian Airlines International, American Airlines, Delta Airlines, Northwest Airlines, United Airlines and K.L.M. all have regular flights to the airport. Regional companies also serve Calgary International.

There is a shuttle from the Calgary airport to the major downtown hotels; the **Airporter** (☎*403-531-3909 or 800-661-6161; www.cardinal-cal.com*) charges $9 one-way and $15 return, while a taxi will run about $25.

By Train

Via does not service Calgary. The train passes through Edmonton. There is a bus connection between the two cities.

The only rail service from Calgary is offered by **Rocky Mountain Railtours** (☎*403-221-8224 or 800-665-7245*).

By Bus

Calgary Greyhound Bus Depot
850 16th St. S.W.
☎*(403) 260-0850*
☎*800-661-8747*
www.greyhound.ca
Services: restaurant, lockers,
tourist information.

**Brewster Transportation and
Tours**
☎*(403) 221-8242*
☎*800-661-1152*
www.brewster.ca.
Offers coach service from
Calgary to Banff departing
from Calgary International
Airport.

Public Transit

Public transit in Calgary consists of an extensive bus network and a light-rail transit
system known as the **C-Train**.
There are three C-Train
routes: the Fish Creek-
Lacombe C-Train follows
Macleod Trail south to Fish
Creek Park, the Whitehorn C-
Train heads northeast out of
the city and the Brentwood C-
Train runs along Seventh
Avenue and then heads northwest past the University of
Calgary. The C-Train is free in
the downtown core. You can
transfer from a bus to a C-
Train, tickets are $1.75 for a
single trip or $5.60 for a day
pass. Tickets books of 10
tickets can also be purchased
at convenience stores for
$16.50. For bus information
call **Calgary Transit** (☎*403-
262-1000, www.calgarytransit.
com)*; you can tell them where
you are and where you want
to go and they'll gladly explain
how to do it.

By Foot

A system of interconnected
enclosed walkways links many
of Calgary's downtown sights,
shops and hotels. Known as
the **+15**, it is located 15 ft.

above the ground. The malls
along Seventh Avenue SW are
all connected as are the Calgary Tower, Glenbow Mu-
seum and Palliser Hotel.

Practical
Information

Area code: **403**

Information on everything
from road conditions to movie
listings to provincial parks is
available from the **Talking
Yellow Pages**. In Calgary call
☎*521-5222*. A series of recorded messages is accessible
by dialling specific codes. The
codes are listed in the front of
the yellow pages phone book;
telephone booths usually have
a telephone book.

Tourist Information

Visitor Centre Calgary
220 Eighth Ave.S.W. (Inside Riley &
McCormick Store)
☎*263-8510*
☎*800-661-1678*

B&B Association of Calgary
1462 Main Str.
☎*277-0023*
⇄*295-3823*
www.bbcalgary.com

Internet

There is no shortage of Internet cafés in Calgary. The
cost is usually $10/hr to con-
nect to the web. **Wired** *($$;
1032 17th Ave. SW, ☎244-
7070, www.wired-cafe.com)* is
close to downtown.

Exploring

Tour A: Downtown

We recommend starting your
tour of Calgary at the 190m,
762-step, 55-storey **Calgary
Tower ★★** *($7.95; every day,
summer 7:30am to midnight,
winter 8am to 10pm; Centre
Ave, corner of Centre St SW,
☎508-5808)*. The city's most
famous landmark offers a
breathtaking view of the city,
including the ski-jump towers
at Canada Olympic Park, the
Saddledome and the Canadian
Rockies through high-power
telescopes, a revolving restau-
rant and a bar. Photographers
should take note that the
specially tinted windows on
the observation deck make for
great photos.

Across the street, at the cor-
ner of First Street SE, is the
stunning **Glenbow
Museum ★★★** *($11; Tue to
Sun 9am to 5pm; 130 Ninth
Ave. SE, ☎268-4100, www.
glenbow.org)*. Three floors of
permanent and travelling
exhibits chronicle the exciting
history of Western Canada.
The displays include contem-
porary and Aboriginal art, and
an overview of the various
stages of the settling of the
West, from the First Nations
to the first pioneers, the fur
trade, the North West
Mounted Police, ranching, oil
and agriculture. Photographs,
costumes and everyday items
bring to life the hardships and
extraordinary obstacles faced
by settlers. There is also an
extensive exhibit on the Ab-
original peoples of the whole
country and an extensive new
permanent exhibit on the local
Blackfoot First Nations. Check
out the genuine teepee and
the sparkling minerals, both
part of the province's diverse
history. A great permanent

Calgary

exhibit documents the stories of warriors throughout the ages. The museum also hosts travelling exhibitions. Free gallery tours are offered once or twice weekly. Great museum shop and café.

The **Cathedral Church of the Redeemer** *(every day 11:30 to 1:30; 604 First Street SE, ☎269-1905)* brings calm and serenity to the feverish pace of the business district on Seventh Avenue SE (the C-Train street). The Victorian-style sandstone church, which was built in 1905, has an array of stained glass windows. Silence and reflection reign here.

Exit onto Eighth Ave. SE and head to the Olympic Plaza and City Hall.

Built for the medal presentation ceremonies of the '88 Winter Olympics, **Olympic Plaza** ★★★ *(205 Eighth Ave. SE)* is a fine example of Calgary's potential realized. This lovely square features a large wading pool (used as a skating rink in winter) surrounded by pillars and columns in an arrangement reminiscent of a Greek temple. The park is now the site of concerts and special events, and is frequented by street performers throughout the year; it is also a popular lunch spot with office workers. Each pillar in the Legacy Wall commemorates a medal winner, and the paving bricks are inscribed with the names of people who supported the Olympics by

purchasing bricks for $19.88 each!

Across from the Olympic Plaza is **City Hall** *(Second St. SE, corner of Macleod Tr.)*, one of few surviving examples of the monumental civic halls that went up during the Prairies boom. It was built in 1911 and still houses a few offices.

At this point head west along Stephen Ave.

Stephen Avenue Mall *(Eighth Ave. between First St. SE and Sixth St. SW)* is an excellent example of the contrasts that characterize this cowtown metropolis—the mall is part vibrant pedestrian meeting place, part wasteland and unsavoury hangout. It has

---

● ATTRACTIONS

Tour A: Downtown
1. Calgary Tower
2. Glenbow Museum
3. Olympic Plaza
4. City Hall
5. Stephen Avenue Mall
6. Devonian Gardens
7. Calgary Science Centre
8. Mewata Armoury

Tour B: Along the Bow River
9. Eau Claire Market
10. Prince's Island Park
11. Crescent Road Viewpoint
12. Chinese Cultural Centre
13. Fort Calgary
14. Deane House (R)
15. Calgary Zoo, Botanical Gardens and Prehistoric Park

Tour C: Southeast and Southwest
16. Stampede Park
17. Saddledome
18. Grain Academy

(R) establishment with restaurant (see description)

○ ACCOMMODATIONS

1. Calgary City Centre Hostel
2. Calgary Marriott Hotel
3. Fairmont Palliser (R)
4. Hawthorn Hotel & Suites
5. Hyatt Regency Calgary
6. Inglewood Bed & Breakfast

7. Plaza Regis Hotel
8. Riverpath Bed and Breakfast
9. Riverwynde Bed and Breakfast
10. Sandman Hotel

11. Sheraton Suite Eau Claire
12. Tumble Inn

(R) establishment with restaurant (see description)

● RESTAURANTS

1. 1886 Café
2. Arden Diner
3. Barley Mill
4. Buchanan's
5. Caesar's Steakhouse
6. Cannery Row
7. Casablancan Chef at the Sultan's Tent
8. Catch
9. Drinkwaters Grill
10. Fiore Cantina
11. Galaxie Diner
12. Good Earth Café

13. Heartland Café
14. Hy's Steakhouse
15. King & I Thai Restaurant
16. La Caille on the Bow
17. Latin Corner
18. Marathon
19. Mescalero
20. Mongolie Grill
21. Moti Mahal Restaurant
22. Nellie's Kitchen
23. Old Spaghetti Factory
24. Owl's Nest
25. Passage To India

26. Pongo
27. River Café
28. Rose Garden
29. Schwartzie's Bagel Noshery
30. Silver Dragon
31. Stromboli Inn
32. Sukiyaki House
33. Sumo Lounge
34. Teatro
35. Wicked Wedge Pizza

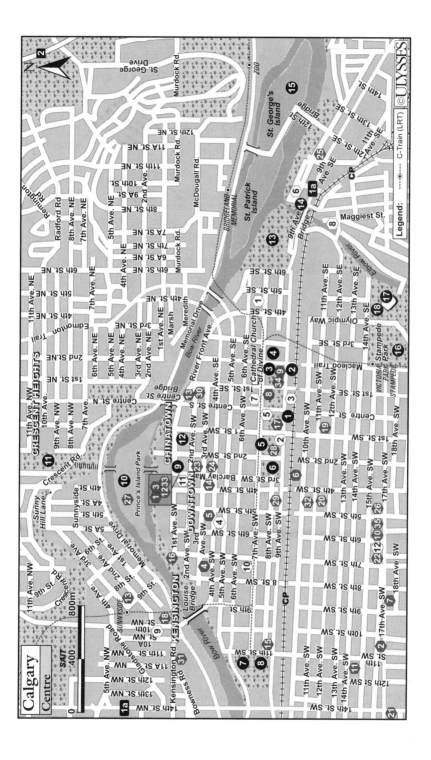

Calgary
Centre

SAIT

0   400   800m

CRESCENT HEIGHTS

KENSINGTON

SUNNYSIDE

DOWNTOWN

CHINATOWN

Prince's Island Park

Bow River

Memorial Drive

River Front Ave.

Cathedral Church of Divine

St. George's Island

St. Patrick Island

Zoo

BRIDGELAND

Elbow River

STAMPEDE

VICTORIA PARK

Stampede Park

Olympic Way

Maggiest St.

MacLeod Trail

St. George Drive

Murdock Rd.

McDougall Rd.

Remington Rd.

Edmonton Trail

Kensington Rd.

Bowness Rd.

Crescent Rd.

Sunny Hill Lane

Gladstone Road

Legend:
- - - - C-Train (LRT)

© ULYSSES

N

fountains, statues, benches, cobblestone, restaurants and shops and the boarded-up storefronts and cheap souvenir and T-shirt shops that characterized it in recent years have to some degree been redeveloped. Historic buildings were restored and there are now some art galleries, several new upscale restaurants and some high end shopping in this district, as well as the recently expanded **TELUS Convention Centre** *(120 Ninth Ave. SE, corner First Ave. SE, ☎261-8500 or 800-822-2697)*. The beautiful sandstone buildings that line the Avenue are certainly a testament to different times, as are the businesses they house, including an old-fashioned shoe hospital and several western outfitters. One of these buildings is the **Alberta Hotel**, a busy place in pre-prohibition days, which now houses a restaurant on the second floor and a clothing store on the main level. Other buildings house trendy cafés and art galleries, as the street is a meeting place for oil tycoons and the who's who of Calgary.

West of First Street SW, you might opt for the **+15 walkway system**, which provides an aseptic alternative to the street below. Purists may scoff at the city's system of interconnected walkways that can take you just about anywhere you want to go, but it is a wonderful alternative to the underground passages found in many large cities. And you certainly won't scoff on cold winter days, when the +15 provides warm, bright and welcome relief.

Among the city's stately buildings along the walkway is the **Hudson's Bay Company** department store, at the corner of First Street SW. Across First Street is **A+B Sound** at 140 Eighth Avenue, a music store housed in the gor-

geously restored former Bank of Montreal building.

Interconnected malls line the street west of First Street SW, including the Scotia Centre, Penny Lane, TD Square, Bankers Hall and Eaton Centre. Though this type of commercialism might not appeal to everyone, hidden within TD Square is a unique attraction— Alberta's largest indoor garden, **Devonian Gardens ★★** *(free admission, donations accepted; every day 9am to 9pm; 317 Seventh Ave. SW, between Second and Third Sts. SW, Level 4, TD Square, ☎221-3782)*. For a tranquil break from shopping, head upstairs, where 1ha of greenery blossoms and ponds teeming with tropical fish await. Stroll along garden paths high above the concrete and steel and enjoy the art exhibitions and performances that are often presented here.

Head west on foot along Eighth Ave SW. If you are tired you can take the LRT free of charge all along Seventh Ave SW to the end, then walk a block to the Calgary Science Centre, although the walk is easy and more interesting.

The peculiar looking concrete building on 11th Street SW is **The Calgary Science Centre ★★★** *($9; Tue to Thu 10am to 4pm Sat and Sun 10am to 5pm Sep to May Closed Mon ; 701 11th St. SW, ☎268-8300, www.calgary science.ca)*, a wonderful museum that children will love. Hands-on displays and multimedia machines cover a whole slew of interesting topics. The museum boasts a planetarium, an observatory, a science hall and two theatres that showcase mystery plays and special-effects shows. The 220-seat domed theatre features an exceptional sound system, all the better to explore the wonders of the scientific world.

South on 11th Street SW is the **Mewata Armoury**, a historic site that is now home to the King's Own Calgary Regiment and the Calgary Highlanders. For more information on Calgary's international military history, visit the Museum of the Regiments (see p 332).

Tour B: Along the Bow

Starting in trendy Kensington, this tour includes a lovely stroll along the Bow River.

Kensington is a hip area that is hard to pin down. To get a true sense of the alternative attitude that pervades the coffee shops, bookstores and boutiques, explore Kensington Road between 10th and 14th Streets NW.

From Kensington, cross the Louise Bridge and take the pathway along the Bow River to the Eau Claire Market.

Eau Claire Market ★★ *(Mon to Wed 10am to 6pm, Thu and Fri 10am to 8pm, Sat 10am to 6pm, Sun 12pm to 5pm; next to the Bow River and Prince's Island Park, ☎264-6460)* is part of a general initiative in Calgary to keep people downtown after hours. The large building houses specialty food shops selling fresh fruit, vegetables, fish, meats, bagels and baked goods; neat gift shops with local and imported arts and crafts; clothing stores; fast-food and fine restaurants; a movie theatre and a 300-seat **IMAX** *(☎974-4629)* theatre.

The area around the market has seen a considerable amount of development, including the construction of a beautiful new YMCA and seemingly countless yuppie condominiums, plus the renovation of several buildings into restaurants and bars. It is quite an appealing area to explore.

Take the Second Street Bridge to **Prince's Island Park** ★, a picturesque green space with jogging paths and picnic tables. You'll also find the lovely River Café (see p 340), which serves a delicious weekend brunch. Continue across the island and over the next bridge to the north side of the Bow. A long stairway leads up to the **Crescent Road Viewpoint** ★ atop McHugh Bluff, a zigzagging path to the left also leads up to the viewpoint for those who prefer to avoid the 160-odd steps. Great view of the city.

Cross Prince's Island once again and continue walking east along the pathway to the stone lions of the Centre Street Bridge. Calgary's Chinatown lies to the south.

Calgary's **Chinese Cultural Centre** ★★ *(free admission; every day 9:30am to 9pm;*

197 First St. SW, ☎262-5071) is the largest of its kind in Canada. Craftspeople were brought in from China to design the building, whose central dome is patterned after the Temple of Heaven in Beijing. The highlight of the intricate tile-work is a glistening golden dragon. The centre houses a gift shop, museum *($2, open 11am to 5pm every day)*, gallery and restaurant.

Calgary's small **Chinatown** lies around Centre Street. Although it only has about 2,000 residents, the street names written in Chinese characters and the sidewalk stands selling durian, ginseng, lychees and tangerines all help to create a wonderful feeling of stepping into another world. The markets and restaurants here are run by descendants of Chinese immigrants who came west to work on the railroads in the 1880s.

Though the pathway continues along the Bow all the way to Fort Calgary, it is a long walk and not necessarily very safe. From Chinatown walk down to Seventh Ave. and take bus #1 or #411 to the fort.

Fort Calgary ★★★ *($6;50; May to mid-Oct every day 9am to 5pm; 750 Ninth Ave. SE, ☎290-1875, www.fortcalgary. ab.ca)* was built as part of the March West, which brought the North West Mounted Police to the Canadian west to stop the whisky trade. "F" Troop arrived at the confluence of the Bow and Elbow rivers in 1875, and chose to set up camp here either because it was the only spot with clean water or because it was halfway between Fort Macleod and Fort Saskatchewan. Nothing remains of the original Fort Calgary—the structures and outline of the foundations on the site today are part of an ongoing project of excavation and discovery undertaken mostly by volunteers. In fact, the fort will never be completely rebuilt as that would interfere with archaeological work underway. An excellent interpretive centre includes great hands-on displays (the signs actually say "please touch"), woodworking demonstrations and the chance to try on the famous, scarlet Mountie uniform. Friendly guides in period costume provide tours.

Right on the other side of the Elbow River, across the Ninth Avenue Bridge is **Deane House** *(Mon to Sat 11am to 2pm an Sun 10am to 2pm, 806 Ninth Ave. SE, ☎269-7747)*, the last remaining house from the garrison. It was built in 1906 for Richard Burton Deane, the Fort Post Commander at Fort Calgary who was later in charge of the jail in Regina where Louis Riel was held. The house originally stood next to the fort, across the river from its present location, and has been moved three times. Used in the past as a boarding house and as an artist's co-op, it has been restored and is now one of the city's better tea houses (see p 339).

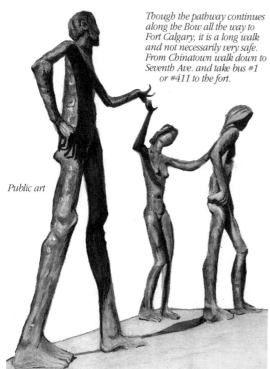

Public art

Take the Whitehorn C-train from downtown northeast to the Calgary Zoo north entrance, or walk across the 12th St. Bridge to St. George's Island and the south entrance.

The **Calgary Zoo, Botanical Gardens and Prehistoric Park** ★★ *($12, every day 9am to 5pm, St. George's Island, 1300 Zoo Rd. NE, ☎232-9300 or 232-9372)* is the second largest zoo in Canada. It opened in 1920 and is known for its realistic re-creations of natural habitats, now home to over 300 species of animals and 10,000 plants and trees. Exhibits are organized by continent and include tropical birds, Siberian tigers, snow leopards and polar bears, as well as animals indigenous to this area. The Prehistoric Park recreates the world of dinosaurs with 27 full-size replicas set amidst plants and rock formations from prehistoric Alberta.

Beyond these two riverside attractions is an area known as **Inglewood**. Interesting shops, especially antique shops, line Ninth Avenue SE just beyond the Elbow River.

Tour C: Southeast and Southwest

This tour explores Calgary immediately south of downtown, which for the purposes of this guide, we will delineate by the CPR tracks between Ninth and 10th Avenues.

The Southeast is Calgary's industrial area, but it is also home to the largest urban park in Canada, Fish Creek Provincial Park (the park also stretches into the Southwest, see p 333), not to mention the site of the "Greatest Outdoor Show on Earth," the Calgary Stampede. At the intersection of Ninth Avenue SE and the Bow, lies the Inglewood Bird Sanctuary, a good spot for strolling and bird-watching (see p 334). The Southwest is home to the city's more attractive neighbourhoods, most of them overlooking the Elbow River. In ritzy Mount Royal, for example, the lots and houses are much bigger than elsewhere in the city. The earliest settlement in this area was the Mission District, established by Catholic missionaries in the 1870s and known as Rouleauville at the time.

From downtown take the Fish Creek-Lacombe C-Train south to the Victoria Park/Stampede stop.

Unless you're in town during the Stampede, **Stampede Park** *(14th Ave. and Olympic Way SE)* has a limited appeal. The park is best known as the site of the famous Calgary Stampede, which takes place every year in July. If you are around at this time of year, get out your Stetson, hitch up your horse and get ready for a rompin' good time, Ya-hoo! See the Entertainment section, p 343.

The aptly named **Saddledome** has the world's largest cable-suspended roof and is a giant testimony to the city's cowboy roots. Apparently, there was some controversy over its name, though it is hard to imagine what else they could have called it! It is home to the city's National Hockey League team, the Calgary Flames, and is also used for concerts, conventions and sporting events. The figure skating and ice-hockey events of the 1988 Olympics were held here. Tours are available in summer *(☎777-1375)*. Also on the park grounds is the **Grain Academy** ★ *(free admission; year-round Mon to Fri 10am to 4pm also on the +15 level of the Round-Up Centre, Sat make resevations; ☎263-4594)*, which traces the history of grain farming and features a working railway and grain elevator. Finally, thoroughbred and harness racing take place on the grounds year-round and there is also a casino.

After exploring the Stampede grounds make your way west along 17th Avenue on foot or by catching bus #7 at First Street.S.W. Once at the corner of 17th Avenue SW and Fourth Street SW, a detour is called for. Whether you continue west or decide to head north, the cafés, boutiques and galleries lining these two streets will draw you in.

Continue along 17th Avenue by car or on bus #2 to 24th Street and the Naval Museum.

Believe it or not, Canada's second-largest naval museum, the **Naval Museum of Alberta** *($5; early Sep to end Jun Tue to Fri 1pm to 5pm Sat and Sun 10am to 5pm, early Jul to end Aug every day 10am to 4pm; 1820 24th St. SW, ☎242-0002)*

Saddledome

Calgary

Nose Hill Dr.
1a
Edgemont Blvd.
Shaganappi Trail
John Laurie Blvd.
Sarcee Trail
Crowchild Trail

Nose Hill Park

80th Ave. NE
72nd Ave. NE
64th Ave. NE

Calgary International Airport

N

Bow 48th Ave. NW
Bowness Park
Banff
6
?
1

Bowness Rd.
River
Shaganappi Trail
Brisebois

McKnight Blvd.

McKnight Blvd.
2 **6**
10
32nd Ave. NE
9

40th Ave. NW **15** **12**
32nd Ave. NW **3**
7 **11**

Northmount Dr.
4th St. NW
Centre St.
Edmonton Trail
Deerfoot Trail

Medicine Hat

Old Banff Coach Rd.
13 **14**
16th Ave. NW **4**

16th Ave. NW **5** **4**
8th Ave. NE
1st Ave. NE

5

Memorial Drive
Bow Trail
19th St. NW
14th St. NW
10th St. NW

4th Ave. SW

Memorial Dr.

Barrow Trail

See map of Calgary Centre

17th Ave. SW **?**
85th St. SW
89th St. SW
Sarcee Trail
45th St. SW
37th St. NW
29th St. NW
1
28th Ave SW
33rd Ave. SW
8
1
6
17th Ave. SE

Inglewood Bird Sanctuary
26th Ave. SE

Richmond Rd. SW
Sarcee Rd.
16th St. SW
14th St. SW
Crowchild Trail
2
46th Ave. SW
Glenmore
1
42nd Ave. SE
Ogden Rd.
Macleod Trail
Peigan Trail
2
50th Ave. SE

Elbow River
66th Ave. SW **8**
Elbow Dr.
58th Ave. SE **4**
Deerfoot Trail
18th St. SE
61st Ave. SE
72nd Ave. SE
76th Ave. SE

3
Glenmore Reservoir
Heritage Dr.
70th Ave. SW
14th St. SW
Macleod Trail
90th Ave. SW
Blackfoot Trail
8
8 Glenmore Trail
Shepard Rd.
Barrow Trail

SARCEE INDIAN RESERVE No. 145
Southland Dr.
Elbow Dr.
Southland Dr.
2

4
24th St. SW
Anderson Rd.
Macleod Trail
Deerfoot Trail
Bow River
114th Ave. SE

0   2   4km

Legend: -------- C-Train (LRT)
Fish Creek Provincial Park **5**
©ULYSSES

⬤ ATTRACTIONS

Tour C: Southeast and Southwest
1. Naval Museum of Alberta
2. Museum of the Regiments
3. Heritage Park Historical Village
4. Tsuu T'ina Museum
5. Spruce Meadows

Tour D: Northeast and Northwest
6. Canada Olympic Park (R)

(R) establishment with restaurant

ACCOMMODATIONS

1. Best Western Calgary Centre Inn
2. Best Western Port O' Call Inn
3. Best Western Village Park Inn
4. Blackfoot Inn
5. Coast Plaza Hotel
6. Country Inn and Suites
7. Econo Lodge Banff Trail
8. Elbow River Manor
9. Executive Royal Inn
10. Greenwood Inn
11. Holiday Inn Express
12. Quality Inn Motel Village
13. Red Carpet Inn
14. Sweet Dreams and Scones Bed and Breakfast
15. University of Calgary

RESTAURANTS

1. 4th Street Rose
2. Blue House Café
3. Mamma's Restaurant
4. Peter's Drive-In
5. Pho Kim/Kim's Vietnamese Noodle House
6. Wildwood Grill

is over 1,000km from the ocean. It salutes Canadian sailors, especially those from the prairie provinces. The story of the Royal Canadian Navy unfolds from 1910 through photographs, uniforms, and models, as well as actual fighter planes.

To reach the Museum of the Regiments, take Crowchild Trail south or bus #63.

The **Museum of the Regiments** *($5; Mon to Thu 10am to 9pm Fri to Sun 10am to 4pm; 4520 Crowchild Trail SW, ☎974-2850)*, Canada's second largest military museum, was opened by Queen Elizabeth in 1990. It honours four regiments: Lord Strathcona's Horse Regiment, Princess Patricia's Canadian Light Infantry, the King's Own Calgary Regiment and the Calgary Highlanders. Uniforms, medals, photographs and maps of famous battles are displayed. Sound effects like staccato machine-gun fire and the rumble of far-off bombs create an eerie atmosphere as you tour the museum. Vintage tanks and carriers can be viewed on the spotless grounds of the impressive building that houses the museum.

To reach Heritage Park continue south on Crowchild, then take Glenmore Trail, turn right on 14th St.SW. Heritage Drive leads into the park.

Heritage Park Historical Village ★ ★ *($11, May to Sep every day 9am to 5pm, Sep to early Oct weekends and holidays only 9am to 5pm, Oct to Nov limited operations; 1900 Heritage Dr. SW, ☎259-1900)* is a 26ha park on the Glenbow Reservoir. Step back in time as you stroll through a real 1910 town of historic houses decorated with period furniture, wooden sidewalks, a working blacksmith, a teepee, an old schoolhouse, a post office, a divine candy store and the Gilbert and Jay Bakery,

known for its sourdough bread. Staff in period dress play piano in the houses and take on the role of suffragettes speaking out for women's equality in the Wainwright Hotel. Other areas in the park recreate an 1880s settlement, a fur trading post, a ranch, a farm and the coming of the railroad. Not only is this a magical place for children, with rides in a steam engine and a paddlewheeler on the reservoir, but it is also a relaxing place to escape the city and enjoy a picnic. Free pancake breakfast (9am to 10am) is included in the admission charge.

Continue south on 14th Street SW and turn right on Anderson Road to reach the Tsuu T'Ina Museum, or take the Fish Creek-Lacombe C-Train south to the Anderson Station and then bus #92 or #96.

The **Tsuu T'Ina Museum ★** *(donation; Mon to Fri 9am to 4pm, reservations required; 3700 Anderson Rd. SW, ☎238-2677)* commemorates the history of the Tsuu T'Ina First Nation, who are Sarcee. Tsuu T'Ina means "great number of people" in their language. Nearly wiped out several times in the 1800s by disease brought by Europeans, the Tsuu T'Ina were shuffled around reserves for many years but persevered and were eventually awarded their reserve on the outskirts of Calgary in 1881. They held on to the land, spurning pressure to sell it. Some of the pieces on display were donated by Calgary families who used to trade with the Tsuu T'Ina, whose reserve lies immediately to the west of the museum. Other items, including a teepee and two headdresses from the 1930s, were retrieved from the Provincial Museum in Edmonton.

If show jumping is your thing you may want to take a little trip even farther south to **Spruce Meadows** *(Marquis de*

Lorne Tr., ☎974-4200). Four equestrian events take place here during the months of June, July and September. The rest of the year, visitors are welcome to look around.

Tour D: Northeast and Northwest

North of the Bow River, the biggest draws in the Northwest are Canada Olympic Park, Nose Hill Park (see p 334) and Bowness Park (see p 333); The Northeast has grown considerably in recent years and now has many hotels and restaurants, in addition to the airport.

To reach Canada Olympic Park take Bow Trail, Sarcee Trail and 16th Ave. NW northwest.

Canada Olympic Park ★ ★ ★ *(museum $10 self guided, $15 guided tours $10; Apr to mi-Oct every day 9am to 9pm, mid-Oct to early Nov every day 10am to 8pm, early Nov to Apr Mon to Fri 9am to 9pm Sat and Sun 9am to 5pm; on 16th Ave. NW, ☎247-5452)*, or COP, built for the 1988 Winter Olympic Games, lies on the western outskirts of Calgary. This was the site of the ski-jumping, bobsleigh, luge, freestyle skiing and disabled events during the games, and it is now a world-class facility for training and competition. Artificial snow keeps the downhill ski slopes busy all winter. The park offers the chance to try the Road Rocket (Bobsleigh on wheels) in the summertime *($45/person)* on the Olympic track and the luge and Bobsleigh Bullet in winter *(luge $13, Bullet $45, limited schedule)*.

Visitors to COP have the choice of seven different guided tour packages ranging from a self-guided walking booklet to the Grand Olympic Tour for $15, which includes a guided bus tour, chair-lift ride,

The Rodeo

Rodeos are serious business in Alberta. In some schools, cowboy skills are part of the sports program and are on a par with football and hockey.

There are essentially six official events in a rodeo. In the **bare-back-riding**, **saddle-bronc-riding**, and **bull-riding** events, the cowboy must stay on the bucking animal for eight seconds to even qualify, at which point he is given a score based on style, rhythm and control. In bare-back and saddle-bronc riding, the animal is a horse, and in all three cases a cinch is placed around the animal's hind quarters which causes him to

buck. The bull-riding event is of course the most exciting, with the bulls weighing in at around 820kg.

In the **calf-roping** event the cowboy must lasso the calf from his horse, race to the animal and tie three of its legs. This is a timed event, and the time includes a final six seconds during which the calf must remain tied.

Big cowboys are the usual participants in the **steer-wrestling** event where the cowboy slides off his horse onto the steer, grabs its horns, twists them and throws the steer to the

ground. Again the fastest time wins.

The **barrel-racing** event is the only one for cowgirls. Riders must circle three barrels in a clover-leaf pattern, and there is a five-second penalty for knocking one over. The fastest time wins.

Other entertaining events and rodeo clowns keep the crowd happy in between the official events. One of the most amusing crowd-pleasers is **mutton busting**, where young cowpokes are strapped to sheep and sent flying around the corral.

the Olympic Hall of Fame and the tower. It is worth taking the bus up to the observation deck of the 90m ski jump tower visible from all over the city. You'll learn about the refrigeration system, which can make 1,250 tonnes of snow and ice in 24hrs, the infamous Jamaican bobsleigh team, the 90- and 70m towers and the plastic-surface landing material used in the summer. If you do decide to take the bus, sit on the left for a better view of the towers and tracks. The **Naturbahn Teahouse** (☎247-5465) is located in the former starthouse for the luge. Delicious treats and a scrumptious Sunday brunch are served, but be sure to make reservations. The **Olympic Hall of Fame and Museum** (*admission included with self guided ticket; mid-May to Sep every day 8am to 9pm Sep to Apr 10am to*

5pm; ☎247-5452) is North America's largest museum devoted to the Olympics. The whole history of the games is presented with exhibits, videos, costumes, memorabilia and a bobsleigh and ski-jump simulator. You'll find a tourist information office and a gift shop near the entrance.

Parks

Prince's Island Park lies across the bridge at the end of Third Street SW. It is a small haven of tranquillity that is perfect for a picnic or a morning jog, and just 2min from downtown.

Fish Creek Provincial Park (*from 37th St. W to the Bow*

River) lies south of the city. Take Macleod Trail south and turn left on Canyon Meadows Drive then right on Bow Bottom Trail. The information centre is located here (☎297-5293). It is the largest urban park in Canada and boasts paved and shale trails that lead walkers, joggers and cyclists through stands of aspen and spruce, prairie grasslands and floodplains dotted with poplar and willow trees. An abundance of wildflowers can be found in the park as can mule deer, white-tailed deer and coyotes. An interpretive trail, artificial lake and beach, playground and picnic areas are some of the facilities. Fishing is exceptional; you are virtually guaranteed to catch something. Horses may also be rented.

Bowness Park (*off 85th St. at 48th Ave. NW*) has always

Calgary

been a favourite escape for Calgarians. You can paddle around its pretty lagoons in the summer, while in the winter they freeze up to form the city's largest skating rink.

Nose Hill Park *(off 14th St. between John Laurie Blvd. and Berkshire Dr. NW)* has an area of 1127ha, just 26ha less than Fish Creek Provincial Park. This windswept hill rises 230m and is covered with native grasses and a few bushes. There is a handful of pretty hiking trails.

Outdoor Activities

Golf

The **Mapleridge Golf Course** *($29/18 holes; 1240 Mapleglade Dr. SE, ☎974-1825)* **Shaganappi Point** *($29/18 holes; 1200 26th St. SW, ☎974-1810)* and **Lakeview Golf Course** *($10.50/18 holes; 5840 19th St. S.W., ☎974-1815)* are three of the nicer municipal golf courses in Calgary. Tee times for all City of Calgary courses can be booked up to four days in advance by calling ☎221-3510. For the more refined golfer, about 10min south of the city limits, **Heritage Point Golf Country Club** *($110/18 holes; Heritage Point Dr., ☎256-2002)* boasts 27 holes, and is one of best golf courses in Canada. In the southeast, **McKenzie Meadows Golf Club** *($47.50/18holes; 17215 McKenzie Meadows Dr. SE, ☎257-2255)*, is more affordable and is still a pretty course.

Skating

For the chance to skate on Olympic ice, head to Calgary's **Olympic Oval** *($4.50; University of Calgary, 2500University Dr.N.W., ☎220-7890).* This world-class facility, built for the '88 Winter Olympics, is now used as a training centre. The public skating hours vary, but generally the rink is open to the public in the afternoon from noon to 1pm and in the evenings. It is a good idea to call ahead.

For outdoor skating, nothing beats the frozen lagoons of Bowness Park.

Hiking

Calgary's trail system is extensive. There are marked paths all along the Bow River, the Elbow River, Nose Creek, around the Glenmore Reservoir and in Nose Hill Park.

Bird-Watching

Inglewood Bird Sanctuary *(donation; May to end Sep everyday 10am to 5pm,Oct to end Apr Tue to Sun 10am to 4pm; 2429 Ninth Ave. SE, ☎269-6688)* is 32ha of riverside land where more than 250 species of birds have been spotted over the years. There is an interpretive centre for information on these species and on Calgary's other wildlife. Walking tracks open everyday during day light hours.

Accommodations

There are often two rates for Calgary hotels and motels: a Stampede rate and a rest-of-the-year rate. The difference between the two can be substantial in some cases. Weekend rates are also lower in many hotels, as many are catered to corporate travellers who stay during the week.

The **Bed and Breakfast Association of Calgary** *(☎543-3900, ≈543-3901)* can help you find accommodation in one of the 40-odd bed and breakfasts of the city.

Tour A: Downtown

Calgary City Centre Hostel
$
520 Seventh Ave. SE
☎269-8239 or 866-762-4122
≈266-6227
www.hihostels.ca
The Calgary International Hostel can accommodate up to 120 people in dormitory-style rooms. Four family rooms are also available in winter. Guests have access to laundry and kitchen facilities, as well as to a game room and a snack bar. Reservations are recommended. The hostel is advantageously located two blocks east of City Hall and Olympic Plaza in a rather seedy—although safe—part of town. If the hostel is full, there are others in the area to chose from. However, be aware that these places are not very pleasant. Their only redeeming feature is their price.

Plaza Regis Hotel
$$
124 Seventh Ave. SE
☎262-4641
≈262-1125
The Plaza Regis Hotel moves into the superior category.

The 100 rooms are spacious, the beds are comfortable and the decor is attractive.

The Fairmont Palliser
$$$-$$$$
ℜ, ≡, △, ⊘, ℑ, ≈, ☺, ✕, ℝ
133 Ninth Ave. SW
☎*262-1234 or 800-441-1414*
⇄*260-1260*
www.fairmont.com
The Palliser offers distinguished, classic accommodations. The hotel was built in 1914, and the lofty lobby, retains its original marble staircase, solid-brass doors and superb chandelier. The rooms are a bit small but have high ceilings and are magnificently decorated in classic styles.

Hyatt Regency Calgary
$$$$
≡, ☺, ⊘, ℂ, ≈, ☺, ℜ, △
700 Centre St. S
☎*717-1234 or 800-233-1234*
⇄*537-4444*
www.hyatt.com
This latest addition to Calgary's service-oriented downtown hotel scene opened in May 2000 with 355 rooms on 25 floors. It has an enviable location just off the bustling Stephen Avenue, even if the modern new building does contrast a bit with Calgary's old sandstone. Rooms and suites are available, and you will be well taken care of by an army of staff. The hotel has a great original collection of Western Canadian art.

Calgary Marriott Hotel
$$$
ℜ, ≈, ≡, △, ⊘
110 Ninth Ave. SE
☎*266-7331 or 800-896-6878*
⇄*262-8442*
www.marriotthotels.com
The business-class Calgary Marriott Hotel is one of the biggest of the downtown hotels. Its spacious rooms are decorated with warm colours and comfortable furnishings.

Tour B: Along the Bow

Riverpath Bed and Breakfast
$$ bkfst incl.
R, ⊙
1011 Maggie St. SE
☎*262-1191*
It's not your traditional Victorian bed and breakfast, but the Riverpath is a good choice for bikers and the budget conscious looking to stay a bit out of the downtown area. Just 5min from Inglewood and 15min from downtown, this tall tan-coloured home has hardwood floors and a contemporary look. The high wooden beds are great, as is the view offered of the city. It's a stone's throw from Calgary's great bike path system, and there are bicycles available for guests.

Riverwynde Bed and Breakfast
$$-$$$ bkfst incl.
✕, sb/pb, ℑ
220 10A St. NW
☎/⇄*270-8448*
www.riverwynde.com
The Riverwynde is a great old Victorian cottage-style home, just behind trendy Kensington Road and close to the Sunnyside C-Train stop. The Sun Room, as its name would imply, is a bright little chamber with salmon walls and red brick. The Earth Room is the cheapest option, at $90 per night. The lovely Forest Room has earth tones and a full balcony. The street is quiet, as there is no through access for traffic, and the Kensington district is probably the coolest area of the city to stay in.

Inglewood Bed & Breakfast
$$-$$$$ bkfst incl.
1006 Eighth Ave. SE
☎*262-6570*
⇄*262-6570*
www.inglewoodbedand breakfast.com
One of the most charming places recommended by the Bed & Breakfast Association of

Calgary is the Inglewood Bed & Breakfast. Not far from downtown, this lovely Victorian house is also close to the Bow River's pathway system. Breakfast is prepared by Chef Valinda.

Sandman Hotel
$$$
ℜ, ≡, ≈, ⊘
888 Seventh Ave. SW.
☎*237-8626 or 800-726-3626*
⇄*290-1238*
www.sandmanhotels.com
Travellers in search of a hotel with facilities and quality rooms should check out the Sandman Hotel. The heated parking and 24hr food services can come in handy.

Hawthorn Hotel & Suites
$$$ bkfst incl.
ℜ, △, ⊘, K, ✕, ℑ, ≡
618 Fifth Ave. SW
☎*263-0520 or 800-661-1592*
⇄*298-4888*
www.hawthorncalgary.com
The weekly, corporate and group rates of the all-suite Hawthorn Hotel & Suites make this perhaps the least expensive hotel accommodation right downtown. The fully equipped kitchens also help keep costs down.

Sheraton Suites Eau Claire
$$$-$$$$$
≡, ⊘, ℜ, ≈, ☺, ☺, ℂ
255 Barclay Parade SW
☎*266-7200 or 888-784-8370*
⇄*366-1300*
www.sheratonsuites.com
Sheraton Suites has a light-filled, stained-glass lobby, and is a hop away from Eau Claire Market. Suites are roomy and feature a writing desk and small kitchen area with a sink and microwave. For those needing to work, there are high-speed Internet connections in rooms and a business centre. Kids will like the water slide in the pool area. Unfortunately, front desk service can be a bit uppity.

Calgary

Tour C: Southeast and Southwest

Southeast

Blackfoot Inn
$$$-$$$$
≡, ✖, ☺, ≈, ✪, ℜ, △
5940 Blackfoot Trail SE
☎*252-2253 or 800-661-1151*
⇄*252-3574*
www.blackfootinn.com
This independently owned hotel looks terrible from the outside, but don't let that turn you off, as a lobby with great stonework and a roaring fireplace will welcome you to pleasant accommodations. Being independent, the hotel has to offer excellent service to compete with the many Calgary hotel chains, so you will be well taken care of during your stay. They pride themselves on being pet friendly, and the K-9 Centre—a kind of doggy daycare—is just three blocks down the road. Yuk Yuk's, a cabaret with international stand-up comedy acts, is also here.

Southwest

**Tumble Inn**
$$ bkfst incl.
✖, sb
1507 Sixth St. SW
☎*228-6167*
⇄*802-1955*
When the hostel fills, they send people to Arlene Roberge's Victorian House just off of 17th Avenue SW. The quality to price ratio is excellent here—a stay costs just $60 per night and the house is wonderfully situated in a trendy area within walking distance of downtown. There are three comfy rooms available and a great claw-foot bathtub in the bathroom. Arlene, who has a friendly old dog named Casey on the premises, speaks English and French.

Elbow River Manor Bed and Breakfast
$$-$$$ bkfst incl.
☺, ℝ
2511 Fifth St. SW
☎*802-0799 or 866-802-0798*
⇄*547-9151*
www.elbowrivermanor.com
Elbow River Manor is a gorgeous establishment, with four rooms overlooking the small, meandering Elbow River. Great bed and breakfast options are few and far between in corporate Calgary, and this is the crème de la crème. The house has been restored to its early days of 1908, using all of the original wood and incorporating coffered ceilings. It looks like a funky Cape Cod-style home, with purple cedar shingles and bright yellow window frames. Guest rooms have hardwood floors and some have terrific four post beds. The loft, which goes for $150 per night, has a pool table and claw foot bathtub.

Best Western Calgary Centre Inn
$$$
≡, ☺, ☺, ≈, ℝ, ✪
3630 MacLeod Trail S
☎*287-3900 or 877-287-3900*
⇄*287-3906*
The name's a bit deceiving, but this Best Western is just a 5min drive south of downtown Calgary. It went up in 1999, so the furniture and decor are still in good shape, and the service is excellent. It's on busy MacLeod Trail, so ask for a room on the east side of the hotel. With the do-it-yourself continental breakfast and great rates, it's a good value.

Tour D: Northeast and Northwest

Northeast (Near the Airport)

Executive Royal Inn
$$
≡, ☺, ☺, ✪, ℜ, △
2828 23rd St. NE
☎*291-2003 or 877-769-2562*
⇄*291-2019*
A domed, sky-lit lobby and stone hallways welcome you to perhaps the most reasonably priced of Calgary's many airport-accessible hotels. There are 201 rooms here, and they have a slight country feel to them. There are plenty of amenities including free shuttle service to and from the airport.

Best Western Port O' Call Inn
$$-$$$
ℜ, ≡, ≈, ☺, ☺
1935 McKnight Blvd. NE
☎*291-4600 or 800-661-1161*
⇄*250-6827*
This Best Western was renovated in 2000, so the rooms and hallways are very fresh looking. There are 201 rooms with queen- and king-sized beds, as well as three main suites. The standard rooms feature earth tones. There is a 24hr shuttle bus to the airport, as well as a racquetball court.

Country Inn and Suites
$$$ bkfst incl.
≡, ☺, ≈, ℝ, ✪
2481 39th Ave. NE
☎*250-1800*
⇄*250-2121*
The Country Inn and Suites is the best airport hotel, with its very warm floral linens and wooden decor. It's as charming as a well-priced, service-oriented hotel can be, and there is a noticeable lack of business-like stuffiness. The beds are very comfortable, and as would be imagined, its rooms and 50 suites are decorated in a country style.

Greenwood Inn
$$$
≡, 🐾, ☺, C, ≈, ℜ, ✿, ℜ, △
3515 26th St. NE
☎*250-4575 or 888-233-6730*
⇌*250-8050*
www.greenwoodinn.ca
This four-storey charmer has a comfortable feel to it. Prices are great at $139 per night year round, and the rooms, with a dark wood decor, are appealing. It's a very clean establishment which has won a number of housekeeping awards. Twenty-sixth Street runs adjacent to Barlow Trail.

Coast Plaza Hotel
$$$$
ℜ, ≡, ≈, ◉, △, ☺, 🐾
1316 33rd Street NE
☎*248-8888 or 800-663-1144*
⇌*248-0749*
www.calgaryplaza.com
The Coast Plaza Hotel offers luxurious accommodations near the airport and is located a short distance from the C-train. The 248 rooms are spacious and comfortable, and the service is impeccable.

Northwest

Calgary's Motel Village is quite something: car-rental offices, countless chain motels and hotels, fast-food and family-style restaurants and the Banff Trail C-Train stop. The majority of the hotels and motels look the same, but the more expensive ones are usually newer and offer more facilities. Most places charge considerably higher rates during Stampede Week.

University of Calgary
$-$$
K (suites only), ℜ, *sb/pb*
2500 University Dr. NW
☎*220-3203*
www.ucalgary.ca/residence
An inexpensive accommodation option, only available in summer, is to stay at the residences of the University of Calgary.

The Red Carpet Inn
$$
≡, ℜ
4635 16th Ave. NW
☎*286-5111*
⇌*247-9239*
www.ctdmotels.com/red carpetinn
The Red Carpet Motor Hotel is one of the best values in Motel Village. Some suites have small refrigerators.

Econo Lodge Banff Trail
$$
≡, 🐾, K, ≈, ℜ
2231 Banff Tr. NW
☎*289-1921 or 800-917-7779*
⇌*282-2149*
www.econolodgecalgary.com
The Econo Lodge is a good place for families. The laundry facilities and large units with kitchenettes are very practical while service is outstanding. There are 62 rooms.

Sweet Dreams and Scones Bed and Breakfast
$$-$$$ bkfst incl.
2443 Uxbridge Dr. NW
☎*289-7004*
www.sweetdreamsand scones.com
Owner Karen MacLeod has been renting out rooms at her lovely home since 1992, and doesn't seem to be tiring of it. There are antiques and crafts everywhere throughout the three guest rooms, including some lovely pine antiques from Ontario. The handmade headboards on the beds are a great touch, as are the winding paths in the backyard garden. The house is in a residential area near the university.

Holiday Inn Express
$$$ bkfst incl.
≡, 🐾, ≈, △, ☺, ◎
2227 Banff Tr. NW
☎*289-6600 or 800-HOLIDAY*
⇌*289-6767*
www.holidayexpress.com
The Holiday Inn express offers quality accommodations at affordable prices. Rooms are furnished with king- and queen-size beds, and a complimentary continental breakfast is served.

Quality Inn Motel Village
$$$ bkfst incl.
ℜ, ≈, ≡, △, ☺, 🐾
2359 Banff Tr. NW
☎*289-1973 or 800-661-4667*
⇌*282-1241*
www.qualityinnmotel village.com
The Quality Inn has a nice lobby and an atrium restaurant and lounge. Both rooms and suites are available. Good value for the price.

The Best Western Village Park Inn
$$$
ℜ, ≡, ≈, ℜ, 🐾
1804 Crowchild Tr. NW
☎*289-0241 or 888-774-7716*
⇌*289-4645*
www.villageparkinn.com
Another member of this well-known chain. Guests enjoy many services, including Budget car-rental offices. Rooms are nicely furnished with up-to-date colour schemes. This is the classiest of the Motel Village options.

Restaurants

Tour A: Downtown

Schwartzie's Bagel Noshery
$
Eighth Ave. SW
☎*296-1353*
If you don't think you'll last until dinner, grab a bagel to go from Schwartzie's Bagel Noshery. Imagine the most typical and the most original bagels you can and they probably have one. You can also eat in; the interior is inviting and comfortable.

Rose Garden Thai Restaurant
$$
207 Eighth Ave. SW
☎*263-1900*
The Rose Garden is a popular Thai restaurant with a small statue of Buddha overlooking patrons. There are also some Chinese, Indian and Pacific

influences on the menu and lots of seafood. Calgary food critics are in love with the place and its Southeast Asian stir-fries, curries and salads. The decor isn't stunning but the customers who regularly pack the place don't seem to care.

The Silver Dragon
$$
106 Third Ave. SE
☎*264-5326*
This is one of the best of the many Chinese restaurants in Chinatown. The staff is particularly friendly and the dumplings particularly tasty.

Latin Corner
$$-$$$
Mon to Sat dinner, Mon to Fri lunch
109 Eighth Ave. SW
☎*262-7248*
The Latin Corner offers central South American cuisine in a narrow, sky-lit dining room with brick walls, candlelight and live Latino music on weekends. The chef is from Venezuela, the server might call you amigo and Chilean, Spanish and Argentinean vintages are on the wine list. You might want to give dinner here a miss if you're dining alone, as much of the menu is made up of shared entrées for two like paella with calamari, mussels, shrimp and a lobster tail over saffron rice. There is a tapas menu though, with samples for $8 to $12.

Grand Isle
$$$
128 Second St. SE
☎*269-7783*
Grand Isle prepares many of the favourites of Cantonese cooking but prides itself on its fresh and light dishes and its Szechuan-inspired flavouring. The decor is understated and the staff particularly friendly.

Drinkwaters Grill
$$$-$$$$
237 Eighth Ave. SE
☎*264-9494*
Its self-billing as "contemporary" is appropriate. The huge sky-blue-coloured columns, modern tableaux, classic dark wooden chairs and upholstered banquettes are appealing. They specialize in Alberta beef with seasonally inspired daily specials and, of course, a range of very acceptable sirloins, strips and other fine cuts, each with original accompaniments. They have theatre specials and a Happy Hour from 3:30pm to 7pm, Monday to Friday.

Catch
$$$-$$$$
100 Eighth Ave. SE
☎*206-0000*
Catch's dining room has bright, cream-coloured walls, hardwood floors, wine racks along the wall and modern iron chandeliers that look like collections of fishhooks. There's a reason for that, with a menu specializing in seafood and dishes like lobster and fine herb risotto or pinot noir braised Queen Charlotte halibut. The dining room is on the second floor, but there's a more reasonably priced oyster bar on the ground floor with entrées going for around $15. There's a 20-item menu of oysters from eastern and western Canada and a 26-page-long wine list with recommendations for each type of oyster. The oyster bar is also open for lunch.

Teatro
$$$-$$$$
200 Eighth Ave. SE
☎*290-1012*
Right next to Olympic Plaza in the old Dominion Bank Building, Teatro features a great setting and stylish atmosphere. Traditional "Italian Market Cuisine", prepared in a wood-burning oven, becomes innovative and exciting at the

hands of chef Andreas Wechselverger.

Caesar's Steakhouse
$$$$
512 Fourth Ave. SW
☎*264-1222*
and 10816 Macleod Tr. S
☎*278-3930*
One of Calgary's most popular spots to dig in to a big juicy steak, though they also serve good seafood. The elegant decor features Roman columns and soft lighting.

Hy's Steakhouse
$$$$
316 Fourth Ave. SW
☎*263-2222*
Hy's, around since 1955, is the other favourite for steaks. The main dishes are just slightly less expensive than Caesar's and the atmosphere is a bit more relaxed, thanks to wood panelling. Reservations are recommended.

Owl's Nest
$$$$
In the Westin Hotel, Fourth Ave. and Third St. SW
☎*266-1611*
Fine French and European dishes are artfully prepared at the Owl's Nest. Some are even prepared at your table and flambéed right in front of you. All of the ladies get a rose at this fancy dining establishment.

The Rimrock
$$$$
In the Palliser Hotel, 133 Ninth Ave. SW
☎*262-1234*
The Palliser Hotel's Rimrock Restaurant serves a fantastic Sunday brunch and of course healthy portions of prime Alberta beef. The Palliser's classic surroundings and fine food coalesce into one of Calgary's most elegant dining experiences.

Tour B: Along the Bow

 Good Earth Café
$
at Eau Claire Market, 200 Barclay Parade SW
☎237-8684
Good Earth Café is a wonderful coffee shop with tasty wholesome goodies all made from scratch. Besides being a choice spot for lunch, this is also a good source of picnic fixings. You'll love it if you're vegetarian.

 Marathon
$-$$
Mon to Sat lunch and dinner, Sun dinner only
130 10 St. NW
☎283-6796
Marathon has made a splash in meat-and-potato Alberta by offering affordable Ethiopian cuisine in a small Kensington café beneath that nation's flapping flag. Ethiopian cuisine is a delicious hands-on experience with lamb, beef and veggie dishes arriving on the traditional injera bread plate. You then roll up your crepe-like plate and dip it in the often-spicy stew-like courses, called wats. Marathon is very affordable, and the food is great.

Old Spaghetti Factory
$-$$
222 Third St. SW
☎263-7223
The Old Spaghetti Factory is located outside the Eau Claire Market, and while not a spectacular place, its prices and atmosphere are good. It's a vast and raucous dining hall in a red-brick building, and, unsurprisingly, there are six different ways to have your spaghetti: with tomato sauce, rich meat sauce, spicy meat sauce, clam sauce, mushroom sauce or browned butter and mizithra cheese. Despite the lack of intimacy, the restaurant still has some charm, and all entrées come with soup/salad, bread, ice cream and coffee or tea.

 The 1886 Café
$-$$
every day 6am to 3pm; breakfast only
187 Barclay Parade SW
☎269-9255
The 1886 is right next door to the market and located in the old Eau Claire & Bow River Lumber Company building. Buffalo heads and a large collection of old clocks decorate the interior. Huge breakfast portions are served all day long.

Heartland Café
$$
corner of 940 Second Ave. NW and Ninth St. NW
☎ 270-4541
The *café au lait* whipped up by the Heartland Café is one of the best in town. They also have cinnamon buns and delicious soups, served in a warm decor accented by old varnished wood.

The Barley Mill
$$
201 Barclay Parade SW, next to the Eau Claire Market
☎290-1500
The Barley Mill is located in what appears to be a historic building, but is actually a new construction. An old-fashioned interior is successfully achieved with worn-down hardwood floors, a grand fireplace, an old cash register and a bar that comes all the way from Scotland. The menu includes pasta, meat and chicken dishes, as well as several imported beers on tap.

Deane House Restaurant
$$
11am to 2pm
806 Ninth Ave. SE, just across the bridge from Fort Calgary
☎269-7747
The Historic Deane House Restaurant is a pleasant tea-room located in the house of former RCMP commanding officer Richard Burton Deane. Soups and salads figure prominently on the menu.

Sumo Lounge
$$-$$$
136 Eau Claire Market, 200 Barclay Parade SW
☎290-1433
The Sumo Lounge is a hip and trendy sushi bar and restaurant in the hip and trendy Eau Claire Market. For purists, the menu isn't full Japanese…it's more fusion-style with some Thai and Chinese influences. The sushi bar and sake however, are straight from the Land of the Rising Sun. The massive rotating sushi bar is surrounded by booths and closed-off tatami rooms. Every night you can feast on all-you-can-eat raw seafood for around $20.

Stromboli Inn
$$$
1147 Kensington Cresc. NW
☎283-1166
The Stromboli offers unpretentious service and ambiance and classic Italian cuisine. Locals recommend it for its pizza, though the menu also includes handmade gnocchi, plump ravioli and a delicious veal gorgonzola.

La Caille on the Bow
$$$-$$$$
Mon to Fri lunch and dinner, Sat and Sun dinner
100 LaCaille Place, First Ave. and Seventh St. SW
☎262-5554
La Caille has been a long-standing fine-dining institution right on the Bow River. The restaurant has the feel of a European chalet, with a series of intimate, brick-walled and hardwood-floored dining rooms. The food is French-inspired with some Canadiana additions like seared venison and scallop ragout in an apple cider glaze. The service is perfect and formal, but the portions can be quite small…fine dining style. The wine list is strong in French Californian and Australian wines, and includes Okanagan ice wine. There is a more informal and less expensive

Calgary

dining area on the ground floor.

The River Café
$$$$
closed Jan
Prince's Island Park
☎*261-7670*
The River Café is only open during warm summer months, when brunch or lunch can be enjoyed outdoors in beautiful Prince's Island Park. Located in an old boathouse, this gem of a restaurant is the perfect escape from urban downtown Calgary, just across the Bow River. Reservations are highly recommended.

 Buchanan's
$$$$
738 Third Ave. SW
☎*261-4646*
Buchanan's gets the nod not only for its innovative steaks and chops in blue cheese sauce, but also for its excellent wine list (fine choices by the glass) and impressive selection of single malt scotches. This is a power-lunch favourite of Calgary's business crowd.

Tour C: Southeast and Southwest

 Nellie's Kitchen
$
73813 17th Ave. SW between Seventh and Sixth St. SW
☎*2444-4616*
Everything is made from scratch at the informal Nellie's Kitchen, a neat little *rendez vous* for lunch and people-watching. Breakfasts here are outstanding, with lineups down the street on weekends.

Wicked Wedge Pizza
$$
618 17th Ave. SW
☎ *212-1024*
The best slice of pizza south of the Bow River is served at Wicked Wedge Pizza. They concoct three different kinds of pizza every day using a variety of ingredients – from Mexican hot peppers, to tahini

sauce, to marinated artichoke hearts. It's very popular with the after-bar crowd.

Galaxie Diner
$
Mon to Fri 7am to 3pm, Sat and Sun 8:00am to 4:00pm
11th St. SW, near 15th Ave. SW
☎*228-0001*
For inexpensive breakfasts served at any time of day, go to Galaxie Diner. The decor doesn't look like it's changed here in 50 years. They serve hearty breakfasts as well as mouthwatering, home-made burgers.

The Arden Diner
$-$$
Mon to Sat lunch and dinner, Sun lunch only
1112 17th Ave. SW
☎*228-2821*
Jann Arden, a Calgary singer-songwriter who has had considerable success nationwide, owns this trendy diner on hip 17th Avenue. The style is earthy funk, with Portishead playing on the stereo and reasonably priced, hearty grub like burgers, salads, fish and chips, New York steak and ahi tuna. This isn't your average diner though—scotch and martinis are also available. The spicy Italian chicken sandwich is notably tasty.

Fiore Cantina
$$
638 17th Ave. SW
☎*244-6603*
Fiore's is a popular little Italian bistro that looks like something out of a Clint Eastwood spaghetti western. And yes, they have spaghetti, as well as dozens of other pasta and sauce combinations. There are some originals here, like the tortellini Bombay, curried tortellini with broccoli. There is also a list of thin crust pizzas, and the minestrone is awesome. The bill won't put much of a dent in your wallet, either.

The Mongolie Grill
$$
1108 Fourth St. SW
☎*262-7773*
The Mongolie Grill is truly a culinary experience. Diners choose meats and vegetables from a fresh food bar, the combination is then weighed (to determine the cost) and grilled right before your eyes. Roll it all up in a Mongolian wrap with some rice and hoisin sauce and there you go!

Passage To India
$$
1325 Ninth Ave. SE
☎ *263-4440*
The owner of Passage To India left India 30 years ago to come to Canada and brought his secret recipes along in his luggage. He recently left his job as a civil servant to devote himself full time to his culinary passion. The great variety of impressive dishes on the menu will definitely satisfy lovers of Indian cuisine (beef, chicken, vegetables, etc.). Even the wine and beer come from India.

Sukiyaki House
$$-$$$
Mon to Fri lunch and dinner, Sat and Sun dinner
517 10th Ave. SW
☎*263-3003*
The very feng shui Sukiyaki House welcomes diners downstairs, over a pond and into a large dining room with intimate paper-walled tatami rooms. Simple, fresh Japanese cuisine has been offered here for the last 28 years—it was Calgary's first Japanese restaurant. You can saddle up to the sushi bar, or take a seat at a table to sample the sukiyaki (Japanese hot pots), tempura, sushi or sashimi.

The King & I Thai Restaurant
$$-$$$
820 11th Ave. SW
☎*264-7241*
The King & I Thai Restaurant features an extensive menu of exotic Thai dishes including delicious Chu Chu Kai. The

ambience is modern and elegant.

Pongo
$$-$$$
524 17th Ave. SW
☎ *209-1073*
Opening onto the street, the Pongo restaurant does not go unnoticed. Its modern Art-Deco design is extraordinary. The round white decorations everywhere create a science-fiction-like atmosphere, and the guests are lulled to the sound of jazz. The oriental cuisine is decent.

4th Street Rose
$$$
2116 Fourth St. SW
☎*228-5377*
The 4th Street Rose is a favourite. The cuisine is very California and features lots of tasty vegetarian selections like Thai stir-fries, pasta dishes and seafood with wonderfully fresh ingredients and sinfully sweet desserts to finish it off. On warm summer days, the terrace is the place to be.

Wildwood Grill
$$$-$$$$
Mon to Sat lunch and dinner, Sun dinner
2417 Fourth St. SW
☎*228-0100*
Wildwood Grill is a fantastic restaurant with a very warm atmosphere. The maple-leaf-rimmed corner fireplace casts a glow on tables, while the meaty menu includes elk steak and linguine bolognese with hog wild boar or bison roulade. There isn't much for you here if you're vegetarian, but the food really is great, and you feel like you're dining in a romantically lit wine cellar. The pub downstairs has lower prices.

Moti Mahal Restaurant
$$
1805 14th St. SW
☎ *228-9990*
The Moti Mahal Restaurant offers good value for your dollar. It is, in fact, an all-you-can-eat Indian buffet. Unlike most restaurants of its kind, the food here is good quality (try the rice pudding at least twice) and the Indian-style decor is elegant. Reservations are recommended if you plan to go there for dinner.

McQueen's Upstairs
$$$$
1705 14th St.SW
☎*269-4722*
has a similar seafood-oriented menu but is slightly more upscale.

Cannery Row
$$$$
317 10th Ave. SW
☎*269-8889*
Cannery Row serves this landlocked city's best seafood with a cajun flair. An oyster bar and casual atmosphere is intended to make you feel like you're by the sea, and it works. Fresh halibut, salmon and swordfish are prepared in a variety of ways.

Mescalero
$$$$
1315 First St. SW
☎*266-3339*
Mescalero serves up an eclectic blend of Southwestern, Mexican and Spanish cuisine. They have a great courtyard, but unfortunately the service can be iffy at times.

The Casablancan Chef at the Sultan's Tent
$$$$
909 17th Ave. SW
☎*244-2333*
This is the place for fine authentic Moroccan cuisine. In keeping with tradition, guests are greeted upon arrival with a basin of scented water with which to wash their hands. The room is decorated with myriad plush cushions and tapestries and the mood is set with lanterns and soft Arabic music. (Remember it is traditional to eat with your right hand as your left one is considered unclean.)

Tour D: Northeast and Northwest

Peter's Drive-In
$
219 166 Ave. NE
☎*277-2747*
Sure, it's fast food, but Peter's has been a Calgary institution for 40 years. Pick up your burgers, fries and shakes to go, or grab a spot at a picnic table on the grass. It's good and greasy, and an order of large fries comes in a box the size of a coffin.

Pho Kim/Kim's Vietnamese Noodle House
$-$$
1511 Centre B St. NW
☎*276-7425*
For cheap, tasty and authentic Vietnamese food, head to Pho Kim just off Centre Street and 16th Avenue NW. It's a popular place with Calgary's Asian community, as well as other locals who have discovered it. The long menu includes pho (noodle soup), spring rolls and lemongrass chicken, and it's all served with the ubiquitous green tea. For a real taste of Vietnam, try the bun; grilled meat, vegetables, lemongrass and fish sauce served on rice vermicelli.

The Naturbahn Teahouse
$$
Sunday brunch and tea
Canada Olympic Park
☎*247-5465*
Located at the top of the luge and bobsleigh tracks at Canada Olympic Park, this is actually in the former start-house. The Naturbahn, which means natural track, no longer serves up luges; nowadays the menu features an interesting Sunday brunch. Reservations essential.

The Blue House Cafe
$$-$$$
3843 19th St. NW
☎*284-9111*
The Blue House doesn't look like much, but the chef's Argentinian creations, espe-

cially the fish and seafood dishes, more than make up for it. Another plus is the flamenco and three-finger guitar performances on some evenings. The mood it fairly casual, but a bit dressier in the evenings.

Mamma's Restaurant
$$$
320 16th St., NW
☎276-9744
Mamma's has been serving Italian cuisine to Calgarians for more than 20 years. The ambiance and menu offerings are both equally refined, the latter including home-made pasta, veal and seafood dishes.

Entertainment

The Calgary Mirror, ffwd and Straight are free news and entertainment weeklies with listings of what's going on around town, including live acts and theatre offerings.

Bars and Nightclubs

Things have changed since the heyday of **Electric Avenue** (*11th Avenue SW*), now boarded-up. The downtown core is picking up, as are 12th Avenue and 17th Avenue. **Crazy Horse** (*1315 First St.SW,☎266-1133*) is popular with young professionals who like classic rock and roll. **The Warehouse** (*733 10th Ave. SW, ☎264-0535*) offers a more "alternative" alternative, as do the **Drum and Monkey** (*1201 First St.SW,☎261-6674*), and **Night Gallery** (*1209 First St.,☎204-4484*).

Also on this First Street strip is the **Castle Pub**, which may well have the coolest jukebox in Western Canada.

Birthplace of the Bloody Caesar

Few people realize that the Bloody Caesar was invented right here in Calgary in 1969 by a man named Walter Chell, when he was beverage manager at the Calgary Inn (now the Westin Calgary). Not only did Chell invent the cocktail, but he was the brains behind its main ingredient as well, a combination of mashed clams and tomato juice, which he called clamato juice. You can even check with the company that later patented the juice as to its true origins.

Others have tried to copy, change and even take credit for Chell's recipe, but true Caesar drinkers know that 1.25 ounces of vodka, 5 ounces of Clamato juice and 3 dashes of Worcestershire sauce, all seasoned with salt, pepper and celery salt and garnished with a celery stalk combine to make the real thing!

Day and night, the terrace of the popular **Ship & Anchor Pub** (*534 17th Ave. SW, ☎245-3333*) is always overflowing with people. It seems that any excuse is good enough for the 20-something crowd to come here and guzzle down one of the many beers on tap. Light fare available.

The cocktail craze has hit Calgary, and the best places to lounge and sip martinis are the **Auburn Saloon** (*200 Eighth Ave. SW, ☎290-1012*), **Mercury** (*801 17th Ave.SW,☎514-1175*), and **Quincy's** (*609 Seventh Ave. SW, ☎264-1000*) which also has cigars.

Boystown (*213 10th Ave. SW, ☎265-2028*) attracts a gay crowd, while **Detours** and **Victoria's Restaurant** (*17th Ave. at Second St. SW,☎244-9991*), both located in the same building, cater to mixed crowds.

Kaos Jazz Bar (*cover charge Wed to Sat; 718 17th Ave. SW, ☎228-9997*) is a popular jazz club with live shows Thursday

to Saturday; it is also a fun café with an interesting menu.

For more music, check out the seedy King Edward Hotel, referred to as the **King Eddy** (*438 Ninth Ave. SE, ☎262-1680*). This is Calgary's home of the blues, with fantastic live acts coming through on a regular basis. The bar, as any blues bar should be, is dirty, but any real music fan will be happy they came. Be careful in this area at night.

If you're itchin' to two-step then you're in luck. Calgary has two great country bars. At **The Ranchman's** (*9615 Macleod Tr. SW, ☎253-1100*), the horseshoe-shaped dance floor is the scene of two-step lessons on Tuesdays and line-dancing lessons on Wednesdays; the rest of the week it is packed. **Outlaws** (*7400 Macleod Tr. SE, ☎255-4646*) is where the real cowboys and cowgirls hang out.

For some downtown night-club action, try **The Drink** (*355 10th Ave. SW, ☎264-*

0202). Owned by the infamous entrepreneur who operated the popular Cowboys (where serving staff were offered… ahem… complimentary surgical enhancements after a certain period of service), it's a decent place to go dancing, if that's what you're looking for.

For a less in-your-face experience, there are two very good Irish pubs in Calgary. The **James Joyce** *(114 Eighth Ave. SW, ☎262-0708)* is a lovely Stephen Avenue establishment, with raucous happy hours for the suit-and-tie types. It's a great place nonetheless. In Kensington, **Molly Malone's** *(1153 Kensington Cres., ☎296-3220)* is another

authentic spot for a pint of Kilkenny or Guinness.

Cultural Activities

Alberta Theatre Projects *(☎294-7402, www.atlive.com)* is an excellent troupe that performs great contemporary plays.

Those in need of some culture may want to inquire about performances of the **Calgary Opera** *(☎262-7286, www.calgary.opera.com)*, the **Calgary Philharmonic Orchestra** *(☎571-0270,www.cpo-live)* and the **Alberta Ballet** *(☎245-4222,www.albertaballet.com).*

Calgary has an **IMAX** theatre in the Eau-Claire Market *(☎974-IMAX or 974-4700).*

The **Uptown** *(612 Eighth Ave., ☎265-0120)* shows a mixture of first run movies and arthouse/European style productions in an old revamped theatre downtown. First-run movies can be seen at movie theatres throughout the city. Pick up a newspaper for schedules and locations, or call the **Talking Yellow Pages** *(☎521-5222)* (see p 325).

Festivals and Events

The **Calgary International Jazz Festival** *(☎249-1119, www.jazzfestivalcalgary.ca)*

The Greatest Outdoor Show on Earth!

The **Calgary Exhibition and Stampede** began in 1912, at a time when many people expected that the wheat industry would eventually supercede the cattle industry. It was originally intended to be a one-time showcase for traditional cowboy skills. Of course, the cattle industry thrived and the show has been a huge success ever since.

Every July, around 100,000 people descend on Stampede Park for the extravaganza. It begins with a parade, which starts at 6th Avenue SE and 2nd Street SE at 9am, but get there early (by 7am) if you want to see anything.

The main attraction is the rodeo where cowboys and cowgirls show off their skills

and vie for nearly one million dollars in prize money. The trials take place every afternoon at 1:30pm, and the big final is held on the last weekend. Reserved seats for this event sell out quickly and you are better off ordering tickets in advance if you have your heart set on seeing the big event. There are also chuck wagon races; heats for the Rangeland Derby are held every evening at 8pm, and the final one is on the last weekend.

Downtown, the **Olympic Plaza** is transformed into **Rope Square**, where free breakfast is served every morning from the backs of chuck wagons. Festivities continue throughout the day in the Plaza.

Back at Stampede Park, an Indian Village and agricultural fair are among the exhibits to explore. The Grandstand Show is a non-stop musical variety spectacular. Evening performances often showcase some of the biggest stars in country music. A gate admission fee of eight dollars is charged, which gives you access to all live entertainment, except shows at the Saddledome, for which tickets must be purchased in advance.

For information on the good rodeo seats write to **Calgary Exhibition and Stampede** *(Box 1060, Station M, Calgary, Alberta, T2P 2L8, or call ☎261-0101 ☎800-661-1260, www.calgarystampede. com).*

Calgary

takes place the last week of June. The **International Native Arts Festival** (☎233-2227) and **Afrikadey** (☎254-9110, *www.afrikadey.com*) take place the third week of August, and both highlight entertainment and art from a variety of cultures from all over the world. **Calgary Winter Fest** (☎543-5480, *www.calgarywinterfest.com*) takes place in late January or February.

Spruce Meadows, located southwest of the city, is Canada's premier equestrian facility. There are actually three annual events here, the National in early June, the North American in July (same time as Stampede) and the **Spruce Meadows Masters** (*www.sprucemeadows.com*) during the second week in September. The winner of the **Du Maurier International** during this last event takes home the biggest purse of any equestrian event anywhere. For information call ☎**947-4200**.

Tsuu T'Ina Nation holds its annual powwow the last weekend of July. This is a more low-key event than the famous Stampede, but also much more intimate. For only $7 you'll see a real rodeo, plus you'll experience Aboriginal culture. For information call ☎**281-4455**.

Spectator Sports

The Canadian Football League's **Calgary Stampeders** play their home games in **McMahon Stadium** (*1817 Crowchild Tr. NW*, ☎282-2044) from July to November. The National Hockey League's **Calgary Flames** play at the **Pengrowth Saddledome** (*555 Saddledome RiseSE*, ☎777-4646 or 777-2177) from

October to April (hopefully longer if they make the playoffs).

Shopping

Eaton Centre, TD Square, Scotia Centre and **The Bay** department stores line Eighth Avenue SW, as does a collection of swanky upscale shops including **Holt Renfrew** and the boutiques in **Penny Lane**.

Eau Claire Market is a wonderful spot to pick up just about anything. Imported goods, including Peruvian sweaters and southwestern-style decorating items, are all sold right next to fresh fish and produce.

Not only are **Kensington Avenue** and the surrounding streets a pleasant place to stroll, but the area is also full of interesting specialty shops that are worth a look. One of these is **Heartland Country Store** (*940 Second Ave. NW*) which sells beautiful pottery.

Another is **Livingstone and Cavell Extraordinary Toys** (*1124 Kensington Rd. NW*, ☎270-4165), which has old-school toys that bring out the child in everyone. It's a great shop with unique train sets, retro wind-up cars and stuffed animals from around the world.

There is a collection of shops, cafés and galleries along 17th Avenue SW, with a distinctly upbeat atmosphere.

Hemporium (*926 17th Ave.*, ☎245-3155) has clothing, hats and even lip balm made out of hemp. Look for the rather familiar leaf design over the

door. A few doors down is **Megatunes** (*932 17th Ave.*, ☎229-3022), a great record store with info on local shows and concerts.

Along Ninth Avenue SE, east of the Elbow River, in Inglewood, gentrified houses now contain antique shops and cafés.

The **Alberta Boot Co.** (*614 10th Ave. SW* ☎263-4623) is the place to outfit yourself for the Stampede, with boots in all sizes and styles, just to make sure you fit in!

The kingdom of records, cassettes and movies in Calgary is called **Recordland** (*1204 Ninth Ave. SE, near 11th St. SE,* ☎262-3839). They have every style of music here—and at unbeatable prices: three CDs for just $25!

Mountain Equipment Co-op (*830 10th Ave. SW,* ☎269-2420) is a co-operative that is essentially open only to its members, but it only costs $5 to join, and it is well worth it. High-quality camping and outdoor equipment, clothing and accessories are sold at very reasonable prices.

Arnold Churgin Shoes (*221 Eighth Ave. SW,* ☎262-3366 *and at the Chinook Centre, Macleod Tr. at Glenmore Tr.,* ☎258-1818) sells high-quality women's shoes at reasonable prices and offers excellent service, a must for those with a weakness for footwear!

Chocolaterie Bernard Callebaut (*1313 First St. SE,* ☎266-4300) makes delicious Belgian chocolates right here in Calgary. They are available throughout the city, but at the head office in the Southeast you can see them being made.

Southern Alberta

When departing Calgary it is difficult to resist the pull of the Rocky Mountains and head south. However, southern Alberta boasts some of the best sights and scenery of the whole province, from Waterton Lakes National Park and the mining towns of Crowsnest Pass to the historic native gathering place at Head-Smashed-In Buffalo Jump, and the edge of the endless prairies.

The vast expanses and sometimes desert-like conditions you'll traverse while making your way from west to east in Southern Alberta are in stark contrast to the looming, snow-capped Rocky Mountains to the west. Neat rows of wheat and other grains, perfectly round bales of hay, and the occasional grain elevator are about the extent of the relief across the slow-rolling terrain of this part of the province.

This chapter is divided into two driving tours:

Tour A: Southern Foothills ★★

Tour B: Lethbridge to Medicine Hat ★★

Finding Your Way Around

By Car

Tour A: Southern Foothills

Although Hwy. 2 is the quickest route from Calgary to Fort Macleod, the superb scenery along Hwy. 22, referred to by some as God's country, is well worth the extra time. This quiet two-lane highway first heads southwest from Calgary through an area synonymous with Alberta's oil-and-gas boom, and then runs through stunning historic ranchlands, with the Rocky Mountains as a backdrop. The community of Crowsnest Pass lies to the west of the junction with Hwy. 3, and beyond it are Crowsnest Pass and British Columbia. To the east, the tour continues down Hwy. 6 to Waterton Lakes National Park before returning north on Hwy. 2 to Fort Macleod and Lethbridge, the starting point of Tour B.

Tour B: Lethbridge to Medicine Hat

There is a quick, fairly scenic way to get from Lethbridge to Medicine Hat, but a detour south to Writing on Stone Provincial Park and then a peaceful drive along Hwys. 501, 879 and 61 is well worth the extra time and promises even better scenery.

Cypress Hill Interprovincial Park lies about 20km south of Medicine Hat on Hwy. 41. The park is also accessible via a gravel road running east from Orion; this road is in fairly good condition, but there are no service stations along it and it is slow going.

Lethbridge and Medicine Hat both have numbered street systems. Most of Lethbridge's hotels and motels are located along Mayor Magrath Drive, on your way into town on Hwy. 5. Medicine Hat's motel and hotel strip is located on the Trans-Canada Highway, east of downtown.

Car Rentals

Lethbridge

Budget
3975 1st Av.S
☎*(403) 328-6555*
☎*800-461-5276*
www.budget.com

Avis
at the airport
☎*800-272-5871*
www.avis.com

National Car Rental
2351 Second Ave. N
☎*(403) 380-3070*
www.nationalcar.com

Medicine Hat

Budget
Airport
☎*(403) 527-7368*
☎*877-283-4389*
Downtown
1566 Gershaw Drive SW
☎*(403) 527-7368*
☎*877-283-4389*
www.budget.com

National Car Rental
Airport, Airport Ave.
☎*(403) 527-5665*
www.nationalcar.com

By Bus

Greyhound
☎*800-661-8147*
www.greyhound.ca

Lethbridge Greyhound Bus Depot
411 Fifth St. S
☎*(403) 327-1551*
services: restaurant, lockers.

Medicine Hat Greyhound Bus Depot
557 Second St. SE
☎*(403) 527-4418*

Practical Information

Area code: *403*

Tourist Information

Lethbridge

Travel Alberta South
2805 Scenic Dr.S
☎*329-6777 or 800-661-1222*
⇥*329-6177*
www.albertasouth.com

Chinook Country Tourist Association
2805 Scenic Dr.S
☎*329-6777 or 800-661-1222*

Medicine Hat

Medicine Hat Tourist Information
☎*527-6422 or 800-481-2822*
⇥*528-2682*
www.albertasouth.com/ town/medhat

Exploring

Tour A: Southern Foothills

Like the tour of the central foothills (see p 372), this tour follows Hwy. 22. These two tours can be joined by following the stretch of Hwy. 22 between Cochrane and Bragg Creek Provincial Park.

★
Bragg Creek

The town of Bragg Creek lies right next to land owned by the Tsuu T'ina First Nation. The eastern extremity of their reserve butts up against the expanding suburbs of Southwest Calgary. There are two very good reasons to visit this community: scenery and pie. The former can be enjoyed at **Bragg Creek Provincial Park**, a pretty place for short walks or picnics and the latter can be had at **Pies Plus** (☎*949-3450*).

Head south on Hwy. 752 to Millarville.

Millarville

Home of the historic **Millarville Racetrack**, this town is the only one left of five that were built to accommodate transient workers of the Turner Valley oil fields. There is not much to see in this hamlet on a weekday, but if you're passing through on a Saturday, be sure to stop at the **Farmer's Market** (*$1 parking; Jun to early Oct, Sat 8:30am to noon; Millarville Racetrack,* ☎*931-2404*). Vendors from throughout the area sell crafts, fresh produce, baked goods and clothing. A three-day Christmas market is

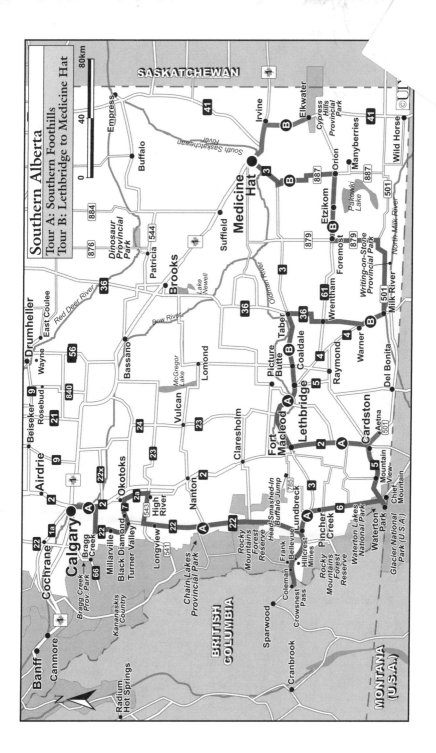

Southern Alberta
Tour A: Southern Foothills
Tour B: Lethbridge to Medicine Hat

also held the first weekend in November, as is an agricultural fair the third Sunday in August. The **races** *($4; first weekend in Jul, Sat and Sun 1pm, ☎951-3411)* take place at the beginning of July. These have been running for 90 years, but betting was only allowed in 1995. Games and festivities accompany the annual races.

Head south on Hwy. 22 to Turner Valley.

Turner Valley

The first major crude oil discovery in Alberta (and Canada), was made in Turner Valley in 1914, but it is natural gas, discovered 11 years earlier that is the claim to fame of Turner Valley. **Dingman No. 1** was Turner Valley's first producing well. It was named after a Calgary businessman who was brought, along with R. B. Bennett, who was later elected prime minister of Canada, to the site by William Herron in 1903. Herron lit a flame using the gas seepage from the earth and cooked the three men breakfast. Dingman and Bennett thus agreed to finance the well, which lasted until 1952. An area known as **burning ground**, where gas flares still burn round the clock, is actually the site of the former Dingman No. 2 well. The seepage was lit in 1977 as a precautionary measure. This unique site is best viewed from the Hell's Half Acre Bridge, which spans the Sheep River.

Black Diamond

Just a few kilometres east of Turner Valley is Black Diamond, another town whose claim to fame lies in its rich natural resources. The false fronts of this town's main street bear witness to the prosperous times when coal was like black diamonds. The mine here was opened in 1899,

and at its peak 650 tonnes of coal a year were extracted.

Head east along Hwy. 7, then north on Hwy. 2A to Okotoks.

Okotoks

Okotoks is the largest city between Calgary and Lethbridge. It is also home to several antique and craft shops. A walking tour map is available at the **tourist office** *(53 N. Railway St., ☎938-3204)* and includes several historic buildings which date from when the town was a rest stop along the Macleod Trail between Fort Calgary and Fort Macleod.

The town's name comes from the Blackfoot word *okatok*, which means rock, and refers to the **Big Rock**, one of the largest glacial erratics found in North America and the town's biggest attraction. This 18,000-ton rock was deposited 7km west of Okotoks during the Ice Age after it landed on an advancing glacier during a landslide in what is now Jasper National Park.

Okotoks is also home to the **Okotoks Bird Sanctuary**, where geese, ducks and other waterfowl can be observed from an elevated observation deck. The sanctuary is an ongoing project of the Fish and Game Association.

High River

Another rest stop along the Macleod Trail, High River, 24km south of Okotoks along Hwy. 2A, was the only place people, horses, cattle and wagons could cross the Highwood River. High River is now a small ranching community with an interesting local museum, the **Museum of the Highwood** *(May to Sep, every day 10am to 5pm, Oct to May, Tue to Sat noon to 4pm, Sun 12:30pm to 4:30pm; 406 First St. W., ☎652-7156).* The North American Chuckwagon

Racing Championships are held here in late June. It is also the birthplace of Canada's 16th prime minister, Joe Clark.

Backtrack from High River along Hwy. 543 then take Hwy. 22 south to Longview and the Bar U Ranch.

Longview

The **Bar U Ranch National Historic Site** ★ ★ *($6.50; mid May to mid-Oct, every day 10am to 6pm; winter, call for group reservations; Longview, Alberta, ☎395-2212 or 800-568-4996)* opened in the summer of 1995 and commemorates the contribution of ranching to the development of Canada. It is one of four ranches that once covered almost all of Alberta, and until recently it was still a working ranch. Now, people are able to wander freely around the ranch and observe ranching operations on a scaled-down, demonstration level. "Bar U" refers to the symbol branded on cattle from this ranch. A beautiful visitors centre features an interpretive display on breeds of cattle, the roundup, branding and what exactly a quirt is. A 15min video on the Mighty Bar U conveys the romance of the cowboy way of life and also explains how the native grasslands and Chinook winds unique to Alberta have been a perpetual cornerstone of ranching. The centre also houses a gift shop and a restaurant where you can savour an authentic buffalo burger.

Continue south along Hwy. 22 for another 100km or so to Hwy. 3.

Chain Lakes Provincial Park ★ (see p 358) is the only real attraction along this stretch of Hwy. It sits between the Rocky Mountains and the Porcupine Hills in a transition zone of spring-fed lakes. There is a campground (see p 361). Farther south, the splendid pale yellow grass-lands, dotted occasionally by deep blue lakes, roll up into the distant Rocky Mountains. There is an otherworldly look about the mountains looming on the horizon.

Head west once you reach Hwy. 3, another stretch of scenic highway. It leads deeper into the foothills and through a series of mining towns to Crowsnest Pass and British Columbia.

★
Crowsnest Pass

The area along Hwy. 3 be-tween Pincher Creek and the continental divide is known as the Municipality of Crowsnest Pass. A number of once thriv-ing coal-mining communities along the highway are now home to a handful of sites offering an interesting historical perspective on the local min-ing industry. Coal was first discovered here in 1845, but it wasn't until 1898, when the CPR built a line through the pass, that towns were really settled. Coal was the only industry in the area, and when the mineral turned out to be of inferior quality and hard to get at, troubled times set in. Local coal fetched lower prices than that of British Columbia, and by 1915 the first mine had closed; the others soon followed. The municipality is Alberta's only ecomuseum and was declared a Historic District in 1988.

The first site you will come across as you head west along Hwy. 3 is the **Lietch Collieries** *(donations accepted; guided tours mid-May to Sep, 10am to 4pm, self-guided Sep to May;* ☎562-7388). This was the only Canadian-owned mine in the Pass and the first to close in 1915. Various information panels explain the extraction process while a path leads through the mine ruins.

Farther down Hwy. 3, follow the signs toward Hillcrest.

On June 19, 1914, **Hillcrest** was the site of the worst min-ing disaster in Canadian history when an explosion ripped through the tunnels of the mine trapping 235 men un-derground. Many that had survived the blast eventually died of asphyxiation from the afterdamp (the carbon dioxide and carbon monoxide left over after the explosion has used all available oxygen), which, along with smoke, also forced back rescuers. The mine has been sealed since it shut down in 1939, and there isn't much to see except the closed-off entrance. The 189 victims of the disaster were buried in a mass grave in a cemetery located 1km along the road from Hwy. 3.

Continue west through Hillcrest, and cross Hwy. 3 to the Bellevue Mine.

The **Bellevue Mine** opened in 1903 and had been operating for seven years without inci-dent, when it was rocked by an underground explosion on December 9, 1910. After-damp poisoning lead to the deaths of 30 miners. The mine reopened and remained operational until 1962. Today visitors are given hard hats and miner's lamps and follow a **guided tour ★ ★** *($6; mid-May to early Sep, tours every half hour 10am to 6pm;* ☎654-4700) through about 100m of dark, cool and damp under-ground mine tunnels. This is the only mine in the Pass open to visitors and is a real treat for both young and old. Bring a sweater, as it can get quite cold in the mine.

Continuing along Hwy. 3, you'll notice a very drastic change in the landscape. Ex-tending on both sides of the highway, covering 3km², de-bris of the Frank Slide creates a spectacular, almost lunar landscape. Consisting mostly of limestone, these boulders are on average 14m deep, but exceed 30m in some places.

The **Frank Slide Interpretive Centre ★ ★** *($6.50; mid-May to Sep, every day 9am to 6pm; mid-Sep to mid-May 10am to 5pm; turn right off highway,* ☎562-7388), located north of the highway on a slight rise, presents an audiovisual ac-count of the growth of the town and of the slide itself. It explains the various theories about what caused the slide on April 29, 1903 that sent 82 million tonnes of limestone crashing from the summit of Turtle Mountain onto the town of Frank, which at the time lay south of the highway at the foot of the mountain. All that remains of the town is an old fire hydrant. The moun-tain's unstable structure, min-ing, water and severe weather are believed to have contrib-uted to the disaster. A self-guided trail through the slide area provides an interesting perspective of the scope of the slide. Sixty-eight of the town's residents were buried, but the disaster might have been worse if it hadn't been for a CPR brakeman who amazingly raced across the rocks to stop an approaching passenger train. Those who dare, can climb Turtle Mountain to examine fissures and cracks near the summit that still pose a threat. The trail is not too difficult and takes between 2 to 3hrs each way.

The town of Coleman lies farther north. The Coleman Colliery closed in 1983, and the town's main street is a testament to the hard times that set in afterward. The **Crowsnest Museum ★** *($3; May to early Sep, every day 10am to noon and 1pm to 4pm; Sep to May, Mon to Fri 10am to 4pm, open for tours by appointment only; 7701 18th Ave., Coleman,* ☎563-5434) recounts the history of the Pass from 1899 to 1950. There are models of coal mining rescues, coal cars from the Greenhill Mine plus a diorama of the fish and wildlife of Crowsnest Pass.

From Coleman, backtrack east along Hwy. 3 to Pincher Creek. Take Hwy. 6 south toward Waterton Lakes National Park.

Pincher Creek is reputed to be the windiest spot in Alberta, which explains all the windmills in the vicinity. This town is a gateway to Waterton Lakes National Park.

★★★
Waterton Lakes National Park

Waterton Lakes National Park, along with Glacier National Park in Montana, is part of the world's first International Peace Park. With stunning scenery, an exceptional choice of outdoor activities and varied wildlife, Waterton is not to be missed. Its main attraction, however, is its ambience. Many say it is like Banff and Jasper of 20 years ago – before the crowds and the mass commercialism. Waterton Townsite is home to restaurants, bars, shops, grocery stores, laundry facilities, a post office and hotels. There is also a marina, from which lake cruises depart. Things slow down considerably in the winter, though the cross-country skiing is outstanding. For more information see p 361.

From Waterton Lakes National Park take Hwy. 5 east to Cardston.

★
Cardston

Cardston is a prosperous-looking town nestled in the rolling foothills where the grasslands begin to give way to fields of wheat and the yellow glow of canola. The town was established by Mormon pioneers fleeing religious persecution in Utah. Their move here marked one of the last great covered-wagon migrations of the 19th century. Cardston might not seem like much of a tourist town, but it

is home to one of the most impressive monuments and one of the most unique museums in Alberta. The monument is the **Mormon Temple** *(free admission, May to Sep; every day 9am to 9pm; 348 Third St. W., ☎653-1696)*, which seems a tad out of place rising from the prairie. This truly majestic edifice took 10 years to construct and was the first temple built by the church outside the United States. The marble comes from Italy and the granite was quarried in Nelson, B.C. When it came time to do renovations recently, a problem arose because there was no granite left in Nelson; luckily, several blocks were found in a farmer's field nearby, having been left there in storage when the temple was built. Only Mormons in good standing may enter the temple itself, but the photographs and video presented at the visitors centre should satisfy your curiosity. A walk on the beautiful grounds adjacent to the temple is also highly recommended.

The unique museum is the **Remington-Alberta Carriage Centre ★★★** *($6.50; mid-May to mid-Sep, every day 9am to 6pm; Sep to mid-May, every day 10am to 5pm; 623 Main St., ☎653-5139)*, opened in 1993. "A museum on carriages?", you may ask. The subject matter may seem narrow, but this museum is definitely worth a visit. Forty-nine of the more than 300 carriages were donated by Mr. Don Remington of Cardston on the condition that the Alberta government build an interpretive centre in which to display them. The wonderfully restored carriages and enthusiastic, dedicated staff at this magnificent facility make this exhibit first-rate.

Take a guided tour through the 1,675m^2 display gallery, where town mock-ups and animated street scenes pro-

vide the backdrop for the collection, one of the best in the world among elite carriage facilities. The interesting film *Wheels of Change* tells the story of this once huge industry, which was all but dead by 1922. Visitors can also learn how to drive a carriage, watch the restoration work in progress, take a carriage ride ($3) and have an old-fashioned picture taken.

Aetna

South of Cardston, just off Hwy. 2, is the once-thriving town of Aetna. **Jensen's Trading Post** *(☎653-2500)* Hwy 501, has an interesting collection of antiques. Hwy. 2 continues to the American border and **Police Outpost Provincial Park**, named after a police outpost set up in 1891 to control smuggling. There is a campground in the park.

Head north of Cardston on Hwy. 2 to Fort Macleod and Head-Smashed-In Buffalo Jump. If it's getting late in the day, you may consider heading north on Hwy. 5, in order to spend the night in Lethbridge. Fort Macleod and Head-Smashed-In are both easily accessible from Lethbridge.

★
Fort Macleod

The town of Fort Macleod centres around the fort of the same name, first set up by the North West Mounted Police in an effort to stop the whisky trade. Troops were sent to raid Fort Whoop-Up (see p 353) in 1874, but got lost along the way, and by the time they got to Whoop-Up the traders had fled. They continued west to this spot by the Oldman River and established a permanent outpost. The original settlement was on an island 3km east of the present town, but persistent flooding forced its relocation in 1882. The fort as it stands

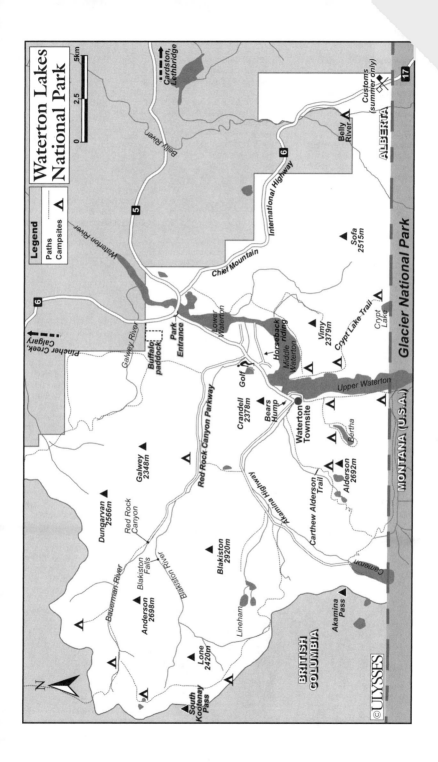

Waterton Lakes National Park

Legend

- ········· Paths
- ▲ Campsites

reconstructed in
[19]57 as a museum. The
...eum ★ ($6; Mar to
end Jun, every day 9am to
5pm; Jul to end Aug 9am to
8pm; Sep to end Dec, every day
9am to 5pm; 219 25th St. at
Third Ave., ☎553-4703)
houses exhibits of pioneer life
at the time of the settlement,
dioramas of the fort, tomb-
stones from the cemetery and
an interesting section of artifacts and photographs of the
Plains, Blood and Peigan
tribes. A Mounted Patrol performs a musical ride four times
a day in July and August.

Fort Macleod's downtown
area is very representative of a
significant period in history.
Most of the buildings were
erected between 1897 and
1914, except the Kanouse
cabin which lies inside the fort
walls and dates from much
earlier.

Walking-tour pamphlets are
available at the tourist office.
The tour includes such notable
edifices as the **Empress Theatre**, which retains its original
pressed-metal ceiling panels,
stage and dressing rooms
(complete with graffiti from
1913). Movies are still shown
here, despite a ghost who
occasionally gets upset with
the way things are run. The
Silver Grill, an old saloon
across the street, has its original bar and bullet-pierced
mirror, while the sandstone
Queen's Hotel still rents
rooms.

*Drive northwest of Fort
Macleod on Hwy. 785 to Head-
Smashed-In Buffalo Jump.*

The arrival of the horse in the
mid-1700s signalled the end of
a traditional way of hunting
buffalo among Plains Indians.
For 5,700 years before this,
the Plains Indians had depended on **Head-Smashed-In
Buffalo Jump ★★★** ($8.50;
mid-May to mid-Sep, every day
9am to 6pm; Sep to May, every
day 10am to 5pm; 15km
northwest of Fort Macleod on
Hwy. 785, ☎553-2731). From
it they got meat: fresh and
dried for pemmican; hides for
tipis, clothing and moccasins;
and bones and horns for tools
and decorations. Head-
Smashed-In was an ideal spot
for a jump, with a vast grazing
area to the west. The Plains
Indians would construct drive
lines with stone cairns leading
to the cliff. Some 500 people
participated in the yearly hunt;
men dressed in buffalo-calf
robes and wolf skins lured the
herd towards the precipice.
Upon reaching the cliff, the
leading buffalo were forced
over the edge by the momen-
tum of the stampeding herd
behind them. The herd was
not actually chased over the
cliff, but rather fear in the herd
led to a stampede. The area
remains much as it was thousands of years ago, though the
distance from the cliff to the
ground drastically changed as
the bones of butchered bison

piled up, 10m deep in some
places.

Today, the jump is the best
preserved buffalo jump in
North America and a
UNESCO World Heritage
Site. Many assume that the
name comes from the crushed
skulls of the buffalo, but it
actually refers to a Peigan
legend of a young brave who
went under the jump to watch
the buffalo topple in front of
him. The kill was exceptionally
good this particular day, and
the brave was crushed by the
animals. When his people
were butchering the buffalos
after the kill, they discovered
the brave with his head
smashed in— hence the
name.

As you approach the jump,
the cliff appears as a small
ridge on a vast plain. Signs of
civilization are few; in fact the
interpretive centre blends in to
the landscape so well that it is
hardly noticeable. You almost
expect to see a herd of buffalo
just beyond the rise, and can
envision what the natural plain
must have been like before
Europeans arrived. There is
something truly mythical about
the place.

The interpretive centre, built
into the cliff, comprises five
levels and is visited from the
top down. Start off by following the trail along the top of
the cliff for a spectacular view
of the plain and the
Calderwood Jump to the left.
Marmots can be seen sunning
themselves on the rocks below and generally contemplat-
ing the scene. Continuing
through the centre you'll learn
about Napi, the mythical creator of people according to
the Blackfoot. The centre
leads through Napi's world,
the people and their routines,
the buffalo, the hunt, the contact of cultures and European
settlement. An excellent film
entitled *In Search of the Buffalo* is presented every
30min. The tour ends with an

Buffalo

archaeological exhibit of the excavation work at the site. Back outside the centre you can follow a trail to the butchering site. The annual Buffalo Days celebrations take place here in July. The centre has a great gift shop and a small cafeteria that serves buffalo burgers.

The city of Lethbridge (see below) is about 20km from Fort Macleod along Hwy. 3.

Tour B: Lethbridge to Medicine Hat

★★
Lethbridge

Lethbridge, known affectionately by locals as "downtown L.A.," is Alberta's third largest city, and a pleasant urban oasis on the prairies. Steeped in history, the city boasts an extensive park system, pretty tree-lined streets, interesting sights and a diverse cultural community. You're as likely to meet ranchers as business people, Hutterites or Mormons on the streets of L.A.

Indian Battle Park ★★, in the Oldman River valley in the heart of town, is where Lethbridge's history comes alive; it is the site of Fort Whoop-Up and was the setting of a terrible battle. On October 25, 1870, Cree, displaced by European settlers into Blackfoot territory, attacked a band of Blood Blackfoot camped on the banks of the Oldman River. In the ensuing battle, the Blood were aided by a group of Peigan Blackfoot nearby; by the end some 300 Cree and 50 Blackfoot were dead.

A year earlier, American whisky traders had moved into Southern Alberta from Fort Benton, Montana. It was illegal to sell alcohol to Aboriginal People in the United

States, so the traders headed north into Canada, where there was no law enforcement. They set up Fort Hamilton nearby, at the confluence of the St. Mary's and Oldman rivers, and it became the headquarters of American activity in southern Alberta and Saskatchewan. This activity involved the trading of a particularly lethal brew which was passed off as whisky to the Aboriginal People; besides whisky, this firewater might also contain fortified grain alcohol, red pepper, chewing tobacco, Jamaican ginger and black molasses.

Fire destroyed the original fort, but a second, called **Fort Whoop-Up ★★**, was built and whisky and guns continued to be traded for buffalo hides and robes. Fort Whoop-Up was the first and most notorious of 44 whisky-trading posts. The American encroachment on Canadian territory, the illicit trading which had a demoralizing effect on the Aboriginal People, and news of the Cypress Hills massacre (see p 360) prompted the Canadian government to form the North West Mounted Police. Led by scout Jerry Potts, the Mounties, under the command of Colonel Macleod, arrived at Fort Whoop-Up in October of 1874. Word of their arrival preceded them, however, and the place was empty by the time they arrived. A cairn marks the site of this fort. The present fort is a reconstruction and houses an interesting **interpretive centre** *($2.50;mid-May to end Sep, Mon to Sat 10am to 6pm, Sun noon to 5pm; Oct to mid-May, Tue to Fri 10am to 4pm, Sun 1pm to 4pm; Indian Battle Park, ☎329-0444)*, where visitors can experience the exciting days of the whisky trade. You can also taste fresh bannock, a round, flat Scottish cake made from barley and oatmeal and cooked on a

griddle. Guides in period costume offer tours.

After peace was restored (so to speak) by the Mounties, attention turned to an exposed coal seam along the east bank of the Oldman River. The first mine was called Coalbanks, and so was the town that eventually sprung up at the opening to the mine. The **Coalbanks Interpretive Site** now stands at the original mine entrance in Indian Battle Park.

With financing from his father, Sir Alexander Galt, Elliot Galt set up a major drift mine. It soon became clear that a railway was needed to haul the coal, and eventually the town of Lethbridge was settled on the benchlands above the river. The town was named after a man who had never even been to Alberta, but was a friend of Galt's and a major financial contributor to the whole operation.

With 62km of walking, biking and horseback riding trails, the recreation possibilities are endless in Indian Battle Park. There are also picnic shelters and playgrounds.

The **Lethbridge Nature Reserve** is also located in Indian Battle Park. This 82ha protected area preserves much of the Oldman River Valley and contains the **Helen Schuler Coulee Centre ★** *(Jun to end Aug, Sun to Thu 10am to 8pm, Fri and Sat 10am to 6pm; early Sep to end Sep, Tue to Sat 1pm to 4pm, Sun 1pm to 6pm; Oct to end Apr, Tue to Sun 1pm to 4pm; early May to end May, Tue to Sat 1pm to 4pm, Sun 1pm to 6pm; Indian Battle Park, ☎320-3064)*, which features hands-on interactive displays and fact sheets on local animals and plant species that are great for kids of all ages—find out if you are a grassland guru or a prairie peewee. Three self-guided trails start from here. The

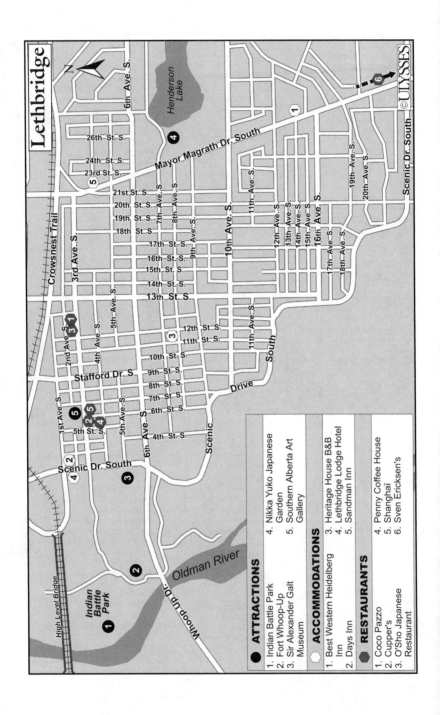

Lethbridge

6th Ave. S.

Henderson Lake

Mayor Magrath Dr. South

26th St. S.
24th St. S.
23rd St. S.

Crowsnest Trail

3rd Ave. S.

21st St. S.
20th St. S.
19th St. S.
18th St. S.

7th Ave. S.
8th Ave. S.

9th Ave. S.

17th St. S.
16th St. S.
15th St. S.
14th St. S.

13th St. S.

10th Ave. S.

11th Ave. S.

12th Ave. S.
13th Ave. S.
14th Ave. S.
15th Ave. S.
16th Ave. S.

7th Ave. S.
18th Ave. S.

19th Ave. S.
20th Ave. S.

Scenic Dr. South

ULYSSES

5th Ave. S.

2nd Ave. S.

4th Ave. S.

Stafford Dr. S

12th St. S.
11th St. S.

10th St. S.
9th St. S.
8th St. S.
7th St. S.
6th St. S.

5th Ave. S.

11th Ave. S.

South

1st Ave. S.

5th St. S.

6th Ave. S.

4th Ave. S.

Scenic Dr. South

Scenic

Drive

Whoop-Up Dr.

Indian Battle Park

Oldman River

High Level Bridge

● ATTRACTIONS
1. Indian Battle Park
2. Fort Whoop-Up
3. Sir Alexander Galt Museum
4. Nikka Yuko Japanese Garden
5. Southern Alberta Art Gallery

◇ ACCOMMODATIONS
1. Best Western Heidelberg Inn
2. Days Inn
3. Heritage House B&B
4. Lethbridge Lodge Hotel
5. Sandman Inn

⬡ RESTAURANTS
1. Coco Pazzo
2. Cupper's
3. O'Sho Japanese Restaurant
4. Penny Coffee House
5. Shanghai
6. Sven Ericksen's

reserve is home to Alberta's provincial bird, the great horned owl, as well as to porcupines, white-tailed deer and prairie rattlesnakes.

The volatile water levels of the Oldman River still wreak havoc on Lethbridge every so often. In the spring of 1995, water levels were so high that the Helen Schuler centre was half-submerged. The CPR High Level Bridge spans the Oldman River. When it was built in 1907-09, it was the longest and highest steel aqueduct in the world.

The **Sir Alexander Galt Museum** *(donation; every day 10am to 4:30pm, closed holidays between Sep and Apr; just off Scenic Dr. at Fifth Ave. S, ☎320-4258)*, overlooking Indian Battle Park, was originally built as a hospital in 1910. Since then it has been expanded to accommodate five galleries that offer an excellent perspective on the human history of the city of Lethbridge. A particularly impressive glazed viewing gallery looks out onto the river valley. The museum outlines the city's development from the discovery of coal to the waves of immigration from many different parts of the world. There are permanent and travelling exhibits, as well as extensive archives.

Paths weave their way through five traditional Japanese gardens at the **Nikka Yuko Japanese Garden ★★** *($5; mid-May to end of Jun, every day 9am to 5pm; Jul and Aug every day 9am to 9pm; Sep to mid-Oct every day 10am to 4pm; Seventh Ave. S and Mayor Magrath Dr., ☎328-3511)*. These aren't bright, flowery gardens, but simple arrangements of green shrubs, sand and rocks in the style of a true Japanese garden — perfect for quiet contemplation. Created by renowned Japanese garden designer Dr. Tadashi Kudo of the Osaka

Prefecture University in Japan, Nikka Yuko was built in 1967 as a centennial project and a symbol of Japanese and Canadian friendship (*Nikka Yuko* actually means friendship). The bell at the gardens symbolizes this friendship, and when it is rung good things are supposed to happen simultaneously in both countries.

The **Southern Alberta Art Gallery** *(free; Tue to Sat; 10am to 5pm, Sun 1pm to 5pm; 601 Third Ave. South, ☎327-8770)* enjoys an international reputation, thanks to the 15 exhibitions it puts on every year. Each of the three art spaces has different architecture. Other events take place here regularly: music, theatre, film and conferences. Call ahead and check this place out.

Head east on Hwy. 3 to Coaldale and then on to Taber.

Prairie falcon

Coaldale

The **Birds of Prey Centre** *($6.50; mid-May to mid-Sep, every day 9:30am to 5pm; 2124 Burrowing Owl Lane, north of Hwy. 3 in Coaldale, ☎345-4262)* is a living museum populated with birds from Alberta and around the world.

The centre is dedicated to the survival of birds of prey like hawks, falcons, eagles and great horned owls. Many of the birds in the centre were brought here injured or as young chicks. Once they are strong enough they are released into the wild.

Taber

Taber is famous for its sweet corn, which is sold all over the province. The city is also a centre for the food-processing industry. Corn season is in August, when the town holds its **Cornfest** celebrations featuring a pancake breakfast, hot-air balloons and all sorts of activities.

Backtrack on Hwy. 3 and head south on Hwy. 36 towards Milk River.

Warner

The town of Warner lies at the intersection of Hwys. 4 and 36. In 1987, an amateur paleontologist discovered a clutch of **dinosaur eggs** containing perfectly formed embryonic hadrosaur bones. There are bus tours to this significant fossil site, and the eggs can also be viewed at the Royal Tyrrell Museum in Drumheller (see p 370).

In Milk River take Hwy. 501, and watch for signs for Writing-on-Stone Provincial Park.

Milk River

The Milk River is the only river in Western Canada on the east side of the continental divide that does not eventually empty into Hudson Bay; it flows south into the Missouri River and on into the Mississippi River and the Gulf of Mexico. As a result the area has been claimed by eight different governments and countries. When France claimed all lands that drained into the Mississippi, this part of

Alberta was under French jurisdiction. The Spanish, British, Americans, and the Hudson's Bay Company have all staked their claim at some point in history.

★★
Writing-on-Stone
Provincial Park

Writing-on-Stone protects fascinating examples of petroglyphs, some of which are believed to date back some 1,800 years. A wealth of animals and plant species call this arid parcel of land home. The province's hottest temperatures are recorded here in this almost desert-like setting. Great hiking is possible, but the best rock drawings lie within a restricted area that is only accessible through guided hikes. To avoid disappointment, call ahead to find out when the hikes are heading out (see p 359).

★★
Across the Prairie
to Medicine Hat

Continue east on Hwy. 501, then go north on Hwy. 879. When you reach Hwy. 61, head east.

The prairies roll on and on as far as the eye can see along this stretch of highway surrounded by golden fields that are empty but for the occasional hamlet, grain elevator or abandoned farmhouse. Towns were set up every 16km because that was how far a farmer could haul his grain. As you drive this road, you will come upon what was once the town of Nemiskam, about 16km out of Foremost. Another 16km down the road is **Etzikom**. With fewer than 100 inhabitants these days, Etzikom's days may be numbered. For a look at the way things used to be, and a chance to stretch your legs, stop in at the **Etzikom Museum ★** *($3;mid- May to early Sep, Mon to Sat 10am to 5pm,*

Sun noon to 6pm; Etzikom, ☎666-3737 or 666-3915). Local museums like this can be found throughout Alberta, but this is one of the best of its kind and makes for a pleasant stop off the highway. The museum is located in the Etzikom School, and houses a wonderful recreation of the Main Street of a typical town, complete with barber shop, general store and hotel. Outside is the Windpower Interpretive Centre, a collection of windmills including one from Martha's Vineyard, Massachusetts, U.S.A.

Continue east along Hwy. 61, then head north on Hwy. 887, and east on Hwy. 3 into Medicine Hat. Cypress Hills Interprovincial Park is accessible along the dirt road running east of Orion, or by taking Hwy. 41 south of Medicine Hat.

★
Medicine Hat

Rudyard Kipling once called Medicine Hat "a city with all hell for a basement," in reference to Medicine Hat's location above some of western Canada's largest natural gas fields. The town prospered because of this natural resource, which now supplies a thriving petro-chemical industry. Clay deposits nearby also left their mark on the city, contributing to the city's once thriving pottery industry. Medicine Hat, like many towns in Alberta, boasts several parks. As for its name, legend has it that a great battle between the Cree and the Blackfoot took place here. During the battle the Cree medicine man deserted his people, and while fleeing across the river he lost his headdress in mid-stream. Believing this to be a bad omen the Cree abandoned the fight, and were massacred by the Blackfoot. The battle site was called Saamis, which means medicine man's hat. When the Mounties arrived

years later, the name was translated and shortened to Medicine Hat.

The **Medicine Hat Museum and Art Gallery** *(donation; Mon to Fri 9am to 5pm, Wed 7pm to 10pm,Sat and Sun 1pm to 5pm; 1302 Bomford Crescent SW, ☎502-8580)* is a National Exhibition Centre with first-rate local, national and international exhibits. The museum has a permanent collection depicting the history of Medicine Hat, the Plains Indians, the NWMP, ranching, farming and the railway.

Continue along Hwy. 1 to the Saamis Tipi and Information Office.

The **Saamis Tipi** is the world's tallest tipi. It was constructed for the 1988 Calgary Winter Olympics, and then purchased by a Medicine Hat businessman following the Games. The tipi symbolizes the First Nations way of life, based on spirituality, the circle of life, family and the sacred home. It certainly is an architectural wonder, though its steel structure and sheer size do seem a bit inconsistent with native traditions. Below the Saamis Tipi is the **Saamis Archaeological Site**. Over 80 million artifacts are believed to be buried at the site. A self-guided walking tour leads through the site of a late winter and early spring buffalo camp and a meat-processing site.

Follow the signs to the Clay Industry Interpretive Centre.

You'll probably have seen the pamphlets for the **Great Wall of China**; this is not a replica of the real thing, but quite literally a wall of china produced by the potteries of Medicine Hat from 1912 to 1988. Though many of the pieces on display are priceless collector's items, the best part of the **Clay Interpretive Centre ★ ★** *($5;mid-May to end Oct 9am to 5:30pm, Nov to mid-May 10am*

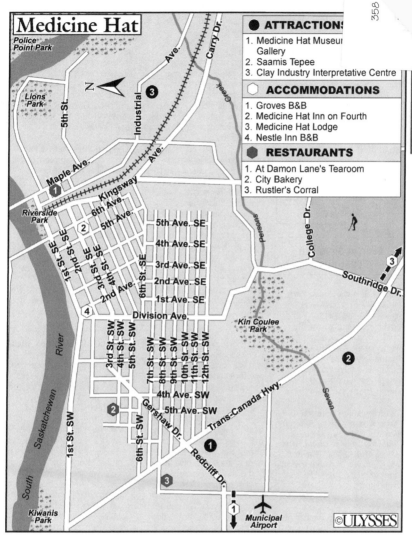

Medicine Hat

Police Point Park

Lions Park

5th St.

Industrial Ave.

Carry Dr.

Creek

Maple Ave.

Kingsway

6th Ave.

5th Ave.

Riverside Park

1st St. SE

2nd St. SE

3rd St. SE

4th St. SE

6th St. SE

2nd Ave.

5th Ave. SE

4th Ave. SE

3rd-Ave. SE

2nd Ave. SE

1st Ave. SE

Division Ave.

Kin Coulee Park

Persons

College Dr.

Southridge Dr.

River

Saskatchewan

South

3rd St. SW

4th St. SW

5th St. SW

6th St. SW

7th St. SW

8th St. SW

9th St. SW

10th St. SW

11th St. SW

12th St. SW

4th Ave. SW

Gershaw Dr.

5th Ave. SW

Trans-Canada Hwy.

1st St. SW

Redcliff Dr.

Kiwanis Park

Municipal Airport

Seven

©ULYSSES

ATTRACTIONS
1. Medicine Hat Museum Gallery
2. Saamis Tepee
3. Clay Industry Interpretative Centre

ACCOMMODATIONS
1. Groves B&B
2. Medicine Hat Inn on Fourth
3. Medicine Hat Lodge
4. Nestle Inn B&B

RESTAURANTS
1. At Damon Lane's Tearoom
2. City Bakery
3. Rustler's Corral

to 4:30pm; ☎529-1070) is the tour of the old Medalta plant and kilns. Medalta once supplied the fine china for all Canadian Pacific hotels. Today, workers' clothes and personal effects remain in the plant, which closed down unexpectedly in 1989. Medalta Potteries, Medicine Hat Potteries, Alberta Potteries and Hycroft China established Medicine Hat's reputation as an important pottery

centre. Tour guides lead visitors through the plant and explain the intricate and labour-intensive work that went into each piece. The tour ends with a fascinating visit inside one of the six beehive kilns outside.

Historic Walking Tour pamphlets are available at the information office for those interested in exploring the turn-of-the-century architec-

ture of Medicine Hat's downtown core.

★ ★
**Cypress Hills
Interprovincial Park**

Cypress Hills Interprovincial Park lies 65km southeast of Medicine Hat, near the Saskatchewan border. These hills were not covered by glaciers during the last ice age, and with a maximum elevation of

.,466m above sea level, they are the highest point in Canada between Banff and Labrador. This was the site of the Cypress Hills massacre in the winter of 1872-3, the result of which contributed to the formation of the North West Mounted Police. Animal and plant species found nowhere else in southern Alberta are the treasures of this park (see p 360).

Parks

Tour A: Southern Foothills

Chain Lakes Provincial Park (☎646-5887) is open year-round and offers all sorts of possibilities for enjoying the outdoors: boating, summer (rainbow trout and Rocky Mountain whitefish) and ice-fishing, summer and winter camping and cross-country skiing. There is a boat ramp.

Waterton Lakes National Park ★ ★ ★ *($5; for information call ☎859-5133 or write Waterton Lakes National Park, c/o Superintendent, Waterton Park, Alberta. Note that reservations are not accepted for campgrounds, http://parks canada.pch.gc.ca)* is located right on the US-Canadian border and forms one half of the world's first International Peace Park (the other half is Glacier National Park, Montana). Waterton boasts some of the best scenery in the province and is well worth the detour required to visit it. Characterized by a chain of deep glacial lakes and upside-down mountains with irregularly shaped summits, this area where the peaks meet the prairies offers wonderful hiking, cross-country skiing,

camping and wildlife-viewing opportunities.

The unique geology of the area is formed by 1.5-billion-year-old sedimentary rock from the Rockies that was dumped on the 60-million-year-old shale of the prairie during the last ice age. Hardly any transition zone exists between these two regions that are home to abundant and varied wildlife, where species from a prairie habitat mix with those of sub-alpine and alpine regions (some 800 varieties of plants and 250 species of birds). One thing to remember, and you will be reminded of it as you enter the park, is that wild animals here are just that—wild. While they may appear tame, they are unpredictable and potentially dangerous, and visitors are responsible for their own safety.

There is one park entrance accessible from Hwy. 6 or 5. On your way in from Hwy. 6, you will come upon a **buffalo paddock** shortly before the park gate. A small herd lives here and can be viewed by visitors from their cars along a loop road through the paddock. These beasts are truly magnificent, especially framed against the looming mountains of the park. Fees must be paid at the gate, and information is available at the information centre a short distance inside the park beyond the gate. Park staff can provide information on camping, wildlife-viewing and the various outdoor activities that can be enjoyed here, including hiking, cross-country skiing, golf, horseback riding, boating and swimming.

There are five scenic drives, including the **Akamina Highway**, which starts near the townsite and runs for 16km to Cameron Lake. About 1km beyond the junction of the park road is a viewpoint over the Bear's Hump, where you have a good chance of spot-

ting some bighorn sheep. You'll find picnic areas as well as the site of Canada's first producing oil well and the city that never was. Mount Custer and the Herbst Glacier in the United States are visible from Cameron Lake, where canoes and pedal boats can be rented. This is the starting point of several trails.

The **Red Rock Canyon Parkway** is another scenic drive. It epitomizes the "prairies to peaks" region as it leads through the rolling prairie of Blakiston Valley to the rusty rocks of the water-carved gorge of Red Rock Canyon. Black bears and grizzlies can often be spotted on the slopes feeding on berries. You can also view the park's highest summit, Mount Blakiston. An interpretive trail leads into the canyon at the end of the parkway.

Another drive, the **Chief Mountain International Highway** leads through the park and into Glacier National Park in Montana. Travellers crossing the border into the United States must report to the Goat Haunt Ranger Station.

Waterton Lakes National Park was initially set aside as a forest reserve in 1895, with John George "Kootenay" Brown as its first warden. Brown got his nickname through his association with the Kootenay First Nation. He led an adventurous life, nearly losing it to the Blackfoot and his scalp to Chief Sitting Bull before turning to more conservationist pursuits.

In 1911, Waterton became a national park, and in 1932 it joined with Glacier National Park to form the first International Peace Park. The park was declared an International Biosphere Reserve in 1979. Waterton's history is also marked by a short-lived oil boom in 1901.

The Chinook Wind

A Chinook occurs when moisture-laden winds from the Pacific Ocean strike the Rocky Mountains and are forced to precipitate their moisture as rain or snow. This leaves the winds cold and dry.

However, as the air descends the eastern slopes it remains dry but is condensed by the increase in atmospheric pressure and warms up. This warm, dry wind brings mild conditions that can melt 30cm of snow in a few hours.

It is essentially because of the Chinook that Alberta's native grasses survive the winter and that cattle can graze on the prairies year-round.

The warm, dry breath of the Chinook is a fabled part of Alberta history. It is the stuff of legend, with stories of farmers rushing home at the sight of the telltale Chinook arch (an archshaped cloud formed when the air pushes the cloud cover to the west), with their horses' front legs in the snow and hind legs in mud!

Unlike Banff and Jasper National Parks farther north, Waterton never had a rail link. This is still the case, with the result that Waterton remains small, pristine and unspoiled. It retains a genuine Rocky Mountain atmosphere, and so far is free of the heavy-handed, touristy commercialism that can mar any adventure into the Canadian Rockies.

The park's trademark **Prince of Wales Hotel** (see p 362) was built in 1926-1927 by Louis Hill, head of the Great Northern Railway, to accommodate American tourists that the railway transported by bus from Montana to Jasper (today, the majority of visitors to the park are still American). Though the hotel has been sold twice, its ownership and operations are still based in the United States; furthermore, the view from the lobby over Upper Waterton Lake remains the same; the

hotel still has 90 rooms and it is still open during the summer months only. The Swiss chalet-style building was proclaimed a National Historic Site in 1994 by the Canadian government and is worth a visit even if you can't afford to stay here.

Tour B: Lethbridge to Medicine Hat

As you approach **Writing-on-Stone Provincial Park ★★** *(free admission; park office ☎647-2877)*, located only about 10km from the U.S. border, you'll notice the carved out valley of the Milk River and, in the distance, the Sweetgrass Hills rising up in the state of Montana. The Milk River lies in a wide, green valley with strange rock formations and steep sandstone cliffs. The hoodoos, formed by iron-rich layers of sandstone that protect the softer underlying layers, appear like strange

mushroom-shaped formations. These formations, along with the cliffs, were believed to house the powerful spirits of all things in the world, attracting Aboriginal people to this sacred place as many as 3,000 years ago.

Writing-on-Stone Provincial Park protects more rock art—petroglyphs (rock carvings) and pictographs (rock paintings)—than any other place on the North American plains. Dating of the rock art is difficult and based solely on styles of drawing and tell-tale objects; for example, horses and guns imply that the drawings continued into the 18th and 19th centuries. Some archaeological sites date from the Late Prehistoric Period, around 1,800 years ago.

Once, buffalo, wolves and grizzly bears could be seen in the park. Though they are gone, a great variety of wildlife and plants still thrive here. Watch for pronghorn antelope, white-tailed and mule deer, yellow-bellied marmots and beavers. Catbirds, mourning doves, towhees and rock wrens also make their homes here. Finally, keep an ear out for rattlesnakes. These venomous critters are not dangerous unless provoked.

The North West Mounted Police also played a role in the history of the park, establishing a post here in 1889 to stop the whisky trade and fighting between Aboriginal peoples. During their time here, many officers carved their names into the sandstone cliffs. The 19th century post was washed away, but a reconstruction stands on the original site. You must participate in a guided tour to view the post.

The Battle Scene, one of the most elaborate petroglyphs in the park, can be viewed along the two self-guided interpretive trails. The scene may depict a battle fought in 1866, but no one is sure. One of the trails, the Hoodoo Interpretive Trail, also leads through the unique natural environment of the park; a self-guiding trail brochure is available from the park office.

The majority of the rock art sites are located in the larger part of the provincial park, which is an archaeological preserve. Access is provided only through scheduled interpretive tours, and for this reason it is extremely important to call the park's **naturalist office** (☎647-2364) ahead of time to find out when the tours are heading out. They are given daily from mid-May to early September, and free tickets, limited in number, are required. These may be obtained from the naturalist office one hour before the tour begins. Wildlife checklists and fact sheets are also available at the naturalist office.

The park boasts an excellent campground (inquire at park office regarding fees). Visitors also have the opportunity to practise a whole slew of outdoor activities, including hiking and canoeing—this is a convenient place to start or end a canoe trip along the Milk River.

Cypress Hills Interprovincial Park ★★ is a wooded oasis of lodgepole pine rising out of the prairie grassland and harbouring a varied wildlife, including deer, elk and moose and some 215 species of bird (including wild turkeys). At least 18 species of orchid also thrive in the park. There are, however, no cypress trees in the park; the French word for lodgepole pine is *cyprès*, and the name *montagnes de cyprès* was mistranslated to Cypress Hills.

This was also the site of the Cypress Hill Massacre. Two American whisky-trading posts were established in the hills in the early 1870s. During the

winter of 1872-3, some Assiniboines were camped in the hills, close to these two posts, when a party of drunken American hunters, whose horses had been stolen, came upon the band of Assiniboine. Believing that they had taken the horses, the American hunters killed 20 innocent Assiniboine.

The incident contributed to the establishment of the North West Mounted Police to restore order. Three-hundred Mounties arrived at Fort Walsh, Saskatchewan, and the men responsible for the massacre were arrested. Though they were not convicted because of lack of evidence, the fact that white men had been arrested gave credence in the eyes of the Aboriginal people to this new police force.

This is Alberta's second largest provincial park and the only interprovincial park in the province. The park is rarely very busy, giving visitors the opportunity to enjoy great hiking and fishing in peace and quiet. It is open year-round. Visitors can rent boats, bicycles, play golf, go downhill skiing and tobogganing. The park is also home to an abundance of stunning fragile orchids. Some bloom throughout the summer but the best time to see them is in mid-June. There are 13 campgrounds here. The visitors centre (*mid-May to early Sep, every day 10am to 5pm, information* ☎893-3833), is close to Elkwater Lake, at the townsite. In the off-season, visit the park administration office, at the eastern entrance to town, or write to Box 12, Elkwater, Alberta, T0J 1C0.

Outdoor Activities

Golf

Paradise Canyon (*$45-$50 for 18 holes; early Apr to end Oct; 185 Canyon Blvd,* ☎381-7500) has a par-71 18-hole course located in southwestern Lethbridge, between the rolling plains and Oldman River.

Waterton Lakes Golf Club (*$30 to $32 for 18 holes;* ☎859-2114) was designed by Stanley Thompson and offers 18 holes of challenging and scenic golf. It is located 4km north of town. There is a pro shop where you can rent clubs and carts.

Canoeing and Rafting

With hot summer temperatures and the possibility of spotting antelope, mule deer, white-tailed deer, coyotes, badger, beaver and cottontail rabbits, as well as several bird species, the Milk River is a great spot to explore by canoe. Set in arid southern Alberta, this river is the only one in Alberta that drains into the Gulf of Mexico. Canoes can be rented in Lethbridge.

Milk River Raft Tours (*Milk River,* ☎647-3586) organizes rafting trips along the river in the vicinity of Writing-on-Stone Provincial Park. Trips last from 2 to 6hrs, cost between $20 and $40 and can include hikes through the coulees.

Hiking and Cross-country Skiing

Waterton Lakes National Park has some of the most exceptional hiking in southern Alberta. Eight trails offer hikers and cross-country skiers the opportunity to explore the far reaches of this park, which lies at the meeting point between the mountains and the prairies. Complete descriptions of the trails are available at the park information centre, but take note that some of the best scenery is along the Crypt Lake Trail (8.7km one way) and the Carthew Alderson Trail (20km one way). There is also the shorter and very popular trail, the Bear's Hump (1.2km one way), which offers great views. Remember, not all of these trails are maintained for cross-country skiing, and you must register at the park office for all back-country exploring in the park, winter or summer (see p 358).

Horseback Riding

The **Willow Lane Ranch** ($25/hr min 2hr, $125/day lunch incl.; ☎687-2284, or 800-665-0284) is a working ranch in the foothills of the Rockies about 20km north of Fort Macleod. City-slickers can join a real cattle drive (two times a year; $600 for 3 nights; reserve several months in advance) or round-up, mend some fences, try their luck at calving and branding or take a day or overnight excursion into the Porcupine Hills. Accommodations are in the main ranch house (private floor) or in a cosy log cabin. Friendly service. Children must be 16 years of age or

older. Enquire about various packages and their rates.

Blue Ridge Outfitters (end Jun to end Aug; Cardston, ☎653-2449) also organizes pack trips. These can be anywhere from two to six days and usually go through the Rocky Mountains close to Waterton National Park. Accommodation is in tipis or tents, your choice. There are many different packages from weekends to excursions on horseback, call for details.

Accommodations

Tour A: Southern Foothills

Chain Lakes Provincial Park

Chain Lakes Provincial Park
$
Hwy. 22 and Hwy. 533
☎646-5887
Chain Lakes Provincial Park has over 120 campsites 27 of which are cleared in the winter ($). Reservations not accepted.

Crowsnest Pass

Rum Runner's Roost
$$
K
2413 23rd Ave.
☎563-5111
The Rum Runner's Roost, on Crowsnest Lake, offer 8 self-contained cabins.

Coleman

Grand Union International Hostel
$
7719 17th Ave.
☎563-3433
⇌563-3433
The Grand Union International Hostel is located in Coleman's original Grand

Union Hotel, built in 1926. The interior was renovated by the Southern Alberta Hostelling Association and now houses standard hostel rooms and all the usual hostel facilities, including laundry machines and a common kitchen.

Kosy Knest Kabins
$
K, 🐾
☎/⇌563-5155
You can stay at the Kosy Knest Kabins looking out over Crowsnest Lake. The 10 cabins are located 12km west of Coleman on Hwy. 3.

Waterton

Things slow down considerably during the winter months, when many hotels and motels close and others offer winter rates and packages.

Waterton Springs Campground
$
≈
Waterton Lakes National Park, Hwy 5, east of park gate
☎859-2247
www.thecowboytrail.com/springs.htm

Townsite Campground
$
Waterton Lakes National Park
☎859-2224
The Townsite Campground is by the lake and close to all the services in town. It is a full-service campground with hookups, showers and kitchen shelters.

Crandell Mountain Campground
$
Waterton Lakes National Park
This campground is 10km up the Akamina Highway; it has 129 sites, no power, flush toilets and kitchen shelters.

Belly River Campground
$
Waterton Lakes National Park
Belly River is more primitive, with pit toilets and shelters.

There are also 13 back-country sites (permit required).

Kilmorey Lodge
$$
℞
117 Evergreen Ave. Waterton Lakes National Park
☎859-2334
⇌859-2342
www.watertoninfo.ab.ca/kilmorey.htm
The Kilmorey Lodge is open year-round. It is ideally located overlooking Emerald Bay, and many rooms have great views. Antiques and duvets contribute to the old-fashioned, homey feel. The Kilmorey also boasts one of Waterton's finest restaurants, the Lamp Post Dining Room (see p 364).

Northland Lodge
$$$ bkfst incl.
sb/pb, ℞
on Evergreen Ave. Waterton Lakes National Park,
☎859-2353
www.northlandlodgecanada.com
Open from mid-May to mid-October, The Northland Lodge is a converted house with nine cosy rooms. Some rooms have balconies and barbecues.

Crandell Mountain Lodge
$$$
K, ℞
102 Mountview Rd., Waterton Lakes National Park
☎859-2288 or 866-859-2288
⇌859-2288
www.crandellmountainlodge.com
The small Crandell Mountain Lodge's rustic, cosy country-inn atmosphere fits right in with the setting and is a nice change from the motel scene. Four three-room suites with full kitchens are available, and four rooms have kitchenettes.

Waterton Lakes Lodge
$$$$
℞, ≈, △, ☺, *K*, ≡, ☉, ✪
corner of Windflower and Cameron Falls Dr.
☎859-2151 or 888-985-6343
⇌859-2229
www.watertonlakeslodge.com
The Lodge at Waterton Lakes is a new resort hotel in the townsite of Waterton Park. Completed in 1998, the complex has 80 rooms in nine two-storey buildings as well as 20 additional rooms affiliated with the YHA youth-hostel network. Each of the nine buildings has a theme (forests, lakes, birds, etc.) and the individual rooms are named and decorated accordingly. There are nature-education programs and a health spa, and some rooms have kitchenettes, whirlpool baths and fireplaces.

Prince of Wales Hotel
$$$$$
mid-May to end Dec
℞
Waterton Lakes National Park
☎859-2231
⇌859-2630
www.princeofwaleswaterton.com
The venerable Prince of Wales Hotel, open from mid-May until the end of September, is definitely the grandest place to stay in Waterton, with bellhops in kilts and high tea in Valerie's Tea Room, not to mention the unbeatable view. The lobby and rooms are all adorned with original wood panelling. The rooms are actually quite small and unspectacular, however, with tiny bathrooms and a rustic feel. Those on the third floor and higher have balconies. Try to request a room facing the lake, which is, after all, the reason people stay here.

Fort Macleod

Red Coat Inn
$$
K, ≈, ≡, ✖, △
359 Col. Macleod Blvd. or Main St.
☎553-4434 or 800-423-4434
⇌553-3731
www.redcoatinn.cm
The Red Coat Inn is one of the most reliable motel choices in Fort Macleod. Clean, pleasant rooms, kitchenettes and a pool make this a good deal.

Mackenzie House Bed and Breakfast
$$ bkfst incl.
1623 Third Ave.
☎/⇌553-3302
The Mackenzie House is located in a historic house built in 1904 for an Alberta member of the legislature at the time the province was founded, in 1905. Tea and coffee are served in the afternoon, and guests are greeted in the morning with a delicious home-made breakfast.

Tour B: Lethbridge to Medicine Hat

Lethbridge

Heritage House B&B
$$ bkfst incl.
sb
1115 Eighth Ave. S
☎328-3824
⇌328-9011
Built in 1937, the Art Deco Heritage House B&B is located on one of Lethbridge's pretty tree-lined residential streets, only a few minutes' walk from downtown. The guest rooms are uniquely decorated in accordance with the design of the house and include many of the house's original features. This house is an Alberta Provincial Historic Resource.

Southern Alberta

Days Inn
$$ bkfst. incl.
≡, ◎, *K*, ≈, ☺, 🐕
100 Third Ave. S
☎**327-6000 or 800-661-8085**
⇄**320-2070**
www.daysinn.com
The newly renovated Days Inn is the best motel choice downtown. The typical motel-style rooms are non-descript, but modern and clean. A free continental breakfast is served. Coin laundry available. You can also take advantage of the new pool.

Best Western Heidelberg Inn
$$
≡, △, ℜ, ☺
1303 Mayor Magrath Dr. S
☎**329-0555 or 800-791-8488**
⇄**328-8846**
www.bestwestern.com/ca/ heidelberginn/
The Best Western Heidelberg Inn is an inexpensive, reliable option along the motel strip south of the city. The recently renovated rooms are spotless, the staff is friendly and you get a complimentary newspaper in the morning.

Sandman Inn
$$
≡, ≈, ℜ, ◎, ☺
421 Mayor Magrath Dr. S
☎**328-1111 or 800-726-3626**
⇄**329-9488**
www.sandmanhotels.com
The Sandman Inn is another safe bet, with a nice indoor pool and clean, modern rooms.

Lethbridge Lodge Hotel
$$$
≈, ℜ, ◎, ☺, 🐕
320 Scenic Dr.
☎**328-1123 or 800-661-1232**
⇄**328-0002**
www.lethbridgelodge.com
The best hotel accommodation in Lethbridge is found at the Lethbridge Lodge Hotel overlooking the river valley. The comfortable rooms, decorated in warm and pleasant colours, seem almost luxurious when you consider the reasonable price. The rooms surround an interior tropical courtyard where small footbridges lead from the pool to the lounge and Anton's (see p 364).

Medicine Hat

Groves B&B
$ bkfst. incl.
≡
☎**529-6065**
Groves B&B is located about 10km from downtown Medicine Hat in a peaceful spot near the South Saskatchewan River. Breakfast, which includes home-made bread, can be taken on the deck outside. There are also walking trails nearby. From downtown take Holsom Road west, turn left on Range Road 70, drive 3.3km and turn right on #130.

Nestle Inn
$$ bkfst. incl.
271 1st St. SE
☎**526-5846**
www.nestle-inn.20m.com
Besides the one central hotel, there is actually another, very pleasant place to stay that is close to downtown, along pretty First Street SE. The Nestle Inn B&B is in a grand western Georgian house with a Victorian interior, and the three rooms are decorated in the arts crafts style, and each with its own bathroom. A large leafy lot surrounds the house. Sourdough pancakes are just one of the breakfast possibilities. Be sure to call ahead.

The Medecine Hat Inn on Fourth
$$
≡, ℜ
530 Fourth St. SE
☎**526-1313 or 800-730-3887**
⇄**526-4189**
The only hotel right downtown is the little The Medecine Hat Inn on Fourth which only has 34 rooms. The rooms are clean and the hotel was completely renovated in 1997.

Medicine Hat Lodge
$$$ bkfst incl.
≈, ≡, ℜ, ◎
1051 Ross Glen Dr. SE
☎**529-2222 or 800-661-8095**
⇄**529-1538**
www.medhatlodge.com
Medicine Hat Lodge offers good value for the money. The newly renovated rooms are standard but surprisingly pleasant with classic dark-wood furniture and pretty bedspreads. Some have sofas, and all have coffee machines and hair-dryers. The hotel also has a waterslide to keep the kids happy. Its restaurant is recommended.

Elkwater

Cypress Hills Interprovincial Park
$
☎**893-3782**
Cypress Hills Interprovincial Park has 12 campsites for both tents and R.V.s, with or without services. Reservations are only required for two sites; Beaver Creek and Lodge Pole, for the 10 others, it's first come, first served.

Restaurants

Tour A: Southern Foothills

Okotoks

La P'tite Table
$$$-$$$$
52 N. Railway St.
☎**938-2224**
La P'tite Table is so *petite* that reservations are a must. The chef once cooked at the Palliser and at La Chaumiere in Calgary. Classic bistro-style French cuisine and Alberta ingredients, including duck and ostrich, are served; perfect pastries and coffee finish the soiree.

Longview

Memories Inn
$$
Tue to Sun
Main St.
☎*558-3665*
Memories Inn has been decorated with the props left behind from the filming of the Clint Eastwood film *Unforgiven*. The atmosphere can get rowdy, especially during the weekend buffets, which feature, among other things, succulent ribs, burgers and home-made pies.

Waterton

Lamp Post Dining Room
$$$$
in Kilmorey Lodge
☎*859-2334*
The Lamp Post offers what some argue is the best dining in Waterton. The traditional charm, coupled with award-winning food and relatively reasonable prices definitely make it one of the best.

Royal Stewart Dining Room
$$$$
☎*859-2231*
The atmosphere at the Royal Stewart Dining Room in the Prince of Wales Hotel is unbeatable. This formal dining room serves a complete menu and daily specials that often include delicious seafood or pasta. Reservations are not accepted. Also in the Prince of Wales, and enjoying an equally elegant ambience and a stunning view are the **Windsor Lounge** and **Valerie's Tea Room**, where afternoon tea and continental breakfast are both served.

Fort Macleod

Silver Grill
$$
24th St. between Second and Third Ave.
☎*553-3888*
The Silver Grill is an interesting alternative to the fast food joints near the motels. This historic saloon serves a medi-

ocre Chinese buffet, called a "Smorg," and typical North American dishes, but it is the interior that makes it worth a stop. The original bar and a bullet-pierced mirror will make you feel like you should be watching your back!

Tour B: Lethbridge to Medicine Hat

Lethbridge

 Penny Coffee House
$
331 Fifth St.S.
☎*320-5282*
Located next to B. Maccabee's bookseller, The Penny Coffee House is the perfect place to enjoy a good book; don't worry if you haven't got one, there is plenty of interesting reading material on the walls. This café serves delicious hearty soups and chilis, filling sandwiches, a wonderful cheese and tomato scone, sodas and of course a great cup of Java.

Shanghaï
$$
610 Third Ave. S
☎*327-3552*
Despite an interior that could use a little freshening up, the Shanghaï restaurant offers a complete Chinese menu. They also serve north-American fare (club sandwiches, steaks, and the like). The chicken dishes are the chef's speciality.

Sven Ericksen's
$$-$$$
1714 Mayor Magrath Dr. S
☎*328-7756*
Sven Ericksen's is a family-style restaurant that stands out among the endless fast-food joints on Mayor Magrath Drive. This restaurant has been in business since 1948 and serves carefully prepared home-made dishes. The vast menu will please everyone.

O'Sho Japanese Restaurant
$$-$$$
1219 Third Ave. S
☎*327-8382*
For a change from Alberta beef try the O'Sho Japanese Restaurant where classic Japanese fare is enjoyed in traditional style from low tables set in partitioned rooms.

Botanica Restaurant
$$$
The Botanica Restaurant is a less expensive alternative in the Lethbridge Lodge with the same lovely surroundings. It is open from 6:30am to 10pm and serves a hearty breakfast, as well as truly divine desserts.

Coco Pazzo
$$$-$$$$
1249 Third Ave. S
☎*329-8979*
The hip Mediterranean decor at Coco Pazzo certainly has something to do with this new Italian café's success, but so does the food. The Strascinati sauce, a tomato cream sauce of their own invention is good, though not too original. It compliments the veal with capicollo nicely in the Modo Mio dish. Another house specialty is fettucine del Pescatore, prepared with scallops, clams and tiger prawns.

Anton's
$$$$
Lethbridge Lodge
☎*328-1123*
The Lethbridge Lodge is home to Anton's, the city's finest restaurant. The pasta dishes are particularly well received, as is the setting, in the hotel's tropical indoor courtyard. Reservations are recommended.

Medicine Hat

City Bakery
$
Fifth Ave. SW, between Third and Fourth St. SW
☎*527-2800*
The City Bakery bakes up wonderful fresh breads and New York bagels.

 Damon Lane's Tearoom
$
10am to 4pm, closed Mon
730 Third St. SE
☎*529-2224*
At Damon Lane's Tearoom you can lunch on simple soups, salads and sandwiches, all home-made on the premises, or just stop in for a spot of tea and a bit of shopping. There are crafts, pottery, and decorative items for the home.

Rustler's Corral
$$-$$$
901 Eighth St. SW
☎*526-8004*
Rustler's is another spot that transports you back to the lawless wild west—the restaurant boasts a blood-stained card table preserved under glass for all to gawk at! The menu features steaks, chicken, ribs, pasta and several Mexican dishes. Breakfasts are particularly busy and copious.

 Mamma's Restaurant
$$$-$$$$
at the Medicine Hat Lodge, 1051 Ross Glen Dr., SE
☎*529-2222*
Mamma's Restaurant offers a varied menu that features fine Alberta steaks and several pasta dishes. The food is

recommended, but unfortunately the noise and chlorine smell from the hotel's waterslides is a little distracting.

Entertainment

Tour A: Southern Foothills

Fort Macleod

Main Street's **Empress Theatre** *(235 24th St., ☎553-4404 or 800-540-9229)* is an original theatre from 1912. In fact, it's one of the oldest theatres in the province. It presents popular films throughout the year. Depending on the time of year, musical concerts, plays and conferences alternate with the program of films.

Every year in mid-July the **Annual Pow-Wow** is held at Head-Smashed-In Buffalo Jump. A large tipi is set up on the grounds where visitors can see traditional native dancing and sample some native food. For information call ☎*553-2731*.

Tour B: Lethbridge to Medicine Hat

Lethbridge

The third week in July is time for **Whoop-Up Days** in Lethbridge. Parades, festivities in the streets, a casino, perfor-

mances every night and, of course, a rodeo are just some of the highlights. For information call ☎*328-4491* or *www.letherbridgeexhibition. com*.

Medicine Hat

The **Medicine Hat Exhibition and Stampede**, held the last weekend in July, is second only to Calgary's Stampede in grandeur and extravagance. For information call ☎*527-1234* or *www.mhstampede. com*.

Shopping

Tour A: Southern Foothills

Lethbridge

B. Macabee's Bookseller *(Fourth Ave. S at 333 Fifth St. S, ☎329-0771)* is a cosy little bookstore adjoining the Penny Coffee House (see p 364). Choose from an extensive selection of books about local issues by local writers. Not only is this a great place to pick up a good book, but it's also a great place to peruse your purchase.

Medicine Hat

The **Clay Interpretive Centre** (see p 356) sells replicas and originals of Hycroft China and Medalta potteries. Copies of the Medalta cauldrons, prized by antique collectors, are available.

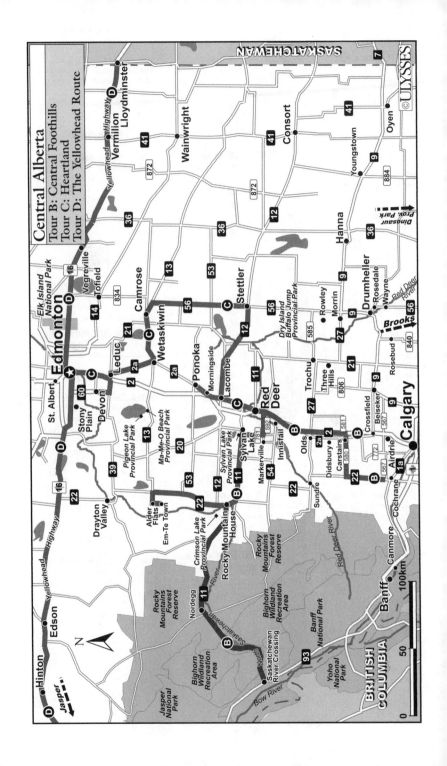

Central Alberta

Tour B: Central Foothills
Tour C: Heartland
Tour D: The Yellowhead Route

© ULYSSES

Central Alberta

Central Alberta encompasses a vast swath of the province that includes the Canadian Badlands, the foothills, the Rocky Mountains Forest Reserve and the heartland.

A region that holds an inestimable amount of natural resources, forestry, farming and oil drive the economy of this region, as does tourism which has been boosted by the occasional discovery of a dinosaur bone or two.

This chapter is divided into four driving tours:

Tour A: Digging for Dinosaur Bones and Other Treasures ★★★

Tour B: The Central Foothills ★

Tour C: The Heartland ★

Tour D: The Yellowhead ★★

Tour A and Tour C of this chapter can be combined loosely to form a meandering route between Alberta's two main cities, Calgary and Edmonton, while Tour B heads north from where Tour A of the Southern Alberta chapter begins.

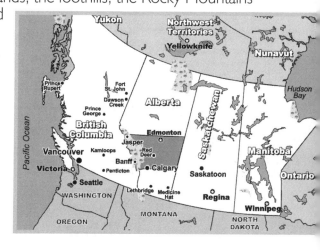

Finding Your Way Around

Visitors who want to go from Calgary to Edmonton have several otions :

One of these, though indirect, consists of passing through the spectacular Rocky montains following Rre. 93. Travellers can take this route there and a more direct route back.

This route also covers parts of the first three tours of this chapter and links up to the last one.

By Car

Tour A: Digging for Dinosaur Bones and Other Treasures

This tour takes in the Canadian Badlands from Dinosaur Provincial Park to the vicinity of Drumheller. Dinosaur Provincial Park is north of the TransCanada (Hwy. 1), off Hwy. 876. From there, head west on Hwy. 550 then Hwy. 1. Head north on Hwy. 56 to Drumheller. To reach Rosebud head west on Hwy. 9 then south on Hwy. 840. The tour continues north of Drumheller on Hwy. 9 to Morrin and Rowley and then west on Hwy. 585 to Trochu.

Tour B: Central Foothills

This tour heads north from where Tour A: Southern Foothills (Southern Alberta chapter) begins. It begins in Cochrane at the intersection of Hwy. 1A and 22, north of the TransCanada Highway 1. From Cochrane head north on Hwy. 22 then east on Hwy. 580 to Carstairs. Next head north on Hwy. 2A to Innisfail, then west on Hwy. 592 to Markerville, then north on Hwy. 781 to Sylvan Lake, and finally west on Hwy. 11 to Rocky Mountain House. Hwy. 11 is the David Thompson Highway and reaches Hwy. 93, the Icefields Parkway through the Rockies, at Saskatchewan River Crossing.

Tour C: Heartland

This tour starts in Olds, heads north toward Red Deer, and continues to Ponoka. From there, it returns towards Lacombe in the south before heading east on Hwy. 12 to Stettler, north on Hwy. 56 to Camrose, west on Hwy. 13 to Wetaskiwin, north on Hwy. 2A to Leduc, and finally west on Hwy. 39 and north on Hwy. 6 to Devon. Edmonton is another 15km north on Hwy. 60.

Tour D: The Yellowhead

The Yellowhead Highway 16 crosses the province from east to west, leading from the Saskatchewan border and the city of Lloydminster to Jasper and the border of British Columbia at Yellowhead Pass.

Car Rentals

Red Deer

Budget
5214 Gaetz Ave.
☎*(403) 346-7858*
☎*800-268-8900*
www.budget.com

National
2319 Taylor Dr.
☎*(403) 347-5811*
☎*800-387-4747*
www.nationalcar.com

Avis
4702 51st Ave.
☎*(403) 343-7010*
www.avis.com

By Bus

Drumheller Greyhound Bus Depot
308 Center St.
☎*(403) 823-7566*
☎*800-661-1145*
www.greyhound.ca

Red Deer Greyhound Bus Depot
4303 Gaetz Ave. at 50th Ave. (across from the Red Deer Inn)
☎*(403) 343-8866*
☎*800-661-1145*
www.greyhound.ca

Wetaskiwin Greyhound Bus Depot
4122 49th St.
☎*(780) 352-4713*
☎*800-661-1145*
www.greyhound.ca

Lloydminster Greyhound Bus Depot
5217 51st St.
☎*(780) 875-9141*
☎*800-661-1145*
www.greyhound.ca

Hinton Greyhound Bus Depot
128 North St., behind the Kentucky Fried Chicken
☎*(780) 865-2367*
☎*800-661-1145*
www.greyhound.ca

By Train

Via trains follow the Yellowhead Route into Edmonton and then on to Jasper. For information on schedules and stops, see "Practical Information" chapter.

Alberta Prairie Railway Excursions: (☎*403-742-2811 for schedule and reservations, www.absteamtrain.com*) operates a scenic train out of Stettler (see p 377)

Practical Information

Unless otherwise indicated, the area code is **403.**

Tourist Information

Alberta Central Tourism Destination Region
☎*888-414-4139*

Red Deer Visitor and Convention Bureau
25 Riverview Park
☎*346-0180 or 800-215-8946*
⇄*346-5081*
www.tourismreddeer.net

Rocky Mountain House
summer only
tourist information in a trailer north of town on Hwy. 11
☎*845-2414 or 800-565-3793*

Rocky Mountain Chamber of Commerce
open year round
In Town Hall
☎*845-5450*

Drumheller

Drumheller Tourist Information
60 First Ave. W.
☎*823-1331 or 866-823-8100*
⇄*823-4469*
www.dinosaurvalley.com

Exploring

Tour A: Digging for Dinosaur Bones and Other Treasures

Where the Red Deer River Valley now lies was once the coastal region of a vast inland sea; the climate probably resembled that of the Florida Everglades and it was an ideal habitat for dinosaurs. After the extinction of the dinosaurs, ice covered the land. As the ice retreated 10,000 years ago, it carved out deep trenches in the prairie; this and subsequent erosion have uncovered dinosaur bones and shaped the fabulously interesting landscape of hoodoos and coulees you'll see on this Dinosaur odyssey.

Brooks

Brooks began as a railway stop in the 1880s, and soon developed a major irrigation system. The **Brooks Aqueduct National and Provincial Historic Site** *($2; mid-May to early-Sep, every day 10am to 6pm; 3km southeast of Brooks, ☎362-4451 or 653-5139)* began operating in the spring of 1915; at the time it was the longest concrete structure (3.2km) of its kind in the world. It was a vital part of the irrigation of southeastern Alberta for 65 years.

South of Brooks on Hwy. 873 is **Kinbrook Provincial Park** ★ (see p 379) and Lake Newell. The wildlife observation possibilities here are excellent.

★★★
Dinosaur Provincial Park

The town of Brooks is also a great jumping-off point for Dinosaur Provincial Park, declared a UNESCO World Heritage Site in 1979. The landscape of this park consists of Badlands, called *mauvaises terres* by French explorers because there was neither food nor beavers there.

These eerie Badlands contain fossil beds of international significance, where over 300 complete skeletons have been found. Glacial meltwater carved out the Badlands from the soft bedrock, revealing hills laden with dinosaur bones. Wind and rain erosion continues today, providing a glimpse of how this landscape of hoodoos, mesas and gorges was formed.

There are two self-guided trails and a loop road, but the best way to see the park is to follow a guided-tour into the restricted nature preserve, though this requires a bit of planning. Unless you plan to arrive early, it is extremely important to call ahead for the times of the tours, to make sure you are there in time and to reserve a spot (see p 379). Visitors can tour the **Field Station of the Royal Tyrrell Museum** ★ (see p 379 for fee and schedule information) for an introduction to the excavation of dinosaur bones, and then head off on their own adventure.

The dinosaur odyssey continues in Drumheller. From Dinosaur Provincial Park take Hwy. 550 west to Bassano and then travel west on Hwy. 1. At Hwy. 56 head north to Drumheller.

★★★
Drumheller

The main attractions in Drumheller are located along the Dinosaur Trail and Hoodoo Trail; they include the

Royal Tyrrell Museum of Palaeontology, the Bleriot Ferry, the Rosedale Suspension Bridge, the Hoodoos, East Coulee, the Atlas Coal Mine and the Last Chance Saloon. Erosion in the Red Deer River Valley has uncovered dinosaur bones and shaped the fabulously interesting landscape of hoodoos and coulees found in Drumheller. Besides the bones, early settlers discovered coal. Agriculture and the oil and gas industries now drive the local economy.

As you arrive in Drumheller via Hwy. 9, one of the first buildings on the right is **Reptile World** *($4.50; mid-May to mid-Sep every day 9am to 10pm, mid-Sep to mid-May Thu-Tue 10am to 6pm; Sun City Market, ☎823-8623)*. It has the greatest selection of reptiles in Canada. You can meet Britney the boa constrictor, among others. Apparently snakes only bite if they feel threatened, but Britney has been handled every day since her birth, so she is completely at ease with visitors.

Located downtown, the **Badlands Historical Centre** *($4; May to Oct 10am to 6; 335 First St. East, ☎823-2593)* is a museum that offers you a chance to learn about First Nations' culture of the Badlands. Dinosaur fossils and skeletons are on display as well as an instructive geological exhibit on the history of the valley.

★★★
Dinosaur Trail

The Dinosaur Trail runs along both sides of the Red Deer River. The first stop on Hwy. 838 (the North Dinosaur Trail), the **Homestead Antique Museum** *($3; mid-May to mid-Oct, every day 10am to 8pm; mid-Oct to mid-May, every day 10am to 5:30pm; ☎823-2600)*, which has a collection of 4,000 items from the days of the early settlers, is not the highlight of the tour. That honour falls on the **Royal Tyrrell Museum of Palaeontology** ★ ★ ★ *($10; mid-May to early-Sep every day 9am to 9pm; early-Sep to mid-Oct every day 10am to 5pm; mid-Oct to mid-May, Tue to Sun 10am to 5pm; 6km west of Drumheller on Hwy. 838, ☎823-7707 or ☎888-440-4240, www.tyrell museum.com).* This mammoth museum contains over 80,000 specimens, including 50 full-size dinosaur skeletons. There are hands-on exhibits and computers, fibre-optics and audio-visual presentations. The Royal Tyrell is also a major research centre, and visitors can watch scientists cleaning bones and preparing specimens for display. There is certainly a lot to thrill younger travellers here; however, the wealth of information to absorb can be a bit overwhelming. Special new displays are always being set up. You can participate in the **Day Dig** *($90, includes lunch, snacks, transportation and admission to the museum, reservations required; Jun Sat and Sun, July to early Sep every day, early Sep to late Sep The, Thu and Sat 8:30am to 4pm),* which offers an opportunity to visit a dinosaur quarry and excavate fossils yourself, or the **Dinosite!** *($12; daily departures from the museum at 10am, 11am noon, 1pm and 2pm),* a 90min guided tour to an actual working excavation site, where you'll see a dig in progress. Call ahead for tour times.

The next stop is the world's largest **Little Church**, which can accommodate "10,000 people, but only 6 at a time." The seven-by-eleven-foot house of worship, opened in 1958, seems to have been more popular with vandals than the devout and was rebuilt in 1990.

Continue along the Dinosaur Trail for breathtaking views over the Red Deer River at

Digging for Dinosaur Bones

The very nature of the Red Deer River Valley means that every time it rains, more dinosaur bones are uncovered. As mentioned, the Royal Tyrrell Museum organizes various digs for budding palaeontologists, but while exploring on this tour you may just make a discovery of your own.

Any items found on the surface and on private land can be kept with the landowner's permission. You can keep what you find as a

custodian (ultimately ownership resides with the Province of Alberta), but you cannot sell the fossil or take it out of the province without permission.

Fossils should never be removed from their original stratigraphic position, however, without first mapping out that position, and you need a permit to excavate fossils. These treasures are an important part of the planet's history and should be treated as such.

the **Horsethief Canyon Viewpoint**. There are paths to petrified oyster beds. The canyon got its name after it became an ideal hideout for horse thieves' booties in the early 1900s. Turn right onto Hwy. 838 to the **Bleriot Ferry**, one of the last cable-operated ferries in Alberta. The ferry was named after the famous French pilot and balloonist Louis Bleriot. The trail continues along the southern shore of the river with another great lookout, the **Orkney Hill Viewpoint**.

★ ★ ★
Hoodoo Trail

Once back in Drumheller, get on the Hoodoo Trail, which heads southeast along the Red Deer River. The town of **Rosedale** originally stood on the other side of the river next to the Star Mine. The suspension bridge across the Red Deer looks flimsy, but is said to be safe for those who want to venture across. Take a detour to cross the 11 bridges

to get to **Wayne**. The bridges are perhaps the best part, as the main attraction in town, the Rosedeer Hotel, with its **Last Chance Saloon** *(☎823-9189),* leaves something to be desired. Rooms are available for rent at $25/night, but settle for a beer and some nostalgia instead. You can also have a good steak cooked up on the grill. The fourth floor is closed because legend has it that the spirit of a murderer from the early 1900s still wanders there.

About halfway between Rosedale and East Coulee you'll see some of the most spectacular **hoodoos** ★ ★ ★ in southern Alberta. These strange mushroom-shaped formations result when the softer underlying sandstone erodes. **East Coulee**, a town that almost disappeared, was once home to 3,000 people but only 200 residents remain. The **East Coulee School Museum** *($3; early May to end Sep, every day 10am to 6pm; Oct to early May Mon to Fri*

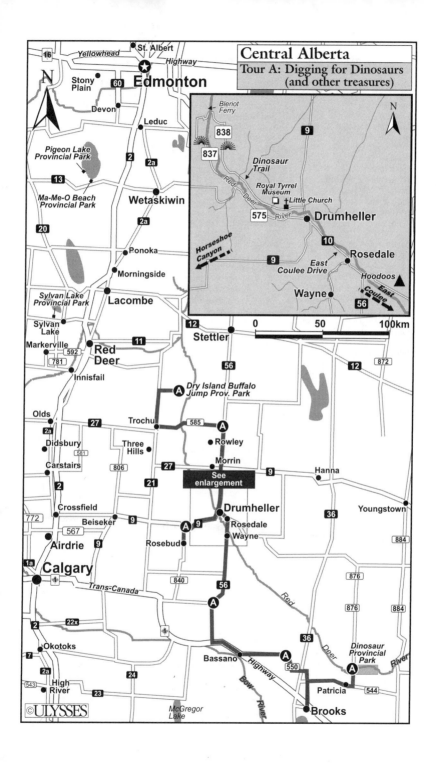

9am to 5pm; ☎822-3970) occupies a 1930s school house. Inside are a small tea room and gallery. Although the Atlas Coal Mine ceased operations in 1955, the **Atlas Coal Mine National Historic Site** *($5; May to early Sep Mon to Fri 9am to 4pm, Sat and Sun 11am to 4pm; ☎822-2220)* keeps the place alive to this day across the river from town. The last standing tipple (a device for emptying coal from mine cars) in Canada stands among the mine buildings, which you can explore on your own or as part of a guided tour. The colourful owner of the Wildhorse Saloon, in front of the mine, was instrumental in saving the School Museum and the Atlas Coal Mine. Don't drink anything that's not bottled in this place.

Horseshoe Canyon *(19km from Drumheller on Hwy. 9)* looks out over Alberta's version of the Grand Canyon. The terrific formations of volcanic and sedimentary rock can be observed up close on easy footpaths leading into the canyon from the lookout.

Continue on Hwy. 9 and turn left on Hwy. 840 to reach Rosebud.

★
Rosebud

This town, which almost disappeared, is becoming a tourist attraction in its own right with the opening of the new Rosebud Country Inn (see p 382) and the increasing popularity of its biggest claim to fame, the **Rosebud Theatre ★ ★ ★** (see p 384). The streets of this tiny town overlooking the Rosebud River are lined with **historic buildings ★** that will take you back in time. Most of these have markers.

North of Drumheller

North of Drumheller on Hwy. 56 are two curious towns. The first is **Morrin**, with its **Sod House and Historical Park** *(donations accepted; early Jul to end Aug, Wed to Sun 9am to 5pm; ☎772-2180).* The earth floor of this replica of the pioneers' original houses underlines the crude conditions they lived in.

Continuing north on Hwy. 56 and turning left on Range Road to **Rowley** is a must for movie buffs. Rowley's main drag looks like a ghost town, all the better for making movies: the street has been featured in several films. Of particular interest are an old country school, a refurbished train station, the Trading Post soda shop and Sam's Saloon, which doubles as the terminus of the Alberta Prairie Railway Excursions tour out of Stettler (see p 377).

Take Hwy. 585 West, then Hwy. 21 North to Trochu.

Trochu

The **St. Ann Ranch and Trading Company ★** *($2; every day 9am to 9pm; on the south-east edge of Trochu, ☎442-3924 or 888-442-3924)* was originally established in 1903 as part of a French-speaking settlement. The community thrived and grew to include a school, church and post office, but the onset of WWI prompted many settlers to return to their homeland of France. The ranch has been restored and is run by a descendent of one of the original settlers. A small museum displays historic pieces, while an adjoining tea room *(open every second weekend in Jul and Aug from 2pm to 4pm)* and *gîte* (bed and breakfast, see p 382) provide an opportunity for an experience *à la française*.

Thirty kilometres north of Trochu off Hwy. 21 you'll find **Dry Island Buffalo Jump Provincial Park**, a day-use park that highlights the dramatic contrast between the Red Deer River Valley floor and the surrounding farmland. The jump, once used by the Cree, is higher than most in Alberta; the buffalo herded over its cliffs fell about 50m and were then butchered by the Cree for their meat and hides.

Red Deer can be reached by heading east on Hwy. 590 and north on Hwy. 2, Calgary is south on Hwy. 2.

Tour B: Central Foothills

★
Cochrane

This friendly town lies on the northern edge of Alberta's ranchlands and was the site of the first big leasehold ranch in the province. Ranching is still a part of the local economy, but more and more residents are commuting into nearby Calgary, just 20min away.

The **Cochrane Ranche Historic Site ★ ★** *(donation; visitors centre: mid-May to early Sep, every day 9am to 6pm; ranche site: open year-round; 0.5km west of Cochrane on Hwy. 1A, ☎932-1193 in summer, or ☎932-2902 in winter)* commemorates the establishment in 1881 of the Cochrane Ranche Company by Québec businessman Senator Matthew Cochrane, and the initiation of Alberta's cattle industry.

The company controlled 189,000ha of sweeping grasslands which, along with three other ranches including the Bar U Ranch National Historic Site (see p 348), covered most of Alberta. Though the ranch failed after two years, its legacy lives on. Travellers can relive those romantic days through interpretive programs at the visitors centre.

The **Studio West Art Foundry Gallery** *(free admission; every day 8am to 5:30pm; 205 Second Ave. SE, ☎932-2611)*, in Cochrane's industrial park, is Western Canada's largest sculpture foundry. Artisans practise the age-old "lost wax", a bronze-casting technique that hasn't changed in 3,000 years. You can see the complete process of sculpting here, from the original concept to the final product. Wildlife and western bronze sculptures as well as woodcarvings and paintings are for sale.

While in Cochrane, don't miss the opportunity to savour some ice cream from **McKay's Ice Cream ★**, rated one of the best in Canada. You may even want to take a trip from Calgary just for a cone or stop in on your way to Banff.

Drive north on Hwy. 22 and then east on Hwy. 580 to Carstairs for a bit of shopping.

Carstairs

Two of Carstairs's most interesting attractions, which are essentially great shopping opportunities, lie on the outskirts of this town, whose streets are lined with grand old houses. The **Pa-Su Farm** lies 9km west of town on Hwy. 580, while the **Custom Woolen Mills** are about 20km est on Hwy. 581 and then 4.5km north on Hwy. 791. See the Shopping section, p 385.

Instead of boring old Hwy. 2, take the 2A, which runs parallel to the 2, then go west on Hwy. 592 to Markerville.

★
Markerville

The town of Markerville began in 1888 as an Icelandic settle-

ment called Tindastoll, whose settlers arrived from Dakota. A year later another group of Icelanders arrived, including poet Stephan G. Stephansson (see below), and settled in a district they called Hola. The area was chosen partly because of its isolation, for the settlers wished to preserve their language and customs.

In 1899, the federal government built the Markerville Creamery, and the village that grew up around it became something of an economic hub, attracting various groups of settlers including Danes, Swedes and Americans. The Icelandic culture nevertheless thrived into the 1920s. Eventually, however, intermarriage and migration changed things. Today less than 10% of the region's population is of Icelandic descent.

Once a leader in Alberta's dairy industry, the **Markerville Creamery ★★** *($2; mid-May to early Sep, every day 10am to 5:30pm; Creamery Way, Markerville, ☎728-3006)* is the only restored creamery in the province. It was opened in 1899 by the federal Department of Agriculture. An association of local Icelandic farmers maintained the building, and the government kept the books and hired a buttermaker. The buttermaker paid farmers depending on the butterfat of their cream. The creamery was the mainstay of the local economy until it closed in 1972, producing 90,000kg of butter at its peak. It is now a Provincial Historic Resource and has been restored to circa-1934. Visitors can take a guided tour to learn about the operation of the creamery and its equipment, which includes old pasteurizers. Adjoining the building are two neat gift shops, as well as the "Kaffistofa", where you can sample *vinarterta*, Icelandic layer cake.

To reach Stephansson House, continue west on the 364A across the Medicine River; shortly after the river turn right on an unnamed road. Follow this road to the 371, turn right, cross the river again, and you'll soon see the entrance to the house on your left.

Stephansson House ★ *($2; mid-May to early Sep, every day 10am to 6pm; ☎728-3929)*. Stephan G. Stephansson was among the second group of Icelandic settlers who came to the area now known as Markerville from Dakota in 1889. Few people have heard of Stephansson, perhaps one of Canada's most prolific poets, because he wrote in his native Icelandic.

His original log house quickly proved too small, so a study, front room, upstairs, kitchen and front bedroom were gradually added. The house, with its newspaper insulation and attempts to copy the picturesque style, is representative of a typical struggling Canadian farm family.

Stephansson, like the other Icelandic settlers, was particularly concerned with preserving his native culture and he perpetuated it with his strong views and mastery of the language. The most famous of his works to have been translated is *Androkur*, or *Wakeful Nights* (Stephansson was an insomniac). Guides give tours of the house and light the stove every day to bake delicious Icelandic cookies called *astarbollur*, "love buns."

Head north on Hwy. 781 to Sylvan Lake.

★
Sylvan Lake

This lakeside town, with its marina, beach, souvenir shops, hotels, waterslide and shingled buildings, looks almost like an Atlantic coast beach resort. **Sylvan Lake**

Provincial Park ★ (☎340-7683) is a day-use area for sunbathing, swimming and picnicking.

Jarvis Bay Provincial Park (*camping reservations* ☎887-5522) is also located on Sylvan Lake and, like the former, is popular on weekends. Hiking trails lead through the aspen parkland, and provide some good bird-watching.

You may want to overnight in Red Deer, which has a lot of hotels, before continuing west, if so head east on Hwy. 11, otherwise head west to Rocky Mountain House.

Rocky Mountain House

Despite its evocative name, Rocky Mountain House is not a picturesque log cabin in the woods but rather a gateway town into the majestic Rocky Mountains. The town, known locally as Rocky, is home to just under 6,000 people and represents a transition zone between the aspen parkland and the mountains. The exceptional setting is certainly one of the town's major attractions, which otherwise offers the gamut of services—hotels, gas stations and restaurants. Just outside Rocky lies the town's namesake, Rocky Mountain House National Historic Site, along with a wealth of outdoor possibilities, including river trips in voyageur canoes and fishing, hiking and cross-country skiing at Crimson Lake Provincial Park (see p 379).

The **Rocky Mountain House National Historic Park ★★** (*$2.50; mid-May to end Sep, every day 10am to 5pm, call for winter hours; 4.8km southwest of Rocky on Hwy. 11A,* ☎845-2412) is Alberta's only National Historic Park and the site of four known historic sites. Rocky Mountain House is interesting because it exemplifies, perhaps better than any other trading post, the inextricable link between the fur trade and the discovery and exploration of Canada.

Two rival forts were set up here in 1799, Rocky Mountain House by the North West Company and Acton House by the Hudson's Bay Company. Both companies were lured by the possibility of establishing lucrative trade with the Kootenay First Nation, west of the Rockies. It was after the merging of the Hudson's Bay Company and the North West Company in 1821, that the area was called Rocky Mountain House.

David Thompson

David Thompson began at the Hudson's Bay Company in 1784 as a clerk stationed at several posts on Hudson Bay and the Saskatchewan River.

While laid up with a broken leg, he took an interest in surveying and practical astronomy. After years of exploring and surveying much of present-day northern Manitoba and Saskatchewan, he decided to switch camps and go to work for the North West Company in 1797.

The company enlisted his services in the "Columbia Enterprise," the search for a route through the Rockies. In 1806-07, Thompson made preparations to cross the Rockies at Rocky Mountain House. However, the Peigan First Nation, who frequented the post, opposed the project; if trade extended west of the Rockies, their enemies, the Kootenay and Flathead, would acquire guns. Thompson thus moved up-river from Rocky Mountain House to the Howse Pass in 1807.

In 1810, the race to the mouth of the Columbia came to a head when news of an American expedition reached Thompson. He immediately headed west but was blocked by the Peigan. He headed north again, skirting Peigan territory.

In 1811, he crossed the Athabasca Pass and reached the Pacific and the mouth of the Columbia River four months after the Americans had set up their post there.

Thompson later settled in Terrebonne, near Montreal, and worked on the establishment of the boundary between Upper and Lower Canada. He was unsuccessful in business and died in 1857, in poverty and virtual obscurity.

Trade with the Kootenay never did materialize; in fact, except for a brief period of trade with the Blackfoot in the 1820s, the fort never prospered, and actually closed down and was then rebuilt on several occasions. It closed for good in 1875, after the North West Mounted Police made the area to the south safe for trading. The Hudson's Bay Company thus set up a post in the vicinity of Calgary. An interesting aside: the Hudson's Bay Company, today the cross-Canada department store The Bay, makes more money on its real estate holdings than on its retail operations.

The visitors centre presents a most informative exhibit on the fur-trading days at Rocky Mountain House, including a look at the clothing of the Plains Indians and how it changed with the arrival of fur traders as well as artifacts and testimonies of early explorers. Visitors can also choose to view one of several excellent National Film Board documentaries. Two interpretive trails lead through the site to listening posts (in English and French) along the swift-flowing North Saskatchewan River. Stops include a buffalo paddock and demonstration sites where tea is brewed and a York Boat, once used by Hudson's Bay Company traders, is displayed (the North West Company traders preferred the birchbark canoe, even though it was much slower). All that remains of the last fort are two chimneys.

Rocky Mountain House was also a base for exploration. David Thompson, an explorer, surveyor and geographer for the North West Company who played an integral role in the North West Company's search for a route through the Rockies to the Pacific, was based at Rocky Mountain House for a time. Ultimately beaten by the

Americans in his pursuit, he travelled 88,000km during his years in the fur trade, filling in the map of Western Canada along the way.

A detour north on Hwy. 22 leads to the tiny town of Alder Flats.

Alder Flats

Alder Flats itself is of little interest to visitors. A few kilometres south, however, is another town that is full of attractions, a place ironically called **Em-Te Town**. Here you'll find a saloon, jailhouse, harness shop, schoolhouse, church and emporium, located in a pretty setting at the end of a gravel road. Built from scratch in 1978, this is a neat place to experience life the way it was in the old west, with trail rides and home-cooked meals at the Lost Woman Hotel. Some may find the whole experience a bit contrived. In addition to the attractions, there are campsites and cabins for rent, as well as a restaurant.

★★★
David Thompson Highway

The drive west from Rocky Mountain House runs along the edge of the Rocky Mountain Forest Reserve. Stunning views of the Rocky Mountains line the horizon. Hwy. 11, the David Thompson Highway, continues west from Rocky Mountain House up into the Aspen Parkland and on into Banff National Park (see p 272). The town of **Nordegg** lies at the halfway point of the highway. In addition to the interesting Nordegg Museum, the town offers access to great fishing, the Forestry Trunk Road and camping and is also home to the Shunda Creek Hostel (see p 382). The only services available west of Nordegg before Hwy. 93 are at the David Thompson Resort (see p 382).

Tour C: The Heartland

Olds

Located about 30km south of Red Deer, Olds is a small agricultural town. For those interested in agriculture, it's worth checking out. Olds is also the site of the **Agricultural College** (*4500 50th St., ☎556-8281 or 888-661-6537*), where you can learn more about agriculture by visiting the greenhouses as well as the various research areas scattered around the enormous premises.

★
Red Deer

Red Deer, a city of 60,000 people, began as a stopover for early commercial travellers along the Calgary Edmonton Trail. Red Deer is an erroneous translation of *Waskasoo*, which means elk in Cree. The shores of the river were frequented by elk, and Scottish settlers thought the animals resembled red deer found in Scotland. During the Riel Rebellion of 1885, the Canadian militia built Fort Normandeau at this site. The post was later occupied by the North West Mounted Police. The railway, agriculture, oil and gas all contributed to the growth of Red Deer, at one point the fastest growing city in Canada.

Red Deer is another Alberta city whose extensive park system is one of its greatest attractions. The **Waskasoo Park System** weaves its way throughout the city and through the Red Deer River valley with walking and cycling trails. The Great Red Deer Visitor Centre is located next to the **Heritage Ranch** (*mid-May to early Jul every day 9am to 6pm, early Jul to early Sep Mon to Thu 9am to 6pm Fri, Sat and Sun 9am to 7pm, early*

Central Alberta

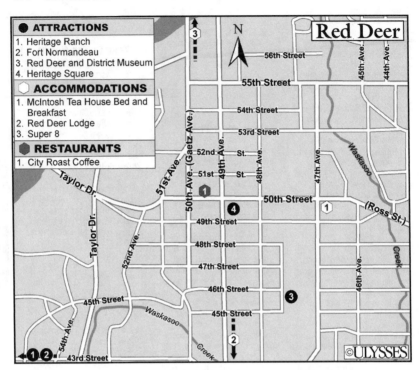

Sep to mid-May Mon to Fri 9am to 5pm Sat and Sun 10am to 5pm; 30 Riverview Park, at the end of Cronquist Dr., ☎346-0180) on the western edge of town; take the 32nd Street Exit from Hwy. 2, left on 60th Street and left on Cronquist Drive. Heritage Ranch also features, among other things, an equestrian centre, picnic shelters and access to trails in the park system.

Fort Normandeau ★ *(free; late May to end of Jun, every day noon to 5pm; Jul to early Sep, every day noon to 8pm; ☎347-2010)* is located west of Hwy. 2, along 32nd Street. The fort as it stands today is a replica of the original. A stopping house next to the river was fortified and enclosed in palisade walls by the **Carabiniers de Mont Royal** under Lieutenant J.E. Bédard Normandeau in anticipation of an attack by the Cree during

the Louis Riel Rebellion of 1885. The fort was never attacked. An interpretive centre next to the fort describes Aboriginal, Metis and European settlement of the area. Visitors can see wool being spun, and rope, soap, candles and ice cream being made.

In downtown Red Deer, the **Red Deer and District Museum** *(donation; Mon, Tue and Fri 10am to 5pm, Wed and Thu 10am to 9pm, Sat and Sun 1pm to 5pm, mid-May to early Sep, extended hours, Sat 10am to 5pm; 4525 47A Ave., ☎309-8405)* boasts different galleries featuring international and Canadian art, plus permanent exhibits dealing with the history of the area from prehistoric times. Walking tours of historic Red Deer depart from the museum.

Heritage Square, next to the museum, encloses a collection of historic buildings, including

the unique Aspelund Laft Hus, a replica of a 17th-century sod-roofed Norwegian home. Northwest of Heritage Square is **City Hall Park ★**, a lovely garden filled with 45,000 blossoming annuals.

Head north of Red Deer on Hwy. 2A, turn right on Hwy. 12 East to reach Stettler, make a brief stop in the town of Lacombe.

Lacombe

Lacombe is a small agricultural town typical of central Alberta. At the turn of the century it was larger than Red Deer. Today, its population is only 8,000.

There are over 25 restored buildings in Lacombe's historic downtown. The town even has its own distinctive **Flat Iron Building** *(50th Ave.)*. A block over is the **Mitchener House Museum** *(donations* appreciated; mid-May to early Sep, every day 10am to 4pm; 5036 51St., ☎782-3933), the birthplace of the governor general of Canada from 1967-1974. The house has been restored and furnished with family heirlooms, period pieces and old photographs.

The museum also manages the **Blacksmith Shop Museum** (donations welcome; Jun to Sep, Mon to Fri, 10am to 4pm or by appointment; 5020 49th St., ☎782-3933), located two streets away. It's one of the rare original blacksmith workshops remaining in Alberta. You can watch as the blacksmith carefully moulds the hot iron the same way it was done in the early 1900s. At that time, the blacksmith workshop was essential since it repaired heavy machinery and made the shoes for horses.

Two other attractions are found on the way to Stettler. The **Ellis Bird Farm** (donation, $2.50 tour; mid-May to early Sep; drive 8km towards Stettler on Hwy. 12, then 8km south on Prentiss Road, ☎346-2211) has looked after endangered species of birds for nearly 50 years. The protected wildlife reserves on this interesting property ensure the survival of the flora and fauna, and the many hiking trails offer an opportunity to appreciate its beauty.

Continue down Hwy. 12 east for a few minutes (instead of turning on Prentiss Road) and you arrive at **Doug's Exotic Zoo** ($5; early May to early Sep every day 10am to 9pm, early Sep to early May every day 10am to 6pm; ☎784-3400). There are 54 different kinds of animals here, from the hedgehog, to the zebra, to the Siberian tiger. Unfortunately, some of the cages are cramped.

Ponoka

If you are travelling through this region in late June or early July make a detour to Ponoka

(north of Lacombe on Hwy. 2A), home of the province's second largest rodeo after the Calgary Stampede. **The Ponoka Stampede ★** (☎783-0100) takes place the last weekend in June and first weekend in July, just as it has for more than 60 years.

Return toward Lacombe and take Hwy. 12 East to Stettler.

Stettler

For a trip across the wonderful prairie landscape **Alberta Prairie Railway Excursions ★** (47th Ave. and 47th St.; ☎742-2811 for schedule and reservations) organizes trips aboard a vintage 1920s steam locomotive, which departs from Stettler for small towns like Halkirk, Castor and Coronation to the east or even Big Valley to the south. Full and half-day excursions include one or two meals, and special trips include murder-mystery trains and casino trains. The trains run from May to October and on selected weekends from November to April.

Take Hwy. 56 north to Camrose.

Camrose

Alberta's Littlest Airport (donation; Jun to Aug, Wed to Sun, noon to 8pm; from Camrose, 22km east on Hwy. 13 then 4km south on Kelsey Rd., ☎780-373-3953) has mini-runways where radio-controlled planes land and take-off. Camrose is also the setting for the Big Valley Jamboree in early August, a terrific country music festival with big names from the United States and Canada.

Take Hwy. 26 west to Wetaskiwin.

★ Wetaskiwin

The city of Wetaskiwin is home to one of the finest museums in the province. Like the Remington-Alberta Carriage Centre in Cardston (see p 350), the Reynolds-Alberta Museum proves again that there is more to Alberta than Calgary, Edmonton and the Rockies. Though there isn't much to see in Wetaskiwin besides the Reynolds-Alberta and the Aviation Hall of Fame, this pleasant city has an interesting main street, and respectable restaurants and hotels.

The **Reynolds-Alberta Museum ★ ★ ★** ($6.50; late Jun to early Sep, 10am to 6pm; Sep to Jun, Tue to Sun 10am to 5pm; west of Wetaskiwin on Hwy. 13, ☎361-1351 or 800-661-4726, www.machine museum.com) celebrates the "spirit of the machine" and is a wonderful place to explore. Interactive programs for children bring everything alive. A top-notch collection of restored automobiles, trucks, bicycles, tractors and related machinery is on display.

Among the vintage cars is one of about 470 Model J Duesenberg Phaeton Royales. This one-of-a-kind automobile cost $20,000 when it was purchased in 1929. Visitors to the museum will also learn how a grain elevator works, and can observe the goings-on in the restoration workshop through a large picture window. Daily tours of the warehouse, where over 800 pieces are waiting to be restored, are offered twice daily (call ahead for times, sign up at front desk); pre-booked 1hr guided tours ($50) are also available.

Canada's Aviation Hall of Fame, located on the site of the Reynolds-Alberta, pays tribute to the pioneers of Canadian aviation. Photographs, artifacts, personal

Central Alberta

memorabilia and the favourite aircraft of the over 140 members of the Hall of Fame are displayed. These people include military and civilian pilots, doctors, scientists, inventors, aeronautical engineers and administrators.

Continue north on Hwy. 2A to Leduc, site of the biggest oil discovery in the world.

Leduc

Alberta came into its own when crude oil was discovered south of Edmonton. **Leduc Oil Well #1** *($4; mid-Apr to mid-Sep 10am to 6pm; 2km south of Devon on Hwy 60, ☎780-987-4323)* blew in on February 13, 1947, signalling the start of the oil boom. The oil was actually discovered on a farm northwest of Leduc in what was to become the town of Devon. A replica of the original 174-foot conventional derrick now stands on the site. Visitors get a firsthand look at equipment by climbing down to the drilling floor.

Head west on Hwy. 39 and then north on Hwy. 60 to Devon.

Devon

Devon and its **University of Alberta Devonian Botanic Garden** *($5.50; early May to mid-Sep, every day 10am to 7pm; mid-Sep to mid-Oct, every day 11am to 6pm; Hwy. 60, ☎780-987-3054)* are named for the Devonian rock formation in which oil was struck in the 1940s. Native species, a Japanese garden and the Butterfly House, full of fluttering tropical beauties, occupy 110 acres.

Edmonton (see p 387) is 30min north on Hwy. 60.

Tour D: The Yellowhead

The scenic **Yellowhead Route** follows Hwy. 16 west from Winnipeg, Manitoba and across the prairies through Saskatoon, Saskatchewan, before reaching the Alberta border at Lloydminster. It crosses Alberta, passing the provincial capital, Edmonton, and Jasper along the way. Once in British Columbia it splits, heading south on Hwy. 5 to Merritt and continuing on the 16 west all the way to Prince Rupert.

Lloydminster

Lloydminster was settled in 1903 when the region was part of the vast Northwest Territories. In 1930, 25 years after the creation of the provinces of Saskatchewan and Alberta, the two communities merged to form the only city with a single corporate body in two provinces. The different costs of living in each province make life interesting in Lloydminster: there is no sales tax in Alberta; the minimum wage is higher in Saskatchewan, but so are the income taxes; the drinking age in Saskatchewan is 19, in Alberta it is 18, and so on.

The **Barr Colony Heritage Centre** *($4; mid-May to early Sep Wed to Fri noon to 5pm, Sat and Sun 1pm to 5pm; Hwy. 16 at 45th Ave., ☎306-825-5655)* recalls the original settlement of Lloydminster in 1903 when 2,000 British colonists arrived with Reverend Isaac Barr. It houses five art galleries.

Bud Miller Park *(every day 7am to 11pm; 59th Ave., south of Hwy. 16, ☎780-875-4499)* is 81ha of nature trails and aspen stands. There are also lawn bowling greens, beach volleyball courts, outdoor waters park, a tree maze, a formal

garden and Canada's largest sundial.

Head west on Hwy. 16 through Vermillion, named for the reddish deposits of the river, and on to Vegreville.

Vegreville

Vegreville was first settled by French farmers migrating from Kansas. These days it is better known for its Ukrainian community and its rather curious landmark, the world's largest pysanka. The traditional Ukrainian Easter egg is 7m long and it actually turns in the wind, like a giant weathervane.

Continuing west on Hwy. 16, you will soon come upon the **Ukrainian Cultural Heritage Village ★ ★** *($8; mid-May to early Sep every day 10am to 6pm; Sep to mid-Oct Sat and Sun 10am to 6pm; on Hwy. 16 about 30km east of Edmonton, ☎780-662-3640)*, where the fascinating story of the region's Ukrainian settlers is brought to life. Life at the Bloc settlement in East Central Alberta from 1892 to 1930 is recreated with staff in period costume and a whole historic townsite. Driven from their homeland, these settlers fled to the Canadian prairies, where land was practically being given away. They dressed and worked as they had in the old country, thereby enriching the Canadian cultural landscape. Late August is the time for the **Harvest of the Past**, featuring *tsymbaly* entertainment and pirogi (potato dumpling) eating contests.

★★
Elk Island National Park

Heading west on Hwy. 16 (the Yellowhead Highway) the next stop is Elk Island National Park. This island wilderness in a sea of grass preserves two herds of buffalo, plains bison and the rare wood bison. It is also home to a multitude of animals species. There are campgrounds, while trails and a lake offer the possibility of all sorts of outdoor activities (see p 380).

Edmonton (see p 387) lies 27km west. Continuing on the Yellowhead, Stony Plain is 40km west of the provincial capital.

The Yellowhead West to Jasper

Another 160km west of Stony Plain is the town of **Edson** – not much to look at but nonetheless home to two small museums on the history of the region, the **Galloway Station Museum** *($1; mid-May to early Sept,every day 10am to 5pm; 5425A 3rd Ave., ☎780-723-5696)* and the **Red Brick Arts Centre and Museum** *(Mon to Fri 9am to 4:30pm; 4818 Seventh Ave., ☎780-723-3582)*, in a 1913 schoolhouse.

Hinton lies on the Jasper National Park's doorstep and offers an inexpensive alternative for accommodations and services (see p 383). The **Alberta Forest Service Museum** *(free admission; Mon to Fri 8:15am to 4:30pm; 1176 Switzer Dr., ☎780-865-8220)* covers the forestry industry in Alberta. Spectacular wilderness surrounds Hinton including the **Cadomin Caves** *(excursions can be arranged in town)*, the best known and most accessible in the province.

Parks

For more information on Alberta's Provincial Parks:
www3.gov.ab.ca/env/parks/

Tour A: Digging for Dinosaur Bones and Other Treasures

★
Kinbrook Island Provincial Park

The shores of Lake Newell, the largest artificial lake in the province, are home to over 250 species of birds and fowl. Colonies of double-crested cormorants and American white pelicans occupy several of the protected islands on the lake. The best wildlife viewing is from the eastern shore. There are also walking trails through nearby Kinbrook Marsh. For information and reservations: ☎*362-4525.* Camping avaible.

★★★
Dinosaur Provincial Park

Dinosaur Provincial Park offers amateur palaeontologists the opportunity to walk through the land of the dinosaurs. Declared a UNESCO World Heritage Site in 1979, this nature preserve harbours a wealth of information on these formidable former inhabitants of the planet. Today, the park is also home to more than 35 species of animals.

The small museum at the **Field Station of the Tyrell Museum** *($6.50; mid-May to early Sep, every day 9am to 9pm; Sep to May, Mon to Fri, 9am to 4pm; ☎378-4342 or 378-4344 for bus tour reservations)*, the loop road and the two self-guided trails (the **Cottonwood Flats Trail** and the **Badlands Trail**) will give you a summary introduction to the park. Two exposed skeletons left where they were discovered can be viewed. The best way to see the park, however, is on one of the guided tours into the restricted nature preserve that makes up most of the park. The 90min **Badlands Bus**

Tour leads into the heart of the preserve for unforgettable scenery, skeletons and wildlife; the **Centrosaurus Bone Bed Hike** and **Fossil Safari Hike** offer close-up looks at excavation sites. Places for these tours are limited, especially during July and August, so to avoid missing out, visitors are advised to call ahead to find out when tours leave and even to reserve tickets.

The park also features campgrounds and a Dinosaur Service Centre with laundry, showers, picnic and food.

The cabin of John Ware, an ex-slave from Texas who became a well-respected Albertan cattle rancher, lies near the campground.

Tour B: Central Foothills

Crimson Lake Provincial Park

Crimson Lake Provincial Park *(information and camping reservations ☎866-427-3582, for emergencies, call the warden's office at ☎845-2340)* is located just west of Rocky Mountain House and features peaceful campsites and good fishing for rainbow trout. Extensive hiking trails become cross-country trails in the winter.

Ma-Me-O Beach and Pigeon Lake Provincial Parks

Ma-Me-O Beach Provincial Park *(day use only; park office ☎780-586-2645)* and Pigeon Lake Provincial Park *(park office ☎780-586-2645, camping reservations ☎780-586-2644)* are for those who have had enough of the mountains and are up for a day at the beach. Both offer excellent access to the great swimming (said to be the best in Alberta) and fishing on Pigeon Lake. Boats can be rented at the

Central Alberta

Zeiner campground in Pigeon
Lake Provincial Park.

Tour D: The Yellowhead

★★
Elk Island National Park

Magnificent Elk Island National
Park *($4; open year-round;
park administration and
warden Mon to Fri 8am to
4pm,* ☎780-992-5790) pre-
serves part of the Beaver Hills
area as it was before the
arrival of settlers when Sarcee
and Plains Cree hunted and
trapped in these lands. The
arrival of settlers endangered
beaver, elk and bison populations, prompting local residents and conservationists to
petition the government to set
aside an elk reserve in 1906.
The plains bison that live in the
park actually ended up there
by accident, having escaped
from a herd placed there
temporarily while a fence at
Buffalo National Park in Wainwright, Alberta was being
completed. The plains bison
herd that inhabits the park
began with those 50 escaped
bison.

Elk Island is also home to a
small herd of rare wood bison, North America's largest
mammal. In 1940, pure wood
buffalo were thought to be
extinct, but by sheer luck a
herd of about 200 wood
buffalo were discovered in a
remote part of the park in
1957. Part of that herd was
sent to a fenced sanctuary in
the Northwest Territories.

Today the smaller plains bison
are found north of Hwy. 16,
while the wood bison live
south of the highway. While
touring the park, remember
that you are in bison country
and that these animals are
wild. Though they may look
docile, they are dangerous,

unpredictable and may charge
without warning, so stay in
your vehicle and keep a safe
distance (50 to 75m).

Elk Island became a national
park in 1930 and is now a
195km^2 sanctuary for 44 kinds
of mammals, including moose,
elk, deer, lynx, beaver and
coyote. The park offers some
of the best wildlife viewing in
the province. It is crossed by
major migratory fly ways; be
on the look-out for trumpeter
swans in the fall.

The park office at the South
Gate, just north of Hwy. 16,
can provide information on
the two campgrounds, wildlife
viewing and the 12 trails that
run through the park, making
for great hiking and cross-
country skiing. Fishing and
boating can be enjoyed on
Astotin Lake, and the park
even boasts a nine-hole golf
course.

Beaches

Believe it or not, land-locked
Alberta has a handful of
beaches that are great for
swimming and suntanning. In
central Alberta and northern
Alberta, countless lakes left
behind by retreating glaciers
now provide water fun for
summer vacationers. **Pigeon
Lake Provincial Park** has a
long sandy beach with showers and picnic tables, while
Ma-Me-O Provincial Park at
the other end of Pigeon Lake,
is a day-use area that's great
for picnics and for catching
some rays. **Sylvan Lake ★** is a
veritable beach resort town. A
beautiful beach lines one of
Alberta's most spectacular
lakes. Windsurfers and pedal-
boats can be rented.

Outdoor Activities

Canoeing and Rafting

**Alpenglow Mountain Adven-
tures** *(R.R. 1, Rocky Mountain
House* ☎/≈844-4715) organizes
rafting, kayaking and canoeing
trips along the North Saskatchewan River between
Nordegg and Rocky Mountain
House. Full-day trips range
from $39 to $64, while overnight trips from two to three
days range from $149 to
$249. This outfit also orga-
nizes trips along the Athabasca
River. They also offers ice-
climbing excursions in winter.

Also based in Rocky Mountain
House, **Voyageur Adventure
Tours** *(*☎845-7878) organizes
trips of one to several days in
eight passenger voyageur
canoes.

Hiking and
Cross-Country Skiing

Elk Island National Park
offers the opportunity to view
an exceptional variety of
wildlife. The **Shoreline Trail**
(3km one way) and **Lakeview
Trail** (3.3km round trip)
explore the area around
Astotin Lake, where beavers
are occasionally seen. The
Wood Bison Trail (18.5km
round trip) does a loop
around Flying Shot Lake in the
area of the park south of
Hwy. 16, where wood buffalo
roam. These three trails are
maintained as cross-country
trails in the winter.

Paragliding

Located 30min west of Calgary, just before the town of Cochrane, **Muller** *(Bigg Hill Road, ☎/≈ 932-6760)* offers hang-gliding and para-gliding classes. The beginners' course costs $100 and includes a few flights. Apparently the sensation of flying is incredible! The young instructor grew up on the slopes and today he participates in international competitions.

Accommodations

Tour A: Digging for Dinosaur Bones and Other Treasures

There are campsites at **Kinbrook Island Provincial Park** *($; ☎362-4525)* as well as at **Dinosaur Provincial Park** *($; ☎378-3700)*. The latter has more facilities, including a snack bar, showers and a laundry.

Brooks

Tel-Star Motor Inn
$$
ℜ, ≡, ℝ, *K*
813 Second St. W., on the way into town,
☎*362-3466 or 800-260-6211*
≈*362-8818*
About 30min down the highway from Dinosaur Provincial Park is the town of Brooks and the Tel-Star Motor Inn. The rooms don't have much to recommend them aside from the fact that they are clean and each has a microwave and a refrigerator. The hotel also doesn't charge for local calls and has freezer facilities for your catch.

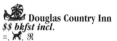 Douglas Country Inn
$$ bkfst incl.
≡, 𝕏, ℜ
☎*362-2873*
≈*362-2100*
The Douglas Country Inn is 6.5km north of town on Hwy. 873. A casual country atmosphere is achieved in each of the seven beautifully appointed rooms and throughout the rest of the inn. The only television is in the small TV room, which is rarely used.

Drumheller

Pope Lease Pines Bed and Breakfast and RV Resort
$-$$ bkfst incl.
≡, 𝕊, *sb*
Range Rd. 22-1, 21km west of Drumheller via Hwy. 575
☎*823-8281*
≈*572-2370*
www.popeleasepines.com
Pope Lease Pines can be found in an oasis of pine trees in the middle of Alberta's Prairies. It's a quiet country home with three guest rooms and 14 full hook-up sites for RVs. The home dates back to the 1940s and Kent and Janice Walker have tried to recreate the era with hardwood floors, period antiques, four-poster beds and floral linens. Two sunny rooms have queen beds, while there is a much smaller room with two twin beds. Ask to see Kent's collection of dinosaur bones, which he found himself in the area.

Badlands Motel
$$
≡, ℜ, ℝ, *K*, 🐾
on the Dinosaur Trail
☎*823-5155*
≈*823-7653*
The Badlands Motel lies outside of town, along the scenic Dinosaur Trail. Rooms are typical, but the pancake restaurant next door is particularly noteworthy.

Taste the Past B&B
$$ bkfst
⊗
281 Second St. W.
☎*823-5889*
The fittingly named Taste the Past B&B is a 1910 Victorian house decorated with antiques. Guests enjoy a large yard and veranda and a choice of breakfasts. They also have the use of a cosy bathrobe and slippers. This establishment has three very private rooms. Each room now has its own private bathroom.

The Inns at Heartwood Manor
$$$
⊗, ≡, 𝕏, *K*, 𝕁
320 Railway Ave. E
☎*823-6495 or 888-823-6495*
≈*823-4935*
www.innatheartwood.com
By far the prettiest place to stay in town is the Inns at Heartwood Manor, a bed and breakfast in a restored heritage building, where a striking use of colour creates a cosy and luxurious atmosphere. Nine of the ten rooms have whirlpool baths, and five even boast fireplaces. A spacious cottage and a two-bedroom suite is also available. Yummy homemade fruit syrups are served with the pancake breakfast. French and English spoken.

Central Alberta

Best Western Jurassic Inn
$$-$$$
≡, ≈, ℜ, ⊛, ℝ
1103 Hwy. 9 S
☎*823-7700* or *888-823-3466*
⇔*823-5002*
www.bestwestern.com
The Best Western has 49 guest rooms. They are standard, but very clean and very well equipped: they all have a fridge, microwave and hair dryer. Continental breakfast is included.

Trochu

St. Ann Ranch
$$ bkfst incl.
☎*442-3924* or *888-442-3942*
⇔*442-4264*
Once the ranch of French cavalry men, the St. Ann Ranch country bed and breakfast offers travellers the chance to experience a true French *gîte*. Guests of the B&B have the choice of seven private, antique-furnished rooms (five with private baths) in the rambling 30-room ranch house or in the Pioneer Cottage and the use of a parlour with a fireplace, a library and patios. While you're here visit the tea house and museum (see p 372).

Rosebud

Queen Regent Guest House
$$
pb/sb
one block north of Rosebud Theatre
☎*677-2451*
www.experiencerosebud. com
The Queen Regent Guest House is an absolutely lovely inn with artfully painted walls and bright colours. Young Alana Bowker has done a fabulous job with the home, which is the community's old teacherage. From the outside it may not look like much, but inside, there are seven lovely guest rooms with handmade quilts. The Angel Room and Queen's Chambers are especially exquisite, with netting draped romantically over canopied beds.

Rosebud Country Inn
$$$
≡
☎*677-2211*
⇔*677-2106*
Rooms at the Rosebud Country Inn feature queen-size sleigh beds, designer linens, pedestal sinks and balconies. Rose colours brighten up the interior space throughout. This inn boasts first-rate facilities and spotless accommodations. The tea room serves breakfast, Sunday brunch, lunch, supper and, of course, afternoon tea. There are no televisions (by choice) and children are not permitted.

Tour B: Central Foothills

Rocky Mountain House

Voyageur Motel
$$
≡, *K*, ℝ
on Hwy. 11 S
☎*845-3381* or *888-845-3569*
⇔*845-6166*
www.voyageurmotel.com
The Voyageur is a practical choice with spacious, clean rooms, each equipped with a refrigerator. Kitchenettes are also available. Each room has a VCR.

Walking Eagle Motor Inn
$$
≡, ℜ, ⊛, *K*, ℝ
on Hwy. 11
☎*845-2804*
⇔*845-3685*
The log exterior of the Walking Eagle Motor Inn encloses 63 clean and large rooms decorated in keeping with the hotel's name. The hotel owes its attractive appearance to a complete renovation and paint-job. In addition, a brand new 35-room motel (*$80*) was built right next door. There's a microwave and refrigerator in each one of the clean – but rather drab – rooms.

Nordegg

Shunda Creek Hostel
$
sb
west of Nordegg, 3km north of Hwy. 11, on Shunda Creek Recreation Area Rd.
☎/⇔*721-2140*
www.hihostels.ca
Set against the stunning backdrop of the Rocky Mountains in David Thompson Country, surrounded by countless opportunities for outdoor activities is the Shunda Creek Hostel. The two-storey lodge encloses kitchen and laundry facilities, a common area with a fireplace and 10 rooms able to accommodate a total of 48 people; it also adjoins an outdoor hot tub. Hiking, mountain biking, fishing, canoeing, cross-country skiing and ice-climbing are possible nearby.

David Thompson Resort
$$
≡, ≈, ℜ, ⋈
Cline River
☎*721-2103*
⇔*721-2267*
www.davidthompsonresort. com
This is more of a motel and RV park than a resort, but regardless it is the only accommodation between Nordegg and Hwy. 93, the Icefields Parkway, and you can't beat the scenery. The resort rents bicycles and can organize helicopter tours of the area.

Tour C: Heartland

Red Deer

Many conventions are held in Red Deer, and as a result weekend rates in the many hotels are often less expensive.

The Super 8
$$
≡, ℜ
7474 Gaetz Ave.
☎343-1102
⇥341-6532
The Super 8 is one of the many hotels between Gaetz Avenue and downtown. To justify sleeping in one of these pleasant rooms overlooking the parking lot, bring your car.

McIntosh Tea House Bed and Breakfast
$$ bkfst incl.
4631 50th St.
☎346-1622
This is the former home of the great grandson of the creator of the McIntosh apple. Each of the three upstairs rooms of the red-brick historic Victorian is decorated with antiques. Guests can enjoy a game of apple checkers in the private parlour. Tea and coffee are served in the evening and a full breakfast in the morning.

Red Deer Lodge
$$$
≡, ≈, ℜ, ⊚, ☺, ⛵
4311 49th Ave.
☎346-8841 or 800-661-1657
⇥341-3220
www.reddeerlodge.net
The Red Deer Lodge is a favourite with convention-goers because of its modern and extensive amenities. As one would expect, the rooms are comfortable and spotless. The rooms surround a cheerful tropical courtyard.

Wetaskiwin

Rose Country Inn
$$
≡, ℜ, ℝ, K
4820 50th St.
☎(780) 352-3600
⇥(780) 352-2127
Close to the Reynolds-Alberta Museum, on 50th Street, the Rose Country Inn is one of the best deals in town. Each of the recently renovated rooms has a refrigerator and microwave oven.

Tour D: The Yellowhead

Elk Island National Park

Elk Island National Park
$
Site 4, RR1, Fort Saskatchewan
☎780-992-5790
Elk Island National Park has two campgrounds. The park office at the South Gate, just north of Hwy. 16, can provide information on registration and the sites.

Hinton

Black Cat Guest Ranch
$$$$, fb
☎(780) 865-3084
☎800-859-6840
⇥(780) 865-1924
www.blackcatguestranch.ca
The Black Cat provides a peaceful retreat and lots of family fun, ideal for family get-togethers. There are guided trail rides, hiking trails and cross-country skiing in the winter. The accommodations are rustic and homey and each room has a mountain view. The scenery can be enjoyed from the outdoor hot-tub. The ranch also offers theme weekends and organizes excursions as well as spa weekends.

Restaurants

Tour A: Digging for Dinosaur Bones and Other Treasures

Drumheller

Whif's Flapjack House
$
every day 6am to 3pm
801 North Dinosaur Trail
☎823-7595
This popular breakfast spot, located in the Badlands Motel, serves up flapjacks, crêpes, Belgian waffles and the usual array of omelettes and egg combos. It's a simple country affair, with pinewood decor. The coffee's fresh and you'll be able to face a day of dinosaur bone hunting on a full stomach. For lunch there's an assortment of burgers and sandwiches.

The Whistling Kettle
$
Mon to Sat 7:30am to 5pm
☎923-9997
The sunny Whistling Kettle café offers an ever-changing menu. It lies beyond the Heartland Office of Alberta Travel. Soup and biscuits figure on the menu along with hot dishes, chicken salad, egg salad and pastrami sandwiches. The yellow walls of this bright establishment are covered with local art. If you have a sweet tooth, satisfy it with the famous sour cream and rhubarb pie.

Yavis Family Restaurant
$$
249 Third Ave.
☎823-8317
This restaurant has been around for years. The interior is fairly non-descript, and so is the menu. The selections are nonetheless pretty good, especially the great big breakfasts.

Athens Cafe and Greek Restaurant
$$
71 Bridge St. N
☎823-9400
Athens Cafe and Greek restaurant that serves a bit of everything, including steaks and pasta dishes. The Greek selections are the best – they are a bit on the greasy side but come in huge portions with tsatziki on the side (i.e. don't order more!). The interior was recently redone and, along with the background music, is faintly reminiscent of the Mediterranean.

Sizzling House
$$
160 Centre St.
☎823-8098
The Sizzling House serves up tasty Szechuan, Pekin and Thai cooking, and is recommended by locals. A good place for lunch, the service is quick and friendly.

Corner Stop Family Restaurant
$$$
15 Third Ave. W
☎823-5440
The Corner Stop Restaurant is located in the middle of the city. The Greek-style décor is meticulous, and the menu includes salads, pizza, pasta, seafood and steaks.

Rosebud

Rosebud Dinner Theatre
$$$$
☎677-2001 or 800-267-7553
The Rosebud Dinner Theatre is an entertaining way to spend an evening. The food is simple, but the plays are always well presented. Reservations are mandatory (see below).

Tour B: Central Foothills

Cochrane

Mackay's Ice Cream
$
220, First St.
☎932-4126
Mackay's scoops up what many claim is the best ice cream in the country. Be sure to stop in to see for yourself!

Home Quarter Restaurant & Pie Shoppe
$$$
216 First St. W
☎932-2111
Cochrane's friendly Home Quarter Restaurant is the home of the ever-popular Rancher's Special breakfast with eggs, bacon and sausage. Home-made pies are available all day long to eat in or take out. The lunch and dinner menu includes filet mignon and chicken parmesan.

Tour C: Heartland

Red Deer

City Roast Coffee
$
4940 50th St.
☎347-0893
The City Roast serves hearty soup, sandwich lunches and good coffee. The walls are decorated with posters announcing local art shows and events.

Wetaskiwin

The MacEachern Tea House & Restaurant
$-$$
Mon to Fri until 4pm, early Jun to end Aug also open Sun 10am to 4pm
4719 50th Ave.
☎780-352-8308
Home to specialty coffees and over 20 teas. The menu boasts hearty home-made soups and chowders, as well

---

as sandwiches and salads. Reservations recommended.

Entertainment

Drumheller

The Canadian Badlands Passion Play
$25
Last two weeks of Jul
for tickets write to Box 457, Drumheller, T0J 0Y0
☎823-2001
www.canadianpassionplay.com
The badlands make an eerily fitting background for this moving open-air portrayal of the life, death and resurrection of Jesus Christ.

Rosebud

The **Rosebud Dinner Theatre**, is a splendid way to spend a fun evening with friends. Amusing plays are presented every day except Sunday, alternating from one day to the next between matinee and evening performances. Reservations are mandatory; for schedules and information call **☎677-2001 or 800-267-7553**. Rosebud is located about an hour from Calgary on Hwy. 840 about halfway to Drumheller.

Shopping

Tour B: Central Foothills

Markerville

Two gift shops can be found in the vicinity of the Markerville Creamery (see p 373), the **Gallery and Gift Shop** adjoins the creamery and sells pretty

Freshly cut bundles of hay dot Prairie fields, with the Rockies rising up in the distance.
- *Troy & Mary Parlee*

Like other western capitals, Edmonton boasts a magnificent parliament.
- *Troy & Mary Parlee*

Diverse landscapes, such as these sandy plains in Saskatchewan, stretch across Western Canada.
- *M. Michaelnuk*

bric-a-brac and gifts. Next door the **Butterchurn** features a remarkable collection of wood-worked items, from small shelves to benches and tables.

Carstairs

Pa-Su Farm *(9km west of Carstairs on Hwy. 580, follow the signs,* ☎*337-2800)* is a working sheep farm with a collection of rare and endangered breeds of sheep. A 280m² gallery displays weavings from Africa and local sheepskin and woolen products. The working part of the farm is only open to scheduled tours. The Devonshire Tea Room serves delicious warm scones with tea.

On the other side of Carstairs, the **Custom Woolen Mills** *(21km east of Carstairs on Hwy. 581, then 4.5km north on Hwy. 791,* ☎*337-2221)* is a curious little spot. Raw wool is processed on machines that in some cases are more than 100 years old. Yarn and ready-made knitted articles can be purchased.

Tour C: The Heartland

Lacombe

The Gallery on the Main *(4910 50th Ave., 3rd floor,* ☎*782-3402)* exhibits an impressive variety of creations by local artists. The gallery represents 45 artists who use diverse mediums such as acrylic, oil, woodcarving and pottery. Come check out these fine works of art.

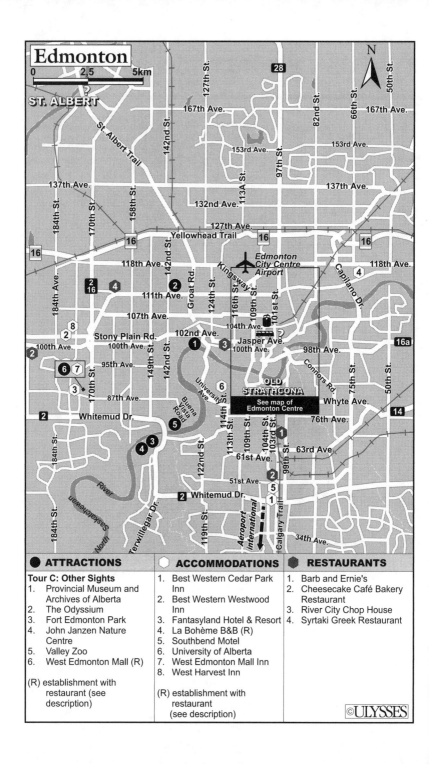

Edmonton

0   2,5   5km

N

ST. ALBERT

St. Albert Trail

167th Ave.   153rd Ave.   153rd Ave.

137th Ave.   137th Ave.

132nd Ave.

127th Ave.

Yellowhead Trail

118th Ave.   **Edmonton City Centre Airport**   118th Ave.

Kingsway

111th Ave.

107th Ave.

Stony Plain Rd.   104th Ave.

102nd Ave.

100th Ave.   Jasper Ave.   98th Ave.
                     100th Ave.

95th Ave.   **OLD STRATHCONA**

87th Ave.   See map of Edmonton Centre   Whyte Ave.

Whitemud Dr.   76th Ave.

Buena Vista Road

University Ave.

63rd Ave.

61st Ave.

51st Ave.

Whitemud Dr.   Barb and Ernie's

North Saskatchewan River

Terwillegar Dr.

Aeroport international

Calgary Trail

34th Ave.

● ATTRACTIONS

Tour C: Other Sights
1. Provincial Museum and Archives of Alberta
2. The Odyssium
3. Fort Edmonton Park
4. John Janzen Nature Centre
5. Valley Zoo
6. West Edmonton Mall (R)

(R) establishment with restaurant (see description)

⬡ ACCOMMODATIONS

1. Best Western Cedar Park Inn
2. Best Western Westwood Inn
3. Fantasyland Hotel & Resort
4. La Bohème B&B (R)
5. Southbend Motel
6. University of Alberta
7. West Edmonton Mall Inn
8. West Harvest Inn

(R) establishment with restaurant (see description)

⬡ RESTAURANTS

1. Barb and Ernie's
2. Cheesecake Café Bakery Restaurant
3. River City Chop House
4. Syrtaki Greek Restaurant

©ULYSSES

Edmonton

Edmonton ★ ★ seems to
suffer from an image problem, and undeservedly so.

People have trouble getting past the boomtown atmosphere and the huge mall! Admittedly it is a boomtown: a city that grew out of the wealth of the natural resources that surround it. But this city has grown to become one of the world's largest northerly cities, encompassing an attractive downtown core, Canada's largest urban parks system and numerous cultural facilities, including theatres and many festivals (see p 400). With all this going for it, though, the city's biggest attraction still seems to be its gargantuan shopping mall. You be the judge!

Edmonton has actually experienced three booms: the first in fur, the second in gold and the third in oil. The area had long been frequented by Aboriginal peoples who searched for quartzite to make tools and who trapped abundant beaver and muskrat. However, it was the supply of fur that attracted traders to the area in the late 18th century. The Hudson's Bay Company established Fort Edmonton in 1795 next to the North West Company's Fort Augustus overlooking the North Saskatchewan River where the Legislative Building now stands. Trading at the fort

involved Cree and Assiniboine from the north as well as Blackfoot from the south. These normally warring peoples could trade in safety essentially because the fierce Blackfoot were more peaceable when they were outside their own territory to the south.

Edmonton's fortunes rose and fell until the next boom. Merchants tried to attract prospectors of the Klondike Gold Rush to pass through Edmonton on their way to Dawson City. Prospectors were encouraged to outfit themselves in Edmonton and use this "All-Canadian Route," which was an alternative to the Chilkoot Trail, thereby avoiding Alaska. The

route turned out to be something of a scam, however, proving arduous and impractical. None of the some 1,600 prospectors lured to Edmonton actually reached the goldfields in time for the big rush of 1899. Some perished trying and some never left. Six years later, on September 1, 1905, the province of Alberta was founded and Edmonton was named the capital. Citizens of cities like Calgary, Cochrane, Wetaskiwin, Athabasca and Banff, among others, all claimed that this distinction should have been bestowed on their cities, but Edmonton prevailed. In 1912, the cities of Strathcona and Edmonton merged, pushing the total population over 50,000.

Agriculture remained the bread and butter of Alberta's capital until the well at Leduc (see p 378) blew in and the third boom, the oil boom, was on. Since then Edmonton has been one of Canada's fastest growing cities. Pipelines, refineries, derricks and oil tanks sprang up in farmer's fields all around the city. Some 10,000 wells were drilled and by 1965 Edmonton had become the oil capital of Canada. As the population grew so did the downtown core in order to accommodate the business community, which is still very much centred around oil though the boom is over. Fortunately the city took care not to overdevelop, and today this boomtown has an unusually sophisticated atmosphere (despite the shopping mall), with fine restaurants and a thriving arts community. Edmonton has become the technological, service and supply centre of Alberta.

Finding Your Way Around

By Car

Edmonton's streets are numbered; the avenues run east-west and the streets run north-south. The major arteries include **Gateway Boulevard**, known until recently as the Calgary Trail Northbound; **Calgary Trail**, formerly known as Calgary Trail Southbound, runs south from the city; **Whitemud Drive** runs east-west: it lies south of the city

centre providing access to West Edmonton Mall, Fort Edmonton Park and the Valley Zoo; **Jasper Avenue** runs east-west through downtown where 101st Avenue would naturally fall; Hwy. 16, the Yellowhead Highway, crosses the city north of downtown, providing access to points in the tour of northern Alberta (see also Tour D in Central Alberta, p 378).

A collection of hotels line Calgary Trail south of downtown and Stony Plain Road west of the city centre.

Car Rentals

Budget
Airport
☎*(780) 448-2000*
☎*800-661-7027*
Downtown
10016 106th Street
☎*(780) 448-2001*

Hertz
Airport
☎*(780) 890-4435*
☎*800-263-0600*
Downtown
10048 103rd Street NW
☎*(780) 423-3431*

National
Airport
☎*(780) 890-7232*
☎*800-387-4747*
Downtown
10133 1100th Street NW
☎*(780) 422-6097*

Avis
Airport
☎*(780)890-7596*
☎*800-879-2487*
Downtown
Sheraton Hotel, 10235 101st Street
☎*(780) 448-0066*

Discount
Downtown
Hotel Macdonald, 9925 Jasper Avenue
☎*(780) 448-3892*
☎*800-263-2355*

Thrifty
Airport
☎*(780) 890-4555*
Downtown
10036 102nd Street
☎*(780) 428-8555*

By Plane

Edmonton International Airport is located south of the city centre. Recently expanded, it offers many services and facilities, including restaurants, an information centre, hotel courtesy phones, major car-rental counters, currency exchange and a bus tour operator.

Air Canada, WestJet, American Airlines, Delta Airlines, Northwest Airlines, United Airlines and Lufthansa all have regular flights to the airport. Regional companies (Smart Air, Peace Air and Quik Air) fly in and out of Edmonton City Centre Airport, located north of the city.

The **Sky Shuttle** (☎*465-8515*) travels to downtown hotels and to Edmonton's municipal airport. It passes every 30min on weekends and every 20min during the week. The trip is $11 one-way and $18 return.

A taxi from the airport to downtown costs about $40.

By Train

Via Rail's (☎ *888-VIA-RAIL*) transcontinental railway passenger service makes a stop in Edmonton three times a week, continuing west to Jasper and Vancouver or east to Saskatoon and beyond. The VIA train station is at 12360 121st Street, about 15min from downtown.

By Bus

Edmonton Greyhound Bus Depot
10324 103rd St.
☎*(780) 413-8747*
☎*800-661-8747*
Services: restaurant, lockers.

Edmonton South Greyhound Bus Depot
5723 104th St., 2 blocks north of Whitemud Dr. on Calgary Trail
☎*(780) 433-1919*
☎ *800-661-8747*

Public Transit

Edmonton's public transit also combines buses and a light-rail transit system. The LRT runs east-west along Jasper Avenue, south to the university and then north to 139th Avenue with only 10 stops, and in the city centre the train runs underground. The LRT is free between Churchill and Grandin stops on weekdays from 9am to 3pm and Saturdays from 9am to 6pm. The fare is $2 for adults and a day pass is $6. Route and schedule information is available by calling ☎*496-1611*.

By Foot

Edmonton's downtown core has its own system of walkways known as the pedway system. It lies below and above ground and at street level and seems complicated at first, though is very well indicated and easy to negotiate once you have picked up a map at the tourist information centre.

Practical Information

Area code: **780**

Tourist Information

Edmonton Tourism Information Centre
Shaw Conference Centre, 9797 Jasper Ave. NW also in Gateway Park, south of downtown (Hwy. 2)
☎*496-8400 or 800-463-4667*
www.tourism.ede.org

Bed and Breakfasts

Alberta Bed & Breakfast Association
15615 81st St.
☎/≈*456-5928*
www.bbalberta.com
Represents various regional B&B associations across the province.

Edmonton Bed & Breakfast
13824 110A Ave.
☎*455-2297*

Guided Tours

If you prefer to be escorted through the streets of Old Strathcona (Tour B), the **Old Strathcona Business Association** offers a variety of options (☎*737-4182*), while **Edmonton Ghost Tours** (☎ *469-3187*) provides tours of a different sort.

Exploring

Tour A: Downtown and North of the River

Begin your tour of Edmonton with a visit to the **Edmonton Tourism Information Centre** *(Mon-Fri 8am to 5pm)*, located in the **Shaw Conference Centre** *(9797 Jasper Ave. NW)*. The hours may not be very practical, but the staff is very friendly and helpful. While there, pick up a *Ride Guide* to help you figure out the public-transportation system.

The impressive **city hall** *(99th St. and 102A Ave.)* is the centrepiece of the **Edmonton Arts District**, which occupies six city blocks and includes the Stanley A. Milner Library, the Edmonton Art Gallery, Sir Winston Churchill Square, the Law Courts Building, the Shaw Conference Centre and the Citadel Theatre. With its impressive eight-storey glass pyramid, the city hall opened in 1992 on the site of the old city hall.

From the information centre, head up 97th Street.

While the city hall may be the centrepiece of the Edmonton Arts District, its biggest star is the **Francis Winspear Centre for Music** ★ ★ *(4 Sir Winston Churchill Square, corner of 99th St. and 102 Ave.)*. Built with a $6 million gift from Edmonton businessman Francis Winspear, the 1,900-seat hall is considered an acoustic wonder and as a result, attracts a wide range of musicians. It is faced with Manitoba tyndall limestone to match the city hall and is now the home of the Edmonton Symphony Orchestra.

On the eastern side of Sir Winston Churchill Square lies the **Edmonton Art Gallery** ★★ *($5, free Thu after 4pm; Mon-Wed and Fri 10:30am to 5pm, Thu 10:30am to 8pm, Sat and Sun 11am to 5pm; 2 Sir Winston Churchill Square,99th St. and 102A Ave. ☎422-6223)*. The Gallery houses an extensive collection of Canadian art, which is complemented by various travelling exhibits throughout the year.

Walk up 97th Street.

The stretch of 97th Street from 105th to 108th Avenue is Edmonton's **Chinatown**, home to plenty of shops and restaurants.

The focal point of Edmonton's Chinatown, is the **Chinatown Gate** at 97th Street and 102nd Avenue. The gate is also a symbol of the friendship between Edmonton and its sister city Harbin in China. Roll the ball in the lion's mouth for good luck.

From the Chinatown Gate at 97th Street and 102nd Avenue, proceed north along 97th Street to the heart of Chinatown, and then along 107th Avenue from 97th Street west to 109th Street which is known as the "**Avenue of Nations**." This area is home to a great many Chinese, Vietnamese, and other ethnic restaurants and shops. Notice the telephone booths and light standards, themed in a Chinese motif, along 97th Street.

At the corner of 97th Street and 108th Avenue is **St. Josephat's Ukrainian Catholic Cathedral** ★. Among Edmonton's several Ukrainian churches, this is the most elaborate and is worth a stop

for its lovely decor and artwork. One block to the east, 96th Street is recognized in *Ripley's Believe It or Not* as the street with the highest concentration of churches (16). It is appropriately known as Church Street.

At 110th Avenue and 95th Street you'll find the **Ukrainian Canadian Archives and Museum of Alberta** ★ *(donations; Tue-Fri 10am to 5pm, Sat noon to 5pm; 9543 110th Ave., ☎424-7580)*, which houses one of the largest displays of Ukrainian archives in Canada. The lives of Ukrainian pioneers in the early 1900s are chronicled through artifacts and photographs. About 10 blocks to the west, the smaller **Ukrainian Museum of Canada** ★ *(free admission; mid-May to late Aug, Mon-Fri 9am to 4pm, Sep to mid-May by appointment;*

● ATTRACTIONS

Tour A: Downtown and North of the North Saskatchewan River
1. Francis Winspear Centre for Music
2. Edmonton Art Gallery
3. St. Josephat's Ukrainian Catholic Cathedral
4. Ukrainian Canadian Archives et Museum of Alberta
5. Ukrainian Museum of Canada
6. Chinatown Gate
7. Alberta Legislature Building

Tour B: Old Strathcona and South of the North Saskatchewan River
8. Rutherford House
9. John Walter Museum
10. C&E Railway Museum
11. Telephone Historical Information Centre
12. Strathcona Farmer's Market

Tour C: Other Sights
13. Muttart Conservatory

○ ACCOMMODATIONS

1. Alberta Place Suite
2. Best Western City Centre
3. Days Inn Downtown
4. Delta Edmonton Centre Suite Hotel
5. Econo Lodge
6. Edmonton House Suite Hotel
7. Fairmont Hotel Macdonald
8. Grand Hotel
9. Hostelling Internation Edmonton
10. Inn on Seventh
11. Thornton Court Hotel
12. Union Bank Inn Hotel
13. Varscona
14. Westin Edmonton Hotel

⬡ RESTAURANTS

1. Bagel Tree
2. Bee-Bell Health Bakery
3. Bistro Praha
4. Block 1912
5. Café de la Gare
6. Café Select
7. Chianti Café
8. De Vine's Restaurant & Lounge
9. Funky Pickle Pizza Co.
10. Hardware Grill
11. Hy's Steakloft
12. Julio's Barrio
13. Packrat Louie Kitchen & Bar
14. Symposium
15. Turtle Creek
16. Unheard of Restaurant

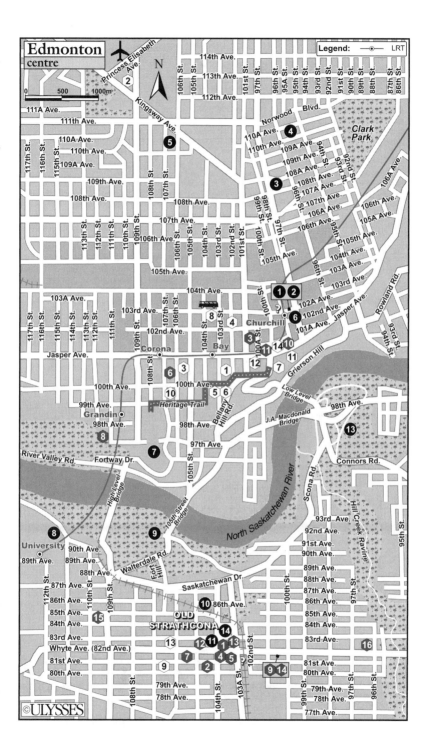

10611 110th Ave., ☎466-4216) displays a collection of Ukrainian costumes, Easter eggs, and household items.

Retrace your steps along 97th Street and make your way over to 100th Street, below Jasper Avenue.

In true Canadian Pacific tradition, the Chateau-style **Fairmont Hotel Macdonald** ★★ *(10065 100th St.)* is Edmonton's ritziest place to stay (see p 396) and was for many years the place to see and be seen in Edmonton. Completed in 1915 by the Grand Trunk Railway, it was designed by Montréal architects Ross and MacFarlane. The wrecker's ball came close to falling in 1983 when the hotel closed. A $28-million restoration, however, brought the Macdonald back in all its splendour. If you aren't staying here, at least pop in to use the facilities, or better yet, enjoy a drink overlooking the river from the hotel's suave bar, Confederation Lounge.

The next stop on the tour is the Alberta Legislature Building. It is a fair walk to get there from the Hotel Macdonald, but a pleasant one nevertheless, along the tree-lined **Heritage Trail** ★★★. This historic fur-traders' route from Old Town to the site of Old Fort Edmonton is a 30min walk that follows the river bank for most of its length. A red-brick sidewalk, antique light standards and street signs will keep you on the right track. The river views along Macdonald Drive are remarkable, especially at sunset.

The 16-storey vaulted dome of the Edwardian **Alberta Legislature Building** ★★ *(free admission; May to mid-*

Oct Mon-Fri 8:30am to 5pm, Sat and Sun 9am to 5pm; mid-Oct to Apr weekdays 9am to 4:30pm, weekends noon to 5pm; guided tours every hour in the morning and every 30min in the afternoon; 107th St. at 97th Ave., ☎427-7362) is a landmark in Edmonton's skyline.

Sandstone from Calgary, marble from Québec, Pennsylvania and Italy, and mahogany from Belize were used to build the seat of Alberta government in 1912. At the time, the Legislature stood next to the original Fort Edmonton, but today it is surrounded by gardens and fountains. Be sure to visit the government greenhouses on the south grounds. Tours begin at the Interpretive Centre where Alberta's and Canada's parliamentary tradition is explained.

Tour B: Old Strathcona and South of the River

Cross the High Level Bridge, continue along 109th Street, turn right on 88th Avenue, turn right again on 110th Street, and then left on Saskatchewan Drive to Rutherford House.

Rutherford House ★ *($3; mid-May to early Sep every day 9am to 5pm; Sep to May Tue to Sun noon to 5pm; 11153 Saskatchewan Dr., ☎427-3995)* is the classic Edwardian former home of Alberta's first premier, Dr. A.C. Rutherford. Guides in pe-

riod costume bake scones in a wood stove, offer craft demonstrations, lead visitors through the elegantly restored mansion and operate a tea room in the summer *(☎422-2697)*.

If it is Sunday, return to 88th Avenue and head east. It becomes Walterdale Road; follow it to Queen Elizabeth Park Road and turn left into the parking lot of the John Walter Museum.

The **John Walter Museum** *(free admission; Sun 1pm to 4pm, until 5pm beg Apr to late Aug; 10627 93rd Ave., Kinsmen Park, ☎496-4852)* is in fact made up of three houses, each built by John Walter between 1874 and 1900. Walter manned a ferry across the North Saskatchewan River, and his first house was used as a rest spot for travellers. Exhibits outline the growth of Edmonton over this period.

Continue your tour by heading to **Old Strathcona** ★★★. Once a city independent of Edmonton, Strathcona was founded when the Calgary and Edmonton Railway Company's rail line ended here in 1891. Brick buildings from that era still remain in this historic district, which is the best-preserved in Edmonton. While the area north of the North Saskatchewan River is clean, crisp and new with the unfinished feel of a boom town, south of the river, in Old Strathcona, a sense of character is much more tangible. Here an artistic, cosmopolitan and historic atmosphere

Alberta Legislature Building

prevails. Walking tour brochures are available from the **Old Strathcona Foundation** *(Mon-Fri 8:30am to 4:30pm; 10324 Whyte Ave., suite 401, ☎433-5866).*

Three other interesting stops along the way are the **C&E Railway Museum** *(donation; Jun to early Sep Wed to Sun 10am to 4pm; 10447 86th Ave. NW, ☎433-9739),* housed in a replica of the original railway station; the **Telephone Historical Information Centre** ★ *($3; Tue-Fri 10am to 4pm, Sat noon to 4pm; 10437 83rd Ave., ☎441-2077),* housed in the original telephone exchange, where you'll get the real story behind switchboards and manholes; and finally the **Strathcona Farmer's Market** ★ *(year-round, Sat 8am to 3pm; 10310 83rd Ave., ☎439-1844)* on 83rd Avenue between 104th Street and 103rd Street, where fresh produce, crafts and plenty of little treasures can be bought. On the corner of Whyte Avenue and 103rd Street is the **Caboose Tourist Information Centre** where you can pick up brochures for walking tours of historic Old Strathcona.

Next take a stroll along **Whyte Avenue** *(82nd Avenue)* to explore the shops and cafés and soak up the atmosphere.

Tour C: Other Attractions

The city has a handful of other sights that merit a visit and are best reached by public transit or by car.

The four glass-pyramid greenhouses of the **Muttart Conservatory** ★★★ *($5; Mon to Fri 9am to 6pm, Sat and Sun 11am to 6pm; 9626 96A St., off 98th Ave., ☎496-8755)* are another of the landmarks of Edmonton's skyline. Flourishing beneath three of these pyramids are floral displays of arid, temperate and tropical climates, respectively. Every month a new, vivid floral display is put together under the fourth pyramid. The conservatory is accessible from bus no. 45 or 51 south on 100th Street.

About 6km west of downtown is the **Provincial Museum and Archives of Alberta** ★★ *($7; Sat to Thu 9am to 5pm, Fri 9am to 9pm; 12845 102 Ave., ☎453-9100, www.pma.edmonton.ab.ca).* The natural and human history of Alberta is traced from the Cretaceous period and through the Ice Age to the pictographs of the province's earliest Aboriginal peoples. The Syncrude Gallery of Aboriginal Culture explores the 11,000-year history of Aboriginal people in an interesting multi-media exhibit. The habitat gallery reproduces Alberta's four natural regions while the Bug Room is abuzz with exotic live insects. Travelling exhibits complement the permanent collection.

Government House ★ *(Sun 11am to 4:30pm; closed mid-Dec to end Jan; free guided tours every half-hour, ☎427-2281),* the former residence of Alberta's lieutenant-governor, is located beside the Provincial Museum. The three-storey sandstone mansion features the original library, oak-panelling along with newly renovated conference rooms. Take bus #1 along Jasper Avenue, or bus #116 along 102nd Avenue.

Also north of the river is the **Odyssium** ★ *($9.95; Sun-Thu 10am to 5pm, Fri and Sat 10am to 9pm; 11211 142nd St., ☎451-3344, www.odyssium.com),* formerly the Edmonton Space and Science Centre. All sorts of fascinating interactive exhibits are sure to keep the young and old busy in this newly expanded science museum. You can experience how our bodies work through 3-D models or solve a crime by collecting clues and analysing them in a lab. You can even explore all aspects of space exploration or experience the science of sport. The Forensics Gallery is now home to the collection that was formerly displayed in the Edmonton Police Museum (now closed). The gallery traces the history of law enforcement in Alberta through uniforms, handcuffs and other artifacts. The Margaret Ziedler Star Theatre presents multimedia shows. An IMAX theatre is also on site (see p 400).

In the North Saskatchewan River Valley, off Whitemud and Fox drives, lies **Fort Edmonton Park** ★★★ *($8; mid-May to late Jun Mon-Fri 10am to 4pm, Sat and Sun 10am to 6pm; late Jun to early Sep every day 10am to 6pm; Sep Sun only 10am to 6pm; open other days for wagon tours, ☎496-8787).* This is Canada's largest historic park and home to an authentic reconstruction of Fort Edmonton as it stood in 1846. Four historic villages recreate different periods at the fort: the fur-trading era at the fort itself; the pre-railway era on 1885 Street; the municipal era on 1905 Street; and the postwar era on 1920 Street. Period buildings, period dress, period automobiles and period shops, including a bazaar, a general store, a saloon and a bakery, will bring you back in time.

Reed's Bazaar and Tea Room serves a "proper" English tea with scones from 12:30pm to 5pm. Theme programs for children are put on Saturday afternoons. New additions to the park, such as a reproduction of the Selkirk Hotel, originally built downtown in the 1920s, and a reproduction of a 1920s midway and exhibition, are scheduled to open by the end of 2005. Admission is free after 4:30pm, but don't arrive any later in order to catch the last train to the fort,

Edmonton

and take note that you'll be tight for time if you choose this frugal option, so it depends how much you want to see.

For a lovely walk through the North Saskatchewan River Valley, follow the 4km-long self-guided interpretive trail that starts at the **John Janzen Nature Centre** *($1.50; mid-May to Jun Mon-Fri 9am to 4pm, Sat and Sun 11am to 6pm; end Jun to beg Sep Mon-Fri 10am to 5pm, Sat and Sun 11am to 5pm; rest of year Mon to Fri 9am to 4pm, Sat and Sun 1pm to 4pm; next to Fort Edmonton Park, ☎496-2939).* The Centre has hands-on displays and live animals, including a working beehive.

The Fort Edmonton Valley Zoo Shuttle operates from the University Transit Centre and between these two sights on Sundays and holidays between Victoria Day (3rd Sunday in May) and Labour Day (early September). Fares (one-way) are $1.60. Alternatively, bus #12 drops you at Buena Vista and 102nd Ave., from where you must walk 1.5km to the zoo.

North of the river is the **Valley Zoo ★** *($6; May to Jun every day 9:30am to 6pm; Jul and Aug until 8pm; Sep to mid-Oct Mon-Fri 9:30am to 4pm, Sat and Sun 9:30am to 6pm; mid-Oct to early May every day 9:30am to 4pm; at the end of Buena Vista Rd., corner 134th St., ☎496-6912),* a great place for kids. It apparently began with a story-book theme but has since grown to include an African veldt and winter quarters which permit it to stay open for that season. The residents include Siberian tigers and white-handed gibbons along with indigenous species. Kids enjoy run-of-the-mill pony rides and more exotic camel rides for a small extra charge.

Last, but certainly not least, is Edmonton's pride and joy, the **West Edmonton Mall ★ ★ ★**

(87th Ave. between 170th St. and 178th St., ☎444-5200 or 800-661-8890, www. westedmall.com), the world's largest shopping and amusement complex. You may scoff to hear that some visitors come to Edmonton and never leave the West Edmonton Mall. Then you may swear that you won't give in to the hype and visit it, but these reasons alone are enough to go, if only to say you've been.

There are real submarines at the Deep-Sea Adventure; the world's largest indoor amusement park; a National Hockey League–size rink where you can occasionally watch the Edmonton Oilers practise; an 18-hole miniature-golf course; a waterpark complete with wave pool, waterslides, rapids, bungee jumping and whirlpools; a casino, bingo room and North America's largest billiard hall; fine dining on Bourbon Street; a life-size, hand-carved and painted replica of Columbus's flagship, the *Santa Maria*; replicas of England's crown jewels; a solid ivory pagoda; bronze sculptures; fabulous fountains, including one fashioned after a fountain at the Palace of Versailles; and Playdrum, an entertainment centre featuring 150 games and attractions. Finally, the Fantasyland Hotel & Resort (see p 396) is a lodging option that truly lives up to its name...and, oh yeah, we almost forgot, there are also some 800 shops and services—this is a mall after all! It seems it is possible to come and never leave! Subject of more than a few doctoral theses examining postmodern culture, the West Edmonton Mall simply has to be seen and therefore merits its three stars!

If you can't afford the extra money to stay in an igloo or a horse-drawn coach, at least take a tour of the theme rooms at the **Fantasyland Hotel & Resort** *(free tour;*

every day 2pm; reserve ahead ☎444-3000, see p 396).

Parks

The **River Valley Parks System** *(Edmonton Community Services, ☎496-4999)* lies along the North Saskatchewan River and consists of several small parks where you can bicycle, jog, go swimming, play golf or just generally enjoy the natural surroundings. The amount of land set aside for parks per capita is higher in Edmonton than anywhere else in the country. Bicyclists are encouraged to pick up a copy of the map *Cycle Edmonton* at one of the tourist information offices.

Outdoor Activities

Golf

Edmonton is enjoying a golf boom of late, with a number of new courses opening. Among them is **Northern Bear** *(51055 Range Rd. 222, Sherwood Park, ☎922-2327),* the third Jack Nicklaus signature course in Canada.

The **Riverside Golf Course** *(8630 Rowland Rd., ☎496-4914),* overlooking the North Saskatchewan River in Edmonton, is one of the city's more than 30 courses.

Cycling

With its relatively flat terrain (besides, of course, the Rocky Mountains), Alberta is an ideal place to explore by bike. The **Alberta Bicycle Association** (*11759 Groat Rd.*, ☎*427-6352 or 877-646-2453*) can provide more information about bicycle touring in the province. There is also a map for bicycling in Edmonton called **Cycle Edmonton**, which is available at the tourist office.

Accommodations

Tour A: Downtown and North of the River

Downtown

Days Inn Downtown
$$
≡, ℜ, 🐕
10041 106th St.
☎*423-1925 or 800-267-2191*
⇥*424-5302*
www.daysinn.com
The Days Inn Dowtown boasts comfortable, modern rooms. This is downtown spot has a good quality to price ratio.

Grand Hotel
$$ bkfst incl.
10266 103rd St., corner of 103rd Ave.
☎*422-6365*
⇥*425-9070*
At the Grand Hotel you will be fascinated by Edmonton's cowboy past. With its tavern, diner, dance hall and 75 anonymous dark rooms, the Grand Hotel seems right out of one of Lucky Luke's comic strips. Despite its minimal comfort and lacklustre appearance, people come here for the price and location (the Grey-

hound bus terminal is right across the street).

Econo Lodge
$$
≡, ℜ, ⊛, 🐕
10209 100th Ave.
☎*428-6442 or 800-613-7043*
www.choicehotels.com
This Econo Lodge has 73 rooms including some suites featuring whirlpool baths. Parking and an airport shuttle service make this a good deal for those looking for lodging downtown. Rooms are nothing special, however.

Inn on Seventh
$$
≡, ℜ, ⊛, ⊘
10001 107th St.
☎*429-2861 or 800-661-7327*
⇥*426-7225*
www.innon7th.com
Fifteen of the nearly 200 clean and modern rooms at the Inn on Seventh are "environmentally safe," though this just means they are non-smoking rooms on non-smoking floors. Weekend rates are available. Facilities include coin-laundry machines.

Best Western City Centre
$$$
≡, ≈, ℜ, ⊛
11310 109th St.
☎*479-2042 or 800-666-5026*
⇥*474-2204*
www.bestwestern.com
This Best Western is not quite in the city centre and has a rather dated exterior. The recently renovated rooms are nevertheless very comfortable and pleasantly decorated with wooden furniture.

Thornton Court Hotel
$$$ bkfst incl
ℝ, ℜ, ⊘, 🐕
One Thornton Court (99th St. & Jasper Ave.)
☎*423-9999 or 877-588-9988*
⇥*423-9998*
www.thorntoncourt.com
Edmonton's newest downtown hotel boasts incredible views of the river valley and an outdoor terrace that literally hangs over the side of the valley. Its 200 rooms are

spacious and well-appointed and they sometimes have special promotions that make it a great value. Small pets are permitted in the hotel's smoking section for a $10 surcharge.

🐾 Union Bank Inn
$$$ bkfst incl.
ℜ, 🍽, ⊛, ⊘
10053 Jasper Ave.
☎*423-3600 or 888-423-3601*
⇥*423-4623*
www.unionbankinn.com
Edmonton's only boutique hotel is housed in the old Union Bank, built in 1911. This unique historic property is centrally located and has 34 individually designed rooms. Special touches like wine and cheese delivered nightly to your room, a business centre, and a full continental breakfast make this hotel a great place to stay.

Alberta Place Suite Hotel
$$$$
K, ≡, ⊘, 🐕, △, ≈
10049 102nd Street, near Jasper Avenue
☎*423-1565 or 800 661-3982*
⇥*426-6260*
www.albertaplace.com
As the name indicates, the Alberta Suite Place Hotel offers mini-apartments with kitchenettes and work areas. With its friendly staff and unpretentious, tastefully decorated rooms, this establishment is a perfect compromise between impersonal, luxury hotels and budget accommodation.

Westin Edmonton Hotel
$$$$
≈, ≡, ℜ, ⊘
10135 100th St.
☎*426-3636*
⇥*428-1454*
www.thewestinedmonton.com
The Edmonton Westin Hotel was built on the site of the first post office in Edmonton. This modern facility with 413 rooms is located in what is now the heart of the business district. The guests, mostly

from the business district, enjoy the restaurant, pool and enormous terrace – all of which exude luxury.

Edmonton House Suite Hotel
$$$$
ℜ, K, ≈, △, ☉, 🐾
10205 100th Ave.
☎**420-4000 or 800-661-6562**
⇌**420-4008**
The Edmonton House is actually an apartment-hotel with suites that boast kitchens and balconies. This is one of the better apartment-hotel options in town. Reservations are recommended.

Delta Edmonton Centre Suite Hotel
$$$$
ℜ, ◉, △, ≡, ☉
10222 102nd St.
☎**429-3900 or 800-661-6655**
⇌**426-0562**
www.deltahotels.com
This Delta is part of the downtown Eaton Centre shopping mall. This means that apart from the hotel's extensive facilities, guests have access to shops and cinemas. Rooms are comfortable and the suites are lavishly decorated.

Fairmont Hotel Macdonald
$$$$
≡, ℜ, ≈, ◉, △, ☉, 🐾, 🛏,
10065 100th St.
☎**424-5181 or 800-441-1414**
⇌**429-6481**
www.fairmont.com
Edmonton's grand chateaustyle Hotel MacDonald is stunning. Classic styling from the guest rooms to the dining rooms make this an exquisite place to stay. A variety of weekend packages in the summer are available, including golf packages and romantic getaways. Call for details.

West of Downtown

West Harvest Inn
$$
≡, ℜ, ◉
17803 Stony Plain Rd.
☎**484-8000 or 800-661-6993**
⇌**486-6060**
www.westharvest.com
The West Harvest Inn is an inexpensive choice within striking distance of the West Edmonton Mall. This hotel is relatively quiet and receives quite a few business travellers.

Best Western Westwood Inn
$$$
≡, △, ☉, ≈, ℜ, ℝ, ◉
18035 Stony Plain Rd.
☎**483-7770 or 800-557-4767**
⇌**486-1769**
The Best Western Westwood Inn is also close to the mall. The rooms are more expensive here but they are also much larger and noticeably more comfortable and more pleasantly decorated.

West Edmonton Mall Inn
$$$
≡
17504 90th Ave.
☎**444-9378 or 800-737-3783**
⇌**423-4623**
www.westedmall. com
Owned by the same company as the mall, this new hotel's best asset is that it is located across the street from the mall. All of the hotel's 88 rooms are comfortable and have two queen-size beds as well as all the other standard hotel amenities, such as coffee makers and hair dryers.

Fantasyland Hotel & Resort
$$$$
☉, 🐾, ≡, ℜ, ◉, △
17700 87th Ave.
☎**444-3000 or 800-737-3783**
⇌**444-3294**
www.fantasylandhotel.com
Travellers on a shopping vacation will certainly want to be as close to the West Edmonton Mall as possible, making the Fantasyland Hotel & Resort the obvious choice. Of course, you might also choose to stay here just for the sheer delight of spending

the night under African or Arabian skies or in the back of a pick-up truck!

East of Downtown

La Boheme B&B
$$$ bkfst incl.
K, ℜ
6427 112th Ave.
☎**474-5693**
⇌**479-1871**
www.laboheme.ca
Set on the second floor of the historic Gibbard Building and upstairs from the restaurant of the same name, La Boheme B&B occupies the rooms of a former luxury apartment building. All the rooms are charmingly decorated and equipped with kitchenettes, but you will find it hard to resist the gastronomical delights at the restaurant downstairs (see p 398).

Tour B: Old Strathcona and South of the River

The cheaper hotels are situated in Strathcona. We found two that we liked. With its 40 rooms located in one of the oldest wooden buildings in Edmonton, the **Strathcona Hotel** *($; sb/pb, 10302 82nd Ave, near 103rd Street;* ☎*439-1992)* is less expensive and more attractive than its neighbour across the street, the **Commercial Hotel** *($; sb/pb; 10329 82nd Ave.;* ☎*439-3981)*, which is clean and comfortable, but sometimes noisy. In both of these establishments, expect to pay extra for a private bathroom.

Hostelling International Edmonton
$
10647 81st Ave.
☎**988-6836 or 877-467-8336**
⇌**988-8698**
This 88-room member of Hostelling International Canada is located in the heart of Edmonton's Old Strathcona neighbourhood. It offers a spacious lounge, common

kitchen and parking, as well as Internet access and laundry facilities for members. There are both dorms and semi-private rooms available at a slightly higher rate. Its location near the North Saskatchewan River provides access to walking and cycling trails; bicycle rentals available. During the summer, the hostel organizes trips and barbecues and will take bookings for local attractions and recreation.

University of Alberta
$
116th St. at 87th Ave.
☎*492-4281*
⇄*492-7032*
www.ualberta.ca
Student residences at the University of Alberta are available May to August only. They have pleasant youth hostel style dormitories. Reservations recommended.

Southbend Motel
$-$$
K, 🐾, ≈, ℜ
5130 Calgary Tr.
☎*434-1418*
⇄*435-1525*
www.southbendmotel.ca
For a very reasonable rate, guests can stay at the Southbend Motel, where rooms are admittedly a bit dated, and for no extra charge use all the facilities at the Best Western Cedar Park Inn next door (see below). These include a pool, a sauna and an exercise room.

The Best Western Cedar Park Inn
$$$ bkfst incl.
ℜ, ≈, 🐾, ≡, △, ☺
5116 Calgary Tr..
☎*434-7411 or 800-661-9461*
⇄*437-4836*
www.bestwestern.com
The Cedar Park Inn is a large hotel with 190 equally spacious rooms. Some of these are called theme rooms, which essentially means there is a hot-tub for two, a king-size bed, a living room and a fancier decor. Weekend and family rates are available, and there is a courtesy limo ser-

vice to the airports or the West Edmonton Mall.

🌴Varscona
$$$ bkfst incl.
≡, ℜ, 🐾, ☺, ℝ
8208 106St.
☎*434-6111 or 888-515-3355*
⇄*439-1195*
www.varscona.com
The Varscona offers guests king-size beds, wine and cheese is served Mon-Sat 5:30 to 6:30 and a cosy fireplace for those cold Edmonton winters. In the heart of Old Strathcona, it is easily one of the city's best-located hotels.

Restaurants

Tour A: Downtown and North of the River

The **West Edmonton Mall's** Bourbon Street harbours a collection of moderately priced restaurants. **Café Orleans** *($$$; ☎444-2202)* serves Cajun and Creole specialties; **Sherlock Holmes** *($$; ☎444-1752)* serves typical English pub grub; and **Albert's Family Restaurant** *($; ☎444-1179)* serves Montréal-style smoked meat.

🌴 De Vine's Restaurant & Lounge
$$
9712 111th St.
☎*482-6402*
De vine's is located in a converted house overlooking the North Saskatchewan River Valley. Innovative and delicious dishes are served in its several small dining rooms and, in the summer, on the terrace, from which you can enjoy great views and spectacular sunsets. Service can be slow if they are really busy, but the chocolate pecan pie on

the dessert menu is worth the wait!

Syrtaki Greek Restaurant
$$$-$$$$
16313 111th Ave.
☎*484-2473*
The whitewashed and blue decor of the Syrtaki Greek Restaurant is enough to make you forget you are in Edmonton. Belly dancers animate the evening on Fridays and Saturdays. Fresh game, seafood, meat, chicken and vegetables are all prepared according to authentic Greek recipes.

Bistro Praha
$$$
10168 100A St. NW
☎*424-4218*
Edmonton's first European bistro, Bistro Praha is very popular and charges in accordance. Favourites like cabbage soup, Wiener schnitzel, filet mignon, tortes and strudels are served in a refined but comfortable setting.

River City Chop House
$$$
11811 Jasper Ave.
☎*482-1140*
Alberta is well known for its beef and this is one of the best places to sample it. A broad menu selection of various meat and fish dishes is complemented by one of the most elegantly modern dining rooms in Edmonton.

The Hardware Grill
$$$$
9698 Jasper Ave.
☎*423-0969*
Located in a historic building that once housed the city's most popular hardware store, this upscale restaurant specializes in seasonally inspired Canadian prairie cuisine. It has received a number of international awards for its extensive wine cellar consisting of more than 500 wines and has been recognized as one of Canada's finest restaurants.

Edmonton

Madison Grill
$$$$
10053 Jasper Ave.
☎421-7171
The Madison Grill is the Union
Bank Inn's (see p 395) magnificent restaurant. The dining
room is as impeccably decorated as the rooms. Its high
quality food, from the four
corners of the globe, has
earned it a place among the
top 100 restaurants in the
country.

La Bohème
$$$$
6427 112th Ave.
☎474-5693
La Bohème is set in the splen-
didly restored Gibbard Building. A delicious variety of
classic yet original French
appetizers and entrées are
enjoyed in a romantic setting
complete with a cosy fire. Bed
and breakfast accommodation
is also offered upstairs (see
p 396).

Café Select
$$$$
10018 106th St.
☎423-0419
The posh ambience at the
Café Select is deceiving. The
atmosphere is actually elegantly unpretentious, all the
better to enjoy the delicious
entrées featured on the evening menu of the week. With
a 2am closing every day, this is
the place for a fashionably late
meal.

Hy's Steakloft
$$$$
10013 101A Ave.
☎424-4444
Like its Calgary counterpart,
Hy's Steakloft serves up juicy
Alberta steaks done to perfec-
tion. Chicken and pasta dishes
round out the menu. A beautiful skylight is the centrepiece
of the restaurant's classy decor.

Tour B: Old Strathcona and South of the River

Bagel Tree
$
10354 Whyte Ave
☎439-9604
As one would expect, the
Bagel Tree makes its own
bagels, but it also sells bagels
imported from Fairmount
Bagels in Montréal, arguably
the best bagels around.

Bee-Bell Health Bakery
$
10416 80th Ave.
☎439-3247
Wonderful breads and pastries.

Block 1912
$
10361 Whyte Ave.
☎433-6575
Block 1912 is a European café
that won an award for its
effort to beautify the
Strathcona area. The interior
is like a living room, with an
eclectic mix of tables, chairs
and sofas. Lasagna is one of
the simple menu's best offerings. Soothing music and a
relaxed mood are conducive
to a chat with friends or the
enjoyment of a good book.

Café La Gare
$
10308A 81st Ave.
☎433-5138
Among the many cafés in Old
Strathcona, the Café La Gare
seems to be the place to be.
Outdoor chairs and tables are
reminiscent of a Parisian café.
The only food available is
bagels and scones. An intriguing intellectual atmosphere
prevails.

Funky Pickle Pizza Co.
$
10041 Whyte Ave.
☎433-3865
At Funky Pickle Pizza Co., the
art of pizza making is brought
to unparalleled heights. Of
course, at $3.75 a slice, it's
not cheap. But the price is
quickly forgotten as soon as

your teeth sink into the
whole-wheat crust, home-
made sauce, blend of cheeses,
fresh vegetables and spices—
a sheer delight. Since the
place is not much bigger than
a counter, it's best to take out.

Barb and Ernie's
$-$$
9906 72nd Ave.
☎433-3242
This is an exceptionally popular diner-style restaurant with
good food, good prices and a
friendly, unpretentious ambience. Breakfast is a particularly
busy time, expect to have to
wait a bit for a table in the
morning, though you can
always come later since breakfast is served until 4pm.

Chianti Café
$$
10501 82nd Ave.
☎439-9829
More than 40 varieties of
pasta are served at Chianti
Café located in Old
Strathcona's former post of-
fice. Reservations are recom-
mended on weekends.

Turtle Creek
$$
8404 109th St.
☎433-4202
Turtle Creek is an Edmonton
favourite for several reasons,
not the least of which are its
California wines and its relaxed ambiance. The dishes
follow the latest trends in
Californian and fusion cuisine
very well, though a little pre-
dictably. The weekend brunch
is a good deal. Free indoor
parking.

Julio's Barrio
$$-$$$
10450 82nd Ave.
☎431-0774
Julio's boasts an original
Mexican-Southwest decor
with *piñatas* hanging from the
ceiling, cactus coat racks and
soft leather chairs. The menu
features a good selection of
nachos and soups, plus all the
regular Mexican fare. Servings

are huge and the service is quick.

Packrat Louie Kitchen & Bar
$$-$$$
10335 83rd Ave.
☎433-0123
A good selection of wines and a nice atmosphere are mixed with interesting music. The menu offerings are varied and generally well prepared.

Symposium
$$$
10039 Whyte Ave.
☎433-7912
Right above Funky Pickle Pizza is Symposium, a Greek restaurant whose pleasant terrace opens onto Whyte Avenue. The friendly staff serves dishes that go far beyond simple souvlaki and Greek salad.

The Unheardof Restaurant
$$$$
9602 82nd Ave.
☎432-0480
The name fits and it doesn't. This restaurant is no longer unheard of, yet it is an exception to Edmonton's dining norm. Recently expanded, it offers both à la carte and table d'hôte menus. The menu changes every two weeks, but usually features fresh game in the fall and chicken or beef the rest of the year. Inventive vegetarian dishes are also available. The food is exquisite and refined. Reservations are required.

Entertainment

Vue Weekly and See Magazine are free news and entertainment weeklies that outline what's on throughout the city.

Bars and Nightlife

Barry T's (☎438-2582) on 104th Street is a nightclub that attracts a young crowd with a mix of R&B and dance music. **Urban Lounge** (*8111 105 St.*) attracts a casual crowd to its live shows and multiple activity rooms. **The Iron Horse** (*8101 103 St.*) has a great terrace attached to the old converted train station it occupies, with lots of room for the inevitable crowds. There is always something happening at the **Sidetrack Cafe** (*10333 112th St.*, ☎421-1326) resto-bar with its mix of comedy, rock and jazz acts.

The **Sherlock Holmes** (*10012 101A Ave.*, ☎426-7784) has an impressive choice of British and Irish ales on tap. The relaxed atmosphere seems to attract a mixed crowd. Other popular Irish pubs include **O'Byrnes** (*10616 Whyte Ave.*), the **Druid** (*11606 Jasper Ave*) and **Ceili's** (*10338 - 109th St.*). The **Yardbird Suite** (*11 Tommy Banks Way.*, ☎432-0428) is the home base of the local Jazz Society, with live performances every night of the week. A small admission fee is charged. **Blues on Whyte** (*10329 82nd Ave.*, ☎439-5058) showcases live acts.

The **Parliament Club** (*10551 Whyte Ave.*) is a popular dance bar among the college crowd while the **New City Likwid Lounge** (*10161-112 St.*) attracts a broad variety of live acts and an eclectic crowd of all ages.

The **Roost** (*10345 104th St.*, ☎426-3150) is one of the few gay bars in Edmonton.

Well known as Edmonton's premiere country bar, the **Cook County Saloon** (*8010 103rd St.*, ☎432-2665) offers lessons for amateur line-dancers and a mechanical bull for those closet cowboys looking for a wild eight seconds.

Casinos

Those who like to live dangerously can choose from Edmonton's five casinos, including **Casino Edmonton** (*7055 Argyll Rd.*, ☎463-9467); **Casino Yellowhead** (*12464 153 St.*, ☎424-9467); and **Palace Casino** (*West Edmonton Mall, Upper Level, Entrance 9 off 90th Ave.*, ☎444-2112). Horse racing takes place from March through October at the **Northlands Spectrum** (*Northlands Park*, ☎471-7378 or 888-800-7275, ext. 7378).

Cultural Activities

The **Citadel Theatre** is a huge facility with five theatres inside. A variety of shows are put on from children's theatre to experimental and major productions. For information contact the box office at ☎**888-425-1820** or **425-1820**, *www.citadeltheatre.com*.

The **Northern Light Theatre** (☎471-1586, *www.northern lighttheatre.com*) stages innovative and interesting works.

For some more classical culture, check out the offerings of the **Edmonton Opera** (☎424-4040, *www.edmontonopera.com*), the **Edmonton Symphony Orchestra** (*in the Francis Winspear Centre for Music, box office* ☎428-1414) and the **Alberta Ballet** (☎428-6839, *www.albertaballet.com*).

First-run movies are shown throughout the city; for locations and schedules pick up a newspaper or try *www.edmovieguide.com*.

Edmonton has a couple of large cinema complexes that have comfortable, modern theatres showing the latest productions. **Silver City** (*West Edmonton Mall*, ☎444-2400) has an IMAX cinema in addition to 13 comfortable theatres, and **South Edmonton Common** is located at the extreme southern end of the city. A number of smaller first-run movie theatres are scattered throughout the city as well as two repertory cinemas; **Princess Theatre** *(10337 Whyte Ave.)* and **Garneau Theatre** *(8712 109th St.).*

More spectacular cinematic events occur at the giant **IMAX** *($10; 11211 142nd St.,* ☎*451-3344)* theatre at the **Odyssium.** (see p 393).

Calendar of Events

Edmonton is touted as a city of festivals, and **Edmonton's Klondike Days** is possibly the city's biggest event. During the Yukon gold-rush, gold diggers were attracted to the "All-Canadian Route," which departed from here. The route proved almost impassable and none of the prospectors made it to the Yukon before the rush was over. This tenuous link to the gold rush is, nevertheless, reason enough for Edmontonians to celebrate for 10 days in July. Starting the third Thursday in July, festivities, parades, bathtub road races, sourdough raft races and a casino bring the city to life. Every morning, free pancake breakfasts are served throughout the city. For information ☎*471-7210* or *888-800-7275, www.klondike days.com.*

Other festival highlights include the **Jazz City International Festival** *(*☎*433-4000)*, which takes place during the last week in June. In late June and early July, **The Works Visual Arts Celebration** *(*☎*426-2122, www.theworks.ab.ca)* sees art exhibits take to the streets. The **Edmonton Heritage Festival** *(*☎*488-3378, www.edmontonheritagefest.ca)* features international food, crafts and entertainment during the first week in August. The **Edmonton Folk Music Festival** *(*☎*429-1899, www. edmontonfolkfest.org)* takes place the second weekend in August and tickets are recommended. The **Fringe Theatre Festival** *(*☎*448-9000, www. fringe.alberta.com)* is one of North America's largest alternative-theatre events; it takes place throughout Old Strathcona starting the second Friday in August for ten days.

Sports

The National Hockey League's **Edmonton Oilers** play at the **Northland Coliseum** *(118th Ave. and 74th St.,* ☎*471-2191 or 414-4400)*; the season lasts from October to April.

Shopping

Besides the obvious, the **West Edmonton Mall** (see Exploring, p 394) and its 800 shops and services located at 87th Avenue and 170th Street, there are regular malls scattered north, south and west of the city centre.

Downtown, the **Edmonton City Centre** was recently refurbished and now boasts an expanded variety of stores providing the downtown core a needed boost.

Old Strathcona makes for a much more pleasant shopping experience, with some funky specialty shops, bookstores and women's clothing stores along **Whyte Avenue** *(82nd Avenue)*, including **Avenue Clothing Co.** *(*☎*433-8532)* and **Etzio** *(*☎*433-2568)*, and along 104th Street. **Strathcona Square** *(8150 105th St.)* is located in an old converted post office and boasts a bright assortment of cafés and boutiques all set in a cheery market atmosphere.

High Street at 124th Street *(124th St. and 125th St. between 102nd Ave. and 109th Ave.)* is an outdoor shopping arcade with arts galleries, cafés and shops located in a pretty residential area.

Northern Alberta

N orthern Alberta, as described in this chapter, covers more than half the province.

This vast hinterland offers excellent opportunities for outdoor pursuits as well as the chance to discover some of Alberta's cultural communities. Distances are so great, however, that it is inconceivable to imagine touring the whole region unless you have all sorts of time and a car.

The following three tours explore the northern frontiers of Alberta, passing major attractions along the way. They run northeast to Cold Lake at the Saskatchewan border; north to Fort McMurray with its Oil Sands Interpretive Centre and then on to Wood Buffalo National Park; and northwest, to the valley of the Peace River and then up the Mackenzie Highway or into northern British Columbia (see p 231).

Tour A: Northeast to Cold Lake

Tour B: North of Edmonton ★

Tour C: Valley of the Peace ★

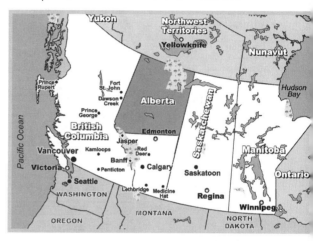

Finding Your Way Around

By Car

Tour A: Northeast to Cold Lake

From Edmonton head north on Hwy. 15, then Hwy. 45. Continue on the 45 and then north on Hwy. 855 to the Victoria Settlement Historic Site and Smoky Lake at Hwy. 28. Remain on Hwy. 28 all the way to St. Paul. At Hwy. 41 head south to Elk Point. Head back up Hwy. 41 to the 28 and on to Bonnyville and Cold Lake.

Tour B: North of Edmonton

This is an ambitious tour that cannot be done entirely by car. Fort McMurray is accessible by car, but Wood Buffalo National Park is best reached from the communities of Fort Chipewyan, Alberta or Fort Smith, Northwest Territories. The tour starts on Hwy. 2, north of Edmonton. At Hwy. 55 it splits, with one leg heading east and north to Lac La Biche and Fort McMurray and the other heading west for a scenic drive to High Prairie.

Tour C: Valley of the Peace

This loop tour follows Hwy. 2 from High Prairie to Grande Prairie, the circle being completed by Hwy. 32 and 43. The Mackenzie Highway (35) heads north from Grimshaw, while Hwy. 2 is the scenic route to Dawson Creek in northern British Columbia, where you can join the tours of the Alaska Highway outlined in the Northern British Columbia chapter (see p 231).

By Bus

Athabasca Bus Depot
Teg's Store
☎*(780) 675-2112*

Lac La Biche Greyhound Bus Depot
Almac Motor Inn
☎*(780) 623-4123*

Cold Lake Greyhound Bus Depot
5504 55th St.
☎*(780) 594-2777*

Slave Lake Greyhound Bus Depot
Sawridge Truck Stop, Hwy. 88
☎*(780) 849-4003*

High Prairie Greyhound Bus Depot
4853 52nd Ave.
☎*(780) 523-3733*

Peace River Greyhound Bus Depot
9801 97th Ave.
☎*(780) 624-2558*

Grande Prairie Greyhound Bus Depot
9918 121st Ave., north of the Prairie Mall
☎*(780) 539-1111*

Practical Information

Area Code: **780**

Alberta North
☎*800-756-4351*
www.travelalbertanorth.com

Mighty Peace Tourist Association
9309 100th St., or in the old NAR Station at town entrance
☎*624-2044 or 800-215-4535*

Grande Prairie Regional Tourism Association
11330 106th St.
☎*539-7688 or 866-202-2202*

Fort McMurray Visitors Bureau
400 Saskitawaw Trail, just north of Oil Sands Centre
☎*791-4336 or 800-565-3947*
www.fortmcmurrayvisitors.com

Athabasca Country Tourism
3602 48th Ave.
☎*675-2273 or 4035*
www.athabascacountry.com

Exploring

Tour A: Northeast to Cold Lake

Fort Saskatchewan

Established by the North West Mounted Police in 1875, Fort Saskatchewan, overlooking the North Saskatchewan River, was demolished in 1913, when it was taken over by the city of Edmonton. Fort Saskatchewan became an independent city in 1985.

The **Fort Saskatchewan Museum** *($2; Jan to Mar Mon to Fri 11am to 3pm; Apr to Jun and Sep to Dec every day 11am to 3pm; Jul and Aug, every day 10am to 6pm; 10104 101st St., ☎998-1750)* takes you back to the old town. It features nine buildings dating from 1900 to 1920, including the original courthouse, a schoolhouse, a country church, a blacksmith's shop and a great old log farm. There are tours in the summer.

Drive north on Hwy. 855 to the Victoria Settlement Provincial Historic Site and Smoky Lake, on Hwy. 855.

Smoky Lake

Before reaching Smoky Lake itself, watch for signs for the Victoria Settlement Provincial Historic Site, about 16km south of Smoky Lake.

Victoria Settlement Provincial Historic Site ★ *($2; mid-May to early Sep every day 10am to 6pm; 5025 49Ave., StPaul; ☎656-2333).* A Methodist mission was established here in 1862, and two years later the Hudson's Bay Company set up Fort Victoria to compete with free traders at the settlement. This wonderfully peaceful spot along the Saskatchewan River, once a bustling village, was also the centre of a Metis community.

The town was called Pakan, after a Cree chief who was loyal to the Riel Rebellion. When the railway moved to Smoky Lake, all the buildings were relocated; only the clerk's quarters were left behind. Exhibits and trails point out the highlights of this once thriving village that has all but disappeared. The tranquil atmosphere makes this a nice place for a picnic.

The little **Smoky Lake Museum** *(donation; mid-May to Sep, Mon to Sat 10am to 4pm, Sun 10am to 5pm; located in the Agricultural Complex)* holds a quaint and curious collection of pioneer artifacts that puts faces on all those courageous settlers. Photos, old dresses and linens, early farm equipment and stuffed, mounted wildlife are proudly displayed in an old rural school.

A drive east on Hwy. 28 toward the Saskatchewan border leads through a region of francophone communities. These include **St. Paul**, **Mallaig**, **Therien**, **Franchère**, **La Corey** and **Bonnyville**.

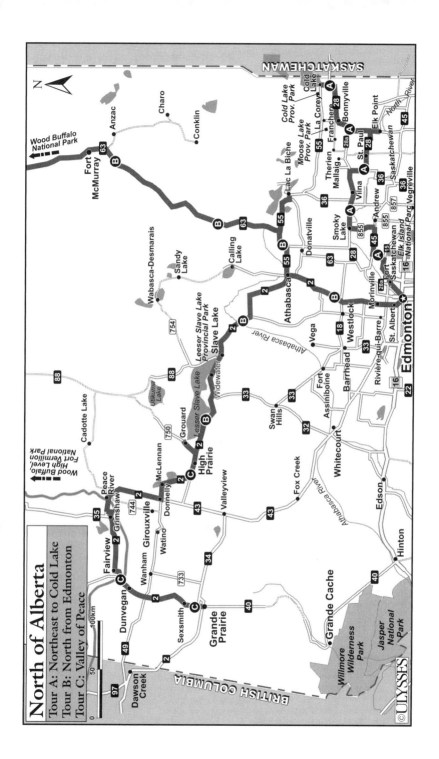

North of Alberta

Tour A: Northeast to Cold Lake
Tour B: North from Edmonton
Tour C: Valley of Peace

N

© ULYSSES

0   50   100km

★
St. Paul

The town of St. Paul began in 1896 when Father Albert Lacombe established a Metis settlement here hoping to attract Metis from all over Western Canada. Only 330 Metis, who had been continuously ignored by the government, responded to his invitation. Eventually settlers from a variety of cultural backgrounds arrived. The **St. Paul Culture Centre** *(Mon to Fri 8:30am to 4:30pm; 4537 50th Ave.,* ☎*645-4800)* examines the area's diverse cultural background. The **old Rectory** still stands a few blocks away *(5015 47th St.)*.

These days, residents of St. Paul are attempting to attract a whole other kind of visitor to their part of the world, something that may someday diversify the cultural make-up of St. Paul even more, that is if the **UFO Landing Pad ★** *(every day 9am to 5pm; near the tourist information centre at 50th Ave. and 53rd St.)* in town is ever put to use!

Continue east on Hwy. 28 then south on Hwy. 41 to the junction of Hwy. 646 and Elk Point.

Elk Point

For an idea of this town's history and culture one only needs to check out the colourful **100 Foot Historical Mural** *(west of Hwy. 41 on 50th Ave.).* From the mural drive east on Hwy. 646 to **Fort George - Buckingham House Provincial Historic Site ★** *($3; mid-May to Sep every day 10am to 6pm;* ☎*724-2611),* which marks the location of two rival fur-trading posts. Both built in 1792, the North West Company held the former and the Hudson's Bay the latter. They were abandoned shortly after the turn of the century and there isn't much to see today, save a few depressions in the ground

and piles of stones. An interpretive centre does a good job, nonetheless, explaining the excavations and the posts' histories. The North Saskatchewan River is close by and short trails lead around the site.

Drive north on Hwy. 41 to the 28, turn right toward Bonnyville.

Perogi (Ukrainian potato and onion dumpling) fans might want to take a jog left to **Glendon** where that increasingly popular fashion for huge sculptures of inane objects has struck again: Glendon is home to the world's largest perogi!

Bonnyville

Bonnyville used to be known as St. Louis de Moose Lake and today provides access to lovely natural areas. **Jessie Lake** is a wetland area that is great for bird-watching (see p 408) and **Moose Lake Provincial Park** (see p 408) has swimming, boating, walking and fishing.

Cold Lake

Home to Canadian Forces Base Cold Lake, this town actually relies on the nearby oil sands for its economic well-being. The nearby town of Medley is really just the post office, while Grand Centre is where all the shops are.

The lake is the seventh largest in the province with an area of 370 km². Its name is fitting when you consider that the surface remains frozen for five months of the year. The 100m depths are home to some prize fish (see p 409).

The **Kinosoo Totem Poles** are two 6.7m totems carved out of cedar trees by Chief Ovide Jacko. They overlook Kinosoo Beach, a popular picnicking spot on the shores of Cold Lake.

Cold Lake Provincial Park (see p 408) has fishing, wildlife viewing, beaches and camping.

★
Tour B: North of Edmonton

★★
St. Albert

Just north of Edmonton lies the community of St. Albert, the oldest farming settlement in Alberta. It began as a small log chapel in 1861, built by the Mary Immaculate Mission and Father Albert Lacombe. Born in Québec in 1827, Albert Lacombe began his missionary work in St. Boniface near present-day Winnipeg. He convinced Bishop Alexandre Taché of the need for a mission dedicated to the Metis population, and St. Albert thus came into existence.

Father Lacombe only stayed at the new mission for four years, and then continued his work throughout the prairies. Bishop Vital Grandin moved his headquarters to St. Albert in 1868 and brought a group of skilled Oblate Brothers with him, making St. Albert the centre of missionary work in Alberta. Grandin played an important role in lobbying Ottawa for fair treatment of Aboriginal people, Metis and French Canadian settlers.

The **Father Lacombe Chapel ★★** *($2; mid-May to early Sep every day 10am to 6pm; St. Vital Avenue,* ☎*459-7663)* is the oldest known standing structure in Alberta. This humble log chapel, built in 1861, was the centre of the busy Metis settlement. It was restored in 1929 by being enclosed in a brick structure. In 1980 it was once again restored and moved to its present site on Mission Hill, where it enjoys a sweeping view out over the fields and the Sturgeon River Valley. Mission Hill is also the site of the residence of Bishop Grandin, now known as the Vital Grandin Centre.

The **Musée Heritage Museum** ★ *(free admission; Jul and Aug Mon to Sat 10am to 5pm, early Sep to Jul Mon to Sat 10am to 5pm and Sun 1pm to 5pm; 5 St. Ann St., St. Albert; ☎459-1528)* is located in an interesting, contoured brick building called St. Ann Place. The museum houses an exceptional exhibit of artifacts and objects related to the history of the first citizens of St. Albert, including the Metis, Aboriginal people, missionaries and pioneers. Tours are available in both French and English.

Continuing north on Hwy. 2, you'll soon reach another area of francophone communities, some with poetic names like Rivière Qui Barre, before arriving in **Morinville**. The **St. Jean Baptiste Church** *(☎939-4412 for tours)* in town was erected in 1907, while the original chapel was built in 1891 under direction of Father Jean Baptiste Morin. There are a Casavant organ and large murals adorning its interior.

★
Athabasca

A little over 100km farther north is the town of Athabasca, located close to the geographic centre of Alberta. The Athabasca River, which flows through the town, was the main corridor to the north, and the town of Athabasca was once a candidate for provincial capital.

The town began as Athabasca Landing, a Hudson's Bay Company trading post, and a point along one of the river trails that led north. Traders and explorers headed west on the North Saskatchewan River to present-day Edmonton,

then overland on a hazardous 130km portage, cut in 1823, to the Athabasca River at Fort Assiniboine, southwest of the present-day town of Athabasca.

It was this pitiful trail that spelt disaster for Klondikers in 1897-98 on the "All-Canadian Route" from Edmonton (see p 387). A new trail, the Athabasca Landing Trail, was created in 1877. It soon became the major highway to the north and a transshipment point for northern posts and Peace River.

Hudson's Bay Company scows built in Athabasca were manned by a group known as the Athabasca Brigade, composed mainly of Cree and Metis. This brigade handily guided the scows down the Athabasca River through rapids and shallow waters to points north. Most scows were broken up at their destination and used in building, but those that returned had to be pulled by the brigades. Paddle-wheelers eventually replaced these scows.

The town was known as a jumping-off point for traders and adventurers heading north, and to this day, it is still a good jumping-off point for outdoor adventurers as it lies right on the fringe of the northern hinterland, yet is only 1.5hrs north of Edmonton. Cross-country skiing in winter, river adventures, fishing and even golf on a beautiful new 18-hole course in summer are some of the possibilities. A pamphlet featuring a historic walking tour is available at the tourist office, located in an old train car on 50th Avenue *(mid-May to mid-Sep every day 10am to 6pm)*. Athabasca is also home to Athabasca University, Canada's most northerly university, reputed for its distance-education programs.

Lac La Biche

East on Hwy. 55 lies Lac La Biche, located on a divide separating the Athabasca River system, which drains into the Pacific, and the Churchill River system, which drains into Hudson Bay. This portage was a vital link on the transcontinental fur-trading route and was used by voyageurs to cross the 5kms between Beaver Lake and Lac La Biche. The North West Company and the Hudson's Bay Company each built trading posts here around 1800, but these were both abandoned when a shorter route was found along the North Saskatchewan River through Edmonton.

In 1853, Father René Remas organized the building of the **Lac La Biche Mission** *($2, May to Sep every day 9am to 6pm, on the Mission Old Trail, ☎623-3274)*. The present restored mission lies 11km from the original site, having been moved in 1855. The original buildings, including the oldest lumber building in Alberta, are still standing. The mission served as a supply centre for voyageurs and other missions in the area and expanded to include a sawmill, gristmill, printing-press and boat-yard. An hour-long guided tour is available.

★★
Fort McMurray

About 250km north on Hwy. 63 lies the town of Fort McMurray, which grew up around the Athabasca oil sands, the largest single oil deposit in the world. The oil is actually bitumen, a heavy oil whose extraction requires an expensive, lengthy process; the deposits consist of compacted sand mixed with the bitumen. The sand is brought to the surface, where the bitumen is separated and treated to produce a lighter, more useful oil. The one trillion barrels of bitumen in the sands promise a vital supply future energy needs.

The **Fort McMurray Oil Sands Interpretive Centre** ★★ *($3; mid-May to early Sep, every day 9am to 5pm; early Sep to mid-May, Mon to Sat 10am to 4pm; 515 Mackenzie Blvd., ☎743-7167)* explains the extraction process, and much more, through colourful hands-on exhibits. The sheer size and potential of the operations are evident from the mining equipment and seven-storey bucketwheel extractor on display. Tours of the **Suncor/Syncrude Sand Plant** are also possible *($18; Apr to mid-Oct, Fri and Sat 12pm to 3:30pm; contact Visitors Centre, 400 Saskitawaw Trail, ☎791-4336 or 800-565-3947).*

★★
Wood Buffalo National Park

The boundary of Wood Buffalo National Park is approximately 130km due north as the crow flies. Though this does not seem that far, the park is difficult to access. Furthermore, only people with back-country experience should consider such a trip. Resourceful travellers who choose to venture to Wood Buffalo should do so from the communities of Fort Chipewyan, Alberta, or Fort Smith, Northwest Territories. For more information see p 408.

Back in Athabasca, take Hwy. 2 west to Slave Lake.

★
Slave Lake

Lesser Slave Lake, with an area of 1,150ha is Alberta's largest lake, accessible by car; on its southeastern shore lies the town of Slave Lake, once a busy centre on the route towards the Yukon goldfields. There isn't much to see in town, except of course the spectacular scenery across the

lake, which seems like a veritable inland sea in this landlocked province. Its shallow waters are teeming with huge northern pike, walleye and whitefish. Drive to the top of Marten Montain for a spectacular view. Lesser Slave Lake Provincial Park (see p 408) is the main attraction on the east side of the lake.

Continue west on Hwy. 2 to Hwy. 750 and Grouard.

Grouard

Founded in 1884 as the St. Bernard Mission by Father Émile Grouard, the village of Grouard, with a population fo under 400, lies at the northeastern end of Lesser Slave Lake. Father Grouard worked in northern Alberta as a linguist, pioneer missionary and translator for 69 years. He is buried in the cemetery adjoining the mission *(for a tour call the Grouard Native Art Museum, see below).* A display of artifacts lies at the back of the church, which has been declared a Historic Site.

The **Native Cultural Arts Museum** *(donation; Mon to Fri 9am to 4pm; in Moosehorn Lodge Building, Alberta Vocational College, ☎751-3306)* is an interesting little museum whose aim is to promote an understanding of North America's Aboriginal cultures through arts and crafts exhibits. Artifacts on display include birch-barkwork, decorative arts and contemporary clothing.

Tour C: Valley of the Peace

*From Grouard, the final stop on Tour B, continue on Hwy. 2 through **High Prairie**, home to great walleye fishing (see p 409), and **McLennan**, the "bird capital of Canada" (see p 408), to Donnelly.*

Donnelly

Donnelly is home to the **Société Historique et Généalogique** *($5; Mon to Fri 10am to 4pm, Main St. ☎925-3801)* which has traced the history of French settlement in Alberta. There isn't much to see, except perhaps an interesting map of the province that indicates the principle French settlements. Extensive archives are available for anyone who wants to trace their family tree.

Continue north on Hwy. 2 to Peace River.

★★
Peace River

The mighty Peace River makes its way from British Columbia's interior to Lake Athabasca in northeastern Alberta. Fur trappers and traders used the river to get upstream from Fort Forks to posts at Dunvegan and Fort Vermillion. Fort Forks was established by Alexander Mackenzie in 1792 where the town of Peace River now stands. Mackenzie was the first person to cross what is now Canada and reach the Pacific Ocean. Exceptional scenery greets any who visits this area, and legend has it that anyone who drinks from the Peace will return.

In town, the **Peace River Centennial Museum** *(donations; mid-May to end Aug Mon to Sat 9am to 5pm, end Aug to mid-May Mon to Fri 9am to 4pm; 10302 99th St., near the corner of 100th St. and 103rd Ave., ☎624-4261)* features an interpretive display on the Abroiginal Peoples of the area, the fur trade, early explorers and the growth of the town. All sorts of old photographs do a good job of evoking life in the frontier town.

Aboriginals, explorers, shipbuilders, traders, missionaries

and Klondikers all passed through what is now the town of Peace River when they took the **Shaftesbury Trail** which follows Hwy. 684 on the west side of the river. Take the **Shaftesbury Ferry** *(May to Dec, every day 7am to 11:30pm, ☎624-1753)* from Blakely's Landing to the historic Shaftesbury settlement.

Twelve Foot Davis ★ was not a 12-foot-tall man, but rather a gold-digger and free-trader named Henry Fuller who made a $15,000 strike on a 12-foot claim in the Cariboo Goldfields of British Columbia. He is buried on Grouard Hill, above the town. A breathtaking view of the confluence of the Peace, Smoky and Heart Rivers can be had from the **Twelve Foot Davis Historical Site** accessible by continuing to the end of 100th Avenue. Another lookout, called the **Sagitawa Lookout** *(Judah Hill Road)* also affords an exceptional view of the surroundings.

The Mackenzie Highway starts in the town of **Grimshaw** and continues through the larger centres of **Manning** and **High Level** where a variety of services including gas and lodging are available.

Fort Vermilion is the second oldest settlement in Alberta. It was established by the North West Company in 1788, the same year Fort Chipewyan was established on Lake Athabasca. Nothing remains of the original fort.

Beyond this, the towns of **Meander River**, **Steen River** and **Indian Cabins** do not have much in the way of services besides campgrounds; the next big centre is **Hay River,** near the shores of Great Slave Lake in the Northwest Territories.

Heading west of Peace River, Hwy. 2 leads eventually to historic Dunvegan.

★
Dunvegan

With Alberta's longest suspension bridge as a backdrop, **Historic Dunvegan** ★ *($3; mid-May to early Sep every day 10am to 6pm; off Hwy. 2 just north of the Peace River, ☎835-7150 or 835-5525)* peacefully overlooks the Peace River. Once part of the territory of the Dunne-za (Beaver) First Nation, this site was chosen in 1805 for a North West Company fort, later a Hudson's Bay Company fort. Dunvegan became a major trade and provisioning centre for the Upper Peace River and later the Hudson's Bay headquarters for the Athabasca district.

By the 1840s Catholic missionaries were visiting Dunvegan, including a visit by the eminent Father Albert Lacombe (see p 404) in 1855. In 1867, the Catholic St. Charles Mission was established, and in 1879 the Anglican St. Savior's Mission, making Dunvegan a centre for missionary activity. The missions were ultimately abandoned following the discovery of gold and the signing of Treaty No. 8, at which point the Dunne-za began leaving the area.

The fort operated right up until 1918, when homesteading became more important than trading, hunting and trapping. The mission church (1884), the rectory (1889) and the Hudson's Bay Company factor's house (1877) still stand on the site, as does an informative interpretive centre that is unfortunately housed in a rather ugly modern building. Dunvegan also has some camping sites.

Continue south to the town of Grande Prairie.

★★
Grande Prairie

As Alberta's fastest growing city, Canada's forest capital and the Swan City, Grande Prairie is a major business and service centre in northern Alberta, thanks to natural gas reserves in the area. The town is so named because of *la grande prairie*, highly fertile agricultural lands that are exceptional this far north. Unlike most towns in Alberta's north, Grande Prairie is not what was left behind when the trading post closed. From the start, homesteaders were attracted to the area's fertile farmland.

The **Pioneer Village at Grande Prairie Museum** *($3; early May to end Sep every day 10am to 6pm, early Oct to end Apr Sun to Fri 1pm to 4pm; corner of 102nd Ave. and 102nd St., ☎532-5482)* offers a glimpse of life in Peace Country at the turn of the century with historic buildings, guides in period dress, artifacts and an extensive wildlife collection.

The museum is located near **Muskoseepi Park**, a 446ha urban park with an interpretive trail and some 40km of walking and cycling trails.

The landmark design of **Grande Prairie Regional College** *(10726 106th Ave.)*, with its curved red brick exterior, is the work of aboriginal architect Douglas Cardinal.

The **Prairie Gallery** ★ *(Mon to Fri 10am to 5pm, Sat and Sun 1pm to 5pm; 10209 99th St., ☎532-8111)* exhibits a very respectable collection of Canadian and international art.

The town of **Dawson Creek** (see p 240) is kilometre/mile zero (0) of the Alaska Highway. It is reached by continuing west on Hwy. 2.

Northern Alberta

Parks

Tour A: Northeast to Cold Lake

Moose Lake Provincial Park

There was a Northwest Company post on the shores of this shallow lake in 1789. Trails skirt the shoreline and small beach, and a small marshy area is home to lots of birds. You can also fish for walleye and pike in the lake. Camping is possible (*$5 vehicle entry fee;* ☎437-2285).

Cold Lake Provincial Park

This is a small park on a spit of land south of town. Mostly forested with balsam fir and white spruce, it is the domain of moose, muskrats and minks. Hall's Lagoon in the park is good for birding. Camping is possible (*$15 per night;* ☎639-3341).

Tour B: North of Edmonton

★★ Wood Buffalo National Park

Wood Buffalo National Park is accessible from the communities of Fort Chipewyan, Alberta, and Fort Smith, Northwest Territories. Fort Chipewyan can be reached by plane from Fort McMurray twice a day, Sunday through Friday; in summer, motorboats travel the Athabasca and Embarras Rivers; there is a winter road open from December to March between Fort McMurray and Fort Chipewyan but it is not recommended; and finally, for the really adventurous, it is possi-

ble to enter the park by canoe on the Peace and Athabasca Rivers.

The park is home to the largest, free-roaming, self-regulating herd of bison in the world; it is also the only remaining nesting ground of the whooping crane. These two facts contributed to Wood Buffalo being designated a World Heritage Site. The park was initially established to protect the last remaining herd of wood bison in northern Canada. But when plains bison were shipped to the park between 1925 and 1928, due to overgrazing in Buffalo National Park in Wainwright, Alberta, the plains bison interbred with the wood bison, causing the extinction of pure wood bison. Or so it was thought. A herd was discovered in Elk Island National Park (see p 380), some of which were shipped to Mackenzie Bison Sanctuary in the Northwest Territories. As a result, there are actually no pure wood buffalo in Wood Buffalo National Park.

Those who make the effort will enjoy hiking (most trails are in the vicinity of Fort Smith), excellent canoeing and camping and the chance to experience Canada's northern wilderness in the country's largest national park. Advance planning is essential to a successful trip to this huge wilderness area and a Park Use Permit is required for all overnight stays in the park. Also remember to bring lots of insect repellent. For more information contact the park (*Box 750, Fort Smith, NWT, X0E 0P0,* ☎867-872-7900, *or Fort Chipewyan* ☎697-3662, *www.parkscanada.pch.gc.ca/p arks/NWTW/wood-buffalo*).

Beaches

Tour B: North of Edmonton

Lesser Slave Lake Provincial Park ★, next to Alberta's third largest lake, offers all sorts of opportunities for aquatic pursuits, including Devonshire Beach, a 7km stretch of beautiful sand.

Outdoor Activities

Golf

The **Athabasca Golf & Country Club** (*$30/18holes; mid-Apr to mid-Oct; just outside Athabasca, on the north side of the Athabasca River,* ☎675-4599 or 888-475-4599) is a new course with beautiful scenery and 18 challenging holes.

Bird-Watching

McLennan is the bird capital of Canada. Three major migratory fly ways converge here, giving birdwatchers the chance to see over 200 different species. The town has an interesting interpretive centre and boardwalk that leads to a bird blind.

The town of Bonnyville lies on the north shoes of **Jessie Lake**. These wetlands harbour more than 230 species of birds. The Wetlands Viewing

Trail leads through them to a series of viewing platforms. In the spring and fall, the best time to birdwatch here, you may spot osprey, bald eagles and golden eagles.

Fishing

Real fans may want to try their luck in the Golden Walleye Classic, which takes place in **High Prairie** the third week in August. With thousands of dollars in prize money it just may be worth your while. Anyone can join. For information call **☎751-3906** or *www.walleyesinc.com*.

Northern pike, walleye and trout are the catches of the day in **Cold Lake**. Boats and tackle can be hired at the Cold Lake Marina at the end of Main Street.

To fish **Lesser Slave Lake**, your best bet is to head out onto the lake. Boats can be hired at the Sawridge Recreation Area on Caribou Trail.

Accommodations

Tour A: Northeast to Cold Lake

St. Paul

King's Motel
$$
≡, ℜ, ℝ
5638 50th Ave.
☎645-5656 or 800-265-7407
⇆*645-5107*
King's Motel offers decent, clean rooms, most of which have refrigerators.

Cold Lake

Harbour House B&B
$$ bkfst incl.
ℑ, ℜ
615 Lakeshore Dr.
☎639-2337
⇆*639-2338*
The Harbour House is a lovely spot on the shores of Cold Lake. Each room has a theme, ask for the one with the fireplace and canopy bed. A real gem! There is also an adjoining tea room (see p 410). Each room now has its own bathroom, and a family restaurant offers breakfast, lunch and dinner.

Tour B: North of Edmonton

Athabasca

Best Western Athabasca Inn
$$
≡, ℜ, ☺, 🐾
5211 41 Ave.
☎675-2294 or 800-567-5718
⇆*675-3890*
www.bestwesternathabasca inn.com
The Athabasca Inn features rooms with filtered air. Business people make up the bulk of its guests. Rooms are clean and spacious.

Donatville

Donatberry Inn B&B
$$ bkfst.incl,
△
R.R. 1, Boyle
☎689-3639
⇆*689-3380*
Located about halfway between Lac La Biche and Athabasca on Hwy. 63 is the small town of Donatville, home of the Donatberry Inn B&B. This newly built house is set on a large property with a northern berry orchard nearby (home-made preserves of these berries are served at breakfast). The large, bright rooms all have private

bathrooms, and guests also have access to a whirlpool and a steam room.

Lac La Biche

Parkland Motel
$$
≡, K, ⊛
9112 101 Ave.
☎623-4424 or 888-884-8886
⇆*623-4599*
the Parkland Hotel features regular rooms and kitchenette suites, some of which have fireplaces and lofts. Good value.

Fort McMurray

Quality Hotel & Conference Centre Fort McMurray
$$$
≡, ≈, ℜ, ⊛
424 Gregoire Dr.
☎791-7200 or 800-582-3273
⇆*790-1658*
www.qualityhotel-fort mcmurray.com
With a good restaurant and lounge as well as a pool and a Billards Pub, the Quality Hotel and Conference Centre is the most reliable hotel or motel choice in town. It is located about 4km south of the centre of town.

Slave Lake

Sawridge Hotel
$$
≡, ℜ, △, ⊛, ℝ
just off Hwy 2 on Main St.
☎849-4101 or 800-661-6657
⇆*849-3426*
www.sawridge.com
The rather interesting exterior of the Sawridge Hotel houses some rather ordinary rooms that are just a tad outdated. Several of the rooms have refrigerators.

Northwest Inn
$$
ℝ, ≡, ℜ, ⊛, △, ☺
☎849-3300 or 888-849-5450
⇆*849-2667*
www.northwest-inn.com
Farther along Main Street towards town is the Northwest Inn. The rooms, though clean and modern, are un-

fortunately very plain and bare. Some of them are equipped with refrigerators.

Tour C: Valley of the Peace

Peace River

The Best Canadian Motor Inn
$$
≡, *K*, ℜ, ≈
9810 98th St.
☎*624-2586 or 888-700-2264*
⇰*624-1888*
www.bestcdn.com
The Crescent Motor Inn is located close to the centre of town and offers clean, rather ordinary rooms. Family suites with kitchenettes are certainly an economical choice.

Traveller's Motor Hotel
$$
≡, ℜ, *K*, △, ⊙, 🐎
☎*624-3621 or 800-661-3227*
⇰*624-4855*
www.travellershotel.com
The Traveller's Motor Hotel offers ordinary hotel-motel rooms as well as suite rooms. With a nightclub in the hotel, this isn't the quietest place in town. All rooms are newly renovated. Note that the price includes a special pass allowing free access to the golf course, municipal pool and the Peace River Sports Club.

Grande Prairie

Canadian Motor Inn
$$
≡, ℜ, *K*, ⊛, 🐎
10901 100th Ave.
☎*532-1680 or 800-291-7893*
⇰*532-1245*
www.canadianmotorinn.com
Grande Prairie's best hotel and motel bet is the Canadian Motor Inn, where each room has two queen-size beds, a refrigerator and a large-screen television. Rooms with fully equipped kitchenettes are available (*$89*) and there is also an executive suite with a whirlpool bath (*$150*). The rooms offer spotless, modern,

yet very comfortable accommodations.

Fieldstone Inn B&B
$$ bkfst incl.
☎*532-7529*
⇰*513-8752*
Set on a secluded lakeside property, the Fieldstone Inn B&B is a great find, as long as you have no problem with their new "celebrating marriage" policy whereby unmarried couples must stay in separate rooms. This newly built fieldstone house has a homey feel, thanks to the old-fashioned decor and classic styling. Some rooms have whirlpool baths or fireplaces. The balcony is an ideal spot to contemplate the rose garden and, if you're lucky, the northern lights.

Quality Hotel & Conference Centre Grande Prairie
$$
≡, ℜ, *K*
11201 100th Ave
☎*539-6000 or 800-661-7954*
⇰*532-1961*
www.qualityhotelgrandeprairie.com
The Quality Hotel and Conference Centre lies north of the city centre with services and shops nearby. The decor of the rooms and lobby is slightly outdated.

Restaurants

Tour A: Northeast to Cold Lake

St. Paul

King's Motel Restaurant
$-$$
5638 50th Ave.
☎*654-5656*
The motel's restaurant serves hot pancakes and French toast breakfasts, as well as lunch and dinner. The atmosphere is

nothing special, but the food is good and inexpensive.

Cold Lake

🖼 **Harbour House Tea Room**
$
615 Lakeshore Dr.
☎*639-2337*
The Harbour House serves light fare like sandwiches and cakes each afternoon.

Sun Flower Café
$$
902 Eighth Ave.
☎*639-3261*
While not recommended as a place to stay, the Marina View Hotel serves standard fare all day long.

Tour B: North of Edmonton

Athabasca

Green Spot
$$
4820 51st St.
☎*675-3040*
The Green Spot is open from breakfast to dinner and serves a bit of everything, from healthy soups and sandwiches (as its name suggests) to big juicy burgers.

Fort McMurray

Garden Café
$
9924 Biggs Ave.
☎*791-6665*
This is a fresh and cheery place to enjoy soups, sandwiches and good desserts. It is open all day and all night.

Athabasca Grill
$$$
424 Gregoire Dr.
☎*791-7200*
This restaurant at the Quality Hotel and Conference Centre is known for its huge Sunday brunch.

Slave Lake

 Joey's Incredible Edibles
$$
at the corner of Third Ave. and Main St.
☎849-5577
Joey's is a pleasant family-style restaurant with a complete menu including a wide choice of juicy hamburgers.

Tour C: Valley of the Peace

Peace River

Peace Garden
$$
10016 100th St.
☎624-1048
The best of the handful of Chinese restaurants in town,
the Peace Garden serves good seafood dishes, as well as North American standards like steak and pizza.

Grande Prairie

Java Junction
$
9931 100th Ave.
☎539-5070
Java Junction is a funky spot in the small downtown area with hearty and inexpensive muffins, soups and sandwiches.

 Earl's
$$$-$$$$
9825 100th St.
☎538-3275
Grande Prairie is home to one of Alberta's several Earl's restaurant outlets. With its outdoor terrace and reliable
and varied menu, it is a favourite in town.

Entertainment

Grande Prairie

The **Grande Prairie Live Theatre** *(10130 98Ave., ☎538-1616.www.gplt.ab.ca)* is a small, but popular, theatre company.

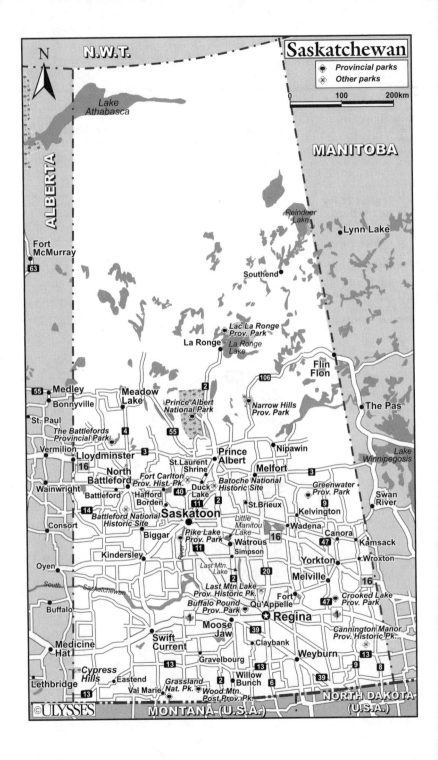

N

N.W.T.

Saskatchewan

◈ Provincial parks
⊛ Other parks

0   100   200km

ALBERTA

MANITOBA

Lake Athabasca

Reindeer Lake

Lynn Lake

Fort McMurray

63

Southend

Lac La Ronge Prov. Park

La Ronge

La Ronge Lake

Flin Flon

106

55 Medley

Meadow Lake

2

The Pas

Bonnyville

Prince Albert National Park

Narrow Hills Prov. Park

St. Paul

The Battlefords Provincial Park

4

55

Lake Winnipegosis

Vermilion

Lloydminster

3

Prince Albert

Nipawin

Melfort

3

North Battleford

16

St.Laurent Shrine

Fort Carlton Prov. Hist. Pk.

Batoche National Historic Site

Greenwater Prov. Park

Swan River

Wainwright

Battleford

Hafford Borden

40

Duck Lake

2

9

Kelvington

Consort

14

Battleford National Historic Site

11

Saskatoon

St.Brieux

Wadena

Little Manitou Lake

Canora

Biggar

Pike Lake Prov. Park

Watrous

16

Kamsack

Oyen

Kindersley

11

Simpson

Wroxton

Last Mtn. Lake

20

Yorkton

Melville

16

South Saskatchewan

Last Mtn. Lake Prov. Historic Pk.

Crooked Lake Prov. Park

47

Buffalo

Buffalo Pound Prov. Park

Fort Qu'Appelle

47

Medicine Hat

Moose Jaw

★ Regina

Cannington Manor Prov. Historic Pk.

Swift Current

39

Claybank

Weyburn

13

Cypress Hills

13

Gravelbourg

13

9

8

Lethbridge

13

Eastend

Grassland Nat. Pk.

2

Willow Bunch

6

39

Val Marie

Wood Mtn. Post Prov. Pk.

©ULYSSES

MONTANA (U.S.A.)

NORTH DAKOTA (U.S.A.)

Saskatchewan

In the popular
imagination, Saskatchewan is but one continuous wheat field, a place with little topography or cultural diversity.

And the traveller passing through parts of southern Saskatchewan in late summer can hardly be forgiven for thinking otherwise: this is Canada's breadbasket, after all, producing a full 60% of the nation's wheat in acres of golden fields that literally stretch to the horizon.

It is for this reason that the place is usually portrayed as nothing more than a cold monotonous patch of grassland between the lakes of Manitoba and the mountains of Alberta. And it's true: the entire province is subject to such bitterly cold winters that "plug-ins" – electric connections that keep a car battery warm overnight – are standard at a good hotel.

However, a little probing reveals a much richer identity than the stereotype indicates. The spectacular Qu'Appelle Valley cuts across two thirds of the province, slicing into the level plain with deep glacial creases running down to the river. Venture to Saskatchewan's two major cities and surprising architectural touches are revealed. In other areas, a preponderance of Eastern European churches crop up – painted church

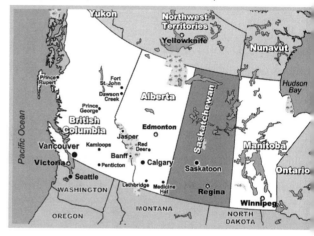

domes rising from the prairie like delicately painted Easter eggs, testifying to the province's solid Ukrainian influence.

Farther north, the prairies abruptly give way to foothills and then genuine mountains, woods and lakes – making it a bit less surprising to learn that there is more forest here – half a province worth, in fact – than farmland. Most of the major rivers in the province flow east into Manitoba, eventually emptying into Hudson Bay.

Saskatchewan's original First Nations include the Assiniboine and the Blackfoot. The Cree took on the most active

role during early European settlement, pushing aggressively westward to satisfy traders' voracious appetite for furs. Later, Sitting Bull came to southern Saskatchewan after routing General Custer of the United States Army at Little Big Horn. Eventually, most First Nations land in the province was sold or ceded to the government by treaty.

Louis Riel and the Metis, descendants of French voyageurs and Aboriginal people, made a significant mark on prairie history here in the hills and valleys of Saskatchewan. In 1884, after fighting for the rights of the Metis and being exiled to the United States, Riel was called up by the settlers of present-day Saskatchewan, which at the time was part of the vast Northwest Territories. Riel's small band, fighting for provincial status for Saskatchewan and better treatment of Aboriginals and Metis, defeated Dominion troops in several early skirmishes. But Riel never wanted a military conflict; rather, he hoped for negotiation.

The Canadians, led by General James Middleton, waited for the victory that seemed inevitable, since they outnumbered Riel's force – especially since a new coast-to-coast railroad was now capable of bringing reinforcements quickly. The Metis were finally defeated at Batoche in the last armed conflict on Canadian soil, and Riel was hanged as a traitor; he is still a hero in some quarters of the province because of his unwavering determination to retain his people's sovereignty. Saskatchewan joined Confederation in 1905. Today, Riel's efforts have been recognized with the renaming of Highway 11 from Regina, through Saskatoon, to Prince Albert, "The Louis Riel Trail."

Since Riel's time, few other individuals have made such a personal mark on the province, save John Diefenbaker. Diefenbaker, who grew up in a tiny homestead near the Saskatchewan River, rose from the post of a country lawyer to become Prime Minister of Canada in the early 1960s. His law office, boy-hood home, adult home and university office are all well-visited attractions. A lake also bears his name. Popular folk singer Joni Mitchell (born Joan Anderson) is probably the most famous contemporary daughter of the province: her formative years were spent in Saskatoon, and she is still known to drop by and sing an occasional set in a local club there.

Generally speaking, however, time still moves slowly in Saskatchewan. Today, farmers are diversifying and growing such crops as flax, and the mining of potash and the damming of rivers provide steady jobs, though wheat and oil continue to power the economy. The province's two major cities both contain just over 200,000 residents and strive to fill the short summer with festivities. Regina is the elegant capital, so English it appears never to have left the Crown, while Saskatoon has a large university and a thriving cultural scene, as well as proximity to many of the province's natural attractions.

Finding Your Way Around

By Plane

The province's two largest airports are located in Regina and Saskatoon; several major carriers serve the province, shuttling to and from Calgary, Toronto, Vancouver and other Canadian cities.

Air Canada's offices in Regina (☎888-422-7533, *www.aircanada.com*) and Saskatoon (☎306-652-4181) are both located at the city airport.

To get to **Saskatoon's John G. Diefenbaker Airport**, head directly north of the city approximately 7km. A chain of motels marks the approach. It is about a $12 taxi ride from downtown.

Regina Airport lies just southwest of the city, about 5km away; a cab costs about $10.

By Bus

Greyhound Canada (☎800-661-8747, *www.greyhound.ca*) serves the province's major destinations. In Regina, the bus depot (☎306-787-3340) is located at 2041 Hamilton St. In Saskatoon, the depot (☎306-933-8000) is at 50 23rd St. E, corner of Pacific Avenue.

The **Saskatchewan Transportation Company** also serves lesser-visited parts of the province. In Regina, STC buses (☎306-787-3340, *www.stcbus.com*) depart from the same depot at 2041 Hamilton St.; in Saskatoon, call ☎**(306) 933-8000** to reach the company.

By Train

VIA Rail's (☎800-561-8630 *from western Canada, www.viarail.ca*) cross-country Canadian service passes through the province during the night, making a stop here difficult, although not impossible; coming from the east, for example, the thrice-weekly train stops in Saskatoon at 2:40am. Eastbound trains pass through at 2:45am.

The Saskatoon station (☎800-561-8630), located in the extreme southwest of the city at Cassino Avenue and Chappell Drive, is the largest station and the usual point of embarking or disembarking in Saskatchewan; the cross-country train no longer runs through Regina. Smaller stations exist at Watrous and Biggar, stopping only on passenger request.

There is no train service to Regina.

Public Transportation

Regina Transit (*333 Winnipeg St., ☎306-777-7433, www.reginatransit.com*) serves the capital city and offers discounts if you buy a booklet of tickets.

Saskatoon Transit (*301 24th St. W, ☎975-3100, www.stnbiz.com/saskatoontransit/*) operates buses around that city.

Taxis

Capital Cab (*☎306-791-2225*) operates throughout Regina. In Saskatoon, try **Radio Cabs** (*☎306-242-1221*).

Practical Information

Area Code: *306*.

Tourist Information Offices

Tourism Saskatchewan (*1922 Park St. Regina, ☎787-2300 or 877-237-2273; www.sasktourism.com*) can be reached year-round. Provincial tourism information centres, scattered around the province on major highways, are only open during the summers; the lone exception is the centre in Regina (*1922 Park St., ☎787-2300*), which remains open all year.

Local tourism office hours vary a great deal, but the larger ones are open year-round.

Tourism Regina (*Trans-Canada Hwy. 1, ☎789-5099 or 800-661-5099; www.tourismregina.com*) is way out on the eastern fringe of the city, impossible to reach except by driving; it is well-stocked and friendly.

Tourism Saskatoon (*#6-305 Idylwyld Dr. N., ☎242-1206 or 800-567-2444; www.tourismsaskatoon.com*) is located downtown and remains open weekdays all year. In summer months, it is open on weekends as well.

Post Offices

The main **post offices** are located at 202 Saskatchewan Dr. in Regina and at the corner of Fourth Avenue N in Saskatoon.

Safety

The province is quite safe, even in its few urban areas. In case of mishaps, the **Regina Police Station** (*1717 Osler St., ☎777-6500*) and **Saskatoon Police Station** (*130 Fourth Ave. N, ☎975-8300*) are the places to call. There is also a **Royal Canadian Mounted Police** (*1721 Eighth St. E, Saskatoon, ☎975-5173*) and (*1601 Dewdney Ave. W, Regina, same telephone no.*).

The **Canadian Automobile Association** (*☎800-564-6222, www.caa.ca*) maintains offices in the province's most populous areas, offering roadside assistance and information to members.

Climate

Summers are generally warm and dry, with a great deal of sunshine. Temperatures frequently reach 30° C. Winter, however, can bring dangerously low temperatures and blinding snowstorms; Temperatures can plunge to below -30°C, with the windchill making it feel even colder. Travellers should take the appropriate precautions.

For updated weather forecast information in Regina, call ☎*780-5744*; in Saskatoon, call ☎*975-4266*.

Exploring

Regina

Though it's hard to see from downtown, the **Wascana Centre** ★ ★ ★ is a huge green space – reputedly the largest urban park in North America; even larger than New York City's Central Park – and the logical spot from which to begin exploring the city. This nearly 400ha complex includes a lake, a university, bridges, lawns, gardens, a convention centre and even a bird sanctuary. Walking trails and bike paths wind throughout, and there is ample parking and well-kept public washrooms.

A particularly interesting local institution here is **Speaker's Corner** ★ ★, a podium on the lakeshore where opinions may be proffered to the public. This is a serious podium: the gas lamps and birches come from England.

Saskatchewan's cruciform **Legislative Building** ★★★ *(free admission; May to Sep every day 8am to 9pm; Oct to Apr every day 8am to 5pm; Albert St. and Legislative Dr.,* ☎ *787-5358),* facing Wascana Lake and landscaped gardens and lawns, may be Canada's most impressive provincial capital building. Its huge dome rises above the city; at the entrance, the fountain is one of a pair from London's Trafalgar Square (the other is now in Ottawa).

Inside, ministers transact the business of the province – and in session, it's possible to sit in on the legislative machinations. An Aboriginal heritage gallery and architectural flourishes such as a rotunda also occupy the building; guided tours leave every half hour from the front reception desk.

Wascana Waterfowl Park ★ is home to swans, pelicans and geese; some migrate while others live here year-round. The small size of the pond allows visitors to get quite close to many of the birds.

The **MacKenzie Art Gallery** ★ *(free admission; every day 10am to 5:30pm; Thu and Fri until 10pm; 3475 Albert St.,* ☎ *522-4242),* located in the Wascana Centre at the corner of Albert St. and 23rd Avenue, showcases travelling exhibitions and a permanent collection. The gallery, funded by the bequest of a local attorney, includes a painted bronze

statue of John Diefenbaker standing on a chair.

Moving across the Prince Albert Bridge toward downtown, the **Royal Saskatchewan Museum** ★ *(free admission; every day 9am to 4:30pm; College Ave. and Albert St.,* ☎ *787-2815 or 787-2810)* occupies a nice corner of parkland. This is Regina's natural history museum and it was recently renovated; the exhibits are heavy on sandbox-style dioramas of dinosaurs accompanied by stentorian voiceovers, and there's more Saskatchewan geology here than a visitor could ever want or need to know. Still, this is the best place in town to see aboriginal Canadian artifacts and hear recorded Aboriginal voices. An impressive selection of black-and-white photographs of native leaders, along with videotape of some dances and ceremonies, makes a fitting closing to the walk.

A few blocks north of the museum, toward downtown, you will come across lovely **Victoria Park** ★★★ – an outstanding urban green space, the best on the prairies, right in the centre of Regina with a fantastic view of downtown's modern skyscrapers. A series of pathways radiate like spokes of a wheel outward from the war memorial at the centre; spruce trees add a lovely

contrast to the grass and gardens.

Nearby, Regina's **city hall** ★★ *(free admission; Mon to Fri 8am to 4:45pm; 2476 Victoria Ave.,* ☎ *777-7003)* is also worth a look while downtown. The lights on the roof are designed to resemble a queen's crown at night; tours, which must be booked in advance, offer a glimpse of the council chambers, foyer and forum. There is also a souvenir shop on the premises.

Scarth Street is downtown's pedestrian mall, which ends at a large forgettable shopping centre called the Cornwall Centre. Just a few doors before the centre, the **Regina Plains Museum** ★★ *(free admission; end-Jun to end-Aug Tue to Sat 10am to 4pm; Sep to end-Jun Mon to Fri 10am to 4pm; 1835 Scarth St.,* ☎ *780-9435 or 780-9434)* is a bit hard to find but worth the trip. Located four floors up in the same downtown building that houses the Globe Theatre, this stop makes a good introduction to life on the plains.

The museum contains the obligatory recreations of a plains chapel, schoolhouse, bedroom and post office. More interesting are a small display describing the migrations of Aboriginal people through the province; *"The Glass Wheatfield"* by Jacqueline Berting, a sculture of 14,000 individually crafted waist-high

Legislative Building

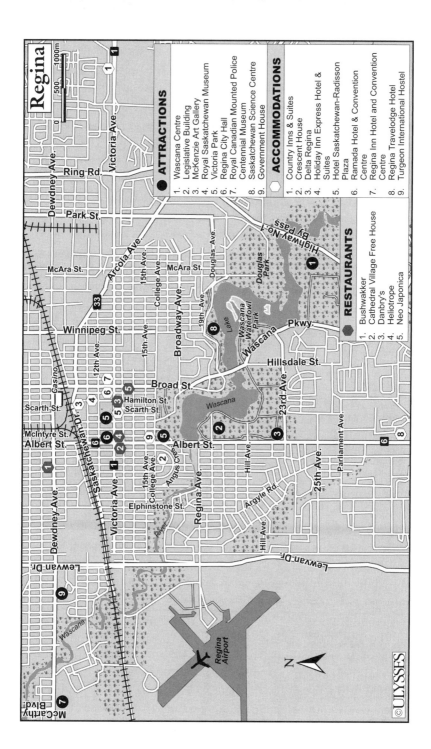

Regina

0   500   1000m

● ATTRACTIONS

1. Wascana Centre
2. Legislative Building
3. McKenzie Art Gallery
4. Royal Saskatchewan Museum
5. Victoria Park
6. Regina City Hall
7. Royal Canadian Mounted Police
   Centennial Museum
8. Saskatchewan Science Centre
9. Government House

⬡ ACCOMMODATIONS

1. Country Inns & Suites
2. Crescent House
3. Delta Regina
4. Holiday Inn Express Hotel &
   Suites
5. Hotel Saskatchewan-Radisson
   Plaza
6. Ramada Hotel & Convention
   Centre
7. Regina Inn Hotel and Convention
   Centre
8. Regina Travelodge Hotel
9. Turgeon International Hostel

⬢ RESTAURANTS

1. Bushwakker
2. Cathedral Village Free House
3. Danbry's
4. Heliotrope
5. Neo Japonica

© ULYSSES

wheatstalks; a display on Louis Riel's trial; period surveyor's tools that were used to carve up the prairie (on paper, at least); and an old police mug book containing criminals' photographs. The cons' offenses, described in cursive handwriting as "cheating at cards," "resident of a bawdy house," and the like, make for entertaining reading.

The only two major sites requiring a drive are just a few minutes west of downtown and nearly adjacent to each other. The **Royal Canadian Mounted Police Centennial Museum** ★ ★ ★ *(free admission; mid-May to early-Sep every day 8am to 6:45pm; early-Sep to May every day 10am to 4:45pm; Deudney Ave. W, ☎ 780-5838)* is a popular, well-laid-out attraction located on the grounds of the RCMP's training academy. Exhibits at this walk-through museum include many rifles, red-serge uniforms and other police artifacts dating from the formation of the R.C.M.P. force in 1873 to keep order and quell bootleggers in the Canadian Northwest. The story of the force's creation, the march west across the prairies – their inaugural 3,200km walk from Montreal – and eventual relocation to the Regina post, are all traced in detail here.

The museum is obviously strong on military items from all historical periods, but as a bonus it also contains some truly interesting material relating to the darker side of the pioneers' resettling of the west: First Nations land treaties, a buffalo skin incised with victories, Sitting Bull's rifle case, a buffalo skull paired with an ironic quote about the native buffalo hunt, the personal effects of Louis Riel, and so forth. On Thesday (Jul and Aug) there is a flag-loweting exercise, the Sunset Retreat Ceremonies, wich recall the RCMP'S military roots.

Government House ★ *(free admission; Tue to Sun, 10am to 4pm; 4607 Dewdney Ave. W., ☎ 787-5773)*, near the RCMP training grounds, has been home to some of the province's highest officials since the late 19th century. It is still the private home of Saskatchewan's lieutenant governor, but tours are offered. The rea room is open from March to December one weekend per month from 1pm to 4pm. Call ahead for specific dates.

The **Saskatchewan Science Centre** ★ *($7 IMAX, $12 IMAX and Powerhouse; Mon 6pm to 9pm, Tue to Thu 12pm to 9:30pm, Fri and Sat 12pm to 10:30pm, Sun 12pm to 9:30pm; at Winnipeg St. and Wascana Dr., Wascana Centre, ☎ 522-4629 or 800-667-6300)* is best known for its 17m IMAX cinema with sourround-sound. Another section of the museum, the **Powerhouse of Discovery** *($6.50; closed Mon, Tue to Thu 9am to 5pm, Fri 9am to 8:30pm, Sat and Sun 12pm to 5pm)*, presents exhibits and live talks, which are great for kids.

Southern Saskatchewan

The Trans-Canada Highway runs east to west through southern Saskatchewan, crossing wheatfields and the occasional town. East of Regina, it gives no hint of the spectacular vista lying just a few kilometres to the north, in the Qu'Appelle Valley, which runs parallel to it at this point. West of Regina the land is perfectly flat; this is the scenery for which Saskatchewan is best known, making humans feel, as the popular saying goes, like a fly on a plate.

★★★
Qu'Appelle River Valley

The Fort Qu'Appelle River Valley makes for a surprising detour: the river has cut a little valley in the otherwise flat countryside. **Route 247** *(north of the Trans-Canada between Whitewood and Grenfell)*, barely known by tourists, runs along the river as it dips through the brown and green hills. It passes **Round Lake** ★ ★ and then **Crooked Lake Provincial Park** ★ ★, beautiful lakes for swimming, fishing and sightseeing. A string of tiny tree-shaded resort towns provides campgrounds and the odd country store.

Continuing along the very poorly maintained Rte. 22, which takes you to a worthwhile, if isolated, destination: the **Motherwell Homestead National Historic Site** ★ ★ *($4; May and Jun every day 9am to 5pm, Jul and Sep every day 10am to 6pm; Abernethy, ☎ 333-2116)*. This impressive Victorian fieldstone house with gingerbread trim was built by W.R. Motherwell, famous for developing innovative dryland farming techniques at the turn of the century. The property, which more or less amounts to an estate, does not lack for anything: the grounds encompass a tennis court, croquet lawn, arbours, a herb garden and barnyard. The interior of the house is just as astonishing an example of high living in the midst of deserted prairie. Visitors can tour the house and grounds, and are even invited to help with the farm chores. There is a food concession stand on the premises.

At a bend in the valley, where the river feeds into a series of lakes, the small town of **Fort Qu'Appelle** charms visitors with its setting – tucked among hills – as well as a smattering of historic sites. The tourist information centre is situated inside a former train station. A former Hudson's Bay Company log cabin for which the town is named is now a small **museum** ★ *($2; early June to late Aug 10am to 5pm; Bay Ave. and Third St., ☎ 332-6443 or 332-4319)*. The fort was the site of a historic treaty ceding vast tracts of First Nation lands in Saskatchewan to the Canadian government. Fort Qu'Appelle is now home to the large tipi structure of the Treaty 4 Governance Centre.

Moose Jaw

Moose Jaw (pop. 30,000), a former bootlegging capital during US prohibition years, sprouts up in the flatlands west of Regina and offers visitors a glimpse into little-known aspects of the province's past. While it is now a sleepy little town where the parking meters still accept nickels, impressive bank buildings and the ornate city hall attest to its more glamorous past.

The Moose Jaw **Western Development Museum : The History of Transportation Museum** ★ *($6; every day 9am to 6pm; Jan to Mar Mon closed; 50 Diefenbaker Dr., ☎693-5989 or 693-6556)*, in a somewhat forlorn location north of downtown, serves up the history of Canadian transportation – everything from canoes, Red River carts and pack horses to vintage rail cars, automobiles and airplanes. A narrow-gauge railway runs behind the museum on weekends and holidays from late May to Labour Day. Also popular is the **Snowbirds Gallery**, devoted to Canada's national aerobatic team. The airplanes' artful manoeuvres come to life on a big movie screen in the flight simulator, in the museum's cinema.

Crescent Park ★, just east of downtown, is on the banks of the Moose Jaw River and is a pleasant place for a short walk beneath trees and over a picturesque bridge.

The secret underground passages of Moose Jaw were but a rumour until a car plunged through the pavement and wound up 4m

below street level in what are now referred to as the **Tunnels of Moose Jaw** ★ ★ ★ *($12; May to Jun, Sun to Thu 10am to 5:30pm Fri and Sat 12pm to 8pm, Jul to early Sep Mon to Thu 9am to 7pm Fri and Sat 9am to 8pm, call ahead for operating times during the remainder of the year; 18 Main St. N., ☎693-5261 or 693-7273)*. Today, visitors can take two guided tours of the newly renovated underground passageways. During the "Passage to Fortune" tour, interpreters explain how they were built by the Chinese labourers who had come to work on the railway and decided to go "underground," in this case literally, when Canada went back on its promise to grant them citizenship once the task was completed. The tour evokes the abysmal living conditions endured by the Chinese in these dark, cramped quarters. You'd better bring along your Tommy Gun for the second tour, "The Chicago Connection." The tunnels were later used as hideouts of a different kind, as bootlegging operations were set up here and gangsters from as far away as Chicago slipped into town, evading the long arm of the law. Guides in period costumes—and attitudes—take visitors through this 1920s bootlegging operation, with a twist.

It is said that the illustrious Al Capone himself made appearances here when things heated up strong south of the border. The tour brings to life the scintillating era of speakeasies and corruption. While the adjacent museum is less interesting, the tours of the tunnels are excellent ways to become immersed in the history of this once-electrifying town.

Claybank

Southeast of Moose Jaw, on Hwy. 339, is little Claybank

and its historic **Claybank Brick Factory National Historic Site** ★ *($3; Jul to Aug Sat and Sun 10am to 4pm; ☎868-4774)*. The plant operated from 1914 until 1989, one of Canada's two major plants of this kind during that time; its bricks were used in such buildings as Quebec City's Chateau Frontenac. The complex of high chimneys and dome-like kilns can be toured by arrangement, and there is also a tea room on the premises.

Gravelbourg

Southwest of Moose Jaw, a 115km detour off the Trans-Canada down Rtes. 2 and then 43, Gravelbourg is the acknowledged centre of French culture in Saskatchewan. A French-Canadian cultural centre and dance troupe both make their homes here. Most prominent among downtown buildings is the **Our Lady of Assumption Co-Cathedral** ★ ★ *($2; every day 9am to 5pm, guided tours Jul and Aug, ☎648-3322)*. Built in 1918, the church is a historic property and features wonderful interior murals painted by Charles Maillard, its founding pastor, over a 10-year period.

Nearby, on Fifth Avenue East, the **Musée de Gravelbourg** ★ *(early Jul to end-Aug 1pm to 5pm, 5th Ave. E., ☎266-5526 or 648-3349 off season)* preserves mementos from the original French-speaking settlers of the region, including the missionary Father L.P. Gravel, for whom the town is named.

Other Sights

Nearby, **Wood Mountain Post Provincial Historic Park** ★ ★ *(donation; Jun to mid-Aug everyday 10am to 5pm; ☎694-3659)*, a former Mountie post, is interesting particularly for its association with the Sioux chief Sitting Bull and his people. Sitting Bull came here in the spring of 1877 after defeating the United States Army at the battle of Little Big Horn; as many as 5,000 Sioux were already hiding in the surrounding hills.

The chief quickly forged a friendship with police Major James Walsh, but political pressure from both the Canadian and United States governments replaced Walsh with another officer who began a siege against the Sioux. The two buildings here, staffed with interpreters, recount the story in more detail.

Sitting Bull's former camp is located near the village of Willow Bunch in **Jean-Louis Legare Park ★**. Legare, a Metis trader, supplied food to the Sioux during their exile and also provisioned them for their long march back to the United States in 1881.

Approximately 40km north of Regina on Rte. 20 is **Last Mountain House Provincial Park ★** *(free admission; Jul to Sep, ☎787-2700)*, a small but interesting recreation of a short-lived Hudson's Bay Company fur post. Built of wood and local white clay, the post was established near a buffalo herd in the adjacent river valley in 1869. However, the buffalo moved west the following year, never to return.

Today the windswept park's displays include a fur press, trading store, icehouse for preserving meat, bunkhouse quarters for trappers and the more spacious quarters of the officers. During the summer, park interpreters are on hand to recreate the experience. Some 350km southwest of Regina, literally in the middle of nowhere, lies the town of **Eastend**. It was here that the nearly complete skeleton of a 65-million-year-old Tyrannosaurus rex was found in 1991. Excavation of this rare find, nicknamed "Scotty," began in 1994. Today, this

15m-high, 5.5-tonne T. rex is housed in the **T.rex Discovery Centre** *($3; summer every day 9am to 6pm, early Sep to summer Mon-Fri 9am to 5pm, Sat and Sun 11am to 4pm; ☎395-4009)* in Eastend, along with hands-on displays and educational programs for children. Scotty is sharing the premises with a 37-million-year-old brontothere, whose 2-tonne, 2m-tall skeleton was found in a nearby riverbed. Unlike Scotty's remains, which are still being worked on by experts from the Royal Saskatchewan Museum, the brontothere is fully assembled and on display.

Saskatoon

Set on the banks of the South Saskatchewan River, Saskatoon is Saskatchewan's hip address. Home to a large university, and a world leader in agricultural biotechnology, the city also offers a host of outdoor activities and cultural events year-round, including a jazz festival, fringe and folk festivals, and the famous Shakespeare on the Saskatchewan theatre series. Once a major stop on the trans-Canadian rail network, the downtown still has some impressive buildings from that era.

Among the city's most striking buildings is the castle-like railway hotel, the **Bessborough**, which was built by relief workers during the depression era, as were the graceful arched bridges that span the river from downtown.

While the Bessborough is Saskatoon's best-known hotel, the **Hotel Senator** *(243 21st St. E.)* is its oldest. Built in 1908 as the Flanagan Hotel, it boasted such extravagances as steam heating, hot and cold running water, and a telephone in

each room. Although the Senator can no longer be considered a luxury hotel by any stretch of the imagination, some of its former glory is still in evidence; the marble pillar at the foot of the staircase, the wood-panelled dining room with its original chandelier, and the marble floor of the lobby recall a more prosperous era in the hotel's history.

Saskatoon's most interesting commercial street is **Broadway Avenue**, south of the river. Downtown, **Second Avenue** is lined with small shops selling everything from CDs and LPs to books, pottery and international crafts. It intersects with **21st St. E**, which boasts the major banks, a few slightly more upscale shops, and some attractive older storefronts including the Art Deco facade of the former Eaton's department store (now housing military surplus store).

At the corner of 21st St. E and First Ave. is an interesting sculpture commemorating a chance meeting of two of the most prominent figures in Canadian history; it depicts Sir Wilfrid Laurier buying a newspaper from a young John Diefenbaker, circa 1910.

Historical sites are harder to find. The city is, in fact, rather short on cultural attractions. Nearly all of the good ones are concentrated downtown along the river. It's possible to see everything of note in a single busy day.

The **Ukrainian Museum of Canada ★★** *($2; Mon to Sat 10am to 5pm, Sun 1pm to 5pm, closed Mon, mid-May to mid-Sep; 910 Spadina Cr. E, ☎244-3800)* is a surprisingly good history lesson beneath a small roof. Through a series of walk-through rooms, the museum uses texts and simple articles to describe the Ukrainian people's Eastern European origins and persecution, their migration to North

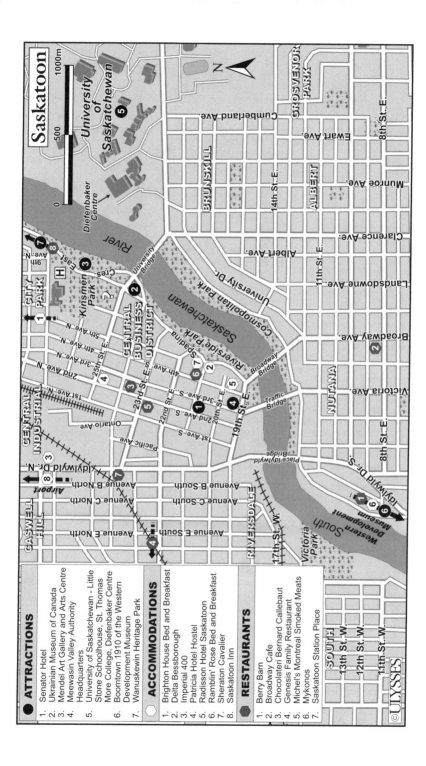

Saskatoon

0   500   1000m

N

University of Saskatchewan

Diefenbaker Centre

River

● ATTRACTIONS

1. Senator Hotel
2. Ukrainian Museum of Canada
3. Mendel Art Gallery and Arts Centre
4. Meewasin Valley Authority Headquarters
5. University of Saskatchewan - Little Stone Schoolhouse, St. Thomas More College, Diefenbaker Centre
6. Boomtown 1910 of the Western Development Museum
7. Wanuskewin Heritage Park

⬡ ACCOMMODATIONS

1. Brighton House Bed and Breakfast
2. Delta Bessborough
3. Imperial 400
4. Patricia Hotel Hostel
5. Radisson Hotel Saskatoon
6. Ramblin' Rose Bed and Breakfast
7. Sheraton Cavalier
8. Saskatoon Inn

⬣ RESTAURANTS

1. Berry Barn
2. Broadway Cafe
3. Chocolateri Bernard Callebaut
4. Genesis Family Restaurant
5. Michel's Montreal Smoked Meats
6. Mykonos
7. Saskatoon Station Place

© ULYSSES

America, their settlement of the prairies, and their subsequent endurance as a people. Highlights among the displays include a large section on the deep religious significance of the beautiful art of *pysanka* (Easter-egg decoration), a careful explanation of the distinctively domed Ukrainian churches and a delineation of where and why the Ukrainians settled where they did. Some intricate ornamental breads and examples of *rozpys* – the decorative painting of furnishings, walls and doors – are also nice touches.

The **Mendel Art Gallery and Arts Centre** ★★★ *(free admission; every day 9am to 9pm; 950 Spadina Cr. E, ☎975-7610)* is the province's best art museum. Its exhibits rotate quite regularly, and whether drawn from the permanent collection or just on loan, they're always interesting; concurrently showing might be American James Walsh's astonishingly thick acrylics in one gallery, several different multimedia installations occupying another and a collection of modern prints, paintings and other media works by First Nations artists sprinkled throughout. The museum also contains such amenities as a children's room, coffee shop, a good gift shop and a small but lovely conservatory.

A footpath from the back of the centre leads down to the river, hooking up with an extensive network of trails running north and south along both river banks. The **Meewasin Valley trails** ★★ *(www. meewasin.com)* extend more than 50km along the river, a joy for cyclists and walkers. The valley's other amenities include an outdoor skating rink and an urban grassland reserve. The **Meewasin Valley Authority Headquarters** ★ *(402 Third Ave. S, ☎665-6888)* provide an introduction to the river and the city.

Southeast, across the river, lies the large and pretty **University of Saskatchewan** ★★ campus. Several attractions of historic interest are found here, though some are only open during the summer when school is out of session. Especially quaint is the **Little Stone Schoolhouse** ★ *(☎966-8384)*, Saskatoon's first schoolhouse – it dates from 1887. The **St. Thomas More College chapel** ★ *(☎966-8900)* is worth a look for its mural by Canadian artist William Kurelek, and the university **observatory** *(☎966-6429)* opens to the public Saturday evenings.

Also not to be missed, the **Diefenbaker Centre** ★ *($2; Mon to Fri 9:30am to 4:30pm,Sat and Sun 12pm to 4:30pm; ☎966-8384)* preserves many of Diefenbaker's personal papers and effects, and his gravestone is located nearby on the university campus. Other displays include replicas of the former Prime Minister's office and Privy Council chamber. The centre – splendidly located with a view of the river and the downtown – is also famous for housing what is probably the most renowned piece of furniture in the province: a simple maple desk that once belonged to John A. Macdonald, the man considered the father of Canadian confederation.

On the outskirts of town sits the **Western Development Museum's Boomtown 1910** ★ *($6; every day 9am to 5pm; 2610 Lorne Ave. S., ☎931-1910)*, which reconstructs a typical western mining town's main street in movie-set fashion. More than 30 buildings make up the complex; like many of the province's museums, its exhibits lean toward agricultural equipment and farm implements. Also outside the city, about 4km away, is **Valley Road**, an agricultural drive leading to a number of

fruit, vegetable and herb farms in the area.

Finally, a 10min drive to the north leads to the wonderful **Wanuskewin Heritage Park** ★★★ *($6; mid-May to early Sep every day 9am to 9pm; early Sep to mid-Oct every day 9am to 5pm, mid-Oct to end Mar Wed to Sun 9am to 5pm, early Apr to mid-May, every day 9am to 5pm; ☎931-6767)*, perhaps the best native museum in the prairies. The area around Saskatoon was settled continuously for thousands of years before the first white settlers arrived; a river valley just north of the city was long used as a "buffalo jump" where local First Nations hunted and established winter camps. Now the property is open to the public as a series of archaeological sites – ancient tipi rings and a medicine wheel, for instance, can be walked to – plus an indoor museum and interpretive centre dealing with the history of First Nations people here.

"A people without history is like wind in the buffalo grass," says a panel in the museum, and the museum does indeed throw much light onto the Aboriginal peoples of the Plains. The differences among Cree, Dene, Lakota, Dakota and Assiniboine are carefully explained in one display, and their recorded voices can be heard by pressing a button. Other rooms in the centre host art exhibits and slide shows; talks and conferences; and an Aboriginal-foods café. Ongoing archaeological research is also conducted on the grounds.

Yellowhead Highway

Yorkton

Yorkton's main attraction is the **Western Development Museum's "Story of People" Museum** ★★ *($6; May to Sep every day 9am to 6pm; Hwy.*

16, ☎783-8361), which traces the history of the various immigrant populations that have made the province as colourful as it is.

Yorkton is also the site of western Canada's first brick Ukrainian church. **St. Mary's Ukrainian Catholic Church ★★** (*155 Catherine St., ☎783-4594*), built in 1914, is topped with a distinctive 21m-high cathedral dome. The dome was painted in 1939-41 by Steven Meush and is considered one of the most beautiful on the continent. Inside, there is beautiful icon work by Ihor Suhacev. If the church is not open, visitors can ask at the adjacent rectory for a look inside. The church also hosts an annual "Vid Pust" (Pilgrimage Day) celebration each June.

Veregin

Approximately 50km north off the Yellowhead, Veregin houses the **National Doukhobour Heritage Village ★★** (*$3; mid-May to mid-Sep every day 10am to 6pm; mid-Sep to mid-May prior booking only ☎542-4441*), an 11-building complex that throws light on one of the province's most intriguing immigrant groups. The Doukhobours came to Saskatchewan in 1899 and established a short-lived community here, eschewing meat, alcohol and tobacco in favour of an agrarian existence. They soon moved farther west, but this museum preserves the original prayer home and machinery shop. Also on display are a brick oven, bath house, agricultural equipment and blacksmith's shop.

Canora

Just 25km west of Veregin, Canora welcomes travellers with a 7.6m statue in Slavic dress. A tourist booth next to the statue operates from June until September to orient

visitors to local attractions. This little village is also home to a fine restored **Ukrainian Orthodox Heritage Church ★** (*Jun to mid-Sep every day 8am to 6pm; 710 Main St., ☎563-5482 or 563-5211*) Built in 1928, the church displays Kiev architecture and stained glass; visitors can obtain a key next door at 720 Main St. when the church isn't open.

Wroxton

Wroxton is some distance from the Yellowhead – 35km north – but interesting for its two Ukrainian churches on opposite ends of the village. Both domes are visible just north of the main highway, and can be reached by driving along one of the town's several dirt roads.

Around Wadena

In the Wadena area, **Big Quill Lake** and various other marshes on both sides of the Yellowhead offer good opportunities to view birds. The advocacy group Ducks Unlimited helps preserve many of these lands and interprets them for the general public. **Little Quill Lake Heritage Marsh ★**, best reached from Hwy. 35, was designated an international shorebird reserve in 1994 and is open year-round. This marsh hosts more than 800,000 migrating and resident shorebirds each year; visitors can hike, learn from interpretive signs and climb an observation tower.

St. Brieux

St. Brieux features a little **museum ★** (*donations accepted, early Jun to end Aug everyday 10am to 4pm; 300 Barbier Dr., ☎275-2229*) in a former Roman Catholic rectory. It contains artifacts of early settlers from Quebec, France and Hungary; tours here are conducted in both English and French.

Muenster

Continuing west, also near the Yellowhead, the small town of Muenster is notable for a beautiful twin-towered cathedral and adjoining monastery. **St. Peter's Cathedral, ★★** (*off Hwy 5; donations accepted; early Mar to end Dec, mid-May to mid-Sep every day, mid-Sep to end Dec and early Mar to mid-May 9am to dusk; closed Jan and Feb, ☎682-5484*), built in 1910, features paintings by Berthold Imhoff, a German-born count who later moved to St. Walburg, Saskatchewan, and became an artist. Approximately 80 life-sized figures grace the cathedral, with saints and religious scenes making up the interior. **St. Peter's Abbey ★★** (*Mar 1 to Dec 31, 8am to dusk ☎682-1777*) gives a sense of what the monastic life is like: a self-guided tour reveals the abbey's farm, gardens, print shop and so on. It's also possible to sleep a night in the monastery for a small donation.

★
Little Manitou Lake

For centuries, travellers have been making a trip to Little Manitou Lake to "take the waters." This lake is so high in natural mineral salts that a person swimming can't sink. In fact, the water is three-and-a-half times saltier than normal ocean water. These briny waters are unique to the western hemisphere, possessing natural therapeutic properties found only at a few places in the world—Karlovy Vary in the Czech Republic and the Dead Sea in Israel. The salts are reputed to have restorative powers. That's why a strange little tourist town has sprung up around the lake, itself oddly placed among barren hills.

The Battlefords

Battleford (pop. 4,000), former capital of the Northwest

Territories, was once important but is today overshadowed by its twin city of North Battleford across the Saskatchewan River. As usual, railway politics decided the fate of the twin towns. **Fort Battleford National Historic Site** *($4; mid-May to early-Oct every day 9am to 5pm; ☎937-2621)* recalls the original impetus for the townsite – a Mountie post – complete with four restored period buildings. The barracks house contains additional displays of historical interest, explained by guides in period police costume.

North Battleford (pop. 14,000) is often visited for the **Western Development Museum's Heritage Farm and Village** ★ *($6; early- May to early Sep every day 9am to 5pm; Oct to Apr 12:30pm to 4:30pm, closed Mon, Tue and holidays; ☎445-8033)*, a mostly agricultural museum featuring plenty of period farm machinery.

The town is also famous as home to artist Allan Sapp. The **Allan Sapp Gallery** ★ *(free admission, donations accepted; Jun to Sep every day 10:30pm to 5:30pm; Oct to May Wed to Sun 1pm to 5pm; ☎445-1760)* showcases the work of the prairies' best-known and loved Aboriginal artist. Sapp's paintings, recollections of Aboriginal life from a half-century ago, hang in the important museums of Canada and are displayed and sold here; the gallery, located on the ground floor of a restored Carnegie library, also contains hundreds of works by Sapp's mentor Allan Gonor.

West Central Saskatchewan

Poundmaker Trail

Highway. 40, also called Poundmaker Trail, is the former stronghold of the

Poundmaker Cree Nation. **Cut Knife** sports what is said to be Canada's largest tomohawk, a suspended sculpture of wood and fiberglass whose fir handle is more than 16m long and supports a six-tonne blade. The surrounding park contains the obligatory small museum. The legendary **Chief Poundmaker's grave** *(www.poundmaker.com)* is also in town, on the Cree Reserve. It is a testament to a man who favoured peace over war and surrendered his force of natives to the Mounties rather than continue to shed blood. There is an interpretive centre and you can even spend a night in a teepee.

Hafford

Just northeast of Saskatoon, near the village of Hafford, the **Redberry Lake Biosphere Reserve Highway 40** ★ *(☎549-2400 or 549-2258)* maintains one of the province's best waterfowl projects in a federal migratory bird sanctuary on Redberry Lake. It was named a UNESCO World Biosphere Reserve in 2000. Their motto is "we have friends in wet places," and the specialty here is pelicans. More than 1000 American white pelicans nest on the lake's New Tern Island; it's just one of 14 colonies of these birds in Saskatchewan. Boat tours are also available *(mid-May to mid-Sep; ☎549-2452 or 888-747-7572)*, and cost about $25 for approximately 1.5hrs.

Prince Albert

Prince Albert (pop. 39,000), the oldest city in the province, is a gateway in more ways than one. It is the largest town near **Prince Albert National Park** ★★★ *(☎663-4512)*, the site of a huge mill that converts the northern forests into pulp and paper, and the birthplace of three Canadian

Prime Ministers (see p 426). Though the town began as a fur post for Northwestern explorer Peter Pond in 1776, the town as it exists today was established nearly a full century later by the Reverend James Nisbet as a mission for local Cree.

The **Diefenbaker House Museum** *(free admission, donations welcome; mid-May to early Aug Mon to Sat 10am to 6pm, Sun 10am to 8pm; 246 19th St. W., ☎953-4863 or 764-2992)* is probably the most famous stop in town. It contains many of the former Canadian Prime Minister's personal effects and furnishings, and describes his relationship to the city.

The **Prince Albert Historical Museum** *($1; River St. and Central Ave.; mid-May to early Sep Mon to Sat 10am to 6pm, Sun 10am to 8pm, winter tours available by appointment; ☎764-2992)* brings local history into focus, beginning with native and fur-trader culture from the mid-1800s. There is also a second-floor tearoom with a balcony overlooking the North Saskatchewan River.

Several other museums in Prince Albert are also worth a look. The **Evolution of Education Museum** *(free admission; mid-May to early Sep every day 10am to 6pm; 3700 2nd Ave. W., ☎764-2992)* is located in a former one-room schoolhouse, and the **Rotary Museum of Police and Corrections** *(free admission; mid-May to Sep 10am to 8pm; ☎922-3313)* is inside a former North West Mounted Police guardhouse and includes a fascinating display of weapons fashioned by prisoners trying to break out of provincial jails.

Around Duck Lake

Southwest of Prince Albert, **Duck Lake** was the site of one of the most famous events in Saskatchewan history: the battle between Louis Riel and his band of Metis and the North West Police. The **Duck Lake Regional Interpretive Centre ★ ★** *($4; 5 Anderson Ave.; mid-May to early Sep every day 10am to 5:30pm; ☎467-2057)* describes the events as they unfolded, displaying artifacts from the Metis Resistance campaign, you can also climb a viewing tower of the battlefield grounds. A series of painted outdoor murals welcome the visitor.

About 25km west of Duck Lake, **Fort Carlton Provincial Historic Park ★ ★** *($2.50; mid-May to early Sep; every day 10am to 6pm; ☎467-5205)* dates from 1810, another in the string of Hudson's Bay Company posts in Saskatchewan. An important land treaty was also signed here. Today the site consists of a reconstructed stockade and buildings; a Visitor Centre with displays and interpretive trails explain how the fort was a Mountie post until the Battle of Duck Lake. Just outside the fort, a Plains Cree encampment – three tipis furnished in typical late-19th-century fashion – give a sense of what and how the natives traded with the English. The objects in these tipis include robes, skins, pipes, weapons and other ceremonial objects.

St. Laurent

St. Laurent Shrine ★ *(donations accepted; May 1 to early-Sep; ☎467-4447 or 467-2060)* makes for an enjoyable side trip in the area. Built in 1874 as an Order of the Oblate mission right on the South Saskatchewan River, and quite similar to the Our Lady of Lourdes shrine in France, it holds Sunday services at 4pm during July and August. Annual pilgrimmages also take place during those months; the tradition dates back to 1893, when one Brother Guillet's leg miraculously healed after he prayed to the shrine.

Batoche National Historic Park ★ ★ ★ *($5; early May to end-Sep 9am to 5pm every day; ☎423-6227)* is where Riel's story came to its end in March of 1885. The site, a peaceful agricultural valley where the Metis had settled after moving westwards, became capital of the Metis resistance when Riel challenged the English. Today, a walking path, museum and interpretive staff guide visitors through the remains of the village of Batoche, including the restored St. Antoine de Padoue church and rectory. There are also trenches and rifle pits used by the Mountie forces during their four-day siege of Batoche.

Parks

For futher information on Saskatchewan provincial parks: ☎*800-205-7070* or *www.serm.gov.sk.ca/saskparks*.

For further information on national parks, contact Parks Canada at *www.parks canada.pch.gc.ca/parks*.

Southern Saskatchewan

Cannington Manor Provincial Historic Park ★ *($7; May to Sep 10am to 6pm; ☎577-2622 or 739-5251)* recounts a short-lived experiment by the Englishman Captain Edward Pierce. Pierce tried to form a utopian colony based on agriculture here, and for a while it worked. Days consisted of a combination of working the fields and diversions such as fox hunts, cricket, horse races and afternoon tea. The experiment did not survive, but the manor features period antiques and farm tools used on the site. Six other buildings – some original, some reconstructed –

complete the park. Camping available.

Buffalo Pound Provincial Park ★ *($7; ☎694-3659)*, 23km northeast of Moose Jaw, presents a variety of recreational choices, including – most popularly – a chance to view grazing bison. A number of hiking trails wind through the dips and rises of the Qu'Appelle Valley: the trail tells the story of the Charles Nicolle Homestead, a stone dwelling built in 1930; another proceeds through a marsh; yet another traverses the junction of two rivers, an area rich with such wildlife as painted turtles, deer and great blue herons. The river is a popular beach and boating destination, as well. Camping avaible.

Last Mountain Lake National Wildlife Area ★ ★ *(free admission; May 1 to Oct 31; ☎836-2022)*, occupying the northern end of the lake of the same name, is believed to be the oldest bird sanctuary on the North American continent. More than 250 species of bird touch down here during their annual migrations south, including the spectacular whooping crane. These migrations are most spectacular during spring (mid-May) and fall (September); visitors either choose to follow a scripted tour by car or climb the observation tower and take the two hiking trails on foot. The preserve is best reached by turning east off Hwy. 2 at the town of Simpson, then following signs to the lakeshore. There is talk that the site's administrators may soon begin charging a fee to visit the preserve.

Grasslands National Park ★ ★ *(free admission; year-round; between Val Marie and Killdeer, south of Hwy. 18, ☎298-2257 or 298-2042)* was the first representative portion of original mixed-grass prairie set aside in North America. Among the variety of habitats represented here are grass-lands, buttes, badlands and the Frenchman River Valley; spectacular views can be had from some of the butte tops, while the wildlife includes the rare swift fox, pronghorn antelopes, burrowing owls, and golden eagles. Most interesting, though, is the unique **prairie dog town ★ ★**, where colonies of black-tailed prairie dogs still live in their natural environment. Guided hikes are given from the park office in Val Marie on summer Sundays, and wilderness camping is permitted in the park – but permission must be obtained from private land-owners to access certain parts of it.

Cypress Hills Interprovincial Park (☎662-441), which straddles the Saskatchewan/Alberta border, is described in the Southern Alberta chapter. (See p 345)

The Yellowhead Highway

Duck Mountain Provincial Park ★ ★ (☎542-5500) sits 25km east of Kamsack, right on the Manitoba border. Open year-round, the park completely surrounds popular Madge Lake. The mountain itself rises 240m above the surrounding terrain, covered with aspens. Full recreational facilities are here, including a campground, golf course, mini-golf course, fishing gear and beach. A lodge within park grounds provides accommodations.

Cumberland House Provincial Historic Park ★ ★ ★ ($7; ☎888-2077), on an island in the North Saskatchewan River, North of the Yellowhead Highway near the Manitoba border, was quite important historically: it was the first Hudson's Bay Company fur post in western Canada. Later, it served as a port for steamboat traffic along

the river. An 1890s-era powderhouse and part of a sternwheeler paddleboat are all that remain, but it's still a fascinating stop.

Greenwater Lake Provincial Park ★ ($7; ☎278-3115) is on Hwy. 38, north of Kelvington in the province's eastern Porcupine Forest. There is a marina with boat rentals and fishing gear in the summer, as well as tennis, golf, and horseback-riding facilities; in winter, the park becomes a destination for cross-country skiers. Nice log cabins are available for rent, too.

Pike Lake Provincial Park ★ (☎933-6966), a small recreational park about 30km southwest of Saskatoon, is a popular day trip for residents of Saskatchewan's largest city. The terrain here includes lawns shaded by aspen, ash and birch trees, a good beach and lots of wildlife. Watersports facilities include a pool, waterslide and canoes for hire; hiking trails, tennis courts, golf and mini-golf are also available here.

The Battlefords Provincial Park ★ ($7; ☎386-2212) is considered one of the recreational jewels of the province. Its location on the northeast shore of Jackfish Lake provides easy access to fishing and sailing. Equipment is available for these watersports; there are also a golf course and mini-golf course on premises, as well as a store and year-round resort-style accommodations.

West-Central Saskatchewan

Prince Albert National Park ★ ★ ★ ($4; ☎663-4522), encompassing 400,000ha, is one of Saskatchewan's finest parks. Entering from the south entrance on Rte. 263, you will pass

through grassland and fields, then aspen parklands and finally forests.

Scenic **Anglin Lake ★ ★**, southwest of Prince Albert Park, has at least one particularly distinguishing feature: it harbours the continent's largest nesting loon population.

Waskesiu Lake is the park area's largest and most popular body of water, and is where most of the services, beaches and activities are located. Farther off the beaten track, the park is noted for several good canoe routes and hiking trails that provide access to bird and plant life: bird enthusiasts, for instance, come to glimpse Canada's second-largest colony of American white pelicans, who nest on Lavallee Lake. Wolves, elk and buffalo also live here. Hikers often choose to explore Boundary Bog Trail, which penetrates the park's muskeg territory and includes carnivorous pitcher plants and dwarf stands of larch more than a century old, or the Treebeard Trail which winds through tall, aromatic groves of balsam fir and white spruce.

The park is most famous, however, for wise old Archibald Bellaney, an Englishman who came here in 1931, took the name of Grey Owl, and lived on a remote lake. **Grey Owl's Cabin ★**, a one-room log cabin on Ajawaan Lake, can only be reached by boat, canoe or – during summer – on foot via a 20km trail. Grey Owl lived here for seven years. Tours are available from park staff.

Lac La Ronge Provincial Park ★ ★ ★ ($7; ☎425-4234 or 800-772-4064) lies just north-east of Prince Albert Park on Rte. 2, providing similar scenery – and more of it, as this is the province's largest provincial park – than its more well-known neighbour. There are more than

100 lakes here, including enormous Lac La Ronge, dotted with what are said to be more than 1,000 islands. Cliffs, rock paintings and sand beaches can also be found in the park. Camping available.

Additionally, Lac La Ronge Park contains one of the province's showcase historic sites, the **Holy Trinity Anglican Church Historic Site ★ ★ ★** – Saskatchewan's oldest standing building, an enormous structure in an oddly remote location. Built in the late 1850s from local wood, then completed with stained-glass windows shipped from England, the church was part of the historic Stanley Mission.

Narrow Hills Provincial Park ★ ★ *($7; ☎426-2622)* lies just to the east of Prince Albert Park, although there is no direct connecting route; it can only be reached by a series of roads. It is famous for its eskers – the long, narrow glacially deposited hills that give the park its name – and more than 25 bodies of water, harbouring a number of species of game fish. One esker is topped by a fire tower, and its main building includes a small museum. Camping available.

Accommodations

Regina

Turgeon International Hostel
$
close end-Dec to end-Jan
sb
2310 McIntyre St.
☎*791-8165*
⇛*721-2667*
www.hihostels.ca
A great value for the guest who enjoys interacting with other travellers, this friendly hostel provides dorm rooms, a family room with space for

five and a room for groups. The house once belonged to William Turgeon, an Acadian from New Brunswick who came to Regina and ran a successful law practice for many years; it was later purchased by Hostelling International and moved on a flatbed trailer.

Its location is superb – the Royal Saskatchewan Museum is visible at the end of the street – and the family room is a super bargain. There's also a huge self-catering kitchen, delightful travel library, airy television room and great manager. The neighbourhood is within walking distance of all the city's major attractions and restaurants, as well. The office is closed during the day, however, and the facility closes completely during January.

Crescent House
$$ bkfst incl.
sb, ≡, 𝄐
180 Angus Cr.
☎*352-5995*
Crescent House is a bed and breakfast located on a crescent-shaped street just minutes on foot from most of Regina's major attractions. Special touches include a fireplace, three friendly terrier dogs, and a backyard shaded by 17m ash and elm trees.

Country Inns & Suites
$$ bkfst incl.
≡, *K*, 𝄐
3321 Eastgate Bay
☎*789-9117 or 800-456-4000*
⇛*789-3010*
www.countryinns.com/reginask
This hotel chain strives to offer a more homey atmosphere than most chains; rooms are done up with brass beds and guilt-like bed covers. Most rooms have mini-bars on the honour system; all guests receive free newspapers and can make free local calls. Suites come with a sitting room, sofa bed and microwave as well, and continental breakfast is included. Located

just off Hwy. 1, at the eastern edge of town.

Holiday Inn Express Hotel and Suites Regina
$$
≡, ⊘, ℝ, *K*
1907-11th Ave.
☎*569-4600 or 800-667-9922*
⇛*569-3531*
www.sixcontinentshotel.com
The newly renovated Holiday Inn rents out attractive and very spacious suites that come fully equipped with kitchenettes, desks and couches, everything you could need for a longer stay. The attractive red brick building and large windows give it a distinctive look.

Regina Travelodge Hotel
$$
≡, ℜ, ≈, ⊘
4177 Albert St. S
☎*586-3443 or 800-578-7878*
⇛*586-9311*
www.travelodgeregina.com
Unlike many other hotels in this chain, Regina's Travelodge has a unique character; a California theme pervades the building, from the attractive pastel lobby with its glitzy chandelier to the fake rocks and greenery in the pool area. The rooms provide exceptional comfort, and the Hollywood-themed restaurant is sure to be a hit with the kids and star(let)s-in-the-making.

Delta Regina
$$$
⊛, △, ≡, ℜ, ≈
1919 Saskatchewan Dr.
☎*525-5255 or 800-209-3555*
⇛*781-7188*
www.deltahotels.com
The Delta Regina Hotel offers guests luxurious accommodations, right near downtown. The rooms have a muted yet stylish decor, and most offer fine views of the city. The friendly and professional service, complete list of amenities, attractive pool area and overall elegance combine to pamper business travellers and vacationers alike.

Saskatchewan

Radisson Plaza Hotel Saskatchewan
$$$
≡, ℜ, △, ☺, ⊛
2125 Victoria Ave.
☎522-7691 or 800-333-3333
⇆757-5521
www.hotelsask.com
This hotel's fabulous location along one side of pretty Victoria Park, facing the city skyline, is only the beginning of the luxury that makes it Regina's crown jewel of accommodations. Built in 1927 by the Canadian Pacific Railroad, the hotel features such decorative notes as a chandelier from the Imperial Palace in St. Petersburg. More touches were added during a $28-million renovation in the early 1990s. There's also the original barbershop, a health club, massage therapists and an elegant dining room. How classy is it? Queen Elizabeth and Richard Chamberlain stay here whenever they're in town – not at the same time, of course – in the $995-per-night Royal Suite, where a special device heats towels as occupants bubble in the tub and the windows are fitted with bulletproof glass. It's 3,000 square feet of luxury and history.

Ramada Hotel and Convention Centre
$$$$
≡, ℜ, 🐾, ≈, △, ☺, ⊛
1818 Victoria Ave.
☎569-1666 or 800-667-6500
⇆525-3550
www.ramada.ca
Formerly the Sands Hotel, the Ramada was extensively renovated in 1999, making this centrally located hotel one of the most appealing places to stay in Regina. The rooms are attractively decorated, with all the usual amenities expected of an upscale hotel, plus additional perks such as suites with whirlpool bath.

Regina Inn Hotel and Convention Centre
$$$$
≡, ℜ, ⊛, ☺; 🐾
1975 Broad St.
☎525-6767 or 800-667-8162
⇆525-3630
Another centrally located luxury hotel, its amenities include a dinner theatre, suites with whirlpools, a health club and winter plug-ins. Guests can choose from four on-site restaurants and lounges catering to fine or casual diners. All rooms have balconies.

Southern Saskatchewan

Swift Current

Swift Current Heritage Bed and Breakfast
$$ bkfst incl.
sb, ≡
Hwy. 4 bypass to Waker Rd., Swift Current Sq.
☎773-6305 or 866-773-6305

Archaeologists and equine enthusiasts like this small bed and breakfast for its horses and Swift Current Petroglyph complex – both located on the property. There are three rooms in the house itself, and there is also a separate "barn" which houses three additional rooms, each with its own private bathroom.

Fort Qu'Appelle

Country Squire Inn
$$
≡, ℜ
Hwy. 10
☎332-5603
⇆332-6708
Probably the best affordable hotel-motel in the Fort Qu'Appelle Valley. Big clean rooms, cheerful help and a good restaurant (see p 430) all add up to an enjoyable experience. Short hiking trails beginning behind the place climb to the top of surrounding hills. There are a lounge, a bar and 'offsales' – on-premises sale of beer – here, as well.

Moose Jaw

Temple Gardens Mineral Spa Hotel and Resort
$$
≡, ℜ, ≈, △, ☺, ⊛, ✪
24 Fairford St. E.
☎694-5055 or 800-718-7727
⇆694-8310
www.templegardens.sk.ca
This resort, tucked improbably down a sidestreet off Moose Jaw's slow-moving main drag, offers true luxuries to the dusty prairie traveller. The big open lobby gives a hint of what's to come. Regular hotel rooms here are roomy enough, with big sofas, but the 25 full suites are the real hit: king-sized beds, cotton robes, tables, enormous walk-in bathrooms and a two-person mineral water whirlpool create a romantic experience in each. Furthermore, all resort guests have free access to the resort's fourth-floor, $2000m^2$ mineral waterpool. There is also a small health club featuring Nautilus machines and treadmills, a poolside café and a restaurant.

Saskatoon

Patricia Hotel Hostel
$
sb, 🐾
345 Second Ave. N.
☎242-8861
⇆664-1119
For hostel prices, visitors get very basic accommodations in a hotel that has frankly seen better days. The advantage here is the low, low price and the location close to downtown. However, there are no kitchen facilities or special touches, save a local bar beneath the dorm rooms. Rooms are very basic, with two bunkbeds and shared washrooms. Some single rooms are available, however; these are in slightly better condition and all have a television and private bathroom (*$30 per person, $34 for two*).

Ramblin' Rose Bed and Breakfast
$ bkfst incl.
sb/pb, ◯, 🐾
☎668-4582
Located south of Saskatoon, near popular Pike Lake Provincial Park, this cedar home offers two private suites with private baths and two with shared baths. Extras are plentiful – a whirlpool, tv/vcr, video and book library among them. Pets are welcome here, and guests are also welcome to hike any of several nature trails on the property. Rooms are comfortable, but try to book one on the main floor, rather than in the semi-basement.

Brighton House Bed and Breakfast
$$ bkfst incl.
sb/pb, ◉, ≡
1308 Fifth Ave. N
☎664-3278
⇔664-6822
The Brighton House Bed and Breakfast is in a lovely white clapboard house with blue and pink trim, located outside the downtown area and surrounded by a well-tended garden. All the rooms are delightfully furnished with floral prints and antiques, and the "honeymoon suite" comes with a private bathroom and sun porch. Hosts Barb and Lynne are sure to make you feel right at home. Extra touches include the family suite on the top floor, which provides ample space for children to play, and the outdoor hot tub and croquet set at guests' disposal.

Imperial 400
$$
🐾, K, ≡, ℜ, ≈
610 Idylwyld Dr. N
☎244-2901 or 800-781-2268
⇔244-6063
www.imperial400motels.com
This 176-room motel features an indoor recreation complex with a whirlpool and (leaky) water-slide, and in-house movies, making it a good deal for families. Even more attractive are kitchenettes in some rooms. There is also a restaurant on premises.

Radisson Hotel Saskatoon
$$$
≡, ℜ, ≈, ◯, ◉, ⊘
405-20th St. E,
☎665-3322 or 800-333-3333
⇔665-5531
www.radisson.com
This elegant and newly renovated high-rise luxury hotel caters to everyone: there are three executive floors and six meeting rooms, not to mention waterslides, a sauna, whirlpool and gym. Its location right on the South Saskatchewan River means good access to outdoor recreation. It includes 14 deluxe suites complete with a bar and an extra telephone connection and modem hook-up for your computer.

Delta Bessborough
$$$
≡, ℜ, ≈, ◯, ◉, ⊘
601 Spadina Cr. E
☎244-5521 or 800-268-1133
⇔653-2458
www.deltahotels.com
One of Saskatoon's most distinguishing landmarks, the Delta Bessborough is a former CN hotel in the *faux* French *château* style, with many turrets and gables. While the renovated lobby and restaurant do not do justice to the grand old edifice, the newly restored guest rooms are comfortable, if somewhat dark, and have retained such luxurious touches as the original bathroom fixtures and deep ceramic tubs. Modern conveniences such as in-room coffee makers, voicemail and hairdryers have, of course, been added. The elegant ballrooms and extensive river property are among Saskatoon's most prized sites for all kinds of functions and receptions.

Saskatoon Inn
$$$
≡, ≈, ◉, 🐾, ⊘
2002 Airport Dr.
☎242-1440 or 800-667-8789
⇔224-2779
www.saskatooninn.com
Conveniently located right by the airport, the Saskatoon Inn offers spacious, attractive rooms with all the comforts and conveniences, as well as a unique recreation area with a swimming pool and ping pong table set amid a profusion of greenery traversed by winding walkways. The adjoining restaurant and lounge elaborate on the tropical theme, providing a sort of indoor oasis that is especially welcome in the dead of a northern Saskatchewan winter!

Sheraton Cavalier
$$$
≡, ℜ, ≈, ◯, ◉, ⊘,
621 Spadina Cr. E
☎652-6770 or 800-325-3535
⇔244-1739
www.sheraton.com
Beautifully set on the river, the newly renovated Sheraton Cavalier is a glamorous hotel with a sophisticated contemporary style. The rooms have all the comforts and conveniences, and the friendly and efficient service ensures a pleasant stay. The hotel's amenities include two indoor waterslides, a ballroom, a cigar lounge and mountain bike rentals.

The Yellowhead Highway

Manitou Beach

Manitou Springs Hotel and Mineral Spa
$$
≡, ◉, ⊘
MacLachlan Ave.
☎946-2233 or 800-667-7672
⇔946-2554
*www.manitouspringsspa
.sk.ca*
An old and well-known resort in western Canada, this facility is famous for its three pools of

heated mineral water drawn from Little Manitou Lake. Other services at the resort include massage therapy, reflexology, and a fitness centre.

West Central Saskatchewan

North Battleford

Battlefords Inn
$$
≡, ℜ, 🐕
11212 Railway Ave. E
☎445-1515 or 800-691-6076
≈445-1541
Known for spacious rooms, this inn provides king- and queen-size beds, free local phone calls and free in-room coffee. Meals can be taken in the on-site restaurant, and alcohol can be purchased in the licensed beverage room.

Prince Albert

South Hill Inn
$$
≡, ℜ, ⊛, 🐕
3245 Second Ave. W
☎922-1333 or 800-363-4466
≈763-6408
www.southhillinn.com
Highlights of this conveniently located inn include big comfortable rooms, televisions with the option of in-house movies and free coffee. There is also a licensed restaurant on the premises.

Restaurants

Regina

Bushwakker
$-$$
closed Sun
2206 Dewdney Ave.
☎359-7276
A fun brewpub on the edge of an industrial area. Locals don't think twice about motoring over here to try the latest batch of Harvest Ale or some other concoction, buffered by a fancy hamburger or other typical bar fare. The bar also offers offsales (small and very large bottles of the brewery's beer) in addition to the usual taps.

🚢 Heliotrope
$$
2204 McIntyre St.
☎569-3373
Heliotrope is the only vegetarian restaurant in Saskatchewan, and quite possibly one of the best in all Canada. The chairs and tables in this brick house are cozy. In the winter a fireplace keeps things warm, and in summer there's a great outdoor patio. Entrees are expertly handled, everything from lunches of falafel, vegetables and burgers to dinners of Thai curries and *gado gado*. Dessert is a real stunner, with in-season fruit cheesecake and homemade gelato that consists only of fresh fruit and water.

Cathedral Village Free House
$$$
2062 Albert St.
☎359-1661
Filling contemporary fare from all over the map – a concept that doesn't always work, but satisfies some of the time. Lunch might consist of straightforward buffalo burgers, salads, stir-fried vegetables, wood-fired oven pizza and the like; dinner leans toward pasta and other Italian dishes. The place gets extra points for having eight beers on tap. The crowd here is young and hip despite the stodgy name, possibly explaining the erratic service; at least the location is central, and the decor, with bold colours and tiled floor, is welcoming.

🚢 Neo Japonica
$$$
2167 Hamilton St.
☎359-7669
The all-around most charming restaurant in Regina, Neo Japonica serves exquisite Japanese cuisine in a small, unassuming house with an inviting decor. The food's artistic presentation is matched only by its expert preparation. If you order the special plate you can sample the teriyaki chicken, tempura, nigri sushi and Japanese tea for under $12. Homemade green tea and ginger ice cream are the perfect finale for any meal.

Southern Saskatchewan

Fort Qu'Appelle

The Country Squire
$$$
Hwy. 10
☎332-5603
Attached to the inn of the same name, this restaurant serves tasty, hearty portions in a convivial atmosphere; locals often drop by for a bite of grilled salmon, burgers (choose from elk, buffalo or hamburger), salad or fish and chips.

Caronport

The Pilgrim
$$$
7am to 10pm
Trans-Canada Hwy. 1
☎756-3335
Yet another restaurant in a gas station, this one is located in the small town of Caronport, just west of Moose Jaw. This place serves family fare and a salad bar. Its reputation for hearty prairie cooking and a 60-item salad and soup bar is solid.

Saskatoon

Michel's Montreal Smoked Meats
$
101-129 Second Ave. N
☎*384-6664*
Fortuitously placed right next to Saskatoon's Belgian choco-late shop, this enterprising French-Canadian tries to match Montréal quality from 3,000km away – and nearly succeeds. The peppery smoked meat, stuffed be-tween two slices of rye bread and embellished with gener-ous squirts of mustard, doesn't have quite the bite of its Qué-bec counterpart, but it's still very good. Other great touches include homemade sour pickles, a very basic (and therefore good and crunchy) coleslaw, and black-cherry cola.

Broadway Café
$-$$
814 Broadway Ave.
☎*652-8244*
This restaurant is located right in the heart of Saskatoon's hippest district. However, that's a bit misleading: this is merely a diner that serves up burgers, eggs and the like to swarms of locals. The snappy service is cheerful but a bit off-putting out here in laid-back Saskatchewan, and daring entrées should definitely be avoided. Nevertheless, an authentic local experience.

Wanuskewin Café
$$
R.R 4
☎*931-6767 ext. 223*
Located in the native heritage park of the same name, just north of Saskatoon, this little café offers a good quick sam-pling of native-style cookery. Entrées aren't large here but they are tasty; the fare ranges from a warming, hearty cup of bison stew with a side of bannock (bread), to bison with wild rice. Dessert offerings include pastries while the line of First Nation water– bottled

by an Aboriginal-owned com-pany – are among the bever-ages offered.

Berry Barn
$$
830 Valley Rd.
☎*978-9797*
Located approximately 10km south of the city, the Berry Barn makes for a pleasant excursion to the country. Saskatoon berry bushes line the parking lot, hinting at the delights to come: berry pies, waffles, syrup and tea accom-pany hearty meals of perogies and farmer's sausage. The rustic pine-finished dining room has a great view of the river. After your meal you can browse in the gift shop for still more berry products or pick some berries yourself at the you-pick farm. Reservations recommended.

Genesis Family Restautant
$$
901D 22nd St. W.
☎*244-5516*
Widely acclaimed as Saskatoon's best healthy food, the menu leans toward Chinese food cooking. Dim sum is available at lunchtime.

Mykonos
$$$-$$$$
416-21st St. E.
☎*244-2499*
Mykonos serves the usual kebabs, seafood, lamb and moussaka, but the overall flavour is not exactly authentic. The formal dining room has a mediterranean décor that is attractive, though, like the food, not exactly Greek. Overpriced, but still one of the better restaurants in town. The friendly service adds to the dining experience.

Saskatoon Station Place
$$$-$$$$
221 South Idylwyld Dr.
☎*244-7777*
Saskatoon Station Place draws guests with its railway motif; plush dining cars with mahog-any trim surround a mock

train station. While the Belle Epoque reigns supreme in the decor, the restaurant service and menu is more family-style, and dishes cover the basics of ribs, steak and sea food. Still, a good choice for an evening out. Be sure to stop in at the lounge for a pre-dinner drink.

West Central Saskatchewan

North Battleford

DaVinci's Ristorante Italiano
$$$
1001 Hwy. 16
☎*446-4700*
Even Leonardo himself might be surprised that the menu here is not exclusively Italian as the name suggests; traditional Louisiana flavours and conti-nental European dishes are served.

Prince Albert

Amy's on Second
$$
2990 Second Ave.
☎*763-1515*
Fresh ingredients and a healthy approach to cooking make this restaurant a popular switch from the many local fast-food joints. Salads are made to order, and come with home-made soups. Also featured are steak, chicken and pasta dishes.

Entertainment

Regina

There are a great many annual events in Saskatchewan. Check out Tourism Saskatche-wan's web site, ***www.sasktourism .com/events*** for details.

The **Buffalo Days** festival (☎781-9200 or 888-734-3975) occupies one week each summer, usually beginning in late July and lasting into early August. Festivities kick off with a Sunday picnic in lovely Wascana Park; from there, it's on to a raft of shows and, eventually, fireworks.

Southern Saskatchewan

Saskatoon

Most of the pubs and clubs in Saskatoon are concentrated along Second Avenue South.

The **SaskTel Saskatchewan Jazz Festival** (☎652-1421, www.saskjazz.com) brings world-class jazz, gospel and world music to Saskatoon's riverbanks for 10 days each June. Musicians range from international stars to local artists. Some performances are held in the Delta Bessborough Gardens, adjacent to the landmark hotel.

The **Great Northern River Roar** is either an abomination or a great time, depending on your opinion of powerboats tearing up and down the river.

Either way, there's no avoiding these races when they arrive in Saskatoon each July. Some 60,000 spectators are said to watch as the powerboats charge around courses at speeds of up to 225km/h.

Second Avenue South is the place to go for all the pubs, clubs and street life.

Shopping

Regina

Shopping is concentrated on the south end of Albert Street and east end of Victoria Avenue (respectively the south and east sides of town). The Corwall Centre and Scarth Street Mall, both downtown, are also good locations.

Saskatoon

Shopping in Saskatoon is easy, with several downtown malls and streets dedicated to the activity. Perhaps the most popular area is the **Bayside Mall** (225 Second Ave. N), next to and including The Bay department store. The **Midtown Plaza**, on First Avenue South between 22nd St. E and 20th St. E, is another good option.

The Original Bulk Cheese Warehouse
732 Broadway Ave.
☎652-8008
The Original Bulk Cheese Warehouse is the place to load up on picnic provisions like samosas, quiche, salads, fresh shrimp cocktails, desserts, and, of course, an impressive selection of cheeses, including a local buffalo mozzarella.

Chocolatier Bernard Callebaut
125 Second Ave. N.
☎652-0909
Right in the centre of downtown Saskatoon, a small Canadian chain based in Calgary serves up artful cream chocolates and bars of baking chocolate made of all-natural ingredients. A special treat here are the hand-dipped chocolate ice cream bars – delicious beyond words, and only a few dollars apiece.

Manitoba

There's much more to Manitoba than meets the eye. While the mention of its name may elicit a blank stare from tourists who flock to some of Canada's better-known corners, Manitoba has plenty of surprises in store.

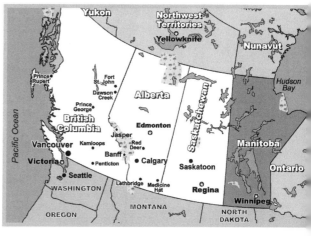

In fact, visitors have been coming to Manitoba – and staying – for more than a century, swelling its capital city of Winnipeg into Canada's eighth-largest city and creating a surprising mix of immigrant culture more diverse than anywhere else between Vancouver and Toronto.

In the beginning, the province was occupied by several Aboriginal groups. It was they who gave the province its name: Manitou was a highly revered spirit among the First Nations who lived there, and the rapids of Lake Manitoba were believed to be his voice.

Once the English and French arrived, however, the story of Manitoba swiftly became the story of a running feud between two rival fur-trading companies: the English-owned Hudson's Bay Company on the one hand and the French-Indian North West Company – which emerged later and, for a time, successfully competed against the British – on the other.

The French-Canadian explorer Pierre de la Vérendrye made quite a mark on the region's fur trade. La Vérendrye was the first European to penetrate the grasslands of Manitoba; his trading posts established populations in what would eventually become the communities of Dauphin, The Pas, Selkirk and Portage la Prairie. This French influence is still evident today; in fact, the eastern Winnipeg suburb of St. Boniface, which was a separate city before it was amalgamated in 1972, is the largest French settlement in Canada west of Québec.

The Metis made up a considerable part of this French-speaking population. The descendants of French trappers and Aboriginal people, the French-speaking, Catholic Metis lived at the forks of the Red and Assiniboine Rivers, in settlements which were annexed to Canada in 1869. Fearing for their language, education, land and religious rights, they were led by Louis Riel in their pursuit of responsible government for the territory. What little they had was slowly being taken away, leading settlers, both white and Metis, to set up their own provisional government. The outrage over the trial and execution of Ontarian Orangeman Thomas Scott for defying the authority of the said government forced Riel into exile in the United States. He did return to Canada, to Saskatchewan this time, to continue his fight and lead the Northwest Rebellion. Riel, the man who might have been the first premier of Manitoba, was executed for treason in 1885 and has been seen as a martyr by many ever since.

There are also considerable Ukrainian and Mennonite influences in Manitoba, as well as a sizeable population of Icelandic immigrants. The beginning of the latter influx can be precisely dated: in 1875 a string of volcanic eruptions drove Icelanders to North America in search of another home. Many of them settled in the Interlake district, on the shores of Lakes Winnipeg and Manitoba, where they traded in their skills at saltwater fishing for the taking of whitefish. Manitobans have gone to great lengths to preserve all these immigrants' stories, keeping their history alive through numerous museums and historic parks.

It is certainly true that the southern portion of the province is flat, levelled by great glaciers during the most recent Ice Age. Where thousands of square kilometres of uninterrupted tallgrass prairie once rolled under the press of the wind, colourful fields of hard wheat, flax, canola and sunflowers thrive today. In wet areas, pocket marshes teeming with resident and

migrating waterfowl replace the fields.

But whatever Manitoba lacks in varied topography it makes up for with its fertile farmland and immense lakes that are home to countless birds. In fact, only about 40% of the province is flat. The rest is comprised of hills and waterways carved out of the Canadian Shield, a mass of hard ancient rock surrounding Hudson Bay that surfaces most obviously here and in northern Ontario. This land is shot through with deep pine forests, cliffs, and lakes; it is not unusual to see elk, deer, moose and bears in this rugged landscape.

In the sparsely populated far north, tundra becomes predominant and the wildlife grows more spectacular still, with the singular light of the luminous sub-Arctic summers, white whales and polar bears.

Finding Your Way Around

By Plane

Winnipeg International Airport is situated surprisingly close to the downtown area, only about 5km away.

Air Canada (☎888-247-2264, *www.aircanada.ca*), handles traffic from both coasts.

By Bus

Greyhound Canada (☎800-661-8747) runs to the major towns and cities. In Winnipeg, the terminal is located at the corner of Portage Avenue and Colony Street.

By Train

VIA Rail's (☎800-561-8630 in *Canada*) cross-country Canadian service passes through the province, usually stopping in Winnipeg around 4pm (westbound) or 11am (eastbound); if the train is on time, it can be an excellent way to arrive in Winnipeg before dinner. Winnipeg's grand **Union Station** (*132 Main St.*), located right in the centre of downtown at the major intersection of Broadway and Main Street, is the largest station in Manitoba and the usual stopping point.

Smaller stations are located in Brandon, Portage la Prairie and other towns roughly parallel to the Trans-Canada Highway.

Public Transportation

Winnipeg Transit (☎986-5717), located in an underground facility at the corner of Portage and Main, runs a decent bus system around the city; rides cost $1.65, slightly less if purchased in bulk-ticket blocks.

The city also maintains a transit information line (☎986-5700).

Taxis

Unicity (☎925-3131) is the main taxi company in Winnipeg.

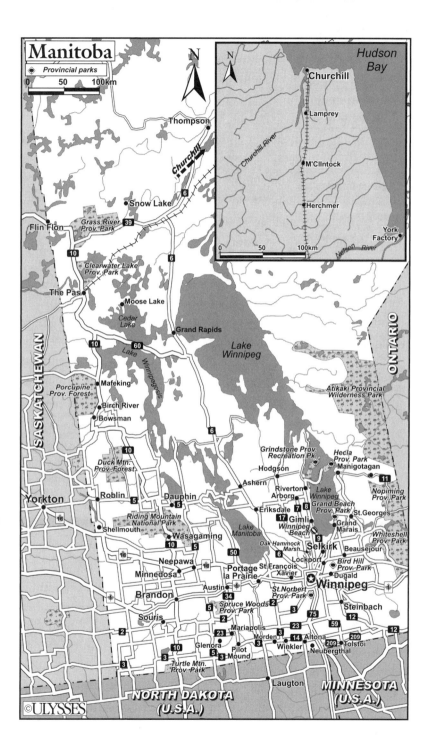

Manitoba

Provincial parks

0   50   100km

N

Hudson Bay

Churchill

Lamprey

M'Cllntock

Churchill River

Herchmer

York Factory

Nelson River

N

0   50   100km

Thompson

Churchill

Snow Lake

Flin Flon

Grass River Prov. Park   39

Clearwater Lake Prov. Park

The Pas

Moose Lake

Cedar Lake

Grand Rapids

Lake Winnipeg

SASKATCHEWAN

Lake Winnipegosis

Porcupine Prov. Forest

Mafeking

Birch River

Bowsman

ONTARIO

Atikaki Provincial Wilderness Park

Duck Mtn. Prov. Forest

Roblin

Yorkton

Dauphin

Riding Mountain National Park

Shellmouth

Wasagaming

Neepawa

Minnedosa

Brandon

Austin

Souris

Mariapolis

Glenora

Pilot Mound

Turtle Mtn. Prov. Park

Grindstone Prov. Recreation Pk.

Hecla Prov. Park

Manigotagan

Hodgson

Nopiming Prov. Park

Ashern

Riverton

Arborg

Lake Winnipeg

Grand Beach Prov. Park

St. Georges

Eriksdale

Gimli

Winnipeg Beach

Grand Marais

Lake Manitoba

Whiteshell Prov. Park

Oak Hammock Marsh

Selkirk

Beausejour

Lockport

Portage la Prairie

St. François Xavier

Bird Hill Prov. Park

Dugald

Winnipeg

St. Norbert Prov. Park

Spruce Woods Prov. Park

Steinbach

Morden

Altona

Winkler

Neubergthal

Tolstoï

Laugton

NORTH DAKOTA (U.S.A.)

MINNESOTA (U.S.A.)

©ULYSSES

Practical Information

Area Code: **204**.

Tourist Information

Winnipeg Tourism
279 Portage Ave., Winnipeg
☎*943-1970 or 800-665-0204*
www.tourism.winnipeg.mb.ca
Winnipeg Tourism runs a year-round information centre that is open weekdays all year, and seven days a week during the summer months. There is also an office at the airport (☎982-7543).

Explore Manitoba Centre
Travel Manitoba, 24 Forks Market Rd.
☎*945-3777 or 800-665-0040*
www.travelmanitoba.com
The Explore Manitoba Centre, beside The Forks Johnson Terminal (10am to 6pm), is open year round. In other parts of the province, tourism office hours vary a great deal, but the larger ones are open year round.

Post Office

The main **post office** *(266 Graham Ave.,* ☎*987-5054)* is located right downtown.

Safety

Manitoba is generally safe, although much of downtown Winnipeg becomes deserted after dark, so some caution is advised. The city's police department maintains 17 stations in six districts around the city; dial **911** for emergencies. There is also a **Royal Canadian Mounted Police** detachment *(1091 Portage Ave.,* ☎*983-2091)* in the city.

The **Canadian Automobile Association** *(☎800-222-4357)* maintains offices in the province's most populous areas, offering roadside assistance and information to members. Its offices are located at:

Winnipeg
870 Empress St.
☎*987-6100 or 6166*

501 St. Anne's Rd.
☎*987-6200*

1353 McPhillips St. ☎*987-6222*

Brandon
20-1300 18th St.
☎*727-1394*

Altona
61 Second Ave. NE
☎*324-8474*

Climate

Summers are warm and dry. Winter, however, can bring dangerously low temperatures and blinding snowstorms; temperatures can plunge to below -30°C, with the windchill making it feel even colder. Thus, you should take the necessary precautions, especially if you are planning to drive outside of town in the winter. For updated weather forecast information in Winnipeg, call ☎*983-2050*.

Exploring

Winnipeg

Winnipeg, a bona fide metropolis of more than 680,000 inhabitants, rises improbably from the plains at the convergence of two rivers; it is the likely starting point for most

visitors' journeys around the province.

The name of Manitoba's capital city was derived from the Cree name *(Win-nipi)* for the lake situated 65km north of the city.

The city was settled by a Scotsman named Thomas Douglas, fifth Earl of Selkirk, as a 187,000km[2] settlement called the Red River Colony (a monument at the end of Alexander Avenue marks the exact spot). Douglas was an emissary of the Hudson's Bay Company.

All roads in Winnipeg seem to lead to **The Forks** ★★ *(behind Union Station, corner of Mark St. And Broadway Ave.,* ☎*943-6757)*, which have always been a focal point in the province: this fertile confluence of the Red and Assiniboine rivers was the original camping ground of the region's Aboriginal peoples, and later the base camp for the North West Company, the area's original fur-trapping concern. The company's headquarters *(77 Main St.)* still stand across a busy street from the original site. Today, however, The Forks is synonymous with the covered market of the same name.

Inside, dozens of stalls house purveyors of everything from fresh fish, candy and Ethnic food to frozen yogurt and handmade jewellery. There's even a fortune teller.

The riverwalk takes you on a lovely stroll along the banks of the Red River, and gives you a superb view of St. Boniface, including its famous cathedral (see p 439), which lies just on the other side. There are many picnic-perfect green spaces and a small marina that rents canoes and pedal-boats in the summer, and lots of green spaces perfect for a picnic. Many events take place on the plaza just outside the

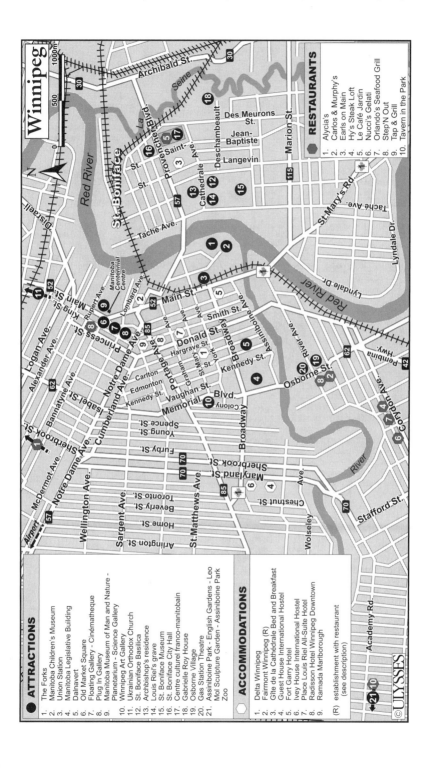

Winnipeg

© ULYSSES

market, in the summer as well as winter, and several restaurants have terraces here, which are extremely pleasant on hot summer nights.

In the adjacent Johnson Terminal, a former rail station, the province's tourism office dispenses plenty of useful information. The **Explore Manitoba Centre ★** is short on information but long on inspiration, especially for kids, who love the intriguing (if strangely juxtaposed) dioramas. The Terminal also contains more stores and coffee shops.

In the same complex but a different building is the **Manitoba Children's Museum ★★★** *($5.50; Sun-Fri 9:30 am to 4:30am and Sat 9:30am to 8pm; Forks Market Rd., ☎924-4000)*, the only children's museum in western Canada. The building was once a railway facility, containing an engine house and train repair shops as well as a blacksmith's shop. Today, there's a whimsical hand at work, creating such displays as a fully functioning television studio and a diesel engine from the 1950s.

The most recent addition to the Forks are the CanWest Global ballpark and the Manitoba Theatre For Young People, an imaginatively designed building on Forks Market Road. Inquire within about their family-oriented activities.

Adjacent to the Forks complex and facing downtown sits **Union Station ★** *(132 Main St.)*, designed by the same team of architects that designed Grand Central Station in New York City. The station was built during Winnipeg's golden age, when the city was considered the "Gateway to the West," and thus an important

Legislative Building

economic centre. Today, its impressive grandeur seems a little out of place. The station features a huge dome plastered inside in pink and white, pierced with arching half-moon windows. The walls are covered with the famous local Tyndall limestone.

It is only a few blocks west up Assiniboine Street or along the river to Manitoba's **Legislative Building ★★★** *(free admission; Jul to Aug every day, 9am to 6pm, Sep to Jun Mon to Thu 9am to 3pm by appointment; 450 Broadway, ☎945-5813)*. This is where the province's parliamentary business is taken care of, and it's an impressive property, full of interesting touches like limestone walls embedded with fossils, two bronze bisons, a bust of Cartier and more. Up top, the dome is capped with the 5.25m-tall **Golden Boy**, a French sculpture of a boy covered in gold leaf carrying a sheaf of wheat underneath

one arm and extending a torch toward the sky with the other. Guided tours in English an French are available throughout the day during the summer. Behind "the Leg" are landscaped gardens containing a fountain and a statue of Louis Riel. The original and more controversial sculpture of this Metis leader now stands across the river, behind St. Boniface College (see p 440).

Just down Assiniboine Avenue, **Dalnavert ★** *($4; closed Mon and Fri, Jun to Aug 10am to 4:30pm, Sep to Dec and Mar to May noon to 4:30pm, Jan and Feb Sat and Sun noon to 4:30; 61 Carlton St., ☎943-2835)* is an old brick Queen-Anne-Revival-style home built for Sir Hugh John Macdonald, son of former Prime Minister John A. Macdonald, and former premier of Manitoba. Its interest lies mainly in its period furnishings, and in the fact that it was among the very first homes in the city to be built with such amenities as indoor plumbing.

The best way to get acquainted with downtown Winnipeg's history and architecture is to take one of the **Exchange District Walking Tours** *($5; May to Sep weather permitting; ☎942-6716)*. The tours are 1.5 to 2 hours long.

The **Exchange District ★★★**, close to downtown, northwest of Portage and Main, is Winnipeg's former warehouse district — though today the smart industrial buildings have been given fresh coats of paint and new occupants, such as print shops, bookstores, theatre companies and the like. The federal government designated the area a National Historic Site in 1997.

The district surrounds **Old Market Square**, a small park with a stage for outdoor performances. The Fringe Festival (see p 455) is one of the events that makes use of this urban greenspace each year.

Some of the most striking buildings can be found by walking in the area of Albert Street and Notre Dame Avenue. The **Paris Building** *(269 Portage Ave.)* features many architectural flourishes such as scrolls, urns, Cupid figurines and other ornamental terra cotta work. The nearby **Birks Building**, across Portage *(at Smith St. and Portage Ave.)* displays an Egyptian mosaic. The building was restored in 2000.

Around the corner, away from the busy traffic of Portage Avenue, the **Alexander Block** *(78-86 Albert St.)* was the first Edwardian-style construction in the neighbourhood and the only residence built here in that style; it was once a businessman's home. Finally, a few paces up Albert, the spectacular **Notre Dame Chambers** *(213 Notre Dame Ave.)*, also known as the Electric Railway Chambers Building, is a terra cotta building with arches along the top, lit up brightly with some 6,000 white lights at night.

The Exchange District is also home to a number of small, independent galleries that specialize in contemporary art. Among these, the **Floating Gallery** *(free admission; Tue to Sat 12pm to 5pm, 218-100 Arthur St.; ☎942-8183)* is notable for its photograph exhibits. The gallery is located right on Old Market Square, in the Artspace building which also houses the **Cinematheque**, a venue for independent films. You can always find truly avant-garde multimedia installations in the no-frills warehouse space at the **Plug In Gallery** *(free admission; Tue to Sat 11am to 5pm; 286*

McDermot Ave., ☎942-1043, www.plugin.mb.ca), only a few blocks away.

The city's finest museums are also very close to the Exchange District. Located within a complex of science attractions in the same downtown building, the **Manitoba Museum of Man and Nature ★★★** *($6.50; mid-May to early Sep 10am to 6pm; rest of the year, Tue to Fri 10am to 4pm, Sat, Sun, holidays 10am to 5pm,closed Mon; 190 Rupert Ave., ☎956-2830 or 943-3139, www.manitoba museum.mb.ca)*, is Winnipeg's showcase museum, a tour-de-force emphasizing Manitoba's natural and social history. Separate galleries teach the visitor about the province's geology, grasslands ecology, Arctic ecology – a polar bear diorama is the star here – and Aboriginal history. Other special exhibit rooms describe the voyage of the English ship the **Nonsuch** (which established the Hudson's Bay Company's presence in western Canada in 1670) with a replica of the ship, which visitors can board to explore the cabins and deck, and the construction of the railroad to the far northern Manitoba port town of Churchill.

The tour ends with a very popular and well-designed two-storey recreation of late-1800s downtown Winnipeg, including a cobbler, chapel, movie theatre and much more. The new Hudson's Bay Company Gallery showcases an impressive number of Hudson's Bay Company items. This museum is a must-see. Other attractions on the lower floor of the same building include a **Planetarium** *($5; mid-May to early Sep every day 11am to 6pm, winter weekends and holidays noon to 4pm; ☎956-2830)* and the **Gallery** *(same hours as museum; $5)*, where visitors can learn about science and technology through "hands-on" activities.

It is especially popular with children.

Housed in a striking triangular building of pale limestone, the **Winnipeg Art Gallery ★★** *($6, free admission Wed 5pm to 7pm and Sat; every day 11am to 5pm mid Jun to early Sep at 10am, winter closed Mon; 300 Memorial Blvd., ☎786-6641, www.wag.mb.ca)* is best known for its vast collection of Inuit art and sculptures. Founded in 1912, the museum boasts everything from 16th-century Flemish tapestry to modern art; it is particularly strong on Canadian artists, decorative porcelains and silver, and collections acquired from the Federal Department of Indian and Northern Affairs and the Hudson's Bay Company. Aboriginal works are displayed in changing exhibits on the mezzanine level. There is an interesting gift shop, as well as a pleasant rooftop restaurant with a terrace.

In the city's north end, on north Main Street, the **Ukrainian Orthodox Church ★★** is one of the city's most distinctive landmarks, decked in handsome burgundy and gold paint and possessing the trademark Ukrainian dome. The building houses a collection of Ukrainian folk art exhibits, a library and a gift shop *(donations welcome; Jul and Aug Mon-Sat 10am to 4pm; 1175 Main St., ☎582-1018)*.

St. Boniface

Just across the Red River in St. Boniface, the distinctive ruins of the **St. Boniface Cathedral ★★★** *(190 Ave. de la Cathédrale)* are a must-see. The walls are all that remain of the church, which burned in 1968, but they are still very impressive. This was actually the fourth cathedral to stand on this spot. No wonder it remains a kind of shrine for Canada's largest French-speaking population outside of Quebec. The giant circular opening in the stone once contained a giant roseate stained-glass window. The beautiful **Archbishop's residence** (*141 Ave. de la Cathédrale*) right next door is one of the oldest remaining stone buildings in western Canada.

In the cemetery in front of the basilica, **Louis Riel's grave** is marked by a simple red stone that belies the renown of the man who lies beneath it. Other stones on the lawn mark the graves of French settlers and Metis, including Chief One Arrow. There's also a glorious view of the river and the city skyline from this vantage point.

Behind the cathedral stands the silver-domed **St. Boniface College** (*200 Ave. de la Cathédrale*), established in the 1800s. A scultpure of Louis Riel stands at its northern entrance.

Next door to the cathedral, the **St. Boniface Museum** ★★ (*$3; year round Mon to Fri 9am to 5pm, plus Mar to May, Oct and Nov Sun 12pm to 4pm, Jun to Sep Sat 10am to 4pm Sun 10am to 8pm; 494 Tache Ave., ☎237-4500*) was built as a convent in 1846 and tells a number of fascinating stories about the city's French roots; it is the oldest building in Winnipeg and its largest log structure. Of particular note is the tale of the four Grey Nuns (*Les Soeurs Grises*) who founded the convent – they travelled some 2,400km by canoe from Montréal, taking nearly two full months to complete the arduous journey.

Other highlights in the museum include holy-water vessels and church objects, and western Canada's oldest statue, a papier mâché Virgin

Mary, decked in a blue shawl. It was crafted by the artistic Sister Lagrave, one of the original Grey Nuns.

Strolling north along the river brings you to the Provencher Bridge where you can stop for a snack at the crêperie located right in the middle of the bridge, in the former gatehouse. The bridge leads onto Provencher Boulevard, the main shopping and entertainment area in St. Boniface, lined with some interesting shops and locales. The old **St. Boniface City Hall** (*219 Provencher Blvd.*) and the modern **Centre Culturel Franco-manitobain** (*340 Provencher Blvd.*) are located on this street.

Fans of Gabrielle Roy can see the house in which she grew up and where several of her works, including one of her most famous novels, *Rue Deschambault*, are set. Distinguished by a commemorative plaque, the **Maison Gabrielle Roy** (*Fri and Sat 10am to 5pm and Sun 1pm to 5pm; 375 Rue Deschambault, ☎231-8503*) offers a unique glimpse into the life of this famous French-Canadian author. The 10 rooms of Roy's childhood home are being completely restored with period furnishings, and an interpretive centre is being added in the basement. Activities and events are also scheduled. After years of neglect, this historic place will finally assume its position as a true landmark on the Rue Deschambault.

East of St. Boniface, on the edge of the city, sits the ultra-modern **Royal Canadian Mint** ★ (*$2, early May to end Sep Mon to Fri 9am to 5pm, Sat 10am to 2pm; free admission end Sep to early May Mon to Fri 10am to 2pm; 520 Lagimodière Blvd., ☎983-6429*), where all of Canada's circulation coinage is minted. Tours and observation areas give insight into the process.

Greater Winnipeg

South of the Assiniboine River but easily accessible from Memorial Boulevard by crossing the Osborne Bridge, **Osborne Village** is considered by some the city's hippest address, with its trendy shops and restaurants. People come here to browse or meet for coffee, or to take in one of the varied shows at the **Gas Station Theatre** (*454 River Ave., ☎284-9477*) which hosts everything from live theatre to music, contemporary dance and improv comedy.

Assiniboine Park ★★ is a popular walking and cycling destination. Its extensive tree-lined paths wind along the river of the same name, and are surrounded by wide open lawns where families come to picnic or play frisbee. During the winter, you can skate to piped music on the **Duck Pond**, or use the cross-country ski trails.

The park's **English Gardens** are a wonderful surprise when in bloom: colourful carpets of daisies, marigolds, begonias, and more, artfully arranged beneath dark, shaggy columns of spruce trees. This garden blends almost seamlessly into the **Leo Mol Sculpture Garden** ★★, an adjacent area containing the works of a single sculptor. Mol, a Ukrainian who immigrated to the city in 1949, has created whimsical bears, deer and nude bathers, among other forms. A glass-walled **gallery** (*free; Jun to Sep 10am to 8pm; ☎986-6531*) displays hundreds more pieces of his work, while a reflecting pool catches the grace of several posed figures. Mol's studio, moved to a new home just behind the gallery, can be viewed.

The park's most popular feature is the **Assiniboine Park Zoo** ★★★ (*$3; every-*

day 10am to 4pm, Sat and Sun 10am to 6pm; ☎986-2327). More than 1,600 animals live here, including Russian lynx, a polar bear, kangaroo, snowy and great horned owls – even imported residents like the *vicuña* (a kind of South American camel) and Siberian tigers. A statue of "Winnie-the-Bear" on the zoo grounds honours the famous Pooh's origins as a bear cub purchased by a Winnipeg soldier in Ontario and carried to England, where author A.A. Milne saw it and brought its story to a worldwide audience of children.

The **Prairie Dog Central** *($18; May, Jun and Sep Sun and holiday Mon 10am to 3pm, Jul and Aug Sat-Sun and holiday Mon 10am to 3pm; 0.5km north of Inkster Blvd. on Prairie Dog Trail, ☎832-5259 or 888-780-7328)* is a vintage steam train dating back to circa 1882 that welcomes visitors aboard for a unique 2.5hr excursion to Warren, northwest of Winnipeg.

Living Prairie Museum, in a suburb west of downtown, is said to contain the last significant pocket of tallgrass prairie in Canada. If so, these 12ha are a stark testament to the loss of the once vast prairie, for this is a rather small plot surrounded by an airfield, a school and housing developments, making it hard to imagine the wide open plains. However, the adjacent **Interpretation centre** ★ *(free entry, $2 for guided hike; Jul and Aug every day 10am to 5pm, Apr to Jun Sun only; 2795 Ness Ave., ☎832-0167)* does an adequate job of explaining and recapturing what once existed here. An annual festival, in August, draws further attention to the ecosystem.

Southwest of downtown, the **Fort Whyte Nature Centre** ★★ *($5; Mon to Fri 9am to 5pm, Sat and Sun 10am to 5pm, extended hours in summer; 1961 McCreary*

Rd., ☎989-8355) is a pocket of wilderness that's a bit more vital: its animal life includes foxes and muskrats; a number of birds are also present. An interpretive centre on the premises features an aquarium, demonstration beehive and other exhibits designed with children in mind.

Tiny **Riel House** ★★ *(suggested donation $2; mid-May to early Sep every day 10am to 6pm; 330 River Rd., just south of Bishop Grandin Blvd., St. Vital; ☎257-1783)* is set on a narrow river lot along the Red River. This building was home to famous Metis leader Louis Riel (see p 17) and his family for several years, and belonged to his descendants until 1969. Riel's body lay in state here after he was executed for treason in 1885. In addition to its connection with Riel, the museum paints a vivid picture of what life was like for the Metis in the Red River Settlement. Guided tours are available.

The **St. Norbert Farmers Market** *(late Jun to mid-Oct Sat 8am to 3pm, Jul and Aug Wed 3pm to dusk; ☎275-8349)* is just south of the perimeter, on the east side of Pembina Highway. During the summer, people come from all over southern Manitoba to sell their products at the outdoor stalls. Locally grown fruits and vegetables, home-made bread and baking, plants, crafts and traditional Mennonite farmer's sausage are all sold here.

Eastern Manitoba

Dugald

Just east of Winnipeg, in the small town of Dugald, is the **Costume Museum of Canada** ★ *($5; Jun to Aug 10am to 5pm, Apr to mid-Nov Tue to Fri 10am to 5pm, Sat and Sun noon to 5pm; at the intersection of Hwy. 15 and Dugald Rd., ☎853-2166)*, the

first of its kind in Canada. A 35,000-piece collection of costumes dating back to 1765 is displayed in tableaus, housed in an 1886 pioneer home. Special exhibits illustrate aspects of costume; one recent exhibit, for instance, explained the long history of the silk trade. The museum somehow has also acquired some of Queen Elizabeth I's linen napkins dating from the late 16th century.

Oak Hammock

Birds are the most satisfied visitors to **Oak Hammock Marsh and Conservation Centre** ★★ *($4; every day May to Aug 10am to 8pm, Sep and Oct 8:30am to dusk, Nov to Apr 10am to 4:30pm; head north on Hwy. 8, then east on Hwy. 67, ☎467-3300 or 800-665-3825)*, a protected wetland (it was once farmland) a few kilometres north of downtown Winnipeg. Among the annual arrivals are Canada geese, ducks and more than 250 other species; mammals like the park, too, and all are visible while walking the centre's boardwalks (constructed so as not to disturb the marsh) and dikes. Special guided tours and canoe excursions are also available.

An excellent **interpretive centre** ★ on site explains the value of the wetland and allows visitors to see it via remote-controlled cameras installed in the marsh. The Canadian headquarters of Ducks Unlimited are also located here.

★★ Red River Heritage Road

From Rte. 9 heading north, the Red River Heritage Road makes a nice meander off the beaten track. This territory once formed the heart of Thomas Douglas's "lower settlement" of Hudson's Bay Company charges; the dirt heritage road is beautifully laid out along the river banks and is well-marked with historic sites. It passes a number of old limestone buildings, including the William Scott farmhouse and the **Captain Kennedy Museum and Tea House** ★★ *(free admission; early May to end Sep Mon to Sat 10:30am to 4:30pm, Sun 10:30am to 6pm;* ☎*334-2498),* built by trader Captain William Kennedy in 1866 with three restored period rooms, English gardens and a superb view of the river. There is a pleasant restaurant where you can have a lovely English-style tea with scones.

Near the end of the road, the **St. Andrews-on-the-Red Anglican Church** ★★★ is the oldest stone church in western Canada still being used for public worship. It is handsome, with typical English pointed windows – the stained glass was supposedly shipped in molasses from England to protect it from breaking – and massive stone walls. Inside, benches are still lined with the original buffalo hide.

Just south of the church is **St. Andrews Rectory** ★★ *(*☎*334-6405 or 785-6050),* a striking little building that is now a national historic park. Signs on the grounds tell the story, and interpreters are available during summertime to discuss the rectory's function.

Selkirk

On Rte. 9A, Selkirk, a small river town marked by a giant green fish, is home to several important attractions. **Lower Fort Garry National Historic Site** ★ *($5.50; mid-May to early Sep, 9am to 5pm; off Hwy. 9, just south of Selkirk,* ☎*785-6050 or 877-534-3678),* just south of town, is a recreated trading post. It recalls the former importance of this post, built to replace the original Fort Garry in Winnipeg after it was carried away by flood waters. Exhibits include a recreated doctor's

office, powder magazine, Aboriginal encampment and blacksmith's shop. The main attraction, however, is the big stone house at the centre of the property, constructed for the governor of the Hudson's Bay Company. It displays many interesting artefacts, including housewares and an old piano transported here from Montréal by canoe. Costumed characters interact with visitors while baking, trading and otherwise acting out their roles.

Several bridges across the Red River provide good views of the surrounding landscape. Downtown, hugging the river, lies **Selkirk Park** (see p 448). The world's largest Red River Ox Cart (6.5m high and 13.7m long) stands here, and the **Marine Museum of Manitoba** ★★ *($3.50; May to Sep Mon to Fri 9am to 5pm, Sat and Sun 10am to 6pm; 490 Evelyn St.,* ☎*482-7761)* occupies six ships – including Manitoba's oldest steamship – at the park entrance. An actual lighthouse that once stood on Lake Winnipeg is also located here.

St. Peter's Dynevor Church ★ sits just across the Red River, and has a lovely view of it. The stone church, built in 1854, is a reminder of the first agricultural colony in Western Canada; it employed a combination of missionaries and First Nations. **Chief Peguis** is buried in the churchyard, as are other settlers of the colony.

North of Selkirk on Rte. 9, the **Little Britain Church** ★ is one of just five surviving Red River Settlement stone churches that remain standing in the province. It was constructed between 1872 and 1874.

Lockport

East of town, in Lockport at the foot of the large bridge, a park is home to the **Kenosewun Centre** *(free ad-*

mission; mid-May to mid-Sep 11am to 6:30pm; ☎*757-2902).* The name means "there are many fishes" in the Cree language; the centre displays Aboriginal horticultural artifacts and material on the history of the town, and offers tourist information. Pathways lead to the St. Andrews lock and dam.

Driving northeast from Selkirk, you will reach a series of beautiful white sandy beaches; some of the province's finest, including Winnipeg Beach (see p 447) and Camp Morton.

Gimli

Situated on the shores of Lake Winnipeg, Gimli is still the heart of Manitoba's Icelandic population; a Viking statue welcomes visitors to the centre of town. The town was once the capital of a sovereign republic known as New Iceland. A maritime ambiance still pervades the streets, though today it is mainly sailboats and windsurfers that set out from the marina and beach, while the history of the town's fishing industry and the lake's geological formation are recounted at the **Lake Winnipeg Visitor Centre** *(1 Centre St. at the harbour,* ☎*642-7974).*

The region's Icelandic heritage is commemorated with an annual festival (see p 455) and is also on display at the **New Icelandic Heritage Museum** *($4; Mon to Fri 9am to 5pm, Sat and Sun noon to 4pm;* ☎*642-7974),* located at the Betel Waterfront Centre. The museum recounts the history of the first Icelandic settlers to arrive on the shores of Lake Winnipeg and the collection will include interesting historical artifacts.

Around Lake Winnipeg

On the eastern side of Lake Winnipeg, Rte. 59 passes through resort towns located on some of the province's best beaches: **Grand Beach ★★★**, **Grand Marais** and **Victoria Beach ★** are the places to go during the summer for stunning white sand. Turning southeast again on Rte. 11, angling toward the Ontario border, the province's seemingly endless flatlands suddenly drop away and are replaced by rocks, rushing rivers and trees. As the road proceeds east, the towns become increasingly woodsy, while the fishing, canoeing and hiking become truly spectacular.

Pine Falls is known for its paper mill and a festival celebrating paper, hydroelectric power and fish. A string of increasingly remote provincial parks compete for the attention of the traveller seeking off-the-beaten track Manitoba.

Southern Manitoba

Directly south of Winnipeg, between the city and the United States border, lies the Pembina Valley – the province's Mennonite country. The drive is absolutely flat, and the endless fields are interrupted only by the leafy oases of towns such as **Altona**. The town is famous for its fields of sunflowers and an annual festival that celebrates them (see p 455).

Steinbach

Southeast of Winnipeg, Steinbach is the largest town in the region and features the popular **Mennonite Heritage Village ★★** (*$5; May to Sep Mon to Sat 10am to 5pm Sun noon to 5pm, Oct to Apr Mon to Fri 10am to 4pm; Hwy. 12, ☎326-9661*). A 17ha village is laid out in the traditional pattern. The buildings focus on the lives of Mennonites, people of Dutch origin who emigrated to the province from Russia beginning in 1874.

Attractions include a restaurant offering authentic Mennonite food (plums and meat are featured); a general store selling such goods as stone-ground flour and old-fashioned candy; sod and log houses; an interpretative building; exhibition galleries, and a windmill with 20m-high sails.

Mariapolis

In Mariapolis, an unusually beautiful church reminds visitors of the strong French and Belgian culture in the province. **Our Lady of the Assumption Roman Catholic Church ★★★** combines careful brickwork with a striking steeple whose alternating bands of black and white draw the eye upward to a simple cross.

Morden

Morden, another Mennonite stronghold, is known for its attractive agricultural research facility and streets of graceful fieldstone mansions; various local tour operators will point out the homes for a small fee. The **Morden and District Museum ★** (*$2; May to Sep every day 1pm to 5pm, Oct to Apr Wed to Sun 1pm to 5pm; 111B Gilmour St., ☎822-3406*) displays a good collection of prehistoric marine fossils, reminders of the vast inland sea that once covered North America. Also in town, the **Agriculture Canada Research Station** (*open daily dawn to dusk, arboretum closes at 5pm weekdays and all day week-*

ends; ☎822-4471) has impressive ornamental gardens.

Winkler

A bit farther east on Rte. 14, Winkler is home to the unusual **Pembina Thresherman's Museum ★** (*$3; May to Oct Tue to Sun 1pm to 6pm; ☎325-7497*), filled with tools and machines from another era.

Neubergthal

Just southeast of Altona, Neubergthal is one of the province's best-preserved Mennonite towns, with its distinctive layout (just one long street lined with houses) and equally distinctive architecture, featuring thatched roofing and barns connected to houses.

Tolstoi

Just east of the small town of Tolstoi on Rte. 209, a 128ha **patch of tallgrass prairie ★★** (*☎945-7775*) is maintained by the Manitoba Naturalists Society; this is the largest remaining tract of this kind being protected in Canada.

Central Manitoba

Two main routes pass across central Manitoba. The **Trans-Canada Highway** (*Hwy. 1*) is the faster of the two; though less visually rewarding, it does pass through the major population centres of Brandon and Portage la Prairie. The **Yellowhead Highway-Trans**

Canada *(Hwy. 16)* is a somewhat more scenic journey.

St. François-Xavier

Taking the Trans-Canada west from Winnipeg, it's not far to St. François-Xavier, a solidly French-Canadian village featuring one of Manitoba's most interesting restaurants (see p 454) as well as an intriguing Cree legend of a white horse. This is the oldest Metis settlement in the province, established in 1820 by **Cuthbert Grant**. Grant, legendary for his acumen at hunting buffalo, is buried inside the town's Roman Catholic church. The picturesque setting along a bow of the Assiniboine River makes this an excellent destination for a short excursion out of the city.

From here, **Rte. 26** makes a short scenic detour along the tree-lined Assiniboine River, once home to a string of trapping posts.

Portage La Prairie

A little farther west lies Portage la Prairie (pop. 20,000), founded in 1738 by French-Canadian explorer Pierre Gaultier de la Vérendrye as a resting stop on the riverine canoe journey to Lake Manitoba. The town's most interesting natural attraction is the crescent-shaped lake, a cutoff bow of the Assiniboine River that nearly encircles the entire downtown.

Island Park ★ sits inside that crescent, providing beautiful tree-shaded picnic spots by the water and a host of attractions, including a golf course, playground, deer and waterfowl sanctuary (watch for the Canada geese), fairgrounds and a "you-pick" strawberry farm. Canoeing is excellent here. Good relief from the heat and glare of driving.

The limestone **city hall** ★ ★, a former post office right on the main street, was designed by the same architect who planned Canada's first Parliament Buildings. It is surprisingly ornate, and has been declared a federal historic site.

Fort la Reine Museum and Pioneer Village ★ ★ ★ *($5; May to mid-Sep every day 9am to 6pm, Hwys. 26 and 1A,* ☎857-3259) is not, in fact, a fort, but rather an eclectic mix of old prairie buildings set on a small lot just east of town. This is not to say that it is not worth a visit; in fact, its small size makes the museum more manageable, and the varied collection is often surprising. Finery, such as mink stoles and gramophones ,tells of the aspirations of the people who once lived in this small prairie city and forms a stark contrast to the wash tubs, well-worn highchairs and rusted gas pumps found elsewhere in the museum, which give an excellent sense of the typical life of the average settler. It includes everything from a small trading post, trapper's cabin, school, church and barn to weathered houses like those prairie travellers see standing abandoned and on the verge of collapse in the flat, endless landscape.

Perhaps the museum's most remarkable piece is the luxurious and well-equipped railway car specially fitted for William Van Horne of the Canadian Pacific Railway, who traveled in it while overseeing the construction of the rail line. Next to it is one of the humble cabooses which are fast disappearing from the ends of trains across Canada. Children especially will enjoy climbing into the lookout dome of this relic from the past!

Austin

The highway west then passes through more fields and towns, reminders of the richness of the local farmland. A

short distance south of the one-street town of Austin, the **Manitoba Agricultural Museum** ★ *($5; mid-May to early Oct every day 9am to 5pm;* ☎637-2354) is particularly strong on farm equipment and old vehicles; John Deere tractors and implements and ancient snowmobiles are typical of the collection, which is the largest of operating vintage farm machinery in Canada. An old prairie schoolhouse, train station, general store and amateur radio museum have also been moved here to add atmosphere.

Every July, the **Thresherman's Reuninon and Stampede** brings the place alive for a weekend with farm contests and a race between a turtle and an old-fashioned tractor. (Sometimes the turtle wins!).

Glenboro

A detour 40km south of the Trans-Canada takes you to Glenboro, gateway to Spruce Woods Provincial Park (see p 449) Located near Baldur, 23km south of Glenboro **Frelsis** ★ is the oldest Icelandic Lutheran church in Canada. Manitoba's last remaining cable ferry still crosses the Assiniboine River here.

Brandon

Brandon (pop. 42,000) is Manitoba's second-largest city, a city so tied to the fortunes of the surrounding wheatfields that wheat is still grown experimentally right near the centre of town. Many gracious Victorian homes stand in the residential area just south of downtown. The handsome 1911 **Central Fire Station** ★ *(637 Princess Ave.)* and neoclassical **Courthouse** *(Princess Ave. and 11th St.)* are both on Princess Avenue, one of the city's main streets.

Turn right on 18th St. to reach the **Daly House Museum** ★ ★ *($3; Tue to Sat 10am to 5pm,*

Sun noon to 5pm; 122-18th St., ☎727-1722) the best place to get a feel for Brandon's history. Once home to Brandon's mayor, the house today includes a grocery store, recreated City Council chamber and research centre. A little farther is the attractive campus of **Brandon University**.

Heading north along 18th St. leads you to Grand Valley Road, which takes you to the **Agriculture and Agri-Food Canada Research Centre ★ ★** *(May to Sep Mon to Fri 8am to 4pm; Grand Valley Rd., ☎822-4471)*, whose scenic grounds and striking modern glass building are set in an idyllic location with a view of the valley. Guided tours are available Tuesdays and Thursdays at 1:30pm and 3:30pm.

Finally, there's an interesting aircraft museum housed in Hangar No. 1 of the city airport on the northern outskirts of Brandon. The **Commonwealth Air Training Plan Museum ★** *($5; May to Sep every day 10am to 4pm, Oct to Apr 1pm to 4pm; ☎727-2444)* features vintage planes from WWII Royal Canadian Air Force training schools that were held here; some of the more interesting articles include a restored vintage flight simulator, memorials, official telegrams announcing casualties and losses and biographies of flyers.

Souris

Southwest of Brandon, Souris is known for its **swinging suspension bridge ★**, Canada's longest at 177m; the bridge was constructed at the turn of the century and restored after a 1976 flood swept it away. The adjacent **Hillcrest Museum** *($2; May and Jun Sun 2pm to 5pm, Jul to early Sep every day 10am to 6pm; 26 Crescent Ave.E; ☎483-2008 or 483-3138)* preserves

items of local historical interest.

Neepawa

Another choice for touring central Manitoba is the Yellowhead Highway (Hwy. 16). Lying to the west of Winnipeg, Neepawa touts itself as the "World Lily Capital". This is no idle boast, especially in lily season, when this pretty little town blooms. The oldest operating courthouse in Manitoba is here, as is the **Margaret Laurence Home** *($2; May and Jun Mon to Fri 10am to 6pm Sat and Sun noon to 6pm, Jul and Aug every day 10am to 6pm, Sep to mid-Oct every day noon to 5pm; 312 First Ave., ☎476-3612)*, dedicated to the beloved author who was born here. Laurence's typewriter and furniture are the highlights.

Minnedosa

Minnedosa, a tiny town to the west, surprises with its Czech and Slovak populations. A series of prairie potholes, glacier-made depressions in the earth that later filled with rainwater, lie south of town on Rte. 262 and provide optimum conditions for waterfowl such as drake, mallards and teal. Continuing north of Minnedosa on Rte. 262, the road enters a valley good for spotting white-tailed deer; a wildlife viewing tower provides even better opportunities to do so.

Dauphin

Just north of the Yellowhead, Dauphin is transformed into the famous **Selo Ukrainia** ("Ukrainian Village") during the **National Ukrainian Festival** (see p 456) each summer. The event draws thousands to the town in late July.

Also in Dauphin, the **Fort Dauphin Museum ★** *($3; May to Sep Mon to Fri 9am to 5pm,*

also on weekends Jul and Aug; 140 Jackson St., ☎638-6630) recreates one of the area's French-run North West Company trading posts, showcasing fur trapping and other pioneer activities. The displays and buildings include a trapper's cabin, blacksmith's shop, one-room rural schoolhouse, Anglican church and the trading post. There's even a birch-bark canoe made entirely from natural materials, and a collection of fossils such as a bison horn, mammoth tusk and an ancient canine skull.

Western Manitoba

Inglis

As the "sentinels of the prairies" rapidly disappear from the landscape, the **Inglis Grain Elevators ★** *(Railway Ave.; May to Sep Mon-Fri 9am to 4pm, Sat and Sun 1pm to 4pm, ☎564-2243)* stand as a reminder of the golden era of the Canadian West. A row of five standard wooden grain elevators is being preserved as a National Historic Site, allowing visitors to see for themselves these impressive wooden structures. One of the elevators contains an interpretive centre, and the others are being remodelled for various uses.

Northern Manitoba

The Pas

The so-called Woods and Water Rte. shows another side of Manitoba. The Pas, home to a large Aboriginal population, hosts an important annual gathering of trappers and has an exceedingly clear lake. Most visitors head for the **Sam Waller Museum ★ ★** *($2; mid-May to mid-Sep every day 10am to 5pm; Sep to mid-May every day 1pm to 5pm; 306 Fischer Ave., ☎623-3802)*.

Manitoba

Getting to Northen Manitoba

Special arrangements are required to reach Manitoba's far north. VIA Rail runs regular trains from Winnipeg to Churchill three times a week, taking a full day and two nights each way.

Canadian Airlines and its partner **Calm Air** (☎632-1250) operate regularly scheduled flights from

Winnipeg everyday except Saturday year-round; in autumn, during polar bear season, there are additional flights on weekends.

Once in Churchill, a variety of charter air and bus services can be hired for excursions out onto the tundra.

Built in 1916 and occupying the town's former courthouse, it covers local natural and cultural history, based on the eclectic collection of Sam Waller. Walking tours are offered.

A wall of **Christ Church ★★** (*Edwards Ave.*, ☎623-2119) is inscribed with the Ten Commandments in the Cree language. The church was built in 1840 by Henry Budd, the first Aboriginal in Canada ordained to the Anglican ministry, and still retains some furnishings fashioned by ships' carpenters and brought here during an 1847 expedition.

Flin Flon

Flin Flon is Canada's most whimsically named municipality and greets visitors with a jumble of streets climbing the rocky hills. Located mostly in Manitoba, with a smaller part spilling over into Saskatchewan, Flin Flon is the most important mining centre in this part of the country, and has grown to become the province's sixth-largest city.

Flin Flon was named by a group of gold prospectors in

1915 who found a copy of the mass-market science fiction paperback of the same name during a northern Manitoba portage. Later, on a lakeshore near here, they staked a mining claim and named it for the book's main character, Josiah Flintabbatey Flonatin or "Flinty" to locals. Thus, the green 7.5m-tall **Josiah Flintabbatey Flonatin statue** presides over the city's entrance. It was designed for the city by the renowned American cartoonist Al Capp.

A walk around town reveals old boomtown-era hotels, bright red headframes indicating mine shafts, and historic redwood cabins. Of all these historic sites, though, the **Flin Flon Station Museum ★★** (*$2; early Jun to end Aug every day 10am to 8pm;* ☎687-2946) might be the best. It has a small collection of local mining artifacts, including a diving suit and helmet for underwater prospecting, a Linn tractor, a train sweeper and an ore car. The collection also includes a stuffed 29kg lake trout that was caught near here.

Churchill

Special arrangements are required to reach the far north of Manitoba. Isolated and cold, Churchill nevertheless beguiles travellers with its remoteness and stunning wildlife. The place is important historically as well, having helped the English first establish a foothold in Manitoba. They chose the site because of a superb natural harbour, so it's fitting that the town's dominant feature today is a huge **grain elevator** beside the docks.

The townsite is also located right in the middle of the migratory path of the area's **polar bear** population, which is a mixed blessing for the town's inhabitants. While these majestic animals attract visitors from around the world to this remote spot every autumn, they also wander right into town occasionally, posing a potential risk to anyone who crosses their path. In addition to the bears, people also come here. They come to see caribou, seals, birds and especially white **beluga whales** in summer. And there is always the possibility of an astonishing display of the aurora borealis, or northern lights.

The **Parks Canada Visitor Reception Centre** (☎675-8863), orients visitors with an overview of the fur posts and forts. **Prince of Wales Fort ★★** (*$5; early Jun to early Sep, times are dependant on tides and wearther permitting,* ☎675-8863), an enormous, diamond-shaped stone battlement located at the mouth of the Churchill River, is historically interesting: after four decades of steady construction by the English it was surrendered to Canadian forces without a fight. The fort can only be reached by boat or helicopter; in summer, park staff lead interpretive tours of the site.

Sloop's Cove National Historic Site ★ ★ *($5, early Jun to early Sep; ☎675-8863)*, 4km upstream from the fort, is a natural harbour that provided safe haven for huge wooden sailing ships at least as far back as 1689. When the Hudson's Bay Company set up shop here, its sloops were moored to these rocks with iron rings. Some of the rocks still bear inscriptions from the men posted there – men like explorer Samuel Hearne, who presided over the company in its heyday. Like Fort Prince of Wales, the site can only be reached by boat or helicopter. Call ahead for times and booking.

Across the river, **Cape Merry National Historic Site** ★ *(Jun every day, Jul to Sep Sat; ☎675-8863)* preserves a gunpowder magazine, the only remnant of a battery built here back in 1746. It is reached via the Centennial Parkway.

The **Eskimo Museum** ★ ★ ★ *(free admission; Jun to Mid Nov Mon 1pm to 5pm, Tue to Sat 9am to noon and 1pm to 5pm; mid-Nov to Jun Mon to Sat 1pm to 4:30pm; 242 La Vérendrye Ave., ☎675-2030)* maintains one of the world's pre-eminent collections of Inuit artifacts. Founded in 1944 by the local Roman Catholic Diocese, it contains artifacts dating from as far back as 1700BC. A set of ornately carved walrus tusks is among its most impressive pieces.

The **Northern Studies Centre** *(Launch Rd., ☎675-2307)*, 24km east of Churchill proper, is located in a former rocket test-range. Today, students come here to study the northern lights, Arctic ecology, photography and ornithology.

York Factory National Historic Site ★ ★ ★ *($5; mid-May to mid-Sep; ☎675-8863)*, 250km southeast of Churchill, is what remains of the Hudson Bay Company fur-trade post

that first established the English in western Canada. A wooden depot built in 1832 still stands here, and there are ruins of a stone gunpowder magazine and a cemetery with markers dating back to the 1700s. Access can only be gained by charter plane or canoe, however; some guided tours are also offered in summer through Parks Canada.

Finally, there are the spectacular **polar bears** ★ ★ ★, easily Churchill's premier attraction. Autumn is the time to observe them, and the only way is as part of a guided tour (see p 450).

Parks

For information on Manitoba's Provincial Parks : ☎*800-214-6497* or *www.gov.mb.ca/natres/parks*.

Greater Winnipeg

Birds Hill Provincial Park, just north of Winnipeg, sits on a gentle rise deposited by retreating glaciers. It makes for easy and popular cross-country skiing. In summer, visitors bike and hike the park's trails (one of which is wheelchair-accessible) to view prairie wildflowers – including several species of rare orchid – or head for a small beach. The park is also the site of the city's annual folk-music extravaganza (see p 455).

Grand Beach Provincial Park is the most popular beach in Manitoba, hands down. Situated 100km north of Winnipeg on Lake Winnipeg's eastern shore, it consists of lovely white sand and grassy 8m-high dunes that seem to have been lifted directly from Cape Cod. As a bonus, the beach is wheelchair-accessible. Three

self-guiding trails wind through the park – Spirit Rock Trail, Wild Wings Trail and the Ancient Beach Trail – enlightening beach-goers before they even slap on the sunblock. This is a good spot for windsurfing, as well. There are full tourist facilities here, including a restaurant, campground and outdoor amphitheatre for concerts. A golf course lies just outside the park.

St. Norbert Provincial Heritage Park *(free; every day mid-May to Sep 11am to 7pm; Museum Jun Mon to Fri, Jul to Sep Thu to Mon 8:30am to 3:30pm; 40 Turnbull Dr.)* is a 6.8ha, south-Winnipeg complex of buildings, a former Metis and then French-Canadian settlement at the juncture of the Red and La Salle rivers. The restored gambrel-roofed Bohémier farmhouse and two other homes are on display and there is also a self-guided trail.

Eastern Manitoba

Winnipeg Beach Provincial Park ★ ★ *(☎389-2752)* has long been a favourite summer getaway for Winnipeg residents. Besides the well-known beach and a boardwalk, the park's grounds also include a marina, campground and bay that's a favourite with windsurfers.

Whiteshell Provincial Park ★ ★ ★ *(from Winnipeg, take Hwy. 1 east to Falcon Lake or West Hawk Lake, or, farther north, take Provincial Rd. 307 to Seven Sisters Falls, or Hwy. 44 to Rennie)* is Manitoba's largest and best. Occupying some 2,720km^2, it is rich in lakes, rapids, waterfalls, fish and birds. There's something for everyone: **Alf Hole Goose Sanctuary** ★ *(☎369-5470)* is among the best places in the province to see Canada geese, especially during migration; the rocks at **Bannock Point** ★, laid out by local First

Nations to resemble the forms of snakes, fish, turtles and birds, are of archaeological interest; the cliffs of **Lily Pond ★** are 3.75 billion years old. West Hawk Lake is the location of the province's deepest lake, which is popular with scuba divers. **Hiking** is also good in Whiteshell. Hikes include the Forester's Foot-steps Trail, an easy walk through jackpine forest and then up a granite ridge, the Pine Point Trail, which is suited for cross-country skiing in winter, and the White Pine trail. A **Visitor Centre** and the **Whiteshell Natural History Museum** *(free; May to Sep every day 9am to 5pm;* ☎*348-2846)* help orient travellers and explain the park's ecology, geology and wildlife.

Nopiming Provincial Park *(from Winnipeg, take Hwy. 59 North to Hwy. 44; continue east along Hwy. 11, before turning onto Provincial Rd. 313 North and finally taking Provincial Rd. 315 East to Bird Lake, which lies just south of the park)* shows a whole different side of Manitoba; a place of huge granite outcrops and hundreds of lakes. The sur-prising presence of woodland caribou here is an added bo-nus, as are the fly-in and drive-in **fishing lodges** scattered through the park. "Nopiming" is an Anishinabe (Ojibwa and Cree) word meaning "en-trance to the wilderness."

Atikaki Provincial Wilderness Park ★★★ *(from Winnipeg, take Hwy. 59 North, then turn onto Provincial Rd. 304)*, in the east of the province along the Ontario border, consists of a 400,000ha hodgepodge of cliffs, rock formations, pris-tine lakes and cascading rivers. It is extremely difficult to get to, however, requiring a ca-noe, floatplane or a hike of several days to reach its inte-rior; as a result, it contains the most unspoiled wilderness in the province's major park-lands. Fly-in lodges are found

throughout the park region. Among the highlights are a series of rock murals painted by Aboriginals and a 20m waterfall well suited for white-water canoeing. As Atikaki means "country of the cari-bou," moose and caribou sightings are quite possible.

Hecla Provincial Park ★★ *(from Winnipeg, take Hwy. 8 North along Lake Winnipeg to Gull Harbour)* is a beautiful and interesting park, combin-ing lake ecology with dramatic island geology and the colours and creatures of the forest. Interpretive programs take place year-round, and there is a tower for viewing and photographing wildlife. The park's **Hecla Village ★** adds a short trail with points of historical interest relating to Icelandic culture and architec-ture and a **heritage home museum ★★** *(Thu to Mon 11am to 5pm)*, a restored 1920s home. Adjacent **Grind-stone Provincial Park ★★** is still being developed, and therein lies its beauty: it is not nearly as busy as Hecla.

West of Lake Winnipeg, the **Narcisse Wildlife Manage-ment Area** on Rte. 17 be-comes wildly popular late each April and May when thousands of resident red-sided garter snakes emerge from their limestone dens to participate in a visceral mating ritual.

Selkirk Park, a riverside park in downtown Selkirk, has lots of recreational opportunities. There are campgrounds, boat-launching pads and an outdoor swimming pool. Snowshoeing and ice fishing are possible in winter; in spring and summer, the park is home to a bird sanctuary with an observation deck for view-ing Canada geese and other birds.

Prairie Dog

Central Manitoba

Grand Valley Provincial Park ★ *(just west of Brandon on Hwy. 1)* is best known for the **Stott Site ★★**, a desig-nated provincial heritage site. Bones and artifacts from at least 1,200 years ago have been discovered here. A bison enclosure and camp have been reconstructed.

North of Portage La Prairie, on the shore of Lake Mani-toba, lies the 18,000ha **Delta Marsh**, one of the largest waterfowl staging marshes in North America, stretching 8km along the lake and a great place to bring binoculars. At Delta Beach, a waterfowl and wetlands research station studies ecological questions in a natural environment.

Approximately 23km south of Roblin, the **Frank Skinner Arboretum Trail** commemo-rates the work of Dr. Frank Leith Skinner, a famous Cana-dian horticulturist. This farm served as Skinner's laboratory for breeding new strains of plants; visitors can walk atop a former dike, visit Skinner's greenhouse, and walk the Wild Willow Trail.

Western Manitoba

The "Spirit Sands," a desert landscape of immense sand dunes in **Spruce Woods Provincial Park** ★★ *(take the Trans-Canada Hwy. 1 west to Carberry, then take Hwy. 5 South)* never fails to take visitors by surprise. Self-guided trails take hikers through the dunes and the surrounding spruce forests and prairie, and to the "Devil's Punch Bowl," an unusual pond created by underground streams. Campgrounds and a sandy beach for swimming make this large park popular in the summer.

Turtle Mountain Provincial Park ★★ *(from Brandon, travel 100km on Hwy. 10 South until you reach the park)*, composed of compacted coal and glacial deposits, rises more than 250m above the surrounding prairie land. Explorer La Vérendrye called it the "blue jewel of the plains," and its gentle hills lend themselves to mountain biking, horseback riding and hiking. There is also, of course, a considerable population of the beautiful painted turtles that give the mountain its name. Camping is available at three lakes here.

Riding Mountain National Park ★★★ *(☎848-7275 or 800-707-8480)* rises majestically from the plains with aspen-covered slopes that are habitats for wild animals such as elk, moose, deer, wolves and lynx. The largest black bear ever seen in North America was killed here by a poacher in 1992, and bison are contained within a large **bison enclosure** ★★ near Lake Audy. Rte. 10, running north-south, passes directly through the heart of the park and past the shores of its most

beautiful lakes. The 12m-high wooden Agassiz lookout tower here gives a superb view of the surrounding territory. The remains of an old sawmill also fall within park boundaries, as does a series of geological formations called beach ridges – former edges of a giant lake.

The local Aboriginal people own and operate a traditional **Anishinabe Village** *(Southquill Camp; ☎925-2030; On site May 15 to Sep 15; ☎848-2815)* in the park which offers visitors the opportunity to learn about Anishinabe culture. The camp features tipi accommodations and campsites, walking tours, traditional teachings, performances and local crafts.

Rte. 19 begins in the centre of the park and travels a switchback path up (or down) the park's steepest ridge. The naturalist Grey Owl, an Englishman who passed himself off as an Aboriginal person, lived here for six months, giving talks with his two tamed beavers (he spent most of his time in Prince Albert National Park, however, see p 426); his remote **cabin** ★ is located 17km up a hiking trail off Rte. 19. More than 400km of trails have been cleared at Riding Mountain National Park, including the North Escarpment Loop, best for views, Whitewater Lake, giving a history of the prisoner-of-war camp that was once here, and the Strathclair Trail, formerly a fur trappers' route. through the wooded hills. The park is also dotted with a number of pristine lakes superb for swimming. The sand beach at Wasagaming on **Clear Lake** ★★ is a hub of activity. There is also a superb **golf course**.

Duck Mountain Provincial Park ★★★ *(from Dauphin, take Hwy. 5 West, then Provincial Rd. 366 North)* rises in long hills near the Manitoba-Saskatchewan border; forests,

meadows and lakes appear where the land has wrinkled upward in the Manitoba Escarpment formation. This is the home of **Baldy Mountain** ★★, the highest mountain in the province at 831m (there is also a tower at the top to get a still better view), as well as six hiking trails and a lake so clear the bottom, 10m below, can be seen from its surface.

Northern Manitoba

At **Clearwater Lake Provincial Park** ★ *(from The Pas, take Hwy. 10 North to Provincial Hwy. 287, then head east to the park)*, the lake water is so clear that the bottom is visible 11m below the surface, making it one of the clearest lakes in the world. It is well known for its lake trout and northern pike. Also interesting is a series of enormous limestone slabs on the south shore; known as "the caves," they splintered off from the nearby cliffs and can be reached by a trail.

The **Wapusk National Park** lies within the **Cape Churchill Wildlife Management Area** ★★ which, together with the **Cape Tatnam Wildlife Management Area** ★★, takes in the coastline of Hudson Bay from Churchill to the Ontario border – a tremendous stretch of wild country, nearly 2.4 million hectares of land in all, harbouring polar bears, woodland caribou and many more birds and animals. They are accessible only by plane.

The region of **Grass River Provincial Park** ★★ *(from Flin Flon, take Hwy. 10 South, turn left onto Hwy. 39 which takes you to the park)* was used by the Aboriginal peoples for thousands of years, then explored anew by the English. Countless islands and some 150 lakes interrupt the river. A Karst spring, which gushes from a rock cliff is one of the park's most fascinating sites.

Outdoor Activities

Polar-Bear-Watching

Churchill

Churchill is famous for its polar-bear-watching tours, which can be arranged through local outfitters, such as the following:

Tundra Buggy Tours (☎675-2121 or 800-544-5049) has vehicles specially outfitted to accommodate photographers.

Seal River Heritage Lodge (☎675-8875 or 888-326-7325) runs ecotours out of a remote wilderness lodge in the north country. Sights include caribou, polar bears, beluga whales and seals.

Churchill Nature Tours (☎636-2968) specializes in nature-study tours of the Churchill region.

Bird-Watching

Eastern Manitoba

The **Netley Marsh ★** *(Rte. 320, 16km north of Selkirk)* is one of the most frequented spots in the country for migrating birds, and said to be one of the most important waterfowl nesting areas in North America. At least 18 species of ducks and geese flock here each autumn to feed before heading south for the long winter.

Oak Hammock Marsh *(year-round; north of Hwy 67 on PR220,* ☎467-3300) is one of the best bird-viewing areas in North America, with more than 295 species of birds, 32km of hiking trails, canoe excursions and more.

Northern Manitoba

Bird Cove ★, 16km east of Churchill, might be the area's best spot for observing the hundreds of bird species that pass through here, including possibly the rare Ross Gull. The wreck of the Ithaca, which sank in a storm on its way to Montreal in 1961 with a load of nickel ore, sits at the western tip of the cove.

For addresses of polar bear-observation outfitters see above.

Polar bear

Water Sports

Eastern Manitoba

Gimli's best rental agency for water and land sports is **H2O Beach and Adventure Sports** (☎642-9781), located right on the sandy beach of **Lake Winnipeg**. It rents bicycles, in-line skates, sailboats, kayaks, beach volleyballs, windsurfing equipment and just about everything else one could want or need.

It's purely manufactured fun, but **Skinner's Wet 'n' Wild Waterslide Park** *(mid-May to mid-Sep* ☎757-2623) in Lockport keeps drawing crowds anyway. The attraction contains four giant waterslides, two smaller slides, a giant hot tub, mini-golf, bumper boats, arcade and lots more. It's impossible to miss the complex, situated at the west end of the Lockport bridge.

Downhill Skiing

Western Manitoba

The **Asessippi Ski Area** *($32; Asessippi Provincial Park, off Hwy. 83 near Russell and Inglis,* ☎564-2000) boasts the biggest ski hill between Regina and Winnipeg, sculpted for challenging, if somewhat short, downhill runs. The slopes cater to beginner and more advanced skiers, and include a snowboard terrain park. The new lodge offers cafeteria-style dining, an arcade and a bar, with beautiful views of the valley. Ski rentals, lessons and night skiing available.

Accommodations

Bed and Breakfast of Manitoba
893 Dorchester Ave.
☎*661-0300*
www.bedandbreakfast. mb.ca
Bed and Breakfast of Manitoba coordinates reservations for approximately 81 member B&Bs throughout the province.

The Manitoba Country Vacations Association
☎/≈*667-3526*
www.countryvacations. mb.ca
The Manitoba Country Vacations Association in Winnipeg, provides a similar service but a different experience, booking rooms at farms or other rural vacation destinations.

Winnipeg

Guest House International Hostel
$
sb, ≡, 🐾
168 Maryland St.
☎*772-1272 or 800-743-4423*
≈*772-4117*
This is a quirky old house in a residential neighbourhood very close to downtown Winnipeg. However, be cautious when walking in this area at night. Walls feature art by Aboriginal children, and there are all kinds of rooming options. A game room in the somewhat crowded basement adds appeal, and the price is right.

Ivey House International Hostel
$
sb, ≡
210 Maryland St.
☎*772-3022*
≈*784-1133*
www.bihostels.ca
This extremely friendly and well-run Hostelling International-member facility is

situated close to downtown (and very close to the other hostel). A classy operation, featuring a big kitchen, great staff and rooms that sometimes include desks.

Ramada Marlborough Hotel Winnipeg
$$
≡, 𝕽, 🐾
331 Smith St.
☎*942-6411 or 800-667-7666*
≈*942-2017*
www.ramada.com
With its central location and beautiful facade, the Ramada Marlborough makes a stunning first impression. While the sophisticated style is carried through in the hotel's wood-panelled dining room and the pleasant breakfast room, the guestrooms don't quite measure up, tending to be somewhat gloomy and cramped. Nevertheless, the place is comfortable.

Hotel Fort Garry
$$$ bkfst incl.
≡, △, 𝕽, ≈, ☺
222 Broadway
☎*942-8251 or 800-665-8088*
≈*956-2351*
www.fortgarryhotel.com
One of the most recognizable hotels on the city's skyline, this big-shouldered, recently renovated neo-Gothic building was built by the Canadian National Railway in 1913. The impressive lobby and function rooms welcome guests in high style, though the rooms themselves are somewhat disappointing for a hotel of this calibre. Extensive renovations were just being completed at press time.

Fairmont Winnipeg
$$$
☺, 🐾, ≡, 𝕽, ≈, △, ⊛
2 Lombard Place
☎*957-1350 or 800-441-1414*
≈*956-5527*
www.fairmont.com
This landmark is among the top posh digs in the city. It's where the Rolling Stones stay when they're in town, though

they sometimes get bumped by business conventions. Located at the busy and famous corner of Portage and Main.

Radisson Hotel Winnipeg Downtown
$$$$
🐾, ≡, 𝕽, ≈, △, ⊛
288 Portage Ave.
☎*956-0410 or 800-333-3333*
≈*947-1129*
www.radisson.com
Smack in the downtown business district, this posh hotel features an haute-cuisine restaurant, child-care services and laundry service. Elegantly remodelled, the tastefully decorated rooms offer every comfort and excellent views. Very friendly and professional service make this one of the best places to stay.

Place Louis-Riel All-Suite Hotel
$$$$$
≡, *K*, 𝕽, 🐾, ☺
190 Smith St.
☎*947-6961 or 800-665-0569*
≈*943-3574*
www.placelouisriel.com
Every unit in this downtown high-rise is a suite, comprising several rooms and usually a kitchenette. Seventeen of the suites have two bedrooms. Ideal for longer visits.

Delta Winnipeg
$$$$
☺, ≡, *K*, 𝕽, ≈, ⊛, △, 🐾
350 St. Mary Ave.
☎*942-0551 or 800-268-1133*
≈*943-8702*
www.deltahotels.com
This centrally located hotel comes with all the frills: four restaurants, a dry cleaning service, a beautiful pool and recreation area and an attractive lobby. It even offers aerobic classes!

St. Boniface

Gîte de la Cathédrale Bed and Breakfast
$ bkfst incl.
sb
581 Rue Langevin
☎233-7792
Gîte de la Cathédrale Bed and Breakfast is located right across from Provencher Park in old St. Boniface. Five pleasant, flowery bedrooms are available; all have ceiling fans. Hostess Jacqueline Bernier's traditional French-Canadian breakfast might include pancakes with maple syrup, an omelette, or delicious French toast, served at a beautifully set table. Service is available in French and is very friendly.

Greater Winnipeg

Birds Hill Provincial Park

Birds Hill Provincial Park Campground
$
Late Apr to mid-Oct
Birds Hill Provincial Park, 24 km north of Winnipeg, on Hwy. 59
☎948-3333 or 888-482-2267
www.manitobaparks.com
Birds Hill Provincial Park offers family and group camping with numerous activities close by. Bicycling and walking trails, a riding stable and beach are all available in the park, and downtown Winnipeg is only a 40-minute drive away.

Eastern Manitoba

Selkirk

Selkirk Inn Banquet & Conference Centre
$$
🐾, K, ℜ, ≡
162 Main St.
☎482-7722 or 800-930-3888
⇒482-8655
The Selkirk Inn Banquet & Conference Centre offers reasonably priced accommodations in central Selkirk, not

far from several important local attractions. Rooms with kitchen units cost only $10 extra, and videocassette players are also available for an extra charge.

Whiteshell Provincial Parks

West Hawk Lake Campground
$
Mid-May to mid-Oct
off Hwy. 1
☎948-3333 or 888-482-2267
www.manitobaparks.com
West Hawk Lake offers camping in a beautiful setting, with all the amenities. Campsites are separated by birches and pines and offer varying degrees of privacy, from tucked-away single lots to clusters of serviced sites. The campground is within easy walking distance of two beaches, three restaurants and tennis courts. Also an excellent base for hiking and canoeing.

Hecla Provincial Park

Gull Harbour Resort
$$-$$$
≡, ℜ, ≈, △, ℝ, ℨ
☎279-2041 or 800-267-6700
⇒279-2000
A beautiful resort on the tip of an island. This convention centre is especially well known for the golf courses nearby, as well as the natural scenery of Hecla and Grindstone parks. It's also located close to the Hecla Island Heritage Home Museum.

Gimli

Lakeview Resort
$$$
🐾, ≡, ℜ, ≈, △, ℝ, ☉
10 Centre St.
☎642-8565 or 877-355-3500
⇒642-4400
www.lakeviewhotels.com
The Lakeview Resort is right on the harbour in Gimli. Guests can choose a country-style suite or a room overlooking the small town or the large lake from which the town derives most of its busi-

ness. Breaking with the tradition of impersonal rooms in most big hotel chains, rooms here feature quilts, a fresh scent, and refrigerators; there is a cozy fireplace in the lobby. Each room has a balcony.

Southern Manitoba

Winkler

Winkler Inn
$$
≡, 🐾, ℜ, ≈, ⊛, K
851 Main St.
☎325-4381 or 800-829-4920
⇒325-9656
www.winklerinn.com
The fertile Pembina Valley draws visitors to Winkler, and the Winkler Inn accommodates them with a wide variety of amenities, including queen-sized beds and a view of the pool. Also on site are a bar, restaurant, pool, and 10-person hot tub.

Central Manitoba

Wasagaming

The New Chalet
$$
≈, ≡, K
☎848-2892
⇒848-4515
www.newchalet.com
The New Chalet is open year-round and offers some of the best accommodations in the area. Pleasant and newly renovated, this well-kept establishment is centrally located and offers guests the use of its outdoor swimming pool. It should be noted that since the hotel lies within park boundaries, guests must pay the park admission fee.

Roblin

Harvest Moon Inn
$$ bkfst incl.
K, ≡, ℝ
25 Commercial Dr.
☎*937-3700 or 888-377-3399*
⇄*937-3701*
The Harvest Moon Inn is a
new all-suite hotel with lots of
room. Each suite includes a
microwave, refrigerator,
television and videocassette
recorder; a small selection of
free movies is available at the
front desk. As a bonus, the
family that runs the business is
full of fishing advice and inter-
esting stories about their
travels.

Brandon

Comfort Inn
$$
≡, 🐾
925 Middleton Ave.
☎*424-6423 or 800-228-5150*
⇄*727-2246*
www.choicehotels.com
The Comfort Inn offers super
rooms and professional management right on the Trans-
Canada north of downtown
Brandon. Rooms here feature
work tables and sofas, a bonus
for business travellers; the
only drawback is the place's popularity: it is often booked up
months in advance.

Northern Manitoba

Churchill

Polar Inn and Suites
$$$
K, 🐾, ≡
15 Franklin St.
☎*675-8878 or 877-765-2733*
⇄*675-2647*
www.cancom.net/polarinn
The Polar Inn and Suites offers
one-bedroom apartments,
kitchenette suites and standard
rooms. Mountain-bike rentals
are a real bonus for outdoor
types, and shoppers will find
the on-site gift shop pleasant.

Northern Nights Lodge
$$$$
🐾, ℜ, △, ⊛
☎*675-2403*
⇄*675-2011*
This northern outpost caters
to those in search of the polar
bears who can usually be seen
frolicking on the shores of
Hudson Bay.

Restaurants

Winnipeg

Alycia's
$
559 Cathedral Ave.
☎*582-8789*
This is likely the most popular
of Winnipeg's half-dozen or so
Ukrainian eateries. "It sticks
with you," say customers of
the food here; and, indeed,
the place is well-known
around town for thick soups,
hearty perogies, cabbage rolls
and other warming fare. Red
creamy sodas and decora-
tions, such as Ukrainian Easter
eggs and pictures of the Pope,
add to the festive mood, and
the owners also run a deli
next door that offers takeout
meats and side dishes.

Nucci's Gelati
$
643 Corydon Ave.
☎*475-8765*
On a hot summer night, this
ice cream parlour is the place
to be. Don't be put off by the
long line-up: the 30 flavours of
delicious home-made gelato
are well worth the wait! The
huge servings will keep you
cool as you stroll along Winni-
peg's Italian strip, which
comes alive with a festive
atmosphere at night.

Carlos & Murphy's
$$
129 Osborne Ave.
☎*284-3510*
Right beside the Tap & Grill
(see below), this small, dark
restaurant has a real frontier
feel to it – rough wooden
boards are nailed to the wall in
the pattern of a sunset, and
saddles and other western
gear decorate the interior.
The Tex-Mex food comes in
large portions, and is good
with a lime Margarita or a
Mexican beer.

Tap & Grill
$$
137 Osborne St.
☎*284-7455*
Located in the trendy
Osborne Village, this restau-
rant has a relaxed Mediterra-
nean atmosphere. Wicker
chairs, shutters and ceramic
tile floors create a cool, south-
ern interior. There is an out-
door terrace in the back,
surrounded by trellises and
plants; an idyllic and very pop-
ular spot in the summertime.
The menu includes meat
dishes, seafood, pasta and a
selection of fresh salads.
Lemon, garlic and sun-dried
tomatoes are the dominant
flavours.

Hy's Steak Loft
$$$-$$$$
216 Kennedy St.
☎*942-1000*
The brick-warehouse appear-
ance of this downtown institu-
tion is quite deceiving; it's one
of those places where smoky
backroom deals are forged
over Alberta prime beef. Poli-
ticians and other bigshots head
for the wood-panelled steak
room to watch the beef char-
grilled to order on an open
grill right before their eyes.
Those with real clout ask for
one of the Loft's private dining
rooms and discuss changes in
insurance laws or whatever
else needs to be arranged out
of the public's earshot. There's
a lounge on the premises,

good for relaxing before and after the big meal.

 ### Orlando's Seafood Grill
$$$$
709 Corydon Ave.
☎477-5899
For something a little more upscale, try this elegant Portuguese restaurant with a contemporary indoor decor and a charming deck patio. It is known for its expertly prepared fish dishes, such as, on occasion, delicacies like shark. Attentive and knowledgeable service.

The Velvet Glove
$$$$
2 Lombard Ave.
☎985-6255
Located in the prestigious Fairmont Winnipeg Hotel, this restaurant caters to Winnipeg's high rollers. Entrees might include choices of the chef's latest creations in beef, seafood or lamb; whatever's cooking, all meals begin with a simple soup and salad.

St. Boniface

Le Café Jardin
$
lunch only
340 Provencher Ave.
☎233-9515
Attached to the Centre Culturel Franco-Manitobia, this café serves French-Canadian cuisine as well as light meals and pastries baked on-site. The outdoor terrace is popular in summertime.

Eastern Manitoba

Gimli

Seagull's Restaurant
$$$
10 Centre St.
☎642-4145
This restaurant's biggest draw is its patio located right on the beach. Items like battered fish and gyros are served in a large dining room, and you can try

some Icelandic Vinetarta for dessert. Although there is nothing special about this place, it's the best sit-down restaurant in town.

Central Manitoba

Brandon

Humpty's
$
Hwy. 1
☎729-1902
This restaurant, located in a gas station on a Brandon service road running parallel to the Trans-Canada, serves up solid stick-to-your-ribs food such as burgers, eggs and lots of filling sandwiches. Locals swear by it.

Casteleyn Cappuccino Bar
$
closed Sun
908 Rosser Ave.
☎727-2820
This place is an oasis on the prairie, well worth a detour to Brandon. The Belgian Casteleyn family has been making hand-dipped chocolates here for seven years; they also serve a gelato, Italian sodas and coffee in their cappuccino bar. This place is more of a coffeehouse than a restaurant, but there's a tasty selection of meat and vegetable focaccia sandwiches each day. Other dessert options include Grand Marnier truffles, amaretto cheesecake and peach chocolate gateau. A wonderful lunch or snack experience.

St. François-Xavier

The Medicine Rock Café
$$$
990 Hwy. 26
☎864-2451
Located in a large, new log building with comfortable booths and lots of windows, this place features one of the most interesting menus in the province. Dishes include ostrich, emu, boar and rabbit.

Reservations are recommended, as this restaurant is often crowded.

Wasagaming

T.R. McKoy's Italian Restaurant
$$
on Wasagaming St.
☎848-2217
This is an unexpected gem, serving well-prepared pasta, pizza and grill dishes in a friendly and relaxed ambiance.

Shellmouth

The Church Caffe
$$
head north 25km from Russell on Hwy. 83, 10km west on Hwy. 482 and north again on Hwy. 549
☎564-2626
Housed in a former United Church, this place serves Austrian dinners in a scintillating lakeside location. It takes a bit of searching to find it, but the reward is a selection of beef, pork and turkey entrees that come with soup and salad. The restaurant won the Flavour of Rural Manitoba Award in 1995.

Entertainment

Winnipeg

Bars and Pubs

Times Change Blues Bar
Thu to Sun
234 Main St.
☎957-0982
Little seems to have changed at the Times Change Blues Bar, a small, intimate club that keeps on playing... the blues.

Centre Culturel
340 Provencher Blvd.
☎233-8972
A lively crowd gathers Tuesdays at the Centre Culturel for

Manitoba

an evening of Mardi Jazz. Live music is also presented on Friday nights.

King's Head Pub
120 King St.
☎957-7710
This might be Winnipeg's best bar. Located in the Exchange District, it features lots of imported beers and a wide selection of scotch, plus darts and pool. Food is also available.

Toad in the Hole
112 Osborne St.
☎284-7201
In funky Osborne Village, this is a good pub with plenty of pints of various imported brews. Darts and pool are available here, as well.

Cultural Events

Royal Winnipeg Ballet
380 Graham Ave.
☎956-2792 or 800-667-4792
www.rwb.org
The Royal Winnipeg Ballet is Canada's best-known dance company, housed in its own performance building right downtown. The ballet company won a gold medal at the International Ballet Competition and sometimes hosts tours of its facility, in addition to regular performances.

The **Winnipeg Fringe Theatre Festival** (*held in Jul; ☎956-1340; www.winnipegfringe. com*) is one of the largest theatre festivals of its kind, featuring a mix of local talent and international groups who perform in various small downtown venues. Real discoveries are to be made among the wide variety of shows, which range from family entertainment to experimental works. Free outdoor performances are held at Old Market Square (see p 439) throughout the festival.

Folklorama (*☎982-6210 or 800-665-0234; www. folklorama.ca*), Winnipeg's huge annual summer bash,

first two weeks each August, held the covers a lot of ground: representatives of the city's many cultures – French, Ukrainian, Hungarian, Chinese, Japanese, East Indian, to name a few – cook the food, sing the songs and dance the dances of their homelands in the many pavilions that spring up around the city for this event.

Some 30,000 folkies converge on **Bird's Hill Provincial Park** (see p 447) for one fun-filled weekend each July to sing, dance, or simply enjoy the **Winnipeg Folk Festival** (*☎231-0096; www.winnipegfolk festival. com*), one of North America's finest festivals of its kind. The extravaganza draws talented musicians from around the world to play on outdoor stages for enthusiastic crowds of all ages.

Gaming

Club Regent
1425 Regent Ave. W.
☎957-2700
Palm trees and waterfalls set a Caribbean theme for the Club Regent casino. The emphasis here is on electronic gaming: bingo, poker and Keno. There are slot machines here, as well.

McPhillips Street Station Casino
484 McPhillips St.
☎957-3900
Monte Carlo it's not, but the McPhillips Street Station Casino may appeal to visitors looking for a night of light entertainment. Short on games but long on theme, VLTs, slot machines and bingo make up the bulk of gaming activities, although there is also Keno and blackjack. The real draw here are the "extras," namely the historic railway theme evoking Winnipeg's splendid past, including the now-demolished Royal Alexander Hotel. A scaled-down "replica" of the "Chattanooga Choo Choo" (an imaginary

train immortalized by Glenn Miller) also chugs through the casino. More historically correct is the "Manitoba Millennium Express," a multi-media presentation that brings to life Manitoba's past.

St. Boniface

The **Festival du Voyageur** (*768 Ave.Taché; ☎237-7692; www.festivalvoyageur.mb.ca*) held in St. Boniface each February, celebrates winter and the fur trade era of the voyageurs who settled the province. Action at the big outdoor pavilion includes dog-sled races, snow sculptures and children's activities, while musical performers entertain the crowds at night.

The **Cercle Molière** (*340 Provencher Blvd. and 825 Rue St-Joseph; ☎233-8053*) is Canada's oldest operating theatre company, staging four major productions in the Théâtre de la Chapelle, an intimate Café-style venue. Performances are in French.

Eastern Manitoba

Gimli

Islendingadagurinn (the Icelandic Festival of Manitoba) takes place during three days in early August, celebrating the local heritage from that far-off land right in downtown Gimli. The festival includes a parade, music, poetry, Icelandic food and more.

Southern Manitoba

Altona

The **Manitoba Sunflower Festival** (*☎324-6468; www. townofaltona.com/events*) celebrates the tall yellow flower for three days each July in Altona with Mennonite foods, parades, dancing in the street and the like.

Morris

The **Manitoba Stampede and Exhibition** *(☎746-2552; www.manitobastampede.ca)* turns Morris, an otherwise slowpoke town, into rodeo-central for five days in mid-July. It is Canada's second-largest rodeo (after Calgary), and features chuckwagon races, an agricultural fair, and (of course) bullriding and other rodeo contests.

Central Manitoba

Dauphin

The hugely popular **National Ukrainian Festival** *(119 Main St. S., ☎622-4600; www.cnuf. ca)* takes place in Dauphin for three days each August, beginning on a Friday morning. Heritage village festivities include a bread-baking competition, embroidery contests, an Easter-egg decorating competition, folk arts, lots of dancing and a beer garden.

Northern Manitoba

The Pas

The **Northern Manitoba Trappers' Festival** *(☎623-2912, www.trappersfestival. com)* in The Pas runs for five days each February. Festivities here include a famous dog-sled race.

Shopping

Winnipeg

Shopping is concentrated in the downtown area: The Eaton Place, Hudson's Bay Company and the North West Company – are within a few blocks of each other. They are connected by a series of covered elevated walkways that are especially appreciated in wintertime. The library and other buildings are also linked via these "skywalks."

Winnipeg's **Hudson's Bay Company** *(Portage Ave. and Memorial Blvd., ☎783-2112)* was once the flagship of the illustrious chain, founded as a trading company in 1610. Now a modern department store, it still sells the original Hudson's Bay blankets and other unique merchandise.

Eaton Place *(downtown at 234 Donald St.)*, has more than 100 shops connected by the walkways. **Corydon Avenue** is a popular shopping district with plenty of restaurants and a European atmosphere created by gaslights, hanging flower baskets and street festivals. The district is sometimes referred to as Winnipeg's Little Italy. **Portage Place** is another downtown mall spanning three blocks; it contains 160 shops or so, and an IMAX theatre. **Polo Park**, *(1485 Portage Ave., on the way to the airport)*, contains more than 180 shops and leans toward upscale department stores. Among other stores downtown, The **Bayat Gallery** *(163 Stafford St., ☎475-5873 or 888-88-INUIT)* is particularly interesting; it is the city's best Inuit art gallery.

Osborne Village has a number of great little boutiques that should not be left unexplored. Jewellery, paperware, gifts, clothes, cookingware and more can be found in shops along Osborne Street between River and Stradbrook Avenue.

Toad Hall *(54 Arthur St., ☎956-2195 or 888-333-TOAD)* is a place that most children can only dream of. Shelves brimming with quality toys, both contemporary and traditional, line the walls of this store, which has a whimsical atmosphere that will transport children and adults alike into the magical realms of the imagination. Everything from complete hand-made Czech puppet theatres to electric train sets, colourful kites and magic sets are sold.

McNally Robinson *(1120 Grant Ave., ☎475-0483)* is by far the best bookstore in the city. It has a huge selection in every field, with special emphasis on prairie writing. A spiral staircase winds around a massive tree trunk, leading to the children's section on the second floor. Its restaurant, Café au Livre, serves light lunches and desserts.

Index

Index

Index

Index

Queen Charlotte Islands Museum
   (Skidegate) 250
Quesnel (Northern British Columbia) 236
   Accommodations 254
   Restaurants 260
Quesnel & District Museum (Quesnel) 236
Quinsam Salmon Hatchery
   (Campbell River) 148
Quw'utsun' Cultural and Conference
   Centre (Duncan) 140
Radium Hot Pools (Radium Hot Springs) .. 288
Radium Hot Springs (Rocky Mountains) .. 288
   Accommodations 310
   Restaurants 317
Rafting
   Central Alberta 380
   Northern British Columbia 253
   Rocky Mountains 296
   Southern Alberta 360
   Southern British Columbia 207
Railway & Forestry Museum
   (Prince George) 237
Rectory (St. Paul) 404
Red Brick Arts Centre and Museum
   (Edson) 379
Red Deer (Central Alberta) 375
   Accommodations 382
   Restaurants 384
Red Deer and District Museum
   (Red Deer) 376
Red River Heritage Road (Manitoba) 441
Red Rock Canyon Parkway
   (Southern Alberta) 358
Redberry Lake Biosphere Reserve
   Highway 40 (Hafford) 424
Regina (Saskatchewan) 415
   Accommodations 427
   Entertainment 431
   Restaurants 430
   Shopping 432
Regina Plains Museum (Regina) 416
Remington-Alberta Carriage Centre
   (Cardston) 350
Reptile World (Drumheller) 369
Restaurants 41
Restrooms 46
Revelstoke (Southern British Columbia) . 186
   Accommodations 215
   Restaurants 223
Revelstoke Dam (Revelstoke) 186
Revelstoke Railway Museum (Revelstoke) . 186
Reynolds-Alberta Museum (Wetaskiwin) .. 377
Rhododendron Lake (Vancouver Island
   and the Gulf Islands) 142
Riding Mountain National Park
   (Manitoba) 449
Riel House (Greater Winnipeg) 441
River Valley Park System (Edmonton) 394
Riverside Park
   (Southern British Columbia) 203
Roblin (Manitoba)
   Accommodations 453
Robson Square (Vancouver) 69

Robson Street (Vancouver) 69
Rocky Mountain House (Central Alberta) .. 374
   Accommodations 382
Rocky Mountain House National
   Historic Park (Rocky Mountains) 374
Rocky Mountains 265
   Accommodations 301
   Economy 269
   Entertainment 319
   Exploring 272
   Fauna 267
   Finding Your Way Around 269
   Flora 266
   Geography 265
   Glaciers 266
   History 268
   Outdoor Activities 292
   Practical Information 270
   Restaurants 314
   Shopping 320
Roderick Haig-Brown Provincial Park
   (Southern British Columbia) 186
Roedde House Museum (Vancouver) 71
Rogers Pass (Revelstoke) 186
Rogers Pass Discovery Centre (Revelstoke) 186
Roonay Bay (Skidegate) 250
Rosebud (Central Alberta) 372
   Accommodations 382
   Entertainment 384
   Restaurants 384
Rosedale (Central Alberta) 370
Ross Bay Cemetery
   (Victoria and Surroundings) 118
Rossland (Southern British Columbia) 200
   Accommodations 220
   Restaurants 226
Rossland Historical Museum (Rossland) .. 200
Rotary Centre for the Arts (Kelowna) 197
Rotary Museum of Police and Corrections
   (Prince Albert) 424
Round Lake
   (Fort Qu'Appelle River Valley) 418
Rowley (Central Alberta) 372
Royal Bank (Vancouver) 68
Royal British Columbia Museum
   (Victoria and Surroundings) 115
Royal Canadian Mint (St. Boniface) 440
Royal Canadian Mounted Police Centennial
   Museum (Regina) 418
Royal Centre (Vancouver) 68
Royal London Wax Museum
   (Victoria and Surroundings) 115
Royal Saskatchewan Museum (Regina) 416
Royal Tyrrell Museum of Palaeontology
   (Dinosaur Trail) 370
Rutherford House (Edmonton) 392
Saamis Archaeological Site
   (Medicine Hat) 356
Saamis Tipi (Medicine Hat) 356
Saanich Historical Artifacts Society
   (Victoria and Surroundings) 120
Saanich Peninsula
   (Victoria and Surroundings) 120

Index

Index

Index